Alexandria in Late Antiquity

*Ancient Society and History*

# Alexandria in

CHRISTOPHER HAAS

# *Late Antiquity*

## *Topography and Social Conflict*

The Johns Hopkins University Press
Baltimore and London

Printed in the United States of America on acid-free paper
06 05 04 03 02 01 00 99 98 97 5 4 3 2 1

The Johns Hopkins University Press
2715 North Charles Street
Baltimore, Maryland 21218-4319
The Johns Hopkins Press Ltd., London

Library of Congress Cataloging-in-Publication Data will be found
at the end of this book.

A catalog record for this book is available from the British Library.

ISBN 0-8018-5377-X

*for Barb,*
*". . . both now and forever"*

Listen to me, old thing: this is the first time in my life that I've had a real chance to yield to the temptations of a great city. What's the use of a great city having temptations if fellows don't yield to them? Makes it so bally discouraging for the great city. Besides, mother told me to keep my eyes open and collect impressions.

"Motty" Pershore in
"Jeeves and the Unbidden Guest," in
P. G. Wodehouse, *Carry on, Jeeves*

# Contents

# Illustrations

*Maps*



*Plans*



*Figures*

# Acknowledgments

Books tend to thrive near the intersection of experience, thought, grace, and friendship. This one has taken a decade to come to fruition, having begun as a dissertation at the University of Michigan. Since the project's inception, I have benefited from the kindness and wisdom of a number of individuals. They have generously contributed to this project, either by commenting on portions of it or by steering me toward further avenues of inquiry: Roger Bagnall, Robert Bianchi, Peter Brown, Alan Cameron, Michael Carr, Elizabeth Clark, Andrew Ehrenkreutz, Zbigniew Fiema, Gary Johnson, Zsolt Kiss, Ludwig Koenen, Jean Marc Lepillez, Adele Lindenmeyer, Birger Pearson, Elzbieta Rodziewicz, Doreya Said, Gregg Schwendner, Pete Tjapkes, Ray Van Dam, and Robert Wilken. I benefited also from the expertise of Kim Gavin, who drew the maps. Needless to say, the shortcomings that remain are entirely the fault of a sometimes stubborn author.

The long-term nurture of a book often requires various forms of financial support. I have benefited from the generosity of the University of Michigan's Rackham School of Graduate Studies, the National Endowment for the Humanities, and Villanova University. In particular, I wish to mention the kind support offered by Fr.

Lawrence C. Gallen, O.S.A, Villanova's former vice-president for academic affairs—blessed in memory.

During this book's gestation, earlier drafts of several sections have appeared as journal articles: "The Arians of Alexandria," *Vigiliae Christianae* 47 (1993): 234–45; "Patriarch and People: Peter Mongus of Alexandria and Episcopal Leadership in the Late Fifth Century," *Journal of Early Christian Studies* 1.3 (1993): 297–316; and "The Alexandrian Riots of 356 and George of Cappadocia," *Greek, Roman and Byzantine Studies* 32.3 (1991): 281–301.

Special thanks must be given to my mentors at Michigan: John Eadie, who always urged me to ask interesting questions, and Chester Starr, who taught me how to answer them. Also to John Fine, who enthusiastically adopted the project midstream and shepherded it through to the end. I am grateful for Kathy Ehmann's inestimable help with various texts. Dan Ehmann first challenged me to look at cities in new ways and he provided an entrée into urban design theory. For over a decade, Bill Barry shared his expertise in classical social conflict and his enthusiasm for a city that has enchanted us both. The theoretical basis for this book owes much to him, as it is the fruit of hours of sometimes heated discussion, "as iron sharpens iron." In addition, I owe an incalculable debt of gratitude and love to my late parents, William and Helen Haas.

This project could not have been possible were it not for the untiring assistance of Mieczyslaw Rodziewicz. His experience of over thirty years of archaeology in Alexandria and in the Mareotis made him an invaluable resource. Professor Rodziewicz's generosity in putting at my disposal his intimate knowledge of Alexandrian archaeology has enriched my work at every turn.

This book is the product of the support and encouragement of my wife, Barb, who shared me with the ancient city that claimed so much of my attention. I lovingly dedicate this book to her.

Alexandria in Late Antiquity

PHAROS
MEDITERRANEAN SEA
N
PHAROS ISLAND
GREAT HARBOR
LOCHIAS
HEPTASTADION
EUNOSTOS HARBOR
MARTYRIUM OF ST. MARK?
BOUKOLIA
BRUCHION
CIBOTOS
CAESARION
THEATRE?
NICOPOLIS
AGORA
VIA CANOPICA
GATE OF THE MOON
CHURCH OF THEONAS
GYMNASIUM?
KŌM EL-DIKKA
GATE OF THE SUN
HIPPODROME?
R-4
SERAPEUM
NECROPOLIS
RHAKOTIS
SCHEDIA CANAL
LAKE MAREOTIS

# ALEXANDRIA

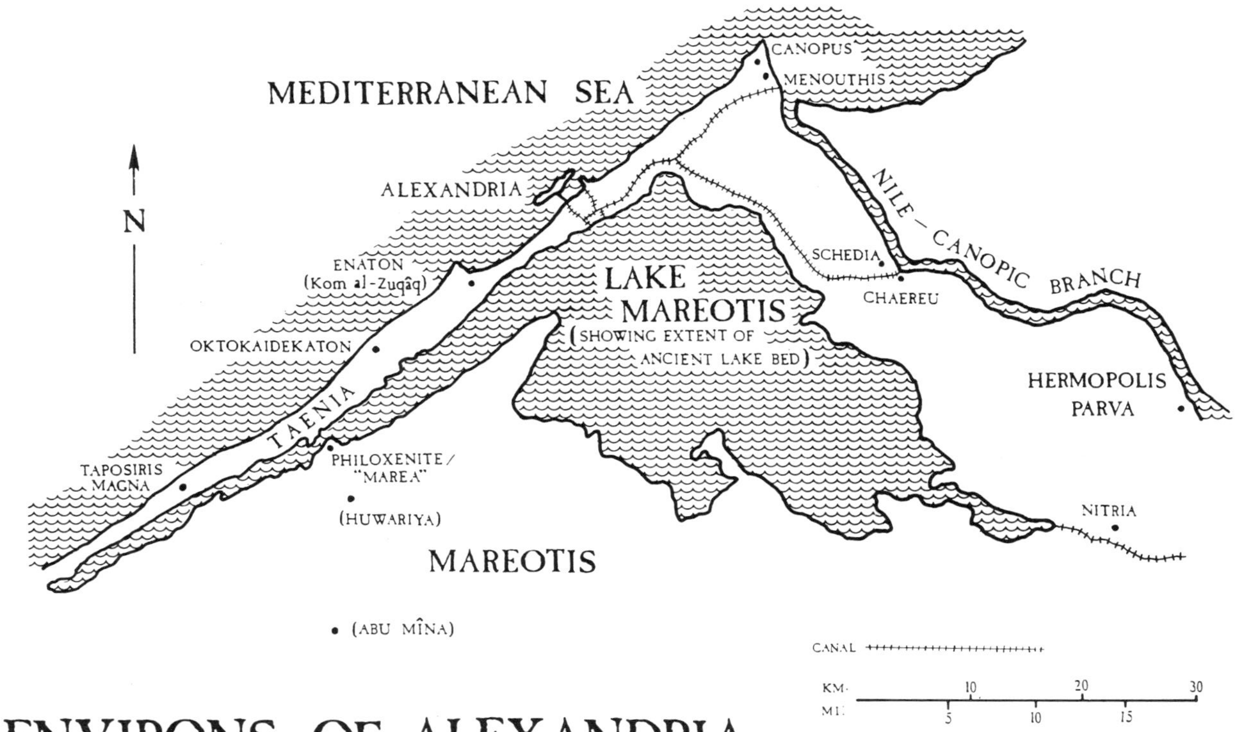
MEDITERRANEAN SEA
N
CANOPUS
MENOUTHIS
ALEXANDRIA
NILE – CANOPIC BRANCH
SCHEDIA
CHAEREU
ENATON
(Kom al-Zuqâq)
LAKE
MAREOTIS
(SHOWING EXTENT OF
ANCIENT LAKE BED)
OKTOKAIDEKATON
TAENIA
HERMOPOLIS
PARVA
TAPOSIRIS
MAGNA
PHILOXENITE/
"MAREA"
(HUWARIYA)
NITRIA
MAREOTIS
(ABU MÎNA)
CANAL
KM.
MI.
10
20
30
5
10
15

# ENVIRONS OF ALEXANDRIA

MEDITERRANEAN SEA
(RASHID)
ALEXANDRIA
PELUSIUM
SCETIS
CANAL
PETRA
BABYLON/
(FUSTAT)
MEMPHIS
CLYSMA
KARANIS
SINAI
FAYYÛM
OXYRHYNCHUS
N
ANTINOOPOLIS
NILE
RED
SEA
PHBOW
NAG
HAMMADI
COPTOS
ROMAN
EGYPT
THEBAID
APOLLINOPOLIS
MAGNA
BERENIKE
SYENE/
ELEPHANTINE
FIRST
CATARACT
PHILAE
KM.
100
MI.
50
100

# One

# Introduction

Justinian was furious. For nearly ten years he had promoted careful administrative reforms in the empire's provinces. Yet one region in his vast domain still seemed to ignore the emperor's directives. Even though the all-important tax revenues continued to flow uninterruptedly into the imperial treasury in Constantinople, Justinian complained to his praetorian prefect that the situation in Egypt and its capital of Alexandria was completely disordered—so much so that he did not know what was going on in the province.[1]

We should not minimize the Byzantine emperor's frustrations in trying to understand one of the most important cities of his empire. The cities of late antiquity have long intrigued modern historians, since they bring into sharp relief the factors that transformed the fabric of society between antiquity and the Middle Ages. For the past three decades a flowering of urban histories has re-created for us the quality of life in these Mediterranean cities. Among the more notable of these "urban biographies" are Dagron's and Mango's on Constantinople, Foss's on Ephesus, Liebeschuetz's on Antioch, and Lepelley's study of the cities of North Africa. Recently, the archaeologist's spade has revealed the splendors of Aphrodisias in Caria, resulting in a handful of studies of this fascinating Anatolian site.

These admirable urban histories have done much to deepen our understanding of the empire's cities during a time of great cultural transition. Yet, they have also shown how difficult it is for us to grasp late antique cities on their own terms, separated in time as we are by more than a millennium and a half.[2]

Alexandria, the commercial hub of the eastern Mediterranean, especially invites our scrutiny. In the period spanning the empire's restoration under Diocletian (284–306) and the conquest of the Near East by Arab armies in the seventh century, Alexandria figured prominently in late imperial politics, socioeconomic developments, and religious history. Alexandria entered the late Roman period as the center of a concerted rebellion against imperial authority which had to be suppressed by the emperor Diocletian himself. Arianism, the great heresy that rocked the late imperial church, had its origins in the preaching of an Alexandrian presbyter. The monastic movement, which radically altered the way late antique man related to his society, his classical heritage, and even to his own body, was nurtured in the deserts near Alexandria. In addition, one of the most dramatic episodes in the bitter Mediterranean-wide struggle between paganism and Christianity was the violent conflict that erupted in 391 over the temple of Serapis in Alexandria. By the late fifth and sixth centuries, Alexandria was also a major center of opposition to the Christological theology of the imperial capital, creating the so-called Monophysite controversy.[3]

Despite the city's importance during late antiquity, the modern study of Alexandria has often fallen into the cracks between the disciplines of ancient history and papyrology. Evelyne Patlagean touches on an important factor that dissuades historians from studying late antique Alexandria when she states that Alexandria and Egypt possess "la documentation trop riche et les réalités trop particulières."[4] Consequently, discussions of Egypt and Alexandria frequently are relegated to papyrological journals, a "backwater" that historians of the broader Mediterranean world seldom enter, doubtless fearing the complexities of material as labyrinthine as the marshes of the Nile Delta.[5] In the case of late antique Egypt, the situation has been redressed considerably by Roger Bagnall's nuanced survey of society and culture in the Egyptian countryside.[6]

Despite Bagnall's enumeration of the links between city and hinterland, most papyrologists consider Alexandria as somehow separate from Egypt, belonging more to the classical world of Mediterranean cities than to the more familiar villages and metropoleis of the Egyptian *chōra* (countryside).[7] From the standpoint of papyrology, the city is considered *Alexandria ad Aegyptum* (that is, "next to" or "toward" Egypt) rather than *in Aegypto,* thereby echoing the phraseology of the ancients.

One of the chief difficulties in discussing Alexandria during this era is the relative absence of a detailed archaeological context. This lack of material evidence is due principally to the modern city having been situated atop the ancient one. Added to this is the woeful disregard given by the builders of modern Alexandria to the city's ancient monuments and sites, resulting in their almost complete obliteration during the last century and a half. Even today, rescue archaeologists are forced to work round the clock in their effort to keep the bulldozers at bay. Rome presents an instructive contrast, where the ancient monuments were often incorporated into the design of the city by urban planners and architects from the Renaissance to the present day.

Consequently, we are often in the dark as to the precise location of many important Alexandrian sites, including the much-revered tomb of Alexander the Great and the celebrated Museon, the great research institute and library established by the Ptolemies. This all-too-slender basis for scholarly reconstruction can be seen by perusing the pages of Achille Adriani's compendium of Alexandrian topography, *Repertorio d'arte dell'Egitto greco-romano.* In this indispensable reference tool, Adriani assiduously collects every possible snippet of information on each site within the city.[8] Despite Adriani's unmatched skill at collecting and analyzing the extant evidence, his conclusions regarding particular topographical problems are often tenuous at best. Bearing in mind that Adriani is one of the great lights of twentieth-century scholarship on ancient Alexandria, how much more should we cast a skeptical eye on the detailed maps confidently published in atlases and general histories?

The absence of a clearly discernible archaeological setting is especially regretted for Alexandria, since it was the home of many of late antiquity's most brilliant writers, philosophers, and theologians. Philo, Origen, Arius, Athanasius, Hypatia, and John Philoponus (to name but a few) have all been the subjects of specialized studies in recent years. Seldom, however, do these otherwise valuable intellectual biographies place the Alexandrian thinkers within their particular social context. It is hardly conceivable that Alexandria's bustling urban milieu failed to influence profoundly the development of these intellectuals. In the pages that follow, I attempt to provide this context. While very little is said about theology and philosophy, I focus on the lives of these theologians and philosophers, and seek to restore them to their social world.

We are aided in our quest to re-create this city by the animated depictions of Alexandrian life presented by ancient writers. Strabo leads us on a leisurely walking tour of the city during the age of Augustus, and his outline is supplemented in the late antique period by writers as diverse as Herodian, Achilles Tatius, Ammianus Marcellinus, and John of Nikiu.[9] This classical fascination with the city is not surprising, in light of Alexandria's position as the major commercial entrepôt of the eastern Mediterranean. Even during the closing years of Byzantine rule in Egypt, accounts of visiting Christian pilgrims provide vividly detailed descriptions of everyday life in the city. For in the words of a certain Antoninus, one of these later pilgrims from Italy, "Alexandria is a magnificent city. Its people are very frivolous, but they are fond of pilgrims."[10]

Clement of Alexandria, writing circa 200, describes Jews, pagans, and Christians as belonging to three separate peoples (*laoi*).[11] Although pagan critics had long derided Christians as a "third race," this characterization was picked up by Christian writers during the second century, and was developed with particular verve by Tertullian.[12] Clement's use of this theme, however, is far more than mere imitation. Indeed, Clement's taxonomy reflects his own experience of urban life, since a noteworthy feature of Alexandria's social organization during the late Roman period is the prominence of well-defined ethno-religious communities within the city. While other Mediterranean cities had their respective pagan, Jewish, and Christian communities, in very few of these cities do we find such a distinctive communal consciousness separating the various groups. Moreover, a prominent strand running through much of fourth- and fifth-century Alexandrian history is the competition of these ethno-religious groups for cultural hegemony.

Comparing Alexandria with other late antique cities throws the competitive nature of Alexandrian social dynamics into sharp relief. Rome was in decline, and the unquestioned status of its entrenched aristocracy guaranteed that the history of socioreligious change in the Urbs Aeterna would be written as the conversion of the senatorial order. Constantinople, the product of a Christian emperor's act of will, likewise lacked strongly defined communities, save for rival factions within the Constantinopolitan church. The integration of the wealthy and powerful parvenu, and the stormy relationship between emperor and bishop (and, by extension, between emperor and populace), are the major themes in Constantinople's social development. In Antioch, the contest for cultural hegemony among the city's ethno-religious communities had been won early in the fourth century. Despite the protestations of Libanius and the incredulity of Julian, Antioch at midcentury was largely a Christian city. Although it possessed an influential Jewish community, Antioch's major intercommunal conflict, the Judaizing controversy, sprang up within the Christian community and resulted from the fluid nature of communal life in the Syrian capital. When episodes of popular violence erupted in Antioch, they did not arise from tension among Jews, pagans, and Christians. Instead, they took the form of bread riots or faction-led insurrections against imperial authority.

The story of Alexandria's communal groups in the fourth and fifth centuries is dominated by the growing ascendancy of the Christian community.[13] In fact, the history of the city during this period is, in large part, demarcated by events directly concerned with the church. Diocletian's reign and administrative reforms can be seen as bringing to an end the political instability that plagued the empire (including Egypt) during the third century. Yet, his accession in 284 also marked in Egypt the beginning of the "Era of the Martyrs," the benchmark of the Coptic calendar to this day. Moreover, the major watershed in Alexandrian history between

Diocletian's reign and the Arab capture of the city in 642 is also related to the church. In 451, rioting broke out in Alexandria when news arrived of the deposition of the patriarch Dioscorus by the Council of Chalcedon. This upheaval ushered in a new period largely characterized by adherence to Monophysite theology and by sustained opposition to imperial authority.[14] Further, the church's emergence from a persecuted status to one of unquestioned hegemony by the first quarter of the fifth century is personified by the increasing power of the Alexandrian patriarch, whom contemporaries could style (not without reason) a "new Pharaoh."[15]

Unfortunately, the church's expanding role in Alexandrian society is usually traced by analyzing the development of ecclesiastical institutions or by providing thumbnail sketches of the remarkable personalities within the Alexandrian church who naturally capture our attention. Individuals like Athanasius or Cyril tend to dominate discussions of Christianity in the city during the fourth and fifth centuries. As a result, the rank and file of the Christian community are easily overlooked. Moreover, these approaches do violence to the broader context of Alexandrian history, and relegate the city's other communal groups to the status of mere foils for the eventually dominant Christian community.

A far more balanced perspective can be gained by first focusing on these other communities, analyzing their social composition and internal organization, and only then proceeding to discuss the city's Christian community. An examination of both the pagan and Jewish communities in Alexandria provides an important corrective to a Christian-oriented analysis, since the changing status of these two communal groups within the city helps to delineate the contours of the city's social history. The pagan community began this period as the hegemonic group in Alexandria and gradually was forced into a subservient status by the early part of the fifth century. The Jewish community, on the other hand, always remained a minority in Alexandrian society, but its socioeconomic position in the city dictated that it be treated as an essential component of the Alexandrian social dynamic. Consequently, these communities serve as two of the important missing players in the sometimes-violent drama that took place on the stage of late antique Alexandria.

Our literary sources, ranging from Josephus and Dio Chrysostom to Ausonius and Socrates Scholasticus, unite in their condemnation of the Alexandrians as a people naturally prone to outbursts of mob violence. Typical of these comments is Ammianus Marcellinus's observation that Alexandria is a city "which on its own impulse, and without ground, is frequently roused to rebellion and rioting." This propensity toward violence is often coupled with an innate frivolity, a characteristic noted even by our Italian pilgrim to the Holy Land.[16] However, it should be pointed out that the typicality of Alexandrian violence appears to be more of a literary topos, reinforced and embellished by successive writers, than an accurate depiction of social behavior in the city. There is no evidence that Alexandria was any more violent than other large Mediterranean cities—at least in the early Roman period.[17] The third century witnessed a number of conflicts within the city, but these struggles appear to have been out-and-out revolts against Roman authority rather than incidents of intercommunal violence. However, the situation changes dramatically in the fourth century, when factionalism and popular violence become far more frequent.[18] This climate of violence covers a wide spectrum of social unrest: carefully orchestrated revolts against imperial authority, rioting between rival communal groups in the city which occasionally reached the level of prolonged *stasis* (civil war), and sporadic acts of violence directed against a particularly detested individual—altogether, a social environment that would appear to be a strange breeding ground for the sensitive souls of philosophers and theologians.[19]

Although outbreaks of violence were a prominent feature of the city's life during late antiquity, Alexandrian social history should not be interpreted solely with reference to riots and bloodshed. Such an approach subordinates the everyday life of the various communities to atypical, though occasionally pivotal, events in their relations. As an organizing principle for understanding Alexandria in the late empire mob violence is inadequate, since such episodes merely stand at one end of a broad continuum of intercommunal relations within the city. At the other end were the daily contacts between members of the different communities characteristic of a diverse cosmopolitan urban setting. Legal and papyrological texts reveal a complex network of social and economic relationships, ranging from intermarriage and slaveholding to everyday commercial transactions—relations often ignored by ancient chroniclers and their modern commentators in favor of the riots and violence which make for much more exciting reading.

How are we to understand the incidents of popular violence which punctuate Alexandrian history across late antiquity? At the outset, we need to part company with the ancient sources in their condemnation of the Alexandrians as frenzied madmen who possess an inborn propensity to senseless violence. While acts of popular violence do occur, in every case it can be demonstrated that the violence resulted from some specific breakdown in the normal structures of urban conflict resolution. Frequently, popular riots occur as a means of reasserting some threatened aspect of the traditional social, political, or religious order. At times, mob violence occurs when some prominent figure (an imperial official or a newly installed churchman) violates the carefully scripted protocols of civic ritual. Thus, in many cases, mob violence can be seen as a drastic means for restoring the city's stability.

Clearly, each incident of popular violence needs to be examined on its own merits and, if possible, placed within the broader currents of Alexandrian history. Even though the city's ethno-religious communities engaged in a fierce competition for cultural hegemony, this type of intercommunal competition does not necessarily lead to violence. For popular violence to occur, certain distinct factors need to be present: communal leadership committed to violence, the careful mobilization of the crowd, the absence of alternative means for expressing disaffection, the weakness of counteracting social controls, an accessible target, and a precipitating event. It is quite possible for there to be a climate of intercommunal tension without outbreaks of violent collective behavior.

Also, we should note that acts of popular violence have the ability to reflect back upon urban social structure. The preoccupation of ancient observers with riots and hostile outbursts results in social descriptions of the participants which we would not have otherwise. Consequently, we may view the various manifestations of intercommunal violence as flashpoints that illuminate the internal structure of the respective communities. They also highlight the changing roles of the major ethno-religious communities in the social world of late Roman Alexandria. Although violent incidents are analyzed frequently in the following pages, a methodological choice dictated in part by the nature of the source material, we need not subscribe to the ancient opinion that mob violence was an essential element in Alexandrian social relations.

In a more comprehensive model, popular violence in Alexandria becomes just one form of a broader structure of intercommunal competition during late antiquity. Extending beyond the simple question of who could gain the most adherents in the city, such competition included other issues of more potential significance. Who controlled the symbols of civic consciousness in Alexandria and the tokens associated with the city's founding? Who controlled the sites that dominated the city's landscape? Who managed the arenas of public discourse, like the town council, the agora, the hippodrome, and the theater? Who orchestrated and presided over the public rituals that embodied the established social and political order? And who could lay claim to representing the city to outsiders, especially to the emperor?

It is in this broader context that the Alexandrian violence of the fourth and early fifth centuries becomes comprehensible. Prior to the fourth century, the pagan community was undisputed in its cultural mastery of the city. For the pagans, Alexandrian identity was so intertwined with paganism, that the two were inseparable. This identification was called into question by the Jewish community during the early empire, occasionally with the backing of the Roman overlords. The pagans responded to this perceived threat with violence. By the early second century, however, the Jewish community was crushed and the pagans were able to reassert their hegemony. Although there were incidents of violence during the third century, these were the by-product of relations with an outside power—the imperial government. Caracalla's massacre of the citizenry in 215, the government's persecuting policies during the 250s, and the usurpations and civil conflicts of the 260s all come under this rubric.

Not until the early fourth century were intercommunal relations seriously destabilized by the growing power of the Christian Church. In the ensuing century and a quarter, cultural hegemony in Alexandria was sharply contested. During this period of intense intercommunal competition, diverse factors conducive to mob violence came together on the urban stage and were frequently exacerbated by the intervention of imperial power on one side or another. After this conflict was finally resolved, and Alexandrian society achieved a certain reintegration, the Christians emerged as the hegemonic community. Once again, we find the virtual identification of Alexandrian civic consciousness with the ideology of one ethnoreligious community, testifying to the success of this social reintegration. Just as Antioch had been renamed *Theoupolis* (the City of God), so Alexandria became known as "the most glorious and Christ-loving city of the Alexandrians."

In placing the city's communal groups within a coherent urban milieu, we need not be shackled by a rigid form of materialistic determinism. Nevertheless, careful attention should be paid to the various elements composing Alexandria's urban environment, such as the city's physical setting, its economic life, demographic structure, civic institutions, and administrative apparatus. More than a vague background for the events of these centuries, this urban environment demonstrably affects and in part shapes the course of historical developments.[20]

For these reasons, I eschew a strictly chronological approach to Alexandrian history as well as a rigidly thematic approach. Both of these methodologies have their own particular virtues, as can readily be seen in two very different books on Antioch: Glanville Downey's *History of Antioch in Syria* (1961) and J. H. W. G. Liebeschuetz's *Antioch: City and Imperial Legislation in the Later Roman Empire* (1972). Despite the laudable qualities of these two traditional approaches to urban history, they are unable to capture an essential element in the history of Alexandria: the constant interplay among the built environment, the socioeconomic and political structures of the city, and the ongoing competition for cultural hegemony.

In order to explore this interplay as fully as possible, I first sketch the city's physical setting and then proceed to a general discussion of the economic and social structures of Alexandrian life. Another crucial element is the issue of political authority in Alexandria and its division between local and imperial officials. Only then do I turn to a social description of the city's ethno-religious communities. For each community, I not only examine its internal structure and governance but also give attention to the community's topographical and social location within the city. Finally, I address the question of intercommunal competition by examining three critical flashpoints in their relations.

Another way to view the structure of this presentation is to compare it to a play. I first bring the audience into the theater (the urban setting) and examine the stage (the economic and social background). Next, I introduce each of the dramatis personae and explore the nature of their individual characters. Only then do the house lights dim and the play begin—the competition for cultural hegemony. By no means do I wish to minimize the importance of the theater's layout and the arrangement of the stage. They focus the action in very specific ways. Nonetheless, "the play's the thing." Only by bringing together the totality of this theatrical experience can I hope to re-create some hint of what it was like to live in Alexandria during this period. I make no claims of presenting a comprehensive history of late antique Alexandria. Instead, I highlight certain features of Alexandria's social dynamic which seem to outline best the city's rich history during the twilight of antiquity.

Given the uneven quality of our ancient sources and the fragmentary nature of the city's material remains, is it possible for us to do more than merely catch a stray glimpse of life in Alexandria? One profitable avenue of inquiry utilizes recent work in the field of urban design and morphology. Edmund Bacon, a leading figure in modern theories of urban design, has challenged architects and urban planners to "see" their cities in heretofore neglected ways. For Bacon, cities are more than just a random collection of structures. They are made up of discernible units of mass and space, linked together by "movement systems" into a coherent whole.[21] These movement systems can be defined as "paths along which city dwellers move" and the architectural forms that articulate these principal urban arteries. Bacon goes on to explain that "as the movement systems of a city become clearly defined and are used by more and more people over a span of time, they establish themselves deeply in the collective psychology of the community." Eventually, a strongly articulated movement system can evolve into "a powerful influence, capable of seizing men's minds and developing loyalties around it. Of itself it becomes a major political force."[22] Although Bacon's "movement systems" cannot completely do justice to the complexities of urban life in a city like Alexandria, his observations help to animate our understanding of ancient cities in a way that mere site plans are unable to do.

Bacon's theories have important ramifications for urban historians. The design systems of cities reflect conscious decisions on the part of their inhabitants concerning the emphasis of some topographical points at the expense of others, and the organizing principles for their cities. In support of this view, Bacon points to classical Athens, where the Panathenaic Way is easily seen as the city's principal "movement system" leading to the city's focal point—the Acropolis. It would not be an exaggeration to say that all of Athens's subsequent urban development in antiquity was predicated on this one movement system and point of reference.[23] Bacon's influence can be seen in other recent works on urban planning, notably those of Mark Girouard, James Vance, and Spiro Kostof, all of whom examine the growth and decline of urban forms by focusing on the subtle relationship between the cities and the societies that produced them.[24] The second volume of William MacDonald's *Architecture of the Roman Empire* applies this perspective more vigorously to the cities of antiquity and investigates the role played in urban life by systems of well-defined, connected spaces, such as fora and colonnaded streets.[25]

Urban topography serves as both the ground and the articulation of the lives of city dwellers. The constant experience of particular urban places is bound to effect the ways in which the inhabitants organize their social, political, economic, and religious worlds.[26] This is certainly true of late Roman Alexandria, a city that possessed a distinctive configuration marked out by sweeping urban corridors and imposing monuments. As a result, episodes in the city's history may be illuminated by constantly referring to the question of location, in the belief that the changing fortunes of individuals and groups were shaped by the topography of Alexander's magnificent city.

Late antique Alexandria is a city particularly suited to the careful application of recent theories in urban design. Yet attempts at employing these methods of "seeing" the city would offer little reward were it not for the richness of newly available sources for the reconstruction of the Alexandrian urban setting. And even though the ongoing discovery of new sources necessitates the caveat that a scholarly reconstruction of any ancient city will always be provisional, the number and variety of new sources concerning Alexandria makes such an attempt worthwhile. Recently edited papyri in the form of letters, poems, receipts, contracts, and edicts continue to enhance our understanding of Alexandrian topography and provide important data concerning economic and social relations during late antiquity.[27] Relevant texts have also been isolated and reattributed to an Alexandrian provenance. Prominent among these is a fourth-century listing of housing and urban amenities, contained in a Syriac chronicle of the twelfth century.[28] During this past century, building projects throughout the modern city have turned up a wealth of new inscriptional evidence which also sheds light on the ancient metropolis.

Undoubtedly the most important new discoveries relating to late antique Alexandria are in the field of archaeology. This is the result of extensive work carried out by Polish excavators during the past three decades in an area of the city's center known as Kōm el-Dikka (see plan 1 in chapter 6). A portion of the excavated site, which today lies between the railway station and the Greco-Roman Museum, consists of an inhabited quarter dated to the fourth through seventh century. This quarter is especially noteworthy as it provides our first archaeological window onto urban life in late antique Alexandria. Workshops and street-front stores as well as private dwellings complement the depictions in literary sources of the city's varied commercial and social life. An elegant theaterlike structure was uncovered, along with a large imperial bath complex and lecture halls, the latter being unprecedented archaeological evidence for the city's intellectual reputation. Unexpected discoveries from the inhabited quarter include frescoes and other wall decorations that provide clear evidence for the development of Coptic artistic forms in a cosmopolitan urban setting—not just in the chora of Middle and Upper Egypt. Inscriptions from the theater supply data concerning the sixth- and seventh-century factions of the hippodrome, a topic of perennial interest to historians of the early Byzantine period. Moreover, the quarter's workshops grew up around several public buildings (including the theater and baths) which were newly erected during the fourth century. These late Roman building projects reflect the renewed vigor of urban conditions following Diocletian's siege and eventual capture of the city in 297/98.[29]

However, it is exceedingly difficult to harmonize the topography of the excavated areas with the descriptions found in ancient writers. The mound of Kōm el-Dikka had long been considered to be the site of the Paneion, an artificial hill surmounted by a shrine to Pan which commanded a wide view of the city.[30] Instead, we now know that the excavated hill was composed of medieval rubbish atop a layer of Muslim graves, which, in turn, covered the late Roman inhabited quarter. Thus far, there has been no Troy found under this Hissarlik. Nonetheless, the modifications made to scholars' former configurations of the ancient city, not to mention the vast quantity of new data regarding late antique Alexandria, will ensure that the site of Kōm el-Dikka will long be regarded as the most important Alexandrian excavation undertaken during the twentieth century. These archaeological discoveries, combined with our other sources, provide the materials for a preliminary reconstruction of the Alexandrian urban milieu during late antiquity. This diverse cosmopolitan setting, in turn, helps to illuminate the social organization and intercommunal relations that took place in what Ammianus Marcellinus unabashedly called "the crown of all cities."[31]

# Two

# The Urban Setting

Throughout the autumn and spring of 297/98, the anxious inhabitants of Alexandria looked out from their eastern walls onto the standards and tents of Diocletian's siege camp. The emperor, on his part, was attempting to crush a rebellion in Egypt which centered on the important trading center of Coptos and the region's great metropolis of Alexandria. These two cities had supported Lucius Domitius Domitianus in his bid for imperial power. Upon his death, they transferred their allegiance to his lieutenant, Aurelius Achilleus. By the early part of 298, the revolt in Coptos had been suppressed, but Alexandria continued to defy the emperor, even though he had raised siege mounds and had cut the important canal running to the city from the Canopic branch of the Nile. It was unlike this energetic emperor to wait out a protracted siege. The literary sources for his reign bear witness to Diocletian's wide-ranging activities, from Italy and what is now Hungary to Syria. In this case, however, the emperor knew that Alexandria was a jewel well worth his long wait. Eventually, Diocletian found his chance. The city was betrayed from within, and the emperor's troops poured through one of the gates, initiating a great slaughter within the siege-weary metropolis. Diocletian trumpeted this great victory by

Fig. 1. Diocletian's victory column, erected 298 atop the hill of the Serapeum. It was originally surmounted by a large porphyry statue, fragments of which were found around the base. Dedicated to Diocletian "the Invincible" by Aelius Publius, prefect of Egypt, 298/99. Total height of column and base is twenty-six meters.
(From *Description de l'Égypte,* Planches, Antiquité, Paris, 1822, vol. 5, pl. 34)

erecting a lofty column atop the hill of the Serapeum, where it can still be seen to this day (figure 1).[1]

The emperor had spent half a year encamped before the walls of Alexandria because he recognized its strategic importance, and the danger that it posed were it to persist in rebellion. After all, in July of 69, Vespasian was first acclaimed as emperor in Alexandria, and the third century had witnessed a number of imperial usurpations originating in the city. Egypt was one of the empire's most important granaries, and Alexandria served as the conduit for this vital grain supply as well as for much of the empire's trade with the east.

## *"The Most Glorious City of the Alexandrians"*

The city's importance in the region as well as in the empire was due, to a large degree, to its remarkable geographical setting, which defined the course of Alexandria's urban development and helped shape its economic and social evolution.[2] Although the city's development was not governed by an inexorable geographical determinism, a combination of unique geographical factors interacted with Alexandria's institutions and history in a fashion perhaps unparalleled in other Mediterranean cities of antiquity.

Alexandria possessed one of the very few favorable sites along the marshy coast of Egypt which allowed for the construction of a major port. Building foundations dating from the Ptolemaic era almost uniformly rest upon a bed of limestone, part of a kilometer-wide limestone ridge that runs intermittently along the coast from Canopus to a point some fifty-six kilometers west of the city. This ridge also permitted much of Alexandria to be built on an elevation that would catch the refreshing sea breezes especially noted by ancient writers.[3] The city's mild Mediterranean climate is such that Alexandria's population today doubles during the summer months, when many Egyptians seek relief from Saharan temperatures in Cairo and regions farther to the south.

In addition to the natural advantages of the city's site, Alexandria developed at a point located near the intersection of two continents, and possessed easy access to the many lands surrounding the Mediterranean. This location did not in itself ensure Alexandria's prosperity; Caesarea and Berytus could lay claim to similar advantages. However, Alexandria alone was linked to the Nile, which fertilized and irrigated the rich agricultural region along its banks and which served as cheap and reliable transport for Egypt's abundant resources. A network of canals ran from the Canopic branch of the Nile and permitted river traffic to sail directly to Alexandria. These canals utilized another of Alexandria's geographical advantages, Lake Mareotis, a vast freshwater lake whose waters delimited the southern boundaries of the city. Washed by both the Mediterranean and by the Nile-fed Lake Mareotis, Alexandria's unique location led the anonymous fourth-century author of the *Expositio Totius Mundi* to marvel that the city's inhabitants could partake of "something no other province has: river fish, lake fish, and saltwater fish." This remark is confirmed by the excavations at Kōm el-Dikka, where the surviving graffiti depict in equal numbers seagoing ships and river craft (figure 2).[4]

A glance at a map shows that the city was designed to maximize the benefits of these geographical factors, particularly those promoting regional and long-distance trade. This linkage between Alexandria's topography and its socioeconomic structure was widely recognized by ancient writers.[5] Even at the end of antiquity, John of Nikiu (writing in the seventh century) ascribes commercial motives to the builders of the canals, the Heptastadion, and the Pharos.[6] Perhaps the best testimony to the interrelationship of Alexandrian commerce and topography is the oft-repeated legend of the city's foundation by Alexander the Great in 331 B.C. According to this story, the architects accompanying Alexander ran out of chalk while they were tracing the future course of the city's walls. For lack of a better substitute, they used barley meal to complete the outline. Almost immediately, however, a great flock of birds descended from the sky and eagerly devoured the grain. This naturally troubled the Macedonian conqueror, who turned to his augurs for an explanation of the portent. They assured him that, rather than presaging misfortune, the incident foretold the city's great abundance and its ability to feed many nations.[7]

Modern descriptions of the Ptolemaic and Roman city closely follow the account found in Strabo's *Geography*. André Bernand goes so far as to entitle one of his main chapters on Alexandrian

Fig. 2. Alexandrian trade. Graffito of seagoing vessel at dockside, with six sailors. Found at House D, Kōm el-Dikka, late sixth or early seventh century.

(M. Rodziewicz)

topography "Promenade avec Strabon." This is not surprising, since Strabo's first-century B.C. geographical compendium provides us with the most complete description of Alexandria found in any ancient source. Yet Strabo omits certain topographical features from his account: the eastern necropolis, the Agora, and the buildings that housed the city government. Consequently, his walking tour of Alexandria should be treated with a measure of caution. The need for caution is especially compelling in the context of this study, since the city in which Strabo strolled is as distant in time from late Roman Alexandria as the New Amsterdam of Peter Stuyvesant is from modern New York. Perhaps a more important reason for departing from Strabo's itinerary in Alexandria is the tendency of his catalog-like description at times to obscure those elements that gave unity to the city's topography, as well as the ways in which those distinct unifying features highlighted certain focal points within the urban landscape. By contrast, an analysis of the city's design which takes into account these "movement systems" and "urban foci" need not be an exercise in the esoterica of modern theories of urban planning and architecture. As Edmund Bacon and William MacDonald ably demonstrated, a sensitivity to these factors only helps to articulate the common urban experience of the person in the street. Strabo himself bears witness to the utility of this method. Being an astute observer of geography, he naturally relies on certain of these catagories which serve as organizing principles for his description—for example, the Via Canopica and the harbor area.[8]

As we begin our own tour of the metropolis, it should be noted that Alexandria was a planned city.[9] This characteristic, most clearly seen in the regular grid pattern of the streets, set it apart from such cities as Athens or Rome, both of which grew and evolved over the course of centuries.[10] Since the greater part of Alexandria's design was executed within a relatively brief period after the city's foundation, a certain unity of design to the urban landscape prevails, much like L'Enfant's Washington, D.C. There were important accretions to the original design (for instance the Serapeum, the Caesarion, and the extramural necropoleis), but these later additions only tended to enhance the strong and forceful lines of the city's original conception.

The design of Alexandria clearly accorded pride of place to the city's twin harbors. Indeed, Alexandria's design can best be understood as an expression of the city's function as a port. At the time of its foundation, Alexandria possessed only one large harbor, but one of the early Ptolemaic rulers constructed a causeway seven stadia long (hence Heptastadion), linking the mainland with the island of Pharos. This created two distinct harbors, which were more easily protected from the force of the strong coastal currents: the Eastern or Great Harbor and the Western Harbor, also known as the Eunostos Harbor.[11] A third-century Alexandrian bishop speaks glowingly of "our smooth and waveless harbors."[12] Maritime commerce was further promoted by digging a number of canals, which brought the waters of the Nile to the city via the Canopic branch of the river at Chaereu and Schedia. An important canal seems also to have joined the Nile-fed Lake Mareotis on the south of the city with the Western Harbor.[13]

The crown of Alexandria's harbors was the great lighthouse erected on the eastern edge of the Pharos island. This immense structure, rising just above the height of the Statue of Liberty, acted as a beacon to sailors still some dozens of miles out to sea, and guided their course among the treacherous reefs that lay just beyond the city's harbors (figure 3).[14] This was accomplished by means of a fire which blazed at the summit during the night and a mirror which

Fig. 3. Ships leaving Great Harbor while passing in front of Fort Qayt Bey, built circa 1500 on the remains of the Pharos. The fort, which is only as tall as the very lowest reaches of the great lighthouse, nonetheless conveys a sense of the earlier structure's massive scale—especially as it was experienced by maritime travelers.

(From *Description de l'Égypte*, Planches, État Moderne, Paris, 1817, vol. 5, pl. 87.3) reflected the sun's rays by day. Achilles Tatius likens the structure to "a mountain, almost reaching the clouds, in the middle of the sea. Below the building flowed the waters; it seemed to be as if it were suspended above their surface, while at the top of the mountain rose a second sun to be a guide for ships." One can only imagine the profound effect such a huge building had on the consciousness of Alexandria's inhabitants, surely every bit as great as that of the Acropolis in Classical Athens, or the Eiffel Tower in fin-de-siècle Paris.[15]

The primacy of the harbor area in the topography of ancient Alexandria was further accentuated by a number of subsidiary buildings related to the activities of a busy international port. As one would expect, various dockyards and warehouses could be found all along the twin harbors. Toward the western end of the Great Harbor sat the Emporion, where duties on imports and exports were collected, and which also served as the Bourse for merchandise passing through the port. Nearby, stood a massive temple to the imperial cult known as the Caesarion (or Sebasteum), which dominated the waterfront of the Great Harbor. Originally constructed by Cleopatra VII (reigned 51–30 B.C.), the precinct of the Caesarion eventually included stoas, a library, and gardens. On the seaward side of the Caesarion two graceful obelisks were erected, plundered by Augustus from Pharaonic temples at Heliopolis (figure 4). These two monuments would have captured the attention of travelers who had just passed by the Pharos and entered the Great Harbor, immediately drawing their vision toward the temple of the Divine Augustus.[16] Philo strikingly captures the central place these buildings occupied in the city's design:

> For there is elsewhere no precinct like that which is called the Sebasteum, a temple to Caesar on shipboard, situated on an eminence facing the harbors famed for their excellent moorage, huge and conspicuous, fitted on a scale not found elsewhere with dedicated offerings, around it a girdle of pictures and statues in silver and gold, forming a precinct of vast breadth, embellished with porticoes, libraries, chambers, groves, gateways and wide open courts and everything which lavish expenditure could produce to beautify it—the whole a hope of safety to the voyager either going into or out of the harbor.[17]

Just east of the Caesarion was the former quarter of the Ptolemaic

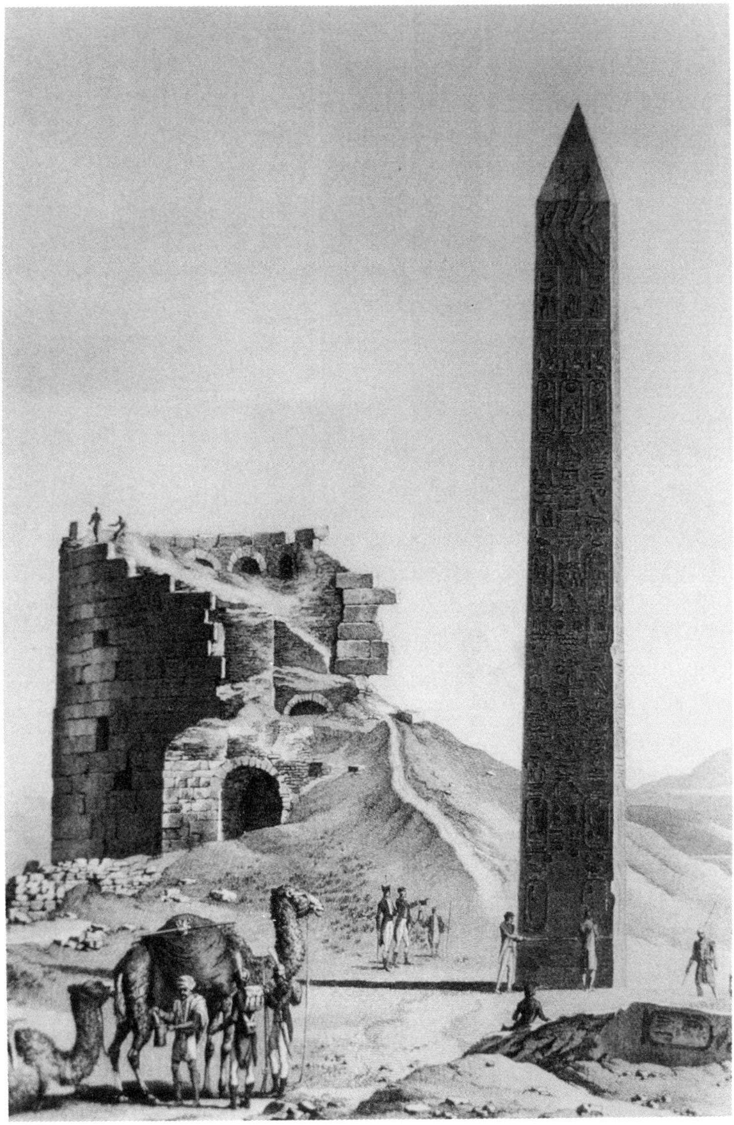

Fig. 4. Obelisks ("Cleopatra's Needles") at Caesarion and the "Tower of the Romans" along the shoreline of the Great Harbor. The standing obelisk is now in New York's Central Park, and the fallen one is now on the Thames Embankment, London.

(From *Description de l'Égypte,* Planches, Antiquité, Paris, 1822, vol. 5, pl. 32) palaces (called Bruchion during late antiquity), which extended from the ridge above the harbor out onto Cape Lochias (today al-Silsilah). Bruchion at one time was made up of palaces, parks, the royal docks, and the pyramidal tomb of Alexander the Great (known as the Sema or Soma). It also included the world-renowned Museon, where scientists, academics, and writers forged a unique and celebrated intellectual environment under the often-fickle patronage of Ptolemaic rulers. By late antiquity, however, this entire quarter lay in ruins, destroyed during civil conflict in the 270s.[18]

The importance of Alexandria's twin harbors was also emphasized by certain aspects of the city's design and architecture, which established a north-south "movement system" leading from Lake Mareotis to the harbors. In urban design, hills and gradual slopes lend themselves to architectural exploitation, and the broken limestone ridge on which Alexandria was built suited this role admirably. Toward the eastern sector of the city, a great theater was built into the side of the ridge, allowing the spectators to gaze down upon the Great Harbor and the Pharos. In the southwestern corner of the city, the temple of Serapis also made use of the limestone ridge, which only added to the temple's "massive and lofty dimensions." In this way, the Serapeum commanded a wide view over the whole city, particularly the vicinity of the Western Harbor. It appears that Diocletian chose to erect his victory column on this elevation in order to exploit these topographical advantages, rather than in a more central location in the city. The Paneion also was built on this limestone ridge, rising to a still greater height by sitting atop an artificially constructed hill, so that "from the summit one can see the whole of the city lying below it on all sides." It is no wonder that Ammianus Marcellinus, in the last decade of the fourth century, described Alexandria's skyline as having "temples pompous with lofty roofs."[19]

Man-made elements also contributed to this strong north-south sense of movement in Alexandria's design. Heavily traveled canals crossed the city, from the Canopic (or Schedia) canal south of the city to the Great Harbor, and from Lake Mareotis to an inner port in the Western Harbor. A broad colonnaded avenue bisected Alexandria, extending from Lake Mareotis to the Great Harbor in the vicinity of the Caesarion. Other streets ran parallel to this avenue, "practicable for horse riding and chariot driving." Two of these secondary streets from the later Roman period have been uncovered at Kōm el-Dikka: street R4 with an average width of 4.5 meters, and the colonnaded "rue thêâtral" averaging 7.5 meters in width.[20]

The pronounced north-south orientation of the city's configuration was more than offset by an equally strong east-west axis centered on the Via Canopica, Alexandria's principal boulevard. The dynamic tension produced by these two opposing movement systems in the city's design recalls the balance of contrasting forces so often expressed as a fundamental element in classical art and architectural design: vertical pottery shapes containing horizontal narrative designs, or tall fluted columns offsetting the crushing horizontal lines of entablature and stylobate.

It would be difficult to exaggerate the importance of the Via Canopica as the one architectural element that defined and tied together Alexandria's entire urban design. Extending in a straight line from one end of the city to the other, the Via Canopica perfectly fits William MacDonald's definition of an "armature," that is, "a clearly delineated, path-like core of thoroughfares and plazas that provided uninterrupted passage throughout the town and gave ready access to its principal public buildings." It was clearly the architectural axis for the city's entire design, and its width (30.5 meters) was four times that of Alexandria's other streets. It endowed Alexandria with "directional and spatial unity, an indivisibility underwritten by fluid, unimpeded connections."[21] In this respect, the design of Alexandria resembled that of other large cities of the Roman east. The Via Canopica performed the same function as the great colonnaded street of Palmyra, the street of Herod and Tiberius in Antioch, or the "Street called Straight" in ancient Damascus. Even more evocative is the similarity of Alexandria's design with another late antique port—Thessaloniki. Both cities were largely the creations of Hellenistic urban planners who laid down a great boulevard (the Via Egnatia in Thessaloniki) which bisected the city, running parallel to the harbor area and the upper city.[22]

In order to invoke some sense of the effect the Via Canopica had on Alexandria's inhabitants, we may turn to the famous description found in Achilles Tatius:

> I entered [Alexandria] by the Sun Gate, as it is called, and was instantly struck by the splendid beauty of the city, which filled my eyes with delight. From the Sun Gate to the Moon Gate—these are the guardian divinities of the entrances—led a straight double row of columns, about the middle of which lies the open part of the town, and in it so many streets that walking in them you would fancy yourself abroad while still at home. . . . I tried to cast my eyes down every street, but my gaze was still unsatisfied, and I could not grasp all the beauty of the spot at once; some parts I saw, some I was on the point of seeing, some I earnestly desired to see, some I could not pass by; that which I actually saw kept my gaze fixed, while that which I expected to see would drag it to the next. I explored therefore every street, and at last, my vision unsatisfied, exclaimed in weariness, "Ah, my eyes, we are beaten."[23]

Even after allowance is made for hyperbole and rhetorical inventiveness, this account vividly depicts the sense of architectural movement generated by the Via Canopica. This lengthy colonnaded avenue so impressed one later pilgrim that he took nearly nine hours to traverse it from end to end—no doubt, taking in all the sights along the way.[24]

The extent of the Via Canopica was confirmed archaeologically by soundings undertaken by Adriani, establishing the existence of a parallel street (L2 in el-Falaki's plan) just to the north of the Via Canopica. These soundings, which consisted of a pavement, wall, and mosaics datable to the late Roman or early Byzantine period, were located in the vicinity of the English Girls' School, and extend an intramural street well beyond the city plans previously suggested by Hogarth and Breccia. The original line of Via Canopica was first established at the beginning of the nineteenth century by Mayer, an Englishman, whose drawings of a ruined line of columns are reproduced in Adriani's *Repertorio*. This ancient colonnade coincided almost exactly with the modern Shari el-Horeyya.[25]

Most travelers coming to Alexandria from Egypt, either by land or by canal, entered the city at its eastern gate, the Gate of the Sun. Built by Antoninus Pius (emperor 138–61), this gate marked the formal boundary of the city and was strong enough to withstand repeated sieges from the time of Diocletian to the Arab conquest under ʿAmr ibn al-ʻAs. Just within the Gate of the Sun, a weary traveler could find accommodations at one of the many hostels that clustered in this district.[26]

Proceeding along the Via Canopica, one would pass by the Bruchion district with the remains of its palaces and stoas. Toward the center of the city, the street broadened into the spacious Agora surrounded by porticoes with a four-sided monumental arch at one end. Legal petitions were often posted in the Agora since the city lawcourts were located nearby. In addition, imperial edicts were proclaimed in the Agora, with the result that it served as the ceremonial heart of the city, bustling with activity from the wrangling of merchants and the cries of beggars to the imprecations of itinerant philosophers and teachers.[27] As one beggar implored his benefactor, "Crowds are what I need—I want to go back to the Agora!"[28] The size of the Agora permitted large groups of people to gather there for political purposes, to the extent that "those of the Agora" became a synonym for "the multitude" in late antiquity.[29] The gymnasium, possessing "porticoes more than a stadium in length," either adjoined the Agora or was situated nearby. Evidence for this gymnasium, the focal point of Hellenism in Alexandria, does not extend in time past the beginning of the third century.[30] However, the district around the Agora continued to boast numerous public buildings throughout the late Roman period. It is quite possible that the baths, lecture halls, and small theater located close-by at Kōm el-Dikka were designed, in part, to take over the social role formerly held by the gymnasium.

Beyond the two main gates of the city were a number of important extramural districts. A western necropolis grew up on the other side of the New Canal, and this region saw a gradual encroachment of suburban dwellings throughout late antiquity. Alexandria's eastern suburbs developed around two prominent sites: the hippodrome, and Augustus's garrison camp at Nicopolis. The position of the legionary camp took advantage of the east-west axis of the Via Canopica, allowing for the rapid intervention of Roman authority into the city via the Sun Gate. The camp's proximity to the hippodrome also facilitated the enforced maintenance of order during occasionally turbulent gatherings in this all-important Alexandrian locale. Moreover, Augustus must have recognized the strategic location of Nicopolis since he established the garrison on the only broad landward approach to the city.[31]

Athanasius, who knew Alexandrian topography as well as anyone in the fourth century, presents a marvelous picture of the city's configuration in a passage condemning the violent persecutions instituted by the Arians:

> Where is there a house [*oikon*] which they did not ravage? Where is there a family they did not plunder on pretence of searching for their opponents? Where is there a garden [*kēpon*] they did not trample underfoot? What tomb [*taphon*] did they not open, pretending they were seeking for Athanasius, though their sole object was to plunder and despoil all that came in their way? How many men's houses [*oikoi*] were sealed up! The contents of how many persons' lodgings [*xeniais*] did they give away to the soldiers who assisted them! Who had not experience of their wickedness? Who that met them but was obliged to hide himself in the marketplace [*agoran*]? Did not many a person leave his house from fear of them, and pass the night in the desert [*ermias*]? . . . And who, however inexperienced of the sea, did not choose rather to commit himself to it, and to risk all its dangers, than to witness their threatenings? Many also changed their residences, and removed from street to street [*lauras eis lauran*], and from the city to the suburbs [*apo tēs poleōs eis ta proasteia*].[32]

In this account, Athanasius describes the full range of topographical variation found in Alexandria: from center (Agora) to periphery (gates/hostels, suburbs, and necropoleis) and beyond (the desert). He also makes a rudimentary attempt at a hierarchical differentiation of the city's topography, by referring to houses, neighborhoods, and public areas.[33] Even the dangers of the reefs lying just beyond the Pharos are not neglected in this comprehensive summary, all the more remarkable for the genre of literature in which it is presented.

While not as detailed as Strabo's travelogue, this passage from Athanasius strikingly conveys a sense of Alexandria's urban landscape in the fourth century, complementing the account of Achilles Tatius with its strong feeling of sequential architectural impressions.

*Civitas Opulenta*

Despite Alexandria's many architectural glories evoking expressions of wonder from both visitors and inhabitants, the city would have remained the sleepy fishing village of Alexander's day were it not for its rich hinterland. Alexandria's relatively isolated geographical position earned it the epithet "Alexandria ad Aegyptum," that is, Alexandria "next to" or "toward" Egypt.[34] Even today Alexandrians speak of traveling "to Egypt." However, from the time of the Ptolemies to that of the Arabs, the prosperity of Alexandria was inextricably dependent upon the fertile lands of the Nile Delta and the regions up river. In the words of one anonymous second-century poet: "Seat of the immortal gods, august and wealthy, foundation of Alexander! The gentle climate and fertile soil of Egypt provide you with all good things, happy land! There is abundant grain, infinite flax; from your harbours sail ships with rolls of papyrus and brilliant glass."[35]

In part, this economic relationship was based on the exploitation of the interior as a source of agricultural goods and natural resources. These raw materials were then either directly consumed in the market created by a thriving metropolis or processed into merchandise that could be shipped to ports throughout the Mediterranean.

During the late Roman period (as also in the rest of antiquity), the most famous of these processed goods were papyrus, glass, and linen. An upper-class Roman dilettante described Alexandria at the end of the fourth century as "prosperous, rich, and fruitful, and in it no one is idle. Some are blowers of glass, others makers of paper, all are at least weavers of linen or seem to belong to one craft or another."[36]

These observations are echoed by other, more reliable, literary sources as well as by archaeological material. The finely made glass productions of Alexandrian workshops gained a wide currency, from the tables of emperors to the cupboards of rural villagers in the Fayyūm. One should not imagine, however, that these workshops were vast enterprises employing hundreds of workers. At Kōm el-Dikka, the ground floors of several neighboring residential dwellings were given over to the manufacture and sale of glass beads. The best preserved of these "workshops" consisted of eleven to fourteen small rooms, none more than six meters on a side, which were arranged around a modest courtyard. A more spacious room toward the rear seems to have been used as an office. Directly across the street from this building, a row of small *ergasteria* have been excavated, one of which contained an oven used in the manufacture of glass objects (see plan 2 in chapter 6). Although the scale of this commercial operation was small, it was highly developed. Glass molds made of granite and limestone have been discovered, as well as tubes of unfinished beads, which were formed around an inner shaft of iron when the glass was still pliable. In this way, the tubes of connected beads could be easily cut and strung together, producing delicate necklaces of red, green, dark blue, and yellow beads. It appears that the principal market for the products of these glass-works was not in export trade, but instead was drawn from members of the local populace who frequented the baths and theater nearby.[37]

The anonymous fourth-century author of the *Expositio* informs us that papyrus was manufactured "nowhere but in Alexandria and its region."[38] This is clearly an exaggeration, since papyrus is known to have been made elsewhere in the Delta. Nonetheless, the marshes in the vicinity of Alexandria provided an abundant supply of the slender plant. The limestone ridge lying west of the city, between the narrow arm of Lake Mareotis and the sea, gave its name to one popular brand of papyrus. Whether it was manufactured in the city itself or in the surrounding countryside, "Alexandrian papyrus" was a valued commodity in the bureaucracies of the late antique world—used alike by emperors, popes, and Frankish kings.[39] The production of this papyrus was so profitable that one unscrupulous Alexandrian bishop of the late 350s even attempted to gain a monopoly on the market.[40]

Woven goods, such as linen, tapestries, and embroidered fabrics, were also very popular items of export from Alexandria. During the fourth century, many of the more common Egyptian linens were manufactured in upper Egypt and then were sent to Alexandria as requisitioned goods, either on behalf of the government or for the church. There is also evidence for linen workshops in Alexandria during this period. A late Coptic martyrdom mentions a wealthy merchant who bought up all the flax in his nome with the intention of selling it to the linen workshops in Alexandria. The weavers who manned these looms appear to have been Egyptian fellahin who had migrated to the city, perhaps seeking higher wages. Attractive profits could be gained from the export of Egyptian linen, since we hear of linen merchants leasing their own vessels and also establishing themselves in bases as far away as Sicily. The importance of this trade during late antiquity can be gauged by a casual comment put into the mouth of Gallienus (emperor, 253–68) by the author of the *Historia Augusta,* who exclaims, "What! We cannot exist without Egyptian linen!"[41]

More specialized varieties of fabrics were also produced at Alexandria, which was noted for its manufacture of finely woven tapestries and garments. The poet Claudian and the monk-geographer Cosmas Indicopleustes both mention the fame of Alexandrian tapestries, and the Edict on Maximum Prices enumerates a type of Alexandrian fabric which imitated more expensive garments from Cilicia. A specialized variety of sewing, known as "the Alexandrian mending," occurs in a rabbinic source from the early fourth century. Together, these literary accounts depict a lively industry in luxury woven goods.[42] While more common linens could be manufactured easily in the villages of the Nile Valley, the production of luxury fabrics appears to have required more specialized craftsmen who tended to concentrate in the metropolis.[43]

Aside from these three main Alexandrian commodities, other items either produced in Alexandria or shipped via its harbors were in great demand in many regions of the late Roman world. For the most part, these tended to be luxury goods, since their high prices were able to spur on long-distance trade, even taking into account the many duties and tariffs imposed on them. Alexandria was renowned as the principal market in the empire for spices, perfumes, and exotic candies. Various medicines and drugs were also important exports, perhaps in part because of the fame of Alexandrian doctors. Precious stones, such as porphyry, alabaster, and red-flecked granite from Aswan, were also much sought after, as well as the exquisite creations of Alexandrian gem cutters and metalworkers. Some of these products were derived from Egypt's own natural resources, while others, particularly spices, came from beyond the empire's borders, with Alexandria serving as the main transit point in their long-distance exchange.[44]

Late antique Alexandria was also the conduit for a great variety of agricultural goods. The Egyptian wines that Pliny noted for their excellent quality during the early empire were requisitioned (along with other agricultural staples) in vast quantities by the imperial government in the fourth and fifth centuries. Although the cultivation of olives was relatively rare in Greco-Roman Egypt, radish oil appears to have been used extensively as a cheap substitute in the late Roman period. Barley and dates were other staples that the province exported in bulk to Constantinople and to the imperial armies on the frontiers. The collection, transport, and foreign distribution of these agricultural products was a business that could generate enormous profits for Alexandrian merchants. One trader in vegetables possessed a fleet of Nile barges and a business worth twenty thousand solidi. An Alexandrian merchant named Apollonius gave up his lucrative business in foodstuffs and became a monk at Nitria in the fifth century. However, his business instincts could not be denied, and he soon found himself providing "grapes, pomegranates, eggs, and cakes such as the sick fancy" to over five thousand monks in the monastic community. Not surprisingly, "he found this a very profitable livelihood in his old age."[45]

Even though the Nile facilitated inexpensive and efficient transport of agricultural goods, the principal supplier of these products to Alexandria was its immediate hinterland within a radius of some forty to sixty kilometers.[46] In this way, Alexandria followed a pattern of agricultural supply common to other large cities of antiquity, including Antioch, Ephesus, and, to a lesser degree, Rome itself. Alexandria's immediate hinterland may be divided, for the sake of convenience, into two distinct geographical areas: Mareotis, comprising the lands to the south and west of the lake, and the "territory [*chōra/regio*] of the Alexandrians," which extended from the lake's eastern shore as far as the Nile. This latter district became a separate nome sometime in the early Roman period with its metropolis at Hermopolis Parva (today Damanhūr). Throughout antiquity, the region contained extensive landholdings of Alexandrians, and helped to furnish the city's needs in meats and vegetables.[47]

Nonetheless, of the two districts subordinate to Alexandria, Mareotis was clearly the more important, not only because of its abundant output of agricultural goods, but also owing to its closer political and economic ties to the city. Mareotis, in fact, was made up of two regions, which need to be distinguished very carefully when the term is encountered in the ancient sources.[48] The first of these refers to the lake itself, which covered approximately three times its current area during antiquity.[49] A good measure of its size can be found in Palladius, the mid-fifth-century hagiographer, who informs us that it took him a full day and a half to cross from Alexandria to the monastic settlement of Nitria at the lake's southernmost shore.[50] During the late Roman period, its waters teemed with fish and waterfowl, and it was noted for its many papyrus marshes.[51] The inhabitants of Lake Mareotis carried on an existence not too much different from that of today's lake dwellers: living in reed huts either along the shoreline or on islands, and maneuvering among the maze of reeds in shallow-draft boats.[52] However, the lake's inhabitants in antiquity supplemented their income from fishing and papyrus gathering with another form of economic activity—piracy. Throughout the Roman era, brigandage was rife in the lake's regions, doubtless owing to the quantity of valuable Nile traffic plying its waters and the innumerable hideouts afforded by the marshes. It was only with difficulty that the authorities (both the government and the church) were able to suppress this piracy and redirect the energies of the lake's inhabitants.[53]

In late antiquity, the name Mareotis also referred to "a district of Alexandria, in which are contained very many villages, and an abundant population."[54] This semirural region south and west of the lake possessed ten or more villages and a larger urban center named Marea around which there was a countryside dotted with prosperous villas. The wealth of this district was largely due to viticulture, and the fame of Mareotic wine endured from the time of Strabo and Virgil to the Arab conquest and beyond. Archaeological remains from the region supply striking confirmation of the vital role held by wine production in the economy of Mareotis, since an elaborate wine "factory" has recently been discovered at a site some thirty kilometers from Alexandria. Made up of a series of presses and basins of various depths, this well-preserved complex measures approximately 16 by 9 meters, and has been dated by one of its excavators to the fifth or sixth century.[55] The Mareotis district also boasted a number of pottery kilns (factories?) during antiquity. One of these kilns, located near Taposiris Magna, measures at least 7.5 meters in diameter, making it clearly one of the largest in the Mediterranean basin.[56] Huge amphorae were found near the kiln, used either for export trade in Alexandria, or employed in the shipment of Mareotic products such as wine or oil.

The long westward arm of the lake and a series of canals provided for the easy transport of agricultural wares from the region.[57] The huge mounds of pottery sherds which stand near Alexandria's ancient lakeside port area attest to the volume of goods which crossed the lake. The intimate connection between Mareotis and Alexandria is also apparent from the ruins of an extensive port facility with several quays, discovered at a site not far from the wine factory in Mareotis (figure 5). Late antique hagiographical sources depict a busy harbor economy and the sometimes dangerous atmosphere of a port town. This same port also possessed a number of shops and storage facilities, as well as a church, which served the needs of another important sector of the region's economy—pilgrims.[58] After disembarking, these pilgrims proceeded a day's journey into the desert in order to visit the healing shrine of Saint Menas, which developed into a veritable city during the fifth and sixth centuries. A huge basilica, a baptistery, episcopal offices, several baths, and pilgrim hostels have all been found at this remote site, which is reminiscent of other healing shrines of antiquity, such as Epidauros and the Asclepeion at Pergamum.

Approaching the city from the chora, a traveler to Alexandria

Fig. 5. Shops and harbor facilities, Philoxenite. This port, about 30 kilometers southwest of Alexandria, was located on the long western arm of Lake Mareotis, and flourished during the sixth and early seventh centuries. It served as the principal link for pilgrims traveling from Alexandria to the shrine of Saint Menas.

might observe two very different forms of economic activity vital to the city's well-being. Just beyond the suburbs, various quarries and mines could be found which helped supply Alexandria's needs in building materials (particularly limestone from the area known as Mex) as well as more valuable minerals such as alabaster. The scale of these quarrying operations can be gauged by fourth-century papyrus receipts for requisitioned laborers who were recruited from as far away as the Fayyūm.[59] East of Alexandria and beyond the extramural necropolis was a sparsely inhabited region populated mainly by herdsmen and their flocks of sheep and cattle.[60] Portions of this area were so untamed that wild animals apparently scavenged at will there.[61] This district is known in the sources as Boukolia, or "the pasturage." Although grazing took place all along the shores of Lake Mareotis and extended as far as the Nile, the focus of the region's economic activity appears to have been an important cattle market just outside Alexandria's walls, not far from the camp at Nicopolis. The proximity of the troops to this pastureland was more than coincidental, since the shepherds and herdsmen of Boukolia were notoriously rough characters, known for assaulting travelers, murdering one another, and, on at least one occasion, breaking out into open rebellion against the Roman authorities. During the fourth century, various factions within the city recruited these violent men to attack political and religious opponents with their clubs and shepherds' staves.[62]

As we have seen, the economic relationship between Alexandria and its hinterland during late antiquity displayed great variation and could spill over into areas often regarded as strictly religious or social. The economic importance of the city was also predicated on exchanges of goods and services with the Egyptian countryside which could be either monetary or in kind. The great diversity of these exchanges is not surprising, especially given the volume of wealth flowing like the Nile to the city. On occasion, payments in kind are made to Alexandrians who have performed some service for individuals up river, such as an Alexandrian carpenter paid for his skills with wine in the early sixth century, or the Alexandrian businessman who arranged a loan and then received back the interest in the form of hemp.[63] However, the overwhelming majority of payments going to Alexandria in the late empire were taxes levied in both cash and in goods. These latter payments could take many forms, usually as grain, wine, meat, and clothing. More rarely, we hear of taxes paid in coal, wax, flax, and unprocessed wool. A measure of the church's growing dominance in the secular realm during the fourth and fifth centuries can be seen in the sending of "whole shiploads of wheat and clothing" to the patriarchate in Alexandria for the poor. Labor was also a valued commodity taxed by the Roman authorities, as is shown by a revealing document from Theadelphia in the Fayyūm which mentions construction workers, bakers, and carpenters who are compelled to perform requisitioned labor in Alexandria.[64]

A large proportion of the surviving papyri that mention Alexandria are concerned with the business dealings of persons from the towns and villages of the Egyptian countryside. These letters and documents show Alexandria to have been the source of a broad range of merchandise, from food items and books to purple dye and axles for waterwheels. A number of letters simply refer to unstated "business," perhaps relating to the city's vital role as a center of banking, moneylending, and currency exchange in late Roman Egypt. The courts of the prefect attracted a host of petitioners hailing from towns as far away as the Thebaid. In the early fourth century, one petitioner named Trophimus wrote to his father up river, and refers both to money he sent home as well as to unspecified luxury items, which he intended his family to sell. Alexandria's many goods and services were not restricted to purely economic categories. Trophimus, our young petitioner, seems to have acquired a lover in Alexandria whose moral reputation reached even the ears of his indignant father in Oxyrhynchus.[65]

As a center of higher education, the city also attracted large numbers of eager students. The importance of Alexandria's religious shrines further ensured a steady stream of tourists and pilgrims drawn from many different religious persuasions.[66] The broad spectrum of people from the chora who visited the city is well illustrated by the famous letter of Caracalla in 215. After mentioning, among others, "pig dealers and river boatmen and the men who bring down reeds for heating the baths," the emperor then speaks of "those who congregate here with the object of viewing the glorious city of Alexandria or come down for the sake of enjoying a more civilized life or for incidental business."[67] Despite these lofty motives, it appears that Alexandria was most commonly viewed as a large market town, where a peasant from the chora might find a buyer for some odds and ends.[68]

Of all the diverse economic activities joining late Roman Alexandria with the Egyptian countryside, none was greater than the vast network of supply and transport which embraced Alexandria's grain trade. This one enterprise is not only the most fully articulated and detailed commercial activity in the ancient sources, but it is also the one that best exemplifies the prosperity of the city during late antiquity.

Although this copious supply of grain could be shipped from Alexandria to various corners of the empire in times of special need, such as for extended military campaigns, the grain trade primarily was organized to supply in an efficient manner the requirements of the late empire's great cities—including Alexandria itself.[69] The efficiency of this system can be gauged by the astounding volume of grain shipped annually to Rome and later to Constantinople. During the height of the empire, Rome received upward of 13 million modii or 83,000 tons of grain per year from Egypt alone.[70] Under the late empire, when Egypt bore the responsibility for provisioning the rapidly growing population of Constantinople, 36 million modii or approximately 220,000 tons of grain were sent annually to the new capital.[71] This comes to roughly 5.5 million sackfuls, which would require 647 average-sized grain ships to sail annually from Alexandria's harbors. Factoring in the Egyptian harvest period and the sailing season for these cumbersome grain ships, over thirty-two fully loaded vessels would have sailed weekly from Alexandria over a period of four and a half months.[72]

Before it could be shipped to Rome or Constantinople, this incredible volume of Egyptian grain had to be first collected and then transported downstream to storage facilities in Alexandria. Our knowledge of this complicated network is illuminated by scores of surviving papyrus receipts required by the Roman government in order to document carefully each stage of shipment.[73] After threshing, the wheat was collected in granaries by the banks of the Nile. From these collecting points, fleets of river barges would then carry the grain down to the city. Sealed samples of each shipment were sent along to ensure its quality and guarantee that the grain was "unadulterated, with no admixture of earth or barley, untrodden and sifted."[74] Once in Alexandria, the barge captains unloaded their precious cargo at huge granaries located south of the city, near the shore of Lake Mareotis.[75] All of this was done under the watchful eyes of various Roman officials, acting on behalf of the administrative head of this vast network, the praefectus annonae Alexandrinae.[76] Only after the completion of this detailed cross-checking of accounts and shipments was the grain transported by canal across the city to the Western Harbor where the grain fleet rode at anchor. The manpower required to accomplish the transfer of this mountain of grain, sackful by sackful, must have been enormous.

Consequently, Alexandria's bustling wharves and dockyards were a beehive of activity, not only servicing the all-important grain fleet but also fitting out other merchant ships bound for an array of Mediterranean ports. Having filled the holds of their ships with an assortment of luxury goods, Alexandrian merchants plied a number of trade routes, which carried them along the coast of North Africa or up into the Adriatic. Some ventured even as far as Spain and Britain. In Strabo's day Alexandria's port on Lake Mareotis handled more goods than the harbors on the sea, thus indicating the high volume of trade coming from Egypt itself, as well as from regions farther south and east. This influx of merchandise continued unabated during late antiquity, for in the words of an anonymous geographer living some 350 years after Strabo, "Beyond the borders of the Thebaid, there are the peoples of India, and having received all manner of things from there, [Alexandria] exports them everywhere."[77]

Trade with regions to the east was conducted over caravan routes from Coptos or Edfu to the Red Sea port of Berenike, and then to the spice-producing lands of Arabia and India by means of the monsoon winds, the use of which in facilitating trade had been recently discovered.[78] From the second century to the Arab conquest, an alternative route was also employed which made use of a Ptolemaic canal dredged during the Antonine period, linking the Nile to the Red Sea at Clysma (Suez).[79] This latter route became commercially important during the third and fourth centuries, because of both the threat of marauding desert tribesmen along the caravan routes of the eastern desert, and also the destruction of Coptos during the insurrection of Achilleus in 298. Moreover, trade routes connecting the Roman world with kingdoms to the south and east were used by missionaries and diplomats alike—although Constantius in 356 had to admonish his ambassadors to curtail lengthy layovers in Alexandria and continue on with their diplomatic journeys![80]

Doubtless, the attractions of such a cosmopolitan entrepôt tended to outweigh the rigors of long-distance travel. These highly developed routes of trade and travel contributed to Alexandria's vital role as a channel of goods in the late Roman world, and its equally important function as antiquity's melting pot of ideas and philosophies drawn to the city from the entire *oikoumenē*.[81]

# Three

# The Social World

Alexandria's prosperity during late antiquity resulted from its role as an important center of production and international trade. As a consequence, the city was able to sustain a population which could rival that of the Urbs Aeterna, and surpass that of many other great cities of the late empire. The poet Ausonius ranked Alexandria on a par with Antioch, the other major city of the eastern Mediterranean in the fourth century.[1] However, it becomes a much more difficult task to discuss Alexandria's relative size and population in precise quantitative terms. This difficulty is exacerbated by the tendency of ancient writers to cast such questions in florid rhetorical language, designed to glorify the city rather than portray it with any precision. Achilles Tatius typifies this style when he describes Alexandria's size and population: "For the former was larger than a continent, the latter outnumbered a whole nation. Looking at the city, I doubted whether any race of men could ever fill it; looking at the inhabitants, I wondered whether any city could ever be found large enough to hold them all. The balance seemed exactly even."[2]

Diodorus Siculus informs us that the free population of Alexandria in 40 B.C. was 300,000. It is nearly impossible to assess the reliability of this figure, and when we consider the untrustworthy character of many such quantitative statements from antiquity, Diodorus's population figure may not take the inquiry much further than the comment of a ninth-century monk, Adamnan, that Alexandria "is an exceedingly populous city." Nevertheless, a reasonable estimate of the city's population throughout late antiquity is still possible on the basis of rough calculations regarding the city's size. Even though the exact course of the ancient walls can no longer be determined, it is still possible to arrive at some idea of Alexandria's total area and, by extension, of the city's population.

Several writers from the first century concur that Alexandria was approximately 30 stadia long from east to west and 10 stadia from the harbors to the canal. As confirmation of these figures, it is about 5,500 meters, or 30 stadia, from the western branch of the Mahmoudiya Canal to the site of the former Bab Rashid in the east (near the Gate of the Sun). Thus, the approximate area of the classical city was in the vicinity of 1,000 hectares. By multiplying the area by 200 persons per hectare (a figure less dense than that for Rome, but comparable with that of other contemporary cities) one arrives at a population of approximately 200,000—a conservative figure that could easily be pushed higher given reasonable modifications to any one of the variables.[3]

This calculation is virtually meaningless if it is required to stand alone. The population of a major city fluctuates over time, subject to unpredictable factors like famine, earthquake, plague, or invasion. This figure also does not take into account seasonal population shifts, suburbs like Nicopolis and Canopus, or the populated area spilling over the defined walled precinct. We know, for example, that in late antiquity, suburban villas began to dot the region to the city's immediate west, an area previously set aside for necropoleis. On the other hand, portions of the city's intramural area were reserved for agriculture, principally for the gardens and orchards of the wealthy, and the proportion of this urban agriculture steadily increased during late antiquity.[4]

Nonetheless, there are other checks on this rough estimate of population. A Syriac document which goes back to a Greek original of the fourth century A.D. lists the total number of Alexandria's private houses and courts (that is, common areas with small dwellings or apartments fronting on them).[5] Multiplying these totals by household averages furnished by papyri from other towns such as Oxyrhynchus and Karanis, we come to a total approaching 180,000.[6] Two literary sources from opposite ends of late antiquity tend to confirm these estimates. A papyrus dated to the second century mentions a figure of 180,000. Though fragmentary, many commentators believe it refers to Alexandria's population. Finally, in the ninth century, Ibn Abd al-Hakam estimated that the population of the city at the time of the Arab conquest stood at approximately 200,000.[7] While any one of these estimates may seem to be less than trustworthy, their cumulative voice may provide an indication of Alexandria's population in the later Roman period, at least within the city itself. In the last analysis, however, one must bear in mind that population estimates for ancient cities are often exercises in weaving insubstantial strands of gossamer, given the imprecision and fragmentary nature of the ancient sources. Alexandria fares only slightly better than other cities in this regard, but perhaps it is best to employ the scattered data on urban population simply to reinforce our image of Alexandria as one of antiquity's largest cities.

The populace of this teeming metropolis developed a highly elaborate social structure. Some patterns of social organization were imposed upon the Alexandrian population by the governing authorities—early on by the Ptolemies and later by the city's Roman masters. However, these often artificial systems of ordering (and controlling) the Alexandrians are not as instructive as the patterns of social organization which emerged spontaneously from the populace itself, since a certain degree of self-organization often occurs within large clusters of people. Further, the various ways in which Alexandria's inhabitants organized themselves provide fascinating insights concerning the all-important bonds of loyalty and association among the populace, the self-understanding of different subgroups, and finally the perimeters of group consciousness in late antique Alexandria—that is, the vital boundaries of "us" and "them."

Perhaps the most obvious of the imposed systems of social organization was the division of the city into various quarters (*grammata*) named for the first five letters of the Greek alphabet, as well as the further division of the five quarters into smaller subdistricts. This geographical division was carried out sometime in the third century B.C. and was in use up through the fourth century A.D.[8] A familiar parallel to this arbitrary division of Alexandria by the Ptolemies was Augustus's allotment of Rome into 14 *regiones* and 265 *vici*. Hadrian also applied this type of imposed social organization onto his new foundation at Antinoopolis, and carried the system further by enumerating blocks (*plintheia*) within each quarter. The practice continued in the late empire with the division of the New Rome, Constantinople, into named regions and smaller subdistricts.[9]

This artificially imposed structure was not likely to engender significant loyalties on the part of Alexandria's inhabitants. As Ramsay MacMullen observes, "Who, after all, would want to lay down his life for Letter B?" Moreover, by the time of Diocletian, the division of Alexandria's citizen body into tribe and deme had all but disappeared. This system, based partially on ancestral habitation within the city, was modeled on similar systems found in the Greek homeland. It was used extensively by Alexandrians in legal documents and contracts, thereby attesting its importance as a means of identification among the citizenry. This mark of citizenship also was closely related to membership in the Alexandrian gymnasium, a cultural institution that embodied the ideals of Hellenism and perpetuated the separateness of the Hellenized elite. Yet, while the gymnasia of Alexandria and other Hellenized towns in Egypt continued into the late empire, the twofold citizenship indicators of tribe and deme had fallen out of use over the course of the third century.[10]

Geography, however, remained an important determinant in the self-identity of Alexandrians throughout late antiquity. This can be observed on a smaller scale than that of the alphabetical quarters, especially at the level of neighborhoods and other narrowly defined geographical districts in the city—a level described by urban sociologists as comprising the "primary communities" within a given city. The strength of associative bonds in neighborhood communities is illustrated by an edifying tale from the mid-sixth century told by John Moschus. It seems that the orphaned daughter of some wealthy Alexandrians gave away most of her patrimony through an act of charity. Reduced to extreme poverty, she turned to prostitution. She became quite ill, returned to her old neighborhood and remorsefully asked her former neighbors to take her to the patriarch for baptism. They scorned her request and were appalled when she later returned from church dressed in the robes of the newly baptized. They rejected her story that two beings of augustal rank had served as her sponsors, and they demanded an investigation. The scandal reached the ears of the patriarch himself. He wisely discerned that it had taken two angels to override the rigid boundaries of decorum upheld by a neighborhood community.[11]

As in many other large Mediterranean cities, the neighborhoods of late antique Alexandria tended to focus on a particular trade, distinguishing topographical feature, or ethnic identity. Although the evidence is not as extensive as at Rome or Pompeii, it appears that Alexandrian streets and neighborhoods were even named, on occasion, after the commercial activity clustered in the area.[12] This pattern is confirmed by the excavations at Kōm el-Dikka, where street R4 was populated largely by glassworkers during the late Roman period, and a similar pattern can be seen to this day among the suqs and bazaars of the modern city. Other Alexandrian neighborhoods took their identity from prominent features in the urban landscape such as temples, baths, or fountains. Scraps of papyrus which preserve street directions speak of dwellings "beside the Iseum," "opposite the Nanaion, where the bath of Claudianus was," or "in the lane opposite the well."[13]

More commonly, Alexandrian neighborhoods were distinguished from one another by the ethnic communities that dwelt in them. The most famous of these was the so-called Jewish quarter, thought by some to be conterminous with the "Delta" district in the early Roman period. The city also contained other communal enclaves, such as Lycians and Phrygians. The southwestern sector of the city, known as Rhakotis from the village on Alexandria's original site, seems to have been populated by a concentration of Egyptians who had migrated to the city from the countryside.[14]

Many of the inhabitants of the Rhakotis district were employed as linen weavers, and the area was in all likelihood relatively poor, as it still is today. This brings up the question of geographical differentiation among Alexandria's social classes; that is, the degree to which certain sectors of the late antique city could be characterized by the socioeconomic standing of their inhabitants.[15] During the Ptolemaic and early Roman period, at least one region of the city, Bruchion, contained wealthy palaces and villas. However, by the fourth century the splendors of this district were only memories. Aside from designating certain obvious sectors as commercial (the harbors and markets), any labeling of particular zones as wealthy or poor can be only tentative at best.[16]

The need for caution in this regard can be well illustrated by the stratigraphy of certain areas at Kōm el-Dikka. The zone containing the "rue théâtral" was the site of spacious urban villas in the initial period following the Roman occupation. In the fourth century, these dwellings were cleared and a parklike zone of public buildings was built in their place. Less than a hundred meters away, a densely inhabited block of workshops and houses grew up. This entire region, in turn, was filled in and used as a cemetery or built over with rural-type dwellings in the Arab period.[17] Consequently, it is perilous to make confident assertions regarding the character of a particular region, barring careful archaeological investigation. And all the more should sweeping generalizations be avoided which would pigeonhole an area over the course of nearly a millennium of continuous habitation.

## *The Social Hierarchy*

Geographical considerations aside, however, there are other methods of exploring the social world of the Alexandrians in late antiquity. In recent years, scholars who have analyzed the nature of Roman society have tended to approach the topic using two broad interpretive models. The more traditional of these perspectives sees ancient society as being highly stratified, with distinct levels of social classes, each rigidly separated from one another by status indicators such as dress, education, political rights, and especially wealth. The other model does not entirely discount these factors, but instead emphasizes the bonds and loyalties between members of different classes. Further, this interpretation does not view the exploitation of the lower orders by the upper class as the leitmotif of social relations. On the contrary, the "vertical" ties formed by the exchange of mutually advantageous *beneficia* between patron and client are seen as the strands that bind together the social world—whether between emperor and senator, general and soldier, or landowner and tenant.[18]

For the purposes of understanding Alexandria's ethno-religious communal groups, the latter interpretation illuminates far better the forms of association which gave each group its communal identity during this period. Athanasius shares a great deal more in common with his supporters in the imperial grain fleet or in the monasteries of the desert than with the rabbis or philosophers leading the other communal groups in the city. Nonetheless, a "horizontal" or stratified approach to Alexandrian society in the late Roman period does illustrate certain aspects of this society which might otherwise be overlooked. While Jewish, pagan, and Christian merchants have very different perspectives on their world and their roles in it, they still inhabit the same niche in the social landscape and share common problems as they go about their businesses. The particular lines of patronage in the various communities might never cross in the normal course of events, but they would form along similar principles in a common urban environment. Consequently, by employing this stratified approach in a brief survey of Alexandria's socioeconomic classes, it is possible to elucidate further the city's complex social organization.

Urban society in late antique Alexandria appears to have been fundamentally two-tiered, with a small number of wealthy *honestiores* standing in contrast to the poorer bulk of the urban populace, or *humiliores*. This pattern is typical in many regions of the late empire, producing a social hierarchy that roughly parallels several of the rigidly stratified societies found in modern Central American nations rather than the more diversified industrial societies of the West. It might be objected that this is an inappropriate parallel, in the sense that modern Central American societies are primarily agrarian, whereas Alexandria's social organization grew up in a varied commercial environment—an economic setting that is often conducive to the growth of a middle class. However, there is very little evidence of what we might call a true middle class in late antique Alexandria. Wealth and poverty are relative terms, and it is not difficult to discover the "middle class" if we include within this group all those who were not destitute and could eke out an adequate living. This is hardly a serviceable definition, however, and falls short of identifying a distinct class of "participants in the urban economy of production, distribution, and services, owners of establishments of one sort or another rather than workers for others."[19] These individuals are easily distinguished in the towns of the Egyptian chora. Where are their Alexandrian counterparts? Unfortunately, Alexandria lacks the rich papyrological documentation that casts such a vivid light on the social world of the middle class in the countryside. This loss is offset only in part by archaeological material from Kōm el-Dikka, which hints at a social grouping immersed in workshop production. Another major factor limiting our knowledge of an Alexandrian middle class is the social bias of the surviving literary sources, most of which come from the pens of aristocratic writers.[20] For these elite authors, everyone not of their privileged status is easily consigned to the *ochlos*—the mob.

Yet the snobbery of the upper class is partially borne out by the social and economic realities of the day. While certain members of the Alexandrian middle class undoubtedly flourished, they were far closer to their poor neighbors than to the city's aristocracy. Despite subtle gradations in prosperity and poverty among the lower orders, the opulent and privileged life-styles enjoyed by the Alexandrian elite in late antiquity placed this class on a vastly different social level than that of most Alexandrians. Even the housing above the ergasteria in Kōm el-Dikka was extremely modest in size compared with villas both within the city and in the suburbs.

The Alexandrian upper class is most often identified in our sources by the holding of civic magistracies. Yet the perimeters of this urban elite may be expanded to include those Alexandrians eligible for local offices, usually denoted by a seat in the Alexandrian senate/council or *boulē*. Since patterns of office holding tend to be hereditary, it is thus possible to speak of a "bouleutic class" made up of these *bouleutai* and their families, equivalent for the most part to the *ordo decurionum* in the more familiar *municipia* of the Roman West. The continuity of this group was further reinforced in 436 by an imperial edict that prolonged the liability to hold office and perform compulsory public services to a period of thirty years or more. Gradations appear among the Alexandrian bouleutic class, since we hear frequently of the five chief councillors of the boule, as well as certain members of the council known as *honorati* who were freed from otherwise obligatory (and costly) civic duties. Alexandrian bouleutai of these higher ranks were also exempted from "corporal indignities" (*a corporalibus iniuriis*), the increasingly widespread practice of corporal punishment to which ordinary local senators were liable.[21]

Although office holding was a vital status indicator for the Alexandrian elite, a particular cultural or religious allegiance does not seem to have been a determining factor in class identity. Athanasius would have us believe that a large percentage of the Alexandrian bouleutai in the fourth century comprised pagans, since he refers to them as idolaters and heathens. However, there is evidence that a number of these upper-class Alexandrians acted as powerful patrons of the church. Several of the "chief men of the city" arranged an elaborate burial for the bishop/martyr Peter in 311. A century later, one of the local magistrates was the driving force behind the murder of the pagan philosopher Hypatia, in a period of escalating intercommunal violence. Athanasius himself mentions certain "wellborn men" who were persecuted during the Arian conflict in 339.[22] This inconsistency in Athanasius's characterization of the urban elite is perhaps best explained by the general unwillingness of those in the Alexandrian upper class to hold politically inconvenient opinions during the controversies of the age. Athanasius caustically depicts them changing their allegiance from the Meletian party to the Arian faction,

> and if the emperor should command them to adopt any other profession, they are ready to change again to that also. Their ignorance of true godliness quickly brings them to submit to the prevailing folly, and that which happens to be first taught them. For it is nothing to them to be carried about by every wind and tempest, so long as they are only exempt from compulsory duties and obtain the patronage of men; nor would they scruple probably to change again to what they were before, even to become such as they were when they were heathens.[23]

In light of the frequent reversals in the political and religious controversies of late antiquity, it is no wonder that the social class with the most to lose took pains to embrace positions that would be deemed inoffensive. The political realities of the day called for "easy-natured men" (*eukoloi*).[24] Their nonconfrontational stance was bound to raise the ire of a factious patriarch who had been exiled several times for his views—and who, consequently, presents us with an often tendentious account of Alexandrian history during his episcopate.

These upper-class political chameleons also proved to be especially adroit at a variety of shrewd business activities. Some aristocrats were urban landlords, possessing numerous income-producing properties within Alexandria. Other bouleutai engaged in financial speculation by floating loans on behalf of the Roman fiscal administration in the city. Apparently, while the traditional ideals of the proper aristocratic life excluded the acquisition of wealth through trade and business, the Alexandrian elite during late antiquity did not scorn commerce as a déclassé activity. In this manner, the Alexandrian upper class resembled its counterparts in Rome and Asia Minor who supplied the financial backing for dependent *negotiatores* during the late republic and early empire. Papyri from Upper Egypt indicate that Alexandrian bouleutai carried out their commercial dealings through personal business agents (or *pragmateutai*). In the late third century, one Alexandrian councillor named Calpurnius Horion employed an agent in Oxyrhynchus over the course of fifteen years.[25] The widespread use of business agents by the Alexandrian elite is also reflected in a monastic tale of the early fifth century recounting the ascetic adventures of two upper-class brothers. A strong factor influencing them to renounce the world was the realization that, if a life of commerce was followed, "we would have to entrust our business to others."[26]

Not all wealthy Alexandrians consigned their business dealings to pragmateutai. The sources from our period frequently mention Alexandrians who engage in trade themselves, or are at least described as shipowners (*nauklēroi*). In 334, the latter were specifically exempted from compulsory magistracies in the city by an imperial edict, and it is for this reason that they are seldom referred to as bouleutai. As a result, it is difficult to determine whether these shipowners should be considered, strictly speaking, as members of the "bouleutic class," especially since some of the shipowners were not rich men. The same social ambiguity holds true for those merchants who clearly were more than just petty traders. Because of their successful mercantile ventures, these men were able to amass tremendous fortunes, at times on a scale as great as twenty thousand solidi. One merchant, who acquired his wealth trading in Spain, left an inheritance of five thousand nomismata, luxurious clothes, and a retinue of slaves. Even though these merchants might have been considered nouveaux riches by Alexandrian councillors with more respectable pedigrees, the mere fact of their wealth made them an integral part of the city's upper class. Indeed, John of Ephesus relates that these shipowners were "the most powerful class in that wealthy city."[27]

Despite the commercial proclivity displayed by some members of the Alexandrian upper class, the economic activity most commonly associated with them was the ownership of agricultural land in the chora. For that matter, next to holding magistracies in various towns, the Alexandrian elite is most often encountered in the papyri either buying, selling, or leasing property in Upper Egypt. This, in itself, tells us very little about the relative importance of landholding in the lives of the elite, since Egyptian papyri are largely taken up with matters concerning the ownership of land. Moreover, the survival rate of the papyri is skewed toward receipts, letters, and contracts found in this region.

Nonetheless, the evidence suggests that Alexandrian bouleutai considered landholding to be a vital part of their economic (if not social) well-being. A sampling of the extant papyri reveals a strong pattern of land tenure, which continued well into the fourth century. Some of these upper-class property owners possessed a house (or houses) in Alexandria, a house situated in an up-country nome metropolis, as well as several tracts of agricultural land. In the second and third centuries, Alexandrians are found in the papyri leasing rural land and, in turn, subletting it for a profit to cultivators of wheat or grapes. During the course of the fourth century, documents referring to property ownership increasingly mention ex-councillors from Alexandria or their descendants who had inherited family property. This seems to indicate a trend of former councillors leaving Alexandria and settling in the chora on a permanent basis.[28] Property-owning bouleutai from Alexandria become quite rare in ancient sources from the fifth century up to the time of the Arab conquest. It is only toward the end of the period that we begin to see some of these landed *despotēs* taking up sporadic residence in the city. Yet, under these changed conditions, one cannot speak of a return of bouleutai to Alexandria with all of the connotations of a return to civic life, but instead rural powerbrokers acquiring a base of operations in a city which could provide important goods and services.[29]

During the height of the Arian crisis, Athanasius complained that unworthy men were being consecrated to episcopal office solely "on account of the wealth and civil power they possessed." Elsewhere, he accuses Alexandrian bouleutai "famous for their wealth" of eagerly seeking episcopal appointment throughout Egypt for no other reason than obtaining the clerical exemption from certain taxes and compulsory public duties.[30] In this way, the Alexandrian elite followed a well-established pattern of office holding in the towns and metropoleis of the countryside. Across the first three centuries of Roman rule in Egypt it was quite common for Alexandrian bouleutai to hold metropolitan magistracies, sometimes concurrently in more than one locale. Doubtless, the wealth and influence of these Alexandrians rendered them powerful patrons for their rural clients. By the fourth century, however, Alexandrian bouleutai virtually disappear from lists of magistrates in the chora.[31] In Oxyrhynchus, they vanish altogether. In part, this may result from former bouleutai becoming assimilated thoroughly into the society of rural towns and villages. It may also reflect a general unwillingness to take up previously popular civil posts once it became clear that the financial burdens of office clearly outweighed any possible benefits. In the fourth century, the path to career advancement led to imperial administration or to an increasingly powerful and wealthy church. It was not difficult for the Alexandrian councillors to recognize the opportunity afforded by the shortage of officially sanctioned bishops in the chora. Wealth and political power continued to be the hallmarks of the Alexandrian upper class.

The lower social orders in the city enjoyed neither of these advantages to any appreciable degree during the late empire. Yet their cumulative political and economic importance ensured that faction leaders throughout late antiquity would actively canvass for their support in the various conflicts that racked the city. Unfortunately, the bulk of the information available to us concerning the Alexandrian *plebs* comes from the pens of authors who reflect the prejudices of the educated, aristocratic elite. In the eyes of these authors, the common people of the city are "wholly light-minded, unstable, most seditious," or "extremely frivolous and easily aroused for very trivial reasons." Even the admiring pagan emperor Julian describes them as "lawless," and "incensed." Christian writers, who often come from the same upper-class educated circle as their pagan contemporaries, are no more charitable in their depictions of the Alexandrians—"an irritable race, excited to sedition," in a city "half-crazed with the riots of her frantic populace." It is therefore extremely difficult to get past the stock characterizations found in the literary sources and construct a detailed social description of these lower-class Alexandrians. Just as Athanasius's writings distort our picture of factional conflict in fourth-century Alexandria, the literary topos of a violent Alexandrian *turba* can only obfuscate a proper understanding of a complex urban society.[32]

Some of the contours of this variegated social landscape begin to emerge when one turns to the city's many *collegia/synadoi*. These associations most often developed on the basis of a particular craft or cult. However, Alexandrian collegia could assume innumerable forms, ranging from drinking clubs to the "society of the scrapers"—an athletic association taking its name from grooming implements commonly used in the gymnasia. Other Alexandrian collegia were less flamboyant, although perhaps more important because of their function in Alexandrian society. This is particularly true of the trade and craft associations that were made up of Alexandrian workers from across the entire spectrum of the local economy: sailors, linen workers, carpenters, bakers, gem cutters, shoemakers, gravediggers, water carriers, and an assortment of shopkeepers (figure 6). Since many occupations tended to run in families for several generations in other cities of late antique Egypt, Alexandrian

Fig. 6. In the workshop. Carpenter with plane. Ivory relief, Alexandria, third or fourth century. Princeton, inv. y1956-105

(The Art Museum, Princeton University. Bequest of Albert Mathias Friend Jr.)

trades may have exhibited a similar pattern, thereby serving to strengthen the associative bonds among the collegia.[33]

Within each of the Alexandrian collegia, a hierarchy developed which gave special status to the collegial elders (*archigerontes*) and stewards (*dioecetai*). Even the association of Alexandrian prostitutes appears to have had its own chosen leader. The distinctive role of these officers in the citizen body as a whole is revealed by the chapter title in the *Codex Theodosianus* which refers to them—*de Alexandrinae Plebis Primatibus*. At the other end of the social scale, however, one could also speak of "the poor from the associations." Nevertheless, the bonds uniting members of these collegia could be so strong as to create a quasi-autonomous form of social organization which existed within the city's ethno-religious communal groups; in the Great Synagogue, for example, we find that Alexandrian Jews were seated according to their membership in various craft associations. In addition, corporate identity among the collegia led certain of these associations to address emperors through dedicatory inscriptions. At the close of the second century, the Alexandrian naukleroi offered public congratulations to both Commodus and Septimius Severus.[34]

The Alexandrian collegia were recognized by the Roman authorities as distinct corporate bodies within the urban populace and, as such, were accorded certain rights and duties. In the fourth and fifth centuries, much more is heard of the latter—for example, the requirement that the collegia keep the city's canals properly dredged. These associations were also responsible for collecting the city's portion of the empirewide tax on urban commerce, the *collatio lustralis*.[35]

Further, the ready-made organization afforded by the collegia could be manipulated for political ends. Throughout the late Roman period, the Alexandrian patriarch made frequent use of his ardent supporters among the ship captains and sailors of the grain fleet. These patriarchal clients often carried the bishop's letters and treatises along with the all-important cargoes that filled the holds of their vessels. On numerous occasions, sailors drawn from the Alexandrian grain fleet were mobilized to provide strong-armed assistance for the patriarch at church councils held in ports far from Egypt. The long-standing political support given to the patriarch by these maritime collegia could also be turned against them, since they were singled out for persecution by Arian authorities in several instances during the fourth century. There are also indications that other Alexandrian collegia were mobilized to fight on one side or another throughout late antiquity. During the bloody conflicts attending the Arian controversy in 339, Athanasius's partisans were attacked after "the trades [*ergasiai*] were stirred up against them." These Alexandrian workers are identified as persecutors and are depicted against an undifferentiated background of "the pagan multitude" (*ethnikoi dēmoi*)—offhanded testimony to the effectiveness of the collegia as a means of organizing the urban populace.[36]

Once we look beyond the collegia, it becomes much more difficult to distinguish particular elements among the nonelite social classes of late antique Alexandria. Although one often encounters "the people of Alexandria" (*ho Alexandreōn dēmos*), such a broad, undifferentiated term is virtually meaningless in reconstructing the city's social world. It is of some interest, though, that Alexandrian citizenship appears to have been a desirable indicator of status, even after the Constitutio Antoniniana granted Roman citizenship to all of the empire's free inhabitants in 212. Caracalla himself drew a distinction between true Alexandrians and Egyptians who had migrated to the city. Later in the same century, Alexandrian citizenship was one of the many qualifying marks for recipients of the grain dole in Oxyrhynchus. Individuals who identify themselves as Alexandrian citizens also appear in papyri from the fourth century. Even as late as the fifth century, Macarius, the famous ascetic from Alexandria, was differentiated from his contemporary of the same name by the epithet, *politikos*—"belonging to the city," or even, "the citizen."[37]

The only other stratum of the Alexandrian populace which receives more than cursory notice in the ancient sources is the urban poor. John the Almsgiver is quoted by Leontius as graphically describing the contours of poverty in late antique Alexandria:

> How many are there at this minute grinding their teeth because of the cold? And how many have only a rough blanket half below and half above them so that they cannot stretch out their legs but lie shivering, rolled up like a ball of thread? How many would like even to have a sniff at the wine which is poured out in my wine cellar? How many would like to be filled with the outer leaves of the vegetables which are thrown away from my kitchen? How many strangers [*xenoi*] are there at this hour in the city who have no lodging-place but lie about in the marketplace [*en tē agora*], perhaps with the rain falling on them? How many are there who have not tasted oil for one month or even two? How many have no second garment either in summer or winter and so live in misery?[38]

Determining the proportion of Alexandria's population which could properly be classed among the poor is impossible, since many Alexandrians dwelt along the margins of poverty. However, the number of destitute individuals receiving regular subsidies from the church in the early seventh century was estimated at 7,500. The social location of these "poorest of the poor" may be gleaned from the term commonly used to refer to them—*anexodos*. Although this term usually is rendered as "beggar," the desperate social plight it depicts can be seen better in its other shades of meaning: "unfit for society, unsocial, with no outlet or recourse, unable to escape." To alleviate their condition, both the Roman government and the church organized charitable enterprises such as the distribution of alms and grain, and also set up poorhouses and hospitals throughout the city. It is quite possible that steps were taken in this direction long before the formal establishment of charitable institutions in the fourth century. Beggars had long frequented the Agora of the Caesarion, which might indicate that the temple of the Divine Augustus was a center for public and private donations to the poor, in much the same way that beggars even today congregate at the portals of churches and mosques in Mediterranean cities.[39]

Joining the urban poor on the bottom rung of the Alexandrian social ladder were the city's slaves. This segment of the urban population leaves very little trace in the extant sources. However, the surviving references to slaveholding in Alexandria fit well into the pattern found elsewhere in ancient cities: an occasional wealthy *oikos* with many slaves, and a greater number of smaller urban households possessing no more than a handful at any one time. The precarious daily existence of these slaves varied according to the relative harshness of their masters, with the degree of cruelty perhaps alleviated somewhat by the moral strictures of religious leaders.[40]

### *Civic Institutions: Windows on Alexandrian Society*

This stratified social analysis of late antique Alexandria is helpful in introducing the city's various social classes. Nonetheless, it distorts our view by presenting a static snapshot of these groups, and only rarely does it show them interacting with one another. Perhaps a more useful way to approach this topic would be to examine briefly those instances when the entire spectrum of Alexandrian society gathered together for one reason or another. Riots, violent demonstrations, and intercommunal clashes are an obvious and much studied category of urban gathering. However, such atypical events tell us little about the normal state of social relations in the late antique city and are better described in terms of Alexandria's distinct communal groups—that is, through a "vertical" analysis of Alexandrian society based on community, rather than a "horizontal" approach based on class.

Day-to-day social relations among Alexandria's classes may be illuminated by observing those regular occasions when the city's population gathered together. Here, attention should be paid to the city's major institutions that served as foci for urban gatherings and gave tangible expression to the city's social organization. Some of these institutions were class specific, such as the boule, and consequently do not adequately represent the city's social complexity. Other institutions were even more restrictive, as in the case of the Alexandrian gymnasium, where membership was based on Alexandrian citizenship as well as other status indicators, such as ancestry and adherence to a common Hellenic culture.[41] The city's educational institutions were also class specific, largely restricted to the wealthy and more cultured elements of the populace. Moreover, many of these educational institutions were segregated so that the ideals and traditions of each ethno-religious community could be faithfully transmitted to the young, whether in a synagogue school, a pagan lecture hall, or a Christian catechetical school. As a result, the city's educational institutions were important forces for promoting class consciousness and for solidifying communal differentiation. The far-flung reputation of each of these respective schools was a measure of their success in maintaining communal distinctiveness while jostled together in such a cosmopolitan milieu.

Other institutions in the city could be characterized as both multiclass and multicommunal. As in other late antique cities, the theater and the hippodrome held preeminent positions in the social life of Alexandria. Although the populace enjoyed very different types of entertainment in these institutions, they are best discussed together, since they had similar functions in Alexandria's social world. This connection is also evidenced by the small theater, or *odeion,* at Kōm el-Dikka (figure 7), in which was discovered a variety of inscriptions referring to Alexandrian charioteers and cir-

Fig. 7. Theaterlike structure, Kōm el-Dikka. View from the west. In the foreground, a portion of the colonnaded street. Late antique.
(M. Rodziewicz)

cus factions.[42] In addition, both the Alexandrian theater and hippodrome were wildly popular in late antiquity and provided a convenient forum for government officials to interact with the urban crowd.

The Alexandrians were renowned in the later Roman period for their great (perhaps excessive) devotion to the theater. This form of entertainment drew Alexandrians from every element of the urban population, from Alexandrian Jews who kept their Sabbath by attending dancing exhibitions to Christian grammarians who frequented the mimes of local acting troupes as much as the sermons of the patriarch. Papyri, upper-class literature, and monastic writings all mention the "players of harp and the flute, actors and jesters from the mimes, jugglers, and all kinds of slaves," in whom the Alexandrians took such great pleasure. In this respect, the Alexandrians resembled their contemporaries in Antioch, "who think more of the pantomime dancers than of sun and moon and darkness itself." It is noteworthy that one of the best preserved flutes from antiquity was discovered in Alexandria's Chatby region, not far from the site of the theater. The Alexandrians' fondness for theatrical performances was so great that the emperor Justin (518–27) found it advisable at one point to exempt the city from a general order banishing dancers from the empire. Church canons vainly attempted to prohibit Christians from attending the theater. Even priests were not immune from the allurements of the stage. The hippodrome, however, did not lag behind in popularity among the urban crowd. For as Dio Chrysostom said, the Alexandrians are "a folk to whom you need only throw plenty of bread and a ticket to the hippodrome, since they have no interest in anything else"—echoing the *panem et circenses* so eagerly sought by the Roman populace.[43]

With crowds drawn from every sector of Alexandrian society, these arenas for large public gatherings served as important points of interaction between the Roman authorities and the urban populace. On occasion, the prefect would proclaim imperial edicts in the theater or hippodrome, and might address the crowd on points of policy. Likewise, the crowd might use these opportunities to seek redress from the government, as in 453 when the populace petitioned the prefect Florus in the hippodrome to reopen the baths and restore the city's grain *annona.* As natural foci of public gatherings, the theater and hippodrome might also be the scene of more violent expressions of the crowd's will. In 391, a large portion of Serapis's great statue was burned by a Christian mob in the theater, and a century and a half later, the body of the Chalcedonian patriarch Proterius "was burnt with fire in the hippodrome." This use of the theater and hippodrome as urban gathering places and as channels for public opinion can be paralleled in other large cities of the empire (including Rome, Antioch, and Constantinople), and followed a tradition that may be traced back to Hellenistic or early imperial times.[44]

In many cities of late antiquity, the expression of the crowd's will (whether in approbation or discontent) was institutionalized in the factions of the hippodrome. The nature of these factions has been the subject of intense controversy among scholars during the past half century, especially concerning the degree to which the hippodrome factions were politicized and the ways in which they affected the course of events in the imperial capital of Constantinople.[45] Some commentators view the factions as thinly veiled political parties that actively promoted the interests of various causes and personalities, whereas others maintain that they remained essentially sporting clubs and societies of fans.

These circus factions existed also in Alexandria and engendered deep loyalties among their adherents. The graffiti from the theater at Kōm el-Dikka refer to no less than nine charioteers who are identified with either the Green or the Blue *factio,* and crude inscribed drawings on the theater's walls depict chariots and palm-bearing charioteers.[46] This does not mean, however, that these factions may be properly described as political groups. Despite the quasi-political role assigned to the Alexandrian factions by the editor of the Kōm el-Dikka graffiti, the inscriptions themselves only exhort the charioteers to victory in upcoming races.[47] Further, two early fourth-century papyri provide us with illuminating information regarding the ways in which the faction stables were supplied during this period. Both mention a certain Hephaestion who is described as "the *factionarius* of the Blues at Alexandria" as well as "the horsebreeder of Alexandria"—thereby ascribing to this faction leader a distinctly apolitical role. Moreover, one of the papyri concerns a quantity of barley that was to be sent to Hephaestion on the orders of no less an authority than the prefect himself. During the sixth century, the prefect even contributed 320 solidi of Alexandria's annual budget for the upkeep of thirty-six racehorses. It seems hardly credible that the prefect would subsidize an institution whose activities were inimical to imperial interests and to the often disturbed peace of the city. Only in the changed atmosphere of the seventh century do we find evidence for Alexandrian hippodrome factions taking on unequivocally political characteristics.[48]

Prior to that time, the theater was the primary setting for collective protest and organized demonstrations, both of which could easily escalate into outright political violence. The role of the theater in popular expression is echoed in Dio Chrysostom's comment that "in the theater the people's character is revealed." This character was not always peaceful, as evidenced by the riot of A.D. 66, which broke out when pagans at a public meeting in the theater accused

Jews in attendance of being spies and subsequently burned them alive. A remarkably similar incident took place three and a half centuries later, when a partisan of the patriarch was denounced to the prefect by members of the Jewish community who accused him of having come to the theater "for no other purpose than to excite sedition among the people." The prefect had him flogged on the spot, much to the delight of the audience. As in the early Roman period, the theater remained an important venue for show trials, thereby elevating judicial proceedings to the level of a civic spectacle.[49]

It is tempting to ascribe the violence associated with the Alexandrian theater to organized groups of professional demonstrators and slogan chanters commonly known as the theater claque. These theatrical fan clubs, often in the employ of the performers themselves, became politicized during the late empire and used theater gatherings as a forum for shouting their approval or criticism of government policy. Their success in stimulating public opinion can be gauged by the prominent role played by the theater claque in stirring up the so-called Riot of the Statues which brought Antioch to the brink of revolt and disorder in 387. However, there is no evidence to suggest that Alexandria in the late empire followed Antioch's example with regard to the part played by a professional theater claque. Granted, Nero was much taken by the rhythmic applause and distinctive dress of the Alexandrian claque in the first century—so much so that he recruited over five thousand young men to imitate the "Alexandrian style" of applause when he performed. In 193, a more politicized role was played by the claque when groups in Rome jeered Didius Julianus and called for the accession of Pescennius Niger. Niger had built up a solid base of support in the Roman East, and it is possible that the influence of the Alexandrian claque can be seen in the organized cheers of the Roman crowd. Caracalla undoubtedly recognized the adverse political potential of Alexandria's theater (and, ultimately, of the theater claque) when he abolished all forms of public entertainment in the city at the time of his murderous visit in 212.[50]

Nonetheless, the Alexandrian claque was a factor of little or no importance in the formation of popular opinion within the city during late antiquity. On those occasions when organized demonstrations took place in the theater, the source of the disturbances can be found in the communal organization of Alexandria's distinct ethno-religious groups. In the late 450s, it was an ad hoc group of Monophysite "citizens," not an institutionalized claque, who "prepared the others to cry out, 'Not one of (the Proterians) shall set his foot here, neither shall the transgressors be received!'" The violent incidents of 414/15 took place when members of one Alexandrian community, the Jews, persuaded the prefect to punish the outspoken theatergoing supporters of the patriarch. This "Christian claque" (if we may use the term) was led by a grammarian whom Socrates Scholasticus describes as "a very enthusiastic listener of bishop Cyril's sermons," and one who "made himself conspicuous by his forwardness in applauding." In the aftermath of the events of 415, imperial edicts were issued to regulate another group among the patriarch's supporters—the shadowy *parabalani,* who appear to have had something to do with hospital organization in the city. While not delving into the thorny problems of this group's origin and role as a violent wing of the patriarch's entourage, it should be noted that on two separate occasions the emperor specifically forbade the parabalani "to attend any public spectacle whatever." Thus, these organized groups of vocal and sometimes violent partisans, composed on the basis of communal solidarity, gradually came to usurp the traditional role of the Alexandrian theater claque during late antiquity. Considering the enormous popularity of the theater among all sectors of the Alexandrian plebs, it is easy to understand Socrates' comment that, in this setting, "disorder [was] almost invariably produced."[51]

Other gathering points within the city complemented the important social functions of the Alexandrian theater and hippodrome during the late antique period. Alexandria's ethno-religious communities spawned a host of religious institutions in the form of temples, synagogues, and churches that served as communal foci for these various groups. Other less documented Alexandrian social centers, such as baths or taverns, should be seen as more prosaic gathering points, but they can hardly be called civic institutions in the traditional sense, owing to their sheer numbers and their diffusion throughout the city. One source from the fourth century estimates that Alexandria's various quarters and neighborhoods held no less than 1,561 baths and 845 taverns. A purported letter of the Arab conqueror, ʿAmr ibn al-ʿAs, makes the fantastic claim that the captured city contained as many as 4,000 baths. Even if one accepts Fraser's suggestion that the fourth-century total for Alexandrian baths includes both public and private bathing facilities, most of them were probably rather small, considering the quantity of these establishments. However, some of the public baths must have been quite impressive, in light of the bath complex currently being uncovered at Kōm el-Dikka which measures at least fifty-five meters on a side. During the reign of Justinian, nearly five hundred solidi from the municipal budget were earmarked for the maintenance of Alexandria's large public baths. The city's smaller baths and taverns should best be understood on the level of the neighborhood, and doubtless served as natural gathering places for neighborhood residents. These taverns probably resembled the more familiar *tabernae* or *popinae* of Pompeii and Ostia, and might be better described as corner wineshops. The importance of these local centers can be gauged by Athanasius's irritation over the spread of Arian doctrine in Alexandria via the singing of popular Arian songs in the city's many taverns.[52]

All of these social institutions, from the hippodrome to the taverns, constituted the flesh and bone of the urban experience in late Roman Alexandria. In a certain sense, they defined and articulated the very essence of urban life in the city. This is borne out by a monastic source from the fifth century which recounts the misadventures of a brother who left the monastic community at Nitria (south of Lake Mareotis) and traveled to Alexandria. Palladius tells us that, while in the city, the former monk "fell willfully into a dissolute life and later found salvation against his will. He went to the theater and to races in the hippodrome and haunted the taverns. Eating and drinking to excess, he fell into the filth of lust. And since he was bent on committing sin, he met an actress and had relations with her." To the Egyptian ascetics of late antiquity, city life represented the world and all of its pleasures. And if a monk wished to renounce his quest for salvation and seek the enticements of Vanity

Fair, he knew where to go. Alexandria, with its wide variety of public entertainments and private pastimes, was "the world" par excellence, and stood poles apart from the ascetic furnace of the soul out in Egypt's lonely deserts. Thus we hear that the venerable monk, John of Lycopolis, warned one pilgrim not to turn aside to Alexandria on her return from the Thebaid, "for there you must surely fall into temptation."[53]

## *Administration and Coercion*

The Romans, like the Ptolemies before them, found that this great metropolis was not an easy city to govern. This was particularly true during the fourth and fifth centuries, when intercommunal conflict increased appreciably, to the extent that the author of the *Expositio* claimed "it is a city which imposes its will upon its governors." He goes on to suggest that the imperial authorities in Alexandria were so afraid of the populace that "they entered the city with fear and trembling." This is no doubt an exaggeration, since several officials returned to Alexandria for a succession of administrative positions. Nonetheless, some imperial appointees found the situation in the city so unstable that they took up their posts only with the backing of substantial military force.[54]

The imperial administration of the city can be sketched briefly if we keep in mind a threefold division of authority in Alexandria which emanated from the emperor himself: the emperor's direct relations with the city and with certain of its citizens, the military administration of the city, and the civil administration—often embodied in the person of the prefect. At times these categories overlapped, as when the prefect employed the coercive power of the troops garrisoned at Nicopolis. Still, this threefold division provides a schematic way of understanding Roman administration in the city without becoming entangled in the intricate problems connected with bureaucratic organization.

Although the emperor himself visited Alexandria seldom during late antiquity, he could ill afford to ignore this wealthy and important urban center. Throughout the Roman period, imperial edicts were publicly proclaimed and subsequently recorded in the library of Hadrian and the temple library of the Nanaion. In addition, milestones in an emperor's career were publicly announced in Alexandria, in order to keep the virtues and achievements of the reigning Augustus before the eyes of the populace. Theodosius, for example, sent a special proclamation to Alexandria heralding his victory over Eugenius in 394. A few years earlier, this same emperor dispatched to the city no less an official than the praetorian prefect of the East in order to announce the appointment of Maximus as coemperor and set up statues of the new Augustus. The display of laureled imperial portraits and statues in significant urban places also promoted the emperor's public image. Another form of "public relations" was carried out by the imperial mint located in the Caesarion, which issued coinage bearing imperial titles and attributes. Monumental inscriptions and large sculptural pieces were also continual reminders of imperial authority and beneficence. A colossal seated statue in porphyry of a fourth-century emperor, several times life-size, still retains its original power to awe the beholder even though it has been seriously damaged over the course of sixteen centuries.[55]

To Alexandrians of the later Roman period, the emperor was more than just a distant figure presiding over his far-flung empire from Constantinople. At times, the emperor found it necessary to intervene directly in the internal affairs of the city. Perhaps the best-known example of this type of imperial intervention is the series of letters which initiated and ended Athanasius's numerous exiles during the course of the Arian controversy. Athanasius's writings betray great anxiety among his partisans over the receipt of imperial letters in Alexandria, their publication, and their enforcement.[56]

Clearly, more than theology was at stake in the conflict between emperor and bishop, since Athanasius incurred the wrath of both Homoousion and Arian rulers such as Constantine, Constantius, and Valens, as well as the displeasure of the pagan emperor Julian. One indication of the political ramifications of this conflict is the fact that Constantine supported Athanasius in the face of a variety of accusations, but abruptly turned against him when the patriarch was accused of threatening to interrupt shipments of grain to Constantinople. Given the seriousness of this charge, it is no wonder that Constantine was "vexed unto indignation" against Athanasius and subsequently banished him to Trier in 336. Successive emperors found themselves drawn into the struggle for communal hegemony in Alexandria. Indeed, this theme runs through much of the city's history during the fourth and fifth centuries; bishops were installed and deposed on imperial orders, the stalemated conflict over the Serapeum in 391 was resolved by an imperial rescript from Theodosius, and his imperial namesake in 416 sought to regulate the private army of the patriarch after a period of intense intercommunal violence. All of these imperial directives and orders were carried to Alexandria by court officials such as *palatini, notarii,* and *agentes in rebus* who were charged with the responsibility of seeing that the emperor's wishes were fulfilled to the letter. However, the political realities in the city were such that particularly unpopular orders were often committed into the hands of military men (*comites*) who possessed the force necessary to compel obedience, even if it required violence.[57]

It was natural that military officers should be found at Alexandria, since the suburban camp of Nicopolis was the headquarters for Roman troops in Egypt. Transfer requests had to be processed there as well as petitions seeking exemption from military service. Although Egypt was generally a peaceful province, it was necessary to hold in check marauding tribes from Libya and deal with the more serious threat posed by a tribal grouping known as the Blemmyes, who disrupted caravan trade in the Eastern Desert and carried on occasional razzias in the wealthy agricultural districts of the Thebaid. Egypt's southern defense was entrusted to a seasoned officer known as *dux Thebaidis,* who was under the jurisdiction of the *dux Aegypti,* the senior military commander in the entire provincial diocese. The dux Aegypti (sometimes known as the *comes Aegypti*) was the principal military officer in charge of keeping order in Alexandria and enforcing imperial directives regarding the city. This often led to duties that were not, strictly speaking, of a military nature, such as persecuting out-of-favor factions within the city. In 356, the *dux* Syrianus led an attack on Athanasius and his followers, and after ejecting the intransigent patriarch, he installed an Arian appointee, Gregory the Cappadocian. Four years later, another dux Aegypti named Artemius carried out the wishes of his imperial patron Constantius by torturing Homoousions and offering violence to the temple of Serapis. However, the temple survived another thirty years until troops under the command of another officer, Romanus, settled the dispute over the site by destroying the cult image and tearing down portions of the sacred precinct.[58]

The dux Aegypti did not act alone in carrying out imperial policy in the city. Following the division of military and civil authority in the provinces by Diocletian and Constantine, the dux normally worked in concert with the senior civil administrator in Alexandria, the *praefectus Augustalis.* This official, successor after circa 380 to the *praefectus Aegypti,* was clearly the most important imperial official in late antique Egypt. Although his authority was eclipsed in the late third century by that of the *corrector,* the prefect reemerged in the fourth century with many of the same wide-ranging judicial and administrative powers as formerly possessed by the great prefects of the early principate. Despite the formal restriction of his authority to the reduced province of Aegyptus (which included Alexandria), petitions from all over Egypt inundated the prefectural courts in Alexandria—just as in the early Roman period. Aside from ruling on such routine matters as tax liability, estate division, and civic obligations, the prefect's courts could also be employed to enforce imperial orders regarding proscribed religious opinions and sectarian activity, particularly in Alexandria. We often hear of recalcitrant Alexandrians being "led away to the tribunal of the prefect," frequently with violent consequences (figure 8).[59]

While other administrative dioceses in the post-Diocletianic province of Egypt were governed by subordinate *praesides,* the diocese comprising Alexandria's primary hinterland (Aegyptus proper) appears to have been governed directly by the prefect.[60] Nonetheless, the duties of the prefect were mainly taken up with presiding over the vast administrative bureaucracy centered in Alexandria, which governed nearly every aspect of life throughout the late Roman province of Egypt. Subordinate financial officers such as *logistes, katholikoi,* and the *procurator rei privatae* were concerned primarily with the assessment and collection of taxes, but they also

Fig. 8. The prefect's court. The prefect dispensing justice, seated in his praetorium, with guard and notary. Ivory pyxis, one of three panels depicting the life of Saint Menas. Egypt (Alexandria), sixth century. British Museum, inv. 79,12–20,1. (The Trustees of the British Museum)

supervised the confiscation of goods to the treasury from criminals and subversive groups. For example, during the so-called Great Persecution (303–11), agents of the *procurator rei privatae* sent off to Alexandria the valuables of a village church near Oxyrhynchus. Other prefectural administrators, such as the *procurator Phari* collected harbor dues at the ports of Alexandria, protected shipping lanes near the city, and strictly regulated the flow of persons and goods through this main gateway to Egypt. The prefect was also ultimately responsible for the smooth running of the imperial mint, which was placed under the supervision of a *praepositus monetae*.[61]

Probably the best-documented branch of the prefect's bureaucracy was the complicated administrative machinery set up to facilitate the collection and transport of grain to Alexandria—and eventually to the rest of the empire. This department was put in the hands of the *praefectus annonae Alexandrinae,* an official who rated so high in the administration that he was sometimes of senatorial rank. The holder of this post controlled a wide-ranging network of administrators, and the office seems to have existed until at least the early part of the seventh century.[62] All of these various prefectural *officinae* must have employed a large number of civil servants who further contributed to the strength of the local economy and to the city's role as an important regional center of commerce and administration.

Although this threefold division of imperial authority constituted the main elements of Alexandria's administration, there still remained a limited scope for the exercise of authority by locally elected magistrates. As in other cities of late antiquity, civic magistracies in Alexandria suffered a decline during the third and fourth centuries. This decline was due to the increasingly burdensome costs of holding these offices, so that eligible individuals actively evaded their honors/obligations. In addition, Diocletian's administrative reforms had an effect on the contours of public office in the empire's cities, so that it is not possible to assume continuity for particular magistracies across this period. In Alexandria, the highly esteemed office of *hypomnematographus* was abolished in the early fourth century. Previously, this position was granted to a favored member of the bouleutic class who served as chief of the prefect's chancery. In place of the hypomnematographus, a bureaucrat (normally a katholikos) was appointed by the imperial government. Other offices, such as *archiereus* and even *stratēgos,* seem to have been phased out over the course of the fourth century. Thus it is likely that the *cursus* of Alexandrian magistracies in the later empire differed markedly from the normal succession of civic offices in the first three centuries A.D. Unfortunately, it is difficult to assemble the scattered pieces of the late antique *cursus honorum* in Alexandria, since Alexandrian magistracies are only infrequently attested in the sources from this period. Further, most of the Alexandrian officeholders who appear in papyri are designated as *ex*-magistrates, having exercised their duties in many instances well before the reforms of Diocletian.[63]

Of the lengthy Alexandrian *cursus* from the early principate, there remained two principal offices which continued to function in the fourth and fifth centuries, and in both cases these magistrates are usually seen working in conjunction with other governmental bodies. The most important of these offices was that of the *prytanis,* who acted as the city's chief magistrate and in all probability presided over meetings of the Alexandrian boule. In the sources, the prytanis is sometimes mentioned in the same breath with the prefect and the dux, testifying to the preeminence of this civic magistracy in the later Roman period. Alexandrian *dikastai* or judges also appear as local officials during the fourth and fifth centuries. While their exact role vis-à-vis the judges in prefectural courts remains unclear, their consent was apparently needed in order to torture Alexandrians, and their importance in the city was such that they were singled out and threatened for refusing to hold communion with Arian appointees. Alexandrian dikastai are sometimes found in league with "the people"—perhaps a veiled reference to the assembly or *ekklesia.* Together with the *dēmos,* the dikastai mounted a successful resistance to the violent measures attempted by the imperial *notarius* Diogenes in 355. Despite these infrequent occasions, however, Alexandrian magistrates took a decidedly subordinate position to imperial administrators during the late empire. Though imperial authority had always taken precedence in the city—so much so that the Alexandrians were only permitted a boule in 200—local authorities possessed more than mere honorific status. However, by the fourth century, civic officials found that their tenuous position in the forefront of "the most glorious city of the Alexandrians" was a thing of the past.[64]

The civic magistrates were progressively overshadowed by Roman authorities partially because of the increased efforts necessary to quell disturbances and maintain order during the fourth and fifth centuries. In contrast to local officials, imperial administrators had more effective means of both coercing and persuading the Alexandrian crowd. Still, great care was needed in dealing with a sometimes volatile urban populace. As one late fourth-century author reminds us, "merely because a greeting was omitted, or a place in the baths refused, or meat and vegetables withheld, or on account of the boots of slaves or some other such things, they have broken out into riots, even to the point of becoming highly dangerous to the state, so that troops have been armed to subdue them."[65] Actions that might be seemingly insignificant to modern observers (such as an imperial official neglecting to extend formal greetings to an assembly of the people) could be pregnant with meaning in an Alexandrian context and consequently provoke a violent response from the demos. Food shortages were potentially even more dangerous, as the prefect Theodosius discovered in 516. A scarcity of oil led to the prefect's murder—grim confirmation of the *Expositio.*[66] It should also be noted that, at a time of tension and unrest within the city, it would be difficult for the authorities to anticipate a precise reaction on the part of the crowd to the various means of exercising control at the disposal of the government.

Not surprisingly, a frequent method of maintaining order was through the simple deployment of armed force. The prefect commanded his own contingent of guards who were called upon to enforce his will within the city. At times, these guards (*protiktorai*) were even dispatched on missions into the surrounding countryside, and were noted by the common people for their "savage and ferocious" manner. When the need arose for a more potent display of force, the prefectural guards could also be combined with military detachments serving the dux or comites. Under normal circumstances, however, policing in Alexandria was carried out by two *stratēgoi tōn poleōs* along with their body of militia. This post, to be distinguished from the earlier honorific Alexandrian magistracy of strategos, perhaps could be likened to the role of the *praefectus vigilum* of Constantinople, the fifth-century *nukteparchos* of Antioch, or to the fourth-century *nuktostratēgos* of Oxyrhynchus. The guards of the strategos did not hesitate to employ violent methods in order to maintain compliance with the governing authorities. If it was deemed necessary, they even wielded clubs and rods upon the citizenry. Yet, the strategoi did not act independently of Roman authorities in the city, and often are seen taking their cue from imperial administrators.[67]

Following the exile of the patriarch Dioscorus in 451, there began a period of civic disorders marked by sporadic clashes between the populace and imperial troops sent out from Constantinople. Eventually, an assembly of the Alexandrians was held in the hippodrome with the prefect, Florus, in attendance. Although brute force had failed to quell factional violence within Alexandria, Florus was able to restore a modicum of peace to the formerly tumultuous city. How? By prohibiting spectacles, closing the baths, and, most important, cutting off the long-standing bread ration to the citizenry. This had such an immediate and profound effect upon the populace that their pleadings prompted Florus to reinstate these essential amenities "and the rioting quickly ceased." This was not the first time that a calculated interruption of the bread dole was used by Roman authorities in Alexandria. Ever since the annona had been reorganized by Diocletian and expanded under Theodosius II, the Alexandrian populace had grown increasingly dependent on the nearly one-third of a million modii of wheat distributed annually in the city.[68]

During the third century, a *eutheniarch* administered the Alexandrian grain annona, and it was probably set up along the lines of the better-documented grain dole in Oxyrhynchus, where bread recipients had to meet certain qualifications of residence and citizenship. In 261, the patriarch Dionysius related that Alexandrians "from fourteen to eighty years of age are enrolled and mustered for the public grain dole." In the fourth century, the dole in Alexandria (like so many other aspects of government) was taken over by the prefect's administration, although Alexandrian bouleutai were recruited to purchase food supplies out of a special fund maintained by the Roman authorities, the *alimonikos logos*. In the sixth century, this fund apportioned over 550 solidi annually from the city's budget for the purchase of grain alone. Once the grain was collected in Alexandria, *tesserae* or marked tokens of some sort which could be exchanged for bread rations were issued. A place among the recipients was evidently inheritable, since one set of documents from the mid-fourth century concerns a dispute over the division of an Alexandrian's estate which included one-half of a bread ration.[69]

Questions concerning the precise nature of the grain dole in Alexandria are necessarily intertwined with the socioeconomic status of the recipients. Were these indigent persons for whom bread distributions provided a means of eking out survival at the bottom of the social ladder? The legal and literary sources tend to confirm this view, since the dole was apparently designed by Diocletian to support "the common people lacking the necessities of life." Imperial edicts ensured a steady supply of grain "so that no person may be deprived of that sustenance which he has thus far received." Among those Alexandrians benefiting from the annona, widows and orphans are specifically mentioned.[70]

Nonetheless, there are indications from surviving papyri that the grain dole went to individuals across the entire spectrum of Alexandrian society. One Alexandrian of the fourth century was wealthy enough to have possessed a house in a rural nome as well as "a house and bread in Alexandria"—doubtless referring to a place among the grain recipients. During the reign of Constantius (337–61), the Roman officer Fl. Abinnaeus collected rent on a house he owned in Alexandria, which was paid to him in both cash and bread. The close connection between residence and the bread dole has led some commentators to suggest that grain was distributed in Alexandria, not per capita, but on the basis of house ownership, in a manner similar to the *panis aedium* of Constantinople. This would explain the incidence of fractions of bread issues among testamentary documents. While the extant sources for Alexandria do not allow for a conclusive resolution to this question, it can be established at the very least that the grain annona evolved into a type of honorific civic pension, regardless of the emperor's original intentions. This is further supported by evidence of a cash bounty or *dorēa,* which appears to have been distributed in Alexandria along with the loaves. Moreover, if the social classes represented by the dole recipients at Oxyrhynchus are any indication, the distributions of grain occasionally went to rather wealthy citizens—certainly not those on the margins of society.[71]

How then does one account for the frequent mention of poor and destitute recipients of the dole in late antique Alexandria? On examination, most of the references concerning the support of indigent Alexandrians come from the pens of ecclesiastical authors. The patriarchate appears to have been particularly concerned with the regular distribution of alms in the form of grain, wine, and oil—the staples of the Mediterranean diet in antiquity. These charitable distributions were carefully organized and, by the seventh century, were associated with other charitable institutions run by the church, such as hospitals, poorhouses, and pilgrim hostels.[72] There is an echo of this charitable activity in the archaeological record, since a number of small pottery vessels from Cyprus have been discovered near the theaterlike building at Kōm el-Dikka. Since they date from the early seventh century, one excavator has suggested that these pots might have contained foodstuffs distributed at this location by John the Almsgiver—himself a Cypriot.[73]

By the sixth and seventh centuries, the patriarchate had established its own network of collection and transport in the chora in order to supply the needs of the Alexandrian poor. In an earlier period, stray notices in the literary sources suggest that the state earmarked a portion of the grain annona to be distributed by the church. We find this same distinction between the state-run annona and the charitable work of the church in the distribution of oil within the city. However, church-sponsored distributions during the fourth century tend to show up in the sources only when they have become politicized for one reason or another. At one point, Athanasius's Arian detractors accused him of making a profit off grain entrusted to him by the state for the maintenance of the poor. Later in the patriarch's career, Constantius sent "letters and orders" to the prefect "that for the future, the grain should be taken from Athanasius and given to those who favored Arian doctrines."[74]

This explains the frequent interference of the state in the charitable distributions carried out by the Alexandrian church, since the recipients of this charity were in a particularly vulnerable economic and social position: priests, deacons, virgins, widows, orphans, and the destitute. Interrupting the flow of alms was an important means of disrupting the patron-client relationship that existed between the patriarchate and the Alexandrian lower classes. The political significance of these distributions was clearly understood by the Roman authorities. During the disturbances of 339, agents of the government persecuted Athanasius's followers and "took away their bread for no other reason but that they might be induced to join the Arians and receive Gregory, who had been sent by the emperor."[75]

Disrupting the almsgiving of the church was a frequent occurrence during the turbulent patriarchate of Athanasius. However, other communal groups also suffered from imperial tampering with the Alexandrian annona. Wishing to break pagan resistance to heavy-handed imperial evangelization, Constantius included pagans in his directives concerning the dole in Alexandria, specifying that "their bread should be taken away and their idols overthrown."[76] While these measures failed to achieve their desired results at this time, we have seen how similar prohibitions, coupled with other coercive actions, could drastically affect factional conflict in the city.

In this regard, Alexandria was not unique among the large cities of late antiquity. After the Riot of the Statues in 387, grain distributions in Antioch were stopped and the theaters and baths were closed. Antioch's proscribed amenities were restored only after an imperial pardon was granted by Theodosius to the penitent city. In Constantinople, the grain dole was interrupted in 342 following a riot during which the urban crowd murdered Hermogenes, the *magister equitum,* when he attempted to depose their Homoousion bishop, Paul. Consequently, tight control over public entertainments and food supplies in the cities appears to have been an important facet of imperial policy during this period.[77]

Once Alexandria became largely Christianized, the imperial government was able to employ yet another method of coercion, closing churches. In 539, after a year of unsuccessful efforts at winning over the Alexandrians to a Chalcedonian patriarch, Justinian decided to take more drastic measures. "He commanded that the doors of the churches in the city of Alexandria should by shut and sealed with his seal, and guards set before them, so that no one at all might enter." This action effectively cut off the Alexandrians from the sacraments of the church. Despite their reported "anguish and unbounded sorrow," the Alexandrians persisted in their opposition to the emperor, partly because the Monophysite hierarchy hastily consecrated two unauthorized churches within the city. Justinian responded by ordering that all of the city's churches be opened, and that they be placed under the authority of Chalcedonian clergy. The Monophysite patriarch, Theodosius, knew that open Chalcedonian churches were more dangerous to his cause than closed Monophysite ones. "He sighed and wept, because he knew the people of Alexandria, that they loved pomp and honour, and he feared that they would depart from the orthodox faith, with a view to gaining honour from the prince"—a telling observation on the power of imperial patronage.[78]

The effectiveness of these coercive methods in Alexandria was put to the test time and again during late antiquity as the imperial government sought to preserve a modicum of order and deference in the city. Imperial patronage or repression remained an important external factor in the conflicts between Alexandria's pagan, Jewish, and Christian communities—often tipping the balance in favor of one or another faction depending on the government's perceived interests at any given moment. In addition, the city's topography further delimited the conflicts between the communities, and on occasion, provided a topographical focus for intercommunal rivalries.

## *Topography and Society: The Via Canopica*

At first glance, the products of Hellenistic city planning often appear static and gridlike on modern site maps or in standard textbooks. However, certain architectural elements in a city's design interacted with the dynamics of urban society to such a degree that they seemed to take on a life of their own during Greco-Roman antiquity. This was clearly the case with the broad colonnaded boulevards that bisected many of the principal cities of the eastern Mediterranean. Ancient port cities frequently possessed these colonnaded avenues, which served to link widely separated urban quarters along the length of the harbor area. The chief unifying element in the urban designs of two otherwise disparate Mediterranean ports, Carthage in North Africa and Caesaraea Maritima in Palestine, was a long boulevard extending the length of the late antique city. However, none of the boulevards of ancient Mediterranean port cities could compare with Alexandria's Via Canopica, a thoroughfare that easily ranked alongside Rome's Via Sacra or Athens's Panathenaic Way as one of the great streets of the classical world.

The role of Alexandria's Via Canopica encompassed far more than its obvious architectural function of unifying Alexandria's urban design. As the city's principal artery, it also served as the stage for Alexandria's most important ceremonies and civic rituals. Cultural anthropologists have long recognized that a society's rituals provide an important window on the underlying attitudes of that society, that is, how that society articulates its social order, its disposition toward authority, its view of outsiders, and the ideology that binds it together into a distinct community. Obviously, a civic ceremony expresses *shared* values and, as such, is a much more reliable indicator of communal identity than the opinions of any individual observer—even if that observer is a contemporary. Given this perspective on civic rituals, the setting for the rituals takes on an added importance, especially since the setting determines, to a large degree, the form of the rituals themselves. As one examines the numerous civic ceremonies practiced by the inhabitants of ancient Alexandria, it becomes immediately apparent that the vast majority of these ceremonies took place along the Via Canopica. Consequently, a boulevard that appears to be simply a major street in the city's configuration assumes a sociopolitical role which intrudes upon the very communal consciousness of the city's inhabitants.[79] As a result, a close analysis of the link between one of the city's preeminent topographical features and the society that inhabited it provides us with yet another trajectory across the urban landscape in our quest to understand the social world of late antique Alexandria.

The rituals and ceremonies that took place along Alexandria's principal urban artery, running from Nicopolis through the city to the Gate of the Moon, were, in effect, an echo in Alexandrian society of the flow of this "architecture of passage and connection."[80] They illustrate, in an even more graphic way than the placement of civic religious shrines in the city's center, the vital connection between urban form and sociopolitical function, transforming the street into a "theater of power."[81] These processions and ceremonies embraced a broad spectrum of Alexandrians and often articulated the ways in which the Alexandrians ordered their social, political, and religious world. They also serve as an important supplement to those other much-studied occasions when masses of the urban populace assembled in one place: at chariot races and at theatrical performances. The hippodrome and theater do share one characteristic with the Via Canopica and its plazas—they all consist of well-defined *public* space within the city, thereby lending themselves to expressions of popular will. However, the Via Canopica's function as the principal Alexandrian setting for civic ceremonies can be seen by the broad chronological range of evidence attesting these rituals: from the great religious procession of Ptolemy Philadelphus (285–47 B.C.), celebrating the dynasty's patron god Dionysus, to military parades occurring during the Mamluk period (A.D. 1250–1517).[82]

In the first century of Roman rule, some of these demonstrations were primarily political in nature, such as the adventus of Augustus into Cleopatra's capital in 30 B.C., and the noisy reception accorded Germanicus in A.D. 18. This is also true of the adventus of Titus in 71, whose movements in Alexandria followed a clear itinerary from Nicopolis to the Serapeum and back to the hippodrome.[83]

Claudius's much discussed letter to the Alexandrians indicates that the emperor could take part in official ceremonies without actually being present, since he gives the Alexandrians permission to carry his golden image and a throne in processions which were organized at least once a month. This ceremonial display of imperial images had a long tradition in Alexandria. Nearly 350 years later, the emperor Theodosius sent a praetorian prefect to Alexandria with orders that the images of the Spanish emperor and his erstwhile co-ruler, Maximus, should be publicly received and exhibited in the city. During the Byzantine period, images of venerated past emperors, including Theodosius himself, were carried through the city at the time of an annual festival. A Coptic homily attributed to the patriarch Theophilus states that when these images were not being carried in procession, they were "painted and set up in the midst of the marketplace, becoming a protection to the whole city."[84]

The Severan era opened with the adventus of Septimius Severus into the city in 199, after having defeated Pescennius Niger in the civil wars. Unfortunately, the Alexandrians had backed Niger during the wars, and at the approach of Severus, they poured forth from the city and escorted the victorious emperor along the Via Canopica—all the while chanting expressions of their loyalty. At the time of Caracalla's visit to the city in 215, Herodian tells us that the Alexandrians "prepared a superlative reception for the emperor. Everywhere bands were performing on all kinds of musical instruments and playing a variety of melodies. Billows of perfume and the smoke of incense spread sweet aromas throughout the city. The emperor was honored with torchlight parades and showers of bouquets."[85]

In these instances, the Alexandrians are represented as an undifferentiated mass. We see little or no hint that clearly defined groups within the city took part in these ceremonies honoring the emperors. This absence of social distinctions is unexpected, since other large gatherings of the populace were usually segregated according to status—as at the theater or at the hippodrome.

To find this sort of status differentiation, we have to turn to the late antique period and the ceremonial adventus of the Alexandrian patriarch. On his return from one period of exile (February 362), Athanasius was met outside of the city by huge throngs, which accompanied him back into Alexandria in a manner patterned after Christ's triumphal entry into Jerusalem. Gregory of Nazianzus informs us that Athanasius's return was greeted with "universal cheers, and the pouring forth of unguents, and nightlong festivities and the whole city gleaming with light, and feasting in public and at home." One of the onlookers even speculates that the emperor himself would not have received such a thunderous welcome. The resemblance of this ceremonial welcome to that of Caracalla's earlier adventus takes on a greater significance with Gregory's comment that the crowd was carefully arranged according to birth, age, and profession. Indeed, he goes on to state that the city was usually arranged in this way, whenever a public honor was bestowed on anyone. Thus, it would appear that these processions and ceremonies along the Via Canopica provided the city with yet another opportunity to articulate the urban social order.[86]

We should not exaggerate the significance of this shift from the imperial adventus to ceremonies honoring the patriarch. Although the adventus of the patriarch became a central event in the civic rituals of late antique Alexandria, it did not entirely displace processions that expressed loyalty to the emperor and his family. Indeed, the patriarchal adventus may have grown out of an earlier Alexandrian tradition of honoring private individuals with processions. Philostratus's *Life of Apollonius* recounts the welcome given to the celebrated philosopher/wonderworker: "As he advanced from the ship into the city, they gazed upon him as if he were a god, and made way for him in the narrow streets, as they would for priests carrying holy objects . . . thus escorted with more pomp than if he had been a governor of the nation."[87]

By contrast, these processional demonstrations could also be hostile in character. Perhaps the clearest example of this aspect of Alexandrian ritual may be seen in the events surrounding the expulsion of an Arian bishop, Lucius, in September 367. As an imperial appointee, Lucius suspected that he would not be warmly received in Alexandria, and he entered the city secretly at night—in stark contrast to Athanasius's adventus five years earlier.[88] The following day, both the prefect, Fl. Eutolmius Tatianus, and the military dux, Trajan, became incensed when they were apprised of this highly irregular entry. Their displeasure was just a shadow of the popular feeling aroused when the city's inhabitants heard of Lucius's arrival. As Lucius was taken into custody by the prefect's soldiers, they were followed by "the entire populace of the city, Christians, pagans, and those of other religions [Jews?]." This unusual unanimity on the part of the city's ethno-religious communities suggests that local animosity toward Lucius was fueled by sentiments other than religion. Arian appointees had held sway before in Alexandria, and it appears that Lucius began his short-lived first episcopate by violating traditional Alexandrian scruples regarding the proper adventus of a bishop. The Alexandrians responded with their own style of procession for Lucius. While they escorted him "through the midst of the city [that is, along the Via Canopica], they did not cease from shouting insults and hurling criminal charges, crying: Let him be taken out of the city!"[89] His route *per mediam civitatem* went from the bishop's palace in the western part of the city to the Caesarion, and eventually to Nicopolis. Lucius learned his lesson well. When he returned to Alexandria in 373, he came with a sizable body of imperial troops and a *comes* of the imperial treasury. This time Lucius was careful to follow local protocol, knowing that he "could not make his entrance into the city without a procession."[90] He staged his own adventus, albeit escorted by troops and Arian bishops brought to the city for the occasion.

The funerals of important Alexandrians were also opportunities for ceremonial processions. During the early Byzantine period, the typical pattern was for the deceased to be honored in such a way that "the whole city made a procession for him, including the bishop, with lights and incense." Funerals were formalized to the extent that the bearers of the dead were organized into a craft association, and grand processions through the city could easily attract the attention and participation of passersby.[91]

Religious processions, both pagan and Christian, made use of this well-established route. Achilles Tatius describes for us in picturesque terms a magnificent nocturnal ceremony in honor of the city's patron deity, Serapis: "For this celebration, there was a torchlight procession. It was the greatest spectacle I ever beheld; for evening had come, the sun had set, but night was nowhere to be found, only a second sunrise of light in shimmering fragments, as if Alexandria meant to surpass the heavens in splendor." Philostratus speaks of similar religious pageants as though they were a common occurrence. Religious processions along the Via Canopica might even be organized by one of the city's ethno-religious communities with the object of mocking the religious sensibilities of another community. The climax of pagan-Christian violence in Alexandria occurred in 391, with rioting that eventually resulted in the destruction of the cult of Serapis. The episode appears to have been sparked by the public display of pagan cult objects, discovered during the excavation of a basilica site. The patriarch, Theophilus, exploited the situation by parading the sacred images "through the midst of the Agora" (*dia mesēs tēs agoras*). The city's pagans, enraged by the public mockery of sacred mysteries, began to attack the Christians in the streets. The pagans were forced to withdraw and they occupied the immense temple of Serapis—leading to a shift in the locus of this pagan-Christian conflict to the precinct of the city's great patron divinity.[92]

Lastly, one of the most common types of procession in Alexandria was that of outcasts and criminals who were scourged, placed on camels, and led through the midst of the city, "as is usual with malefactors"—in Evagrius's depiction of an incident from 452. The standardized form of this procession during the course of Alexandrian history suggests that it became a civic ritual intended to cleanse the city from a perceived criminal contagion or impurity. At the time of a persecution in the mid-third century, Christians were treated in this way, being led in procession to their execution "across the entire city, very large in extent." A similar incident occurred during a riot in 361; after the city's inhabitants murdered the Arian bishop George and two imperial officials, their bodies were paraded on camels *per mediam civitatem*, and then burned to prevent any possibility of a later martyr cult. As late as the early seventh century, we find an echo of this punishment in the milder chastisement of an offender who is "scourged and paraded in public by the overseer of the Agora."[93]

The murder of George and his associates introduces us to another element of this Alexandrian civic ritual of expiation—the eventual cremation of the criminal's body. This may be compared with the pattern in Rome, where public enemies were hurled from the Tarpeian rock, dragged down the steps of the Capitol, or thrown into the Tiber. While the burning of a Christian's body may have been designed to preclude the veneration of the remains, ritualistic cremation has the connotation of an especially Egyptian insult, given the meticulous care traditionally bestowed upon corpses.

The sequence of events surrounding George's murder was repeated with slight variation in 457 when the imperial appointee to the patriarchate, Proterius, was murdered by some soldiers who dragged his body to the center of the city. The populace, in turn, dragged Proterius "through the whole city" (*dia pasēs tēs poleōs*) and then burned his remains. This ritualistic dragging of criminals through the streets and their subsequent cremation had a long tradition at Alexandria. During the anti-Jewish pogrom of A.D. 38, individual Jews were seized by roaming pagan mobs, "dragged through the whole city and trampled on." Philo relates that the bodies of these Jews were so maltreated that "not a part of them was left which could receive the burial which is the common right of all." Some two centuries later, Christian martyrs were dragged through the city during the Decian persecution. Late Coptic-Arabic accounts of the martyrdom of Saint Mark (which probably reflect an early Greek original) state that on the occasion of a festival to Serapis, some of the god's followers seized Saint Mark, "fastened a rope around his throat, and dragged him along the ground. . . . His flesh was lacerated, and clove to the stones of the streets." True to the Alexandrian pattern, the pagans then attempted to burn his body and were thwarted only at the last moment by a divinely sent thunderstorm.[94]

The murder of Proterius in 457 demonstrates that pagan Alexandrians did not have a monopoly on the ritualistic extermination of civic enemies and the use of the city's principal boulevard in parading and dragging their enemies. In 373, the Arian patriarch Lucius initiated a brutal persecution against his Nicene opponents, many of whom were dragged or led in procession to their death. The most famous of these murders, that of the philosopher Hypatia in 415, is attributable to virulent antipagan sentiment within the Christian community. Passing over the sociopolitical background of this important juncture in Christian-pagan relations within the city, we may limit ourselves here to the particular form the murder assumed. Coptic and Greek traditions of Hypatia's murder both agree that a Christian mob pulled Hypatia from her chariot, dragged her through the city to the Caesarion where she was murdered. Her mangled body was then taken to another locale and was burned on a pile of brushwood—a sequence of events in accordance with established Alexandrian practice.[95]

As we have seen, the violent struggle between the Alexandrian pagan and Christian communities for control of the Serapeum in 391 began with Theophilus's antipagan procession along the Via

Canopica. The denouement of this episode likewise consisted of a procession—however, one more in conformity with the standard Alexandrian ritual for ridding the city of a public enemy. After the pagans had abandoned Serapis's massive temple, a Christian soldier in the prefect's entourage dared to take up an ax and strike the jaw of the magnificent cult statue. The soldier repeated his bold action until he had hewn the head and limbs from the torso. Significantly, the Christian mob then bore off the head of Serapis's statue "and carried it through all the town in sight of his worshipers." As if to emphasize Serapis's newly ascribed status as a would-be condemned criminal, portions of the statue were dragged into each part of the city and burned. Finally, the torso itself was publicly burned in the theater—one of the city's most important gathering places.[96] Apparently, the Alexandrian ceremony for dealing with criminals was inclusive enough to exterminate even gods.

A similar episode occurred nearly a century later, well after the Christian community had gained cultural hegemony within Alexandria. Zachariah Scholasticus's lively biography of Severus of Antioch relates a series of events involving pagan-Christian violence connected with pagan cults at Canopus and Menouthis, located some twelve kilometers east of the city.[97] A group of zealous Christians, including both laity and monks, were entrusted by the patriarch, Peter Mongus, with the destruction of pagan cults at the suburban shrine. After demolishing the sanctuary, the Christians returned to Alexandria bearing the trophies of their vandalism—the Greco-Egyptian cult objects. In Zachariah's words, "We brought back their priest as well as their idols. In fact, it turned out to be possible, with God's help, for us to capture him too. Twenty camels were loaded by us with various idols, even though we had already burned some at Menouthis, as I have mentioned. We brought them into the midst of the city, on the orders we had received from the great Peter."[98] The patriarch Peter preached a sermon against heathenism, led the crowd in ritualized denunciations of pagan gods, and then ordered the remaining cult objects to be burned in the Agora. Like the destruction of Serapis's statue, this event employed the traditional elements of a religious procession, the ceremonial parading of criminals, and eventual destruction by fire.

For the Alexandrians of the Roman period, ritualized processions were a vital component in the ordering of their complex social world. These processions, focused on the Via Canopica, were so much a part of the urban experience that they sometimes even conflicted with one another. A vivid anecdote in the *Life of Apollonius* relates that his adventus into the city was interrupted at one point by a procession of twelve condemned criminals who were being led off to their execution.[99] This juxtaposition of communal responses (adulation and condemnation) served only to enhance the qualities of each distinct procession. Moreover, this anecdote further illustrates the multifaceted nature of the Via Canopica's social function throughout antiquity—at once a *via sacra,* a *via triumphalis,* and a *via dolorosa.*

As we have seen, Alexandria's design and social realities exhibited certain characteristics found in other urban centers in the late antique world. Yet, the magnificence of its architecture and the city's extraordinary wealth of goods and services continued to astound travelers and excite the interest of both pagan and Christian writers. For as one well-traveled Syrian observer was prompted to remark, "Alexandria is truly a very great city, famous for its configuration, possessing an abundance of all goods, and rich in food."[100] It was against this distinctive urban backdrop that the Alexandrian ethnoreligious communities played out their struggle for survival and hegemony in late antiquity.

# Four

# The Jewish Community

After five centuries of periodic conflict, tensions between Alexandrian Jews and Gentiles reached a violent climax in late 414/early 415. Beginning with a disturbance in the theater, a spiral of threats and intimidation escalated until, one night, a group of Alexandrian Jews set upon their Christian neighbors in a street brawl, with bloody results. The next day, the patriarch Cyril set in motion a series of reprisals which led to the plunder of Jewish synagogues and the wholesale expulsion of the Jewish community.[1]

Regardless of how one wishes to interpret these events, the Alexandrian Jewish community clearly emerges as one of the principal players on the urban scene of early fifth-century Alexandria. In gazing back over the previous three centuries, however, the Jews of Alexandria hardly appear at all in the extant historical sources. Surely the Alexandrian Jewish community did not spring up over night, or become an important factor in city politics in just a few short years. Where were the Jews before the events of 414/15? Is it possible to say something about the social and economic status of these Alexandrian Jews, as well as their political standing and group ideology, during the fourth and fifth centuries?

The prominent role played by the Alexandrian Jewish community in the events of 414/15 tends to focus our attention on this particular outbreak of violence in such a way that any other data concerning the Jews from this period are interpreted solely with reference to the stasis of 414/15. This approach subordinates the day-to-day life of the Jewish community to one atypical, albeit crucial, event. Granted, historical gleanings from the everyday existence of this community may contribute to a proper understanding of the violence in 414/15. Nevertheless, by recognizing the unusual nature of these riots, a better approach might be to argue in the opposite direction and employ the abundant data contained in accounts of the violence to fill out our understanding of the Alexandrian Jewish community. In this manner, the focus of the investigation remains on the Jews themselves, and allows more basic questions concerning the community's composition to be addressed. As a corollary to this approach, our understanding of the violence of 414/15 also will be enhanced, by restoring it to its proper context within the long history of the Alexandrian Jewish community.

### *Tracing an Elusive Presence*

At the outset of any study regarding the Jewish population of late Roman Alexandria a major obstacle presents itself: a scarcity of reliable sources, both literary and archaeological. The volume of Alexandrian source material is far less than that for the Diaspora communities in Syria or Palestine. There is no Egyptian equivalent to the Palestinian Talmud, John Chrysostom's sermons against the Judaizing Christians of Antioch, Libanius's letters to the Jewish patriarch, or the splendid fourth-century synagogues from Galilee. While the extant Jewish papyri somewhat redress this imbalance, they normally concern matters pertaining to the Thebaid or to the Fayyūm, and only rarely mention Alexandria.

Moreover, the deficiencies of the source materials are not simply quantitative but qualitative. The exegetical works of the fifth-century patriarch Cyril, although vital for forming an estimation of his anti-Semitic biases, tell us very little about the social status or economic position of the Jews he so despises. Likewise, monastic sources or ecclesiastical historians seldom refer to the Jews of Alexandria since they figure only peripherally in ascetic tales or in chronicles of the era's many doctrinal controversies. While legal texts are quite useful for analyzing the juridical position of the Jews during the later empire, they provide meager data for discussing the composition of *particular* Jewish communities. The situation improves very little on turning to Jewish source material. Apart from the thorny problems of dating and provenance, talmudic literature displays scant interest in broad historical issues. The nuggets mined from such sources (actually more like fine gold dust) have to be handled very carefully if they are to be used effectively in adorning our mosaic picture of the Alexandrian Jewish community reconstructed from other fragmentary pieces of evidence.

In the face of such source difficulties, it is necessary to utilize a variety of historiographical approaches if one wishes to do more than simply gather stray sherds of seemingly unrelated evidence strewn across the landscape of the primary sources. For example, a comparison of data from Upper Egypt with information regarding other Diaspora communities in the eastern Mediterranean could help supply data lacking for Alexandria. In effect, the missing Alexandrian middle could be created, based on the assumption that Alexandria provided the all-important link between Upper Egypt and the rest of the Mediterranean world. Such an approach is admittedly risky, as it is necessary to keep in mind the often special situation existing in Alexandria. The social world of a small town in the Thebaid may bear very little resemblance to the bustling life of Egypt's cosmopolitan capital, even though they shared certain cultural affinities and a common administrative structure under the authority of the prefect. The choice of the other Mediterranean Diaspora communities needs to be made carefully, selecting primarily those communities of comparable size as well as ones with clearly established ties to the Alexandrian community. Antioch is the most likely choice not only due to its size and its position as the other major seaport in the eastern Mediterranean but also because of the wealth of existing information concerning its Jewish community and the close ties maintained by the Jews of Antioch with their brethren in Alexandria.[2]

A similar approach may employ a chronological rather than a geographical continuum. The presence of virtually identical information in the second century as well as in the fifth century might argue for continuity across the entire period. As one example, the Babylonian Talmud refers to Jewish doctors from Alexandria in a section dating to the late first or early second century. In very different sources, both Socrates Scholasticus and Damascius mention Jewish physicians in fifth-century Alexandria. In light of this evidence, is it possible to speak of a continuity of Jewish medical practice within the city? Such a conclusion seems plausible, bearing in mind the very specific nature of the data and the variety of the historical sources attesting to these doctors.[3]

This chronological methodology, however, must confront a major interpretive issue complicating any survey of the Alexandrian Jewish community. How serious a break occurred in the history of the community at the time of the Jewish revolt (115–17) under Trajan? If the effects of this struggle dealt a mortal blow to the status of Alexandrian Jewry, assertions regarding the continuity of any institution or social entity within the community need to be qualified very carefully.[4] The glories of the Alexandrian Jewish community in the late Ptolemaic and early Roman periods should not blind us to the possibility of radical changes in the community's later fortunes. The Alexandria of Philo may not be the Alexandria of Athanasius. At the same time, an apparent discontinuity in Alexandrian Jewish history may also owe more to a chance clustering of the literary evidence in the early period and again in the fourth century than to any real break in status. The *Letter of Aristeas,* Philo, Josephus, Dio Chrysostom, and the so-called *Acts of the Alexandrian Martyrs* provide us with a dazzling wealth of information which far outshines the stray references found in the chroniclers or papyri of succeeding centuries. A sudden upsurge of evidence during the fourth century may not argue for a parallel renaissance of the community, but may only reflect a general improvement in source material (both in terms of volume and quality) for the empire at large.[5]

### *Philo's World*

Despite the vicissitudes of several centuries, the Jews of late Roman Alexandria could look back and see that throughout much of their history, Alexandrian Jewry had held a preeminent place among the communities of the Diaspora.[6] As early as the reign of Ptolemy I (304–283), there appears to have been some sort of Jewish presence in the city, and Jewish emigration from Palestine throughout the third and second centuries B.C. is reflected in the large number of identifiable Jewish tombs from the eastern suburbs of Alexandria. This population increase resulted from the Ptolemies' extensive use of Jewish mercenaries, the attraction of commercial possibilities in the new capital, and the desire to escape the policies of forced Hellenization instituted by Seleucid kings (notably Antiochus IV) during the third century B.C.[7] By the middle of the first century A.D., the number of Jews in Egypt had grown to such an extent that Philo could estimate the Jewish population at one million or approximately one-eighth of the entire population of Egypt. Although this figure is undoubtedly high, particularly regarding Jewish settlement in Upper Egypt, the ratio is probably close to accurate for Alexandria, which at this time had a population perhaps exceeding 200,000.[8]

As was common in other large Mediterranean cities of the first century A.D., the Jews, like other groups of foreigners, tended to settle in definable enclaves within Alexandria. This concentration of population, however, should not be considered as a ghetto since Philo points out that Jews dwelt in many different sections of the city. Nonetheless, one of the traditional five districts in the city had been given over to them by the Ptolemies, and though the evidence is at times contradictory, it appears that this region was situated beyond Cape Lochias and yet near the governmental quarter of Bruchion. There also seems to have been some aggregation of Jews near the docks of the Eastern and Western Harbors, though this may reflect settlement patterns from the second and later centuries.[9]

The Jews in this early period could be found in virtually every economic level of Alexandrian society. Inscriptions, papyri, and other sources attest the great variety of occupations and social positions held by Alexandrian Jews. These ranged from wealthy merchants and landowners to small shopkeepers, shepherds, and seasonal laborers often numbered among the urban poor. During the Ptolemaic era and perhaps even under the early empire, some of the city's Jews were employed as officials in several sectors of the administrative bureaucracy. Clearly, the communal identity of Alexandria's Jews was not based upon social and economic status. In these respects, they differed very little from their Greek, Roman, or Egyptian neighbors.[10]

Throughout this early period, the Jewish community was organized politically in a fashion similar to other foreign groups resident within the Hellenistic cities of the eastern Mediterranean. Each comprised a sociopolitical unit commonly referred to as a *politeuma*. Smallwood defines this semiautonomous political entity as "a recognized, formally constituted corporation of aliens enjoying the right of domicile in a foreign city, a city within a city; it had its own constitution and administered its internal affairs as an ethnic unit through officials distinct from and independent of those of the host city." While this definition probably gives much more organizational precision than is warranted to an institution for which we possess no formal constitution, it does accurately reflect the degree of self-government and political identity enjoyed by the Jews of Alexandria. The Jewish politeuma was originally administered by an ethnarch who ceded much of his authority to a council of elders, or *gerousia,* sometime during the principate of Augustus. A popular assembly also seems to have existed during this early period, although little is known concerning its composition or activity. Moreover, there were lawcourts whose jurisdiction in matters of Jewish law was recognized as authoritative even in Palestine. Serving as an executive officer for the politeuma was the *hazzan,* who saw to the smooth running of the day-to-day administration within the community.[11]

The office of hazzan, however, was not common to other ethnic politeumata in Hellenistic cities. The hazzan was, in fact, a synagogue official, and much of his authority derived from his role in this all-important institution. For the synagogue, as the setting for various religious rites and festivals, provided the focus for the communal identity of Diaspora Judaism throughout the Hellenistic and Roman world. This also held true for the Jewish community in Alexandria, which could boast of several synagogues serving the politeuma. Chief among these was the so-called Great Synagogue, a richly adorned basilica-like structure, which was so immense that the hazzan had to wave a brightly colored scarf so that the huge congregation, some too distant to hear, could respond with the Amen after a benediction.[12]

One of the most important functions of the synagogue within the life of the Alexandrian community was its role as the assembly place for the various collegia, or craft associations, composed of Jews within the city. A passage in the Babylonian Talmud speaks of Alexandrian collegia of goldsmiths, silversmiths, blacksmiths, and other metalworkers. Mention is also made of collegia specializing in the production of such luxury goods as tapestries and incense. The fame of the Alexandrian incense makers and bakers was such that their goods set the standard for articles used in the Temple ceremony in Jerusalem. These collegia exercised strict control over their respective crafts, and a Jew in the city could only ply his trade by first applying to these groups. Their solidarity is best expressed by the fact that the members of each collegium sat in assigned areas within the synagogue, much the same way that their pagan counterparts occupied assigned seats in many of the theaters of the Greco-Roman world. Further, like their pagan contemporaries, the Jewish collegia of Alexandria could also employ their organizations to voice grievances, express political sentiments, or take collective action.[13]

Although the Jews of Alexandria could boast of wealth and socially varied positions unique within the Diaspora, the Alexandrian community in this early period is chiefly known to us as a result of its remarkable intellectual contributions to the heritage of Jewish culture in antiquity. Rabbis from the city participated in many of the important religious discussions that took place in Palestine during the early talmudic period.[14] In Alexandria, Jewish scholars were largely responsible for the translation of the Jewish scriptures into Greek. This translation, known as the Septuagint, was later regarded by the nascent Christian church as the authoritative text of the Old Testament and served as the vehicle for transmitting many Jewish elements into the developing religion. The translation of the Septuagint is but one example of the ways in which some segments of the Alexandrian community sought to bring about a certain harmony between Judaism and Greek culture in the Hellenistic age and under the early principate. This is best seen in the works of Philo, one of the greatest creative minds of Diaspora Judaism. His blending of Judaism and Platonism as well as his extensive use of the allegorical method in biblical interpretation exerted an enormous influence on later Christian theologians, particularly Clement and Origen.

Even a towering intellectual like Philo, however, could not remain aloof from the bitter conflicts raging between the Alexandrian Jewish community and the Greek inhabitants of the city during the first century A.D. His *Legatio ad Gaium* and *Contra Flaccum,* two apologetical works from this period, attest to the animosity that rent the city and occasionally erupted into rioting and bloodshed. Although many interrelated factors contributed to this tension, two of the most important issues centered on the respective relations of the Jewish and Greek communities with the governing authorities and

Fig. 9. The Jewish community views its surrounding culture. David and Goliath on a simple menorah lamp. David whirls his sling while Goliath holds spear and extends shield. Two airborne stone are above Goliath's shield. Unglazed reddish-brown clay. Alexandria, first–third centuries. Yale, inv. 1913.653.

(Yale University Art Gallery)

the question of political rights for the Jewish community within the city.[15] In order to analyze these complicated intercommunal dynamics, one also has to deal with the problem of determining the extent to which the nationalistic aspirations of the Greek Alexandrians were expressed by militant Hellenism and by what has often been labeled as anti-Semitism (or, more properly, anti-Judaism). Certainly, both the intensity and duration of this strife between the two communities has often been overstated in the past. Nevertheless, the first century A.D. saw some of the most violent manifestations of this conflict, notably in 38 and in 66.

*The Great Divide: The Jewish Revolt of 115–117*

These various incidents, however, pale in comparison with the slaughter and destruction effected by the Jewish Revolt of 115–17.[16] The literary sources detailing this revolt are notoriously sketchy, tendentious, and late.[17] They provide very little indication why the Jews of Cyrenaica, Alexandria, Egypt, and later those of Cyprus, Mesopotamia, and Palestine chose to rise in rebellion during the eighteenth year of Trajan's reign.[18] The timing for this widespread revolt was perhaps occasioned by the emperor's Parthian campaigns and by the consequent reduction of garrison troops throughout the eastern provinces. In Egypt itself, it appears that the normal troop strength was drastically reduced, caused by the transfer to the eastern front of Legio III Cyrenaica, one of the two legions usually stationed in Alexandria's garrison suburb of Nicopolis.[19] Beginning as several local anti-Greek disturbances, the revolt soon took on the proportions of a major war, particularly once the Cyrenaican Jews rallied behind a messianic king named Lucuas.[20] Leaving in their wake a broad swath of destruction, these Cyrenaican Jews marched on Egypt in 116, joining with large numbers of their Egyptian compatriots. It seems likely that the ultimate goal of the rebels was Palestine, thereby transforming a haphazard revolt against Roman authority into an eschatological return of Diaspora Jews to their Promised Land while triumphing over their temporal enemies.[21] Trajan soon recognized the seriousness of the situation, and redeployed a portion of his expeditionary force (including the

Legio III Cyrenaica and its attendant auxiliary units), entrusting the command to one of his most experienced career officers, Q.Marcius Turbo.[22]

Before the arrival of these Roman forces, however, the Jews maintained the upper hand in bloody struggles with Gentiles throughout the entire length of the Egyptian chora. The historian Appian relates how he barely escaped with his life from Jewish rebels near Pelusium in the eastern Delta. Near Hermopolis, Egyptian villagers were recruited to fight the Jews, but after a battle these militia-like troops "were beaten and many were killed." A strategos named Apollonius was forced to abandon the usual ceremonial trappings of his office and take up actual military duties in regions ranging from the upper Thebaid to the Delta. Coin hoards dating from this period as well as papyri written by terrified Gentiles attest the violence and dislocation caused by these disturbances. One such letter has Apollonius's mother imploring the gods on behalf of her son that the Jews "might not roast you."[23]

By the early part of 117 the Romans had regained the troop strength necessary to begin their counteroffensive. Eusebius states that Q. Marcius Turbo "waged war vigorously against [the Jews] in many battles for a considerable time and killed many thousands of Jews." In one engagement, Turbo won an important victory at the head of the Delta near Memphis, a strategic location that provided easy access to the various branches of the Nile and which controlled the routes both to Palestine and to Alexandria. A papyrus letter indicates that Turbo was supported in this battle by the prefect, M. Rutilius Lupus, who probably came from Alexandria with portions of the other garrison legion, Legio XXII Deiotariana. By the summer of 117, Turbo had suppressed the rebellion, and final operations in both Egypt and Cyrenaica were completed by August 117, when Hadrian succeeded Trajan as emperor.[24]

Throughout the revolt, the Jews of Alexandria fared much differently from their brethren fighting in the rest of the Egyptian chora. Although the violence seems to have started almost simultaneously in several regions, the revolt in Alexandria appears to have been bloody but relatively brief. Orosius states that the Jews in Alexandria "were conquered and crushed in a pitched battle." An edict of Lupus preserved on papyrus and dated to October 115 refers to a previous "battle between the Romans and the Jews." This suppression of the revolt in Alexandria occurred as much as a year and a half before Turbo and Lupus were able to put down the revolt in the Heptanomia and in the Thebaid.[25] However, the struggle within the city, though not prolonged, must have been particularly fierce since the depleted garrison troops were unable to overwhelm the rebels as easily as they had during other staseis in the past.[26] At one point, the troops in Nicopolis were unable even to leave their legionary camp, and many soldiers were wounded or killed in the fighting.[27]

During this stage of the conflict, the Jews were able to attack with impunity several pagan shrines in various sectors of the city, including the Nemeseion and the Serapeum.[28] The desecration of pagan temples by Jewish zealots was a common feature in many regions during the revolt, particularly in Cyrenaica.[29] In Alexandria, the rebels may have been motivated in their antipagan attacks by the memory of the systematic desecration of synagogues by their Greek opponents in A.D. 38.[30] Beyond the city, shipping along the Nile was also disrupted and portions of roads connecting the city with its chora were destroyed.[31] The devastation caused by the revolt was so extensive that Hadrian was later said to have "reconstructed Alexandria, demolished by the Jews."[32] Eventually, the garrison troops from Nicopolis met the Jewish rebels in some sort of concerted battle and won a decisive victory, which effectually ended the revolt in Alexandria.

While much of the heavy fighting during the revolt set the Jews against regular Roman army units, evidence from Cyrenaica, Alexandria, and the Egyptian countryside indicates that a substantial portion of the strife also involved armed conflict between the Jews and their Greek neighbors. Eusebius reports that the Jews of Egypt first attacked their Greek countrymen, who were forced to flee to safety within Alexandria. These Greeks, in turn, "imprisoned and slew the Jews who were in the city." Papyrological sources tend to corroborate this account of intercommunal violence within the city and provide a more precise sequence of events. Throughout the conflict between Jewish rebels and Roman troops in Alexandria, the city's Greek population hardly figures at all in the extant sources. Yet, as in A.D. 38, once the main Jewish resistance was broken by Roman troops, the Greek Alexandrians began to initiate violent and destructive reprisals. In his edict addressed to the Alexandrians, the prefect alludes to a number of slaves "provided for by the powerful" who created disturbances provoking bloodshed and incendiarism. There are indications that these incidents occurred after Lupus left the city with a portion of the garrison force in order to join up with Turbo's army in the chora. Fragments from later *Acts of the Alexandrian Martyrs* confirm the important role played by slaves in these disturbances and also add that some sort of farcical mime-show was staged ridiculing Jewish messianic aspirations. Perhaps it was during this period of heightened intercommunal tension that the Greeks "imprisoned and slew the Jews." Moreover, it was probably while the Greeks were carrying out these reprisals against a weakened Jewish community that the Great Synagogue of Alexandria, the glory of Diaspora Judaism, was utterly destroyed.[33]

The brevity of the struggle within the city does not minimize the ferocity that characterized the conflict. Indeed, it would be difficult to exaggerate the effects this violence had on the Alexandrian Jewish community. While it is safe to discount the talmudic claim that "sixty myriads upon sixty myriads" were slaughtered in the city, the loss of Jewish life must have been high during the course of fighting against both Roman troops and Alexandrian Greeks. Compounding this decrease in Jewish population was the subsequent emigration of many Jews, including prominent Alexandrian rabbis, to Palestine.[34] Those Jews who remained were forcibly relocated to a new settlement just outside the walls and to the east of the city by Lupus's successor, Q. Rammius Martialis. The prefect's order was not greeted with enthusiasm by the Greeks of the city, as some of them complained to the emperor that the new extramural Jewish district could become a base from which attacks could be launched against Alexandrian Gentiles. Some commentators have interpreted Martialis's order as the creation of a supplementary Jewish district to house the large number of Egyptian Jews who had fled to the city from the violence in the countryside.[35] Given the tribulations suffered by the Alexandrian Jewish community, it seems doubtful that the city would have held much attraction to Jews from the chora as a refuge from Gentile violence. Instead, it appears that the prefect only wished to maintain public order by separating the two combative communities, establishing them on either side of the governmental quarter of Bruchion. Martialis's program for communal coexistence seems to have been largely successful. However, the success of his policy doubtless owed more to the decimated state of the Jewish community than to Martialis's administrative abilities. It would be many years before the Alexandrian Jewish community would again play an important role in the city's life.[36]

*A Tenuous Recovery*

Although the catastrophe of 115 dealt a severe blow to the status of Alexandrian Jewry, it did not result in the complete annihilation of the community. In the aftermath, it is still possible to observe traces of internal government and communal organization. The most notable instance is the sending of an embassy to Hadrian circa 119 to rebut charges leveled against the Alexandrian Jews by spokesmen of the Greek community concerning incidents that took place during the revolt. The precise composition of this Jewish embassy is difficult to determine, as the details are contained in one of the fragmentary partisan pamphlets making up the *Acta Alexandrinorum*.[37] Nevertheless, the mere fact that the Jews were able to present their case before the emperor argues against the total breakdown of communal life among the Alexandrian Jews.

In another vein, it sometimes has been stated that the lack of a response on the part of Diaspora Jews to the revolt of Bar Kochba in Palestine (132–35) is attributable to the exhaustion of these communities after the war of 115–17. In Alexandria, however, this rejection of Palestinian zealotry may be the result of a conscious decision on the part of the community's leadership. In 72, zealous assassins from Palestine known as the *sicarii* had attempted to incite the Alexandrian community, and the gerousia, in a remarkable display of authority within the politeuma, handed these troublemakers over to the Romans.[38] While we have no exact information regarding the composition or even the formal existence of a Jewish politeuma in Alexandria after 115, the previous stance of the community toward outside agitation may have dictated a similar response to the spread of Palestinian zealotry at this later date. This absence of support for the Bar Kochba rebellion may also point to the reemergence of moderate leadership within the Alexandrian community in the period following the revolt of 115–17. Unfortunately, the lack of specific evidence concerning both the embassy to Hadrian and the response to the Bar Kochba revolt prohibits pressing the argument for continuity in internal governance very far. All that one can say is that, for the next century, the Jewish community fails to maintain its former active role in the city's political life, as Jewish antagonists seemingly disappear from the Alexandrian *Acta,* and Jews likewise take no part in the disturbances occasioned by Caracalla's visit in 215.[39]

For other Jewish communities around the Mediterranean, the remainder of the second century and the entire third century marked off a period of recovery and consolidation, and also witnessed the precarious restoration of the relationship between the Jews and the imperial government which had existed prior to the troubles of A.D. 66 through 135. Once the question of Jewish nationalism had been decisively settled by the bloody suppression of Bar Kochba's revolt, the Roman government seemed content to establish a modus vivendi with the Jews of the empire. Certain restrictions were imposed upon the Jews, such as a prohibition against settlement within Jerusalem, now Aelia Capitolina, and also an attempt to restrict the practice of circumcision. Nonetheless, evidence from the Talmud indicates that many of these legal restrictions were seldom enforced and that Judaism thrived and even expanded through proselytism across this period.[40] Caracalla is remembered as having been particularly favorable to the Jews, and his Constitutio Antoniniana removed any disabilities in their legal status by granting them full Roman citizenship, along with the rest of the empire's inhabitants. Even the attitudes of the Roman literary elite toward the Jews seem to have improved during this period, as there is no echo in Cassius Dio of the vitriolic scorn heaped upon the Jews so characteristic of earlier authors like Tacitus or Juvenal.[41]

In Palestine, the Jewish communities appear to have recovered remarkably well following the upheaval of Bar Kochba's revolt. The Sanhedrin was reconstituted after the war as the supreme governing authority within Judaism, and the office of Nasi or patriarch was likewise revived. The development of compliant and responsible structures of authority within Palestine was looked upon favorably by the imperial government, now that the Jewish Temple, capital, and even the Jewish state itself had ceased to exist. The focus of this revived Palestinian Judaism shifted from Jerusalem to Galilee, as rabbinic academies were set up in both Tiberias and Sepphoris. Far from being a period of slow recovery, this era witnessed the flowering of rabbinic Judaism in Palestine, characterized by profound ethical and theological discussions later enshrined in the Palestinian Talmud. The Jewish communities in Galilee also saw a rapid recovery in their material prosperity, in part enhanced by Jewish immigration from the rest of the Diaspora.

A similar tale of recovery and expansion during the later second and early third centuries could be told of other major Diaspora communities like Antioch and Rome. Even smaller Jewish communities on the order of Sardis or Dura experienced a certain level of prosperity at this time. The same, however, could not be said of the community in Alexandria. The scarcity of information pertaining to the Alexandrian Jews in the latter half of the second century and the majority of the third century cannot be attributed solely to the chance survival (or in this case, the destruction) of the relevant source material. This paucity of evidence from the second and third centuries stands in marked contrast to the extended period prior to 115, as well as to the comparatively abundant material from other contemporary Jewish communities.

Christian sources begin to become a factor during this period, but the evidence they present concerning Alexandrian Jewry needs to be handled very carefully. Although certain echoes of rabbinic exegesis may be found in the works of Clement and of Origen, it is perhaps overstating the case to label this as "definite evidence of the presence of Jews in Alexandria and of contacts between Jews and Christians to discuss exegetical and theological matters." While Clement seems to have been acquainted with at least one Jew in the city, most of his knowledge of Judaism appears to have been acquired at second or third hand. Further, much of the evidence used to establish a "Jewish connection" between Origen and rabbinic teachers is probably attributable to the period after he took up residence in Caesarea.[42]

Better evidence for Jewish-Christian interaction during this period can be seen in two pieces of Christian literature with similar aims. Although some scholars argue for a Syrian provenance for the work, the *Epistle of Barnabas* was a relatively moderate specimen of anti-Jewish literature which was probably produced in Alexandria. This work argues that the Christians now possess God's covenant through Christ's fulfillment of the Law, and that the Jews misunderstood the spiritual intention of the Mosaic regulations. An even more explicit indication of Jewish-Christian relations in Alexandria comes from the *Dialogue of Timothy and Aquila,* dated to the late second century. This anti-Jewish tract was reworked and used extensively by later writers, forming the basis for many polemical works in the *Adversus Judeos* genre. Despite later revisions, however, it seems to have originated in an actual discussion held in Alexandria between a Jew and a Christian, though perhaps not in the form of a public dispute. Like other specimens of the same genre, the names of the figures in the debate may have been altered or added later. Nevertheless, the dialogue attests contacts between Alexandrian Christians and Jews, perhaps even providing evidence for some sort of official spokesman from the Jewish community. It would be misleading to infer from such stray notices in Christian sources, however, that the Alexandrian Jewish community was strong and thriving.[43]

Jewish sources, in fact, depict a community struggling to maintain its identity in a changed environment. In contrast to the preceding period when Alexandrian Jews authored works ranging from philosophy, poetry, and drama to exegesis and philology, only one type of literature is extant from the period following the revolt—apocalyptic. The twelfth and thirteenth books of the *Oracula Sibyllina* may have been written in Alexandria by two different Jewish authors living circa 235 and 265. The dark visions in these works are dominated by images of Rome's incessant wars and eventual chastisement at the hands of its enemies—testimonies of a community alienated and threatened by its surroundings. The only Alexandrian Jewish author known to us by name is a certain Judas, another apocalyptic writer who "thought that the coming of the Antichrist, which was much talked about, was then near." It is instructive to compare this literary activity with that of Jews in nearby Palestine, where rabbinic authors were constructing the earlier portions of the Palestinian Talmud, having already compiled the Mishnah.[44]

In the same period, Jewish life in the rest of Egypt gives the appearance of thriving on a much higher level than that downriver in Alexandria. The papyrological testimony concerning non-Alexandrian Jewish social and economic life is so abundant that one hesitates, at first, to speak even in terms of a "recovery" of these Jewish communities from the devastation wrought by the war of 115–17. As in earlier centuries, Jews are found in every sector of Egyptian economic and social life. Several are landowners, leasing property to tenants, and at least one is involved in the transport of bulk goods on the Nile. The great majority of the Egyptian Jews appear in the papyri as small tenant farmers and tax-paying peasants. There even seem to have been some Jews employed as soldiers, a startling fact so soon after the violence and destruction of the years 115–17. Jewish festivals are still being celebrated regularly in these areas of Egypt, creating a picture of Jewish life which differs little from that found in other regions. Alexandria thus appears to have been an unexpected pocket of Jewish decline between the thriving Jewish communities abroad and the prosperity found among the Jews upriver.[45]

This apparent contrast may be partially attributed to the difference in source materials concerning Jewish communities in the Delta as opposed to the regions farther south. Throughout antiquity the papyrological sources shed very little light on Alexandria and its hinterland since papyri only survive in the dry climate found in the Heptanomia and the Thebaid—though documents of an Alexandrian provenance may find their way into archives upriver. Thus, it is possible to exaggerate the status of the Egyptian Jews at the expense of those in Alexandria.

Further, a more accurate picture of the status of the Jewish communities in Upper Egypt is revealed once the papyri from the second and third centuries are compared with those prior to the revolt of 115–17. The scarcity of the papyri alone attests the effects of the rebellion. There are some sixty-one Jewish papyri from the period after Actium, but only thirty between 117 and 337 which are clearly Jewish.[46] Depopulation in some regions after the revolt must have been severe, as streets formerly identified as Jewish in Egyptian towns reverted to Gentile ownership. In Sebennytos, only one in twenty taxpayers can be identified as Jewish, and in Karanis there appears to have been just one Jewish family in the entire town. Moreover, confiscations of Jewish property were widespread in the period immediately following 115–17. While the image of the Jews improved markedly in literature produced elsewhere, Greco-Egyptian literature in the second and third centuries continues to portray Jews in a bitter and degrading manner. In light of these adverse conditions, some Egyptian Jews apparently chose the route of apostasy, since they are seen in the papyri performing duties clearly incompatible with the practice of Judaism, such as keeping guard at night in a local Serapeum.[47] Only toward the end of the third century is an improvement seen in the fortunes of Egyptian Jews, as synagogues are restored and Jews appear more frequently in higher economic and social positions.[48] In this manner, the Jews of Upper Egypt resemble their brethren in Alexandria much more than the Jews of other Diaspora communities.

Taking into account the disparity in the survival of source materials for Egyptian and Alexandrian Jewry, thereby allowing for a much more detailed picture of the decline experienced by communities in the countryside, one must still conclude that the Jews of Alexandria underwent a much greater reduction in status than their brethren throughout the rest of Egypt. Moreover, the extremely slow recovery of Jewish life in Alexandria, particularly when compared with other Jewish communities in the eastern Mediterranean, would indicate that Alexandrian Jewry suffered a near-fatal blow as a result of the revolt of 115–17. Eusebius seems to attribute this disparity in fortunes to the reprisals of Alexandrian Greeks and Greco-Egyptian refugees from the chora upon Alexandrian Jews at the time of the revolt. A more likely explanation for the devastated state of the Jewish community lies in the conflict between Alexandrian Jews and the legionary forces stationed at Nicopolis during 115. Alexandria's strategic importance as the conduit for Egypt's grain and other wealth made the suppression of armed revolt within the city a vital concern for the prefect and his emperor. Doubtless, the need to restore order as well as the concentration of troops just outside the city resulted in a much more severe treatment accorded to the Jews of Alexandria than that visited upon the Jews of the countryside. This disproportionate punishment accounts for the fact that the recovery of the Alexandrian community occurred only at the end of the third century. As we have seen, between 115 and the early fourth century the community virtually disappears from the historical record. Clearly, the age of Philo was over.[49]

## *The Fourth-Century Community*

After Diocletian's capture of Alexandria in 298 and the final suppression of the revolt of Domitius Domitianus and Achilleus, the administration of both Egypt and Alexandria was reorganized along the lines of Diocletian's reforms of other imperial provinces.One of the main characteristics of this era is a sudden upsurge in the quantity and quality of the extant literary sources, which, in turn, allows for a much fuller historical reconstruction of the institutions and culture of fourth-century society than is possible for the preceding century.

This vast increase in source material also holds true for Alexandria and its Jewish community. In addition to talmudic and papyrological sources, which continue to provide valuable information concerning Alexandrian Jewry, data found in patristic writings (especially ecclesiastical chronicles) and legal texts become much more abundant. This increase in ancient testimonies concerning the Alexandrian community, however, does not necessarily signify a corresponding improvement in the status of Jews in Alexandria. In order to trace changes in the community's fortunes, it is necessary to factor in the across-the-board increase in historical sources at this time, the general improvement of conditions throughout the empire, and the *specific* data found in the sources which pertain to

Alexandrian Jews. Attention must also be given to the bias of the different sources, since their principles of selection and organization may drastically skew our picture of the Alexandrian Jewish community. Mention was made at the beginning of this chapter of several Jewish doctors in the city who became apostates during the course of the fifth century, and the possibility of concluding that there was a continuity of Jewish medical practice in Alexandria from the first century through the end of antiquity. The only reason we know of these doctors is that Christian writers chose to exult in the fact that prominent Jews in the city embraced Christianity. How many other professions and social positions within the Jewish community are we ignorant of only because their enumeration did not fit into the programmatic scheme of some contemporary writer? Yet, for all of the shortcomings of these primary sources, the wealth and variety of information they provide greatly facilitate the historical reconstruction of the Jewish community's social world during the fourth and fifth centuries.[50]

As the Alexandrian community emerges into the light of late antiquity, a logical first topic for investigation would be the organization and internal governance of the community. Was the former Jewish politeuma reinstated, and if so, was it presided over by an ethnarch and gerousia? In reply, it must be said that the sources, abundant as they are, fail to mention any of the traditional offices or institutions associated with the politeuma. The political structures of the Hellenistic and early Roman period seem to be only a memory for the Jews of fourth-century Alexandria.

In place of the former politeuma, the synagogue stands out as the dominant institution within the Jewish community of late Roman Alexandria. Although the synagogue held a vital place in the life of the community prior to the revolt of 115–17, its role in that early period was restricted largely to social and religious functions. In consequence, it was clearly subordinate to the broader political structure provided by the politeuma. By the fourth century, however, the political importance of the synagogue had increased until it became the locus of political authority within the community. The Roman administration recognized this authority and regarded the synagogue as a collegium responsible for paying the *fiscus Judaicus*.

The ethnarch of the former politeuma came to be replaced by an *archisynagogos,* referred to in a fourth-century Hebrew papyrus as "the head of the Kneseth." Archisynagogoi may have existed within the Alexandrian Jewish community as early as the first century A.D., but they do not appear to have functioned as communal leaders until the late Roman period. Since there is evidence for several synagogues existing within the city of Alexandria, it was probably the collective body of these archisynagogoi who were considered "the chief men of the Jews" (*tous Ioudaion proteuontas*), summoned by the enraged Cyril after the theater incident in 414/15. It is tempting to equate this administrative system with the gerousia of the former politeuma, although the only evidence supporting such an identification comes from a Hebrew papyrus found in the Heptanomia which refers to a governing body known as "the elders of the Kneseth." Moreover, it is instructive to note the governing structure of the Jewish community in fourth-century Antioch, where a gerousia of archisynagogoi appears to have been the principal authority within the community. This Antiochene gerousia was presided over by a *gerousiarchos,* attested by the funerary inscription of one such official found at Beth She'arim in Palestine.[51]

It is unwise, given the nature of our evidence, to place too much weight on any reconstruction of the hierarchy and functions of synagogue officials during this period. For example, a recent study has called into question traditional assumptions concerning the actual role of archisynagogoi in Diaspora communities. Epigraphic evidence suggests that archisynagogoi were less religious leaders than patrons and benefactors of their communities. Thus, the office assumes the contours of other honorific titles from Greek cities. All this bespeaks a certain fluidity in communal leadership. The Alexandrian community reflects this Diaspora diversity, since the pattern of leadership seems to be largely collective throughout the later Roman period, with no single official appointed as the head or even as the spokesman for "the chief men of the Jews." Doubtless, the leadership of the Alexandrian community included wealthy benefactors as well as prominent rabbis, like R. Abbahu, an influential *Amora* active in Palestine who had lived in Alexandria at the beginning of the fourth century. This collective mode of leadership certainly would have been best suited to a communal structure based upon the synagogue.[52]

In light of the available sources, it is difficult to determine the precise significance of this shift from a traditional politeuma structure to one oriented exclusively around the synagogue. It is possible that the community's internal organization went through a period of retrenchment after the revolt of 115–17, resulting in the enhanced importance of the basic building-block of Diaspora communities—the synagogue. It could also be argued that the increased emphasis on the synagogue represents a movement away from Hellenism and its attendant political structures and a return to Jewish institutions.[53] The Hebraization of both the Alexandrian and Egyptian Jewish communities becomes pronounced by the last decades of the fourth century, and although the shift toward the synagogue occurs much earlier, this may presage the important cultural changes taking place later in the century. Perhaps the simplest explanation accounting for the growth of the synagogue's political role is that the Jews of Alexandria no longer needed the "separate but equal" status that a politeuma structure gave to them. By the early third century, Jews were permitted to hold municipal office throughout the empire, and Caracalla's universal granting of Roman citizenship to the empire's inhabitants in 212 made other citizenship controversies moot issues. Despite the wealth of information we have pertaining to Alexandrian Jews in the later empire, not once does the formerly predominant citizenship issue raise its head. Since it was no longer necessary to maintain the political structure provided by a politeuma, it comes as no surprise that the mantle of political leadership fell to the institution ranked just below, an institution also benefiting from certain cultural changes occurring within the Jewish community.

Unlike Antioch, where there is specific evidence for at least three separate synagogues in the city and its suburban areas, the Alexandrian community is only known to have possessed *synagogoi*. There are no archaeological remains of the Alexandrian synagogues as there are for the synagogues of other Jewish communities in late antiquity, such as the one constructed in Apamea in 391 or the exquisite Galilean synagogues dated to approximately the same era.[54] Thus, both the number and the location of the Alexandrian synagogues are entirely unknown, even though several fragmentary votive stelai commemorate donations to Alexandrian synagogues. Consequently, it is nearly impossible to estimate the population of Jews in Alexandria. Little faith can be placed in the purported letter of ʿAmr ibn al-ʿAs to the caliph ʿUmar in 642 that he had captured a city boasting "40,000 tributary Jews," since he also reckons that Alexandria possessed "4,000 baths and 400 theatres." In the period under discussion, the only indication of the community's size is Socrates' description of the Jews as a "multitude" (*plethos*), although the term could easily be taken as the pejorative assessment, "mob." Further, there is little information from which one might calculate the ratio of Jewish inhabitants to that of the entire population of the city, beyond the fact that they were able to hold their own in street battles with the Christians.[55]

Although there are no precise figures concerning the number of Jews in late Roman Alexandria, they continue to be found occupying virtually every social status and economic position within the city. During late antiquity, as in the period before 115, Alexandrian Jews even made up a portion of the city's intellectual elite, including such professions as philosophers, mathematicians, and teachers. No less than four Jewish physicians are attested by name in the early fifth century, one of whom, Jacob, went on to become the court physician of the emperor Leo. These doctors undoubtedly represent but a fraction of the Jewish physicians within the city, since they are only mentioned in the sources because of their apostasy from Judaism. It is worth remembering the high esteem accorded to Alexandrian medical practice in late antiquity—Ammianus Marcellinus states that "although a physician's work itself indicates it, yet in place of every testimony it is enough to commend his knowledge of the art, if he has said that he was trained at Alexandria" (figure 10).[56]

The economic status of Alexandrian Jews also appears to have improved markedly during the course of the fourth and fifth centuries, an indication that the community was recovering from the lean years of the previous two centuries. Some Jews attained enough wealth to acquire slaves, and a late source tells of a particularly

A

wealthy Jew named Urbib who converted to Christianity at some time in the fifth century. Jews in the Heptanomia and the Thebaid likewise enjoyed increased prosperity during the late Roman period. Several appear in the extant papyri as landowners or merchants of goods such as alum or wine. A businessman named Josep is even named in a payment order as a banker, the only Jew identified as such in the entire corpus of papyri from Egypt—a collection of source material ranging over nine centuries. One intriguing papyrus letter dating to the late fifth or early sixth century mentions an Alexandrian Jew who was well enough off to bear the cost of travel

B

Fig. 10. Medicine in Alexandria. (A) Ivory medicine box with compartments. (B) Lid depicts Hygieia, the goddess of health, holding a snake. Sixth century. Dumbarton Oaks, inv. 48.15.

(Byzantine Visual Resources, © 1991, Dumbarton Oaks, Washington, D.C.)

upriver in order to participate in some judicial matter. The Gentile author of the letter exhibits great anxiety regarding the effect that the appearance of this wealthy Alexandrian Jew might have on the course of the litigation. Perhaps the Jew's interest in the case was connected with some property he owned in the countryside. Alexandrian Jews are attested as landowners during the period before 115, and patterns of land tenure in late antiquity disclose the long-standing practice of individuals within the city holding land in the chora. At the very least, the papyrus would suggest that the wealth and status of certain members within the Alexandrian Jewish community could be felt well into the city's hinterland.[57]

Perhaps the most telling evidence concerning the improved economic status of Alexandrian Jewry is a well-tooled, late Roman dedicatory inscription set up in one of the city's synagogues "for the safety" (*soterias*) of a woman named Roua.[58] The name itself is not particularly Jewish, there being no parallel from other Jewish inscriptions or papyri from Egypt. However, three other names appear in the inscription: Borouch, Barachias, and Entolios—all three clearly Jewish. Although the relationship of the individuals is not completely clear, it appears that Barouch is the son of Barachias, the former dedicating the inscription to Roua, daughter of Entolios. Inscriptions of this quality do not come cheaply, thus arguing for the existence of one or more wealthy families of Jews in late antique Alexandria. It also speaks of a Jewish community whose social values allowed for the display of such wealth.

The provenance of the Roua inscription may also provide a clue as to the economic activity generating the wealth represented by the inscription. It was carved on a large column base found in the vicinity of the so-called Roman Tower, which was located along the shore of the Great (or Eastern) Harbor between the Heptastadion and Cape Lochias (figure 4). The establishment of a synagogue in this region tells us very little in itself, until it is recalled that the eastern portion of this area was the site of extensive Jewish settlement throughout the history of the city. Strabo relates that in an earlier period this region was also the location of many of Alexandria's dockyards and warehouses, particularly those catering to trade throughout the Mediterranean.[59]

Although it is unwise to make the standard assumption that there was a prominent mercantile element among the Jewish populations of every major port city of the Mediterranean, in the case of Alexandria there is strong evidence for Jewish maritime interests. Aside from the uncertain testimony of the Roua inscription, there are two quite disparate sources which speak of Jewish *navicularii* within the city. An imperial edict issued to the Praefectus Augustalis directs that Jewish navicularii are not to be compelled to perform duties incumbent upon other navicularii, most likely the transport of grain to Rome and Constantinople.[60] This edict, the only mention of Jewish navicularii in a group of some thirty-eight laws pertaining to shipmasters in the *Codex Theodosianus,* seems to attach particular importance to the role of Alexandrian Jews in the commerce of the eastern Mediterranean.

The maritime activities of Alexandrian Jews are also revealed in a vastly different source, a letter written circa 400 by Synesius, the urbane bishop of Ptolemais. In this letter addressed to his brother, Euoptius, Synesius chronicles the disasters he encountered on a voyage he took from Alexandria to Cyrenaica. Synesius booked passage in Alexandria with a Jewish navicularius named Amarantus, whom he describes as "a teacher of the [Mosaic] law." Not only was the ship's captain Jewish but nearly half of the crew as well. Synesius reports how the ship almost suffered shipwreck owing to the religious practices of the captain—who refused to steer the vessel in the midst of a storm because the Sabbath had begun! Synesius is obviously taking liberties with his tale, no doubt to enhance the dramatic qualities of his adventures. Nonetheless, this amusing anecdote corroborates the picture provided by the *Codex Theodosianus,* that there was a variety of Jewish shipping interests in late Roman Alexandria, perhaps constituting an important segment of the economic life of the community.[61]

This may account for at least a portion of the occasionally violent conflict between the Jewish and Christian populations of the city during late antiquity. As we have seen, Jewish settlement was concentrated near the Eastern Harbor, where the majority of the Mediterranean trade was located. The Jews, having been exempted from the compulsory duties of the grain fleet, were thus at liberty to pursue other more profitable trading ventures. The Christian navicularii, on the other hand, were subject to these duties and were required to provide the grain fleet that was based in the Eunostos (or Western) Harbor. These Christian ship captains and sailors were among the most ardent supporters of the Alexandrian patriarch and were willing even to take up arms in defense of their ecclesiastical patron against both local opponents and agents of imperial authority. Perhaps one factor contributing to this strong patron-client bond was a certain amount of economic competition between Jewish shippers and Christian navicularii, who doubtless resented having to bear alone the onerous duties involved in the transport of imperial grain. This is not to say that an economic motive was the sole cause of Jewish-Christian conflict in Alexandria. Other issues were vital in separating the two communities and promoting violence in the city. Yet this neglected economic factor may help provide some of the important context which facilitated the growth of this intercommunal conflict.[62]

One of Alexandria's most renowned exports throughout the Roman period was the cloth produced in the city's workshops, and portions of the Jewish community were involved in this sector of the Alexandrian economy. The numerous linen workshops were manned predominantly by Egyptian fellahin, Caracalla singling out this industry in his expulsion order of 215 as the main source of urban employment for workers from the countryside. Jewish weavers during late antiquity, however, tended to specialize in the production of finely woven garments and tapestries. In the Talmud, Rabbi Hisada forbids pilgrims from using the highly skilled "Alexandrian mending" to repair clothes torn as a sign of mourning over the destruction of the Temple. The rationale for this prohibition is that the advanced techniques used at Alexandria would make the garment look as good as new, thereby nullifying the act of mourning. The beautiful tapestries created in Jewish workshops were celebrated equally by the poet Claudian at the end of the fourth century and by the monk-geographer Cosmas Indicopleustes during the sixth century. Moreover, if there was a degree of continuity in crafts and professions throughout antiquity, Jewish artisans in Alexandria probably continued their trades as silversmiths, incense makers, perfumers, and gem cutters. The production of these exquisite luxury goods would go hand in hand with the marketing of these same goods across the Mediterranean by Jewish merchants based in Alexandria.[63]

Another aspect of Jewish economic life within Alexandria concerns the question of debt, which seems to have been a large problem for some sectors of the community. Synesius's navicularius, Amarantus, "courted death owing to his bankrupt condition." In fact, his crew was unable to replace a torn sail during the storm since the spare one had been pledged as security for a loan. The financial difficulties of one Alexandrian Jew certainly do not demonstrate that there was a problem of widespread debt, but another legal text from the *Codex Theodosianus* implies that Amarantus was not alone in his financial straits. In an edict dating from 397, the emperors prohibit Jews from taking sanctuary in Christian churches in order to escape paying debts or being apprehended "for some criminal charge"—perhaps in connection with their financial obligations. The edict is addressed to Archaleus, the praefectus Augustalis, and therefore argues for the problem of Jewish debt being particularly acute at Alexandria—or at least a problem serious enough for Archalaeus to refer to imperial scrutiny. Otherwise, the emperors would have followed the normal procedure and addressed the edict to the praetorian prefect of the East. It would be unwise, nonetheless, to assume that the question of debt was a major factor in the conflict and violence within the city. The Alexandrian Jews probably differed very little from their Gentile neighbors in this respect, since debt was a common problem in later Roman Egypt. Nevertheless, financial difficulties might well have contributed to the tension in the city, occasionally being manifested in violent incidents.[64]

The recovery of Alexandrian Jewry after the difficult years of the second and third centuries can also be seen in the thriving religious life of the community during the later Roman period. Synagogues were rebuilt and Alexandrian rabbis, like the widely quoted Amora, R. Abbahu, even gained renown among other Diaspora communities. Ties between the Alexandrian community and Palestinian Judaism were strengthened throughout the fourth century, with the *apostoli* of the Palestinian patriarch regularly traveling to Egypt to collect tithes. On one occasion in the fourth century, the Alexandrian community sent questions concerning different feast days to the Amoraim in Palestine. Passages in the Talmud further report that Alexandrian Jews prepared Passover breads in a special manner, and testify to the devoutness with which the Sabbath was observed in the city.[65]

This apparently renewed religious vigor among the Jews of Alexandria raises the question concerning the relationship between Greco-Roman civilization and the cultural values of Alexandrian Jews during the fourth and fifth centuries. In the earlier discussion regarding Jewish political institutions, it was suggested that the abandonment of the former politeuma structure and the increased emphasis on the synagogue represented a movement away from Hellenism and a return to more Hebraic values. This trend toward Hebraization was strengthened during the course of the fourth century, and is evidenced by a number of Hebrew papyri from Oxyrhynchus. Tcherikover considers these papyri to be the most important testimonies of this profound cultural change, since they show "some obscure leaders of two Jewish communities in the Egyptian *chōra* carrying on their correspondence in Hebrew"—a language which perhaps the erudite Philo did not know three hundred years earlier. Tcherikover sees this trend toward Hebraization emanating from Palestine, where Hebraic culture was flourishing during the third and fourth centuries. By employing the methodological model developed at the beginning of this chapter, a natural conclusion would be that the cultural views of at least some Alexandrian Jews were likely to be similar to those of their brethren in Palestine and Upper Egypt, and therefore reflect this increased emphasis on Hebraic culture.[66]

On closer inspection, however, the entire question regarding the "de-Hellenization" of Alexandrian Jewry should probably be reformulated to reflect the fluid nature of cultural change in late antiquity. It is as improbable to assume that Alexandrian Judaism in the age of Philo was thoroughly Hellenized as it is to conclude that Palestinian Judaism in the talmudic period was exclusively Hebraic. After all, the Jewish patriarch Gamaliel V was a friend and frequent correspondent of Libanius.[67] "Alexandrian Judaism" and "Palestinian Judaism" were never monolithic entities, and it is more accurate to view these as ideal types created by modern commentators for the convenience of categorizing cultural phenomena within Judaism. It is far too easy to become mesmerized by Philo and the Septuagint and assume that this large and diverse community was characterized by cultural uniformity. It is even less likely that the various elements within the Jewish community underwent changes in their cultural orientation at the same time or at the same rate. Consequently, the "de-Hellenization" of Alexandrian Jewry may have occurred only within that segment of the community that was Hellenized to begin with. In a different light, this "de-Hellenization" may have been, in fact, a further "Hebraization" of another segment of the community which was already opposed to Greco-Roman culture.

This purported cultural transformation is further called into question by a recently edited papyrus from Oxyrhynchus. The text of the papyrus is in Hebrew and consists of a lamentation over the misfortunes suffered by the Jews "in the days of our oppressors"—which the editor identifies as the period following the revolt of 115–17. Hebrew was also known among the Jews of Antinoopolis in the late second or early third century, attested by a Hebrew funerary inscription for a certain Lazarus. Moreover, it is impossible to speak of a uniform cultural shift away from Hellenism by Egyptian Jews in later centuries, since two early fourth-century papyri from Karanis identify a Jew named Aurelius Johannes as a gymnasiarch. The mixed nature of Jewish culture is further illustrated by an early fifth-century marriage contract from Antinoopolis. Although the contract is written in Hebrew characters and follows a traditional Palestinian formula for such a document, the language of the contract is both Greek and Aramaic, and displays additional influences from the surrounding Greco-Egyptian milieu. If such cultural diversity is found among the Jews of the chora, the cultural life of their brethren in a city as cosmopolitan as Alexandria is likely to have been even more rich and varied. While it has been noted that some Alexandrian Jews were quite devout in their observance of the Sabbath, it is also instructive to recall that large numbers of them spent their day of rest by thronging the theaters for mime shows.[68]

## *The Contours of Jewish-Christian Conflict*

Tcherikover attributes the alleged abandonment of Hellenism by Egyptian and Alexandrian Jews to the growing influence and power of the Christian Church throughout society during the fourth and fifth centuries.[69] As one would expect, however, relations between the Jewish and Christian communities in Alexandria were as multifaceted as the complex urban environment they inhabited. Nor should it be forgotten that Alexandria still boasted an influential pagan community, which figured significantly into the mix of urban social relations. The riot of 414/15 is but one episode in the long history of Jewish-Gentile interaction within the city. Unfortunately, the violence surrounding this one incident has often been taken to characterize the entire relationship between the Jewish and Christian communities.[70] Such was not the case. On closer examination, it appears that violence and bloodshed merely stand at one end of a broad continuum of Jewish-Christian relations in Alexandria.

At the other end of this continuum were the everyday contacts between members of each commmunity, which doubtless took place in a bustling urban setting characterized as a "face-to-face society" by modern commentators.[71] Christian sermons and canon law attest the close social and economic relations that Christians and Jews maintained in Mediterranean cities from Spain to Syria.[72] Given the integral role of Jews within the Alexandrian economy, contact between Jews and their Gentile neighbors would have been both necessary and normal. Such contact could well have moved beyond the realm of economic relations, as there are provisions in the *Codex Theodosianus* that forbid intermarriage between Christians and Jews.[73] These sorts of legal prohibitions often imply the existence of the forbidden activity, since there would have been no need for such laws otherwise. Moreover, successive edicts on the same subject and increasingly brutal punishments attached to the crime belie the reality that enforcement of the central government's directives was haphazard at best. Consequently, it is probable to assume that Jewish-Christian intermarriage in Alexandria was frequent enough to be considered a problem by the authorities.[74] In addition, Christian emperors during the later Roman period attempted to prohibit the ownership of Christian slaves by Jews, yet another form of contact between members of the two communities and one likely to have been common in late Roman Egypt.[75]

Aside from everyday contacts between Jews and Christians in

Alexandria, there were also occasions when representatives of the religious leadership from the two communities were able to meet together, often for formal theological disputations. In this context, it is important to note that the two communities shared a great many things in common, particularly their views of the pagan culture that had surrounded them for centuries. Nonetheless, their very proximity in ideology often exacerbated the differences between them, differences that are especially highlighted in the literature of these disputations known by later scholars as *Adversus Judeos*.[76] It is not always clear whether the works within this genre are actual reports of dialogues that took place, extensive reworkings of such dialogues composed at a later date, or literary pieces that are solely the invention of the author. Yet, even if a given work proves to be invention, such compositions were not created in a vacuum and often expressed views known to have been held by both sides. Mention has already been made of the widely read late second-century dialogue that has survived under the title, *The Dialogue of Timothy and Aquila*. A similar fourth-century work, *The Dialogue of Athanasius and Zacchaeus*, purports to be the text of a dispute held between a prominent Alexandrian Jew and the famous patriarch.[77] Similar discussions appear to have been common throughout the eastern Mediterranean and involved such noted churchmen as Jerome, Epiphanius, and Theodoret of Cyrus. During the early fifth century, Cyril of Alexandria composed his *On the Apostasy of the Synagogue* (no longer extant), which may have reflected the charged atmosphere of Jewish-Christian relations at that time. Fortunately, the existence of discussions between representatives of the two communities rests on more than just these quasi-factual reports. Isidore of Pelusium, on several occasions, gave advice to various Christians engaged in disputes with Jews. Particular topics of debate included the Virgin Birth and the identity of the unnamed prophet of Deuteronomy 18. Isidore's correspondents included a bishop, a grammarian, and a layman of unspecified occupation. The variety of these individuals' backgrounds suggests that discussions between Jews and Christians were not limited to theologians and rabbis, but frequently took place on other levels of contact between the two communities.[78]

These doctrinal discussions were not simply schoolroom exercises allowing the participants an opportunity to air their theological views. The evidence indicates that the stakes were high during late antiquity, since Jewish proselytism appears to have been just as effective as Christian efforts to promote conversions from Judaism. Recent studies have illuminated the seriousness with which various patristic writers regarded Judaism and its attractions for many late antique Christians. Although outright conversions from Christianity to Judaism were infrequent, large numbers of Christians appear to have been drawn to Jewish festivals, certain magical practices, and the solemn rites of the synagogue. These Christians earned the appellation "Judaizers" and constituted a major pastoral concern for the church hierarchy in regions as diverse as Asia Minor, North Africa, and Spain. Undoubtedly the most famous conflict over the status of Judaizing Christians occurred in Antioch during the preaching ministry of John Chrysostom. His series of fiery sermons denouncing the Judaizers has become the standard source for analyzing this intriguing controversy.[79]

Given the large and thriving Jewish community in late Roman Alexandria, one would certainly expect to encounter similar trends in the relationship between the Christian and Jewish communities. Alexandria was every bit as large and cosmopolitan as Antioch, and portions of the Alexandrian church had proved to be attracted to a broad range of religious movements such as Gnosticism, Arianism, and Melitianism. Were some Alexandrian Christians likewise attracted to Jewish practices and beliefs? Despite the extensive body of patristic literature composed by Alexandrian authors, there is no evidence at all of Judaizing tendencies within the Alexandrian church. Clearly this is not because figures like Athanasius and Cyril reserved their ire for Arians and Nestorians.[80] Perhaps a better approach would be to view Judaizing tendencies as evidence of extensive socioreligious intermingling and, more importantly, a nonexclusive communal self-definition. One of the major goals of John Chrysostom's preaching was to make the Antiochene Christians aware of the exclusive claims that the church had over their allegiance: "If the ceremonies of the Jews move you to admiration, what do you have in common with us? If the Jewish ceremonies are venerable and great, ours are lies. But if ours are true, as they *are* true, theirs are filled with deceit."[81] In Alexandria, there was no need for such preaching. The self-identities of the respective communities had been forged over the course of several centuries. The exclusive nature of these ethno-religious groups was well established by the late empire, shaped by a long history of intercommunal animosity. The origins of this hostility can be traced back to Jewish-Gentile conflict that began under the Ptolemies and reached its culmination in the Alexandrian violence during the Jewish revolt of 115. While Antioch could likewise boast of long-standing tension between Jews and Gentiles, the level of conflict in the Syrian metropolis did not compare with that in Alexandria.

The converse of this argument and another useful method for detecting the exclusivity of the Alexandrian Jewish and Christian communities is to examine the evidence for Jewish defection to Christianity during late antiquity. While Jewish conversions to Christianity are relatively common in other portions of the empire, they are virtually unknown in Alexandria throughout the fourth century.[82] There are a number of conversions of Alexandrian Jews attested in later centuries, but significantly, they seem to be clustered in the period immediately following the violence of 414/15. The outcome of this disturbance could thus be seen as the breakdown of Jewish communal identity within the city and resultant gains for Christianity.

It is important, however, to avoid interpreting every point of interaction between the Jewish and Christian communities as a result of a structure of relations predicated on violence. The exclusivity of the two communities is not dependent on widely scattered manifestations of conflict. As we have seen, contact between members of the respective communities in Alexandria was frequent and, at times, decidedly cordial. Consequently, it is necessary to view violent incidents as simply one facet of a many-sided relationship.

Nonetheless, over the course of the fourth century, the church displaced the gymnasium as the locus of opposition to Judaism within Alexandria. Elements within the Jewish community seem to have perceived this shift in the city's power relationships, since some Alexandrian Jews united with virtually every group opposed to the Nicene portion of the Alexandrian church during the fourth century. At the time of the Great Persecution, Jews assisted various Roman authorities in the prosecution and punishment of Alexandrian Christians.[83] During the Arian controversy, portions of the Jewish community gave considerable support to the Arians in their efforts to stamp out Homoousian Christianity within the city.[84] Often, this support took the form of an alliance with the other major group opposed to the Christians—the pagans. On several occasions during the 330s and 370s, Alexandrian churches were looted by crowds of Jews and pagans.[85] While the evidence for this Jewish-pagan linkage is found exclusively in the writings of Christian authors and would thereby give rise to some skepticism on the part of the reader, the sources frequently provide detailed testimony that accords well with the known context of intercommunal tension. During one incident in 374, a crowd of Jews and pagans attacked Christians in the vicinity of the Eunostos Harbor.[86] This would be just the place for such a crowd to find large numbers of Homoousian Christians, since the harbor serviced the imperial grain fleet—manned by staunch supporters of the patriarch. Consequently, these kinds of sporadic and seemingly random acts of Jewish-Christian violence fit well into the broad pattern of intercommunal relations fashioned by daily interaction over the course of centuries.

This is the context vital for understanding the riots and bloodshed of 414/15. Once the Alexandrian church gained imperial favor, won ascendancy over the Arians, and defeated the pagan opposition during the conflict over the Serapeum in 391, the Jewish community was the only major group remaining in the city that challenged the complete hegemony of the church and its patriarch. The outbreak of conflict and its subsequent results could hardly have been otherwise.

Yet, it is worth noting that the Alexandrian Jewish community even survived the violence of the early fifth century. Many commentators have assumed that the expulsion order that followed the riots spelled an end to Alexandrian Jewry. However, other Jewish communities survived despite similar expulsion orders during the course of imperial history, notably that of Rome following Claudius's order circa 49, and the community of Jerusalem *qua* Aelia Capitolina in the years following 135.

The Alexandrian Jewish community had proved its resiliency on previous occasions, and it comes as no surprise that it survived the troubles of 414/15. In the immediate aftermath, there were a large number of conversions to Christianity, as could be expected given the outcome of events.[87] Indeed, after the early fifth century, virtually the only Jews encountered in the literary sources are those who convert to Christianity—thereby serving the programmatic intentions of the Christian authors.[88] However, by the middle of the fifth century, we find Alexandrian Jews petitioning the authorities for permission to rebuild synagogues, clearly a sign of communal recovery.[89] This is further attested by the career of a Jewish philosopher named Acoluthos, who reportedly taught in sixth-century Alexandria. Shortly afterward, John Moschus speaks of Jewish teachers engaging their Christian counterparts in lively debates over the Bible. By the time of the Arab conquest, the Jews had recovered in numbers and importance with the result that the treaty between ʿAmr ibn al-ʿAs and the Byzantine authorities contained special provisions regarding their status.[90] The Alexandrian Jewish community continued to flourish throughout the Middle Ages, making it one of the most influential communities in the Near East. Such resiliency demonstrates the integral role played by the Jewish community in the life of the city, and the tenacity with which it faced an ever changing and occasionally hostile environment.

# Five

# The Pagan Community

By the 480s, the Roman Empire in the west was breaking up into the barbarian kingdoms of the early Middle Ages. In Gaul, Clovis had become king of the Salian Franks. In Italy, the boy-emperor Romulus Augustulus had been deposed by Odovacer at Ravenna. Both Cassiodorus and Boethius, the great intermediaries who conveyed so much of the classical heritage to the medieval world, were born during this decade, as was Benedict of Nursia who conceived a new vision of Christian society. In the East, the *Codex Theodosianus* had been providing the imperial realms with a magisterial summation of Christian Roman law for over fifty years. The Council of Chalcedon had taken place in the previous generation, and the Isaurian emperor Zeno was now attempting to gain assent to his compromise Christological formula, the *Henotikon*. Rabbis in Palestine and Mesopotamia were bringing to completion their respective versions of the Talmud. Near the eastern Serbian town of Naissus (modern Nis), the wife of a Romanized Thracian gave birth in 482 to a boy named Petrus Sabbatius. He later became the emperor Justinian.

In Egypt, the burning issue was adherence to the Chalcedonian creed or loyalty to the Christological traditions of the Alexandrian patriarchate. Athanasius had been dead now for over a century, and the fiery Shenute of Atripe had gone to his rest circa 450. Proterius, the imperial nominee to the throne of Saint Mark, was murdered in 457, and by the 480s the Monophysite patriarch Peter Mongus was seeking some way of placating both the emperor and the staunchly anti-Chalcedonian elements among the Alexandrian populace.

Yet there were Alexandrians in this decade who were seemingly untouched by the developments of the past century and a half. Their careers and their pieties seem to have come from another age. Sometime in the late 480s, a young Alexandrian philosopher named Heraiskos died and was buried by his brother and fellow philosopher, Asclepiades. Heraiskos's passing is, in itself, not especially noteworthy. However, in the social and religious matrix of late fifth-century Alexandria, his funerary rites seem incongruously out of place. Damascius informs us that Asclepiades had his brother's body "wrapped in the shroud of Osiris" and gave him a funeral "as performed at the demise of priests." During the last rites, "secret figures appeared brightly all over the linen cloth, and divine apparitions appeared all around, which clearly showed that his soul had lived in unity with the gods." One can easily imagine such a funeral based on ancient practices handed down from time immemorial: attended by the priests of various Egyptian gods, clouds of incense, and traditional prayers for the deceased as he began his journey in the company of Anubis to the shadowy realm of Osiris. The paintings on the interior of Alexandrian tombs frequently echo this practice. As but one example, the second-century A.D. Tegran Tomb displays a remarkable fusion of Egyptian and Greek funerary motifs, with Egyptian goddesses attending the mummified body of the deceased, all rendered in a distinctly classical manner.[1]

During life, Heraiskos had shown himself to be a faithful devotee of Egyptian and Hellenic gods. He could often be found "lingering at every opportunity in sanctuaries or shrines." Damascius states that Heraiskos possessed an ability to discern the divine presence in statues of the gods. "He simply had to cast his glance upon them and the divine excitement made his heart pound and he entered into a rapture with body and soul, as if the god had taken hold of him." Perhaps this reputation for divine "enthusiasm" contributed to the belief among Heraiskos's circle that "he had formerly been Bacchus." Nor did his brother, Asclepiades, lag behind in "a blessed life devoted to philosophy and service of the gods." Indeed, Asclepiades was better versed in the religious lore of Egypt, since he had spent his days studying the traditional wisdom of Egypt while Heraiskos had visited sanctuaries in Greece, Asia Minor, and Syria. Asclepiades was widely regarded as an expert in the arcana of Egyptian theology. "He had examined its beginnings and development and had devoted himself with zeal to the unlimited spectrum of its furthest branches." He was also famous for a number of hymns which he had composed in honor of the Egyptian gods. Together with his brother, Asclepiades sought to maintain the cults of the traditional gods, and "they lit holy fire on the altars."[2]

*Problems of Definition*

These men were pagans, and lived in a city commonly regarded at this time as "the most glorious and Christ-loving city of the Alexandrians."[3] Thanks to Damascius's *Life of Isidore,* we possess a great deal of information concerning Heraiskos and Asclepiades, since they were two of Isidore's early teachers in Alexandria. It is also possible to flesh out a reasonably detailed picture of their immediate circle, and their links with like-minded philosophers in Athens, Aphrodisias, and Berytus. However, once we look beyond the shaft of light cast by the writings of Damascius, it becomes much more difficult to place the two brothers in their proper Alexandrian social setting.[4] Are they in any way representative of Alexandria's pagan community? What was the nature of this community and how had it evolved during late antiquity?

Unlike Alexandria's Jews or Christians, the city's pagan inhabitants were not organized in small local units like synagogues or parish churches—communal foci that could satisfy the religious needs (and many of the social needs) of their respective adherents. Nor did any kind of defined hierarchy within the pagan community place Alexandria's pagans under a widely recognized authority like the archisynagogoi or the patriarch. Even during the early empire, the "High Priest [*archiereus*] of Alexandria and of All Egypt" did not fulfill this leadership role, since he was primarily a civil bureaucrat concerned with the regulation and taxation of temple properties throughout Egypt. His sole religious function appears to have been in connection with the imperial cult. Likewise, the Alexandrian *archiprophētēs* could not have exercised any effective religious authority, since he was subordinate to the archiereus and was a civil official also concerned with tax collection. Moreover, these two offices are not attested beyond the latter part of the fourth century.[5] Even if these offices had survived, it is doubtful whether their status among the city's pagans would have changed appreciably. During Julian's reign (360–63), the arrogation of a wide range of powers to provincial high priests in Anatolia did not seem to have any discernible effect on their long-term role within Anatolian pagan communities.

Besides having no rigid institutional framework, the pagan community in Alexandria was also fragmented into a multitude of cults and religious sects. However, adherence to these subgroups was by no means mutually exclusive. It was quite possible to belong to any number of religious cults simultaneously, particularly since the gods themselves appeared to practice an easy toleration and often assumed attributes and characteristics of one another. This was part and parcel of the very nature of polytheism in antiquity, and it will be profitable for us to explore the perimeters of these Alexandrian groups in some detail. At this point, we simply note that the fluidity of pagan cult and adherence is both an obstacle to precise categorization as well as an inherent trait of paganism in the city.

The pagan community of Alexandria also embraced a broad spectrum of social positions and cultural orientations. At first glance, there appears to be little common ground between the highly educated philosophers who taught in Alexandria's lecture halls and the fellahin from the countryside who sought seasonal employment along the city's wharves. The sheer variety afforded by such a large and socially diverse city would hinder the formation of strong communal bonds, at least of the same sort in evidence among the Jews and the Christians.

A large part of the problem in definition stems from applying to Alexandria's pagan community categories more appropriate to sects, that is, groups self-consciously organized around religious rites and beliefs opposed to those of the prevailing culture. In contrast to Judaism and Christianity, paganism was not differentiated at all from the city's institutions and social order. In fact, pagan belief and practice were intertwined with the city's foundation myths and legitimized its structures of political authority (figure 11). Paganism was the hegemonic culture of Alexandria at the beginning of our period, and it is only natural that such a dominant world view would feel no pressure to construct rigid communal boundaries or articulate an elaborate self-identity.

Even though Alexandrian paganism did not exhibit the hallmarks of sectarianism, it does not follow that it was not a community. Religious sociologists have long recognized that this sort of "natural" or "undifferentiated" community is an important type of religious community, one in which religious life is barely distinguishable from the patterns and practices that define the culture. One trait of this type of religious community is its facility in spawning and tolerating religious groups that are more specific and voluntary, but which remain within the general perimeters of the hegemonic culture. This holds true of confraternities and religious orders within medieval Christianity as well as mystery cults and philosophical schools within classical paganism. Consequently, it is possible to speak of many overlapping pagan communities existing within the larger community of pagans in late antique Alexandria.[6]

A related difficulty in the analysis of the city's pagan community (or communities) concerns the "self-definition" of Alexandria's pagans. That is, to what extent did they see themselves *as pagans* (or Hellenes), vis-à-vis their Jewish or Christian neighbors? Given the multiform expression of paganism in Alexandria, is there a way of defining what a pagan was without reverting to the catchall of "the set not-Jewish and not-Christian?" A definition of this sort is virtually useless, and cannot take into account the variations in religious sentiment one finds in any social group. Some modern commentators have even defined paganism as a nonexclusive attitude toward religion rather than a particular set of cult practices or beliefs. Yet, such a definition would have to include both Jews and Christians who shared in this tolerant "attitude"—an altogether

Fig. 11. Isis as the Tyche of Alexandria. A forceful identification of the goddess with the city itself. She wears a modius, or grain measure, as crown. In her left arm, she holds a cornucopia surmounted by a small temple of Horus. In her right hand, she holds a merchant vessel. She is surround by dancers, flute-playing *putti*, and a small figure of Pan. Ivory relief, Egypt (Alexandria), sixth century. Aachen cathedral, pulpit of Henry II.

(Aachener Domschatz)

unsatisfactory criterion for demarcating a meaningful social grouping. Another hindrance to precise definition is the difficulty of finding a means to categorize groups and individuals dwelling along the religious borderlands, who invoke with equal veneration Yahweh, Christ, and Osiris, or wear amulets decorated with an amalgam of syncretistic designs (figure 12).[7] Such questions admittedly take us a long way from Heraiskos and Asclepiades, but perhaps closer to the religious sensibilities of the average Alexandrian.

One place where Alexandrian pagans appear in abundance is in the writings of their Christian contemporaries. Athanasius, Socrates Scholasticus, Rufinus, and Sozomen (to name but a few) frequently refer to the *hellēnikoi, ethnikoi,* or *gentiles* of Alexandria. From the depictions of pagans given to us by Christian authors, it would appear that the Alexandrian pagan community, far from being divided and unorganized, was in fact a monolithic body, which often acted with great boldness in its conflicts with the Christian community. This sort of depiction is what one would expect to come from the pens of implacably hostile critics. An emphasis on the might and solidarity of the pagan community only serves to enhance the eventual triumph of Christianity within the city. Consequently, the bias of these Christian authors must be taken into account as well as the programmatic nature of their writings.

The formation of a broad communal consciousness among pagans during late antiquity may be traced to the rising tide of pagan-Christian polemic in the third century. Until confronted by a combative religious alternative, the empire's pagans felt no real need to articulate a distinctive self-identity. All this changed by the third century. Porphyry's concerted attacks upon Christianity may be taken as the high point of this polemic, but it is even possible to find important elements of his arguments as early as the time of Celsus and Galen in the late second century. To the informed pagan critic, Christianity was an aberrant sect of Judaism which despised the gods and threatened the social order. This social order rested upon the *pax deorum,* which was preserved by faithfully maintaining the cults of the gods—not only the gods of the Roman state but also the traditional gods of the empire's many peoples. These arguments gained a wide currency among philosophical circles in the empire and fur-

Fig. 12. The religious borderlands. Dark green jasper magical amulet depicting a snake-legged god with cock's head. The figure wears a military cuirass and holds a whip. A syncretistic solar deity, combining Persian, Syrian, and Egyptian elements. The magical names of the planets are inscribed below the whip. There is also a strong Jewish presence, indicated by the inscribed invocation of four angels, Michael, Raphael, Gabriel, and Ouriel. At the bottom are variants of the name Yahweh, employed as a word of power to ward off evil. Egypt (Alexandria), first–fifth centuries. Bonner no. 172; Kelsey Museum, inv. 26054.

(Kelsey Museum of Archaeology, University of Michigan)

nished an ideology for the persecuting policies of Diocletian, Galerius, and Maximinus Daia. This last emperor explicitly sought to strengthen pagan priesthoods and foster traditional cults, while at the same time persecuting the Christians in the regions under his authority.[8]

Despite the shifting direction of imperial religious policy between the reigns of Diocletian and Constantius II, it appears that the pagan group consciousness first articulated by philosophers in the preceding century did not affect wider circles of the empire's pagans. Indeed, it is not until the reign of Julian that one can begin to speak of a "pagan party"—and even then, one should not envision a seamless political force united behind a handful of spokesmen. To do so would be to subscribe to the Christian interpretation of conflict in this period.[9] However, the gradual emergence of a self-consciously defined pagan perspective may be discerned from the writings of Libanius and Themistius in the middle of the fourth century. In part, the articulation of this viewpoint was due to the official encouragement of the apostate emperor, who expended a great deal of energy combatting the superstitions of "the Galilaeans." Yet, in a broader sense, Julian's reign can be seen as increasing the acerbity and pitch of pagan-Christian polemic in the empire, as well as providing both sides with the necessary vocabulary for articulating conflicts that took place in a local or regional setting.[10]

One by-product of these conflicts was the crystallization of pagan "communities" on a local level. Two centuries earlier, Christian communities derived a large portion of their self-identity from categories employed by the overwhelmingly dominant pagan majority. This was true of both the organization of the nascent communities, and of their particular theological concerns. In the changed landscape of the mid-fourth century, the same kind of interplay was taking place, only this time local communities of pagans began to formulate their self-identity as one of several competing sects from terms long common to Christian discourse. Pagan communities certainly existed prior to the mid-fourth century, but their identification with the larger culture rendered them virtually invisible as religious communities. Now, however, the terms of the debate had shifted and they were forced to adopt sectarian language to defend what had previously been the hegemonic religious culture. As a result, the pagans/Hellenes of Alexandria emerged as a self-conscious (though diverse) group by the 350s, in response to empirewide developments and to particular local conditions. Although distinctions of cult and religious zeal were clearly apparent, the city's pagans began to act in concert as they sought to preserve their status against the encroachments of the Christian community. The changing status of paganism in late antique Alexandria and the course of Christian-pagan conflict during this era allow us to speak of a distinct Alexandrian "pagan community"—a useful descriptive term that portrays the reality of intercommunal relations in Alexandria with increasing accuracy during the second half of the fourth and throughout the fifth centuries.

To see this process of pagan communal self-definition at work, especially vis-à-vis the Christian community, we can turn to a passage of Epiphanius's *Panarion,* in which he describes a religious celebration from the 370s:

> In Alexandria they hold festival in what is called the Koreum, which is a great temple, namely the sacred precinct of Kore. They stay awake the whole night singing hymns to the idol to the accompaniment of flutes. They keep it up the entire night, and after cockcrow torchbearers descend into an underground shrine and bring up a wooden statue seated naked [on] a litter, having a seal of a cross inlaid with gold upon the forehead, and two other such seals on both hands, as well as another two upon the two knees themselves, making altogether five seals impressed with gold. They carry the statue in a circle seven times around the very center of the temple to the accompaniment of flutes, kettledrums, and hymns, and thus reveling carry it back down to the place underground. Asked what the rite means, they say: "Today at this hour Kore—meaning the virgin—engendered Aeon."[11]

The devotees of these rites were certainly kindled by a religious enthusiasm that belies any notion that Alexandrian paganism was moribund by the 370s. This is underscored by the fact that the pageantry of this festival took place during the reign of the staunchly Arian emperor Valens and, even more remarkable, at the close of Athanasius's nearly fifty-year episcopate in Alexandria.[12] Despite the vitality of these pagan rites, their very substance was shaped by contact with Christianity. As Glen Bowersock has demonstrated, both the form of the rites and even the conceptualization of the gods owes a great deal to Christian influences. The festival occurs on the Christian Epiphany, and celebrates the birth of a savior god from a virgin mother. The newborn Aeon is marked with a pagan version of stigmata signifying his role as a saving deity. Though the god Aeon may be identified with the long-revered Osiris, he bears little resemblance to the traditional formulation of the great Egyptian king of the dead. In Bowersock's phrase, Aeon is "presented as the pagan Jesus."[13]

Explicit imitation of Christianity is usually ascribed by Epiphanius to the deceptions of malevolent demons. In this case, though, he posits a more human agency: "The leaders of the idolaters . . . in many places hold a great feast on the very night of Epiphany, so that those who have placed their hopes in what is error may not seek the truth." A decade earlier, Julian attempted to counter Christian influence by appropriating Christian ritual, charity, and diocesan structure. Yet, these imperially patronized reforms received only a lukewarm response from the empire's pagans. The Alexandrian festival of Kore and Aeon, however, appears to have tapped into a vein of deeply felt religious sentiment. This should come as no surprise, since Alexandrians had long demonstrated their ability to worship "newly discovered" gods, like their tutelary deity Serapis, himself derived during the early Ptolemaic period from the cult of Osiris-Apis at Memphis. Alexandrian reactions against Christianity, though shaped in part according to terms defined by the opposition, initiated the process that created a cohesive community of pagans.[14]

## *Urban Topography and Late Antique Paganism*

A Syrian visitor to Alexandria in the 350s has left us a vivid account of the city's religious climate:

> I think that in celebrating [this locale], it owes its particular renown to the gods, because there—as I have already said—the gods are especially honored by [artistic] representations. There, one can see every sort of consecrated shrine and lavishly adorned temple; sacristans, priests,

> attendants, haruspices, worshipers, and the best diviners all abound; and everything is performed according to the proper rites. Thus, you will find altars constantly ablaze with the fires of sacrifices and heaped with incense, as well as garlands and censers filled with perfumes emitting a divine fragrance.

This reputation for devotion so impressed the author of the *Expositio* that he was moved to exclaim, "Nowhere, in fact, are the mysteries of the gods celebrated as they have been here—from ancient times up till the present day."[15]

One can easily imagine the enormous variety of religious expression in a cosmopolitan city like Alexandria, exposed as it was to cultural influences from three continents. Hellenic gods, Near Eastern Baals, and Roman divinities all jostled together in late Roman Alexandria. The ancient gods of Egypt served as a substratum to this religious landscape, and the pervasive influence of Egyptian ideas of the divine had interacted with each of the foreign gods and their devotees to produce a uniquely Greco-Egyptian religious world. Added to this mélange was a number of diverse sects and conventicles, ranging from Gnostics and Orphics to Hermeticists and various theurgists. Considering the tolerant nature of polytheism and its unwillingness to discard any vestige of myth or ritual hallowed by antiquity, paganism in Alexandria was a complex amalgam resembling a medieval palimpsest, with a six-hundred-year accumulation of religious fashions and imported cults superimposed upon earlier ones.

In attempting to sort this jumble of religious practices into a comprehensible outline, the usual procedure is to divide the cults according to their national origin and their successive introduction into the city.[16] This yields the semblance of a chronological progression, a useful framework for historical analysis, but such an approach tends to relegate a particular god to one period in the city's long religious history and cannot take into account the vicissitudes of a cult's popularity over time. Where, for example, would one properly place a god like Serapis, whose cult underwent considerable fluctuation with respect to patronage and popularity during the course of six centuries? Should such a discussion be placed at the time of his introduction under the early Ptolemies, or during the zenith of his cult's popularity in the Roman period? Further, by grouping the city's religions by their national origins, it is all too possible to set up arbitrary boundaries for these groups. This is especially true of the so-called oriental religions, a label which assumes that these gods had more in common with one another than with Greco-Roman gods of similar religious function. Oftentimes, it seems that the major criterion for this category is exclusion from the "theological" works of Hesiod and Ovid.

Although these methods of grouping the city's many religions may be of some utility (particularly in relating cult to ethnicity), they do not allow us to see these religions in their Alexandrian context. A mere catalog of cults grouped according to origin and date of introduction could be devised for other cities of the eastern Mediterranean with very little variation from the religious picture created by such a scheme in Alexandria. In order to appreciate the integral relationship between cult and city, a more profitable method would be to employ a topographical analysis and examine the ways in which Alexandria's religions were organized by their respective locations within the urban setting. This kind of topographical perspective on Alexandrian paganism highlights the function of a given cult within the fabric of the city's social life and also helps to determine a religion's significance in the city based on its diffusion and on the prominence accorded to its temples. A topographical approach may also be of some service in ascribing an identity to a cult for which we only possess an otherwise unknown name—although any such identification must be acknowledged as tentative at best.

There are, however, several limitations to this type of methodology. The most serious difficulty is that we do not always possess sufficient data to create a comprehensive topographical picture of Alexandrian paganism. Only a handful of the city's temples can be identified archaeologically, and many of these temple sites were built over during the unbridled expansion of the past century. Consequently, recourse often has to be made to literary sources for the meager details of religious topography, sources that frequently contradict one another concerning a temple's location. Nor should one equate the presence of temples with worshipers. The mere fact that a temple was erected tells us nothing of the popularity of the cult, only of patronage by the state or by wealthy citizens at some point during the cult's local history. In addition, an analysis based on temple diffusion in the city cannot take into account religious movements for which elaborate places of worship were superfluous—for example, Gnosticism or Hermeticism. While these limitations, in themselves, do not prohibit a topographical survey of paganism in Alexandria, they must be kept in mind while attempting to sketch the outlines of the city's diverse religious life.

The Syriac *Notitia* of the city's buildings, derived from a Greek original of the fourth century, preserves unique statistical information regarding Alexandrian paganism in late antiquity. For five of the city's principal quarters, it gives a careful enumeration of their respective temples, houses, courtyards, baths, taverns, and porticoes. By adding up the figures for temples, we arrive at a total of 2,478 temples in the five traditional quarters.[17] This is an astounding figure, unless the *Notitia* includes under the rubric, "temple," private shrines in the home or subsidiary sanctuaries within larger temple complexes.[18] Small neighborhood shrines, similar to the *lares compitales* in cities like Rome or Pompeii, also should be counted as "temples." The tradition of private shrines within Alexandrian dwellings apparently continued even after the city was ostensibly Christianized, as evidenced by House D at Kōm el-Dikka. The interior court of this house may well have been used as a place of prayer, in light of its strong east-west orientation and a professionally executed fresco of the Virgin and Christ which adorned one of its walls.[19]

Since the Syriac *Notitia* lists the temple totals for each quarter, it is possible to discern some patterns in temple distribution throughout Alexandria. One striking aspect of this distribution is that over 67 percent of the temples are located in just two quarters, Gamma and Delta. This is especially noticeable in the Gamma quarter, which has a great many temples (855), but relatively few houses (2,140).[20] By way of contrast, the Beta district possesses only one-eighth of Gamma's number of temples, one-half the number of its baths, but over three times the number of its houses—perhaps characterizing a quieter, more residential neighborhood. The large number of temples in the Delta quarter (800) can be explained by the apparent size of the entire district, since Delta ranks at least third in the number of each category of urban structure. By seeing the quantity of temples in Delta as a function of a quarter's size, this only enhances the position of the Gamma quarter as the principal district in the city given over to shrines and temples. This also confirms for Alexandria a tendency found in the design of other ancient cities: topographical differentiation within the urban precinct resulting in one particular quarter (or part of a quarter) being set aside as the area devoted to religious functions.

Unfortunately, it is not possible, on the basis of the Syriac *Notitia* alone, to identify the section of the city which contained this conglomeration of religious buildings. Although we know that the original city was divided into five *grammata,* the extant sources tell us very little concerning the precise location of each of these districts. Delta, the best known of the quarters because of its concentration of Jewish inhabitants, has been variously located in the extreme northeast portion of the city and also near the Eunostos Harbor to the west. Gamma appears in just one brief papyrus of the first century without any identifiable geographic clues, and Epsilon is attested solely by a papyrus of the early fourth century.[21] Further, the Syriac *Notitia* simply gives the numbers of temples in the different quarters and is silent concerning the size and importance of these shrines as well as the gods honored in each of them. For this information, we must turn to other sources.[22]

From these sources, primarily papyrological and literary, we may discern a topographical picture of Alexandrian religious life—at least insofar as organized cult is concerned. While such a picture is unavoidably static, we must bear in mind that the popularity of individual gods waxes and wanes. Some temples were undoubtedly half empty while others expanded to accommodate throngs of worshipers. Still, it is not difficult to detect concentrations of temples in distinct sectors of the city which echo the attributes and cult functions of the gods in their midst—for example, Poseidon in the harbor area, dynastic gods near the palaces, gods of commerce along the docks. This relationship may seem obvious, but it serves to underscore the vital interplay between urban topography, socio-economic structure, and religious adherence in Alexandria.[23]

Nowhere is this connection more clearly observed than in the cults that clustered around the ceremonial heart of the city. This region, embracing the central core of the Via Canopica and the main Agora (or Mesonpedion), was the setting for a variety of cults associated with the city's founding. The shrine of the Agathos Daimon, the snake god who appeared to the first builders of Alexander's city, was located prominently on the Agora. Although similar snake gods can be found throughout the Greek world, the Agathos Daimon is often depicted on the city's coinage wearing a *skhent* and a sun disk, indicating native Egyptian elements in the cult. Also "in the midst of the city" was the celebrated Tychaion, a Hellenic-style temple containing statues of many gods, both Greek and Egyptian. Tyche herself was shown holding a rudder and cornucopia, and may have worn a modius—all attributes denoting her role in providing for the bounty and good fortune of the city. Isis and Serapis also possessed a temple along the Via Canopica, thereby ensuring them an equal status with the other important civic gods honored in the center of the city. Although they both had other prominent temples in various sectors of the city, their presence together on the Via Canopica stressed their attributes as civic deities. Similarly located in this region was a temple dedicated to Rhea Kybele, a goddess who seems out of place among her divine neighbors. However, Kybele's temple was built by Septimius Severus, an emperor with close family ties to the eastern provinces and who actively promoted the cults of Syrian and Anatolian deities. Consequently, Kybele's presence among Tyche, Agathon Daimon, Isis, and Serapis may indicate that the emperor was encouraging the worship of this goddess as a civic patroness.[24]

As one approached the Great Harbor from the Agora, the first and most conspicuous religious building encountered was the Caesarion. This structure not only housed the imperial cult in Roman Alexandria, but it also contained a shrine to Aphrodite. In the context of the Caesarion, it is likely that this expression of Aphro-

Fig. 13. Isis Pharia. On reverse of an Alexandrian tetradrachm of Hadrian, 117/18, shortly after the suppression of the Jewish Revolt. Isis is shown as the protectress of sailors, wearing a modius, and holding a large billowing sail. Before her stands a representation of the Pharos, surmounted by a statue of Zeus Soter or Poseidon. A temple of Isis Pharia stood near the Pharos.
(American Numismatic Society)

dite's worship was connected with her role (in the guise of Venus) as the divine ancestor of Julius Caesar and, by extension, of the imperial office itself.

In the vicinity of Alexandria's twin harbors, there was a group of temples dedicated to divinities intimately concerned with seafaring and commerce. The Ptolemaic era saw the construction of two temples to Poseidon, one at the base of the Timonium near the Caesarion, and another at the west end of the Pharos island. This Poseidion on Pharos was the last Alexandrian landmark noted by Synesius as he embarked on his hapless voyage back to Cyrene at the very end of the fourth century. Also on the Pharos island was the temple of Isis Pharia, the patroness of seamen, whose cult statue depicted her holding a billowing sail filled with favorable winds (figure 13). On or near the Heptastadion was a shrine to Aphrodite, perhaps celebrating her birth from the sea-foam (*aphros*) and the fertility and divine plenty she represented. Alexandria's commercial Emporion also hosted the temples of suitable gods, like that of Kronos/Thoth, who in his Egyptian aspect presided over trade and banking. Nearby was the temple of Bendis (sometimes Mendis), located between the Caesarion and the Jewish quarter. This temple (later converted into the church of Saint Michael) was originally dedicated to a lesser-known Egyptian god who was likewise concerned with commerce. Also in this vicinity was the Ptolemaic temple of the Thea Kale, an obscure goddess who nonetheless reveals her beneficent qualities by virtue of her name.[25]

Proceeding to the east, dynastic cults become more common as one enters the palace district of Bruchion. These cults glorified a full panoply of Hellenistic rulers, beginning with Alexander himself and his tomb/shrine known as the Soma (or Sema). The other end of the Hellenistic era was also represented by a temple on the promontory of Lochias dedicated to the goddess Isis, the *temenos* of which incorporated the tomb of Cleopatra VII. It appears, however, that the religious significance of this sector waned during the Roman period, not only because the authority of Rome supplanted that of the Ptolemies, but also because this district suffered greatly during civil disturbances in the later third century. All of the evidence for these shrines predates the violence that is likely to have destroyed them.

Of more lasting significance were the cults of gods whose temples ringed the central core of the city. These fringe areas of Alexandria played host to a wide variety of divinities who were not accorded religious prominence equal to the civic deities of the central city. Many of these gods were familiar Egyptian divinities like Anubis, Hathor, and Thoth, or non-Hellenic savior gods like Mithra. Yet, when we recall that Septimius Severus established Kybele near the Mesonpedion, it appears that this geographical differentiation was merely the result of official patronage by the state and did not reflect the fundamental popularity of these cults among Alexandrians. Moreover, since the temples of these gods were located in regions that were often given over to necropoleis, this may indicate some measure of their importance in Alexandrian conceptions of the afterlife. Consequently, the location of these shrines may be a function of their religious significance to Alexandrian pagans and not simply mirror an official policy to banish non-Hellenic gods to the city's periphery.

To this topographical interpretation it may be objected that these fringe areas also contained cults of deified Ptolemaic rulers whom one would expect to find in Bruchion or in the city center, not in a zone of necropoleis. Yet, it should be recalled that these fringe areas were often the city's original suburbs. Gabbari, to the west, at one time contained a temple to the Theoi Euergetai (Ptolemy III and Berenike) and only in the late Ptolemaic and early Roman periods was this region given over entirely to burials. Siūf, to the east, is said to have been the site of a temple to Ptolemy Philadelphus and Arsinöe (the Theoi Adelphoi), but this area was beyond most of the necropoleis and could better be characterized as a region of suburban residences.

Another factor drawing non-Hellenic cults to Alexandria's periphery was the religious importance of the city's most eastern suburb, Canopus. This settlement, connected to Alexandria by canal from the nearby Nile, was famed for the luxurious life-style of its inhabitants from the time of Strabo to that of Ammianus Marcellinus. However, it was also renowned for a group of revered temples dedicated to Serapis/Osiris, Isis, and Anubis. Worshipers who slept in Serapis's temple reported miraculous cures taking place, naturally drawing large numbers of pilgrims. The festivals surrounding the cults of these Egyptian gods were wildly popular with Alexandrians, who journeyed along the canals by boat to participate in the celebrations. Rufinus informs us that the veneration accorded these shrines in the late fourth century was so great that their fame almost surpassed the reputation of the temples in Alexandria itself. Consequently, the religious aura surrounding this suburb helps to explain the large numbers of shrines dedicated to Egyptian gods dispersed all along the route from Alexandria to Canopus: temples of Isis at Mustafa Pascha and farther east at Ras es Sōda, a shrine to Hermanubis at Ras es Sōda, and a temple of Serapis at Nicopolis.[26]

The other great focus of paganism in late Roman Alexandria was the temple of Serapis in the southwestern corner of the city (figure 14). It would be difficult to exaggerate the importance of the Serapeum in the sacred topography of Alexandria, "for on account of the temple of Serapis, Alexandria itself is a consecrated world." This huge complex of buildings included a library, lecture halls, and subsidiary shrines to Isis and Anubis. Rufinus described the won-

Fig. 14. Serapis, the patron god of Alexandria. This marble bust is possibly a copy of the massive cult statue within the Serapeum. Serapis is crowned with a modius, or grain measure, which symbolizes his care for the city's abundance. Alexandria, first–third centuries.

(Graeco-Roman Museum, Alexandria)

ders of this sanctuary shortly before Serapis's cult was forcibly abolished in 391:

> The whole edifice is built of arches with enormous windows above each arch. The hidden inner chambers are separate from one another and provide for the enactment of various ritual acts and secret observances. Sitting courts and small chapels with images of the gods occupy the edge of the highest level. Lofty houses rise up there in which the priests, or those which they call *agneuontas,* that is, those who purify themselves, are accustomed to live. Behind these buildings, a freestanding portico raised on columns and facing inward runs around the periphery. In the middle stands the temple, built on a large and magnificent scale with an exterior of marble and precious columns. Inside there was a statue of Serapis so vast that the right hand touched one wall and the left the other.

This imposing sanctuary was constructed on an already lofty hill in the Rhakotis sector of the city, prompting Ammianus Marcellinus to exclaim, "Next to the Capitolium, which is the symbol of the eternity of immemorial Rome, the whole world beholds nothing more magnificent."[27]

Aside from the shrines that tentatively can be located thanks to the survival of literary or epigraphic evidence, there are many others which are known to us only by name. Although the list of gods with unlocated temples includes deities of every description, well over half of these gods are Hellenic in origin: Adonis, Athena, Dionysus, Hephaistos, Zeus Meilichios, and Zeus Ouranos. This large number of Hellenic gods may result merely from the random nature of our extant sources from Alexandria. It may, however, represent the diminished status of these gods in the religious consciousness of late antique Alexandrians. Most of the Hellenic gods were introduced very early in the Ptolemaic period by Macedonian settlers, and it may well be that these deities lost much of their appeal as gods of the homeland after several generations. The one exception is Dionysus, whose distinctive cult was still active in the fourth century, perhaps because he was not as easily assimilated to an Egyptian god as, for example, Adonis (Osiris) or Athena (Neith).[28]

Another observation arising from a topographical survey of Al-

Fig. 15. The intimacy of religious devotion. Cultic meal in honor of the goddess Isis. A group of five upper-class women recline on couches, attended by servants. Ivory pyxis. Egypt (Alexandria), sixth century. Sammlung Nassauischer Altertumer, inv. 7856.

(Museum Wiesbaden)

exandrian paganism concerns the status of Isis in the city. One cannot help but be struck by the extraordinary diffusion of Isis shrines in and around Alexandria. The goddess may be found in every sector of the city, from the harbors (Isis Pharia) to the palaces (Isis Lochias), and from the city center (Isis Plusia) to the peripheral regions (Isis Nepheron). In the area to the east of Alexandria, there were at least four shrines to the goddess (at Eleusis, Mustafa Pasha, Ras es Sōda, and Canopus). Still, it would be unwise to conclude that the cult of Isis was far more popular than any other well-attested cult in late antique Alexandria. Isis worship tends to require a smaller, more intimate setting than, say, that of her consort Serapis who was revered in one or two large sanctuaries (figure 15).

Moreover, the chronology of paganism in Alexandria may also skew our vision with regard to the status of Isis. Since her popularity fluctuated throughout the Roman period, it is only natural that we possess more evidence for a cult that was one of the last to die out in Alexandria.[29]

This survey has, by necessity, emphasized temples and shrines —easily the most conducive material for a topographical analysis. However, to get a feel for the remarkable diversity of pagan religious life in Alexandria, we should at least note in passing some other forms of paganism which were not geographically focused but were significant nonetheless. These groups included circles of Gnostics who existed on the borders of Christianity and Judaism during the first three centuries of Roman rule. By the fourth century, though, it appears that most Gnostic groups had either been assimilated or suppressed by the authorities in the Jewish and Christian communities, at least in Alexandria. More overtly pagan groups, like the followers of Hermes Trismegistus, continued to thrive during this period. An archive of letters from early fourth-century Hermoupolis preserves for us some specimens of correspondence emanating from one such circle of Hermetics to several of their co-religionists temporarily resident in Alexandria. In addition, a cell of Manichaeans probably existed in Alexandria from the time of the missionary work of Adda in the 260s. This Manichaean group apparently gained adherents throughout the next century and attracted enough attention to provoke a public debate between a local Manichaean teacher named Aphthonius and Aetius, an Arian theologian who traveled all the way from Antioch for the disputation. Later in the century, the brilliant Alexandrian exegete, Didymus the Blind, felt it necessary to compose a polemical work entitled, *Against the Manichaeans*.[30]

These various sects and schools in the city should be seen against a broad religious background imbued with magic and astrology. The popularity of magic in Alexandria is echoed by a rabbinic tale found in the Talmud concerning R. Ze'iri. The rabbi, newly arrived in the city, was tricked out of some money by certain Alexandrian magicians who had sold him an ass which vanished when the rabbi attempted to water it. Magic was such a leitmotif of religious life in the city that Athanasius was accused of sorcery in connection with the supposed death and mutilation of Bishop Arsenius of Hypselis.[31]

While an interest in magical practices was common during late antiquity, the Alexandrians were singled out by contemporaries for their obsession with predicting the future and for the highly refined methods they developed to satisfy this desire. If the author of the *Historia Augusta* is to be believed, fortune-telling was so universal that it could almost be characterized as a religious lingua franca in Alexandria, with eager practitioners of the art found in religious groups of every persuasion: "There is no *archisynagogus* of the Jews, no Samaritan, no Christian presbyter, who is not an astrologer, a soothsayer, or an anointer." The widely traveled author of the *Expositio* claims that haruspices and "the best diviners" may be found in Alexandria. The broadly based appeal of magical practices and divination can also be seen in several late fourth-century canons of the Alexandrian church. It seems that church authorities found it necessary to explicitly forbid presbyters and other clergy to "go unto them that use augury, neither unto magicians nor wizards, nor sorcerers." At the same time, the ubiquitous nature of the magic arts was such that Alexandrian sorcerers and fortune-tellers routinely frequented church services with no apparent objections from Christian authorities—they were simply required to sit with the catechumens.[32]

The city was especially renowned for the skill of its astrologers, for in the words of Ammianus Marcellinus, "Some, though not many, still keep warm the study of the movements of the earth and the stars. . . . Besides these, there are a few who are expert in the course of the fates." Mastery of these disciplines required advanced mathematical training. Thus, some of the finest minds in fourth-century Alexandria were noted mathematicians who had a decided bent toward astrology, like Hypatia's father Theon and the astrological writer Paul the Alexandrian. In Paul, the close connection between the sciences of mathematics and astrology is clearly manifest, so that one can see why the term *mathematicus* was a synonym for astrologer throughout much of antiquity. Theon himself is credited with a work entitled, *On Omens, the Observation of Birds, and the*

*Voice of Ravens*. When it is recalled that even a casual dabbling in divination could merit the fiercest penalties in the late fourth century (being burned alive or torn by iron hooks), the widespread fame of Alexandrian fortune-tellers seems all the more noteworthy. Some of these practices did not die out with the gradual disappearance of public pagan cult in Alexandria. They simply found a new home in a Christianized culture. A Coptic recension of one of Athanasius's letters contains the bishop's complaint about Christians who continue to consult astrological tables and justify the practice by renaming the stars after famous saints! Moreover, while magicians had to burn their books and do penance for three years prior to receiving the sacraments, professional astrologers simply had to do penance for a year.[33]

## *The Sociology of Paganism in Late Antique Alexandria*

Paganism in late Roman Alexandria was a welter of diverse cults and allegiances, an amalgam of religions with no particular unifying bonds of belief or practice. Nevertheless, the religious history of the fourth century gave rise to a communal consciousness among Alexandria's pagans which enabled them to compete effectively with other communal groups in the city. Although religious practices did not mold Alexandrian pagans into a monolithic community, other indicators help us define the forces of cohesion within the pagan community. One method of exploring the contours of Alexandrian paganism in this period is to examine its social dimensions, that is, the adherence to particular pagan cults of various social and economic strata within Alexandrian society. By analyzing the pagan community in this way, we find that it may be best characterized as a conglomeration of various subgroups associated by a wide range of overlapping social and economic ties.

In the literary sources, the most prominent of these pagan groups consists of philosophers and their circles of students. The profession of philosophy in late antiquity required a high degree of erudition. Consequently, the necessary leisure and the expense of studying under the best teachers determined that philosophical training was restricted to only the wealthy portions of society. One of Isidore's teachers, Asclepiodotus, was an Alexandrian whose family was of bouleutic rank, since we are told that the obligation to perform "civic honors" was "traditional in his family." Although Asclepiodotus's father had amassed great debts, the philosophically inclined son was able to repay many of them through the careful stewardship of the family's estate—another indication of social and economic status. Ammonius, the renowned fifth-century commentator on Aristotle, came from an Alexandrian family that had long enjoyed the great honor of being banqueted at public expense. Further, a papyrus from Aphrodito (Kom Ishqāw) provides a revealing glimpse into the economic status of the family of philosophers which included the brothers Asclepiades and Heraiskos. Fl. Horapollon, the son of Asclepiades and himself a noted Alexandrian philosopher, petitioned a magistrate during the reign of Anastasius (491–518) to prevent his unfaithful wife (and cousin) from taking away the ancestral estate at Phenebythis. Horapollon also sought an injunction that would have prohibited his wife from removing a considerable amount of his movable goods. Besides supplying us with these indications of his family's wealth, Horapollon also gives us otherwise unattested information regarding his social status when he conspicuously proclaims his rank as a *lamprotatos* (= *clarrissimus*). This papyrus, then, confirms the impression given by Damascius that philosophy in late antique Alexandria was largely the preserve of the leisured class.[34]

Although Alexandrians of exalted economic and social status predominated in the city's philosophical circles, it cannot be said that these philosophical groups, in and of themselves, exercised a significant role within the larger pagan community of Alexandria. Garth Fowden has made a strong case for the progressive marginalization of pagan philosophers within late antique society owing to their exclusivist attitudes, their disdain for civic life, and also to a growing misanthropic strain in the life-styles of pagan "holy men."[35] A prime example of this tendency toward marginalization is Isidore's revered teacher, Serapion. This ascetic pagan shut himself up in his small house in Alexandria and was completely unknown to his fifth-century contemporaries, so much so that Isidore's recollections to Damascius are the only evidence of the hermit's existence. Serapion's mode of life stands in contrast to certain contemporary Christian hermits whose well-publicized lives in solitude were frequently disrupted by persons seeking "a word"—even to the point of breaking down the doors of their cells. Serapion was not alone among pagan philosophers in this conscious (and successful) turning away from the world, prompting Themistius to complain about philosophers who do not condescend "to emerge from their couches and secluded spots." The exclusivity of pagan philosophic groups is also illustrated by the inbreeding common among "dynasties" of philosophers, as at Pergamon and Aphrodisias and especially at Alexandria. It is no wonder that Fowden refers to philosophical circles in late antiquity as "asphixiatingly exclusive." Consequently, the position of these intellectuals can in no way be considered comparable with the political and social influence wielded by the philosophers, sophists, and rhetoricians of the Second Sophistic during the second and third centuries.[36]

Despite the marginalization of philosophers in the social world of late Roman Alexandria, the attention they receive in the literary sources imputes to them a significance disproportionate to their real status. It is easy to be beguiled by the richly detailed and personal accounts left to us by Damascius and Zachariah of Mytilene. As a result, the role of these philosophers has been skewed in much of the historiography of the Alexandrian pagan community. While teachers like Hypatia or Olympius could command a devoted (though limited) following, their leadership rested on loyalties derived from bonds of patronage largely unconnected with religious sympathies. A recluse like Serapion can hardly be considered a pagan leader during the *Ausgang* of Alexandrian *Heidentums*.

In addition, philosophical circles in Alexandria were never exclusively pagan during late antiquity. While ardent pagans like Olympius in the fourth and Asclepiodotus in the fifth century could attract groups of pupils, there were also Christian teachers of rhetoric and philosophy like Aphthonius, "who was a Christian and had many students." Indeed, it could be said that a typical form of piety found among the city's educated elite was that of the teacher and his small circle of student-initiates, whether we speak of Origen and the catechetical school, the Palestinian rabbi Abbahu and his followers, the Gnostic cells associated with Basilides and Valentinus, the band of Hermeticists revealed by the archive of Theophanes, or the fifth-century pagan Horapollon and his students.[37]

Moreover, Alexandrian lecture halls were scarcely segregated by religious persuasion. Aetius, an Antiochian who espoused radical Arian theology in the 350s and 360s, had received formal training in Aristotelian logic from an Alexandrian sophist and philosopher. Hypatia's best-known pupil was the Neoplatonist Christian and future bishop of Ptolemais, Synesius of Cyrene. In the fifth century, the Christian sophist Aeneas of Gaza studied under the pagan Hierocles. Horapollon's schoolroom was frequented equally by pagan youths devoted to sacrifice and by Christian zealots who wrecked temples and beat up pagan priests for amusement. As late as the sixth century we find Damascius's pagan teacher, Ammonius, instructing the Christian philosopher (and sometime theologian) John Philoponus.[38]

Even though religious institutions like the patriarchal cathedral or the temple of Serapis sponsored schools, it appears that there were also civic chairs such as the one held by Ammonius. The excavations at Kōm el-Dikka have revealed startling evidence of educational institutions in the late Roman city, with the unearthing of a series of adjoining lecture halls situated just northwest of the large bath complex. The halls were arranged with three or four rows of seats, and each hall could accommodate easily between sixty and eighty people.[39] The location of these spacious lecture halls in a purely secular context suggests that teachers and students of different religious backgrounds mingled freely in a neutral setting especially created by the city (figure 16).

If Alexandria's famed philosophical schools were not the bastions of militant paganism in late antiquity, one would suspect that other social groups requiring a familiarity with classical *paideia* were also not restricted to pagans. And, in fact, rhetors, poets, grammarians, and doctors could be found in virtually every ethnoreligious community of Alexandria. Although Jews do not figure among the professions most closely associated with pagan learning, we have seen that they ranked among the most respected doctors of

Fig. 16. Lecture halls, Kōm el-Dikka. Late antique. These two halls (indicated as halls 2 and 3 on plan of Kōm el-Dikka) could each seat nearly eighty students. The teacher would lecture from a raised seat located in the center rear of each hall. The lecture halls were situated next to the bath complex and just down the colonnaded street from the Kōm el-Dikka "theater" building.

the city. Moreover, few of the city's educated elite could be considered fanatics, except with regard to their shared cultural values. Given what we know of the most prolific of these literati (Palladus, Nonnus, Claudian, and Synesius), culture—not religion—was the determining factor in setting social boundaries.[40] Indeed, it is often difficult to discern the precise religious convictions of many Alexandrian writers in this period. Alexandria cannot boast a Eunapius or a Zosimus.

Although the practice of medicine was not solely in the hands of pagans, the cults associated with the healing arts have left a significant amount of Alexandrian archaeological material from antiquity. The Hellenic healing god Asclepius and his divine daughter Hygeiea (health) are recurring coin types. They are also frequent subjects of Alexandrian statuary ranging from large freestanding sculptures to small figurines in ivory (figure 10B). Although these statues were not necessarily in the possession of Alexandrian physicians, they are eloquent testimonies of the religious dimensions of the city's medical fame.[41]

Just as literary culture cannot be considered a distinguishing mark of paganism in Alexandria, neither can exalted social status or the possession of great wealth. The Alexandrian boule included both pagans and Christians throughout the fourth and much of the fifth centuries. Likewise, the urban populace was made up of individuals of every religious persuasion. Since religion was not class specific, it is clear that communal identity within the city crossed social boundaries and linked together groups of varying cultural orientation and economic status.

As one proceeds down the social ladder, however, it becomes increasingly difficult to perceive the exact contours of belief among the inarticulate bulk of the urban plebs. Considering the paucity of literary testimonies regarding lower-class portions of the populace, reconstructions of popular belief tend to rest almost exclusively on archaeological evidence. Votive offerings, amulets, terracottas, and other material remains are usually grouped in such a way to imply a dichotomy between the Hellenized sectors of the populace and the more strictly Egyptian elements within the urban plebs. While such a methodology is useful for arranging large catalogs of material, it reveals a circular argument when applied to social organization. This Egyptian-Greek dichotomy may have some utility for describing early Ptolemaic society, but even Fraser emphasizes the mingling of the populace which took place within a few generations after the death of Alexander the Great. The opposition between these two cultural elements also has overtones of a rural-urban dichotomy, and is especially evident in discussions of the Christian community with its supposed Coptic-Hellenist tensions. Yet, the assumptions lying behind this Coptic-Hellenist dichotomy rest upon tenuous archaeological evidence, since excavations at Kōm el-Dikka have revealed widespread employment of artistic techniques usually described as both rural and Coptic.

A sharp Egyptian-Greek split in the Alexandrian pagan community may also be largely an illusion created by the arbitrary arrangement of source material. Although it is possible to identify certain sectors of the city as more Greek or Egyptian (as in the area of Rhakotis surrounding the Serapeum), the easy toleration of paganism created an atmosphere that encouraged a pagan Alexandrian to worship a variety of gods, both Greek and Egyptian. An Alexandrian who wore an amulet of a rooster-headed solar deity and adorned his house with terracottas of the pensive infant Harpocrates could very well have been a regular worshiper at a temple of Poseidon—after he had stopped for a brief ceremony at a local Mithraeum. Moreover, eclectic pagans did not even need to frequent a variety of shrines. When the temple at Menouthis was looted by a Christian crowd in the 480s, the zealous mob burned images of Apollo, Athena, and Dionysus—as well as statues of "dogs, cats, apes, crocodiles, and other reptiles."[42]

By the same token, we should not allow the gap between the literary sources and the archaeological material to become prima facie the divide between elite paganism and "popular religion." Alexandrian philosophers may very well have worn magical amulets and kept small good-luck statues of Bes in their homes. One has only to consider the undiscriminating religious interests of the brothers Heraiskos and Asclepiades to see one side of this catholicity of belief in Alexandria. After all, the city's pagan intelligentsia maintained particularly close ties with the cult center in Canopus—which was almost exclusively Egyptian in character. The other side of this issue is the degree to which the mass of Alexandria's pagan inhabitants were affected by the concerns and debates of the city's philosophical circles. Granted, the bulk of the population could not begin to grasp the intellectual arcana of a Hierocles or an Ammonius. Nonetheless, some of the subjects taken up by pagan thinkers, like predicting the future or reflecting on the importance of statues, would have filtered down to the general populace. Although we see this process more clearly within the Christian community (Arius's *Thalia* as well as both pro- and anti-Nicene sloganeering in the marketplace), the same popularization seems to have occurred within the pagan community. Pagan intellectuals were able to rally violence-prone crowds of devoted pagans throughout the fourth century. Once the status of the temples was no longer in doubt, these pagan teachers and philosophers also circulated widely believed prophecies which foretold doom to those who harmed the shrines or their statues.

### *The Downfall of Serapis*

During his ill-fated tenure as Arian bishop of Alexandria, George of Cappadocia (356–61) took forceful measures in his campaign to eradicate pagan cults in the city. His persecution of the old gods and their followers forged these various pagan groups into a broadly based pagan community with common fears and aspirations. His murder at the hands of an Alexandrian crowd in 361 demonstrated the latent strength of the pagan community when faced with an implacable foe who did not enjoy the support of any other major group in the city.[43]

Despite this flare-up of violence, the three decades following the murder of George witnessed comparatively little overt conflict between the pagan and Christian communities in Alexandria. Julian and his attempted revival of state-sponsored paganism proved to be, in the words of Athanasius, "but a cloud which soon is dispersed." During his brief reign, Julian had sought especially to foster the traditional civic cults of the Greek cities, including that of Serapis at Alexandria. Aside from the testimony of his letters, Julian's patronage of the Serapis cult is perhaps best illustrated by the popular story that, upon hearing news of the apostate emperor's death, certain pagan Alexandrians "ran to the temple of Serapis crying out against him [Serapis] and saying, 'If you did not want him, why did you accept his gifts?'" Just as imperial patronage under Constantius played a critical role in maintaining the fragile status of Alexandria's Arian community, the sudden disappearance of imperial support in 363 undoubtedly contributed to the quiescence of the pagan community in the years immediately following Julian's death. During this period, Alexandrian pagans very seldom took any communal initiative unless it was in support of one faction of the Christian community against another. Even in these post-363 instances, however, the pagans tended to side with groups within

Alexandrian society, like the Jews and the Arians, who felt especially threatened by the growing influence of the patriarch and his followers.[44]

Nonetheless, Athanasius and his immediate successors did not have carte blanche to run roughshod over the sensibilities of the pagan community. None of them wished to follow the example of George the Cappadocian. Even Athanasius, for all of his authority within the city, expressed reluctance to assail particular strongholds of pagan sentiment in Alexandria, such as the Serapeum. He could only express the desire to transform, at some point in the future, the site of the temple into a sanctuary of Christian worship. Besides, it was not until 407 that bishops in the empire were granted the legal authority to close or demolish temples. While they and their congregations might provide the impetus for temple destruction in this earlier period, it was essential that they gain the active support of civil authorities (both imperial and local) for their antipagan campaigns. The changing nature of this support can be seen in the career of Bishop Mark of Arethusa, who destroyed a temple and was later martyred when he refused to restore it. Some pagan communities, like that of Gaza, guarded their traditional civic cults so zealously that it was not until the early fifth century that Porphyry, the local bishop, was able to secure imperial assistance and overawe both popular and official resistance in order to demolish the temple of Marnas.[45]

A later Coptic tradition informs us that Athanasius's secretary was sitting with him at table when the aged patriarch uttered his wish to close the Serapeum. The secretary's name was Theophilus. He eventually gained the leadership of the Alexandrian church in 385, and he possessed the good fortune of becoming patriarch in an era when pagan-Christian relations within the empire had changed appreciably from the days of his episcopal mentor. During the period 384–88, Theodosius's compatriot and praetorian prefect of the East, Maternus Cynegius, carried out a determined policy of temple closings while touring the provinces under his care. He has often been identified as the imperial official who oversaw the destruction of temples in Osrhoene, Carrhae, and Beroea. Marcellus of Apamea took advantage of this favorable turn in imperial policy to recruit official aid in his efforts to demolish the local temple of Zeus. Pagan reactions to this changed climate are eloquently expressed by Libanius in his *Pro Templis,* an impassioned plea to Theodosius to reverse this unofficial policy of temple destruction. Libanius argued that these violent acts directed against pagan temples were contrary to a host of long-standing laws. He respectfully hinted that pagans would be forced to "defend themselves and the law" in the course of protecting their temples.[46]

Cynegius made two official trips to Egypt, at the beginning and end of his tenure in office (384–88). Although the first visit was ostensibly for the purpose of announcing the coreign of Theodosius and Magnus Maximus, Zosimus tells us that Cynegius "forbade the worship of the gods and closed the doors of temples in the East, Egypt, and Alexandria." His second trip to Egypt was also characterized by temple closings and the prohibition of sacrifices. After two decades of de facto toleration, the concerted nature of these antipagan attacks, directed by one of the highest officials in Theodosius's administration, undoubtedly came as quite a shock to the pagans of Alexandria. We have no evidence that the Serapeum itself was threatened at this time. Yet, it must have been clear to all parties that the final struggle over public cult in Alexandria would be determined by the future status of the shrine dedicated to the city's patron deity.[47]

When the conflict finally erupted in 391, it did not arise from a premeditated plan on the part of Theophilus (as Socrates and Theodoret imply), or from a popular outburst among the city's Christian inhabitants, "God having sent goads to prick the hearts of that devout people."[48] According to Rufinus, our earliest and fullest source for these events, the incident began when some workmen discovered an underground sanctuary (perhaps a Mithraeum) while renovating a basilica which had been given to the patriarchate by Constantius. The underground shrine still contained a number of cult objects, and Theophilus seized this chance discovery by publicly displaying the pagan "mysteries," even going so far as to parade them "through the midst of the Agora."[49] Seeing such sacred objects exposed to public ridicule, some devout pagans became infuriated. As Rufinus colorfully puts it, "The Gentiles, as though they had drunk a chalice of serpents, all began to go mad and rage openly."[50] These pagans then attacked the Christians, and bloody street battles ensued. One pagan, Helladius, later boasted to Socrates Scholasticus that he had personally slain nine of the sacrilegious Christians. Eventually, the pagans retreated into the citadel-like fastness of the Serapeum. From this easily defended position, they occasionally made sorties against the Christians besieging them. During these sallies, they also were able to take captive a number of Christians, including a distinguished Christian rhetor named Gessius.[51]

A standoff ensued, and the city's civil and military authorities attempted to mediate in this tense situation. Evagrius, the praefectus Augustalis, and Romanus, the *comes Aegypti,* sent messengers to those inside the fortified temple, reminding them of "the power of the Roman Empire, the coercive force of the laws, and the punishments which are accustomed to follow on acts such as theirs."[52] The barricaded pagans responded by strengthening their defenses and refusing to negotiate. Recognizing that the fortress/temple could only be stormed with great loss of life, the imperial administrators referred the matter to Theodosius.

On his part, Theodosius wished to avoid a repeat of the bloodbath that occurred the previous year in Thessalonica, when soldiers responded to a riot and the subsequent murder of a Gothic officer by slaughtering thousands of the city's inhabitants.[53] Accordingly, he sent back a rescript that declared the slain Alexandrian Christians to be martyrs, offered amnesty to the pagans, but also ordered the suppression of the pagan cults responsible for the violence. Evagrius and Romanus appeared before the Serapeum at the head of a number of soldiers and they had the rescript read in the presence of the pagans. Upon hearing the terms of the imperial letter, the attending Christian crowd cheered loudly and the dismayed pagans within the temple either fled or tried to mingle unnoticed among the Christians.

The soldiers occupying the now deserted temple hesitated to harm the cult statue of Serapis, fearing a widely reported legend that if a hand was raised against the image, "the earth would immediately open up, dissolving into chaos, and suddenly the heavens would collapse into the abyss."[54] This magnificent statue of Serapis, the work of the famous Athenian sculptor Bryaxis, was of composite precious materials (notably ivory and gold), a technique known as chryselephantine.[55] One Christian soldier, however, seized an axe and struck the jaw of the beautiful statue, repeating his bold (and unpunished) action until he had hewn the limbs from the torso. To symbolize the overthrow of Serapis's cult in Alexandria, portions of the statue were burned in each part of the city.[56] Finally, the trunk itself was publicly burned in the theater. Theophilus arranged for monks to settle in the precinct of the former temple, transforming some of the buildings into churches, which eventually housed the relics of John the Baptist and Elijah—two saints whose ministries heralded a new dispensation of God's kingdom on earth. During the reign of Julian, the relics of these saints had been rescued from a pagan mob that attacked them in Sebaste, and the irony of their installation with great fanfare on the hill of the Serapeum surely would not have been lost on the city's inhabitants.[57]

This justly famous outbreak of intercommunal violence in 391 helps to illuminate the character of the Alexandrian pagan community during a crucial juncture in the history of the late antique city. After the temple had been abandoned by the pagans, a number of curious Alexandrians wandered about the precinct taking in the wonders of the site. The pagan poet and grammarian Palladas was moved to compose several vindictive epigrams on the fate of the Christian rhetor Gessius, whose tortured and crucified body Palladas saw after it had been tossed into a pit. However, it seems that Gessius was not without some consolation in his death, since his rival pagan rhetors and grammarians were forced to flee the city or give up teaching. Palladas himself abandoned his teaching career at this time.[58]

The cause of this animosity toward pagan teachers is clear: they had served as the leaders of the pagan crowd during the violent defense of the Serapeum. The fact that literary culture could be linked with the pagan cause can be seen in the careers of two grammarians, Helladius and Ammonius, who later became Socrates' teachers in Constantinople. The ecclesiastical chronicler tells us that Helladius had been a priest of Zeus/Ammon and that Ammonius had served as the priest of an Egyptian ape god.[59] Given Helladius's boast regarding the nine Christians he had slain during the riot, it is not surprising that he, along with other pagans sharing his profession, found it politic afterward to leave the city.

The role of teachers in this pagan rioting is further confirmed by a chorus of contemporary sources who state that the pagans "chose a certain Olympius, by reputation and attire a philosopher, to be the leader of their crime and boldness."[60] He was especially suited for leadership within the pagan community, since his admirers noted that "his lips were graced with a gift of persuasion which was something no longer human but divine."[61] His exceptional talents in persuading his listeners rendered him a potent leader, as we are told that "no one's soul was so unyielding and barbaric that he could not be enchanted by the words which flowed out of the holy mouth of this man."[62] He was passionately devoted to the pagan gods, particularly to Serapis, and "he gathered around him those people whom he met, instructed them in the old ways and showed them what great blissfulness was the fruit for those who consciously held them."[63] His preoccupation with religious concerns was so great that he was regarded specifically as a "religious teacher" (*hierodidaskalos*), in an age when such epithets usually were reserved for Christian teachers. Moreover, Olympius did not limit his following to young, wealthy students, but he found ready hearers among all age groups and social levels within the pagan community.[64] A charismatic leader of this stamp could easily shape pagan opinion within the city and channel those previously unarticulated sentiments into a course of action which held the Christian community at bay and intimidated the local administration. No wonder Palladas thought it best to lie low after the pagan cause was crushed.

What of Olympius's followers? It is always difficult to identify faces in a crowd, especially given the limited information imparted to us by our ancient sources. However, several suggestions may be made in light of comparative evidence as well as what we know concerning the topography of Alexandria. The leaders of the pagan crowd were teachers, and it is likely that students made up a significant portion of their following. These students would have been a diverse lot, since Eunapius informs us that large numbers of eager students were drawn to Alexandria from many cities of the empire, flocking around popular teachers whose fame had spread throughout the Mediterranean world. Literary culture in this age had a distinctly international flavor, and many intellectuals from other regions spent a portion of their training in a city long known as a mecca for academic pursuits. Olympius himself had been a native of Cilicia, Plotinus and later Proclus had both studied in Alexandria, and several Alexandrian philosophers traced their origins to Aphrodisias in Caria. In addition, students throughout late antiquity were known for their devotion to the old gods. Antoninus's eager students served as priests at Canopus. As much as a century later, Zachariah of Mytilene encountered students secretly practicing magical arts when he went to study law in Berytus. Since portions of the Serapeum served as lecture halls for the city's teachers, groups of students would have been close at hand during the violence of 391.[65]

Other elements in the pagan crowd may have consisted of pagan inhabitants from the surrounding native quarter of Rhakotis. Bonds of neighborhood were very strong in ancient cities. In the Latin west, neighborhoods or *vici* were even named at times for the gods worshiped in nearby temples and shrines. While the surviving evidence from Roman Alexandria is admittedly scrappy, it would be quite surprising if this kind of neighborhood loyalty did not find a rallying point in the magnificent complex of buildings dedicated to Serapis. Moreover, this widely revered temple always hosted a throng of pilgrims and tourists, though one might wish to dispute Eunapius's claim that "those who resorted to it from all parts were a multitude equal to that of [Alexandria's] own citizens."[66] At any rate, devoted pilgrims, as well as long-time local worshipers of the god would have provided an enthusiastic body of defenders for the threatened shrine. In addition to these devotees, one might wish to include a broader spectrum of Alexandrians for whom the survival of the Serapeum may have been an issue of civic pride in an age noted for competition between cities to gain the greatest glory. For centuries, Serapis's splendid temple had been an important attribute of "the most glorious city of the Alexandrians."

Those days were now just a memory. Shortly after the cult of

Serapis was destroyed, Theodosius sent another rescript to Evagrius and Romanus with much broader application than the previous one concerned with the temple of Serapis:

> No person shall be granted the right to perform sacrifices; no person shall go around the temples; no person shall revere the shrines. All persons shall recognize that they are excluded from profane entrance into temples by the opposition of Our law, so that if any person should attempt to anything with reference to the gods or the sacred rites, contrary to Our prohibition, he shall learn that he will not be exempted from punishment by any special grants of imperial favor.

The implications were clear. This new edict called for the thoroughgoing eradication of public paganism within the city.[67] Pagan critics later considered Theophilus responsible for these events, Zosimus even calling him "the chief traitor against the age-old ancestral rites."[68] The marginal illustrations of a contemporary Alexandrian chronicle depict a victorious Theophilus, gospel book in hand, standing atop the Serapeum with the disconsolate image of Serapis inside (figure 17).[69] Common Alexandrians assisted the authorities in the overthrow of pagan practices in the city, and they were undoubtedly encouraged in this by their bishop. Nonetheless, it seems evident that the actual work of temple closing was carried out by the prefect and the soldiers under his command, thereby at least adhering to the letter of the law.[70]

One of the most significant acts in the dismantling of civic paganism in Alexandria was the removal of the sacred Nilometer from the Serapeum and its subsequent installation in one of the city's churches. For thousands of years, supervision of the cycle of the Nile was considered a religious function. Carved Nilometers may still be found in temples throughout Egypt, as at Elephantine and at Edfu. At Alexandria, the cult of the Nile had long been associated with that of Serapis, and these two gods traditionally oversaw the annual rising of the life-giving waters. Public feasts were celebrated in honor of the Nile, "inducing him to flood the fields, and if these are not performed in due season and by due persons, he too would refuse." Even after these feasts were discontinued and the Nilometer transferred to a church, the importance of the annual inundation ensured that the Nile retained a certain religious status, only now under the control "of the Lord of the waters."[71]

The cults of other traditional gods were discontinued at this time, including that of Tyche, the former protectress of the city's abundance and good fortune. Palladas has left to us three enchanting epigrams depicting the transformation of the Tychaion into a wineshop. In these poems, Palladas plays upon the current misfortune of Fortune, and he notes with some irony that, "Thou who hadst once a temple, keepest a tavern in thy old age, / and we see thee now serving hot drinks to mortals." The statues in the Tychaion, however, escaped destruction and existed at least until the Persian conquest in 619. Other statues of gods and heroes were not so fortunate. Many were overthrown or were melted down and their metal put to other uses. Palladas again exploits the poetic possibilities of one such occurrence, relating that "the smith transformed Eros into / a frying-pan, and not unreasonably, as it also burns."[72]

Popular reaction to this overthrow of public paganism reveals a certain indignation that the gods were powerless to protect themselves. One night shortly after Serapis's temple had been occupied, small busts of Serapis which adorned the doorposts and windows of private dwellings throughout the city were mysteriously torn away and crosses painted in their place.[73] Such acts of religious vandalism, reminiscent of the mutilation of the hermae in Alcibiades' Athens, can reasonably be ascribed to the zeal of certain Christian elements in the populace. While one might expect that Alexandrian Christians would deride the weakness of the fallen gods, it comes as something of a surprise to learn that, when the head of Serapis "was carried through all the town in sight of his worshipers, they mocked the weakness of him to whom they had once bowed the knee."[74] Further, it was widely believed that the Nile would refuse to rise and replenish the land, since sacrifices to it had been suspended. The following year, however, the river rose to such heights that Alexandria and much of the Mareotis district was in danger of flooding. In response, "the pagans of Alexandria, irritated at this unexpected occurrence, exclaimed in derision at the public theaters, that the River, like an old man or fool, could not control his waters."[75] Some might attribute these popular reactions to the traditional "fickleness" of the Alexandrians. It seems more likely, however, that this religious inconstancy arose from an important aspect of religious commitment in antiquity: the notion that the gods intervened in human affairs through acts of power, and that successful challenges to their authority through opposing acts of power demonstrated the superiority of one god over another.[76] In addition, the love-hate relationship often displayed by Alexandrians to rulers placed over them, whether they be Ptolemaic kings, Roman emperors, or their subordinate administrators, may also extend to authorities in the divine realm. This latter explanation, though, should not be pressed too far, since the antiauthoritarian character of the Alexandrian crowd has often been overstated and rests upon a relatively unsubstantiated literary topos from antiquity.

The pagan intelligentsia responded to the overthrow of the Serapis cult by putting forth arguments intended to limit the damage done to their standing as well as to the cause of paganism. It was widely circulated that a number of pagan priests and philosophers had foretold the downfall of the Serapeum. Even Serapis's great champion, Olympius, "was so full of the spirit of God that he predicted to his companions that Serapis would forsake his temple." Antoninus, a renowned philosopher residing at Canopus, prophesied that the gods would soon leave the realm of men and that "a fabulous and unseemly gloom would hold sway over the fairest things on earth."[77] The clear emphasis in these prophecies was that Serapis abandoned his temple of his own volition and that he made known his intentions beforehand to his closest intimates. Although these remarkably accurate prophecies may have been made after the fact, they had the desired effect, since they "greatly increased the reputation of Antoninus."[78] In the face of this pagan propaganda, local Christians felt the necessity to circulate their own prophetic traditions concerning Serapis's downfall.[79] Further, the fame of the pagan predictions was such that, fifteen years later, Augustine felt constrained to address the question of pagan prophetic powers.[80]

Despite these ex post facto pagan attempts to control the ill effects of the Serapeum's capture, the violence of 391 proved to be the linchpin that initiated the downfall of public paganism throughout Egypt. In Rufinus's words, "After the fall of Serapis, could the sanctuaries of any other demon remain standing?"[81] Temples and shrines were subsequently closed in many Egyptian towns, often at the instigation of the local bishop. Yet Christian chroniclers tend to overstate the scope of this victory, caught up as they are in a spirit of triumphalism. Canopus remained an influential center of pagan cult and philosophy, and the great temple at Philae on the borders of Nubia received worshipers as late as the reign of Justinian (527–65). Moreover, it should be remembered that the outcome of the Serapeum conflict was by no means a foregone conclusion. Prolonged violence between the pagan and Christian communities resulted in a standoff that required imperial intervention to decide the issue. Although the forms of public paganism were abolished in the city, many Alexandrians remained committed to the pagan cause, including influential bouleutai.[82] The patriarch found that his efforts to discredit upper-class pagans had very little effect, even though he skillfully manipulated a scandal implicating the elite patrons of Saturn's local cult.[83] It was another twenty-five years before a later patriarch, Cyril, found the means to break the power of influential Alexandrian pagans and their local network of patronage. The murder of the pagan philosopher Hypatia in 415, and the subsequent brutalization of pagan bouleutai, dashed the remaining hopes of Alexandrian pagans that their cultural hegemony in the city might yet be restored.[84]

## *The Pagans of Fifth-Century Alexandria*

In the aftermath of Hypatia's murder, Alexandria's pagans maintained a certain tenuous existence throughout the fifth century. Cyril, though triumphant over public pagan cult and the influence of the pagan elite, still felt obliged to offer a lengthy refutation of the pagan arguments found in Julian's *Contra Galilaeos* circa 438—over twenty years after the death of Hypatia. He also attempted to displace the cult of Isis at Menouthis by transplanting the bones of Saints Cyrus and John to the site.[85] Nonetheless, isolated pockets of pagans remained. Contemporary observers, both pagan and Christian, speak of a variety of traditional rites that were still being practiced in Alexandria as well as in the eastern suburbs of Canopus and Menouthis.[86]

The most vivid portrait we have of fifth-century paganism in Alexandria is contained in Zachariah of Mytilene's *Life of Severus*. Zachariah's recollections of his student days in Alexandria during the 480s contain the narrative of an incident which served to further isolate the city's remaining pagans. His story concerns the adventures of a fellow student named Paralios who began to question the efficacy of sacrifice, the authority of oracles, and the veracity of supposed pagan miracles. Paralios's caustic remarks on the gods earned for him a thrashing at the hands of his pagan fellow students. Once the patriarch, Peter Mongus, learned of these events, the episode mushroomed into a full-scale antipagan pogrom, resulting in the destruction of the cult center at Canopus/Menouthis. Public sentiment against paganism ran so high that several noted teachers were hounded out of the city.[87]

The public nature of this incident portrays vividly the revolution in intercommunal relations which had taken place since the days of Diocletian and the "Era of the Martyrs." It also explains one reason for the marginalization of pagan spokesmen within Alexandrian society after the death of Hypatia. One can easily understand why Isidore's teacher, Serapion, "followed the exhortation, 'Live in obscurity,'" and "did not often leave his house to go into the street."[88] Of course, Serapion's life as an urban hermit was held up as a model for religious reasons connected with the popularity of asceticism in late antiquity. Yet other Alexandrian pagans likewise found it prudent to keep to themselves. During a hiatus in a political career which eventually led to the consulship, Fl. Messius Phoebus Severus turned away from politics with disgust "and devoted himself to a quiet life untroubled by such activity."[89] Severus gave himself to the pursuit of philosophical studies and entertained visiting Brahmans from India, who "had no urge to visit the public baths or to otherwise observe the goings on in the city, but rather avoided everything that occurred out of doors."[90] Although Severus welcomed many other visitors to his house in Alexandria, we are told that these were not influential politicians, but rather educators who wished to consult with him and enjoy his "rich and manifold library."[91]

The epitome of this privatization of Alexandrian paganism can be seen in the career of Damascius's hero, Isidore (fl. 480–510). In Damascius's comparison of the talents of his beloved teacher with those of Hypatia, Damascius calls to mind the murder of the latter: "The Alexandrians still remembered this incident, but this diminished their respect and interest for Isidore only a very little. Despite the well-founded dread which hung over him, everyone still sought frequent company with him and the opportunity to absorb the words which streamed from his mouth."[92] Who were these Alexandrians clamoring to hear the golden words of Isidore? Rather than Hypatia's influential "jumble of steeds and men," Isidore's visitors consisted of "the authorities in rhetoric or poetry" who sought out the philosopher in order to clear up obscure questions in their particular disciplines.[93] Nothing could better illustrate the reversal in fortunes experienced by Alexandrian's pagans in the space of less than a century.

Moreover, the paganism of these highly educated Alexandrians of the fifth century appears to have been antiquarian in nature. With the demise of public cult at the end of the fourth century, the pagans of Isidore's day found themselves largely cut off from an organic tradition. The wide spectrum of religious interests displayed by these pagans, ranging from Egyptian and Hellenic cults to those of Persia, betrays a certain dilettantism. Despite Damascius's assertion that two such devotees of Osiris and Mithras, "still had contact with the earlier ways," the bookish character of their devotion confirms his more accurate assessment: "These men no longer lived under the time-honored institutions, but were part of the generation which directly came afterward."[94] Returning to the traditional funeral rites performed for Heraiskos by Asclepiades, it is worth noting that the mystical hieroglyphics that appeared on the linen shroud were apparently unintelligible to Asclepiades and his fellow latter-day priests of Osiris.[95] Asclepiades' son, Horapollon, later published a two-volume work given over to the interpretation of hieroglyphics, a fanciful allegorical exposition in Greek of a script lost from living memory.[96] Except in isolated centers like Philae on the borders of Nubia, the religious lore of pharaonic times was largely forgotten. Even Hellenism, which had blended so easily with the religious substratum of Egypt, was being absorbed by Coptic Christian culture, although it was to leave an indelible impression on the art and literature of Coptic Egypt. A phase of cultural history was over. Palladas's lament for the pagan cause after the destruction of the Serapeum more aptly describes the status of Alexandria's pagans at the close of the fifth century:

> Is it not true that we are dead and living only in appearance,
> we Hellenes, fallen on disaster,
> likening life to a dream, since we remain alive while
> our way of life is dead and gone?

Even for the triumphant Christian community, the days of unquestioned dominance were numbered. In just a century and a half, ʿAmr ibn al-ʿAs and his conquering Arab army would ride through the gates of Alexandria.

# Six

# The Christian Community: The Interior Landscape and the Civic Landscape

A popular Alexandrian story of the early seventh century told of two men who had been convicted of murder. The older of the two had implicated the younger one. They were led off to execution by the prefect's guard to a place outside the city, near a ruined temple of the god Kronos.

> The youth implored pity from the soldiers saying: "By the Lord, do me the charity of turning me towards the east, so that I may see it when I am killed." The soldiers asked him, "Why do you want that?" He answered them, "In truth, sirs, unhappy man that I am, it has been no more than seven months since I have received holy baptism and I have become a Christian." Learning this, the soldiers wept over this young man. But the old man, becoming enraged, said: "By Serapis, turn me towards Kronos." Then the soldiers, hearing the blasphemy of the old man, left the young man and hanged the old man first. When they had hanged him, behold a horseman sent by the Augustalis said to the soldiers: "Do not execute the young man, but unbind him." Great was the joy of the soldiers and all their assistants. Then having released him, they brought him into the Praetorium, and the Augustalis set him free.[1]

So writes John Moschus, that indefatigable monastic tourist of the early seventh century. By simply altering a few of the names and details, this tale of dramatic reversal might easily pass for one of the enduringly popular stories told by Herodotus, the first great tourist to Egypt nearly a millennium earlier. Despite its stylized structure, Moschus's story illumines several important features of Alexandrian society in the years just prior to the Arab conquest. The prefect's justice still holds sway in Alexandria and evildoers can expect an exacting recompense for their deeds—even if the judicial process is arbitrary enough to catch innocent persons in its net.

What seems most remarkable about this story is how thoroughly Christianity had permeated Alexandrian society by the early seventh century. Surely the scores of Alexandrian Christians executed during Diocletian's persecution in the early fourth century would have been astounded to see how radically the religious landscape had changed since the "Era of the Martyrs"—so much so that the prefect's guards rejoice when a recently baptized Christian is granted a stay of execution. Two and a half centuries earlier, the emperor Julian attempted to flatter the Alexandrian populace by invoking the name of their tutelary deity, Serapis. In Moschus's day, swearing by the name of Serapis was regarded as blasphemy and could elicit not divine aid, but the wrath of the prefect's guard.[2]

The "most glorious city of the Alexandrians" had become the "most glorious Christ-loving city of the Alexandrians."[3] How did this transformation come about? Over the course of several centuries, the Alexandrian Christian community evolved from a persecuted minority in the city to the dominant force in Alexandrian politics, society, and economic life. This chapter will trace some of the ways that the Christian community was encountered by outsiders as well as the growing presence of Christianity in Alexandria's landscape. Even a brief survey of this profound cultural transformation requires that we sketch out the structure and inner life of this increasingly important Alexandrian community, the subject of the next chapter. By examining the forces of communal cohesion and group identity within the Alexandrian Christian community, we will then be in a better position to see how it was able to withstand violent persecutions in the early fourth century, conflicts with imperial authorities and other influential churches throughout late antiquity, and even military occupations of the city, first by the

Sassanian Persians from 619 to 629 and then by the Arabs beginning in 642. Challenges to the community from within the city were no less great, since the eventual supremacy of the Christian cause in Alexandria was by no means a foregone conclusion at the beginning of the fourth century. Both the Jewish community and the diverse groups composing the pagan community mounted sustained and occasionally successful opposition to the growing power of the city's Christians.

A prominent aspect of this struggle was the mobilization of force (both moral and strong-armed) which permitted bishops, from Athanasius in the fourth century to John the Almsgiver in the seventh century, to exercise enormous authority within the city. What were the forms of social and economic patronage utilized by these bishops? Obviously, there were long-standing disputes over the nature and extent of this episcopal authority, manifested by the Melitian schism, the outbreak of Arianism, the Origenist controversy, and the Monophysite-Chalcedonian split within the church. An analysis of the forces of communal cohesion and the factors leading to communal schism—the subject of the final chapter on the Christian community—will enhance further an appreciation of the broader social dynamics at work within this important late antique city.

## *Obstacles to Understanding*

The historical materials available for understanding the Alexandrian Christian community, though of a similar stripe, present entirely different problems than those we employed in looking at the city's pagans or Jews. For Alexandria's other ethno-religious communities of late antiquity, one must either resort to indirect pieces of evidence culled from bitterly hostile sources or sift through meager scraps of information preserved fortuitously through the centuries.

No such difficulty awaits us when turning to the ancient sources for the Christian community. Here, the most immediate problem is the onerous blessing of abundance. Since the days of Saint Paul, Christian leaders and theologians spent much of their time with pen in hand. By the fourth century, the overwhelming majority of the literary output coming from Mediterranean lands was explicitly Christian in character. Further, it should be noted that the Christian tenor of late antique literature was not due solely to the conversion of the traditional literate classes. The ever rising tide of Christian literature throughout the fourth century and beyond (stemmed only slightly in the west by the Germanic migrations of the fifth century) attests to the bookish nature of Christianity in late antiquity. As a consequence, modern scholars in the field of patristics deal with a body of literature even more extensive than that surviving from all of pagan classical antiquity.

As might be expected of one of the empire's most vibrant cities, Alexandria possessed a Christian community whose literary output was every bit as prolific as the other great centers of Christianity, like Antioch, Carthage, or Rome. Moreover, since Alexandria was the scene of some of the most dramatic events of late antiquity, Christian writers from all over the empire frequently directed their attention to the city of Origen, Athanasius, and Cyril. In practical terms, this means that the literary sources alone constitute a volume of material so great that one can easily feel like an archaeologist examining random potsherds atop the mounds of discarded pottery rising along the northern shores of Lake Mareotis. If, in addition, one takes into account the epigraphic and archeological evidence for Alexandria's Christians, it would not be difficult to imagine a comprehensive study of the subject running to several hundred pages.

Two factors combine to limit our present discussion. My aim throughout has been to see the city's ethno-religious communities in their specific Alexandrian context. As much as possible, then, exhaustive treatment has been avoided, with a view toward asking discrete questions of the evidence in such a way that I am able to sketch out the broad outlines of social dynamics in this volatile urban setting.

In addition, the evidence itself restricts the scope of our inquiry, since its historical worth is not at all in proportion to its quantity. Much of the literature is theological in nature, and while some of these homilies and treatises may fittingly serve as the crowning glories of patristic exegesis and theological speculation, they provide scant material for understanding the urban milieu that produced them. Anecdotes and sayings attributed to Egypt's venerable ascetics compose an often entertaining body of literature, but Alexandria and its Christians appear in these stories only in passing—though these occasional glimpses provide a fascinating portrait of rural and ascetic attitudes toward the city. The martyrologies of Egyptian saints, extant in both Greek and Coptic, frequently use Alexandria as the backdrop for the final act in the martyrs' drama of suffering. But what are we to do with a saint like Macrobius—not at all atypical—who continues to witness heroically to the faith while being sliced to ribbons, boiled in oil and pitch, consigned to wild beasts, thrown into the sea with stones tied to his feet, and burned at the stake.[4] Obviously, this is either a resiliency that would make a Rasputin envious, or a type of fictionalized literature which revels in fantastic tortures, miraculous recoveries, and obdurate resistance to imperial authority. Although it may be worthwhile to attempt to glean a historical kernel from the chaff of such tales, often the remaining kernel is no more substantial than the minor piratical raiding party left over from winnowing Homer's *Iliad*. And just as the traditions which constructed the *Iliad* were far more concerned to spin a timeless tale of strife and pride, so too the compilers of the martyrologies wished to entertain their readers with glorious stories of perseverance infused with supernatural wonders.

Perhaps more useful for our purposes are those works that take as their subject matter the conflicts surrounding the Alexandrian church in late antiquity. Ecclesiastical histories, like those of Socrates Scholasticus, Sozomen, Rufinus, Zachariah of Mytilene, and Evagrius, to name but a few, preserve tantalizing details concerning the inner life of the Alexandrian Christian community. Local historical traditions, which frequently escape the notice of these non-Egyptian historians, may be found in the chronicles of John of Nikiu, Saʿid ibn al-Batriq, and the much-redacted *History of the Patriarchs*.[5] With the all-too-few exceptions of eyewitness accounts, most of these historians are only as good as their sources, many of which are tendentious at best. How trustworthy, then, are these sources for reconstructing Alexandrian history?

A prime example of this question of reliability is Athanasius (bishop, 326–73) and his massive literary output. Whatever his contemporaries may have thought of him (and there are sufficient grounds for concluding that these ancient opinions were mixed, at best), the torrent of self-serving literature he penned has ensured that Athanasius's own works have largely created the image adopted by the early church historians and their modern expositors. This image of a selfless shepherd of God's flock, almost single-handedly defending the true faith against heretical teachers, duped bishops, and persecuting emperors, was taken up with enthusiasm by Newman in the nineteenth century and can still be found with little modification up to the present. This image began to show some tarnish at the beginning of this century, when Eduard Schwartz critically reexamined the sources for the controversies surrounding Athanasius's career. More damning was the papyrological evidence published by H. I. Bell, which showed the Alexandrian bishop to be a virtual mafioso who ordered (unofficially, of course) the beating and imprisonment of his ecclesiastical opponents in Egypt.[6] Suddenly, the charges of brutality leveled at the saint at the Council of Tyre appear to be more than simply the ravings of jealous churchmen.[7] The tension between these two portraits of the bishop has continued unabated throughout Athanasian studies over the past eighty years. The treatment of Athanasius in the *Coptic Encyclopedia*—a truly monumental compendium of scholarly information on Christian Egypt—portrays the bishop in a light so favorable that it borders on hagiographic encomium. By contrast, a recent biography of Athanasius sees him as a consummate politician, shrewdly manipulating power and patronage.[8]

To some degree, one is tempted to breathe a sigh of relief when Athanasius passes from the scene in 373, and we can deal with far less formidable personalities like Peter II (373–80) and Timothy (380–85). As T. D. Barnes has pointed out, "Athanasius is so forceful and convincing a pleader that he is certain to get the better of any modern inquirer on some occasions."[9] And yet, as we proceed to his successors, it is possible to regret the absence of the vivid details of Alexandrian life contained in the admittedly tendentious writings of the controversial bishop. However, this process of disentangling polemical diatribe from valuable historical material is repeated again and again with the literary sources for several of Athanasius's more colorful successors on the throne of Saint Mark, like Theophilus, Cyril, and Dioscorus. And as we shall see, often the more bitter the controversy, the more revealing the historical sources are for illuminating the contours of daily life within the Alexandrian Christian community.

The triumphalism that imbues so many of the ancient sources for Alexandrian Christianity also presents a formidable obstacle to understanding. This can manifest itself as either an orthodoxy projected anachronistically into an earlier period of development, or (more importantly for this discussion) as the ever growing and undisputed dominance of the Christian community within Alexandrian society. As but one example, the prolonged and intense struggle that raged between the city's pagans and Christians over the Serapeum in 391 can become, in the eyes of the victors, a foregone conclusion in the progressive Christianization of Alexandria's topography. This attitude is graphically displayed in an anonymous *Alexandrian Chronicle* from the 390s, whose marginal illustrations show a smug Theophilus standing over the pagan temple and its disconsolate deity (figure 17). Nearby, the pagan usurper Eugenius, representing all the hopes of the pagan party in the early 390s, flees in terror from the triumphant Christian emperor Theodosius.[10] In reality, the conflict over urban hegemony is seldom so neat.

This triumphalism can also be turned on its head, to produce in the ancient literature an attitude that is equally deleterious to a balanced view of Alexandrian Christianity. This is the attitude of the persecuted minority, confident in the righteousness of its cause and its eventual vindication in the courts of divine justice. While this may appear in some of the sources originating in the period of pagan persecution in the early fourth century, it becomes more pronounced after the Council of Chalcedon in 451, when much of the Egyptian church took a stand against "the Council and the Tome" (of Pope Leo I), preferring imperial displeasure to the disgrace of submission. By the beginning of the seventh century, a virtual siege mentality had established itself among both the Monophysite and Chalcedonian portions of the Christian community —a stance toward opposition which was to serve the Christians

Fig. 17. Theophilus and the Serapeum. Bishop Theophilus, Gospel book in hand, stands triumphantly atop the Serapeum in 391. The cult image of Serapis, crowned with the modius, is visible within the temple at the bottom. Marginal illustration from a chronicle written in Alexandria in the early fifth century, thus providing a nearly contemporary portrait of Theophilus. *P.Goleniscev* 6 verso.

(From A. Bauer and J. Strygowski, "Eine alexandrinische Weltchronik," *Denkschriften der Kaiserlichen Akademie der Wissenschaften: Wien* 51.2 [1906]: 1–204, fig. 6 verso) well in the coming centuries under Muslim rule. While one may regret the divisions among Alexandria's Christians, the nature of the communal boundaries separating them can tell us a great deal about the ways in which these Christians viewed themselves and those with whom they differed. Not only are communal boundaries themselves revealing, but the appeal Christianity had for outsiders and the process of initiation into the church may help elucidate the reasons for Christianity's eventual success within Alexandria.

Another obstacle to understanding the social dynamics of Alexandrian Christianity is the almost exclusive preoccupation of the literary sources with the leaders of the Christian community: bishops, catechetical teachers, and ascetics. Although their lives were often colorful and well documented, a mere survey of the careers of Athanasius, Theophilus, and John the Almsgiver would provide little insight into the contours of life experienced by the mass of Alexandria's Christians. Admittedly, the bishop with his vast network of patronage and his growing aura of authority often provided the social glue that bound together the entire Christian community. In the end, however, a hierarchy-centered analysis yields a portrait of Alexandrian Christianity lacking background or perspective—a fine procedure for painting an icon, but a less than satisfactory method for understanding the varieties of Christian life within a complex late antique city. The sources' fixation on strong personalities can be somewhat offset by legal and papyrological evidence. Even more telling is the increasing volume of material evidence unearthed in Alexandria over the last thirty years.

## *Modes of Conversion*

According to a tradition long cherished by the Alexandrian church, Christianity came to Alexandria with Saint Mark. As the evangelist entered through one of the city's gates, a strap on one of his sandals broke. He took this everyday annoyance as a sign of God's providence, since it would provide him with a natural point of contact with one of the city's inhabitants—a cobbler. As a nearby cobbler worked at mending the sandal, the awl he was using accidently pierced his hand, and the wounded cobbler uttered the exclamation

"God is one!" After a short prayer, Saint Mark quickly spat upon the ground, took up some clay, and applied it to the cobbler's hand. The hand was at once completely restored, and the grateful cobbler invited the saint home with him in order to hear more about the miraculous power of Mark's God. The cobbler, named Annianus, and his entire household were soon converted, and he eventually became Saint Mark's successor as head of the earliest Christian community in Alexandria.[11]

This pious story relating the first Christian conversion in Alexandria contains several elements that recur through the centuries. Indeed, owing to the nature of the accumulated traditions which make up the Mark cycle, it is quite possible that elements common to conversions in the later history of the Christian community have been read back into the church's primitive origins. Many Alexandrian conversion stories include chance encounters, miraculous events, a potential convert with some concept of monotheism, and a personal witness resulting in the conversion of an entire household. Categorizing these component elements has a certain utility, and yet the danger remains of simply piling up conversion stories and producing a mere collection of anecdotes. Depending on the reliability of the historical sources, many of these tales may owe more to each other than to the events they purportedly describe.

In a city as large and diverse as Alexandria, it is no surprise that conversions to Christianity exhibit the full range of the social landscape, from slaves and prostitutes to philosophers and town councillors. The motives that impel a radical change in religious adherence are notoriously difficult to discern, especially at a distance of a millennium and a half. Pascal's aphorism, "The heart has reasons that reason cannot know," applies to conversions in late antiquity as well as in the seventeenth century. However, Alexandrian conversion accounts frequently take on certain recognizable patterns and sometimes betray a very well reasoned decision.

Alexandrians of differing persuasions all inhabited the same religious landscape. And yet, it is important to recognize that conversion to Christianity required a sharp break from many practices that made up the warp and woof of urban life in antiquity—neighborhood festivals, religious processions, and casual participation in the rites of various cult associations. Religion permeated everyday existence to a degree that is sometimes difficult for a modern Western observer to fathom. The gods were comfortably ensconced in the marketplace, the baths, the taverns, and even the pantry at home. On the other side, adherence to the church demanded a process of initiation which included baptism, explicit renunciation of past religious inclinations, participation in the mysteries of a divine meal, and a course of instruction in the faith which became increasingly lengthy and rigorous. Christianity's exclusive claims (an inheritance from Judaism) served to create a rigidly articulated social boundary between the Christian community and the rest of the city. As Ramsay MacMullen points out: "A sort of invisible mine field, ready to produce scowls and pointed derision aimed in both directions at important parts of a person's culture, and occasionally exploding in violence (always anti-Christian, in the period before 312), thus divided church and town. To cross it required a conscious decision."[12]

How did an inquirer first encounter the Christian message? Unlike churches in much of the rest of the empire, the Alexandrian Christian community acquired a public face by the first portion of the third century. The fame of the Christian catechetical school and its celebrated teachers like Clement and Origen drew large numbers of interested pagans. Despite Eusebius's excessive enthusiasm for Origen, it is not difficult to believe his report that many pagans came to hear Origen and were subsequently converted. At one point, Origen was forced to go underground with his teaching, moving from house to house in order to avoid the enmity of jealous pagan authorities.[13]

Other forms of instruction were intended for an even wider audience, notably the sermons delivered by Alexandrian bishops. Even before the Peace of the Church, Bishop Peter (300–311) gained many adherents for Christianity through his preaching, probably conducted in the newly built church of Saint Dionysius. In the period after Constantine, episcopal sermons continued to be an effective means for converting Alexandrians. Julian became so exasperated at the success of Athanasius's sermons that he ordered him to be banished from the city: "Infamous man! He has had the audacity to baptize Greek women of rank during my reign! Let him be driven forth!" Recognizing the power of sermons to influence public opinion, Cyril (bishop, 412–44) kept several notaries next to his episcopal throne during services in order to take down his exhortations to the people. By the mid-fifth century, a staff of copyists constituted a well-oiled public relations office, which routinely transcribed episcopal homilies, thereby ensuring their dissemination throughout the city.[14]

An unbeliever might also encounter Christianity in forms other than the explicit proclamation of the Christian message. During the troubled years of the mid-third century, the church proved itself to be a successful advocate for the urban populace. When an outbreak of plague occurred in 263, Christians fearlessly ministered to the dying, even when it sealed their own deaths. The stasis that periodically racked the city in the 260s and 270s resulted in the church organizing famine relief, arranging for the safe conduct of refugees, and ultimately playing a role in the negotiations between warring parties. By the fourth and fifth centuries, the church had taken over from traditional civic institutions the maintenance of the poor and infirm. The planting of churches at strategic points in the city's topography also ensured that an unbelieving Alexandrian would be constantly confronted by Christianity. If that were not enough, religious processions between these churches and along the city's principal boulevards further enhanced the public profile of the church in the period after Constantine.[15]

Any of these public expressions of Christianity would have sufficed to bring unbelievers into the church. Sermons and public instruction seem to have been an especially potent tool in sparking conversions. In another setting, one has only to remember the spell that Saint Ambrose's words cast over a young professor of rhetoric to realize the effectiveness of public discourse. The most common feature of Alexandrian conversion accounts, however, is not persuasive rhetorical pyrotechnics but rather vivid demonstrations of divine power that confirm the superiority of the Christian God over any other deity. This is especially true in accounts of mass conversions, usually prompted by some sort of supernatural one-upmanship.

The agent of these wonders was generally a holy man, regarded by both pagans and Christians as uniquely infused with divine power. Athanasius's admittedly self-serving biography of Saint Anthony hints at the evangelistic impact the saint's presence had on the populace during his visit to the city in 338:

> And all the people in the city ran together to see Anthony; and the Hellenes, and those who are called their priests, came into the church, saying, "We ask to see the man of God," for so they all called him. For in that place also the Lord cleansed many of demons, and healed those who were mad. And many Hellenes asked that they might even but touch the old man, believing that they should be profited. Assuredly as many became Christians in those days as one would have seen made in a year.[16]

Here, Anthony is shown to possess a supernatural authority that attracts Alexandrians on both sides of the communal divide, testifying again to the shared religious terrain inhabited by late antique urban dwellers. Quite apart from any divine wonders, the increasing ascetic piety in Christian life during the fourth century itself became a point of attraction for some pagans. Despite the imprecations of literati like Libanius or Eunapius against the "black-robed tribe," Athanasius asserts that the presence of so many women dedicated to ascetic virginity evoked widespread admiration among non-Christians "and it is a very strong argument that the genuine and true religion is to be found with us."[17]

As related by Athanasius, Anthony's purpose in visiting the city (or more precisely, Athanasius's purpose for orchestrating the visit) was to confront the Arian faction within the Alexandrian church. Pagans are converted almost as an afterthought. However, other ascetics came to Alexandria with the sole purpose of confronting unbelievers. One monk who often journeyed to Alexandria was the erudite ascetic Evagrius, who seemed to enjoy challenging pagan philosophers to public disputations. Sometimes these public discussions went beyond mere academic debate, as in the case of the monk Copres, who after debating a Manichaean at length, finally challenged his opponent to commit himself to his deity, that is, throw himself into a huge public bonfire. The Manichaean demurred, and after Copres passed through the flames unhurt, the enraged crowd threw the Manichaean in the fire—and later drove the singed religious teacher out of the city, barely allowing him to escape with his life. Copres' contest with the Manichaean points to the fine line that sometimes divided intellectual arguments from demonstrations of power, and shows how the latter often served as the final arbiter in evoking religious adherence from the populace. In another similar instance, a public disputation between a philosopher named Diogenes and the future bishop, Peter I, ends when Peter heals the eyes of the philosopher's only daughter.[18]

Although bishops were not always noted for their ability to work miracles, they were often able to shape defining moments in the struggle for religious hegemony. Their exercise of brute force against pagan shrines and cult objects served to reveal how powerless the old gods were to defend themselves. Theophilus's destruction of the pagan cult at the Serapeum in 391 convinced many Alexandrians that Serapis was not as strong as the patriarch's God. The Alexandrians, far from exhibiting some native fickleness, easily switched their religious allegiance owing to the demonstrated impotence of Serapis. This hardheaded pragmatism in religious matters extended to devotion to the Nile god. After Theophilus took the sacred Nilometer from the Serapeum to a church, many expected the Nile to hold back its annual life-giving inundation. Instead, the river rose to unprecedented heights. This led many Alexandrians to chant derisively in the theaters that "the river, like an old man or fool, can not control the flow of his waters."[19] The incident became an occasion for many conversions to Christianity. However, such uses of episcopal power had to be employed judiciously. The whole series of events leading up to the destruction of the Serapeum began when Theophilus ordered sacred pagan cult objects to be paraded mockingly through the city. This resulted not in instantaneous conversions but rather in bloody street riots by indignant pagans.

Riots and violent confrontations take us far from the everyday contacts between pagans and Christians which frequently could lead to individual conversions. The evidence for these nondramatic conversions is far more anecdotal than for the occasional flashpoints of intercommunal violence. And yet, it is likely that the type of conversion arising from these mundane encounters better approximates the religious experiences of most Alexandrians: a mother who embraces the newly adopted religion of her son, prostitutes who respond to the piety and kindness of an ascetic, a woman whose illness leads her to repent of a profligate youth, a promising young aristocrat who rejects his parents' religion in favor of a novel faith.[20]

Perhaps the best single document testifying to this type of conversion is Zachariah of Mytilene's *vita Severi*, the first part of which recounts Severus's (and Zachariah's) student days at Alexandria during the 480s. This portion of the narrative centers on the adventures of a fellow student named Paralios, who hailed from Aphrodisias in Caria.[21] Paralios, along with two of his brothers, came to Alexandria in order to study with Horapollon, a noted pagan grammarian. Paralios's two brothers warned him not to speak with a fourth brother named Athanasius. It seems that this Athanasius had studied for the bar in Berytus and had come to Alexandria on some business. While in Alexandria, Athanasius struck up a friendship with Stephen the Sophist. The two of them subsequently abandoned worldly ambition and had become monks at the suburban monastery of Enaton. Paralios's pagan brothers apparently did not want Athanasius to corrupt Paralios's pagan outlook. However, he spurned their warnings and "overcome by his nature, he burned with a desire to see his brother Athanasius."[22]

A reunion with Athanasius provided the former law student with the opportunity to sow seeds of doubt in Paralios's mind regarding the validity of pagan religion. Paralios's wavering led to his becoming a virtual shuttlecock, carrying volleys of religious arguments back and forth between Horapollon's circle of philosophers and the monks at Enaton, especially the erudite Stephen. This wrangling went on for some time, but the occasion which finally led to Paralios's conversion was the debunking of a much reported pagan miracle at the neighboring Isis shrine of Menouthis. Contrary to pagan claims, it was proved that the barren wife of a pagan philosopher did not miraculously conceive, but had simply taken as her own the illegitimate offspring of a priestess. Paralios's newfound resolve to become a Christian was further strengthened by the silence of a renowned oracle to his repeated petitions. One suspects that Paralios did not receive an answer to his petitions because he had already taken the decisive interior step of embracing Christianity.

Paralios's experience weaves together a number of separate strands in the conversion of Alexandria's inhabitants. As a student, Paralios was much influenced by the fierce intellectual border skirmish that went on between the two religious groups for his soul. And yet the catalyst in his conversion was the gods' demonstrated lack of divine power. This outcome should caution us from adopting a rigid two-tiered model of conversion: elite literati persuaded by intellectual arguments and a lower-class populace awed by demonstrations of power. Even Augustine regarded the direction he received from the Bible, after heeding the *tolle lege* of neighborhood children, as nothing short of miraculous. Underneath all of these factors influencing religious conversion lies the foundational substratum of personal relationships. Paralios's fraternal affection for Athanasius provided the all-important stepping-stone from one religious community to another.[23]

But even a source as rich and detailed as Zachariah's *vita Severi* supplies no more than anecdotal evidence for the conversion of Alexandria's inhabitants to Christianity. Do the extant sources allow us to determine when the vast majority of the urban populace adopted Christianity? On a wider scale, historians have recently sought to fix in time the cultural watershed between paganism and Christianity in the Roman Empire. Was it at Constantine's conversion or during the reign of Theodosius? Did the decisive shift in mentalité occur during the late third century, or did pagan forms of worship continue with their old vigor long into the fifth century? Even if one concedes that the struggle for religious hegemony in Alexandria was all but over by the first quarter of the fifth century, control of the city's public cults does not necessarily indicate a general change in the religious adherence of the population.

In the Egyptian countryside, name changes sometimes can signify religious transformation. The tax rolls of the small towns of Egypt provide data for tracing the noticeable shift from names like Serapion and Isidore to Samuel, Dorotheos, and Johannes. On the assumption that the religion of parents is often reflected in the names bestowed on their children, it appears that numerical parity between Christians and pagans was reached sometime in the 320s. Further, the number of pagans shrank to less than a quarter of the rural population by the 350s, and by 400, was probably less than 10 percent.[24] Although numbers alone cannot provide a rounded picture of the influence and status of paganism in the chora, one is left with the strong impression that the Constantinian epoch proved pivotal in the shift from a pagan to a Christian majority.

Can the same be said of Alexandria? Documentation of the sort available from the countryside is nonexistent for the city, at least in the quantity necessary for a statistical base. Names of Alexandrian martyrs under Decius (249–51) bear distinctly pagan-sounding names: Apollonia, Serapion, Besas, Epimachus, Alexander, Ammonarium, Mercuria, Dionysia, Heron, Ater, Isidorus, Nemesion, Ammon, and the like. Lists of Alexandrian clergy subscribing to episcopal letters at the time of the Meletian and Arian controversies are dominated by names betraying a pagan background. An occasional Paul, Timothy, Theodore, or Peter may appear in the lists, but this is no more than one might expect for the ranks of clergy in the first several decades of the fourth century. It is not until the Nestorian and Monophysite disputes of the fifth century that comparable lists of clergy appear—too late to establish any meaningful onomastic shift. Even if evidence were available from the mid to late fourth century, mere lists of clergy can tell us very little about the religious inclinations of a broad spectrum of the urban populace.[25]

Even without such hard evidence to trace the progressive Christianization of the city's populace, a clear picture of Alexandrian religious life emerges—not from the pens of bishops and chroniclers but from the ground itself. Despite interpretive difficulties, the city's archaeological remains free us from an exclusive reliance on literary sources, which can be notoriously untrustworthy. In the case of Oxyrhynchus, it is difficult to determine how much credence one can place in the assertion of the *Historia Monachorum*: "Not one of the city's inhabitants is a heretic or a pagan. On the contrary, all the citizens as a body are believers and catechumens, so that the bishop is able to bless the people publicly in the street."[26] Although such statements strikingly elucidate the ways in which Christian authors envisioned their society, they are less than sure guides to the actual Christianization of a particular city.

### *The Christians of House D*

"Peace be to all."

"And to thy spirit."

> "May God bless you, He who blesses and sanctifies, who defends and preserves us all through the partaking of His holy mysteries; He who is blessed for ever."
>
> "Amen."[27]

With this final blessing and the resounding "Amen" of the people, another eucharistic liturgy concludes in the Great Church (formerly the Caesarion). The throngs of worshipers have received their spiritual sustenance. Singly or in small groups, the people stream out of the huge precinct, an impressive relic of late Hellenistic monumental architecture. On this day, a typical day in the first decade of the seventh century, no riots occur. The days of intercommunal bloodshed are past, and Alexandria is enjoying a respite from factional conflict among the city's Christians or with the imperial authorities. On this day, nothing would capture the gaze of imperial historians or ecclesiastical chroniclers.

Yet this very typicality merits our attention, since it is on this day that we can examine one of Alexandria's most important inhabitants—the Christian layman. As we follow one of the worshipers out of the Great Church, we note that he never began a heresy, never performed dazzling feats of asceticism, never incited a riot. We do not even know his name. However, thanks to the detailed archaeological record at Kōm el-Dikka in the center of the city, it is possible to follow him home and examine the contours of his everyday existence. The Christian layman of Alexandria is a particularly elusive subject for modern investigation, as are the rank-and-file members of the city's other ethnoreligious communities. More often than not, they only appear as faceless crowds in the dramas played out on the stage of late antique Alexandria. We are perhaps better informed about the Christian layman than his pagan or Jewish counterparts through his frequent appearance in hagiographic literature, which (for all its limitations) often provides a richly detailed, everyday context for its saintly subjects. Indeed, hagiographic literature even lets us become acquainted with some of the Christian women of Alexandria in a way which far surpasses our understanding of either pagan or Jewish women. Yet, in spite of the variegated nature of our sources, an admittedly fragmentary picture of the typical Christian may tell us more about the texture of life in Alexandria than would the biographies of Cyril, Dioscorus, or John the Almsgiver.

From the Caesarion, we follow our Christian south along the broad colonnaded street bisecting the city, which extends from the Great Harbor to neighborhoods bordering on Lake Mareotis. He proceeds through the Agora with its elegant Tetrapylon and pauses to see if any new laws that might affect his family or his business are posted. He passes quickly by the imposing statues arrayed outside the former Tychaion, and he recalls rumors he had heard recently that the statues (under the influence of evil demons) had spoken to terrified witnesses in the dead of night, announcing the sudden death of the emperor Maurice.[28] After making the sign of the cross, he hurries on.

He soon strolls along two large blocks of the Via Canopica until he turns south into his own neighborhood. As he does so, he utters a short prayer, repeating a portion of the Anaphora from the service he had just attended: "Guide and direct in all peace the emperor, the army, the chief men, the councils, the populace, and the neighborhoods, and all our goings-out and comings-in."[29] A prayer of this sort probably did not differ markedly from the prayers of classical urban dwellers over the past millennium. Neighborhood shrines of the *lares compitales* (or gods of the crossroads) are well known from the *vici* of Rome and Pompeii, and served as foci for neighborhood loyalty and communal religious devotion. By the seventh century, the old gods were out of favor, but it was still possible to invoke divine blessings on one's neighborhood.

The neighborhood our Alexandrian enters is known today for its longtime designation, Kōm el-Dikka (plan 1). Today, much of the Kōm is gone, the result of nearly thirty years of excavations by Polish teams from the Center for Mediterranean Archeology of the Polish Academy of Sciences. During the early Roman period, this region boasted spacious urban villas, impressive buildings distinguished by their luxurious peristyle layout and fashionable floor mosaics. However, sometime during the late third or fourth century, these dwellings were destroyed and the entire character of the area changed. Since the region of the Kōm seems to have been constructed

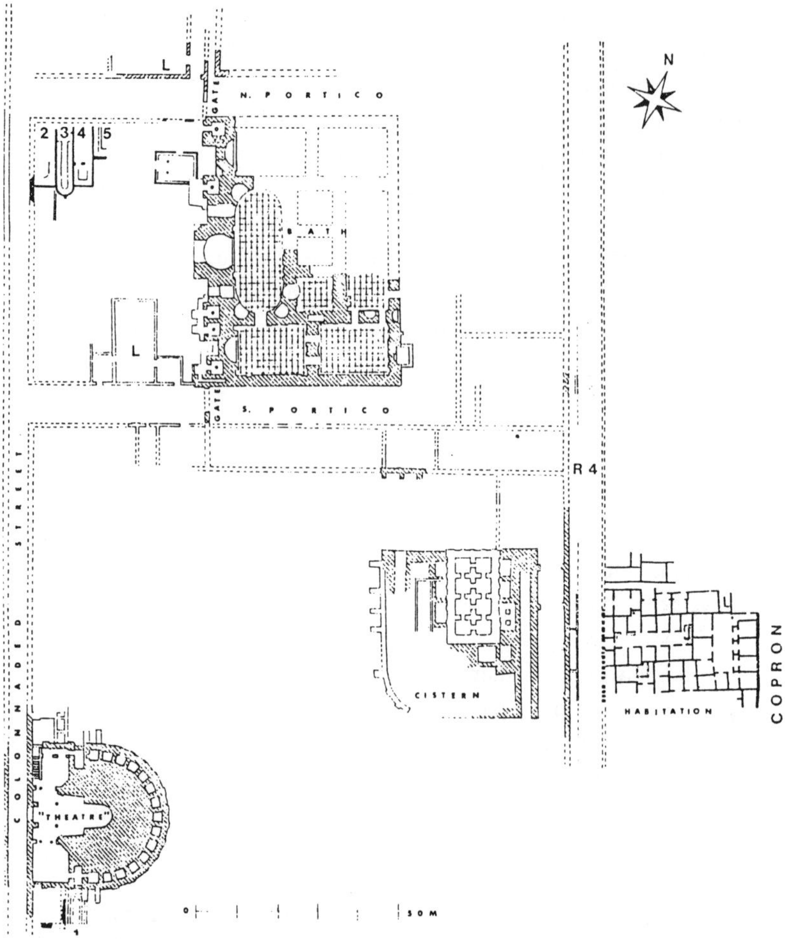


Plan 1. Excavated portions of Kōm el-Dikka, Alexandria. (M. Rodziewicz)

within a relatively short time, it appears that the rebuilt area was designed as a whole—perhaps in the wake of the devastation wrought by Diocletian's siege and occupation of the city in 298, perhaps as late as the earthquake and tidal wave of 365. In place of the urban villas, a large bath complex was built, equipped with hot and warm baths, a bracing cold plunge pool, and adjoining meeting rooms. In keeping with the public nature of this urban renewal project, a theaterlike structure was also erected some seventy-five meters to the south of the baths. Built with locally quarried limestone and accented with marble, this structure probably served as an odeion or (less likely) as a bouleterion (figure 7). Nearby, a series of lecture halls helped to quench the intellectual thirst of the Alexandrians while neighborhood taverns could quench more prosaic kinds of thirst.[3930]

As we follow our Christian layman down his street (designated R4 in el-Falaki's plan of the city), he passes a large complex of cisterns, set slightly higher than street level. These cisterns may have supplied the needs of the baths located nearby. Our primary concern, though, is with the block of multistoried residential buildings on the east side of R4, across the street from the cisterns (plan 2). Our Alexandrian enters one of these dwellings and disappears from view. Before following him inside, let us pause in the street and survey his immediate neighborhood.

Below the cisterns and ranged along the street are a number of long but shallow ergasteria or workshops. Averaging approximately eight meters long and two meters wide, these small workshops should be seen as annexes to the businesses carried on across the street in the residential buildings. Excavated material from the workshop located directly across from the house of our Christian layman—a kiln and bits of unprocessed glass—indicates that his household was engaged in the production of glass objects. The workshop, with its heat and noxious furnace fumes, was located well away from residential dwellings, no doubt to minimize any potential danger. In a contemporary anecdote, John Moschus describes a beggar he found by the Tetrapylon, who became blind as a result of prolonged exposure to fumes from glass kilns. It may be that Moschus's blind beggar had toiled in a cramped workshop not unlike the ones along R4.[31]

That the neighborhood around R4 was also the center of a flourishing cottage industry in small bone and ivory carvings is suggested by the presence of unfinished carved pieces and discarded workshop refuse within deposits of household trash. Large numbers of terracotta figurines have also been found at Kōm el-Dikka, along with nearly 150 ampoules or pilgrim flasks displaying the

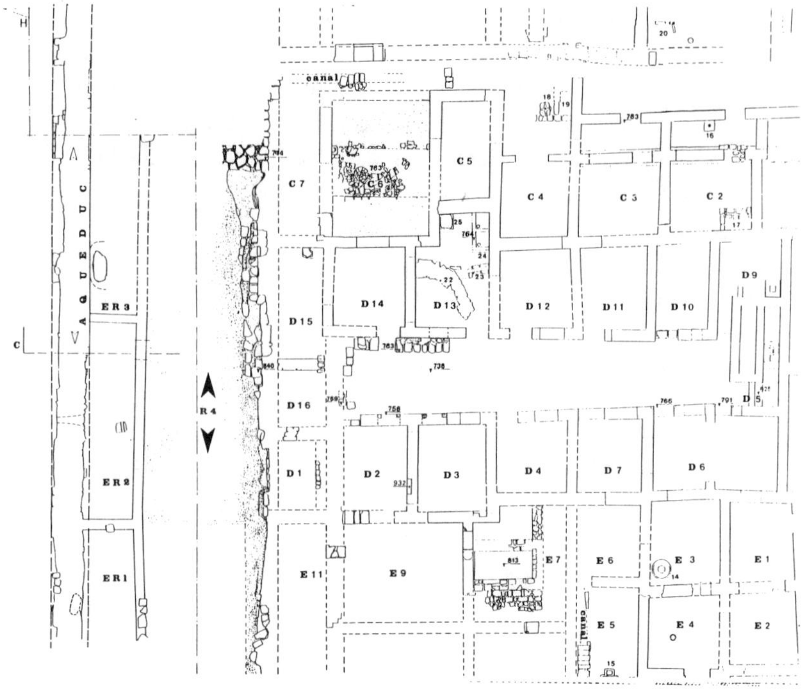

Plan 2. Housing along street R4, Kōm el-Dikka, Alexandria. House D in center, surrounding interior courtyard.
(M. Rodziewicz)

image of Saint Menas (figure 18). The terracottas and the flasks have been attributed to workshops at the shrine of St. Menas, located in the desert some forty kilometers southwest of Alexandria. Yet the sheer abundance of this material in an urban neighborhood suggests that Alexandrian workshops likewise catered to the needs of pilgrims, even imitating models emanating from the shrine itself. After all, it would hardly come as a surprise to learn that the proverbial fondness of the Alexandrians for Christian pilgrims included making a profit from the pilgrim traffic that passed through their city. Even Alexandria's prostitutes found a market among these pious visitors! Nonetheless, one does not have to look far in order to discover the principal market for these manufactured objects, since the nearby baths and theater undoubtedly attracted crowds eager to purchase many of these finely made products.[32]

Turning again to the house of our Alexandrian (labeled House D by its excavator), we note that it sat in the midst of a long block of residential housing with common walls connecting them. In form, the block probably resembled a hybrid between the large *insulae* of late antique Ostia or Rome, as well as the multistoried, mud-brick houses known to us from Egyptian towns like Karanis and Bacchias. The block of housing along R4 probably stood at least two or three

Fig. 18. Ampulla (pilgrim flask) of Saint Menas. Menas is depicted as *orans* and is flanked by two camels. Of a type common throughout the eastern Mediterranean, testifying to the popularity of the healing shrine's patron saint. Found at Kōm el-Dikka, late sixth or early seventh century.

(Z. Kiss, *Les ampoules de Saint Ménas, Alexandrie* 5, Warsaw, 1989, no. 94; M. Rodziewicz)

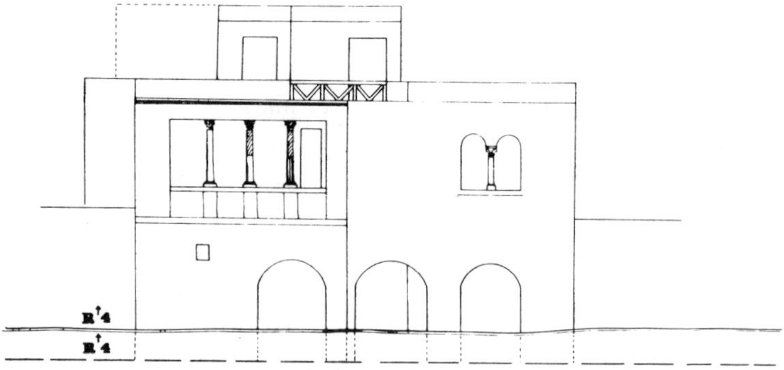

Fig. 19. Reconstruction of House D, Kōm el-Dikka. View of entrance from street R4. (M. Rodziewicz)

stories high, since the ground floor was built of massive limestone blocks from the suburban quarries at Mex—blocks of a size undoubtedly designed to support several stories (figure 19). Sockets on the top of the walls appear to have held stout roof beams, also suggesting a multistoried building. Though the extant remains of House D only reach to the top of the ground floor, it can be conjectured from the surrounding debris that the floors of the upper stories were made of wood, reeds, and palm stalks, covered over with mortar and sheets of limestone. The roof was built of similar material and probably was used as a terrace or open-air room. Fragments of pillars suggest that the inhabitants could look down on the street from a decorated second-floor balustrade. Over the doorway to the house, an inscription on limestone was set into the wall which proclaimed to passersby the religious sentiments of the inhabitants. It read "the pious ones"—an unmistakable (though nonspecific) declaration of faith. This type of acclamation was not uncommon in Alexandria. Other houses in the neighborhood likewise had entry inscriptions, and during an earlier pagan period, busts of the gods adorned niches and doorposts of private dwellings.[33]

As the Alexandrian passed through the small entry hall of House D, flanked by two rooms which may have served as workshops, he emerged into a long inner courtyard open to the sky (figure 20). This design bears some resemblance to modern Egyptian dwellings,

Fig. 20. House D, Kōm el-Dikka. View from the west, with entrance onto street R4 at bottom of photo, courtyard in the center. Sixth century.
(M. Rodziewicz)

with their interior focus on a courtyard supplying light and air to the rest of the house. From the vantage point of the courtyard, the entire design of House D becomes apparent. The courtyard of beaten earth, some sixteen meters in length, was bordered along its sides by two rows of five rooms—each of which measures approximately three meters on a side. At an earlier date, these rows of rooms had belonged to separate dwellings, but they were joined recently to make one larger residence. At the far end of the courtyard, a staircase led to the upper floors, and a balcony running along the inside of the second floor looked down on the courtyard. Stone benches set near the entry to the courtyard served as a convenient meeting place for the inhabitants of the house and could also facilitate the entertainment of potential customers.

The commercial nature of this Alexandrian's house is evident, not only by the workshops along the street, but also by several of the interior rooms fronting on the interior courtyard. The first of these (room D2) was decorated with elaborate geometric patterns incised on the plastered walls. Excavated materials from this room embraced a wide variety of objects, including amphoras, plates, and glass pieces. It may be that this richly appointed chamber, the first room next to the entryway, functioned as a showroom for customers who had come in from the street. Next to this showroom, another room (D3) was similarly decorated with geometric and floral motifs. One of these patterns, made of a series of concentric triangles, formed a large Greek chi, which to the eye of a discerning customer may have revealed itself to be an oblique cross. Granite anvils and numerous small sherds of rock crystal indicate that this room was used as a workshop in semiprecious gemstones, a highly regarded product from late Roman Alexandria.[34] Located further back in the house along the courtyard, room D7 apparently served as a finish workshop for glassware, evidenced by numerous unfinished glass products in the form of long multicolored glass rods, colored pieces of thick glass from the kilns, glass beads, and tessera of glass for mosaics.[35]

The heart of this commercial operation was the office (D6), situated at the far end of the interior courtyard. Our Alexandrian layman probably worked much of his time at a wooden desk set into the room's north wall, underneath a window that let in precious daylight. When this natural light failed, he could continue his work by the light of an oil lamp placed in a semicircular niche in the wall, just above his desk. Supports found in the walls suggest that the office was fitted out with several shelves and small tables. From fragments of rock crystal, unfinished glassware, and some glass beads found in the room, it is not difficult to imagine the proprietor overseeing the quality of his wares during their various stages of production. Several corroded, small bronze coins were also discovered ground into the earthen floor near the desk. Somehow these did not find their way into the office's wooden cash box, of which there are fragments of iron and bronze, and even its well-preserved lock plate.[36]

Obviously, the owner of such an operation was fairly well-to-do by Alexandrian standards. His prosperity is indicated by the extensive renovations in the residence, which were undertaken at some time in the sixth century by either a former owner, the current owner, or by his family. In essence, the size of the house was doubled by joining together two separate residences that had once shared a common courtyard. Moreover, the decorated balustrade which graced the second-floor facade and the carefully wrought interior balustrade both attest the economic status of the owner. Imported pottery from Cyprus, North Africa, and Asia Minor also speak of a certain level of prosperity, as do pieces of jewelry and domestic items of ivory. A final testimony to the standard of living enjoyed by this Alexandrian is the large fresco adorning the courtyard-side wall of D4. This fresco was executed on a scale and level of refinement which stands as a testimony to the artistic patronage generated by the owner's wealth. And while House D clearly cannot qualify as an aristocratic peristyle house or as a luxurious *villa urbana,* nonetheless, its owner was a cut above the urban plebs.[37] Although this economic status may affect the typicality of the Alexandrian, at least it is reasonable to assume that he would not feel too distant from those at either extreme of the Alexandrian social hierarchy.

In order to gain a fuller understanding of the quality of life enjoyed by this Alexandrian, one would naturally like to know the number of persons domiciled in this one residence. Unfortunately, the sources fail us. Stout limestone foundation walls, fragments of upper-story floor supports, and the presence of a staircase in the rear of the courtyard all indicate that House D possessed at least a second—if not a third—story above the ground-floor commercial rooms. Literary sources and artistic representations depict Alexandrian houses of this period reaching as high as four stories (figure 21). However, it is unwise to extrapolate further and estimate the number of upper-story rooms which might have been given over to domestic residence. Even if the precise number of rooms set aside for domestic use were known, it is impossible to quantify the number of inhabitants per room (and thus for the entire house). It is equally difficult to make pronouncements concerning the social structure of such a household. Were they all related (as was the pattern in rural houses), or did many of the residents of House D simply rent out upper-story rooms? Given the likelihood of over a dozen rooms on upper floors, each averaging three meters on a side, one might easily imagine over twenty persons residing in House D. While one principal family probably owned the house and operated the business on the first floor, there were probably other unrelated occupants who rented rooms upstairs, as attested elsewhere in the city by both papyri and by literary evidence.[38]

Such a large number of people in one residence undoubtedly enhanced the importance of the courtyard as a common meeting place. The stone benches near the doorway facilitated the sharing of common meals or, at least, the sharing of some leisure moments. However, much of the household's communal life seems to have been focused several meters farther back in the courtyard, in the open space between rooms D4 and D12. For the courtyard-side

A

wall of D4 displayed a carefully executed fresco of an enthroned Virgin and Child, measuring nearly a meter and a half in width.[39] Though the remains of the fresco are fragmentary, it is possible to discern also the figures of a large archangel and a smaller individual (possibly a saint or the fresco's patron) both standing to the left of enthroned figures. The haloed head of the infant Jesus is clearly visible, as are also fragments of the Virgin's drapery and throne. The modeling and colors employed are paralleled by scenes from the monastery of Apollo at Bawīt (in the Thebaid) and from the cathedral at Faras (in Nubia). This fresco, one of the earliest surviving Christian paintings from Alexandria, is remarkable for its early date (before mid-sixth century), its rejection of traditional Hellenistic modeling in favor of a vigorous style popular in the chora, and for its location—the courtyard of a private house.

B

Fig. 21. The patriarch and the city. (A) Saint Mark enthroned among thirty-five bishops, in all likelihood, his successors. (B) The detail depicts a city gate, with the crowded balconies and rooftops of Alexandria's residential skyline in the upper background. Ivory relief. Alexandria, early seventh century. Louvre, inv. OA.3317. (Département des Objets d'Art, Musée du Louvre)

The purpose of the fresco is indicated by the remains of two iron brackets projecting from the wall, which allowed for oil lamps to be hung by their chains close to the icon. The clear implication is that this fresco had a devotional purpose and probably served as the focus for communal prayers within the household.[40] The care with which the scene was executed, especially compared with numerous Christian graffiti throughout House D, led the site's excavator to conclude that it was painted by a professional painter who was commissioned to copy a large monumental scene originally derived from a church.[41] Thus, we may conclude that the courtyard of House D functioned as a private oratory which could easily accommodate over a dozen worshipers at any one time.

While this elaborately designed oratory illumines the religious life of the inhabitants of House D, it also raises a number of related issues. Archaeologically, private oratories are otherwise unknown from Alexandria at this time, the closest parallel coming from Huwariyya in the Mareotis, some forty-five kilometers southwest of Alexandria. Here, a spacious double-peristyle villa of the fifth century was renovated in the sixth century to include a large chapel.[42] Yet, with the late sixth-century additions of a baptisterium, benches, a large latrine, and a massive stone aqueduct, the Huwariyya villa passes from the private to the public sphere. Elsewhere within an urban context, one would have to look to the church of SS. Giovanni e Paolo at Rome. In this case, however, an entire insula of housing was renovated over the course of several centuries and was transformed into a complex of church buildings.[43] House D remained unmistakably a private dwelling, thereby harkening back to the *domus ecclesiae* model, common in the pre-Constantinian era, when a private house was partially renovated to accommodate liturgical usage.[44] The most frequently cited example of this type is the Christian building at Dura-Europos from the mid-third century.

Yet, virtually all of the known parallels are either buildings that are unmistakably churches or private chapels set up by the wealthy on their rural estates. Alexandria at the turn of the seventh century possessed several large churches (many of which were converted pagan precincts), as well as numerous small parish churches serving the spiritual needs of localized districts within the city. The presence of a well-defined private oratory at Kōm el-Dikka suggests that, in a city which has seen so little systematic excavation, private oratories may not have been uncommon. The impetus for organizing these oratories may have come from the well-documented ascetic impulse within portions of the Alexandrian Christian community, allowing for private devotion and withdrawal from the world. The Chalcedonian bishop, John the Almsgiver (610–19), established oratories for several groups of monks within the city and it is reasonable to conclude that the establishment of oratories also took place under the auspices of less well documented bishops.[45]

Oratories like the one at House D could also facilitate the spread and persistence of belief systems contrary to the one officially sanctioned by the community's leadership.[46] The religious life flourishing within a private chapel is notoriously difficult to regulate. It is easy to imagine a domestic oratory like the one at House D falling under imperial censure as "a private house used for the assembly of superstitious lawlessness," or a heretical conventicle where "the walls of a private house display the likeness of a church."[47] An Alexandrian patriarch contemporary with the oratory at House D, speaking of heretical assembly places, pleaded with his followers, "I implore you earnestly, children: have no contact with such oratories."[48] The later Monophysite patriarch Agathon (661–77) took advantage of the privacy afforded by such oratories in order to shore up Monophysite support during an earlier period of Chalcedonian domination:

> And he used to disguise himself at Alexandria in the days of Heraclius in the garb of a layman, and went about at night, comforting the orthodox who were concealing themselves there, and settling their affairs, and giving them of the Holy Mysteries. And if it was in the daytime, he carried on his shoulder a basket containing carpenters' tools, and pretended to be a carpenter, that the heretics might not hinder him, and that so he might find a means of entering the houses or lodgings of the orthodox, that he might give them of the Mysteries, and encourage them to patience, and console them.[49]

Obviously, this is farther than the archaeological evidence can take us. At most, we can state with some certainty that the oratory, centrally located in the courtyard of House D, was the focal point for communal religious life within the household.

The religious predilections of the inhabitants of House D are also known to us from a host of other excavated materials. As if the entryway inscription and the courtyard fresco were not enough, the graffiti from House D should leave no room for doubt about the spiritual life of our Alexandrian and his household. From the first floor alone, there are no fewer than nine crosses of various design. Several are trifoliate with bells suspended from them, perhaps as apotropaic additions to an already potent symbol.[50] One graffito displays a cross in the midst of two peacocks, a traditional symbol for immortality. And while other graffiti depict genre scenes of seagoing and Nilotic ships, one crudely executed design superimposes a cross upon the prow of a river vessel, thus transforming a prosaic scene into a powerful image of spirituality. Other material remains, excavated from the first floor, are also consistent with this picture of thoroughgoing Christianization. Pilgrim flasks of Saint Menas were found in both the courtyard and in the office (D6). Pottery plates with crosses are also common, and the location of these finds in rooms dedicated to everyday usage (like the kitchen area of D13) reflects the way in which Christian symbols permeated the inhabitants' mundane activities.[51]

When one turns to the carved bone and ivory objects found in House D, a very different picture emerges. In conformity with the iconography of dozens of other pieces from Kōm el-Dikka, these objects display an unmistakable pagan imagery. A bone plaque found in the showroom (D2) shows a reclining nude Nereid similar to other swimming Nereids known from Alexandrian examples. From an early sixth-century level of room D12, there is a carved plaque depicting a seminude male dancer, with hands raised and drapery freely flowing after him—perhaps a Dionysiac scene. In the impression of the wall between the kitchen area and D14, a bone carving was found of a seminude diademed goddess, holding a wreath in her right hand. All of these figures come from a period roughly contemporary to our Alexandrian Christian.[52]

How are these conflicting images to be reconciled? Since these pagan finds emanate from the same levels and rooms as the Christian materials they cannot be explained away by positing a number of inhabitants with varying religious beliefs. Neither are they explained by some sort of religious fickleness, where the inhabitants seek to hedge their bets with the supernatural world, like the roughly contemporary funerary stelae from the chora displaying both ankhs and crosses.

The answer, as suggested by the carvings' excavators, lies in the materials employed—bone and ivory. These small plaques adorned luxury items like jewel boxes and furniture, and the limited repertoire (Dionysiac dancers, lounging goddesses, and bucolic scenes) suggests that these were traditional decorative motifs used over and over for generations.[53] Indeed, it is possible to assemble a stylistic chronology of these carvings across several centuries. Moreover, the fact that the bone and ivory carvers of Kōm el-Dikka were not organized into large workshops, but instead practiced their craft in small cottage industries, would discourage innovation in style and subject matter. It is significant that while most of the other artwork from Kōm el-Dikka (notably the fresco and the graffiti) reflect the vigorous linear style often associated with rural Coptic art forms, the carvings slavishly copy Hellenistic models that have long since lost their inner grace and elegance.[54]

This is not to say that there were no residents of Byzantine Kōm el-Dikka who did not share pagan sentiments. Excavations at House B turned up a stucco statuette of Serapis along with carved images of Dionysus. A handful of terracotta figurines have been discovered in the neighborhood of R4, which have been interpreted as Isis. A sixth-century plate found near the cisterns depicts a traditionally rendered sphinx. Yet these other pagan motifs do not occur in House D. We are safe in concluding that our Alexandrian and the members of his household were Christians.[55]

Despite the wealth of archaeological material surviving from House D, there is still much we would like to know about this Alexandrian layman and his household. How was the workshop and retail business organized? How close were the bonds between the owner's family and the other inhabitants of the house? How was their neighborhood organized? Did they have any business or personal connections with persons in the rest of Egypt or in other Mediterranean cities? What were their feelings toward the divisive theological and political issues of the day? For lack of papyrological evidence, such questions must go unanswered. Nonetheless, the archaeological record from Kōm el-Dikka opens an incomparably vivid window on the daily life of an Alexandrian Christian less than half a century before the Arab conquest. It also illustrates the degree to which Alexandrian society was Christianized by the early seventh century.

Thus far, this discussion has focused on the Christianization of the private realm—the conversion of individuals—and the Christianization of material culture in the private sphere. At times, however, the boundaries between private and public are difficult to discern. The inscription over the doorway of House D is certainly a public statement, proclaiming to the entire neighborhood the piety of its residents. This blending of the private and the public appears as early as the third century, when a handful of private dwellings were used for Christian services and some were eventually given to the church. A bit more problematic is an incident that occurred one night shortly after the cessation of the pagan cult at the Serapeum in 391. Small busts of Serapis that had commonly decorated Alexandrian doorposts were forcibly torn away and were replaced by painted crosses.[56] Who was responsible? This Christian vandalism was so widespread that it is unlikely the owners of the houses decided en masse to express their change of religious sentiments. The perpetrators could easily have been a small band of Christian vandals. The question arises, however, whether these vandals were acting on their own or were sponsored by the leadership of the Christian community, in particular, the patriarch Theophilus. The active encouragement of this type of Christian vandalism is entirely in keeping with the policies of Theophilus, and introduces the crucial role of the bishop in the conversion of Alexandria's urban aspect.

### *The Christianization of Public Space*

Like some ill-fated Midas, it seemed to contemporaries that whatever Theophilus touched turned to controversy. His tenure as Alexandrian patriarch (385–412) was marked by serious disputes, both on a local and on an imperial stage.[57] With the combative temperament of his mentor, Athanasius, yet lacking the political acumen of his nephew Cyril, Theophilus elicited strong opinions from admirers and enemies throughout his stormy career. His contemporaries seem to agree on only one point, his passion for building churches in Alexandria. A popular legend within the Egyptian church credits this building activity to divine guidance. The story relates that a marble slab was found inscribed with three thetas. This slab had a further inscription which promised: "Whosoever shall interpret these three thetas shall receive what is underneath this stone." Without hesitation, Theophilus said that the thetas stood for "Theos, Theodosius, and Theophilus." Removing the stone, he then found a trove of money which he immediately expended on church construction. Others had more difficulty discerning God's hand in Theophilus's building program. A venerable Alexandrian priest named Isidore felt constrained to hide from his bishop a bequest from a widow, designated for poor relief, because he feared it would be appropriated for building funds. As it turned out, his fears were well founded. John Chrysostom and Palladius both compared Theophilus with the biblical Pharaoh, Palladius going so far as to brand him a lithomaniac. A usually mild Isidore of Pelusium echoed these sentiments when he called Theophilus a litholater.[58]

During his episcopate, Theophilus built some nine churches in and around Alexandria, including a church dedicated to John the Baptist and Elijah, founded within the precinct of the temple of Serapis. This temple had been closed in 391 after bloody street battles between pagans and a Christian mob under Theophilus's direction. The patriarch most certainly had a method to his lithomania—nothing less than the complete conversion of Alexandria's urban topography. And yet, despite his notoriety for building activity, Theophilus stands out as but one member of a long line of Alexandrian bishops who actively sought the thoroughgoing Christianization of Alexandria's landscape. Unlike Rome at this time, the Christianization of Alexandria's urban space was not accompanied by a fundamental shift in the city's design, which might have refocused the urban consciousness on new points such as suburban churches and martyria.[59] The topography of Alexandria was too constrained by natural barriers to permit a reconfiguration of the pronounced design system, which dated from the city's foundation by Alexander. Instead, the forceful leaders of the Christian community had a program of converting the existing urban landscape, constructing in stone a reflection of the progressive conversion of the city's populace.

The standard compendia provide useful lists of Alexandria's churches, martyria, and monasteries, known to us from the literary sources and from the spotty archaeological record. Sophisticated discussion of these individual buildings may be found in the recent work of Annik Martin. It is vital, however, to envision the ways that these structures fit into the overall design system of the city, and how they interacted with one another so as to transform the urban landscape.[60]

On the eve of the Peace of the Church, Alexandria already possessed two moderately sized churches and a cluster of smaller parish churches. These churches were undoubtedly the product of the badly documented decades of expansion between the persecutions of the mid-third century and the Tetrarchic period. The most important of these churches was the one named for the sainted Dionysius (bishop, 247–64).[61] While there is no precise information regarding either its origins or location, it may be conjectured that this church was a private donation, perhaps even by Dionysius himself. As a private donation, the church was likely to have been situated on the periphery of the intramural area, since the center of Alexandria had long since been given over to public buildings.[62] In the late 350s, the Arian bishop, George of Cappadocia, established his residence in the church of Dionysius. George's demonstrated aversion to the urban center (with its concentration of pagans and Athanasian supporters) and his predilection for the peripheral regions lend weight to the supposition that the church was situated in a residential district, perhaps near the western gate. The other principal church, that of Pierius, is even more difficult to locate, though it would be reasonable to assume a similar residential location attributed to its likely private foundation.[63]

With the cessation of persecution and the favor shown to Christianity by Constantine, the picture changes rapidly. The episcopate of Alexander (312–28) marks the inauguration of a systematic program of church building which characterizes the next two centuries. Although Alexander is best known for his part in the outbreak of the Arian controversy, he also oversaw the construction of two important Alexandrian churches: the church of Saint Theonas and the church dedicated to the archangel Michael. The church of Theonas may have owed its origins to the bishop of that name who presided over the Alexandrian church from 282 to 300. However, it was Alexander who greatly enlarged and adorned the building, partially in response to the needs of the expanding Christian community. The topographical advantages of the church's location were twofold. Although it was impossible to erect a new church in the built-up center of the city, the church of Theonas was situated along the Via Canopica, Alexandria's principal artery. Also, the new church could be found just inside the western gate of the city, the so-called Gate of the Moon. As one of the first large structures encountered by travelers entering Alexandria from the west, the church of Theonas constituted a topographical indication of the Christian community's enhanced status in the city. This church answered the needs of the growing Christian community as its most important gathering place and also as the episcopal residence until the middle of the fourth century.[64] The church's beauty was such that it was later turned into a mosque, known by its romantic appellation, the Mosque of a Thousand Columns.

If the construction of the church of Theonas reflected Bishop Alexander's intention of appropriating significant foci of Alexandrian topography, his dedication of the church of Saint Michael exhibits the other principal component of the Christian leadership's ongoing policy—the forcible conversion of pagan temples. This church was originally the temple of Kronos (or Saturn), a shrine attested as early as the Ptolemaic period. The temple's lion-headed cult statue is described by Christian sources as having a particularly horrible aspect, and the annual festival in honor of this god consisted of numerous sacrifices and great revelry—at least in the eyes of our Christian sources. In the new regime inaugurated by Constantine in the east after 324, Alexander apparently considered the times propitious for some action to be taken against this offensive cult. A late chronicle informs us that Alexander initially encountered stout popular opposition to his intended destruction of the cult of Kronos. However, he appealed to the crowd to substitute the archangel Michael for Kronos and celebrate the annual festival in honor of the angel. The conversion was an easy one, since Michael, like Kronos, was commonly believed to usher dead souls into the next life, and also to ensure the annual rising of the Nile's floodwaters. A cross was set up in the church, carved from the torso of the broken up cult statue, and the church continued in use until 969.[65]

Significantly, this is the first known instance of a church in Alexandria converted from a pagan temple (or indeed from any public building), and it also marks the introduction of major Christian churches into the monumental center of the city. The location of this new church of Saint Michael is disclosed by attempts made by portions of the Jewish community to burn it down in 415, thus situating the church in proximity to the Jewish quarter in the east-central portion of the city.[66] Even though Alexander's initiative of temple conversion was achieved only through a measure of compromise, a pattern was established for future bishops. Alexander's protégé, Athanasius, followed his lead by forcibly converting the temple of Bendis (or Mendis) into a church in September 369. This temple was located not far from the former temple of Kronos, and fronted on the Eastern Harbor between the commercial area of Emporion and the Heptastadion.[67] It stood next to one of the main points of debarkation for travelers coming to Alexandria by sea.

The patriarchate's twin policies of church construction—the conversion of pagan temples and the appropriation of major topographical sites—combined in the transformation of the Caesarion into the so-called Great Church or Patriarchal Cathedral. This massive precinct was erected during the reign of Cleopatra VII and served as the focus for ruler cult in Alexandria for over three centuries. Constantius II donated the complex of buildings to the church, and it became Alexandria's sole imperial donation in an age when emperors prodigally sponsored construction and/or building conversion projects in the great cities of the empire. Although Constantius originally gave it to his Arian appointee, Gregory of Cappadocia (bishop, 339–46), the Caesarion came into general use as a church under the care of Athanasius.[68]

The conversion of this temple not only gave the Christian community a much needed larger gathering place, it also had the effect of moving the episcopal cathedral from the periphery to the city's center—a process done with great difficulty in other cities of the empire.[69] In some cities, like Rome or Tours, it was never accomplished. Perhaps Athanasius's preoccupation with the conversion of the Caesarion can be explained, in part, by his eyewitness experience in Trier, where he saw a portion of Helena's great palace renovated as the city's cathedral. The transformation of the Caesarion also Christianized an important anchor in the design system of the city. With its twin obelisks and imposing walls, the Caesarion dominated the waterfront of the Eastern Harbor (figure 4). As soon as a seagoing traveler rounded the Pharos, his eye would immediately be drawn to this complex of buildings. By the close of Athanasius's episcopate, the smoke of sacrifice no longer rose from this precinct, only the incense of Christian worship—a powerful statement of the church's growing hegemony within the city.

The destruction of the cult of Serapis, and Theophilus's transformation of the temple into a church, Christianized yet another landmark of Alexandria's topography. This famous complex of buildings crowned the city's most prominent height (sometimes referred to as Alexandria's acropolis). The Serapeum so loomed over the urban landscape that Diocletian chose to set up his victory column here in 297/98. Its conversion into a church presaged the downfall of public paganism in Alexandria and the takeover of several key sites. At the same time, on the island of Pharos, the temple of Isis Pharia was converted into a church, probably the one identified in our sources as Agia Sophia. Isis Pharia, usually depicted holding a billowing sail, had been the protectress of sailors, and we hear of several of these old salts grumbling about the difficulties of entering the harbor without her guidance (figure 13). The eastern gate of the city, the so-called Gate of the Sun, stood near a quarter known for its visitors' hostels. Not surprisingly, this also appears to have been Alexandria's red-light district. A church was established near the gate, dedicated to Saint Metras, an Alexandrian martyr who was dragged out of the city and stoned during the persecution of Decius. In the early seventh century, an ascetic named Vitalios led a remarkably successful (though scandalous) one-man mission to the prostitutes in this quarter. Parishioners at Saint Metras were horrified to find so many prostitutes flocking to their small church. Together with the church of Saint Theonas at the Gate of the Moon and the churches at the city's docks, we find churches planted at the major entry points of Alexandria, much like the churches intentionally planted at each of the gates of Milan.[70]

The Tychaion was the most prominent temple at the city's Agora. This shrine of the patroness of Alexandria's good fortune was not converted into a church. However, following the destruction of the Serapeum, it was transformed into another venerable Alexandrian institution, a wineshop.[71] Although the sources do not speak of any churches being built on the Agora, it became an important public meeting place for the city's Christians. All told, these various acts of deliberate church building and temple destruction speak of a concerted policy to impose Christianity upon the city's distinctive urban configuration.

Thus far we have examined the Christianization of significant foci in the city's topography. How did this official program square with the needs of smaller groups within the Christian community and the establishment of parish churches? Epiphanius states that there were at least six of these smaller churches at the beginning of the fourth century, but he intimates that there were others. Several sources relate that one presbyter was assigned to each of the churches in Alexandria. In Bishop Alexander's letter deposing Arius and his allies, five Alexandrian presbyters were stripped of priestly rank for heresy and sixteen subscribed to their deposition.[72] A total of twenty-one Alexandrian priests seems a bit high, especially since a city of the size of Rome only possessed twenty-five parish churches in the fourth century. Later lists from Athanasius's episcopate average at sixteen Alexandrian presbyters, and so it may be assumed that the replacements for the deposed Arians subscribed to Alexander's letter, thereby producing the higher number.[73] If most of these Alexandrian presbyters presided over separate congregations (and this may be presuming too much of the evidence), a reasonable guess might arrive at some dozen parish churches in fourth-century Alexandria. With one exception, it is impossible to locate the few named parish churches we know of on a map of Alexandria. They probably were not evenly distributed throughout the city's various quarters, clustering instead in the residential districts. Until the outbreak of the Arian controversy these parishes enjoyed a great deal of autonomy, and neighborhood rivalries sprung up among the adherents of various preachers.[74]

In virtually every other city in the empire, extramural cemeteries and martyria became the most important loci in the Christianization of urban space. Rome is, of course, the most obvious example. But others, like Carthage, Ephesus, and Tours, also conform to this pattern. At Alexandria, the situation is a bit different. Although Christians frequently met in suburban cemeteries during the second and third centuries, to our knowledge none of these necropoleis became the site of a later church. The one exception to this general pattern is the martyrium of Saint Mark, located just outside the eastern walls close to the Mediterranean shore. Mark was venerated as the founder of Alexandrian Christianity, and he enjoyed a status analogous to that of Saint Peter at Rome or Saint John at Ephesus. The martyrium of Saint Mark is attested as early as the fourth century, but it is likely that some sort of shrine existed at an earlier date.[75] Why did Mark's tomb not become the center of a major group of church buildings, as was the case at John's tomb in Ephesus? The martyrium was located uncomfortably close to the Roman garrison camp at Nicopolis, and one can understand the reluctance of pre-Constantinian Christians as well as strong-willed fourth-century bishops to provide such a tempting target for official action. The martyrium was also situated in an extramural region called Boucalia, inhabited by herdsmen and brigands whose lawlessness was proverbial.[76] Despite these disincentives for church building, a parish church was erected near Mark's martyrium, known as the church of Baucalis. This is the only Alexandrian parish church whose location is almost certain. We owe our knowledge of this church to the fame of its most important presbyter, Arius. The association of heresy and the church at Baucalis no doubt also contributed to the patriarchate's lack of interest in suburban church building.

Two other martyria figured prominently in the devotion of Alexandria's Christians. However, both were fairly distant from the city—as it were, beyond the gravitational pull of urban church building. The most important of these was the healing shrine of St. Menas, situated some forty-three kilometers southwest of Alexandria in the agricultural region of Mareotis. The other principal martyrium associated with Alexandrian Christianity was that of Cyrus and John. In the early fifth century, their relics were interred with great fanfare by Cyril in the luxury suburb of Canopus, situated some twenty kilometers northeast of Alexandria. Linked by canal with the city, Canopus had long been one of pagan Egypt's most sacred sites, with temples dedicated to both Serapis and Isis. The conversion of Canopus parallels that of Antioch's luxury suburb of Daphne, a distant suburban shrine Christianized by the installation of the relics of the martyr-bishop, Saint Babylas in the mid-fourth century.[77] Like the relics of Saint Menas, those of Cyrus and John achieved wide fame for their healing powers throughout late antiquity. During the Monophysite-Chalcedonian conflict, it appears that the two warring communities each possessed one of the shrines, the Chalcedonians holding Canopus and the Monophysites Saint Menas.

Prior to the installation of the relics of Cyrus and John, Theophilus had planted a community of monks at Canopus.[78] The introduction of monasticism, in many cases, contributed an important element in the transformation of late antique cities. However, like the martyria, the principal Alexandrian monasteries were located at some distance from the city itself, some of them taking their names from the nearest milestone—Pempton (fifth), Enaton (ninth), and Oktokaidekaton (eighteenth).[79] Although several of these monastic houses, notably Metanoia at Canopus and Enaton in the Mareotis, were to play a crucial role in the often-violent ecclesiastical politics of Byzantine Alexandria, their distant locations limited their impact on the Christianization of Alexandria's urban design.

Unlike Ephesus, Alexandria boasted no edifying tale like that of the Seven Sleepers. Had they lived in Alexandria, though, these Christian Rip Van Winkles would have been equally astonished by the transformation of Alexandria's urban landscape by the end of the fifth century. The gradual but unremitting Christianization of the city's topography testified to the Christian community's enhanced wealth and status, and to the power wielded by the bishop. This conversion of urban space meant that unbelievers were constantly confronted by the church's presence, and that it was nearly impossible for "non-Christian people to shut out this noise of Christian exuberance, this din of defeat."[80]

# Seven

# The Inner Life of the Christian Community: Clergy and People

The services marking Holy Week in Alexandria must have been noisy, crowded affairs. To handle the throng of worshipers and encourage their quiet attention during the service, the deacons separated themselves into two groups. One group acted as ushers and discreetly removed crying infants and talkative adults. Another group remained at the door of the nave, ready to assist the doorkeepers at the outer door of the church in case the press of the crowds became too great. Beyond their all-important job of crowd control, the doorkeepers also had to bar entrance to non-Christian "scoffers" as well as those who had been "put forth" from the church for a period of penance.[1]

This picture of the Christian community at worship differs only in its details from depictions of the first-century Jewish community worshiping in the Great Synagogue or the more contemporaneous picture of smoking pagan altars preserved in the anonymous *Expositio Totius Mundi*. The differences among these communities begin to come into view once we pass through the church's outer portals and are able to examine the inner life and structural dynamics of the Alexandrian Christian community. The public face of this community and its incessant expansion on the urban scene has been noted in the previous chapter. This is an important first step in understanding Alexandrian Christianity as it was perceived by outsiders. However, the daily experience of members of this community emerges only with an analysis of the Christian community's composition and structure.

Across late antiquity, this community adapted to changing local circumstances and the varying winds of imperial favor or displeasure. Once the church became the dominant force in Alexandrian society by the late fourth and early fifth centuries, church offices proliferated as did the functions that these administrators performed. Official titles also underwent evolution, most notably in the case of the Alexandrian bishop, who after the 380s was commonly designated as patriarch, thereby signifying his authority over other bishops in his region.[2] Still, most of these changes can be described as the elaboration of a communal structure already in place by the last decades of the third century, and not the development of entirely new institutions. While the following description of the Christian community may take on a certain static quality, it is only because of our desire to provide a clear snapshot of a dynamic community. Despite Heraclitus's assertion that you cannot step into the same river twice, it is still possible to describe some of the essential characteristics of that river.

## *The "Seven Eyes of God"*

As with the Jewish and pagan communities, one profitable method for exploring the Christian community's inner life is to sketch out the contours of its leadership. Although this leadership tended to be rigidly hierarchical, it is noteworthy that whenever contemporaries spoke of the hierarchy of offices within the church, they saw it instead as an integrated web of ministries which derived their collective authority from Christ himself. One monastic source regards five of the church's more visible offices as reflections of Christ's own ministry:

> On one occasion [Christ] was a reader, for "taking the Scriptures in the synagogue, he read to them." . . . He was a subdeacon for "having made a whip out of cords he drove out all from the temple, both sheep

> and cattle, and the rest." He was a deacon, for "having girded himself around the waist, he washed the feet of the brothers." He was a presbyter, for "having sat down in the middle of the elders [presbyters], he taught the people." He was a bishop, for "taking bread and having given praise, he gave it to his disciples."[3]

This vision of leadership is echoed by an Alexandrian source that likens seven of the church's principal ministries to the seven pillars upon which Wisdom rested her house (Proverbs 9:1), the seven spirits before the throne of God (Revelations 1:4), and the seven eyes of God (Zechariah 4:10).[4]

Despite these intimations of egalitarianism, the leadership of the community was strictly hierarchical and developed a command and control system that would make modern strategic military planners envious. The capstone in this structure was, of course, the patriarch.[5] Indeed, it would be difficult to exaggerate the role played by the patriarch as the single element that bound together the Christian community, molded its identity, and expressed its will. Who were these men who defied emperors and shaped church councils? What factors led to their elevation as spiritual leaders for tens of thousands?

A subtle shift takes place over the course of the third and fourth centuries regarding the qualifications for office as patriarch. During much of the third century, the head of Alexandria's celebrated catechetical school was normally designated as the next bishop of the city. This method of promotion seems to have ended with the patriarchate of Theonas (282–300) and the elevation of his successor Peter I (300–311).[6] At the time of Theonas's death, there does not appear to have been any cloud of doubt or suspicion hanging over Pierius, the head of the catechetical school. Indeed, Eusebius portrays him as one who "displayed a wealth of philosophy most rare and inferior to none, and a manner of life that was truly in accordance with the Gospel." The break with tradition occurred as a result of Theonas's long cultivation of Peter as his protégé. Peter's father had been the senior presbyter (*protopresbuteros*) of the Alexandrian church, and Peter's parents had presented him to Theonas for spiritual training at the age of seven. Theonas's "beloved son" had thus found rapid appointment through the ranks as reader, deacon, and priest.[7]

The elevation of Peter I introduces a pattern of episcopal advancement in Alexandria which appears frequently over the next two centuries. A child will come to the attention of the patriarch who will subsequently groom the youth for positions of importance within the church. Such was the relationship between Alexander and Athanasius, and later between Athanasius and Theophilus.[8] These protégés are quickly promoted to high ecclesiastical offices, such as archdeacon or secretary, so that their eventual succession can be claimed on the basis of experience and ability as much as patriarchal affection. Once the former pattern of elevation from the catechetical school was broken, a new one emerged by the end of the fourth century in which the senior presbyter and the archdeacon became the prime candidates. If others were chosen to fill the episcopate, it was due only to some deeper tie with the patriarch or to the direct intervention of imperial authorities. This pattern continued until the sixth century, when the conflict between Monophysites and Chalcedonians led to a competition of holiness, in which both camps nominated respected ascetics to the throne of Saint Mark.[9]

The copious sources on Athanasius's episcopate illumine yet another important criterion for episcopal advancement, the wealth and social status of the candidate's family. A later tradition preserved in the *History of the Patriarchs* relates that Athanasius was born into a wealthy family of Alexandria's upper class. This tradition is borne out by the offhand comment of Sozomen that Athanasius hid, on one occasion, in his family's ancestral tomb, probably located to the west of the city. A family mausoleum would denote a certain level of wealth, and its status is further confirmed by the fact that the family members were easily singled out for persecution by an Arian usurper to the episcopal throne.[10]

While patriarchs and their families after Athanasius were also noted for their wealth, it appears that their prosperity was a result of episcopal election and not a precondition. It is only with the Monophysite-Chalcedonian conflict of the early seventh century that wealth and social status, along with personal holiness, become the critical criteria for election. On the Chalcedonian side, John the Almsgiver (bishop, 609–19) came from an exalted circle of Cypriot landowners, and was nominated to the patriarchate by his half-brother, Nicetas, who was a *patricius* and a dux and who was governing Egypt on behalf of his longtime associate, Heraclius. John's family was of such high rank that his nephew thought an insult offered to him by an Alexandrian shopkeeper merited a public scourging. John reproved his haughty relative and then ordered the market overseer never again to require taxes or rent from the shopkeeper—a beneficence altogether in keeping with John's status and reputation. John's elevation was perhaps a calculated reaction to the Monophysite claimant to the episcopal throne, Anastasius (605–16), a native Alexandrian and a former member of the boule. Not to be outdone by John's fame as an almsgiver, the Monophysites nominated Andronicus (616–22) to succeed Anastasius. He is described as very rich, lavish in his almsgiving, and from a leading family of the city. Moreover, since Andronicus's cousin was *prytanis* of the boule, Andronicus was able to go about his episcopal duties undisturbed by the Chalcedonians. Unfortunately for the Alexandrians, this contest of prodigal beneficence was brought to an abrupt end with the Sassanian occupation of the city in 619.[11]

The criteria of ecclesiastical rank and patriarchal grooming on the one hand and wealth and family status on the other sometimes combined to create virtual dynasties of patriarchs. In this instance, the occupants of the patriarchal see are linked, not only by patronage and background but by blood ties as well. The most conspicuous example of this relationship was the bond between Theophilus and his nephew Cyril. Local historians delight in recounting the tale of the young Theophilus, orphaned along with his little sister, and the faithful Ethiopian slave who recognized the grace of God upon them and delivered them over to Athanasius. A great deal is made of the fact that Athanasius baptized both children, enrolled Theophilus among the readers, and placed the girl in a convent until she reached the age of marriage. After wedding a man from Lower Egypt, she gave birth to Cyril. Thus, a line of patronage and kinship can be drawn from Athanasius down to Cyril, thereby legitimizing the episcopates of both Theophilus and Cyril.[12]

Theophilus, however, tacitly recognized the Alexandrian tradition of consecrating experienced clerics, and he directed his young nephew Cyril to the monastic community at Nitria, where he spent five years in an intensive study of doctrine and the Scriptures. The time at Nitria also allowed Cyril to cultivate ties with Egyptian ascetics, a band of allies he employed time and again when he became patriarch. After this training in the desert, Theophilus made Cyril a reader (as Athanasius had done to him) and relied upon him as his personal attendant. Despite this training and experience, Cyril had not yet attained high ecclesiastical rank by the time of his uncle's death in October 412. As a consequence, the succession was hotly disputed between the supporters of Cyril and those of the archdeacon, Timothy. It took three days for the issue finally to be resolved in favor of the young reader.[13]

The strength of this dynastic principle within patriarchal succession is clearly evidenced by the violent measures taken by Dioscorus after he succeeded Cyril in 444. Dioscorus had been Cyril's archdeacon and had assisted him at the first Council of Ephesus (431). Even though he was Cyril's designated successor, owing to his position within the Alexandrian church, Dioscorus feared the power and influence wielded by the family of Theophilus and Cyril. Immediately upon his elevation to the patriarchal throne, Dioscorus instituted a brutal persecution against the family of his predecessors. The target of much of this animosity was Cyril's nephew, Athanasius, a wealthy Alexandrian priest and a possible rival. Dioscorus hounded the entire family out of Alexandria, including Cyril's elderly sister, and confiscated their wealth and extensive property holdings within the city.[14] In addition, longtime confidants of Cyril were expelled from the city, some of whom had been enrolled among the Alexandrian clergy for nearly two decades.[15] What emerges from the polemical diatribes of these dispossessed, delivered at the third session of the Council of Chalcedon in 451, is that Dioscorus considered his position threatened on several sides and felt constrained to employ drastic measures to shore up his authority within the city.

A later archdeacon was not as successful as Dioscorus and discovered that high ecclesiastical office did not always ensure a smooth road to succession, even when there was no claimant from the former patriarch's family. Upon the death of the Monophysite bishop Timothy III in 535, his personal secretary, Theodosius, was chosen by the assembled bishops, priests, and laity. The archdeacon Gaianus was passed over, perhaps owing to his advanced age. However, a group of disaffected priests won over the aged Gaianus and put him forward as a rival claimant in 537. One of these priests, Theodore, was wealthy enough to spread around "gifts" sufficient to gain the support of the prefect and the military authorities, and Theodosius was duly ousted. Gaianus sat on the patriarchal throne for just over one hundred days, when Theodosius was restored by outside military intervention. This conflict over election led to a long-standing schism within the Monophysite wing of the Alexandrian church. The dispute illustrates that the various traditional criteria for patriarchal election could sometimes come into conflict with one another and that, in this case, the intimacy enjoyed by a secretary may count for more than rank and seniority. Clerics other than the archdeacon or the archpriest might equally contest patriarchal election. For both Theodosius and Gaianus, however, the key element was the extent of their support among clerical circles, the Alexandrian populace, and, most important, imperial officials.[16]

The ritual of patriarchal succession illustrates how vital it was for the new bishop to find his legitimacy in the acclamations of the entire Christian community as well as in his connections with his predecessor. During the first three centuries, the clergy of the city apparently possessed considerable authority in the selection and elevation of their bishop. One might well hesitate to accept the late testimony of Eutychius that Saint Mark established a college of twelve presbyters who would designate one of their number to be the next patriarch. And yet, the presbyters and deacons of the city wielded significant influence in determining episcopal succession, often without the imposition of hands by other bishops. This echoes the relative ministerial autonomy enjoyed by the presbyters in their respective urban parishes. Over the course of the fourth and fifth centuries, however, Alexandria begins to resemble other major cities in that the selection came to be determined by a combination of Egyptian bishops, local clergy, the Alexandrian upper classes, and the assent of the people.[17] One tradition not well attested describes the actual rite of ordination as one in which the designated successor places the right hand of the dead patriarch upon his own head and then takes from his departed predecessor the sacred *pallium* (or *ōmophorion*) of Saint Mark.[18] If there is any truth to the tradition, then this macabre ceremony graphically demonstrates the all-important bond that linked patriarchs in an unbroken chain believed to go all the way back to the Evangelist himself (figure 21A).

Once a patriarch came to power, he found himself at the head of a far-reaching organization whose administrative hub was in the patriarch's own residence. During the fourth century, the bishop resided in several upstairs apartments next to the church of Saint Dionysius, probably situated on the far western end of the city. This location proved useful to Athanasius on several occasions during his turbulent episcopate when he fled from imperial authorities, hastily leaving his apartments and concealing himself in an extramural necropolis or in a suburban villa.[19] Though there are no clear statements as to the precise location of the bishop's residence over the next several centuries, the vita of John the Almsgiver presents a picture entirely consistent with fourth-century sources. Various civic officials and clerics are depicted bustling up and down a narrow staircase, carrying letters and gifts of money to and from the patriarch's rooms.[20] In addition, John himself speaks of coming down (*katerchomai*) to the church for services.[21] And yet, if the seventh-century patriarch still dwelt in the upstairs apartments once occupied by Athanasius, the burgeoning administration of the patriarchate required the use of several other nearby rooms. A private oratory was connected to the bishop's bedchamber, and he often conducted services there. The patriarch regularly met with his clergy or received dignitaries in his council room or consistory (*sēkrēton*), which must have been large enough to accommodate the priests and deacons of the entire Alexandrian church. There are also cryptic references to "the library of Saint Mark at Alexandria," which served as the repository of patriarchal documents and theological writings. And in keeping with the bishop's status as one of the city's leading men, he enjoyed the use of an adjoining private bath and was waited on by his personal bath attendants.[22] By the middle of the fifth century, the entire complex begins to take on characteristics of episcopal palaces known to us archaeologically from around the Mediterranean.

The ecclesiastical organization subordinate to the patriarch grew in proportion to the expanding needs of the Alexandrian Christian community and the ever increasing status of the patriarch within the city. In the three hundred years between the episcopates of Peter I and John the Almsgiver, clerical offices became more numerous and more functionally diversified.[23] Out of a simple corps of priests there emerged the office of senior presbyter (*prōtopresbuteros*), a trusted cleric who ministered on behalf of the bishop during his absence. In light of the indivisible priestly functions of teaching the people, administering the sacraments, and pastoring parish churches, the presbyters of Alexandria grew in number over this period but did not apportion their various duties to newly created officials. This type of functional diversification was reserved for the diaconate. By the end of the fourth century, the Alexandrian diaconate had developed in two directions, with the creation of the office of archdeacon and with the emergence of an entire lower rank of subdeacons. These subdeacons frequently are grouped together with the ushers and doorkeepers of the church, thereby indicating their most noticeable role within the Christian community.[24]

Besides priests and deacons, the other prominent rank within the clergy was that of the readers. The office of reader or lector (*anagnōstēs*) was one of the oldest defined offices in the early Christian church and, by the mid-third century, was considered a clerical, rather than a lay, position. The reader stood on the bottom rung of the clerical *cursus honorum,* and patriarchal protégés were normally first appointed readers. Peter I, Theophilus, and Cyril all began their ecclesiastical careers with this post.[25] There seems to have been nothing unusual about this practice in Alexandria, as we find abundant evidence that other churches considered the lectorate as the starting place for ecclesiastical advancement.[26] One Alexandrian anomaly regarding this office was the ranking of readers above the subdeacons in the church hierarchy—an understandable development given the careers of the influential patriarchs mentioned earlier.

Perhaps one reason for the use of the lectorate as a way to launch an ecclesiastical career was the public role of the reader within the church. It was said of the young Cyril that "the priests and the learned men and philosophers were astonished at him, and rejoiced over him on account of the beauty of his form and the sweetness of his voice . . . and all the people, when they heard him read, desired that he might never cease reading." The visibility of the reader within the church made it imperative that he be free of any taint of heresy or factionalism, and that the bishop periodically certify his orthodoxy. Despite this vital role within the church, readers were ill-paid and had ample opportunity to display the virtues of ascetic poverty. Those who were not so inclined either had to obtain patriarchal patronage or supplement their meager income, as in the case of one seventh-century reader who was also a full-time shoemaker.[27]

The presbyters, deacons, and readers formed a body of clergy charged with the spiritual oversight of the Christian community and they ministered to the city's Christians in both word and sacrament. Originally, the deacons were also concerned with the material needs of the community. By the end of the fourth century, however, the scope of their activity became limited to liturgical functions and to service as the patriarch's personal emissaries. In their place, a new phalanx of clerical officials was created to deal exclusively with the patriarchate's expanding financial responsibilities. At their head was the steward or *oikonomos,* an official chosen with the consent of all the clergy and one who seems to have ranked even higher than the archdeacon in the administration of the patriarchate.[28] For it was through the oikonomos that the patriarch ministered to the physical needs of the community. Every aspect of the church's multiform financial activity was under his authority. He supervised the receipt of tithes and offerings, provided for the sick and for strangers, drew up the list of subsidized poor and widows, and inventoried valuable consecrated vessels. The treasury of the church could be opened only in the presence of both the bishop and oikonomos, and their seals were required (along with that of the archpresbyter) to close it again. Indeed, the patriarch and the oikonomos worked so closely together that "the oikonomos of the church shall do nothing without the bishop and likewise the bishop shall do nothing without the oikonomos."[29]

If the oikonomos held such an exalted position, why then is there not one recorded instance of an oikonomos succeeding to the place of the Alexandrian patriarch?[30] The twenty-fifth canon of the Council of Chalcedon stipulated that "every church having a bishop shall have also an oikonomos from among its own clergy." Although there is at least one case of an Alexandrian oikonomos who also was ordained to the priesthood, the silence of the sources suggests that, in Alexandria, the oikonomos was ranked among a lesser and parallel group of clergy. It appears that the administration of the Alexandrian church was separated into two divisions, liturgical and financial, and that this boundary was seldom crossed. Further, the successor to the episcopate was promoted exclusively from the ranks of liturgical officials (presbyters, deacons, and readers), emphasizing the bishop's function of presiding over the community's eucharistic worship. In some ways, this division echoes secular provincial administration in the late empire, with its strict separation of civil and military authority. There was also the notion that concern with material things could easily corrupt the purity of liturgical ministry. Indeed, one of the explicit reasons for the institution of the office was to ensure "that the ministry of God be free from avarice." Perhaps also it was considered ill-advised to encourage the advancement of an official who closely held the purse strings of the church.[31]

To carry out his financial responsibilities, the oikonomos employed an array of subordinate officials. These ranged from auditors and various treasurers to an almoner who accompanied the patriarch and distributed gifts to the poor. We owe our knowledge of these minor officials to the colorful detail provided by the vita of John the Almsgiver. In most of the anecdotes these officials are depicted as stingy, officious bureaucrats, in contrast to the openhanded, generous patriarch. And yet it is not difficult to sympathize with these conscientious administrators and understand their consternation at the prodigality of their master. How was it possible to responsibly manage the church's wealth when the patriarch ordered the almoner to open his bag of gold and allow an especially petulant begger to take out as much money as he desired? Despite these occasional tensions, the church's lesser financial officials, along with other minor orders like vergers, ushers, and even gravediggers, helped create a patriarchal machinery that was able to permeate nearly every aspect of Alexandrian life.[32]

By the late fourth and early fifth centuries, these Alexandrian clergymen were hedged about by an increasing number of restrictions codified in canon law. These regulations (like the laws of the *Codex Theodosianus*) may not be reliable indicators of actual behavior. Nonetheless, they reflect the goals and ideology of the lawgivers and set forth certain undesirable actions which were at least perceived as occurring among the clergy. More important, these canons illumine some of the boundaries that the church's leadership hoped to erect between the Christian community and "the world," as well as between clerical and lay members of the community itself.

All of the Christians of Alexandria were forbidden, on pain of exclusion from the sacraments, to go to the theater, public assembly places, taverns, brothels, "or any places of the heathen." While these strictures were seldom followed, they established a boundary between sacred and secular, and ranged the church against some of the most central institutions of classical civic life. To the leadership of the Christian community, these institutions were the products of a culture steeped in sin, and they needed to be either carefully avoided or annexed in the name of the church. As was noted in the preceding chapter, many of these institutions and the public buildings housing them were taken over, sometimes forcibly, during the course of the fourth and fifth centuries. At the same time, it is significant that the Christian leadership always convoked large assemblies of Christians on the inside of churches. Until the last quarter of the fifth century, the only public gatherings of the Christian community outside churches occurred in liturgical settings such as in processions or in outdoor services instituted when the size of the churches proved too restrictive for the rapidly expanding community. This is not to say that the Christian populace did not gather and collectively voice its will through acclamations or violence. Nor does this mean that individual clergymen were not present on some of these occasions. Nonetheless, officially convoked assemblies of Christians remained inside of churches until such time as much of Alexandria's topography had become Christianized.[33]

For the clergy, separation from the rest of society was to be even more radical than for the Christian laity. Any of the clergy found frequenting the civic institutions just listed were deposed from the ministry and excluded from eucharistic worship for a full year. Concern about the obscenities of mime shows was so great that if a priest's son went to the theater, the clerical father was barred from the church for a week, "because he hath not trained up his son aright." Unlike the laity, members of the clergy were also forbidden to enter public baths during Lent and on weekly fast days. They were also restricted in their choice of employment for the sake of supplementary income. They could not work at any job that defrauded another (retail trade?), nor could they sell in the marketplace. Their wives must not adorn themselves with costly jewelry or expensive clothing, "for this guise is not for the children of the church." The severest penalties were reserved for priests who practiced augury, consulted magical books, or visited sorcerers. They were to be deposed and excluded from worship for three years, a penalty designed to deter members of the clergy from participating in essentially pagan practices. And if a priest's son engaged in these practices, the father was barred from the church until he delivered his son over to the secular authorities—most likely ensuring the son's death. Altogether, these canons served to broaden the social chasm between the Alexandrian clergy and the members of the city's other ethno-religious communities, doubtless contributing to a climate of conflict rather than accommodation.[34]

## *Laos Theou*

> One day when [John the Almsgiver] determined to stop so many people from leaving the church as soon as the Gospel had been read to spend their time in idle talk instead of in prayer, what did he do? Directly after the Gospel had been read in the church, he slipped away and came out himself and sat down outside with the crowd. And when everybody was amazed, the just man said to them, "Children, where the sheep are, there also the shepherd must be. Come inside and I will come in; or stay

> here and I will stay too. For I come down to the Holy Church for your sakes, since I could hold the service for myself in the bishop's house." . . . He also forbade anyone to make an appointment to meet in the sanctuary, but in the presence of all he would force any such to leave saying, "If you really came here to pray, then occupy your mind and mouth with that; but if you came here merely to meet someone, it is written, 'The house of God shall be called the house of prayer; do not turn it into a den of thieves.'"[35]

The author of John's vita does not tell us whether these attempts at congregational discipline achieved the desired result. Despite the patriarch's annoyance at the people's inattentiveness during services, on another level the mere fact that these problems occurred speaks of the church's ability to forge vital communal bonds among the Alexandrians. Certainly by the early seventh century, if not before, the church service had become such a central element in the lives of Alexandrians that it met needs extending far beyond the desire to worship together. The church had become the locus of more informal, commonplace contacts among members of the same ethno-religious community. The easygoing manner in which these Alexandrian Christians drifted in and out of church services in order to catch up on gossip, meet a friend, or consummate a business deal resembles patterns of Mediterranean worship common alike to classical pagan sanctuaries and to modern expressions of Mediterranean Christianity and Judaism.[36] In the minds of these Alexandrians, the church had eclipsed the agora, stoa, and gymnasium as the preeminent community center.

In such a thought world, the concept of a Christian community incorporated far more than a clerical hierarchy ministering to the needs of the people. The people themselves contributed to the ongoing life of the community and formed themselves into a wide variety of parachurch groups. The inception of these groups during the late fourth and early fifth centuries occurred simultaneously with the crystallization of the clergy and the monks as distinct orders within the church. Both developments reflect the newly won dominance of the Christian community as the hegemonic culture of Alexandria. As we have seen with the pagan community, the proliferation of informal voluntary subgroups tends to occur within a hegemonic culture that is indistinguishable from the general cultural background. At times, some of these subgroups, such as the *parabalani* (ecclesiastical hospital orderlies), took on the aura of religious orders, and even required application to be formally enrolled among them.[37] Others, such as the *philoponoi* (the "zealous ones"), were more casually organized collectives that banded together for specific purposes. Moreover, the "typical" layman, whose outline can be discerned from the archaeological material at Kōm el-Dikka, sometimes joined with thousands of his fellows and made his voice heard, not only in Alexandria, but in the distant halls of the imperial court at Constantinople.

One prominent subgroup of the Christian community, occupying the highest rungs of the sociocultural ladder, was the Christian intellectual elite. Throughout late antiquity, Christian intellectual circles upheld the reputation of Alexandria as a mecca for academic pursuits. The catechetical school appears to have continued well into the fourth century, with Didymus the Blind (d. 398) as its greatest light in the post-Constantinian age. A native Alexandrian, Didymus lost his sight at the age of four, but he went on to acquire vast erudition through his dedication to learning and on account of his prodigious memory. His fame as an ascetic, a theologian, and an exegete was unfortunately later overshadowed by his commitment to the teaching of Origen, and he was posthumously condemned along with his intellectual master. During the fifth and sixth centuries, other Christian intellectuals lived and taught in Alexandria, many of whom are styled grammarians, sophists, and philosophers in the sources. Prior to the indefatigable John Philoponus, the most famous of these was his teacher, Ammonius, a one-time pagan professor of philosophy who lectured on Plato and Aristotle in the early sixth century. Later Christian teachers include the Aristotelian commentators Elias and David, both of the mid-sixth century.[38]

The fourth and fifth centuries saw the ever growing influence of the ascetical movement within Alexandrian intellectual circles. The appeal of asceticism crossed communal lines, and it is possible to find just as many pagan teachers and philosophers leading an austere life-style as their Christian contemporaries. One essential difference between pagan and Christian intellectuals was their response to the ascetical impulse. For the pagan, disdain for material comforts and possessions had the effect of validating his teaching and attracting more disciples. For the Christian intellectual, ascetic practices frequently served as only a way station on the road to total renunciation of the world—including a renunciation of philosophy itself. Typical in this regard was the late sixth-century philosopher Theodore. John Moschus relates that Theodore "owned nothing except for a cloak and a few books; he slept on a bench in any church he entered; later on he renounced the world in the monastery of Samala (at Enaton), and there he finished out his life." Likewise, Zachariah's vita of Severus, set in Alexandria a century earlier, is replete with students, rhetoricians, and sophists who embrace "true philosophy" and spurn the "vain speculations" of classical learning. Before abandoning the lecture hall entirely, many of them served in the front ranks of the philoponoi. These Christian intellectuals, trained in classical paideia and inclined toward monastic zeal, provided a fertile ground for recruitment to ecclesiastical office.[39]

It is commonly noted that a hallmark of the Alexandrian intelligentsia was its easygoing toleration—unless, of course, you came down on the wrong side of an Aristotelian debate with John Philoponus concerning the eternity of the cosmos. Pagans, Christians, and Jews are all found among the intellectual elite of the city, sometimes in the same classroom. This intermingling may give the impression that intercommunal boundaries among intellectuals were virtually nonexistent. If one follows the assumption that these were the natural leaders within their respective communities, then the entire conceptual framework of Alexandrian ethno-religious communities falls away.

However, one should not be beguiled by stray references in the letters of Synesius or in Damascius's *vita Isidori*. Throughout the entire period under examination, intellectuals are found mobilizing students in incidents of intercommunal strife. On the pagan side, Olympius's leadership of the Serapeum's defense in 391 stands out as especially noteworthy. The fifth-century Christian sophist Aphthonius fills a similar role. At the time of the destruction of pagan cult at Menouthis, Zachariah remarks that "Aphthonios ordered the young persons who followed his teaching to go with us and help us."[40] In addition, rival groups of fellow students were not averse to roughing up one another, sometimes even in the lecture halls. Although there were certainly intellectuals whose primary commitment was to their studies rather than to the contest for cultural hegemony, the conjunction of learning and intercommunal strife had a long history in Alexandria. As early as the first century, opposition to the city's Jews was centered in the gymnasium, a bastion of civic tradition and Hellenic culture. Whenever intellectuals are seen interacting with the wider populace, they tend to do so along communal lines. Only those authors who have a deliberate interest in downplaying religious tensions portray an ivory tower world where religious differences melt away in the light of classical paideia.

Rather than taking Hypatia's classroom as a model for Alexandrian intellectual life, perhaps more representative is John Moschus' description of the *scholasticus* Cosmas:

> This admirable man was a great blessing to us, not only through his life and his doctrine, but also because he possessed more books than anyone else in Alexandria and he freely lent them to anyone who so wished. With this he was impoverished: in his entire house one could not see anything else but books, one light, and one table. The whole world could enter, ask for whatever was useful to himself, and read it. I went to be with him every day, and I say it in truth, I never entered without finding him in the act of reading or of writing against the Jews, because he had a great zeal for converting the Jews to the truth. That is why he often sent me to certain Jews in order to discourse with them on the Scriptures, because he did not leave them willingly.[41]

Here, asceticism, erudition, and communal chauvinism are combined to create a bookish piety that thrives on ethno-religious differences.

As we noted in the case of pagan intellectuals, education and culture were often a function of wealth and status within the city. Though there were instances of poor or ascetic scholars like Cosmas, the cultivation of classical paideia was generally the preserve of the leisured classes, and was not especially related to the religious inclinations of the individual. However, the Christians among the city's upper classes, especially the *curiales* or bouleutai, wielded considerable clout within the Christian community and became a factor of major importance in the vicissitudes of urban power politics.

It is nearly impossible to chart the progressive Christianization of Alexandria's aristocracy, at least in the same detail as is possible for other cities like Rome or Antioch. The third century appears to have been the crucial epoch for the penetration of Christianity among Alexandria's elite. The letters of Dionysius, bishop during the trying years of the midcentury persecutions, speak of several Alexandrian aristocrats who were punished for their faith. These bouleutai appear to have been especially susceptible to official pressure. Dionysius mourns the fact that "many of the more eminent [*periphanesterōn*] in their fear came forward [to sacrifice] immediately; others who were public officials [*dēmosieuontes*] were drawn on by their duties; others were urged on by their acquaintances." The persecution under Diocletian brought to light yet more high-ranking Christians, including Philoromus, an imperial official who may have served as *rationalis* in the prefect's administration. Perhaps the most notable of the Alexandrian confessors was "a distinguished and illustrious [*episēmotatē te kai lamprotatē*]" Christian woman named Dorothea. She is portrayed by Eusebius as honorable "on account of wealth and birth and education [*ploutō te kai genei kai paideia*]," and she had the temerity to reject the advances of Maximinus Daia during his sojourn in Alexandria (305/6). Her rank and beauty saved her from a martyr's death, but the spurned emperor exiled her and confiscated her goods.[42]

After the Constantinian revolution, profession of Christianity among the Alexandrian elite becomes fairly commonplace. In the new religious climate it was now possible for these high-ranking Christians to exercise, in a Christian context, the duties traditionally incumbent upon their order—patronage and evergetism. Prior to the Peace of the Church, Alexandrian aristocrats had sometimes offered their financial support to Christian teachers, but by the fourth century the focus of this elite patronage fixed upon ascetics, who often stood outside the regular channels of patriarchal support. Wealthy Alexandrians were known to take individual monks into their households, look after one or more consecrated virgins, or minister to the needs of an ascetic in his suburban hermitage.[43]

In addition, the patronage of monks easily blended with the giving of alms to the poor. Both of these practices were viewed as spiritual disciplines.[44] This can be seen in the careers of Paesius and Isaias, two wealthy heirs to a merchant's fortune. Paesius distributed his share among the monasteries, churches, and hospitals of the city. For his part, Isaias renounced the world entirely, invested his share in the construction of a monastery, and took in "every stranger, every invalid, every old man, and every poor one as well, setting up three or four tables every Saturday and Sunday." Perhaps the most graphic example of the link between aristocratic beneficence and ascetical piety is the tale of one upper-class banker who sought to overcome his native miserliness by ordering one of his slaves to steal secretly five copper coins from him daily and give them to charity. The slave more than fulfilled his master's wishes, eventually stealing gold *trimisia*—all of which God more than recompensed to the banker. The extent of this upper-class almsgiving is difficult to measure, though there are some recorded instances of individuals giving between 30 and 1,500 pounds of gold to charity. The largest sums were expended, not through random acts of almsgiving to individuals, but through the establishment or endowment of charitable institutions. This type of beneficence guaranteed the memorialization of the donor, thereby displaying his or her wealth and virtues, and fulfilling age-old patterns of aristocratic evergetism.[45]

Just as these Christian bouleutai satisfied traditional expectations of upper-class patronage (albeit in Christian forms), so too the Alexandrian aristocracy also performed the class-specific function of acting as mediators between imperial officials and the entire local populace. Their adherence to Christianity further defined their role as spokesmen and representatives for the city's Christian community. As such, they acted in concert with the principal mouthpiece for the community, the patriarch. This public role often resulted in the city's notables being singled out in imperial pronouncements and given the responsibility for implementing unpopular directives. Under the Arian emperor Constantius (337–61), the city's aristocrats were threatened with fines, imprisonment, and confiscations unless they welcomed the emperor's appointee to the throne of Saint Mark. In May 365, the Alexandrian *curia* was threatened by the emperor Valens with a fine of 350 pounds of gold unless it saw to the expulsion of Athanasius. Placed in an untenable position between the emperor's intransigence and the threat of riot among the people, the councillors threw in their lot with the imperial administration and urged Athanasius to quit the city. He complied, but a notarius sent from court three months later secured his reinstatement. Obviously relieved, the bouleutai accompanied the notarius with great fanfare to the suburban villa where Athanasius was staying and enthusiastically ushered him back into the city.[46]

If they felt secure enough in their own local power, or sensed a lack of resolution on the part of the emperor, the bouleutai would not hesitate to take a stand against the emperor's wishes. Two years later, the local magistrates, confident in the support of the prefect and the dux, cast out the universally unpopular Lucius from Alexandria, thus ending the first phase of his bid for the patriarchate. Even during the more volatile reign of Constantius two decades earlier, Christian magistrates were able to assert their authority and resist an imperial notarius named Diogenes who was under orders to transfer churches to the control of Alexandrian Arians.[47]

Although their real power had been largely eclipsed by the patriarch and by imperial administrators, the city's Christian bouleutai still exercised a certain moral leadership, which placed them at the head of the Alexandrian laity. In light of the inherent inertia of sociopolitical change in most ancient cities, it is likely that this leadership role derived from the authority traditionally ascribed to their rank, as well as from habits of deference inculcated over centuries among the lower classes. However, given the realities of power in late Roman cities, the scope of their leadership seems to have been carefully circumscribed and was limited to issues bearing upon the laity of the Christian community. Their ability to resist the notarius Diogenes in December of 356 was due to the leadership they exercised among the laity: "Since the people and the judges strongly resisted Diogenes, Diogenes returned without success." Their prestige was recognized tacitly by the patriarchs, who courted the bouleutai when implementing a major shift of policy within the city, perhaps best seen by Peter Mongus's successful attempts during the 480s to involve the civic aristocracy in his advocacy of Zeno's *Henotikon* and his campaign against paganism. The church regarded the support of the upper classes as crucial. After all, Christian bouleutai were known to interpose their leadership when the unexpected death of a patriarch occurred, to play an active role in the elevation of a new patriarch, and even to provide candidates from among their own ranks.[48]

The social contours of the lower ranks of the Christian populace are nearly impossible to detect, owing to the upper-class prejudices of our sources and their tendency to lump the lower classes together in an undifferentiated mass of "the people." While bishops were able to mobilize specific groups into action, such as the collegia of the sailors and the gravediggers, it is difficult to discern distinguishing marks that would endow these groups with a specifically Christian identity. Their actions and their responses to various authorities frequently seem to be motivated by broadly based socioeconomic interests and the bonds linking clients to powerful patrons. Moreover, in an urban setting which was becoming increasingly Christianized, religious allegiance is less useful to us as a criterion for understanding social dynamics. Should one speak of *Christian* circus factions and trade associations, or simply refer to them as *Alexandrian* phenomena? Did the patriarch Dioscorus redirect monies intended as alms for the poor "to actresses and to the other people of the theater" in order to cultivate a Christian theater claque, or was he simply buying the support of a potent source of mass opinion in a late Roman city?[49]

Two groups whose unmistakable Christian identity distinguishes them from other social collectives in Alexandria by the fifth century are the parabalani and the philoponoi.[50] Of the two, the parabalani are better known, owing to their violent support of the patriarch Dioscorus at the Ephesian Council of 449 (the so-called Latrocinium) and to their reputed involvement in the savage murder of the philosopher Hypatia in 415. As there is no explicit evidence linking them directly to Hypatia's death, the most profitable way to explore their nature and function within the Christian community is to limit the discussion to the few facts clearly known about this group. In an edict issued in the autumn of 416, the emperors Honorius and Theodosius II directed the praetorian prefect to put into effect a series of regulations that would severely limit the Alexandrian parabalani, an action brought on by reports of the "terror" inspired by these ecclesiastical hospital attendants.[51] The two broad areas in which the imperial government sought to restrict their activities fall under the general headings of recruitment and public presence.

With regard to recruitment, the number of the parabalani was cut back to five hundred—backhanded testimony to their numerical importance in the Alexandrian church. Further, decurions and other *honorati* were excluded from their ranks. Only poor men, chosen from the city's collegia, were appointed. Even then, their names had to be approved by both the augustal prefect and the praetorian prefect. Doubtless, this was a means to sift out troublemakers and to appoint only those already enrolled among Alexandrian corporate bodies, that is, those whose identity could easily be ascertained in the event of trouble. Underlying these regulations was a clear attempt on the part of the government to wrest control of the parabalani away from the patriarch and place them in the hands of secular authorities.[52] In addition, their public presence was strictly curtailed. They were expressly forbidden "to attend any public spectacle whatever or to enter the meeting place of a municipal council or a courtroom."[53] These detailed restrictions raise the obvious question—unanswerable, given the evidence—of whether the parabalani had disrupted these civic institutions, and if so, under whose instigation. In any case, the prohibited public institutions were certainly settings far removed from church hospitals.

The parabalani's reputation as a corps of ecclesiastical thugs stems mainly from their role at the second Council of Ephesus in 449, during which they served as a vociferous cheering section for their patriarch and as a menacing squad of rowdies, eager to rough up opponents of their patron's theology. Thirty years earlier, some act of reputed "terror" must have inspired the imperial laws of 416 and 418. While the murder of Hypatia may have been the precipitating incident, it should be pointed out that there is no mention of murder in the edicts and that they repeatedly refer to the parabalani's presence in a municipal courtroom. Because of these cryptic references, the evolution of the parabalani from a dedicated confraternity of hospital attendants to a band of ecclesiastical Brown Shirts is hidden from our view and has consequently spawned more than a little speculation. Perhaps the parabalani were recruited from desperate elements among the population, since their hospital work brought them into dangerous proximity to infectious diseases. In addition, their role as attendants may have had less to do with actually nursing the sick than with transporting their bodies, thereby limiting their number to persons noted for their brute strength.

Their twin functions as hospital attendants and as strong-armed supporters is implied by the denunciation of Dioscorus delivered by the Alexandrian deacon Ischyrion at the third session of the Council of Chalcedon in 451—a neglected text in modern discussions of the parabalani. Ischyrion complained to the assembled bishops that Dioscorus "sent against me a contingent of ecclesiastics [*phallaga ekklēsiastikēn*], or to tell the truth a band of thieves, along with the deacon Peter, Harpocration and the priest Menas, in order to kill me." Failing in this attempt, Dioscorus reputedly dispatched Harpocration and his band against Ischyrion a second time. The persecuted deacon relates:

> I was locked up in a hospital for cripples [*xeneōni tōn lelōbēmenōn*], without being responsible for any crime toward anyone, even though—as I have said—no accusation had been cast against me. But even in this hospital Dioscorus again sent individuals to kill me, as all those know who were residing there. . . . And this illegal imprisonment did not abate until I had promised, in the physical distress which I found myself, to leave very great Alexandria and to do other things which were dear to [Dioscorus's] heart.

Did this "contingent of ecclesiastics" constitute a lower clerical order? While the Codex Theodosianus places the parabalani among the laws regulating clerics, the overall impression is that this was a lay order, in the employ of the patriarchate, and directed by high-ranking clergy.[54]

In light of the problematic nature of the parabalani's clerical status, the only true lay confraternity known from late antique Alexandria is that of the philoponoi. The philoponoi (derived from the Greek for conscientious or industrious) were known especially for their diligence at attending church services.[55] One of Zachariah's student companions among the philoponoi was a certain Menas, whose virtues may be taken as a model for the "conscientious" life: orthodoxy, humility of life, chastity, and almsgiving. Like the parabalani, the philoponoi cared for the sick and the indigent, though this seems to be a minor aspect of their devotion and good works. It appears that many of them assiduously took notes during patriarchal sermons, and even felt free to speak up during the service. In one instance, a group of philoponoi gently reproved John the Almsgiver for leaving his tomb unfinished, thus not bearing in mind the brevity of life. The author of John's vita expresses no surprise at this outburst, which suggests that the philoponoi, virtually alone among the laity, did not regard themselves enjoined to silence in church, perhaps owing to the fame of their religious zeal. Their extraordinary freedom of speech may also reflect their possible function as representatives of the laity to the patriarch.[56]

Their social origins betray an aristocratic background, as many of them were either advanced students or teachers. Indeed, John Philoponus, the erudite philosophical writer of the early sixth century, may have earned his sobriquet because of his association with them while he studied in Alexandria.[57] Their social rank is reflected by the fact that their chosen leaders were often from the urban elite and were occasionally invited to dine at the patriarch's own table. Moreover, their status as a recognized group within the church entitled them to take part, as a corporate body, in patriarchal processions and funerals. Like any good association of like-minded people from antiquity, the philoponoi established a meeting hall, a *philoponion*, which they located next to a church. As with other cult or craft associations, the philoponoi chose a leader and organized themselves into divisions or ranks.[58] Their "humility of life" and high regard for chastity would seem to mark them out as a quasi-monastic order.[59] And yet, the fully monastic life was regarded clearly as a higher calling, since one of Zachariah's fellow philoponoi, a medical student named Stephen, went off one night to Enaton to make a monastic profession—a step taken secretly because Stephen did not want to waver in his resolve, owing to the influence of "weak" Christians like the philoponos Zachariah. As a band of devoted laymen, it was natural that the philoponoi should direct some of their zeal toward the conversion of their fellow townsmen. These "ardent champions [*agōnistai*] of the fear of God" were not especially gentle in their methods. In late fifth-century Berytus, law students who were philoponoi came into violent conflict with fellow students who were clandestinely pursuing divination and magical practices. After several public brawls, the local bishop and various civic officials were drawn into the conflict, with the result that scores of magical books were burned publicly and the remaining pagans were driven underground.[60]

Likewise in Alexandria, the philoponoi were zealous students who had little toleration for the paganism of their classmates. In what became a cause célèbre in the mid-480s, one of Zachariah's fellow students named Paralios began to ridicule pagan oracles, disparage the goddess Isis, and declare his intent to become a Christian. The pagans waited for a day when the Christians in the class were attending church services and then set upon Paralios, exacting brutal retribution for his insults to the gods. In the midst of this bloody beating, Zachariah and two other students/philoponoi unexpectedly showed up at the lecture hall. Despite their vastly superior numbers, the pagans immediately left off with the beating and started offering excuses for their behavior. Zachariah explains the pagans' unwillingness to tangle with even a handful of philoponoi because "we seemed to a certain degree formidable to them." After a brief scuffle, the philoponoi were able to free Paralios from his tormentors. What appears most remarkable about this incident is the force of the philoponoi's reputation among the Alexandrians, almost akin to Augustine's raucous student group in Carthage who aptly called themselves "the Wreckers."[61]

If such was the force of a mere three philoponoi, they could easily disrupt civic life if roused en masse. As a reaction to Paralios's beating, the Alexandrian philoponoi, assisted by several of the clergy, began a virtual riot against pagan practices. Seeking an object for their indignation, they attacked the prefect's assessor who had unwisely boasted of his paganism. It was only with difficulty that the prefect was able to rescue his beleaguered assistant and calm the mob. The philoponoi became frustrated at the prefect's equivocation, and they proceeded to stir up the rest of the people into a pitch of antipagan fervor.[62] Were these philoponoi merely the tools of the patriarch? The evidence suggests that, as at Berytus, the philoponoi took the initiative, and that the patriarch simply placed himself, as it were, at the head of their parade. Despite their close association with the patriarch, the philoponoi remained an independently minded lay confraternity, unlike the parabalani who were unmistakably under the patriarch's direct control.

The mobilization of popular will by various power elites in late Roman cities constitutes a fascinating chapter in the history of urban social relations. A potent gauge of individual authority was the degree to which an urban power broker could orchestrate the lower orders in defense of a particular policy. Like other late antique cities, Alexandria had its share of popular violence, especially the variety spawned by competing religious interests. Although it is imperative not to follow the class-related exaggerations of ancient writers, there is no question that the acerbity and frequency of popular turmoil in late antique Alexandria occurred on a scale far above that of the early Roman period.

Once those incidents resulting from the elite's mobilization of the lower orders are sifted out, is it possible to discern the contours of popular opinion and the collective aspirations of Alexandria's Christian laity? This is a question not easily answered, for it could be argued that expressions of popular will, ranging from acclamations to arson, were always instigated by a cabal of provocateurs, such as a theater claque or a band of ruffians in the Agora. If one sees these agitators as typically the paid agents of some local notable, either secular or religious, then there is little alternative but to embrace the jaundiced view that there was no real vox populi. On closer examination, however, it is abundantly clear that the Alexandrian plebs possessed a mind of its own, quite apart from the manipulations of interested parties. The masses could voice their opposition to a policy approved by both the imperial administration and their own local magistrates, and they were known to lodge formal complaints against their bishop, even when he was a shrewd crowd pleaser like Athanasius. Despite the commonly held view that the Alexandrians always acquiesced to the wishes of their patriarch and were united against imperial authority, they could violently defend the imperial prefect against an attack launched by Cyril's monastic supporters in 415.[63]

How did the laity of Alexandria make its will known? Most commonly, collective opinion on a policy or person was expressed through the use of ritualized acclamations in large public gatherings. The chanting of slogans in unison became a potent force for articulating the mind of the plebs in late Roman cities. Although a claque or faction might "prepare the others to cry out," the enthusiasm with which the crowd took up these chants often reflected deeply held popular sentiments.[64] In effect, acclamations constituted part of a highly ritualized dialogue between ruler and subject, and enabled the masses to comment on specific imperial policies and issues of theological debate. Most commonly, they were employed to honor an individual, from the emperor himself to local magistrates and bishops. However, acclamations could also be hostile, and were a means by which the populace could excoriate a particularly detested individual.

These twin functions of popular approbation and disapproval make it possible to trace the strongly held opinions of the Alexandrian laity. The assent of the people had long been an essential element in the selection of a bishop. Even after the role of the local clergy was diminished in patriarchal elections, it was still necessary to obtain "the consent of all Christian and God-loving people." Indeed, popular participation was such an integral part of patriarchal enthronement that, in 516, the laity clamored for a second consecration of Dioscorus II, even though he had previously been enthroned by bishops, clergy, and the emperor's representatives. If a candidate was favorably regarded by the Alexandrian laity, his elevation likely would be greeted with shouts of "A good pious Christian! An ascetic! A genuine bishop!" On the other hand, an unpopular candidate (usually the emperor's own appointee) could expect chants of "This is the new Judas!" These public denunciations sometimes bordered on more direct action, as in September 367, when the unpopular Arian candidate Lucius was threatened with death at the hands of an angry crowd. Representatives of both the imperial administration and the local government were needed to protect Lucius as he was escorted from the city. The crowd followed the closely guarded Lucius, "and all alike with one breath, and with one mind, and of one accord, did not cease, from the house from which he was led, through the midst of the city, as far as the house of the dux, from shouting and hurling at him insults and criminal charges and from crying out 'Let him be taken out of the city!'"[65]

The laity also made its voice heard by interceding with imperial officials on behalf of its bishop, reflecting the close ties that could grow up between patriarch and people. In 303, the imperial prefect and his staff had a near riot on their hands when they arrested Peter I. Their actions were met with a barrage of stones from the crowd and chants of "Why are you taking away from us our chief priest and good shepherd?" The crowd then followed behind their patriarch and encamped around his prison, holding nightlong vigils and periodically chanting, "First murder us his children, then you can take our father!" In the face of this popular opposition, the authorities were forced to spirit Peter away to a quiet spot before they could venture to execute him. During Athanasius's episcopate, the populace attempted several times to thwart imperial directives or at least appeal to the authorities for a modification in imperial policy. In these circumstances, imperial administrators had to respond carefully to the rhythmic slogans of the populace, since the protocol of late Roman acclamations dictated that the people's chants be forwarded directly to the emperor himself.[66] In most of these cases, it appears that the Christian populace was stirred to action when an established authority in Alexandria was threatened by some intruding force from the outside.[67]

To ensure that its voice was heard in the corridors of power, the populace could even bypass the emperor's representatives and appeal directly to him, as in 458, when the emperor Leo received several petitions on behalf of Timothy Aelurus from "the people [*dēmos*] of Alexandria and their dignitaries [*axiōmatikoi*], senators [*politeuomenoi*] and shipmasters [*nauklēroi*]." If an emperor wished to run roughshod over these expressions of popular will, it was necessary to enforce sanctions designed especially to punish the laity, such as cutting off the grain dole, prohibiting public entertainments, or sealing shut the doors of the city's churches. Such extreme measures were usually avoided. If at all possible, the unpopular bishop (frequently a usurper from the outside) would attempt to win the affections of the populace. Sometimes he was successful, as in the case of John the Almsgiver, a wealthy landowner from Cyprus. More often than not, the usurper failed to win approval and was forced either to withdraw or be content with a tiny following encircled by the protecting spears of the prefect's guard.[68]

As early as the dawn of the fourth century, the passions of the Christian populace ran highest over questions regarding the leadership of the community. It is difficult to overstate the strength of the bonds of affection which grew up between Alexandria's Christians and their patriarch—the one figure who embodied the community's moral, spiritual, and even financial leadership. This position was hedged about with traditions and ceremonial etiquette that went beyond even the age-old decorum of civic leadership in Alexandria. It was absolutely necessary for a new patriarch to follow these conventions to the letter, if he were to be regarded as a worthy successor to the throne of Saint Mark. Gaffes abound and highlight the inauguration of those episcopates regarded as failures: Lucius in 367 ignored the traditional protocol surrounding a patriarchal adventus, Timothy Salofaciolos omitted revered names from the liturgical diptychs in the 460s, and Cyrus had a psalm read out in his first service as patriarch in 631 which was not prescribed for the day's liturgy.[69] This last blunder led to chants of protest among the people: "This is not the proper psalm; it is an evil augury for the patriarch Cyrus; he will not see a second festival of the Resurrection in the city of Alexandria." Even the monks chimed in: "He has acted contrary to what is ordained in the Canons."[70] The laity were a bit more indulgent in matters of proper form when it came to a perceived faux pas committed by a bishop already well known to them. Throughout his patriarchate (300–311), Peter I refused to sit on the episcopal throne, seating himself instead on the footstool. Despite their love for him, the people were disturbed by this breach of protocol and called out to him in church, "Bishop, sit on your throne. Where you were ordained, there you should also sit." Peter still refused, and the laity were forced to accede to his wishes.[71]

Peter's confrontation with the laity serves as vivid exception that proves the rule regarding the integral place of the laity in the smooth administration of the Christian community. Unless a patriarch like Peter could draw upon reserves of goodwill, it was necessary to maintain at least the forms of unity which bound together patriarch, clergy, and people. Perhaps the best illustration of this interplay among various forces within the community is the description in the *History of the Patriarchs* of the elevation of Theodosius I in 535. He was consecrated by "the bishops and priests and chief men of the city, [having] ordained him, and written his diploma of consecration, and promoted him to the degree of primate over the apostolic diocese, and ratified his appointment with the consent of all Christian and God-loving people."[72] At such a precarious moment in the ongoing life of the Christian community, each element in the community played its own, carefully scripted role in the ceremonial transfer of power. To ignore any one of these groups was to invite schism.

# Eight

# Community and Factionalism in the Christian Community

There is no doubt that Peter I's refusal to sit upon the patriarchal throne was the source of considerable consternation among the Alexandrian laity. Why was Peter so resistant to the will of the people? In this instance, the vox populi ran up against the numinous aura of authority which Peter saw residing in the office of patriarch. Later, in his consistory, Peter revealed to the clergy his reasons for opposing the people:

> Do you not know the fear and trembling my heart feels, and how much that oppresses me? For beloved, whenever I ascend the episcopal chair and come near to the throne while standing in prayer—as you see—and I look on the throne and see what radiant and inexpressible power resides there, fear mixed with joy comes over me and mightily crushes my bones, and I am unable to do anything.[1]

How did the Alexandrian episcopate acquire this awesome prestige? In part, this authority derived from the bishop's role of standing in the place of Christ when ministering to his people. For the Christian community, this was made possible by the continuous presence of the Holy Spirit in the bishop's ministry. However, Peter's perception of a *mysterium tremendum* was also predicated on his

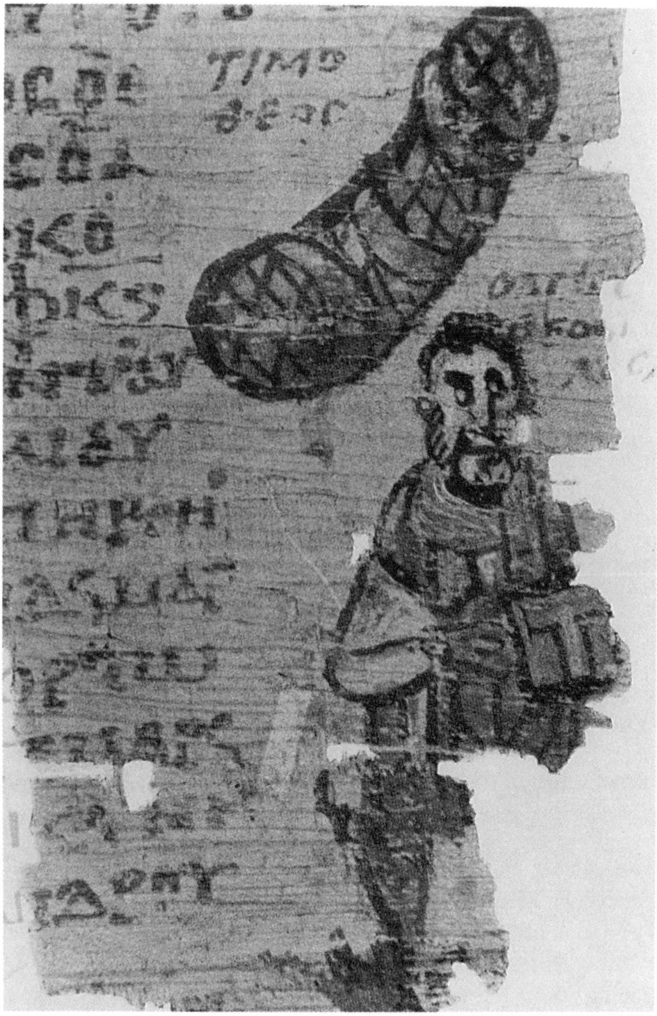

Fig. 22. Patriarchal succession. The mummified remains of patriarch Timothy (d. 385) next to his successor, Theophilus. Marginal illustration from a chronicle written in Alexandria in the early fifth century. *P.Goleniscev* 6 recto.

(From A. Bauer and J. Strygowski, "Eine alexandrinische Weltchronik," *Denkschriften der Kaiserlichen Akademie der Wissenschaften: Wien* 51.2 [1906]: 1–204, 6 recto) realization of an unbroken continuity in the episcopate which extended all the way back to Saint Mark himself. This continuity endowed the patriarchate with an aura of authority comparable with that of Saint Peter in Rome. Mark's successors were buried near the Evangelist's martyrium, and special feasts were appointed in the liturgical calendar to commemorate former bishops. We have already observed how a new bishop might even have received a blessing from the hand of his deceased predecessor. This sense of continuity is also evidenced in a marginal illustration from an early-fifth-century Alexandrian city chronicle which depicts the newly consecrated Theophilus standing beside the mummified body of Timothy I (figure 22). In addition, the unity and collective authority of the succession of Alexandrian bishops can be seen in a seventh-century ivory relief now in the Louvre. Saint Mark is seated on his throne, holding the gospel book and surrounded by several dozen diminutive episcopal colleagues attendant upon him (figure 21A).[2]

### *"Radiant and Inexpressible Power"*

The net effect of this accumulated holiness and spiritual power was to endow the bishop of Alexandria with an authority that extended far beyond that of a traditional urban power broker. It was by reason of this divine authority that a bishop ordained clergy and authorized the ministry of individual priests. Although there was at least an acknowledgment that a charismatic unction might rest upon certain individuals apart from the bishop's authority, it was the bishop alone who could legitimize an independent ministry. A formal list of authorized clergy was kept by the bishop, and periodically he could require written affirmations of clerical orthodoxy and obedience. While these measures may have been motivated by the relatively loose structure of the Alexandrian church in the second and third centuries, by the fifth century a patriarch could control effectively his entire ecclesiastical hierarchy.[3]

This control was exercised through various forms of ecclesiastical discipline. At the dawn of the fourth century, these sanctions usually took the form of penances, exclusion from sacraments, or even deposition from clerical office.[4] With the Constantinian revolution and the resultant enhancement of the bishop's status, other more forceful means of coercion could be employed. As in so many other respects, the episcopate of Athanasius was a watershed in the development of the bishop's powers. In the opening years of Athanasius's episcopate, the Melitians proved to be a thorn in his side, and there are indications that his attempts at using traditional means to curb their activities proved fruitless. Over time, his methods became increasingly brutal. Beatings, confiscations, and imprisonments became the order of the day, but these sanctions came back to haunt him later in the accusations of his enemies. Significantly, however, Athanasius's illustrious successors all followed his lead and offered violence to their perceived ecclesiastical enemies: Theophilus with the Tall Brothers and their associates, Cyril with the Novatians and the Nestorians, Dioscorus with the family of Cyril, Peter Mongus with the Acepheloi. Even so mild a patriarch as John the Almsgiver employed a corps of disciplinary officials (*ekklēsiekdikoi*) to enforce his authority and punish those who violated the canons—with beatings if necessary. The frequency of these acts of ecclesiastical violence bespeaks the increasingly secular authority wielded by the bishops and also echoes the normal forms of cruelty encountered in the courts of their late antique civil counterparts.[5]

The patriarch's possession of a numinous spiritual office, his ability to authorize and regulate clerical ministries, and the coercive powers at his disposal created a highly charged combination that endowed the episcopate with wide-ranging authority over the church's leadership structure. But how did the patriarch translate his monopoly of power over the church's hierarchy into a much broader authority over the entire Christian community? How was he able to extend his sway over a fractious and socially diverse metropolis? From the standpoint of the Christian community (or, at least, the Alexandrian Christians in union with the patriarch), it is crucial not to underestimate the patriarch's role as the channel for the community's sacramental life. The bishop authorized entrance into the community through baptism, and the bishop presided over the community's perceived mystical union with Christ through the eucharist. The patriarch also served as custodian of the relics of local saints, potent dynamos of spirituality in late antiquity. By the bishop's authority, miraculous discoveries of relics were authenticated, and he was entrusted with solemnly installing the relics in their shrines.[6]

As the conduit for dispensing heavenly blessings to his flock, the patriarch was able to move with ease into a similar role as a patron bestowing earthly *beneficia* upon a vast urban *clientela*. Throughout much of the Mediterranean, bishops displaced the municipal elites as the principal "nourisher" of the late antique city. Frequently, they came into conflict with the urban aristocrats over the concomitant issue of who could justly claim to speak for the city with outside authorities.[7] The bishops' newly found role as urban patron could not have occurred were it not for the bishops' acquisition of the wealth necessary to fulfill traditional expectations of civic beneficence.

By the early seventh century, the Alexandrian patriarch was undoubtedly one of the wealthiest men in the empire. When John the Almsgiver succeeded to the episcopate in 609/10 he found 8,000 pounds of gold in the church's treasury, besides quantities of wealth in kind. The patriarchate possessed a fleet of ships which were regularly deployed on trading ventures as far west as Italy. This merchant fleet had been constructed during the tenure of Eulogius (580–607), who carried on a lengthy correspondence with Gregory the Great about securing Italian timber for his shipbuilding program. Some hint of the patriarchate's wealth can be gleaned from John's gifts to Modestus of Jerusalem, who was attempting to recover from the Sassanian sack of the city in 615. If we can believe the figures given by John's biographer, Leontius, the almsgiving patriarch gave Modestus 1,000 gold coins, 1,000 sacks of grain, 1,000 sacks of beans or peas, 1,000 pounds of iron, 1,000 casks of dried fish, 1,000 jars of wine, and 1,000 Egyptian workmen to help assist in the rebuilding of Jerusalem's churches—along with a cover letter begging forgiveness "for sending nothing worthy of Christ's churches."[8]

Such wealth was nothing new to the patriarchate. Nearly two centuries earlier, Cyril sought to ensure the ratification of the Council of Ephesus (431) among the powerful in Constantinople with the generous application of *eulogiae*—the customary "gifts" employed at court as *Schmiergeld*. These bribes came to an approximate total of a half ton of gold, 117 elegantly woven rugs, and 32 ivory chairs and stools. Cyril apparently was willing to expend even greater sums in order to "furnish whatever [was] lacking to their avarice." On a similar mission, Cyril's uncle, Theophilus, arrived in Constantinople in 403 "like a beetle overladen with the dung of the best that Egypt—or even India for that matter—produces." A half century yet earlier, Athanasius was forced to protest to the emperor that he was but "a poor man" despite the accusations of his enemies that he was "a rich man, and powerful, and able to do anything."[9]

The patriarchate's wealth derived from a number of sources, not the least of which was the personal fortune of the bishop and his family.[10] In addition, the favor of the emperor resulted in exemptions from public liturgies and from various kinds of taxation—no small advantage in a competition for wealth and status with overburdened municipal councillors. Constantine directed that the church receive and distribute imperial subsidies of grain and oil, and, if Athanasius's accusers may be believed, the patriarch was also able to requisition linen tunics from Egypt. The patriarchate also profited from tithes given by Egyptian churches and monasteries as well as from revenues derived from lands in the chora owned by the Alexandrian church. These last were so extensive that John the Almsgiver did not feel he was exaggerating when he remarked, "My revenues from Christ-loving persons almost exceed human calculation." Further, beginning in the third century, a rising volume of pious legacies had endowed the Alexandrian church with property and cash. If this were not enough, church offices (along with their exemption from public liturgies) had become such a desirable commodity that an ecclesiastical appointment frequently elicited a "gift" from the new clergyman or his family. John the Almsgiver sought to put an end to this traffic in offices, but despite his opposition to simony, he could still be approached by a landowner who offered him 200,000 modii of grain and 180 pounds of gold for a diaconate.[11]

A key to understanding the patriarch's status within Alexandrian society is the essentially private nature of the patriarch's resources. The wealth of the Alexandrian church was his wealth, administered jointly by the bishop and the oikonomos. While it is true that individual churches possessed wealth in the form of church plate, curtains, and furniture, the patriarchate's cash on hand was strictly under the control of the bishop. Leontius's vita of John the Almsgiver goes so far as to depict the church's treasury as a large money chest kept under the patriarch's bed! Various functionaries are depicted bustling up and down the stairs to the episcopal apartments, carrying jars of gold coins to add to the treasure. Although it is difficult to believe that all of the vast sums belonging to the patriarchate could be conveniently stowed under John's bed, it is worth remembering that even imperial finance was so crude that the funds available to a provincial governor often were limited to what was actually kept in his strongbox.[12]

Like any other great *potentior* of the late Roman Empire, a social distance existed between the Alexandrian patriarch and those of the lower orders who sought his patronage. Even before the Peace of the Church, obtaining access to the bishop was by no means an easy task. Those wishing a patriarchal interview were first questioned closely by a deacon who carefully screened petitioners. Even the wives of Alexandrian presbyters had to proceed through established channels in order to obtain an interview. Over the course of the next several centuries, this social distance increased to the point where petitioners resorted to accosting the patriarch in the streets of Alexandria. Even then, subordinates were quick to interpose and shield the bishop from such breaches of etiquette. As in his opposition to long-established forms of simony, John the Almsgiver also sought to bridge this social distance and be accessible to all comers, especially to those who "were prevented from so doing through fear of the ushers [*kagkellariōn*] and the disciplinary officials [*ekklēsiekdikōn*] and the rest of his retinue." His methods for overcoming these barriers reveal just how formidable they had become. We are told that, twice a week, he sat on a stool before a church, with a gospel book in his hands. In Leontius's words, "He was anxious to give confidence [*adeian*] and ready access [*parrēsian*] to those who wished to consult him." In order to encourage petitioners, he excluded his usual retinue from these proceedings, save for one disciplinary official who was charged with executing the patriarch's judgments so quickly that he was enjoined to fast until the patriarch's wishes had been carried out.[13]

The obstacles erected around a patriarch's accessibility served to heighten the status and wealth of his charmed circle. While some in the circle no doubt were enriched by the "gifts" they exacted from petitioners to the patriarch's justice, it appears that their wealth and status were largely bestowed upon them by the patriarch himself. The *acta* from the third session of the Council of Chalcedon (451) are particularly instructive in this regard. Several of Cyril's relatives and associates detail the private fortunes that Dioscorus had unjustly seized from them. Spacious townhouses, orchards of fruit trees, rental properties, quantities of gold, and retinues of household slaves were all confiscated by the newly elevated patriarch. Several of Dioscorus's victims inventoried their stolen property in the same breath that they speak of the "intimacy and benevolence" (*tēs oikeiotētos kai eumeneias*) with which Cyril had honored them. This phrase crops up conspicuously in the conciliar depositions and seems to define a formal status designation referred to by one former Alexandrian priest, that of the "familiars" (*prosoikeiōthentes*) of Cyril. It is no wonder that an outsider like Dioscorus felt constrained to break up this cozy circle of patriarchal associates.[14]

Patronage exists only insofar as it is actively employed on behalf of a client. In this light, it is useful to observe patriarchal patronage in action, as these instances serve to highlight the contours of the patriarch's influence. Ancient writers continually draw attention to episcopal benevolence toward the poor, the sick, widows, orphans, refugees, prisoners, and cripples. By patronizing these neglected groups, the bishop was able to carve out significant new areas of support within the city, and his resultant patronage of the city's entire social spectrum legitimized his claim to speak for the city as a whole—especially since the masses could convey their wishes to him through the urban rituals of late antiquity. However, care for those normally excluded from polite urban society was also a gospel injunction incumbent upon all clergy. This philanthropy was grounded in a theological understanding that considered the destitute to be deserving of the utmost care, "knowing that God shall enquire concerning them more than concerning the holy vessels;

for they are His image and likeness." Ministry to the downtrodden validated a bishop's holiness and his compassion.[15] Thus, John the Almsgiver called the poor and the beggars his "masters and helpers." It is for this reason that Alexandrian bishops were enjoined by canon law to distribute alms every Sunday and to surround themselves with these marginalized groups at the most important church festivals.[16]

This proclivity toward civic evergetism expressed itself in a number of concrete ways, the most straightforward being the distribution of cash and food items. In the early seventh century, the patriarch supported "out of his own funds" more than 7,500 of the city's poor and beggars (*ptōchous kai epaitas*). John the Almsgiver apportioned one keration of silver apiece to the men and two keratia to the women and children. Further, since the early fourth century, the Alexandrian patriarchs had administered the city's grain dole to the poor, and this became a vital link in a patron-client relationship forged between bishop and people.[17]

The city's destitute were also cared for by the establishment of church-run poorhouses, hostels, hospitals, and homes for the elderly. During the cold and wet winter months, crude wooden dormitories were erected by order of the patriarch in the precinct of the Caesarion to provide shelter for the homeless. In addition, as early as the 260s, victims of plague were ministered to by Alexandrian clerics, and by the mid-fourth century the indigent sick and crippled were cared for in hospitals under the direction of a *hēgemōn* appointed by the patriarch. We should seek for the origins of the parabalani in the context of this charitable activity—despite their later reputation. Given Alexandria's fame as a center for medical studies throughout antiquity, it is not surprising that donations to hospital work served as a traditional focus of patriarchal evergetism. Consequently, in his desire to surpass the charitable work of his predecessors, John the Almsgiver was forced to come up with some creative new services (at least, new to Alexandria), such as hospitals and hostels for refugees and maternity wards for poor women.[18]

While care for the flotsam and jetsam of late antique society endeared a patriarch like John the Almsgiver to the masses and to his hagiographers, it is significant that patriarchal beneficence was not limited to those dwelling along the margins of urban life. Successful bishops developed a keen sense of who counted most in the delicate chemistry of urban power politics. These influential groups were carefully singled out for honors, gifts, and the patriarch's "familiarity." Gifts were lavished on selected members of the civic aristocracy, especially during those times when leadership of the Christian community was being contested—for example, at the time of the Arian controversy in the fourth century and later during the Monophysite conflict. One effective method for courting the upper classes was through gifts of money to impoverished nobles. In one instance, the Chalcedonian patriarch Apollinaris (551–70) actively sought to restore the wealth of a young aristocrat who had fallen on hard times. Apollinaris accomplished his charity through a ruse in which he led the young man to believe that the patriarchate had owed his father a great sum of money. In this way, the patriarch was able to preserve the honor of an Alexandrian grandee and at the same time enable the fame of his own charity to be spread abroad in the right circles.[19]

In a similar vein, not all of the refugees who thronged Alexandria after 615 were indigent and had "no lodging place but were forced to lie about in Agora with the rain falling on them." We know of at least one of the "distinguished foreigners" (*tōn emphanōn epixenoumenōn*) to whom John the Almsgiver gave fifteen pounds of gold—equivalent to a year's subsistence for three hundred persons. Among other influential urban groups, the long-standing ties that bound the patriarch to the maritime classes, particularly to the naukleroi of the grain fleet, were maintained by sustained episcopal patronage. John the Almsgiver also bestowed individual gifts on merchants amounting to as much as twenty pounds of gold. All told, these gifts bespeak a style of patronage more in keeping with traditional forms of civic evergetism, and underscore the patriarch's status as the preeminent patron in the late antique city.[20]

Over time, the new patterns of patronage marked out by the patriarch came to influence even the Alexandrian aristocracy's own style of evergetism. Following the patriarch's lead, wealthy bouleutai widened their horizons and began to care for the destitute, expending quantities of gold in the process. Aristocratic patronage of monks also became quite common, especially since this form of charity secured for the patron a great store of heavenly blessings. In some cases, charitable gifts were funneled through the hands of the patriarch and his representatives, thereby strengthening the communal ties that united the wealthy, the patriarchate, and the poor.[21]

More often than not, however, beneficent nobles engaged in charity without reference to the patriarch. This caused no problem—so long as the methods and the object of the charity coincided with patriarchal policy. These acts of private charity were also deemed inoffensive when they occurred as part of the benefactor's renunciation of the world and adoption of the ascetic life. However, when private almsgiving and patriarchal policy came into conflict, a serious rift could occur. The most notable example of this type of conflict erupted in 398 when an aristocratic widow entrusted one thousand gold pieces to a respected priest (and one-time candidate for the see of Constantinople) named Isidore for the relief of poor women in the city. She made Isidore swear not to divulge this gift to the patriarch Theophilus, whose aggressive policy of church construction was widely regarded as lithomania. Theophilus soon learned of this bequest, however, and used every means at his disposal to expel Isidore from the city and hound him out of Egypt. Although this incident served as but one episode in the larger Origenist controversy and Theophilus's eventual vendetta against John Chrysostom, it vividly illustrates the perceived dangers of private patronage, especially when it was in the hands of a potential rival. In like manner, Dioscorus seized legacies made during the patriarchate of his predecessor, apparently considering lines of patronage established during Cyril's episcopate to threaten his own relatively weak base of support.[22]

What was the net effect of this patriarchal patronage? In light of the resources at the patriarch's disposal, a healthy skepticism should greet Athanasius's special pleadings that he was simply "a poor man, and in a private station," and that he was "not a man that would resist even the *logistēs* of the city, much less (an emperor)." There is no question that the patriarch became, over the course of the fourth and fifth centuries, the single most influential person in the city. He possessed spiritual authority and a great store of wealth, both of which he dispensed liberally in order to create clients and strengthen the associative bonds that united the Christian community. Even Constantius acknowledged Athanasius's success at winning over the crowd and buoying his power on an ever rising tide of popular acclaim.[23]

Compared with the brief tenure of imperial administrators in the city, an average episcopate could extend over many decades and enabled the bishop to cultivate a substantial network of urban support. Constantinople was nearly two weeks away, and a bishop often could force the hand of a bureaucrat who waited for instructions from the imperial court. Thus, the bishops were able to usurp more and more civil authority and "assume the administration of secular matters."[24] By the early seventh century, patriarchs were able to establish standards for weights and measures in the marketplace, determine tax exemptions for shopkeepers, manumit ill-treated slaves, and mediate in feuds between magistrates. It is no wonder, then, that a bishop could be accused of acting "as though this city were his own personal property."[25]

Moreover, with Alexandria and the imperial grain fleet in his hands, the power of the patriarch became a factor in the wider arena of imperial politics. Although this takes us beyond a discussion of Alexandrian affairs, it is worth noting that throughout late antiquity, charges of treason and plotting with usurpers swirled around the patriarchate—often with good cause. Even during the early empire, Alexandria had been a traditional launching-off place for successful attempts at seizing the purple. This explains much of the emperors' anxiety to establish someone loyal and pliable on the throne of Saint Mark. This also underscores the significance of a heavenly vision granted to John the Almsgiver shortly before his death. In this vision, a court eunuch in gleaming robes, holding an official scepter, hailed John and said, "Come, I beseech you, the King of Kings is asking for you"—a ceremonial formulation reserved for the funerary rituals of emperors.[26]

Despite the patriarch's numinous spiritual authority and his ability to dispense almost limitless resources of patronage, religious factionalism rent the Alexandrian Christian community throughout late antiquity. This factionalism was multiform in its expression, ranging from the Melitians and Colluthians at the dawn of the fourth century to the Monophysite-Chalcedonian split that lasted into the Islamic period. Obviously, several structural features of Alexandrian society acted as a powerful undertow, drawing adherents away from unity with the bishop. In order to counteract the sometimes competitive associative bonds that could divide patriarch and people, it was necessary for Alexandrian bishops, beginning with Athanasius, to draw upon alternative sources of authority and patronage.

The only other major base of patronage originating within the city itself was the civic aristocracy. Unlike Antioch, where the copious writings of Libanius allow for a full and nuanced description of aristocratic life, the sources for understanding the bouleutai of Alexandria are relatively meager. It does not follow, however, that the civic nobility was simply eclipsed by the patriarch or by imperial officials. Behind virtually every instance of schism within the Christian community, it is possible to find openhanded upper-class backers who supported the separatists. A story related by Eusebius concerning Origen's youth (c. 200) is typical in this regard. It seems that Origen had made the acquaintance of "a woman of great wealth [*plousiōtatē*], distinguished [*periphanestatē*] in her manner of life and in other respects." Besides caring for Origen's family out of charity, she also "treated with honor" a heretical teacher named Paul from Antioch. This noble lady not only took in Paul, but she sponsored meetings in her home to hear him, and "a great multitude was gathered together, not only of heretics but also of our people, attracted by his apparent skillfulness in speech."[27] This scenario was repeated across the late antique period in conflicts as various as the Arian controversy and the initial split in the church in the wake of the Council of Chalcedon. And yet, from the bishop's standpoint, this aristocratic patronage could cut two ways, thereby allowing bouleutai to support the bishop secretly during times of imperial disfavor, even providing a safe hideout from the prefect's guards.

During the four centuries under review, the imperial prefect often served as an effective counterbalance to the authority of the patriarch within the city. Although he could not claim the same degree of devotion from the people or rely upon a long familiarity with the complexities of the local situation, the prefect more than made up in brute force what he lacked in moral authority. He and other imperial officials, such as *notarii, silentarii*, and various military commanders, were entrusted with executing the emperor's will in the city. These administrators possessed a wide range of coercive powers which could forcibly reshape the structures of patronage in the city by disrupting patriarchal distributions and diverting beneficia to imperial supporters. As could be expected, the methods of these officials frequently lacked finesse—they simply seized churches, appropriated patriarchal wealth, and imprisoned or beat their opponents. Time and again, bishops and other clergy were expelled from the city and were replaced with appointees more malleable to imperial will. Although wide-scale resistance to this outside intervention periodically erupted, some imperially nominated bishops were able to remain on the throne of Saint Mark for decades. On occasion, as in the case of Theodosius I (535–67) or John the Almsgiver, they were eventually able to mollify popular opposition. The mere fact of their association with secular authorities did not automatically prejudice the masses against them. It was necessary, however, that these appointees cultivate the people with all the traditional forms of Alexandrian evergetism, and win the respect and deference of a city habituated to the protocols of power.[28]

## *The Desert and the City: Monastic Opposition to Episcopal Authority*

Both the civic aristocracy and the imperial administration lacked one essential element in establishing an alternative structure of patronage, spiritual authority. Yet, by the later fourth and early fifth centuries, the patriarchate increasingly had to contend with a new locus of spiritual authority which grew up on the outskirts of the city. The appeal of monasticism endowed individual Christian ascetics with an aura of authority which could easily rival that of an established bishop.

City and hinterland played off one another in late antique Egypt to a degree perhaps unparalleled in other regions of the empire.[29] As but one aspect of this interplay, the relationship between the patriarch and the ascetics of the surrounding countryside often intruded upon the urban scene and could influence, in turn, the inner life of the Alexandrian Christian community. Patriarchal-monastic relations were hedged about by a set of expectations, obligations, and fears no less complex than those characterizing the strained relationship between the imperial prefect and the peasants of the countryside. Indeed, it could easily be argued that the patriarch inherited much of the prefect's image in the chora, as he gradually overshadowed the prefect's authority in the largely Christianized society of late Roman Egypt.

A patriarch's success among the desert ascetics was predicated on several factors that remained constant throughout late antiquity. The Alexandrian patriarch, as leader of the entire Christian community of Egypt, stood, as it were, in the place of Christ. This accounts for the pomp and elaborate ceremony of episcopal processions throughout the Egyptian countryside. During one of Athanasius' tours of the towns and monasteries in the diocese of Smoun, he is described as traveling "mounted on a donkey with countless people following him, including bishops, innumerable clerics with lamps and candles, and also monks from various places who were preceding him chanting psalms and canticles."[30] Such was the honor accorded Athanasius on this occasion that Apa Theodore, one of Pachomius's successors, personally led the bishop's donkey by the bridle. Theodore was so overcome with joy in thus serving the bishop that he was "without concern for the crowd which pressed against him or for the flames of the numerous glowing and burning lamps in front of him." Athanasius's visits to the chora were not always carried out with such ceremony. On one occasion he fled to the regions upriver as a fugitive from the violent usurpation of his bishopric. Yet, in this instance also, Athanasius carefully maintained the bishop-as-Christ image—this time as a persecuted shepherd of God's people.

While such posturing could greatly enhance the bishop's image, it alone could not ensure success among the monks of the chora and the desert.[31] It was vital that the patriarch also clearly identify with them and their ascetical ideology.[32] Athanasius, of course, was a master at this—so much so that Saint Anthony bequeathed one of his two garments to the patriarch. Cyril, likewise, courted monastic support, doubtless aided by the experience gained in a five-year sojourn at Nitria and Scetis as a young man. In light of the eremetical tenor of the monastic vocation and the restricted boundaries of rural life, the bishop needed to make the first move in establishing ties with the ascetics of the countryside.[33] This certainly could not be achieved by remaining in Alexandria, a factor that partially explains the failure of the imperial appointees to the patriarchate, both Arian and Chalcedonian, who naturally stayed close to the protection afforded by Alexandria's imperial garrison.[34]

This lack of association with monastic life also helps elucidate the strained relations between the ascetics and patriarchs like Theophilus and Peter Mongus (477–90) who, though orthodox (at least in Egypt), were identified with urban interests. Theophilus's stormy relations with the monks were not touched off by the Anthropomorphic controversy of 399, but were clearly brewing for some years before the controversy erupted. Three quarters of a century later, Peter Mongus succeeded his Monophysite mentor Timothy Aelurus, himself a monk renowned for feats of asceticism. Although Peter Mongus held the same doctrinal position as Aelurus and was likewise persecuted by the imperial authorities, he had virtually no association with the monastic movement. He was a thoroughgoing townsman.[35] This initial lack of sympathy with monasticism contributed to a serious schism originating in the monasteries west of Alexandria, which eventually threatened the very foundations of his authority.[36]

A final factor determining the nature of patriarchal-monastic relations was the relative strength of each of the two parties. During much of Athanasius's episcopate, the monastic movement was in its infancy. While the novelty of the ascetic ideal gave the movement much of its early popularity, the numbers of Egyptian ascetics were still relatively few. By the end of the century, however, the number of monks had grown considerably, to the point where they became a powerful force with which to reckon. This increasing power and influence raised the stakes in patriarchal-monastic relations, accounting for much of the strife that colored their interaction in the fifth century. Not surprisingly, Theophilus's blunt strong-arm tactics were destined to embitter the desert ascetics. Further, it took all of the finesse of a shrewd politico like Cyril to mend temporarily the alliance between patriarch and desert which was originally forged by Athanasius. And yet the issue of episcopal authority in the countryside became moot by the later stages of the Byzantine period, when the imperially appointed patriarch resided in the city and the Monophysite patriarch dwelt first in the suburban monastery of Enaton and, by the late sixth century, in the desert monastery of Saint Macarius. The wider world of imperial politics and ecclesiastical diplomacy had decided this aspect of the perennial rural-urban dichotomy.[37]

Although various styles of Christian asceticism could be found within Alexandria, most of Alexandria's ascetics chose not to dwell within the city itself, but instead established monastic cells in the immediate suburbs. Palladius's first acquaintance with Egyptian asceticism was a sojourn with Abba Dorotheus, a Theban hermit, whose main ascesis was to construct stone cells for the monks who populated Alexandria's suburban region. This localization of Christian sites in the suburbs conforms to a pattern common to other cities in late antiquity, as well as to the long-standing Christian tradition in Alexandria of holding Christian assemblies at the suburban cemeteries. After the legalization of Christianity, these suburban cemeteries frequently became the first retreats of Alexandrian ascetics. In time, we begin to see the gradual development of organized monastic communities just beyond these cemeteries. The popularity of the new monastic foundations grew apace so that by the early 390s, Palladius could speak of "the monasteries in the neighborhood of Alexandria with their some two thousand most noble and zealous inhabitants."[38]

Although hermits were not unknown in the suburbs immediately to the east of the city, a significant concentration of monks could be found some twenty kilometers further, near the luxurious suburb of Canopus. Toward the end of the fourth century, Abba Arsenius dwelt for three years at Canopus, but later left for the desert near Memphis to avoid the visitors who troubled him.

Monks do not seem to have been permanently established at Canopus until the patriarchate of Theophilus. As part of his antipagan campaign (which included the overthrow of Serapis's cult in Alexandria), Theophilus imported monks from Jerusalem to settle at Canopus, which had long been a popular pagan pilgrimage site. The Palestinian monks soon abandoned Canopus, and Theophilus then invited Pachomian monks to establish a community there. This new Pachomian monastery called Metanoia (or Repentance) was further bolstered by the nearby internment of the relics of two popular martyrs, Cyrus and John.[39]

To the west of Alexandria, along the narrow limestone ridge separating the Mediterranean from Lake Mareotis, a number of monasteries sprang up in the late fourth and early fifth centuries. These monasteries, which flourished just prior to the Sassanian and Arab conquests, took their names from the nearest milestone marking the distance from the city—thus, Pempton (fifth), Enaton (ninth), and Oktokaidekaton (eighteenth). In addition, there was a noteworthy monastery named for the nearby settlement and lighthouse at Taposiris Magna.[40] Of these monasteries, the most important was Enaton, which boasted several renowned abbots and miracle workers during the fourth and fifth centuries. Enaton became so large that it eventually comprised a handful of churches and monastic subcommunities all under the hegemony of the larger community. It became an early center of Monophysite opposition to Chalcedonian authority within Alexandria and, for a time, was the seat of the Coptic patriarchate.[41]

Although he is often portrayed as the friend and patron of ascetics, Athanasius made an unequivocal distinction between (in his eyes) orthodox and heretical monks. Orthodox ascetics could confirm the doctrine of the bishop in the eyes of the entire community, most clearly evidenced in the celebrated visit of Saint Anthony to the city in 338—a visit undoubtedly orchestrated by Athanasius with the intention of enlisting a revered holy man on the side of the Homoousian party. This appears to have become a regular policy of Athanasius, since under similar circumstances he also brought Abba Pambo to Alexandria from Nitria. Melitian or Arian monks had no place in Athanasius's Alexandria and could expect to receive rough treatment at the bishop's hands. A set of Alexandrian canons underscores the concern of the Alexandrian hierarchy to place careful controls upon the public activity of ascetics. Monks and nuns were forbidden to frequent martyria within the city, or any public place of amusement or relaxation. Further, any members of the clergy visiting Alexandria were enjoined to go to church every day—doubtless with the intention of monitoring their activities as much as encouraging their piety.[42]

If an ascetically minded bishop like Athanasius could recognize the potential dangers of unrestricted monastic access to the city, the issue became even more acute by the end of the fourth century. By that time, the numbers of monks had grown considerably and they showed a far greater propensity to come en masse to Alexandria and voice their demands. Much ink has been spilled over the stormy relations between Theophilus and the monks in the 390s. Yet, at the beginning of his episcopate, Theophilus seems to have been favorably disposed to the ascetic movement. Not only did he seek out famous ascetics to be his companions, he even attempted to use groups of rural monks for his purposes within the city. One enigmatic apophthegm tells us that "Theophilus the archbishop summoned some Fathers to go to Alexandria one day, to pray and to destroy the heathen temples there." By the end of the decade, however, Theophilus turned against some of his ascetic associates, including the so-called Tall Brothers and Isidore the guestmaster. Previously, he had held Isidore in such high regard that he dispatched him on sensitive diplomatic missions abroad and even pushed for his candidacy to the see of Constantinople. What went wrong? Some commentators have seen this breach as a chapter in the Origenist controversy, a conflict between the Hellenized sophistication of Alexandria and the simple piety of the Coptic countryside. The realities of the situation were not so neat, since even the monks themselves were bitterly divided over the issue of Origenism. As we have seen, there also appears to be an element of a personal grudge that sprang up between Theophilus and several of the other principals, especially with Isidore over the matter of a widow's bequest to the Alexandrian poor. That this grudge could blossom into a full-scale vendetta is not astonishing, in light of Theophilus's combative temperament.[43]

These explanations fail to satisfy entirely, especially when viewed against the earliest stages of the Anthropomorphite (later Origenist) controversy. In late 398 or early 399, Theophilus had learned that large numbers of the desert monks clung to an erroneous view of God's nature, namely, that God possessed a human form (albeit in a spiritual body), with eyes, arms, feet—hence, Anthropomorphism. This doctrine he assailed in his Paschal letter of 399, and he affirmed, as Origen had done before him, that God was incorporeal. Theophilus's letter was received with consternation and fierce opposition in the desert monasteries. Cassian, who was visiting Scetis at the time, tells us "that the majority of the fathers decreed that . . . the bishop ought to be abhorred by the entire body of the brethren as tainted with heresy of the worst kind." Not content with hurling abuse at the patriarch, "they left their monasteries and came to Alexandria; where they excited a tumult [*katestasiazon*] against the bishop, accusing him of impiety, and threatened to put him to death." Recognizing his peril, Theophilus attempted to conciliate the rioting monks, but to no avail. The monks singled out Origen as the author of Theophilus's views regarding God's incorporeal nature, and they demanded in no uncertain terms that he anathematize Origen. They shouted, "If you will not do this, expect to be treated by us as an impious person, and the enemy of God!" Theophilus gave in to their dictates and thus extricated himself from the most life-threatening episode of his entire career.[44]

Almost immediately, Theophilus came into conflict with the Tall Brothers and with Isidore. While there is no doubt that personal animosities came to play an important role in the denouement, Theophilus recognized that these more educated ascetics had admirers among the desert monks. He therefore tarred them with the brush of Origenism and sent letters to the monasteries commanding the monks to break fellowship with the revered ascetics. Socrates informs us:

> A hot dissension was stirred up among [the monks]. Such as had a cultivated mind indeed were not beguiled by this plausibility . . . but the more ignorant who greatly exceeded the others in number, inflamed by an ardent zeal without knowledge, immediately raised an outcry against their brethren. A division being thus made, both parties branded each other as impious. . . . On this account violent altercation arose, and an inextinguishable war [*stasis*] erupted between the monks.[45]

This stage of the controversy is normally glossed over quickly since the condemned monks sought protection from the bishop of Constantinople, John Chrysostom—thereby inaugurating an entirely new phase to the dispute. Locally, however, Theophilus had achieved his goals. He had so divided and weakened the desert monks that they never again posed a serious threat to his episcopal authority.

Even Theophilus's archrival, John Chrysostom, wrestled with the disruptive influences of rural ascetics who ventured into cities. While he staunchly supported monks who stayed within their monasteries and he actively provided for their needs, Chrysostom also vigorously opposed those who went about publicly in cities—to the extent that he incurred the enmity of these monks, "who called him a hard, passionate, morose, and arrogant man." It seems clear that organized bands of rural ascetics had become a problem in many of the cities of the late empire, a problem that eventually called forth a string of imperial enactments seeking to restrict the mobility of monks and nuns. These laws range from a curt edict of Theodosius in 390 to a hyperbolic rescript of Justinian in 519 which sought to expel rural monks from Rome. Typical of these expressions of imperial displeasure is the formulary of Marcian, which decreed that "the monks throughout each city and district should be subordinated to the bishop and should cleave to quiet and should be intent on only fasting and prayer and should not cause annoyance to ecclesiastical and public affairs."[46]

There can be little doubt which monks Marcian had in mind when he thundered against monastic lawlessness. Even though there is no substantive evidence to warrant the often repeated assertion that riotous monks were responsible for the destruction of the

Alexandrian Serapeum in 391 or for the brutal murder of the philosopher Hypatia in 415, Marcian still had good cause to doubt the reception of imperial commands among Egypt's ascetics. In 414/15, a band of five hundred monks from Nitria had mobbed the Prefect Orestes in the streets of Alexandria, and he nearly suffered a fatal stoning at their hands. In this incident, it even appears that the patriarch Cyril, for all his carefully honed political skills, had very little control over the monastic mob and, instead, only reacted to circumstances created by his mercurial ascetic supporters. Small wonder, then, that Marcian directed a letter in 452 to the monks in Alexandria, warning them to "keep your own selves also from unspeakable canons and contrary assemblies, lest in addition to the loss of your souls you should be subjected to legal punishment."[47]

The futility of Marcian's exhortation soon became manifest, for within three years, he sent another rescript that attempted to prohibit heretical assemblies from taking place at Alexandria's suburban estates and monasteries. This enactment serves as a backhanded acknowledgment of the crucial role played by Alexandria's monasteries in ecclesiastical politics during late antiquity, especially in the period between the outbreak of the Monophysite-Chalcedonian controversy and the Arab conquest. Throughout these centuries, the suburban monasteries served as the principal foci of resistance to imperial religious policy. This was true, not only when the monks opposed Chalcedonian appointees on the throne of Saint Mark, but even when a tacitly approved Monophysite patriarch enjoyed a respite from imperial persecution. In the 480s, Peter Mongus had to deal with the schismatic Acepheloi, who congregated in the monasteries west of the city. In the early sixth century, the moderate Monophysite patriarch, Theodosius, faced the schismatic Gaianites and Julianists, who likewise assembled in suburban monasteries. Many of these rifts within the Alexandrian Christian community were not simply the result of urban-rural tensions. Frequently, alliances were forged between the monks and the Christian populace of the city, as in 457, when "the multitude of the monks assembled . . . together with all the believing people of the city of Rhakoti [Alexandria]" and chose the monk Timothy Aelurus to be Dioscorus's successor.[48] Thirty years later, Peter Mongus was able to pull together a coalition of monks from rival monasteries as well as zealous townsmen to extirpate the last remnants of paganism from the shrines at Canopus and Menouthis.

Such ad hoc alliances between rural ascetics and the urban populace seldom lasted beyond any given crisis, thereby reflecting the ambivalence of urban opinion toward the monks of the surrounding countryside. On the one hand, urban opinion was profoundly influenced by the views of rural ascetics. Monks led the initial opposition to the Arian bishop George of Cappadocia (357–61). Not long afterward, the Arian bishop Lucius (367–78) attempted to break Homoousion resistance within the city by trying forcibly to win over famous hermits to his cause. Lucius's persecution of the desert hermits so infuriated the Alexandrian populace that, "apprehensive of a tumult in the city, he suffered the holy hermits to go back to their dens." At the same time, we also hear that many monks in Alexandria "were held in evil repute by laypeople for their foul behavior." Such animosities could result in blows, as in 414/15, when the prefect Orestes was rescued from his monastic assailants by the populace of Alexandria, who put his attackers to flight and delivered over to torture one riotous monk captured in the melee. The loyalty engendered by urban patrons (including certain imperial officials) among the rank and file of Alexandria's populace also could be elicited by the patriarch. Recognizing the depth of this feeling, an imperial representative implored a multitude of schismatic monks in 487 not to enter the city and oppose the patriarch "lest the people should be excited and a civil war should ensue." Despite ties of religion, ties of place sometimes took precedence and brought to the fore deep-seated antirural sentiments.[49]

The monks of Alexandria's suburban monasteries possessed power and influence great enough to sometimes tip the scales of conflict within the urban Christian community. Yet, by themselves, they were seldom strong enough to create long-lasting ruptures among their urban coreligionists. When joined with the civic aristocracy or with the imperial administration of the city (the other two major sources of patronage often opposed to the patriarch), the monks could lend their considerable spiritual authority and their sheer numbers to the outbreak of schism within the Alexandrian church.

### *The Contours of Schism: The Arians of Alexandria*

With these structural features in mind, it is possible to examine more closely the dynamics of factionalism within the Alexandrian Christian community. In order to understand the nature of schism better, a profitable avenue of inquiry is to explore in some detail the contours of one such conflict in its particular Alexandrian context. The course of the Arian controversy in Alexandria stands as a vivid example of the multiform factors that influenced the creation and ongoing life of a schismatic community in Alexandria.[50] Monks, imperial officials, and bouleutai all played their part in the history of this controversy. The later fame of this schism, and its empirewide importance during the fourth century, also prompt a consideration of its Alexandrian origins. Over the past two decades, the stream of scholarly studies on the Arian controversy has risen to a veritable floodtide, resulting from symposia and book-length treatments of Arius's theology (particularly his *Thalia*), his theological antecedents, and the appeal of his teaching as a message of salvation. The majority of these valuable studies treat the outbreak of Arianism within Alexandria as a purely theological phenomenon. If the Alexandrian context of the controversy is considered at all, it is treated as only one factor in the theological and philosophical climate which bred Arius's teaching.

Intellectual history, however, seldom takes place in a vacuum. Arius's teaching gained its first popularity within a socially complex urban environment. Consequently, our understanding of both this outspoken Alexandrian presbyter and his message may be sharpened further by looking closely at the social composition of his first adherents within the city. This, in turn, will serve to elucidate the associative ties that united the Christian community and the centrifugal forces threatening that unity.

Early on, both sides in this local theological dispute appealed to authorities outside Alexandria, thereby embroiling emperors and bishops in over a half century of conflict. The Alexandrian bishop, Alexander (312–28), enlisted the support of various bishops throughout Palestine and Syria. For his part, Arius gained the backing of several high-placed churchmen, including Eusebius of

Nicomedia. Henceforth, the focus of the dispute shifted away from the great Egyptian metropolis. The see of Alexandria became just one of several prizes in the broader arena of ecclesiastical politics fought over by the adherents of various factions. In time, the contentious Alexandrian presbyter became something of a cipher in the complex theologies of the episcopal opponents of Nicaea—lumped together under the derisive epithet "Ariomaniacs" by Athanasius. Some have even argued that eventually, Athanasius's Alexandria became a theological backwater, with the intransigent bishop maintaining positions decades old, out of step with the evolving Trinitarian consensus forged by the Cappadocian fathers in the second half of the fourth century.[51] Despite Athanasius's long tenure as head of the city's Homoousian community (albeit frequently in exile), and his reputation for brutality in suppressing dissent within his church, Arianism continued on as an Alexandrian phenomenon for decades. Who were these Alexandrian Arians? And how did this embattled faction change over time?

The initial focus of Arianism in Alexandria was Arius's parish church of Baucalis or Boukolou. This was a relatively minor church in a parochial organization which, by the beginning of the fourth century, included at least nine churches. The city's most important church, named for the beloved former bishop Theonas, was situated in an area largely consigned to public buildings at the western end of the Via Canopica. Indications are that the episcopal residence and its attached church, that of Saint Dionysius, were likewise located on the fringes of the city's center. As we have seen, Christian buildings on the urban periphery were common on the eve of the Peace of the Church, and it was left to later bishops (notably Athanasius and Theophilus) to fill in the center of the city with large churches. Baucalis was one of a handful of lesser churches which probably could trace their origins back to private donations in the previous two centuries.[52]

It appears as though the church of Baucalis was not in the city at all, but rather was situated in a nearby extramural suburb, on the opposite end of town from the bishop's main church. The church took its name from a larger sparsely inhabited region, just beyond the suburb and the adjacent necropolis, which was inhabited principally by shepherds and their flocks of sheep and cattle. This area, Boukolia or Boukolion (i.e., "the pasturage"), derived its name from the region's predominant economic activity.[53] This zone of pasturage should be distinguished very carefully from the intensely cultivated agricultural area of Mareotis to the city's southwest. The proclivity of Boukolia's herdsmen to violence and brigandage was well known in antiquity. Palladius tells us of one Roman matron, returning from her tour of the holy places, who ordered her boats to be tied up along the canal near Nicopolis while she went into Alexandria. Her entourage was attacked by locals who killed some, maimed others, and tossed one unfortunate bishop into the canal. Not long afterward, Cyril speaks of robbers in this area who placed nets in the canals to rob and murder travelers. And depending upon one's trust in the information provided by Greek romances and by a highly stylized passage in Cassius Dio, the inhabitants of Boukolia may have even broken out in open insurrection against Roman authority in the late second century. In light of the variegated evidence for Baucalis and its adjacent region, it seems reasonable to place the city's cattle market in this suburb, thereby envisioning its economic activity to be roughly comparable to that of early Rome's Forum Boarium.[54]

This excursus into Alexandrian topography sheds important light on the nature of religious factionalism in Alexandria. Epiphanius relates that presbyters were appointed in each of the parish churches of Alexandria to serve the needs of people dwelling in their immediate neighborhood. This structure was common enough in the larger cities of the empire, but he then goes on to explain that, in Alexandria, the parishioners were exceptionally devoted to the style of biblical exposition practiced by their respective presbyters—so much so that a rivalry sprang up between the partisans of these local priests.[55] We have seen that Alexandria had a long tradition of neighborhood pride and competition. In addition, the bishop of Alexandria (for all his authority in the Egyptian chora) had difficulty in the early fourth century asserting his will within his own city. It seems only natural then that religious factionalism in Alexandria would be shaped, at least in part, by the city's topographical divisions.

Thus, in March 339, when the Arian appointee Gregory the

Cappadocian made his violent adventus into the city accompanied by Philagrius, a veteran praefectus Aegypti, the Arian mob which attacked the church of Quirinus included herdsmen and shepherds.[56] Athanasius even tells us that they were armed with clubs—in this case probably shepherds' staves. Two decades later we find a similar topographical connection between Arianism and Alexandria's extramural regions. Before his appointment to the throne of Saint Mark, the Arian bishop George of Cappadocia had spent a portion of his career as a supply contractor (*hupodektēs tamiakōn*) in Constantinople, and had acquired thereby a measure of business acumen and a reputation for ruthlessness.[57] It is instructive to note that during his ill-fated tenure in Alexandria, George sought monopolies on papyrus manufacture and reed cutting, as well as a special tax on the extraction of niter—economic activities concentrated in Alexandria's suburbs. This reliance on the city's peripheral regions is confirmed by George's control over the city's collegia of gravediggers and coffin bearers, who seemed content with giving George a portion of their profits in exchange for the bishop's patronage.[58]

Arius's congregation at Baucalis also included large numbers of ascetically minded Alexandrians. This association between Alexandrian asceticism and early Arianism can be accounted for by several factors. The church at Baucalis appears to have been adjacent to the martyrium of Saint Mark, since all the various recensions of Mark's passion place his execution and eventual burial at a site known as Boukolou. If one discounts the disputed testimony of the *Passio* of Bishop Peter, who was said to have prayed at the tomb of Mark in Boukolou prior to his execution in 311, the earliest mention we have of the evangelist's martyrium dates from the end of the fourth century. It is probable, however, that there was some sort of commemorative shrine for the founder of the Alexandrian church at least as early as the time of Arius, if not before. Several mid- to late fourth-century canons attributed to Athanasius carefully regulate the behavior of ascetics (especially virgins) who frequented the shrines of Alexandrian martyrs. The clear inference from these detailed canons is that the most famous martyrium in the city must have attracted monastic devotees. This connection between Alexandrian asceticism and the Evangelist's martyrium continued until the time of the Sassanian and Arab conquests, when both the shrine and its neighboring monasteries were burned.[59]

Besides this link between ascetics and Saint Mark's martyrium, it is worth remembering that many of Alexandria's earliest ascetics retired to the suburban regions just east of the city. It was here that some of Alexandria's most extensive cemeteries were located, known today by the names of Chatby, Ibrahimiya, and el Hadra.[60] As we have seen, during the middle years of the fourth century, these tombs became the hermitages of numerous Alexandrian ascetics. The necropoleis in and around Boukolia continued to appeal to ascetics until the founding of Alexandria's suburban monasteries toward the end of the fourth century. Saint Anthony himself considered settling in the region of Boukolia before he withdrew to his inner mountain. Boukolia also served as a recruiting ground for monasticism, as seen especially by the conversion of a young shepherd named Macarius, who murdered one of his comrades along the shore of Lake Mareotis and then fled to the desert as a hermit.[61]

Given this context, it is not surprising that Arius, the presbyter charged with the pastoral oversight of this region, was noted for his ascetic demeanor and even a style of dress characteristic of early Egyptian monks. At the time of his excommunication, over seven hundred virgins were expelled along with him—a graphic testimony to the appeal of Arianism among Alexandrian ascetics. In addition, there is also the testimony of Bishop Alexander, who, in a letter to his namesake in Thessalonica, speaks of Arians "troubling us in the lawcourts by the pleas of disorderly women whom they have duped and also discrediting Christianity by the way in which the younger women among them immodestly frequent every public street"—precisely the same immodest ascetic behavior addressed by the Alexandrian canons. A letter of Athanasius, preserved in part by Theodoret, complains of "the impiety of the Arians, [who] block up the gates, and sit like so many demons around the tombs, in order to hinder the dead from being interred." The dating of this fragment is uncertain and may refer to George's monopoly of the funerary collegia. However, it could easily be read as an indictment of Arian ascetics, in a vein not unlike the antimonastic diatribes of a Libanius or a Rutilius Namatianus.[62]

Of course, the bonds between Alexandrian asceticism and Arianism were decisively broken by Athanasius's vigorous courting of the monks, begun as early as the 330s. The clearest expression of this alliance between Athanasius's Homoousion party and the ascetics, both in Alexandria and in the chora, was the visit of Anthony to the city in 338. Anthony was not the only monk brought to the city by Athanasius, and these high profile monastic endorsements of the embattled bishop in Alexandria suggest that his cultivation of the monks was a more multifaceted policy than is usually presented—that is, that the bishop sought to invoke monastic aid to counterbalance Melitian and Arian influence in the chora and also prepare a strategic retreat for himself during moments of imperial displeasure. In light of the makeup of the initial Arian faction in Alexandria, it seems likely that Athanasius also felt a specific need to thwart Arian sentiments among the city's ascetic communities.

However, the complexion of the Alexandrian Arian faction was also changing during the decades following the Council of Nicaea (325). Although Arius's congregation at Baucalis was the most visible center of opposition to the bishop's authority (in part, a function of the literary sources' preoccupation with Arius), it is worth noting that during the episcopate of Alexander (ca. 312–28) at least five presbyters and five deacons were excommunicated for Arianism by the bishop, and that each presbyter probably had authority over an individual church. In light of the often fractious nature of the early Alexandrian clergy, it is unlikely that these "Arians" formed a monolithic party, just as the bishop's party hardly formed a solid phalanx of support. In this context, Athanasius's allegedly brutal methods for enforcing ecclesiastical discipline and doctrinal conformity become much more comprehensible. Despite Epiphanius's enthusiasm for Athanasius, he tells us that Athanasius "kept trying accusations, threats, and admonitions, and no one paid attention."[63]

Among the Arians, there are hints that a more distinctly urban element came to the fore in the thirty some years between Nicaea and the episcopate of George of Cappadocia. Alexander's excommunication of various Alexandrian clergymen suggests that Arian doctrine had found a hearing in several of the city's parishes. In addition, several sources, including a letter of Constantine to the Alexandrians, speak of the spread of Arian sentiments via multiclass urban institutions where the populace would gather, notably the marketplaces, the theaters, and (most frequently) unspecified public assemblies. This may provide at least a partial backdrop for understanding Arius's *Thalia*, and also the well-known comment of Philostorgius on Arius's composition of popular songs designed for sailors, millers, travelers, and others. Perhaps the most telling indication of Athanasius's lack of unquestioned support among the urban populace was the use that his opponents at the Synod of Tyre made of a formal document listing complaints by the Alexandrian *demos*.[64]

During the 340s, when imperial coercion was increasingly brought to bear upon the issue of ecclesiastical factionalism in Alexandria, the urban complexion of the diffuse community labeled as "Arians" by our hostile sources continued to grow. Indeed, there is a direct correlation between official pressure and the morphology of the Arian community, as groups especially vulnerable to outside influence increasingly identified themselves as Arian. These groups tended to cluster at opposite ends of the Alexandrian social spectrum, and their shifting allegiance indicates that the primary issue at stake was patronage, not theology.

With their wealth and status at risk, large numbers of the urban aristocracy took up the Arian cause. On several occasions, the bouleutai of the city were specifically singled out in imperial directives and threatened with fines, confiscations, and imprisonment if they did not renounce Athanasius and accept the imperial nominee. For those who did comply, there were tangible benefits, the most important being the prospect of ordination as bishop and its attendant privilege of exemption from public duties.[65] By and large, it seems that the bouleutic class was eager to embrace positions that would not attract official scrutiny during an age of frequent reversals in imperial policy. No wonder Athanasius denounces so bitterly these irresolute bouleutai, whom he styles "easy-natured men" (*eukoloi*). At the same time, there is also evidence that the Alexandrian upper classes hardly constituted a unified bloc.[66] As with the *curiales* of other large cities, considerable diversity of religious allegiance persisted throughout the entire late antique period—provided that opinions dissenting from those of the emperor were not publicly expressed.

During the summer and fall of 356, in the period just prior to the installation of George of Cappadocia as Arian bishop of Alexandria, groups of Alexandrian young men took a leading role in the violence directed against the supporters of Athanasius. These youths are depicted vandalizing churches, assaulting clergy, and shouting obscenities at virgins.[67] Athanasius describes these young men as thoroughgoing pagans, stating that they cast incense on bonfires of church furniture, sang praises to pagan gods, and even waved tree branches in the church sanctuaries—perhaps an indication of Dionysiac behavior. Later in the same narrative, Athanasius relates that some of these same youths had been ordained, in short order, as Arian bishops throughout Egypt.[68]

Despite Athanasius's characterization of them as belonging to the *agoraioi* (i.e., the lower-class frequenters of the agora) who had attacked the churches, it is more plausible to believe that the young Arian bishops were not agoraioi, but rather belonged to the same class as the other Arian nominees—the Alexandrian bouleutic class. Elsewhere in the sources, these youths are simply styled *neōteroi,* and this may be an echo of upper-class youth organizations known in the early empire as the *neoi,* clubs of young men just past the age for ephebes (seventeen), which often were connected with the gymnasium. These youths elected their own officers and even maintained club treasuries. Their upper-class origins are strongly suggested by a letter of Constantius to the senate and people of Alexandria, wherein he requires the young men "to assemble together, and either to persecute Athanasius, or consider themselves as [the emperor's] enemies." Formal groups of Alexandrian youths appear to have taken an active role in political brawling as far back as the Ptolemaic period. Their importance in urban power politics was tacitly recognized by Caracalla, who assembled them and then ordered their massacre in 215. The youth of Alexandria made up an easily distinguished social group which could be threatened and cajoled by imperial directives. The upper-class elements among the youth would be logical candidates for Arian posts (provided they met the canonical age limit), while their lower-class fellows from the agoraioi could easily be mobilized to riot. By all appearances, both groups of youths had no abiding concern with theological issues but were motivated by class interests and civic pride.[69]

At the other end of the social scale, the recipients of public assistance were also susceptible to the coercive powers of imperial officials. As we have seen, one method of coercion employed time and again was simply to limit the grain dole to those who conformed to imperial dictates. In addition, there is evidence that oil and other regular alms were confiscated from Athanasius's supporters. This may, in part, reflect the government's wish to disrupt the patriarchate's elaborate network of patronage within the city. Widows and the city's destitute (*anexodoi*) suffered most under these measures. Athanasius gives the impression that despite these coercive methods, the lower orders remained faithful Homoousians. However, the veracity of his claim is difficult to determine, in light of the wide success enjoyed by the prefect Florus a century later, when rioting in the city was promptly extinguished after the prefect cut off the bread dole.[70]

Given the attractions of the Arian cause to certain sections of Alexandrian society, one can more easily understand how it was possible for Gregory the Cappadocian to have found a viable local community of coreligionists when, in 339, he entered Alexandria backed by imperial troops. Though diffuse, this Arian "community" possessed enough of a self-identity to insist on the ailing Gregory's replacement in 346 with someone who would promote its interests more vigorously.[71] These Alexandrian Arians wished to present a clear alternative to Athanasius, who had incurred both imperial and ecclesiastical ill-will through his violent methods. Consequently, the Arians found Gregory to be a liability, since his tenure as bishop was marked by violence and arson. The next Arian occupant of the throne of Saint Mark was Gregory's countryman, George. It is only with the disastrous episcopate of George of Cappadocia (357–61) that Arianism lost all appeal among the Alexandrians, because of the association of the Arian cause with this unpopular and inept imperial appointee. George instituted a brutal regime that persecuted indiscriminately pagans, Jews, and Homoousian Christians. These methods destroyed whatever bonds remained between the principal loci of Arian support in the city—suburban ascetics, Alexandrian bouleutai, and imperial officials. Almost inevitably, this led to George's death at the hands of a mob in December 361. The collapse of the Arian cause in Alexandria is clearly evidenced some fifteen years after George's murder, when the support for the Arian Lucius (himself an Alexandrian) extends only as far as the coercion bought by the prefect's spears.[72]

# Nine

# Intercommunal Conflict During Late Antiquity

> The people [*dēmos*] in general are an inflammable material, and allow very trivial pretexts to foment the flame of commotion, and not in the least degree that of Alexandria, which presumes on its numbers—chiefly an obscure and promiscuous rabble—and vaunts forth its impulses with excessive audacity. Accordingly, it is said that everyone who is so disposed may, by employing any casual circumstance as a means of excitement, inspire the city with a frenzy of sedition, and hurry the populace in whatever direction and against whomsoever he chooses.

In this way, the historian Evagrius explains the outbreak of violence leading up to the murder of Chalcedonian patriarch Proterius in 457. Evagrius's biting denunciation of the Alexandrians mimics a long-established topos of classical literature which extends from early imperial times down past the Arab conquest. Indeed, his comments parallel those of the upper-class Roman dilettante who penned the *Historia Augusta* almost two centuries earlier, asserting that the Alexandrians, "like madmen and fools, are led by the most trivial matters to become highly dangerous to the commonwealth."[1]

By employing this hackneyed description of the Alexandrians, secular and ecclesiastical historians alike side-stepped the social complexities of the great Egyptian metropolis. The use of this topos excused them from having to come up with any sort of real explanation for the turmoil that occasionally shook the city. It should be evident by now, however, that the Alexandrians were not frenzied madmen, but rather the inhabitants of a richly textured urban environment. These Alexandrians tended to organize themselves in identifiable ethno-religious communities and articulated their desires to imperial officials according to the rational protocols of a late antique language of power. Having examined the day-to-day realities of life in Alexandria, we can safely demure from the judgment of the *Expositio*'s author that "the city and its region are entirely incomprehensible."[2] Real understanding requires the patient reconstruction of an urban setting, which, even then, can elude our best efforts to "see" the city in a manner approximating that of the ancients.

If we are to avoid the shopworn categories used by the ancient commentators to interpret the city to their fellows, it is necessary to sketch out the basic contours of social life in late antique Alexandria. This is accomplished most effectively by first introducing the major players in this urban drama, and seeking to understand the internal structure and leadership of each major ethnoreligious community. Still, a continuous narrative of the city's history across the late antique period may tend to distort Alexandrian social dynamics, as it may draw the historian toward an easy reductionism.

In the pages that follow, I would like to examine three case studies of intercommunal conflict during this era. Each episode has been chosen for its ability to serve as a flashpoint that illuminates urban social relations. Although these episodes span a period of not quite a century and a half, they embrace a pivotal epoch in the struggle for cultural hegemony among the city's ethnoreligious communities. The events chosen are not, in themselves, the most famous incidents of Alexandrian history during this period, like the conflict over the Serapeum in 391 or the rioting that followed the deposition of the patriarch Dioscorus in 451. Yet, they are potentially more revealing of the city's intercommunal history. Attention to matters of local topography and to the wider context of imperial politics will facilitate our understanding of each episode, and will allow us to see the violence of each incident on its own merits and not according to some innate predisposition of the Alexandrians.

### *The Alexandrian Riots of 356 and George of Cappadocia*

In late June of 346, Gregory of Cappadocia died in Alexandria after a long illness.[3] As the imperial appointee to the patriarchate of Alexandria, Gregory had persecuted the followers of Bishop Athanasius and had generously rewarded his fellow Arians within the city during the six years of his tenure on the throne of Saint Mark. Gregory was not a successful promoter of the Arian cause in Alexandria. Indeed, the growth and viability of the Arian community was largely the work of Gregory's countryman, Philagrius, who, as a veteran praefectus Aegypti, effectively employed all the powers of patronage and coercion in the hands of the imperial administration.[4]

By mid-October of 346, Athanasius returned from exile to a thunderous welcome at Alexandria. Gregory Nazianzus tells us that Athanasius's restoration was greeted with "universal cheers, the pouring forth of unguents, nightlong festivities, the whole city gleaming with light, and both public and private feasting." This return ushered in the so-called Golden Decade of Athanasius's episcopate, during which he vigorously lobbied for support among eastern bishops, launched the missionary initiative to the southern kingdom of Axum, and undertook a major program of church building in Alexandria.[5]

However, after the assassination of Athanasius's imperial patron Constans in 350, the Arian emperor Constantius felt he had a free hand to step up pressure on the recalcitrant Alexandrians. Imperial notarii presented them with a series of admonitions to abandon Athanasius and embrace the theology of the imperial court. One notarius, Diogenes, spent four months in the latter part of 355 trying to effect Athanasius's removal. All in vain, for we are told by the *Historia Acephela* that "since the people and the judges strongly resisted Diogenes, [he] returned [to Constantinople] without success." Constantius, though, was determined to impose his will on the city. In early January of 356, a military dux named Syrianus and yet another notarius, Hilary, arrived in Alexandria accompanied by troops gathered from Egypt and Libya. An uneasy standoff ensued until the night of February 8. Encouraged by Arian elements within the city, Syrianus and his troops made an armed attack on the church of Saint Theonas during a night vigil. Athanasius had been officiating at the service, and only the intervention of his close attendants secured his narrow escape from the subsequent violence. Within a year, Alexandria again had an imperial appointee as bishop, George of Cappadocia, an Arian "who ruled by force rather than by priestly moderation."[6]

This chapter in the tumultuous history of Arian-Homoousian conflict in Alexandria typifies a scenario played out repeatedly within the city's Christian community during the middle decades of the fourth century. Yet, on closer examination, the ongoing violence of 356 and George's subsequent episcopate manifested much broader intercommunal tensions within late antique Alexandria. George's turbulent episcopate marked a milestone in the social and religious history of Alexandria. His unexpected campaign against the city's pagan cults galvanized the diffuse pagans of Alexandria into a recognizable community that defended its religious patrimony with bloodshed. His inept renewal of violent persecution against Athanasius's followers doomed the Arian cause in Alexandria and laid the foundations for the unswerving popular support enjoyed by the Alexandrian patriarchate over the next three centuries in its contests with imperial authority.[7]

Shortly after the followers of Athanasius were expelled from the churches in June 356, a large crowd of pagans looted the newly renovated Great Church in the Caesarion. The pillaging of this church was accompanied by deliberate acts of desecration as well as various sorts of pagan rituals. Although these events are described in great detail by Athanasius (our main source), they are generally ignored in modern accounts of this period, perhaps because modern commentators tend to exhibit a nearly exclusive preoccupation with ecclesiastical matters during Athanasius's patriarchate.[8] Moreover, the year-long interlude between Athanasius's exile and the entry of the Arian bishop, George of Cappadocia, in February 357 is often glossed over by modern scholars, some even denying the existence of this gap in episcopal tenancy.[9] Far from being an isolated incident, the part played by the city's pagans in Alexandrian civic strife only increased during the course of George's episcopate. These tensions culminated in the murder of the Cappadocian bishop and two imperial officials in November 361. The scale of these acts of public violence necessitates a careful assessment of these events in order to evaluate the light they shed on the history of intercommunal relations in Alexandria.

After the defeat of the usurper Magnentius at Mursa in September 351 (and his later suicide in 353), Constantius directed his energies toward eradicating any remaining pockets of dissent which might threaten the unity of his empire. In particular, pagans and Homoousians were singled out and incurred the wrath of the Arian emperor. Against the former, Constantius enacted a series of laws during 353–56 which banned nocturnal sacrifices, closed and demolished a number of temples, and forbade sacrifice. During his sojourn in Rome in 357, the emperor also ordered the removal of the altar of Victory from the Senate house, the first salvo in a decades-long struggle over this important symbol of traditional Roman religion. Against the adherents of Nicaea, Constantius convoked councils at Arles (353) and Milan (355) which resulted in the expulsion of Hilary of Poitiers and Liberius of Rome from their episcopal sees. These two influential churchmen went into exile largely because of their vocal support for the bishop whom Constantius regarded as the villain behind the church's ongoing schism—Athanasius. Constantius's antipathy for the Alexandrian patriarch was also fueled by serious allegations that Athanasius had "subverted all Egypt and Libya" during the revolt of Magnentius and Decentius. Such accusations were apparently more than the malicious whisperings of Constantius's courtiers. Envoys sent by Magnentius to negotiate with Constantius had passed through Alexandria on their way to the emperor.[10]

Four months after the ouster of Athanasius, a *comes* named Heraclius accompanied the new prefect, Cataphronius, when he arrived in Alexandria on 10 June 356. On hand to assist them was an Arian katholikos named Faustinus. These administrators, handpicked by Constantius, immediately instituted a new regime in Alexandria. Unlike their predecessor Syrianus who had directed his attention solely at the city's Christians—on one occasion even setting three thousand soldiers upon a large body of Christians holding prayer services in the cemeteries—the new administrators cast their net much more widely. The pagans of the city were threatened with the destruction of their cult images if they failed to support the imperial nominee succeeding the exiled patriarch. De facto leaders within the loosely structured pagan community (pagan magistrates and ordinary keepers of temples) were especially singled out and forced to swear loyalty to whatever nominee the emperor might send. In this same context, Athanasius informs us that certain of the city's collegia were also coerced into professing loyalty, perhaps indicating their character as cult associations or, less explicitly, as craft associations dedicated to the service of their patron god.[11]

Four days after the arrival of the new imperial administrators, a pagan crowd attacked the followers of Athanasius who were worshiping in the Great Church. Not surprisingly, Athanasius ascribes the ensuing riot to the collusion, if not the active encouragement, of the prefect, the *comes*, and the katholikos. However, his account of this riot suggests that, even if the rioters began their violent demonstration at the prompting of the officials, the riot soon took a course that could not have been orchestrated beforehand. The violence began in the Agora when groups of young pagans (styled *hoi agoraioi* by Athanasius) attacked the Great Church at the Caesarion, the most prominent church in the vicinity.[12] A portion of this former precinct of the imperial cult had been handed over to the church by Constantius during the episcopate of the Arian patriarch Gregory (339–46). However, only after Athanasius's return in 346 was it in general use as a church. The much exiled patriarch even risked imperial displeasure by conducting services there before it could be officially consecrated, attesting the growing needs of the Christian community.[13] The memory of the church's former status as one of the city's preeminent pagan sanctuaries was fresh in the minds of Alexandria's pagans, and it evidently rankled to see this sacred precinct employed in the worship of a condemned Galilean criminal. It was a natural target of their indignation.

After violently disrupting a prayer service, the crowd of young pagans seized the church's furniture and curtains, and used them to fuel a great bonfire in the small forum adjoining the sanctuary. This act of destruction had clear religious overtones, since the pagans then sprinkled incense on the blaze and sang praises to their gods. In addition, they seized the heifer that drew water in the gardens of the precinct, with the intention of sacrificing it, and they relented only upon the discovery that it was female. This episode helps to identify some of the religious leanings of the crowd, as the sacrifice of a sacred bull was clearly associated with the worship of the city's great tutelary deity, Serapis. Another group entered the church shouting religious slogans and waving branches of trees, reminiscent of the worship of Dionysus, the one Hellenic god most closely associated with cults of Serapis and Osiris. A coterie of pagan women, whom Athanasius describes as maenads, also took part in these religious demonstrations. Allowing for some measure of hyperbole on the part of the patriarch, this suggests that the popularity of Dionysus continued beyond the Ptolemaic period, when he appeared as the divine patron of the great religious procession of Ptolemy Philadelphus. Well into the Roman era, Dionysus and Dionysiac imagery frequently appear in tomb decoration; and in the necropolis at al-Anfushi on Pharos, these motifs stand side by side with images culled from the worship of Osiris/Serapis. It comes as no surprise, then, to find devotees of Dionysus and Serapis involved in this popular outbreak of religious violence.[14]

Why did this riot break out when it did—only four days after the arrival of the new administrators—and why did the violence assume such a religious complexion? Two complementary explanations may be offered. Despite the installation of a new prefect and military *comes*, the new administrators were not accompanied by an episcopal replacement for Athanasius—even though he had been ousted from public leadership for over four months. Their only task was to ensure the loyalty of the city's civil leadership for the soon expected Arian appointee. Once these oaths of loyalty were extracted, however, there was a considerable lapse of time before the new Arian patriarch appeared in the city. This gap in ecclesiastical leadership had the effect of creating a vacuum in Alexandria's precariously balanced intercommunal relations.[15] With no strong hand to guide the Christian community, the city's pagans gave free reign to their animosity toward the growing Christian community. By resorting to mass violence, the pagans were not introducing some new element into Alexandrian power politics. After Athanasius's expulsion in 339, pagans joined with Arians in violent demonstrations centered on the churches of Quirinus and Dionysius. Alexandrian pagans, from upper-class bouleutai to paupers in the marketplace, had received tangible benefits from supporting the Arian party under Gregory and Philagrius.[16] Like the riots of 339, this was yet another opportunity for the city's pagans to show their allegiance to their imperial patron and, simultaneously, to attack with impunity their principal rivals within Alexandria.

At the same time, it would not have taken a very discerning pagan to realize that there had been a fundamental shift in Constantius's religious policy over the past five years. Ever since the defeat of Magnentius, the tide of imperial legislation and pronouncements was increasingly antipagan. Not only were new laws enacted against pagan practices, but with the removal of an armed pagan party in the West, Constantius undoubtedly felt as though he had a freer hand to enforce previous legislation. Imperial representatives in Alexandria reflected this shift of policy. While Syrianus had employed armed violence solely against Athanasius's followers and had openly rewarded upper-class Alexandrians with bishoprics, the new administration installed in early June 356 offered only threats to the city's pagans. The pagans had every reason to fear the imposition of a new bishop.

Thus, the rioting at the Caesarion may have taken a form familiar to students of early modern history, that of the "church and king riot," that is, a violent demonstration in support of traditional political and religious usages that are perceived as being threatened. Far from revolutionary, these riots are often carried out in the name of a traditional political authority and with the tacit backing of local administrators. The pagan violence at the Caesarion fits this paradigm exactly, and we even hear of rioting pagans chanting out slogans like, "Constantius has become a Hellene!" and "the Arians recognize our deeds!" while they ransacked the newly dedicated church. This aspect of the violence becomes all the more comprehensible when we recall that the Caesarion had been the focus of ruler cult in the city for nearly four centuries. Clearly, the pagans are reacting against the desecration of their revered shrine and the overturning of traditional notions of divine rulership. Moreover, they likely regarded their Christian emperor with suspicion, since he had not only adjured the role of god-king, but he had now sent out representatives who threatened other ancestral cults that had long maintained the divine order. Alexandrian pagans were widely recognized for their piety to the gods. As the author of the *Expositio* reminds us: "Nowhere, in fact, are the mysteries of the gods celebrated as they have been here—from ancient times up till the present day." Given the intensity of this religious devotion, it is no wonder that the now threatened pagans seized upon the opportunity afforded them by the prefect to restate forcefully their support for traditional usages.[17]

In this atmosphere of heightened intercommunal tension, Constantius's episcopal nominee, George of Cappadocia, entered the city on 30 Mechir (24 February) 357 and took up his post with the backing of imperial troops. George, one of the most intriguing characters in late Roman politics, had begun his career as a contractor of military supplies in Constantinople and, by the 340s, enjoyed a comfortable living in Cappadocia. While there, George lent volumes from his library to the future emperor, Julian, who described his collection as "very large and complete." Unlike his Arian predecessor, Gregory, all the sources agree that George possessed a forceful personality and was a keen opportunist. And although Athanasius might call him an idolater who "exhibited an executioner's temperament," George's imperial patron Constantius praised him in a letter to the Alexandrians as "the most perfect of beings as a guide for your conduct, both in word and deed."[18]

Owing his appointment to Constantius and the Arian bishops surrounding the emperor, George immediately sought to implement the policies of his imperial patron. Like his administrative predecessors who initiated Constantius's new regime in the city and had been overseeing operations against the Homoousians, George directed his energies toward breaking all hints of local opposition—whether Christian or pagan. According to the hostile testimony provided by Athanasius, George instituted a fierce persecution of the followers of the ousted patriarch. Clergy and ascetics were imprisoned, and the grain dole was withheld from the lower-class dependents of the former bishop. Wealthy supporters of Athanasius not only had their property confiscated but, in some cases, even their houses were destroyed—a particularly ruthless method of quelling dissent, as seen in recent years during the attempted suppression of the Intifada in the Palestinian Occupied Territories. Worse followed. In May 357, the soldiers of the dux came upon a band of Athanasius's followers who were praying in one of the city's extramural cemeteries. Those who were unable to escape were caught and beaten severely, so much so that many of them died. The survivors were banished to the Great Oasis.[19]

In many respects, the brutality shown by George to the followers of Athanasius simply followed the policy already put into effect by the prefect and his recently installed administration. Yet, George's antipagan campaign also marked a departure in the official coercion of religious dissent in Alexandria. This carefully orchestrated campaign highlights for us the centers of pagan strength in the city. And it was this new antipagan policy, implemented with enthusiasm by George the Cappadocian, which brought about his eventual downfall.

The main targets of George's antipagan campaign were the temples of Alexandria's civic cults. With the support of the garrison, he attempted to prohibit pagan sacrifices and despoil the temples of their votive offerings and decorations. To sap further the financial resources of the city's pagan cults, George suggested to the emperor that the temples should no longer be exempt from taxation. In this, he specifically mentioned the long-standing civic cults that had enjoyed immunity since the time of Alexander.[20] George also went out of his way to insult the temple of Tyche, at one point asking the crowd, "How long shall this sepulcher be permitted to stand?"[21] Against Serapis, the city's great divine protector, George incited a military strategos/dux to bring in troops and sack the precinct of the Serapeum. The strategos, Artemius, was a virulent antipagan and, perhaps more important, he was a trusted "friend and companion" of Constantius, previously commissioned to bring back the relics of Andrew and Luke to Constantinople. Artemius's attack on the Serapeum provoked a violent reaction from the devotees of the god, resulting in clashes between the garrison and the populace.[22] Also during George's tenure, an imperial mint official named Draconitus tore down an altar, perhaps dedicated to Juno Moneta. Significantly, the mint was located within the precinct of the Caesarion, and this act of sanctioned destruction may have been designed to send a forceful message to the same pagans who had rioted there before George's arrival (figure 23).

Ammianus Marcellinus tells us that an associate of Draconitus named Diodorus, who was a military *comes*, had been overseeing the construction of a church. While he was engaged in this project, Diodorus had arbitrarily cut off the curls of some boys, thinking that the long curls "were an aspect of the worship of the gods."[23] Rows of curls had long been associated with devotion to Serapis, suggesting that this act of antipagan zeal was yet another facet of the campaign against Alexandria's most popular civic cults.

There is, however, another equally plausible interpretation of Diodorus's actions. It may be that the unspecified god mentioned by Ammianus was, in fact, Yahweh. In this case, the boys would have been Jewish youths who had left their side locks (or *pe'ot*) unshorn as a token of respect to the God of their fathers. With both pagans and non-Arian Christians under attack in Alexandria, there is no reason to believe that the city's Jews were excluded from imperial religious coercion. Although Jews had joined with Arians in the rioting of 339, and reappear in the Arian sponsored violence of 373, they are conspicuously absent in the conflicts surrounding the episcopate of George. This Jewish quiescence in Alexandria would reflect their tenuous status in the mid-350s. In the midst of Constantius's struggles with Magnentius, a short-lived Jewish sedition had broken out in Palestine under the leadership of a certain Patricius. This revolt was duly crushed by Gallus in 352. In the aftermath, we find an imperial enactment directed against both the

Fig. 23. Constantius II (337–61). Bronze centenionalis. The reverse depicts the emperor holding the standard with the insignia of Christ (the *labarum*). Reverse inscription: FEL.TEMP.REPARATIO (the restoration of happy times). Minted in Alexandria. Dumbarton Oaks, inv. 48.17.628.

(Courtesy of © 1994 Dumbarton Oaks, Trustees of Harvard University, Washington, D.C.)

"sacrilegious gatherings" (*sacrilegis coetibus*) of the Jews and any Christian who apostatized by joining them. In addition, various taxes were levied against the Jews during Constantius's administration, later rescinded by Julian. Officially sanctioned acts of anti-Jewish violence in Alexandria would not have been out of keeping with this wider imperial context, especially during a period when Alexandria was governed by an administration so closely attuned to the imperial will.[24]

Another avenue for understanding the turmoil of this period is the close connection between religious factionalism and urban topography in late antique Alexandria. All of George's principal enemies had their strongest support in the center of the city. The civic cults that George assailed were all located (with the exception of the Serapeum) in and around the Agora or Mesonpedion. Likewise, the city's most important churches were situated near the Via Canopica, the broad colonnaded boulevard that bisected the city; and some of Athanasius's most ardent supporters could be found among the sailors and dockworkers of the city's twin harbors.[25] In addition, from the little that we know of the Jewish community in the fourth century, it appears that Jewish habitation was clustered near the Eastern (or Great) Harbor.

By contrast, Arianism had for decades found its strongest support in Alexandria's extramural regions. We have seen how Arius's parish church was located in a suburban district, and how ascetics and shepherds numbered among his early followers. Indeed, Gregory and Philagrius had recruited a mob of shepherds to attack

Athanasius's supporters in 339. This topographical connection was not lost on George. As already noted, prior to his ecclesiastical career, George had honed his business skills as a supply contractor in Constantinople. George apparently understood that, because of Alexandria's topographical differentiation, the "business climate" was not favorable in a region dominated by his urban opponents, who were largely concerned with economic activities like maritime trade and workshop manufacture. Consequently, George spent his energies gaining monopolies on economic activities located far beyond the walls of the city, such as niter mining, papyrus production, and reed cutting. This reliance on the city's peripheral regions is confirmed by George's control over the city's collegia of gravediggers and coffinbearers, "keeping them in his own hands, not for humanity, but for profit."[26] One suspects that such a shrewd businessman also took advantage of the fact that gravediggers were granted immunity from taxation by Constantius.[27] In addition, not only was George able to turn a profit on these concerns and set himself up as patron of the suburban inhabitants, but he was also able to keep a close eye on the city's extramural districts—regions where dissent tended to flourish in late Roman cities.

Having antagonized the city's two most influential communal groups (and perhaps also the Jews), George came to rely increasingly on military force to maintain his position. Yet even the prefect's guards were unable to secure George in his see. In late August 358, the plebs attacked him in the church of Saint Dionysius and he barely escaped with his life. By early October, he realized how untenable his position had become and he left the city, "being driven away by the multitude." The Arian patriarch spent the next three years taking an active role in the synods and councils that occupied the imperial church. As frequently happens, a newly dominant ideology soon shows fissures within what was once a solid phalanx of opposition. So too, ascendant Arianism in the 350s evolved into several competing theologies, all of which were opposed to the Council of Nicaea. George, who was very much involved in these debates, tended to follow the lead of Acacius of Caesarea. George's brutal conduct in Alexandria, however, came to haunt him even in Arian circles, as he had to defend himself in 359 at the Council of Arminium against accusations of "plundering and violence"—an echo of similar allegations brought against Athanasius at the Synod of Tyre in 339.[28]

Meanwhile in Alexandria, the prize of control of the churches passed back and forth between the two main parties. Although Athanasius remained securely in hiding, his partisans took possession of the churches nine days after George's departure. The churches remained in their hands for little more than two months until late December 358, when the dux Sebastianus, reinforced with new troops from Egypt, expelled the Athanasians, and restored the churches to George's followers.[29]

In June of the following year, the infamous notarius, Paul (nicknamed "the Chain"), arrived from court with an edict renewing persecution against George's opponents. Paul conducted his investigations under a mandate from Constantius to root out treasonous activity throughout Egypt. Paul was dispatched to the region after Constantius had received stolen petitions directed to an oracle of Bes located at the hallowed shrine of Abydos. Petitions to oracles (especially when made by persons of rank) were deemed treasonous, and, as a consequence, numerous high-ranking pagans were dragged before the notarius's tribunal, both at Alexandria and at Scythopolis in Palestine. Parnasius, a pagan who had been praefectus Aegypti at the time of George's expulsion from Alexandria, was tried and exiled. Andronicus, a town councillor from Hermopolis and a former student of Themistius, was likewise hailed before Paul. An aged Alexandrian philosopher named Demetrius was placed on the rack, but confessed only to making sacrifices at the shrine, and denied having ever consulted the oracle. While Ammianus implies that numerous persons were tried, tortured, and convicted, the harvest from Paul's inquisition was meager. Parnasius is the only named individual who was not eventually acquitted.[30]

However, this hardened imperial policy set the stage in Alexandria for ongoing persecutions directed by Faustinus, the new prefect. Faustinus was an experienced hand in the violent coercion of Alexandrians—it was he who stirred up *hoi agoraioi* in June 356 prior to the assault on the Caesarion. He was now assisted by the dux, Artemius, who eventually became the principal agent of

George's policies during the period of the Cappadocian's absence. The sources depict Artemius ruthlessly harrassing Athanasius's followers as well as continuing a vigorous campaign against pagan cults within the city.[31]

Artemius was seen by the Alexandrians as the mere instrument of George (and, by extension, also of Constantius). All the more reason, then, that George "was regarded with greater aversion than before" when he returned to the city accompanied by imperial troops on 26 November 361. He immediately "commenced a cruel persecution against the pagans." As a consequence, the pagans "had more cause to hate him than any other body of men, especially on account of the insults he offered their images and temples; and having, moreover, prohibited them from sacrificing, or performing the ancestral rites." George felt so confident in his newly restored position that he ignored long-standing Alexandrian protocol, insulted the city magistrates, exiled noted pagans, and imperiously gave orders to both civil and military officials.[32]

To George's misfortune, events were taking shape in the wider world which soon were to alter radically his status in the city. At a posting station in western Cilicia, Constantius contracted a fever and died on 3 November—three weeks before George had even returned to Alexandria. The emperor had been moving his forces west to do battle with his second-cousin Julian, who had been elevated to the purple by his troops the previous year. News of Constantius's death finally reached Alexandria at the very end of November. When the new prefect Gerontius announced to the assembled magistrates and people the transfer of imperial power, a crowd quickly formed and "attacked George with shouts and reproaches as if they would kill him at once." The authorities were able to extricate him from the mob, and he was placed in prison, doubtless to await his extradition to Constantinople for trial.[33]

Although it is clear that George had alienated virtually the entire population of the city, rendering himself "exceedingly obnoxious to all classes," it appears that the driving force behind the riot came from elements within the pagan community.[34] Other antipagan officials in Constantius's local administration were likewise put under detention. These included Draconitus, the director of the imperial mint who had overturned an altar in the sacred precinct of the Caesarion, and Diodorus, the *comes* who had shorn the locks of the Alexandrian boys. Although George's principal military supporter, Artemius, remained unmolested in his post as dux/strategos, he was unable to render any aid to the Arian bishop. Within a year, Artemius himself was recalled by Julian and was subsequently executed in the emperor's presence at Antioch.[35]

Early one morning, less than a month after his imprisonment, George and his companions learned that the walls of their prison could not guarantee their safety. A mob broke into the prison on 24 December, murdered them, and then dragged their bodies through the streets of the city with ropes tied to their feet. Their mutilated bodies were then placed on camels and paraded the length of Alexandria until, having reached the shore, their bodies were burned and the ashes cast into the sea. Their cremation was carried out to prevent the veneration of their relics as martyrs to the faith (such as happened to the bones of Artemius after they were transferred to Constantinople). Moreover, in a land where the careful preservation of corpses had been raised to the level of a highly developed science, the burning of their bodies served as a special insult with unmistakably religious overtones. As we have noted earlier, the entire process (execution or flogging, ceremonial parade and/or dragging of body, cremation) had a long tradition in Alexandria and constituted a carefully structured ritual of civic purgation. Julian reacted to this outburst of mob violence by sending a sharply worded letter to the Alexandrians. He deplored their extralegal use of violence and called upon the law-sanctioning authority of Serapis, while at the same time denouncing George, "the enemy of the gods."[36]

Significantly, the pagan emperor took no punitive measures against the Alexandrians. He simply instructed the new prefect, Ecdicius, to send him George's huge library, which the book-loving emperor had coveted for many years.[37] Several of the Christian historians go out of their way to quash the rumor that Athanasius's followers were responsible for the murders. Although the sources do not state explicitly that the mob of George's murderers was made up primarily of pagans, the wording of Julian's letter, in conjunction with the pagan violence directed at George at the time of his arrest, allows us to ascribe with a measure of certainty the Cappadocian bishop's death to Alexandria's pagans. At the same time, it should be said that both the Athanasians and the city's Jewish community had ample reason to rejoice at George's death.

The ultimate failure of George's episcopate demonstrates that administrators sent out from Constantinople to the great Egyptian port had squandered their effectiveness by attempting to conduct with equal vigor the emperor's antipagan and anti-Homoousian policies. In the end, neither Alexandrian group was sufficiently weakened to ensure long-term conformity to Constantius's wishes. Since the emperor brought about the alienation of both groups, it proved impossible to co-opt one party in the city and tip the scales against the other in favor of imperial policy. In addition, Constantius's enmity ensured that the Jewish community sat on the sidelines during this tumultuous struggle for hegemony within the city.

Even though he lacked the crucial backing of the Alexandrian Christian community, George was the first Christian leader to wage a concerted campaign against paganism in the city. George proved to be an extraordinarily potent antagonist since he possessed the active support of the emperor in the form of imperial edicts and the troops to enforce them. In the eyes of his contemporaries, George was even regarded as the director of imperial policy in Alexandria, denouncing various Alexandrians to the emperor. As Ammianus colorfully puts it, "George poured into the ready ears of Constantius charges against many, alleging that they were rebellious against his authority; and forgetful of his calling, which counseled only justice and mildness, he descended to the informer's deadly practices." Since he had "exasperated Constantius against [the Alexandrians]," in the words of Julian, Constantius gave George a free hand in Alexandria, so much so that military authorities like Artemius and Sebastianus were placed under his control. Once his imperial patron was dead, it was inevitable that George's authority in the city collapsed and he became easy prey for the embittered crowd.[38]

Athanasius's supporters once again seized the churches and expelled the Arians. However, the bishop himself remained in hiding among the ascetic communities for another month or so, until an edict from Julian restored him to his see. Then, in late January or early

February 362, Athanasius entered Alexandria in triumph. Although he found it politic to withdraw discreetly eight months later owing to Julian's hostility, his self-imposed exile was to last only a short while until the death of the pagan emperor. Within Alexandria, Athanasius's place was secure. George's disastrous episcopate spelled an end to the Arian community of Alexandria. When an Arian bishop, Lucius, was installed with military force a decade later, he found no viable group of Arians to welcome him. Mindful of George's example, Lucius never strayed far from the garrison troops.[39]

On their part, activist elements within the pagan community realized that imperial patronage could also work in their favor, especially once a coreligionist had gained the throne. In his letters to the Alexandrians, Julian addressed the city's pagans as a recognizable community—perhaps ascribing to them more communal consciousness than was warranted at the time. Nonetheless, the gap in ecclesiastical leadership in Alexandria, followed by George's antipagan persecution, had the effect of galvanizing the city's pagans into a distinct community that could offer stiff resistance to external threats. The city's pagans demonstrated that they were still an influential factor in the dynamics of Alexandrian power politics. George's episcopate, however, presaged the future course of intercommunal relations in the late antique city. It remained to be seen whether the balance of power would shift in favor of the city's Christians if the throne of Saint Mark was occupied by a virulent antipagan who enjoyed both the unquestioned support of his urban congregation as well as the all-important patronage of a distant, yet potent, imperial power.

### *Cyril and His Opponents, 412–415*

Although some of his contemporaries branded Theophilus as "reckless" and a "hothead," his tenure as bishop of Alexandria (385–412) was a time of relative peace for the city itself.[40] For those outside of Alexandria, notably the Tall Brothers and John Chrysostom, Theophilus's exercise of power unleashed a torrent of unremitting troubles. Theophilus's vindictiveness in dealing with the Origenist monks and with the embattled bishop of Constantinople is well known. And yet, aside from the uproar accompanying the destruction of the Serapeum in 391 and a brief violent incursion of rioting "Anthropomorphite" monks in early 399, Theophilus's episcopate brought to Alexandria a level of public tranquillity unknown during much of the fourth century. The bishop's innumerable building projects must have made him popular with the city's laboring classes. Indeed, it could be argued that domestic peace and prosperity were essential components of the patriarch's overall policy. It was vital for Theophilus to have a secure base of support in his home see, since most of his episcopate was occupied by fierce duels with powerful opponents on an imperial stage. By the time of Theophilus's death on 15 October 412, the Serapeum disturbances were a memory more than twenty years old.

Within a few short years of Theophilus's death, the peace of Alexandria was broken by a series of violent incidents. Rioting attended the election of Theophilus's successor to the episcopal throne. Cyril, Theophilus's nephew and longtime protégé, came to episcopal office amid popular tumult and an open conflict with the dux of the imperial forces in Egypt. Shortly after his election, Cyril deposed the local bishop of the Novatians (a highly respected rigorist Christian sect), shut their churches, and appropriated their church plate. Within a year or two, conflict between the Jewish and Christian communities came to a tragic climax, resulting in intercommunal street brawling, the forcible confiscation of synagogues, and the expulsion of the Jewish community. Soon after, the imperial prefect was assaulted by a band of desert monks, and he responded by torturing to death one of the fractious ascetics. Gangs of partisans disrupted public meetings and courts of law. This spiral of violence culminated in March 415 with the brutal murder of the philosopher Hypatia.[41]

How does one explain this sudden breakdown in the equilibrium of Alexandria's social and political life? The most common procedure is to pin the blame on the newly elevated patriarch, Cyril. Strangely enough, his culpability has often been asserted by two, seemingly contradictory, lines of argument. On the one hand, Cyril can be seen as a ruthless politician who vigorously sought to exterminate every source of authority but his own within the city. On the other hand, the violence that characterized the opening years of his episcopate may be interpreted as the result of the ineptness of a young bishop who was unsure of his status and the workings of urban politics. As we shall see, both lines of reasoning have elements that commend themselves. And yet, both fall short of providing the necessary context for understanding the violence of the period 412–15.

A brief notice in the *Historia Ecclesiastica* of Socrates Scholasticus describes the events surrounding Cyril's election:

> Shortly afterwards, Theophilus, bishop of Alexandria, having fallen into a lethargic state, died on the 15th of October, in the ninth consulate of Honorius, and the fifth of Theodosius (412). A great contest immediately arose about the appointment of a successor, some seeking to place Timothy the archdeacon in the episcopal chair, and others desiring Cyril, who was a nephew of Theophilus. A tumult [*staseōs*] having arisen on this account among the people, Abundantius, the commander of the troops in Egypt [*ho tou stratiōtikou tagmatos hēgemōn*], took sides with Timothy. Whereupon on the third day after the death of Theophilus, Cyril came into possession of the episcopate, with greater power than Theophilus had ever exercised. For from that time the bishopric of Alexandria went beyond the limits of sacerdotal functions, and assumed the administration of secular matters.[42]

Although it is difficult to imagine Theophilus ever having "fallen into a lethargic state," it may be that the sudden onset of illness caught the combative patriarch unawares, before he could make clear provision for his succession. His death exposed a longstanding tension in the procedure for choosing an Alexandrian patriarch. Two factions aligned themselves according to their respective answers to the perennial question, What is the most important qualification in the selection of a patriarch? Some, no doubt appealing to tradition, claimed that high ecclesiastical rank was of prime importance. Therefore, they supported Timothy the archdeacon. Others aligned themselves on the basis of what can only be described as a dynastic principle, that is, the notion that a patriarch carefully groomed an eventual successor who was recognized as having a special unction of grace upon him and who may even be related to the patriarch by ties of blood. At the time of Theophilus's death, Cyril only ranked as a reader, the bottom rung on the ladder of clerical office, but it is clear that Theophilus had long been cultivating him for greater things. As a consequence, "a great contest arose" over the succession, one that turned violent and drew into it the dux of the imperial garrison. It should be noted, however, that unlike disputed episcopal elections in many of the other great cities of the empire, there appears to have been not even a hint of doctrinal controversy attached to the Alexandrian conflict. Despite the influence brought to bear by the dux (armed or peaceful—we are not told), Cyril was elevated to the throne of Saint Mark three days after the death of his uncle.[43]

The *History of the Patriarchs* contains a tantalizing echo of the circumstances of Cyril's election. While the accounts of other patriarchal elections usually speak of the candidate being "appointed," "enthroned," or "seated" by others, Cyril's election is described in unique terms: "When the patriarch Theophilus died, the Father Cyril took his seat upon the apostolic throne."[44] One should not go so far as to envision a process analogous to Jacques David's painting of Napoleon crowning himself and Josephine while prelates meekly stand by. After all, Cyril's elevation was accompanied by the requisite number of bishops praying a consecration blessing over him. Moreover, the author of the *History of the Patriarchs* may have projected back to the ceremony of consecration the self-confidence displayed by Cyril at the height of his power. Nonetheless, the author's formula bespeaks a new bishop who did not approach his office timidly. His actions were soon to underscore this determination.

Socrates informs us that, after his enthronement, Cyril "immediately [*eutheōs*] went and shut up the churches of the Novatians at Alexandria, took possession of all their consecrated vessels and ornaments; and then stripped their bishop Theopemptus of all that he had."[45] Why should the new patriarch take such drastic action against a respected rigorist sect that had weathered persecutions along with the orthodox from the hands of pagans and Arians alike? At this time, Novatianists in Constantinople were on cordial terms with their local bishop. Was the long-standing enmity between Theophilus and the bishops of the New Rome inherited by Cyril, so much so that he felt compelled to take a hard line against anyone favored by the bishop of Constantinople? There is nothing to indicate that Cyril regarded the Novatianists as some sort of Constantinopolitan fifth column within his own diocese.

Instead, his enmity toward the Novatianists more likely sprang from his recent contested election. Despite having their own bishop, the Novatianists may have agitated in favor of Cyril's rival for the throne, the archdeacon Timothy. Like the Arians in the 370s, the Novatianists may have taken sides in the internal quarrels of the Alexandrian church. Cyril was simply settling a score. The Novatianists made an easy target, since a series of imperial laws in 410 placed legal constraints on schismatics, making them liable to compulsory public services. A law issued in January 412 detailed a wide range of sanctions against Donatist clergy, thereby creating a climate in which Cyril could proceed with impunity against another orthodox sect. In Rome, Innocent I (401–17) had provided a precedent by confiscating many Novatianist churches. Moreover, Cyril's five-year stay at the monastic settlement of Nitria may have convinced him that the rigorism of the Novatianists was superfluous in comparison with the asceticism of the desert communities.[46]

Cyril's campaign against the Novatianists should be seen as a piece with his installation of loyal clerics in the churches under his authority. The *History of the Patriarchs* comments that "the first thing that Cyril did was to appoint priests to take charge of the churches throughout his diocese, so that they might not be drawn away from the spiritual food by which they were able to do that which pleases God." Cyril's first festal letter strikes the same chord in his warning against a spirit of division within the church. For a bishop who had emerged from a hotly disputed election, it was vitally necessary that he shore up the unity of his church, especially since there were other opponents with which to contend.[47]

Cyril's conflict with the Jewish community of Alexandria may also be seen in the same context as his vendetta against the Novatianists. Throughout the fourth century, the city's Jewish community could be found siding with various factions in the competition for urban hegemony. Though not in a position to dictate the contours of Alexandria's power relationships, the Jewish community remained large and influential enough to be able to tip the balance in favor of one faction against another. Did the Jews side with Timothy and Abundantius in 412? The sources are silent on this point, but Jewish participation in the fate of George of Cappadocia in 361 and in the Arian persecutions instituted under Lucius and Palladius in 374 may have convinced Cyril that his security was at least partially dependent upon neutralizing Jewish opposition.

Cyril's predecessors, Timothy I (380–85) and Theophilus (385–412), seem to have been largely unconcerned about the sentiments of the Jewish community. Why then did Cyril exhibit such animosity toward the Jews? The answer lies in Cyril's background and orientation as a bishop. Prior to the outbreak of the Nestorian controversy in 428, the overwhelming majority of Cyril's literary output was scriptural exegesis. During his sojourn in the desert, Cyril's ascesis consisted of reading and memorizing lengthy portions of the Bible. By the time he returned to Alexandria and took up his duties as a lector, Cyril was steeped in the scriptures, and it is not surprising that biblical interpretation occupied a great deal of the young bishop's attention. The vigor and elegance of his discourses were quickly recognized and many aristocratic Alexandrians employed copyists to transcribe Cyril's works.[48]

Central to his understanding of the Bible was the place of the Jews after the coming of Jesus. As Robert Wilken has pointed out, Cyril's "opposition to the Arians or the Antiochenes seems like a friendly intramural contest in contrast to the invective against the Jews."[49] By their rejection of Christ, the Jews have shown themselves to be the "most deranged of all men." They are "senseless," "blind," "uncomprehending," and "demented." They are "foolish God haters" and "killers of the Lord"; they are "unbelievers" and "irreligious." Their synagogue is "a leprous house which perpetuates their monstrous impiety." These tirades against the Jews were not confined to Cyril's later works. As early as his first festal letter, issued in the autumn of 413, he engages in a lengthy denunciation of the Jews, whose outlook is "filled with every type of impurity." Cyril's censure of the Jews is replete with quotations from the prophet Jeremiah, and he goes a step further by asserting that the Jews of his day are even worse than their fathers. In light of the events shortly to transpire in Alexandria, an ominous significance may be attached to Cyril's invocation of the passage, "Our end was near, our days were numbered, for our end had come. Our pursuers were swifter than eagles in the sky" (Lamentations 4:18–19).[50]

Clearly, Cyril had assumed a stance of uncompromising opposition to the Jews. As a new bishop, however, he was not in a strong enough position to initiate action against the Jewish community. As we have seen, even though the community was decimated during the second century, it had made a tenuous but steady recovery throughout the third and fourth centuries. The Jewish community was still a force with which to reckon in Alexandrian politics. In addition, Judaism still enjoyed legal protection by the emperors. Ever since the reign of Theodosius I, a rising tide of legislation had limited the civil rights of Jews and sought to curtail Gentile conversions to Judaism. Despite these legal strictures, however, Judaism was still a protected religion. A series of laws affirmed its status and prohibited attacks on synagogues. Moreover, laws of 396 and 404 confirmed the privileges of the Jewish patriarch (*Nasi*) in Palestine, thereby ensuring the autonomous jurisdiction of Jewish communities throughout the empire.[51] The young bishop of Alexandria needed a perceptible change in imperial policy as well as some sort of local cause célèbre before he could proceed against the Jews of Alexandria. He soon got both.

The year 414 saw significant changes in imperial administration in Constantinople. Anthemius, praetorian prefect of the East since 405, was last addressed by an imperial law in April 414. Presumably he died shortly thereafter. Anthemius had served as virtual regent for the young Theodosius II since Arcadius's death in 408. Anthemius had guided the state with a steady hand and formulated policy by carefully building consensus among the powerful.[52] With Anthemius's death there passed from the scene the last of a line of praetorian prefects of lengthy tenure. His successor, Monaxius, was in office for no more than six months. It appears that Monaxius had run afoul of the rising star of the imperial court, Pulcheria, elder sister of the young Theodosius. Though only fifteen years old herself, Pulcheria emerged after the death of Anthemius as the principal advisor to her thirteen-year-old brother. Pulcheria freed herself from the constraints of a future marriage by taking a public vow of virginity and, in July 414, was proclaimed Augusta.

By the end of the year, the turmoil in the corridors of power had settled. Monaxius was sacked and, in his place, the imperial siblings appointed an aged veteran of the Theodosian establishment, Aurelian. Aurelian had engineered the proclamation of Eudoxia as Augusta in 400. He had been deposed and exiled during the coup of Gaïnas the Goth, and was restored after the purge of the Goths in Constantinople in 400. He was a respected elder statesman and a fervent Christian.[53] In his earlier days, Aurelian had been the follower of a renowned Syrian ascetic named Isaac. In 416, after his appointment to the prefecture, Aurelian also built a church in Constantinople to house the recently discovered relics of the martyr Stephen. True to the policies of his earlier masters, Aurelian worked diligently with Pulcheria and Theodosius II to restrict the rights of pagans and heretics. The empire's Jews witnessed the gradual erosion of their status during the prefecture of Aurelian, and it was during his tenure that the Jewish patriarch was stripped of his honorary rank and deprived of much of his judicial powers.[54]

Given the instability of imperial administration during 414 and the strong line taken against dissenters by 415, it is not surprising that Cyril should have acted confidently in his dealings with Alexandria's Jews and pagans. This also goes a long way toward explaining the ineffectiveness of the augustal prefect, Orestes. This chronological context is provided by the notice given by Socrates that Hypatia's murder took place during March 415, not long after news of Aurelian's appointment to the prefecture must have reached Alexandria. Since Hypatia's death signaled the end of a series of violent incidents, precipitated by Cyril's confrontation with the city's Jews, it is reasonable to conclude that the bishop was emboldened by the rapid changes that occurred in imperial administration.

The detailed narrative provided by Socrates makes it clear, however, that Cyril only responded to opportunities that came his way. This was certainly the case with the events leading to the violent expulsion of the Jews from Alexandria.

According to Socrates, the trouble began with disturbances in the theater.[55] For some time, Alexandrians had been wildly enthusiastic about mime and dancing shows. Attendance at the shows was always higher on the Jewish Sabbath, since many of the city's Jews spent their day of rest at the theater. These crowds occasionally got unruly—at least in the eyes of the authorities. Orestes, the prefect, had sought to regulate these performances so as to maintain public order. It appears that he enjoyed support for these restrictive actions from the church's leadership. Socrates informs us that "the Jews continued opposing these measures" and that they found grounds for their animosity toward the Christians "on account of the dancers." This was one of the rare instances when the interests of the imperial administration coincided with those of the church's hierarchy.

Orestes, however, considered the Christian patriarch to be the greatest long-term threat to imperial authority within the city. Jewish crowds attending the dancing and mime shows recognized among the audience an ardent supporter of Cyril named Hierax, and denounced him to Orestes as an instigator of riots and sedition. Hierax had come to the theater along with other partisans (*spoudastai*) of Cyril to learn of the new regulations concerning the shows, doubtless on behalf of their episcopal patron. The prefect seized an opportunity to effect a rapprochement with the Jewish community. Orestes had Hierax flogged on the spot, much to the pleasure of those who had come to the theater for other amusements. Cyril, however, considered such treatment of one of his clients as a personal affront. He also held the Jews in the city responsible for the incident, and summoned "the chief men of the Jews" (*tous Ioudaion proteuontas*), threatening them "with the utmost severities unless they desisted from their molestation of the Christians." Cyril had overstepped the bounds of his authority by dictating to the leadership of the Jewish community. In response to this saber-rattling, some of the Jews decided to unsheathe actual swords, encouraged by the prefect's favor. Indeed, John of Nikiu goes so far as to say that the Jews "gloried in the support of the prefect who was with them."[56]

Shortly thereafter, the populace of Alexandria was awakened one night to cries in the streets that fire had broken out in the church named for the sainted bishop, Alexander. In alarm, the Christians ran out to combat the blaze. Instead of finding fire and smoke, the Christians met with the swords of Jewish zealots who had planned this ruse in order to cut down the defenseless Christians. Although many were killed, at daybreak Cyril was still able to collect "an immense crowd of people" and seize all of the synagogues within the city. Many of these synagogues were converted into churches, thereby providing Cyril with a graphic parallel to his uncle's conversion of pagan shrines a generation before. Many from the Jewish community were summarily expelled from the metropolis while the Christian crowd plundered their homes and belongings. Because of the overwhelming show of force orchestrated by Cyril, Orestes was powerless to assist the Jewish community and had to content himself with sending a lengthy report to Constantinople. Cyril likewise sent his version of the events to the imperial court. Aurelian's administration took no action, save for a vaguely worded directive asserting that disputes between Jews and Christians should be judged by the governor of a province.[57] Perhaps more telling is a law issued in March 415 which sought to curtail unspecified robbery and plunder. These enactments did nothing to assist the once thriving Jewish community of Alexandria. Although the Jewish community survived in Alexandria, it did so in a much reduced status, and it never again held a significant place in the equation of Alexandrian politics. The Jews continued to be a recurring target for abuse in Cyril's works, notably in a condemnation of Jewish "unbelief" which fills the last half of the festal letter for 416, and in a lengthy tirade against circumcision and the Jewish Sabbath in the festal letter for 418.[58]

These events precipitated the ongoing hostility that characterized the relations between prefect and patriarch. According to Socrates' account, Orestes was "excessively grieved" at the expulsion of the Jews, and Cyril's high-handed methods caused the prefect to be "filled with great indignation." Certain Alexandrians, most likely notable bouleutai, recognized that this growing rancor between the city's two most important authorities had the potential of flaring up into yet more violence and bloodshed. They therefore urged the young bishop to be reconciled with Orestes. This is the first indication that Cyril did not enjoy the unanimous backing of the laity. Despite his apparent success in the conflict with the Jewish community, Cyril felt constrained by discordant elements within his own community of coreligionists to effect a reconciliation with the prefect. However, Cyril was determined to do so only on his own terms. Though he made the first move, Cyril's tentative rapprochement was made in the context of a liturgical act, extending toward Orestes the book of the Gospels. Socrates relates that Cyril did this, "believing that respect for religion would induce [Orestes] to lay aside his resentment." This was a shrewd gambit on Cyril's part. For if Orestes accepted this formal act of adjuration by clasping the Gospel book, it could easily be interpreted as his submission to the bishop, not as the reconciliation of two equals. Orestes spurned this offer, no doubt realizing that "respect for religion" in this highly charged atmosphere spelled respect for Cyril.

By employing this potent symbol of reconciliation, Cyril had Orestes in a virtual checkmate. True, Orestes opted not to be seen submitting to Cyril, and "he persisted in implacable hostility against the bishop." However, in light of the symbolic and public nature of late antique protocol, Orestes' refusal to clasp the Gospel book immediately called into question his own religious preferences. His public posture as a Christian was further eroded by his deference toward Hypatia, a high-profile pagan who could dispense equally both philosophical wisdom and civic patronage. Some ardent spirits concluded that the prefect must be a cryptopagan.

News of these proceedings must have reached across Lake Mareotis to the monasteries at Nitria, the most populous monastic retreat in the vicinity of Alexandria until the mid-fifth century.[59] Nearly five hundred Nitrian monks "of a very fiery disposition" streamed into the city determined to fight for the patriarch. They confronted Orestes in his chariot and hurled abuse at him, denouncing him as a pagan idolater. Orestes' vigorous protestation that he was a baptized Christian underscored the prefect's realization of how potentially life-threatening a situation he was in. Indeed, only fifteen years before, a mob of riotous Nitrian monks threatened Theophilus, and it was all he could do to cajole them into withdrawing. Orestes was not as adroit as Cyril's uncle had been at pacifying the monks. Soon, rocks were thrown. A monk named Ammonius cast a stone that struck the prefect on the head, covering him with blood. His hopelessly outnumbered bodyguard fled. This would have been the end of Orestes, but "the populace of Alexandria ran to the rescue of the governor and put the rest of the monks to flight." What induced these Alexandrians to intervene on behalf of the prefect? Socrates does not tell us, but we may surmise that the prefect was saved by the Alexandrians' abiding deference for traditional forms of authority, as well as by the long-standing animosity of the city dweller toward intrusive and disorderly rural elements. Yet again, the Alexandrians asserted their willingness to support the traditional structures of authority, even when this precarious balance disadvantaged their bishop.

Did Cyril unleash the fury of these Nitrian monks against Orestes? Cyril's six-year stay at Nitria may have convinced him not that the monks were potential allies to be exploited, but rather that their inherent volatility made them unsuitable tools in the hands of a bishop. The experience of his uncle may not have been far from Cyril's mind. If he required strong-armed support, the bishop need not have gone out of the city. He had the parabalani, a far more effective and more easily mobilized weapon. It seems reasonable to conclude that the appearance of these monks in Alexandria was not orchestrated by the bishop.

The prefect's unexpected and vigorous show of support among the Alexandrians allowed him to confront this challenge to his authority by publicly torturing the monk who had thrown the stone that wounded him. Torturing ascetics usually was not the way to endear oneself to a city's populace. Such actions by past prefects had merited the Alexandrians' scorn and hatred. However, Orestes knew that he had public support, even when the offending monk died under torture. He would not have embarked on this course of action if he did not sense that the Christian community was wavering in its backing of the new patriarch. As with the events surrounding the Jewish troubles, both Orestes and Cyril sent reports of the recent incidents to Constantinople.

The emperor and his court might believe what they would, but it was imperative to Cyril that he somehow salvage the situation within Alexandria itself. Taking a cue from Athanasius and Peter II, Cyril took steps to transform the public perception of the recent disorders from a mere riot of fanatical monks against the prefect to a grand struggle between the righteous and the ungodly. Cyril laid the body of Ammonius in a church with great pomp, exchanged his pagan sounding name for Thaumasios ("admirable" or "wonderful"), and enrolled him among the martyrs venerated by the faithful. Perhaps in this he was hoping to recall the events of 391, when the emperor proclaimed that the Christians who died in street brawling with the pagan defenders of the Serapeum were martyrs for the faith.[60] In this case, no such edict was forthcoming from the emperor. The violence of 391 had erupted between factions of Alexandrians with the prefect acting as a neutral party. It was not a murderous assault upon the emperor's chosen representative.

Cyril went so far as to eulogize the fallen Ammonius/Thaumasius, praising his magnanimity and his bravery in defending the faith. However, Cyril overplayed his hand. In the words of Socrates: "But the more sober-minded, although Christians, did not accept Cyril's prejudiced estimate of him; for they well knew that he had suffered the punishment due to his rashness, and that he had not lost his life under the torture because he would not deny Christ." Once again the young patriarch discovered that his flock was unwilling to line up unquestioningly behind him in his conflict with the prefect. For a populace often branded with being seditious and restive under imperial authority, the Alexandrians displayed a remarkable sense of decorum. It appears that these Alexandrians, probably led by prominent laypersons, felt that Cyril had gone beyond the bounds of good taste. What could Cyril do? He quietly dropped the whole matter, no doubt hoping that the Alexandrians would have a short memory. His feud with Orestes continued, and "did not by any means subside." It would take a much more dramatic incident to undercut the prefect and irrevocably place the city's cultural hegemony in the hands of the patriarch.

The events surrounding the murder of the pagan philosopher Hypatia have been frequently romanticized, vilified, or rationalized—depending on the cultural outlook of the many writers who have commented on this incident. According to Gibbon, the champion of rationalism over Christianity, the fanaticism of Cyril and his Alexandrian congregation demanded "the sacrifice of a virgin, who professed the religion of the Greeks, and cultivated the friendship of Orestes." Charles Kingsley's lurid rendering of the story owes more to his polemic against Edward Pusey and the Tractarian movement than to a sober assessment of the ancient sources. Cyril's apologists have sought to deflect the blame for the murder away from the patriarch and onto unruly elements in the Alexandrian mob. More circumspect historians have chosen to follow the interpretation of Socrates Scholasticus, who labeled Hypatia "a victim to the political jealousy which at that time prevailed." In Socrates' view, the death of Hypatia was deemed necessary since she was regarded as the principal stumbling block to a reconciliation between Cyril and Orestes.[61]

Socrates, however, is not entirely free from bias in his presentation of the facts, owing to his animosity toward Cyril for persecuting Nestorius.[62] Fortunately, it is not necessary to slavishly follow Socrates, as other perspectives on the events of 415 may be gleaned from the writings of Damascius, in whose *Life of Isidore* Hypatia earns a lengthy treatment. Likewise, we may turn to the chronicle of John of Nikiu, who preserves often neglected Coptic traditions relating to the history of this era. Together, these sources depict the murder of Hypatia not only as the final act in the ongoing conflict between patriarch and prefect but, more importantly, as the culmination of a religious and political power struggle between the predominant communities of the late antique city. Cyril's actions during and immediately following these events transformed a singularly brutal act of political violence into a crucial turning point in the conflict between Alexandria's Christian and pagan communities.[63]

We have seen that Cyril's opposition to the Jewish community grew out of his exegesis of Scripture. Likewise, his vendetta against Hypatia needs to be seen in the broader context of his hostility toward paganism. It is evident from Cyril's early festal letters that he was preoccupied with warding off criticisms of Christianity made by pagan Alexandrians. In the first of these letters, Cyril derides the Hellenes for worshiping the images of beasts in their headlong rush toward "the abyss of death." His attack on paganism becomes more nuanced in his festal letter for 418, foreshadowing many of the arguments he employed later in his *Contra Iulianum*. Although this last work was probably composed in the 430s, Cyril intimates in the introduction that he had long been concerned with the appeal that the pagan emperor's book had among the Alexandrians. Since Julian may have written his *Contra Galilaeos* for Alexandrians who had converted to Christianity, it is easy to see why Cyril thought that the treatise was doing immeasurable harm (*ēdichēsen ou metriōs*) to Alexandrians who were weak in their faith. Cyril was especially irritated by the way in which pagan teachers regarded Julian's arguments to be irrefutable. Moreover, Cyril's opposition to Alexandrian paganism was not confined to literary polemic. In June 414, Cyril solemnly transferred the relics of Cyrus and John to their newly built shrine at Canopus, erected over the former temple of Isis Medica. Thus, Cyril was not one to settle for a modus vivendi with Alexandria's pagans.[64] Hypatia could easily be regarded as the most prominent spokesperson for the pagan community and, as such, she posed a threat to Cyril's authority within both the church and the city.

An Alexandrian by birth, Hypatia had received a thorough training in the mathematical sciences by her father Theon, who was in his own right a celebrated astronomer and mathematician. Hypatia eventually turned to philosophical inquiry, and attained an expertise in Neoplatonic thought.[65] Her teaching appears to have been imbued with the Iamblichan mystical tradition, and she may have even imparted to her students the arcana of the so-called Chaldean Oracles, a second-century collection of purported divine revelations. Judging from the evidence provided by Synesius, her best-known pupil, he probably gained his knowledge of the occult sciences and of Hermeticism from Hypatia. She attracted large numbers of students, and perhaps acquired a municipally endowed chair in philosophy. Her fame was such that Synesius referred to her simply as "the philosopher."[66]

While we must pass over many aspects of her career and teachings, the scope of her influence in the city bears closer examination. It illustrates well the status of pagan intellectuals and their upper-class students during the decades following the disestablishment of public paganism in Alexandria. Hypatia's network of patronage can be observed in three related areas: her role as patroness within the circle of her aristocratic students, her active involvement in the public life of the city, and her relationship with the highest civil authority in Alexandria, the prefect. Together, these realms of influence made her an important source of power within the late Roman city, an island of influence untouched by Cyril and the nearly hegemonic Christian community.

Synesius, who studied with Hypatia circa 393–95, is an eloquent witness to the devotion she engendered in her pupils, as well as to the lasting bonds of loyalty which existed among her circle of students. In one letter, Synesius salutes her as "mother, sister, teacher, and withal benefactress [*euergetikē*] and whatsoever is honored in name and deed." Elsewhere, he styles her "the true guide who presides over the secret rites of philosophy." Synesius's fellow students, whom he calls "the company of the blessed," were drawn to Hypatia from many regions of the eastern Mediterranean. Possessing the requisite *otium* for philosophical pursuits, these students were mostly of an upper-class background. One such student and long time correspondent of Synesius, Herculian, was probably the brother of the later praetorian prefect of the East and consul, Fl. Taurus Seleucus Cyrus. The experience of having been trained under Hypatia united these students into a lifelong circle of friendship, as can be seen in Synesius's voluminous correspondence.[67]

The bonds forged between these young aristocrats and their brilliant teacher could be put to practical political advantage. The status of distinguished rhetors and teachers within late Roman society was such that they were often in a position to provide beneficia to their students and other dependents.[68] Libanius, Themistius, and Ausonius are fourth-century representatives of this patronal tradition, which extends back to the days of Cicero and Pliny the Younger. The correspondence of these literati is replete with letters of recommendation and requests for assistance in obtaining some desired end from higher authorities.[69] Hypatia was no stranger to this widespread practice of patronage, as can be seen in a revealing letter of Synesius:

> . . . all respect which was accorded to me by the mighty of this earth I employed solely to help others. The great were merely my instruments. But now, alas, I am deserted and abandoned by all, unless you have some power [*dunē*] to help. I account you as the only good thing that remains inviolate, along with virtue. You always have power and long may you have it and make a good use of that power [*dunasthai*]. I recommend to your care Nicaeus and Philolaus, two excellent young men united by the bond of kinship. In order that they may come again into possession of their own property, try to get support for them from all your acquain-

> tances, both private individuals and magistrates [*kai idiōtais kai archousi*].[70]

Although Hypatia did not hold a civic magistracy in Alexandria, Synesius recognized that her influence within the city was sufficient to succor his two young friends. Her network of patronage extended to elected magistrates as well as to private citizens—in all likelihood bouleutai who were not currently in possession of elected office. Further, such requests for beneficia do not seem to be extraordinary but simply drew upon her long-standing position of influence.

Rather than retiring to the quiet of the lecture hall, a woman of Hypatia's status chose instead to participate actively in the public life of the city. In Damascius's estimation, "She was not only eloquent and educated, but also practically sensible and inspired with public spirit [*politikēn*]." Socrates informs us that "she not infrequently appeared in public in the presence of the magistrates." In a similar vein, Damascius states, "she wrapped herself in the philosopher's robe and went out into the midst of the city," probably signifying the Agora where much of Alexandria's public life took place. Of course, her actions were especially noteworthy since she was a woman, who by her profession and deportment went contrary to the expectations of her contemporaries. Fortunately, the astonishment she provoked in our male literary sources serves to highlight those aspects of her public career which might have been otherwise overlooked.[71]

The Alexandrians apparently did not consider her status to be an anomaly, since she was frequently bestowed with civic honors. It was even customary for newly elected magistrates to pay her a courtesy call upon taking up their offices. Damascius, in fact, ascribes her death to Cyril's jealousy over the honored position she enjoyed among the city's elite. Damascius vividly describes an occasion when

> Cyril, the bishop of the opposing party, went by Hypatia's house and noticed a great throng at her door, "a jumble of steeds and men" (*Iliad* 21.26). Some came; some went; others remained standing. He asked what this gathering meant and why such a tumult was being made. He then heard from his retainers that the philosopher, Hypatia, was being greeted [*prosagoreuoito*] and that this was her house. This information so pierced his heart that he launched a murderous attack.[72]

Though we are not obliged to accept all of the dramatic details of this anecdote, the setting seems to be plausible enough. The impression conveyed is not one of literary and philosophical types hanging about the residence of their teacher, but rather one depicting men of influence visiting an equal as well as dependents calling upon their benefactress. May we not see the *prosagoreusis* accorded to Hypatia as the traditional *salutatio* given to a patron by *clientes*?

An awareness of Hypatia's role as an influential patroness within late fourth- and early fifth-century Alexandria facilitates an understanding of her relationship with Orestes, the praefectus Augustalis. Though Orestes was a Christian, baptized shortly before his tenure of office by the bishop of Constantinople, he recognized the importance of cultivating the influential pagan philosopher. Accordingly, "he honored her exceedingly" and held frequent consultations with her. All this is what one would expect of an imperial administrator who sought to maintain peace in a sometimes volatile city by establishing ties with the main centers of political power. The cities of the Greek East had a long tradition of philosophers representing their interests before provincial governors. One need not resort to John of Nikiu's explanation that Hypatia "had beguiled him through her magic."[73] Orestes had likewise cultivated a relationship with the city's Jewish leaders and he was evidently held in high regard by the populace. Moreover, as an imperial official, Orestes resented the way in which the patriarchs had previously encroached upon the lawful authority of the emperor and his administration. The leadership of the Christian community had recently been in a state of flux. As a consequence, Orestes felt no urgency in courting Theophilus's young and inexperienced nephew, who was still consolidating his hold upon the throne of Saint Mark.[74]

To make matters worse, at least in the eyes of Cyril, Orestes appears to have made use of his working relationship with Hypatia in order to forge a party of Alexandrians opposed to the patriarch. Not only did Orestes spurn Cyril's offer of reconciliation, he "ceased attending church, as had been his custom." Moreover, "he drew many believers to her, and he himself received the unbelievers at his house."[75] Here, we see two crucial elements in Orestes' bid to counterbalance the influence of the patriarch. The "believers" that

Orestes drew to Hypatia were undoubtedly those same disgruntled Christians who had exhibited more than a little reticence about following the policies of their patriarch. They were probably the very ones who had earlier urged Cyril's reconciliation with Orestes and who had opposed the bogus canonization of the riotous monk, Ammonius. Orestes made it quite clear that, for the Christians of the city, access to his justice and patronage was to be mediated not through the patriarch but via the philosopher Hypatia. Second, there is the notice that he "received the unbelievers at his house." Could this seemingly minor detail indicate a significant shift from the standard practice? It may be that Orestes' reception of prominent pagans at his house, rather than at the prefect's praetorium, emphasized the access and intimacy he accorded to Alexandrian pagans. Orestes hoped to fashion a bond between the Christians alienated from Cyril and the pagan aristocracy. A vital link in this newly forged party was Hypatia. Consequently, the attack upon Hypatia was but one prong of a broader attack on this new coalition.

History has consigned to oblivion any evidence that would directly link Cyril to the murder of Hypatia. We will never know if Cyril himself orchestrated the attack, or if, like the assault upon Orestes, certain partisans unilaterally "resolved to fight for the patriarch."[76] Cyril evidently had retained some supporters among the city's elite. Whether or not at the instigation of the new patriarch, a magistrate named Peter collected a mob and attacked Hypatia. Could Peter's role in the violence betoken a rift between factions of Alexandrian bouleutai? On that fateful day, Hypatia was riding grandly through the city in her carriage, as befitted her public position in Alexandria. She was pulled from her carriage "as soon as she appeared in the street in her usual manner."[77] After dragging her through the streets, the enraged mob tortured her in the Great Church of the Caesarion—the former temple of the imperial cult and the site of the pagan riots of 356. Her mangled body was then taken to another location where it was burnt on a pyre of brushwood. The manner of her death suggests that her attackers viewed her as a disruptive element in the city's recently established structure of authority which revolved around the prefect and the patriarch. Her murder in the Caesarion was a forceful statement of support for this new order, and her cremation followed to the letter the long-standing civic ritual of public purgation. The attack was apparently over before the prefect was able to intervene. As with the Jewish-Christian violence, Orestes was helpless to assist Cyril's enemies. Both Damascius and Socrates denounce the viciousness of the murder, the latter stating: "This affair brought considerable reproach, not only upon Cyril, but also upon the whole Alexandrian church."[78]

It is often assumed that Hypatia's murderers were the parabalani, a group of clerics who served as hospital attendants for the Alexandrian church. And yet, the laws of 416 and 418 in the *Codex Theodosianus* which regulate their recruitment and activities do not include murder among the parabalani's faults. Since the parabalani were under the direct authority of the patriarch, their involvement in Hypatia's death would have warranted a charge of murder against Cyril, not mere "reproach" (*mōmos*). Socrates states that Hypatia's murderers were members of "the Christian populace . . . hurried away by a fierce and bigoted zeal."[79] A crowd of Alexandrian laymen, led by a magistrate, would have far better claim to represent the collective will of the populace than a tightly organized corps of church officials.

While the laws of 416 and 418 do not even allude to the parabalani's participation in Hypatia's murder, there are frequent references to their disruption of "public affairs and matters pertaining to the municipal council." The first and most detailed of these laws goes so far as to state:

> We do not grant to the aforesaid attendants of the sick liberty to attend any public spectacle whatever or to enter the meeting place of a municipal council or a courtroom, unless, perchance, they should appeal to a *judex* separately in connection with their own cases and interests, when they sue someone in litigation or when they themselves are sued by another, or when they are syndics appointed in a cause common to the entire group. The condition shall be observed that if anyone of them should violate the foregoing provisions, he shall be removed from the registers of the attendants of the sick and shall be subjected to due punishment, and he shall never return to the same office.[80]

An edict with provisions as specific as these can only have been issued with a particular problem in mind. In all likelihood, Cyril had used the parabalani to disrupt the municipal council and bully the curial class. This edict was issued just over a year and a half after the murder of Hypatia. Given the slowness of communications and the time needed to formulate policy, the uproar caused by the parabalani in Alexandria's civic institutions must have followed quite closely upon Hypatia's death. It is quite possible that Cyril sought to exploit the rift among the city's bouleutai by overawing Orestes' upper-class allies.[81]

A law issued the very same day as the first parabalani edict (5 October) fills out our understanding of the factionalism that had gripped the Alexandrian council.[82] In this edict, the imperial administration prohibited delegations of decurions from coming to Constantinople with municipal petitions unless they could demonstrate that their embassy was on behalf of the entire council. Municipal decrees and petitions had to be endorsed by a full meeting of the boule, signed by all of the councillors and then forwarded on to the prefect. The prefect alone was given the power to authorize the sending of a particular civic delegation to Constantinople. This edict dovetails with the one concerning the parabalani, since the emperors first learned of the disturbances in Alexandria from an unofficial delegation of bouleutai who complained of "the terror of those called parabalani." This same unofficial delegation requested the emperors to decree "that the Most Reverend Bishop [the patriarch] should not allow certain persons to depart from the city of Alexandria."[83] Apparently, the councillors bullied by the parabalani did not want Cyril's supporters in the boule to be able to present their own version of recent events in Alexandria.

The imperial government responded in a typical fashion. Unity was enjoined upon the Alexandrian council, and all relations between the civic aristocracy and the imperial administration were to be channeled through the prefect. In these edicts, the emperors made a valiant attempt to shore up the authority of the prefect, by granting to him de facto veto power over municipal petitions and embassies. In addition, the prefect alone was authorized to select individuals (other than bouleutai) to serve among the parabalani, now reduced to no more than five hundred.

These efforts were too little and too late. The opposition to the patriarch had been shattered, through the murder of Hypatia and the parabalani's campaign of terror among the civic aristocracy. Even the emperors acknowledged this changed state of affairs, since a law of 418 increased the number of parabalani to six hundred and returned them to the authority of the patriarch. Cyril's partisans among the city's Christians recognized the significance of the recent events. Coptic tradition preserves the detail that "all the people surrounded the patriarch Cyril and named him 'the new Theophilus'; for he had destroyed the last remains of idolatry in the city." The pagan opposition had been broken along with its network of patronage. Even Orestes was never heard from again. It is clear that the balance of power in Alexandria had shifted to the Christian community.[84]

### *Ecclesiastical Stasis and the Marginalization of the Pagans in the 480s*

In the three decades following the death of Hypatia, Alexandria enjoyed a respite from collective violence. Just as Theophilus had employed domestic quiescence after 391 in order to engage in controversies outside of Alexandria, so too Cyril entered the fray of theological conflict once his position in Alexandria was secure. His death in 444 inaugurated another period of instability, since his successor, Dioscorus, did not have as firm a grasp on the reins of authority within the Christian community. Although he had been Cyril's archdeacon, Dioscorus did not belong to the family of Theophilus and Cyril. This wealthy family still wielded considerable influence within the Alexandrian church. Dioscorus eventually was able to hound Cyril's relatives out of Alexandria but, in so doing, he drove them into the arms of his ecclesiastical opponents on the wider imperial stage. The bitter complaints of Cyril's family and other confidants became ammunition for Dioscorus's enemies at the Council of Chalcedon in 451.[85] While the theological issues that ignited the Monophysite controversy played a role in the stance against Dioscorus, theology alone did not motivate his enemies. It could be argued that Dioscorus's fatal mistake was not to pacify dissent within his own church before engaging in controversy elsewhere. His actions at the second Council at Ephesus in 449 (the so-called Latrocinium) created powerful foes, notably Pope Leo I and the supporters of patriarch Flavian of Constantinople. These opponents combined with Dioscorus's Alexandrian enemies to engineer his deposition at Chalcedon.

The evolution of the Alexandrian patriarchate between the deposition of Dioscorus in 451 and the Arab conquest of 642 tends to be ignored by modern scholars who have often viewed this period as one of unbroken Monophysite opposition to imperial religious policy. While all of the bishops who sat on the episcopal throne once occupied by Athanasius and Cyril consciously sought to consolidate their position in the face of threats to their authority, they employed a broad range of tactics with respect to their changing opponents and supporters within Alexandria itself. A close examination of the patriarchate of Peter Mongus (477–90), one of the better known disputants in the wider Monophysite controversy, reveals a resourceful community leader who grappled with various local interest groups—pagans, schismatics, and secular authorities. The literary evidence concerning his patriarchate underscores the primacy of local disputes in determining Peter's stance toward empirewide issues, especially his reaction to the Henotikon espoused by the emperor Zeno. Peter's tenure as Alexandrian patriarch also marks an important watershed in the declining status of the pagan community within the city. Indeed, as a consequence of a series of events capitalized upon by Peter, the pagan community virtually disappears from view by the end of his patriarchate.[86]

In the period immediately following the deposition of Dioscorus (revered by much of the Egyptian church as "the militant Father"), Chalcedonians and Monophysites began to emerge as self-conscious parties within the Alexandrian church, a process marked by violence and intense political jockeying.[87] By 457, the imperial replacement for Dioscorus's patriarchal throne, Proterius, had been assassinated. Proterius's death came after months of bloody street battles between ecclesiastical factions. Eventually, an unnamed soldier of the Roman dux had decided to end the slaughter. On Maunday Thursday 457, he lured Proterius into the street and stabbed him, after which he displayed the bishop's mutilated body in the Agora.[88]

This incident did not put an end to factional conflict in Alexandria. Shortly before the death of Proterius, the supporters of Dioscorus had elevated their own candidate to the episcopal throne, Timothy (popularly called Aelurus—that is, the "cat" or "weasel"—owing to his emaciated countenance from prolonged fasting). The Alexandrians were mistaken, however, in assuming that the new emperor, Leo, would take no action upon hearing of Proterius's murder. Once Leo was able to assert his own authority in the empire, he naturally turned his attention to the troubles in Alexandria. By late 459, Timothy was arrested and exiled to Gangra, a town in northern Anatolia. Many of Timothy's clergy either were exiled or fled before their arrest. Among these was a young deacon named Peter who had been appointed by Dioscorus. In place of Timothy Aelurus, the supporters of the murdered Proterius chose as their patriarch a monk from the Pachomian monastery at Canopus. Unfortunately for those trying to unravel this complicated skein of events, this Chalcedonian monk's name is also Timothy, though distinguished from his Monophysite namesake by his common appellation Salophacialos—"wobble-hat."[89]

For nearly fifteen years, Timothy Salophacialos attempted to govern the faction-ridden church of Alexandria. He was, however, ill-suited to the task of trying to win the allegiance of the Alexandrians, most of whom remained loyal to Timothy Aelurus and looked upon Timothy Salophacialos as an intruder. It was at this time that he earned his appellation of wobble-hat, for the patriarchal miter indeed sat weakly upon his head. Zachariah of Mytilene tells us that Timothy was "soft in his manners and feeble in his actions," being afraid to take forceful measures against the partisans of Aelurus. Although he desperately courted popularity among the Alexandrians and urged them to lay aside their theological differences, Salophacialos took the precaution of never appearing in public without a guard of imperial troops—"because he dreaded the fate of Proterius." In one final bid for support among the urban populace, Salophacialos inscribed the name of the Monophysite Dioscorus in his liturgical Diptych. Unfortunately, all he gained thereby was a writ of excommunication from Pope Leo I.[90]

Despite his best intentions, Salophacialos had never mastered the art of dispensing patriarchal patronage within the complicated social mosaic that made up late antique Alexandria. Previous patriarchs like Athanasius and Cyril had honed these methods of cultivating support. They had shrewdly employed the social, economic, and religious patronage at the church's disposal in their struggles against various opponents in the city. If their examples were too distant, Salophacialos could have taken a lesson from Timothy Aelurus, who proved himself to be as adept as his predecessors in dispensing patronage. Prior to his ejection from Alexandria by imperial troops, Aelurus gave lavish gifts of money to the poor, provided for the city's widows, and supplied the city's numerous pilgrim hostels. Perhaps one reason for Aelurus's exile was the suspicion that some of these charitable funds had been diverted from their original destination—the imperial treasury in the form of tax revenues. Disputes of jurisdiction over the Alexandrian grain dole and other public charities had been a constant irritant in patriarchal-imperial relations since the days of Athanasius. Aelurus's opposition to imperial tax collectors can further be seen after his restoration to Alexandria in 475, when he presented honorific grants of grain to "the great men and rulers of the city" and even sent gifts to the emperor himself—while at the same time, he deliberately snubbed the imperial tax officials. These methods helped to endear Aelurus to both the Alexandrian commons and the civic aristocracy. Aelurus buttressed his support yet further by bringing back the bones of the revered Dioscorus for a solemn funeral, and by conspicuously providing a small pension for Salophacialos when the latter was forced to return to his monastic retirement.[91]

Timothy Aelurus was swept back into the Alexandrian patriarchate on the winds of change in imperial politics. The emperor Leo had died early in 474 and was succeeded by his Isaurian *magister militum* and son-in-law, Zeno (figure 24). Zeno's hold on the imperial purple was tenuous at best, and he was almost immediately faced with a serious revolt led by the former emperor's brother-in-law, Basiliscus. Basiliscus only remained in power for twenty months, but during that time he sought to overturn the decisions at Chalcedon and restore Monophysite bishops to their sees—among them Timothy Aelurus. Basiliscus's coalition of military supporters soon broke down, and by August 476 Zeno was once again emperor

Fig. 24. Zeno (474–91). Gold solidus. The reverse depicts Victory holding a cross. Reverse inscription: VICTORIA AUGGG (the victory of the Augusti). Minted in Constantinople. Dumbarton Oaks, inv. 643.

(Courtesy of The Byzantine Collection, © 1991 Dumbarton Oaks, Trustees of Harvard University, Washington, D.C.)

in Constantinople. Among his first acts, Zeno deposed the anti-Chalcedonian bishops of Ephesus and Antioch. Apparently, Zeno did not feel powerful enough to eject the recently restored Alexandrian bishop, Timothy Aelurus. The emperor had to content himself with "uttering severe threats against Timothy." Before Zeno could take any more substantive steps, Timothy Aelurus died in July 477. Timothy was laid to rest beside his patriarchal predecessors, the solemn rites performed by his trusted deacon, Peter Mongus.[92]

Peter was consecrated patriarch and then awaited the expected reaction from Constantinople. He lacked the political stature of Aelurus, and the announcement of Peter's election to the patriarchate "exasperated Zeno, who judged him to have incurred the penalty of death." Before the year was out, Zeno sent orders that Timothy Salophacialos should be recalled from his monastic retirement in the Alexandrian suburb of Canopus, and that Peter should be arrested. Word of these decisions soon reached Peter. Before the imperial prefect could apprehend him, he went into hiding within the city, "moving about from one house to another"—in the same manner that Athanasius had concealed himself nearly 150 years earlier. Apparently Peter's support among the Alexandrian populace was great enough that he did not consider it necessary to find a monastic retreat in the desert. As a result, he was in a strategic position to organize resistance to Salophacialos. The restored Chalcedonian found Peter to be such an irritant that he wrote letters to Zeno in which he pleaded that Peter be formally sent into exile, "because he lay concealed in Alexandria, and plotted against the church."[93]

During this second tenure as patriarch, Timothy Salophacialos had no more success in winning over the allegiance of the Alexandrians than he had when he was previously installed in opposition to Aelurus. His initial entrance into the so-called Great Church (or patriarchal cathedral) was marked by rioting and bloodshed. Once again, Salophacialos sought to placate the Alexandrian populace with half measures: anathematizing heretics like Nestorius and Eutyches, inserting into the Diptychs the names of Cyril and Dioscorus—but to no avail.[94] Zachariah of Mytilene tells us that "not one believer would consent to hold communion with Timothy and his followers."[95]

Here, Zachariah at least concedes that Salophacialos did have certain followers. Who were they? While there was some sympathy to the Chalcedonian cause among the wealthy of the city (who had been roughly treated by the Monophysite Dioscorus), Salophacialos's principal support came from a tightly organized faction of clergy and monks centered on the Pachomian monastery at Canopus, some twenty kilometers east of the city. Founded during the patriarchate of Theophilus, this monastery called Metanoia (Repentance) came to attract recruits from diverse regions, so much so that Jerome was asked to translate monastic books for the monastery's "many Latins, who did not know the Egyptian and Greek languages in which the precepts of Pachomius, Theodore, and Horsiesios were written." Largely owing to these overseas connections, Metanoia adhered closely to imperial religious policy throughout late antiquity, even when such a policy led to conflict with the local hierarchy. Early in the patriarchate of Dioscorus, a major rift had developed between Dioscorus and the monks at Canopus. One of Dioscorus's most outspoken accusers at the Council of Chalcedon was a presbyter named Athanasius, who later took refuge among the monks at Canopus. Salophacialos himself hailed from this monastery. And when Salophacialos's health began to fail in 481, the Chalcedonian monks at Canopus sent a delegation to the emperor requesting that one of their own party be consecrated as successor to the ailing bishop. This petition was taken to Zeno by a presbyter named John, who is also identified in our sources as one of the Pachomian monks from Canopus.[96]

After his return from Constantinople and the subsequent death of Salophacialos in February 482, John the presbyter intrigued with the prefect to bring about his own elevation to the patriarchate. John's brief tenure during the spring and early summer of 482 was cut short by new directives from the emperor Zeno. John's delegation was not the only one to visit Constantinople in the previous year. Another group of monks, accompanied by some loquacious rhetoricians, had been canvassing support for Peter Mongus throughout the major cities of the east.[97] The presence of these rhetoricians doubtless convinced Zeno that this was more than just another monastic faction, given that rhetoricians frequently served as official ambassadors of cities during late antiquity. Their embassy before Zeno proved to be well timed, since the emperor along with his court bishop, Acacius of Constantinople, had begun to seek out some sort of compromise solution with the Monophysites. I suspect that Peter, who was still in hiding within Alexandria, was using this civic delegation to negotiate indirectly with the authorities in the capital. The newly forged compromise was the so-called Henotikon, and Zeno pinned his hopes for religious concord upon its reception in Alexandria and upon the conciliatory attitude of the still-popular Peter Mongus.[98]

Even before the new directives had reached Alexandria, John fled and took refuge with Simplicius in Rome, there to stir up animosity between the Pope and Peter Mongus's new imperial supporters, Zeno and Acacius.[99] Eventually, John had to content himself with receiving the bishopric of Nola from the hand of Simplicius. In the meantime, Peter Mongus came out from his seclusion and was accorded a thunderous public reception by the Alexandrians. The Chalcedonian party (or Proterians as they are sometimes called) abandoned their control of the Alexandrian churches and withdrew to Canopus under the leadership of a presbyter named Cyrus. Zeno entrusted the implementation of the Henotikon to Pergamius, the newly appointed praefectus Augustalis, and to a new military dux, Apollonius. Although they were also instructed to expel John, Pergamius and Apollonius discovered upon their arrival in Alexandria that John had fled and that Peter was securely in possession of his see. However, even though a successor of Dioscorus now sat unchallenged upon the episcopal throne as sole patriarch for the first time in twenty-two years, factionalism still rent the Alexandrian church.[100]

Zeno, in looking to Peter Mongus and Pergamius, had found two astute individuals who were well able to manipulate urban power politics and employ every symbol in the repertoire of late antique ceremony to bring about religious unity within Alexandria. Both Monophysite and Chalcedonian historians relate how the patriarch and prefect chose the occasion of a public festival to announce the new formula of reunion. In accordance with the protocol of late antique urban ceremonies, the entire Christian populace was assembled together, "the chief men, and the clergy, and the monks, and the sisters, and the believing people," and they accompanied Peter to the Great Church to hear his festival sermon. Peter then read out the Henotikon, and offered his own interpretation of the document—proclaiming that this dogmatic formula tacitly condemned Chalcedon and the Tome of Leo. He concluded his sermon by exhorting the Alexandrians to prayers and thanksgivings on Zeno's behalf, saying, "Now, beloved children, we have the light of the true faith of the holy fathers in this written statement of [the emperor's] orthodoxy." While the original framers of the Henotikon would have been shocked to hear Peter's anti-Chalcedonian interpretation, there is no doubt that Peter knew exactly the tack he had to take in order to gain the Alexandrians' assent. For the first time since the patriarchate of Dioscorus, the majority of the Alexandrian church was in formal union with the emperor and the church of Constantinople—an achievement that had persistently eluded Timothy Salophacialos.[101]

Even with the anti-Chalcedonian slant put on the Henotikon by Peter, the emperor's formula was still broad enough that most of the Chalcedonian party found they could accept its provisions. In addition, Peter offered these Proterian schismatics fully restored communion and status within the Alexandrian church. Consequently, Peter added to his success by persuading the majority of the

Chalcedonians to rejoin their Monophysite brethren. As might be expected, however, there remained a small intransigent faction opposed to reunion with Peter, and they went off to their monastic stronghold at Canopus under the leadership of the presbyter Cyrus and some lectors. Even then, Pergamius the prefect was able to convince some of these Proterians to abandon their cause and rejoin Peter. The intransigent monks at Canopus remained a thorn in Peter's side, though their ranks had been greatly depleted.[102]

Peter and Pergamius had brought about almost complete religious unity in Alexandria. Yet, with the healing of one longstanding breach in the Alexandrian Christian community, another far more serious schism opened up on the other end of the theological spectrum. Part of the success of the Henotikon owed to its deliberate vagueness, stopping short of explicitly condemning the Chalcedonian creed and the Tome of Leo, while at the same time anathematizing those who held unspecified heterodox opinions at Chalcedon. This was not enough for some of the more ardent Monophysites. A group of prominent Alexandrian presbyters, deacons, and some bishops from Egyptian sees upriver lodged a formal complaint against Peter, accusing him of betraying the memory of Dioscorus by now having communion with bishops who had condemned the revered patriarch at Chalcedon.[103]

Besides clergy, this group of dissenters included a large body of monks and abbots. Again we find ascetics set in opposition to episcopal authority within Alexandria. This time, monastic opposition posed an even greater threat than that of the monks at Canopus. This nascent Monophysite resistance centered on the numerous and wealthy monasteries ranged along the coastal ridge to the west of Alexandria, most notably Pempton, Enaton, and Oktokaidekaton. From the first news of the decisions at Chalcedon, the monks of these monasteries banded together in opposition to the council. In 457, the abbot of Enaton had been one of the four individuals to consecrate Peter's predecessor, Timothy Aelurus. Within a few months of Peter's public acceptance of the Henotikon, this informal Monophysite opposition in the Mareotis region had crystallized into a schismatic party. Zachariah tells us that "gradually the number of these Separatists was increased, and they received a considerable accession to their numbers in the monastery."[104]

Peter found himself in a predicament. How was he to reconcile this large and influential body of clergy and monks, while at the same time continue to assent to the Henotikon and maintain communion with Constantinople? Throughout the rest of 482, Peter publicly denounced Chalcedon and upheld his own, distinctly Monophysite interpretation of the Henotikon. Acacius of Constantinople became suspicious of Peter's adherence to the Henotikon and he dispatched a trusted presbyter to conduct a board of inquiry into Peter's orthodoxy. The fact that Peter passed this test only served to exacerbate further his relations with the seceding party.[105]

By early 484 it became clear to Peter that more decisive steps were required if he were to avoid being labeled a second "wobble-hat."[106] In the end, he chose to placate his own church, even if it meant schism with Constantinople—a logical choice, given that his long-standing base of support came from the local Monophysite community. Therefore, Peter placed his signature on his earlier anti-Chalcedonian sermons, he included only Monophysite names on his liturgical Diptychs, and he publicly disinterred the body of Timothy Salophacialos, "casting it outside the city." These acts initiated the slow process that healed this schism within the Alexandrian church, though it took nearly six years for the breach finally to be resolved. Peter went out of his way to welcome back into communion those who had abandoned the schismatics, and at the same time he employed threats and force against the remainder—even going so far as to eject some of the monks from their monasteries. In the meantime, Pope Felix in Rome had excommunicated Acacius for maintaining ties with Peter, and he also wrote to the emperor, exhorting him to "choose between the communion of Peter the Apostle and that of Peter the Alexandrian." In a subsequent letter to Zeno, Felix even insinuated that Peter might take steps to restore paganism in Alexandria.[107]

Peter was soon able to answer these veiled slanders by his actions. In July 484, Zeno's Isaurian compatriot and *magister utriusque militiae*, Illus, raised a revolt in Cilicia, assisted by another Isaurian general named Leontius and the former empress Verina. Within two months, the rebellion was crushed and the leaders fled to a mountain fortress in Isuaria, where they withstood a four-year siege until their eventual capitulation. Illus had been a friend and correspondent of John, the erstwhile Chalcedonian patriarch of Alexandria, and with the collapse of the rebellion Peter probably calculated that the time was right to attack the Chalcedonian faction at Canopus—perhaps as yet a further gesture to the local Monophysite party.[108] In addition, though Illus and Leontius were Christians, their Christianity was not very deeply rooted, and they favored the empire's pagan minority during their short-lived rebellion. This patronage was warmly received by pagans throughout the eastern provinces, and sacrifices were offered on behalf of the usurpers in the hopes that the relatively tolerant policies of the pre-Theodosian era would be restored.[109]

Illus and Leontius even went so far as to consult a noted pagan grammarian, poet, and soothsayer named Pamprepius.[110] Pamprepius himself originally hailed from Egypt, and in 482 or 483 he had made a high-profile visit to the small but wealthy and intellectual pagan community of Alexandria. Although pagan apologists like Damascius take great pains to demonstrate that the Alexandrian pagan intelligentsia "cast off [Pamprepius] and practically loathed him," they still suffered guilt by association in the aftermath of the rebellion. Indeed, a veritable persecution arose when Zeno sent an official named Nicomedes to Alexandria with the authority to hound out and suppress the slightest trace of rebellion. The inquest centered on the circle of the philosopher Ammonius and the grammarian Harpocras.[111] Damascius preserves vivid scenes for us of philosophers hiding in the homes of associates, of their desperate attempts to flee the city (sometimes frustrated at the very wharves of the harbor), of searches among their luggage for incriminating documents, and finally of their torture and imprisonment.[112] Several of these intellectuals sought to avoid imperial displeasure by making hasty conversions to Christianity.[113] Damascius's hero Isidore, though disdainful of such base strivings against ill fortune, "remained constantly worried about his death," and eventually fled to the comparative safety of Athens.[114]

Since paganism was tinged with political rebellion, it seems likely that Peter also judged the times propitious for bolstering his antipagan credentials. As it turned out, events played into Peter's hands in such a way that, by late 484 or early 485, he was able to create a cause célèbre and put himself forward as the champion of Christianity against paganism. By these actions, he was also able to anticipate by several months Zeno's official pogrom against Alexandrian paganism, create a climate of opinion which prepared the way for Nicomedes' brutal actions, and finally underscore his own loyalty to the dynasty. It is no wonder that the pagan Damascius brands him a "reckless and very bad man." Peter, however, had other goals in mind; for the ensuing events provided him with a perfect opportunity to bring Alexandrian Monophysites and Chalcedonians together.[115]

After the destruction in 391 of pagan cult at the Serapeum and the murder of the philosopher Hypatia in 415, Alexandria's pagan minority was greatly reduced in status and yet maintained a certain tenuous existence throughout the fifth century. Among the city's isolated pockets of pagans, mysteries connected with the cults of Persian savior gods were still being performed, as were also the rites of Osiris, Aion, and Isis. Canopus, which had long possessed popular pagan shrines, retained its position as a major focus of pagan religious observances, including sacrifice, incubation, and the promulgation of oracles. The supposed inviolability of this pagan pilgrimage center prompted pagan priests throughout Egypt to deposit at Canopus and at the neighboring shrine of Menouthis their endangered cult objects—even from sites as ancient as Memphis.[116] Zachariah of Mytilene, who studied at Alexandria during the 480s, offers a firsthand account of the latent strength of the pagan party at Canopus and Menouthis and at Alexandria. One of his fellow students, Paralios, learned that it was still possible for a group of infuriated pagan students to defend with blows the honor of Isis in the last quarter of the fifth century.[117]

Paralios, whom we have met in our discussion of Christian conversion, had been searching into the truth of pagan religious claims. One of his pagan teachers sought to convince him by means of a supposed pagan miracle. The barren wife of another pagan philosopher, Asclepiodotus, had given birth to a child after residing at temples in the vicinity of Canopus. Paralios, however, had a Christian brother who was a monk in the monastery of Enaton. This brother encouraged Paralios to inquire further into the miracle by asking whether the new mother also produced breast milk—as one would expect. Eventually it came out that the woman, with the collusion of her philosopher-husband, had taken as her own an unwanted child of a priestess of Isis. As a result, Paralios publicly denounced the hoax and repudiated paganism. This only served to anger some of his fellow students, who began to beat Paralios when he ventured to offer his opinions in class. Zachariah and some other Christian students (styled philoponoi) came upon the scene and, after a violent struggle, rescued Paralios from the pagans.

This incident suggests that militant paganism in fifth-century Alexandria seldom ventured beyond the doorway of the lecture hall. When it did, there were likely to be severe repercussions. Paralios, his monastic brother, and a party of other monks from Enaton appealed to Peter Mongus, doubtless recognizing that a satisfactory resolution of the affair could only be obtained through the patriarch's power. Peter, who realized the opportunity that had fallen into his hands, received them warmly and proceeded to incite the entire Christian populace of Alexandria to an antipagan pogrom. The new prefect conducted a halfhearted inquest and failed to give the Christians the revenge they desired—in part because he was openly sympathetic to the plight of the pagans. Thereupon, Peter Mongus commissioned a party of monks from Enaton and some Christian students (including Zachariah) to extirpate the original cause of the anti-Christian violence—the pagan temples at Canopus and Menouthis. In so doing, Peter directed the vehemence of the Christian crowd away from the city itself and toward a suburb that also contained a conventicle of his opponents. Peter even invited the Chalcedonian monks at Canopus to take part in destroying the temples of their pagan neighbors. It would seem that these monks considered paganism to be a far greater enemy than Peter, and a number of them enthusiastically assisted Peter's expeditionary force. Likewise, the Monophysite monks from Enaton did not shrink from joining with the Chalcedonians in destroying one of the last vestiges of paganism in Alexandria. Peter's shrewd gamble proved a great success. It was possible to unite the Chalcedonians and the Monophysites—if only briefly against a common enemy.

Although the Christian lay inhabitants of Canopus and Menouthis were decidedly lukewarm in their antipagan zeal, perhaps because of the tourist income, Peter's expeditionary force destroyed the temple of Isis and returned to Alexandria the next day with twenty camels loaded with pagan images and cult objects. A remarkable scene followed. The prefect and the patriarch convoked a public assembly in the marketplace, (recalling Peter's earlier use of this urban stage in unveiling the Henotikon). Ordered by ranks were the city's military commanders with their soldiers, the city council, the urban upper class, the clergy, and finally a great throng of the city's populace. Peter then interrogated the frightened priest of Isis, preached a sermon on the deceptions of heathenism, and consigned the idols from Canopus to a huge public bonfire—thus completing this grand auto-da-fé. The crowd, stirred by this public denunciation of paganism, threw into the fire any cult images "found in the baths and in private houses"[118] (figure 25).

In the denouement, Peter still faced monastic opposition. Indeed, the sedition of the Monophysite monks reached its peak two years later in 487, when we are told that the schismatics numbered nearly thirty thousand. Peter, however, had established the groundwork for eventual reunion. As in the days of his concealment from the authorities, Peter's support among the Alexandrian populace remained strong—so much so that an imperial representative pleaded with the schismatic monks not to enter the city "lest the people should be excited and a civil war should ensue."[119] Peter continued to preach against Chalcedon and the Tome of Leo, while trying to maintain relations with the authorities in Constantinople. He entered into a friendly correspondence with Fravitta, Acacius's successor in Constantinople, and felt secure enough to include an explicit condemnation of Chalcedon in one letter to him. Fravitta, however, died in March 490 before receiving this letter and it was passed to his successor, an ardent Chalcedonian named Euphemius. As might be expected, Euphemius denounced Peter as a heretic, but others in Constantinople also saw Peter's letter. A delegation of prominent Monophysite monks and clergy from Alex-

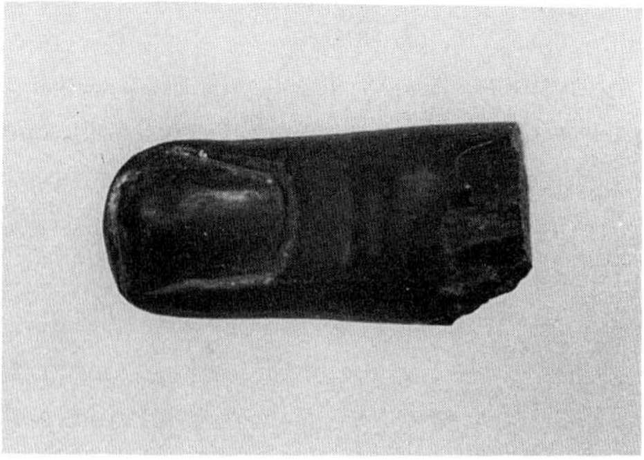

Fig. 25. Religious vandalism. Finger (3 cm) from a chryselephantine (ivory with gold overlay) statue. Part of a cache of destroyed pagan cult objects and religious inscriptions found in 1982 close to the ceremonial center of Alexandria. Statuary fragments probably belonged to figures of Serapis and Isis. The statuary was first sawn or hacked to pieces and then deliberately burned on a limestone pavement. Nearby pottery dates the find to the end of the fourth century through the fifth century. Possible evidence of ritualized destruction of pagan cult images following the end of public cult at the Serapeum in 391, or even as late as the antipagan campaign of patriarch Peter Mongus during the 480s.

(M. Rodziewicz)

andria were in the capital with the intention of petitioning Zeno for Peter's deposition. On seeing Peter's letter, these Monophysites were persuaded that Peter was indeed sympathetic to their cause and they intended to return to Alexandria and reestablish communion with their patriarch.[120]

Peter did not live to see this schism finally healed. Before the Monophysites had returned, Peter died in October 490. It was left to his successor, Athanasius II, to reap the benefits of Peter's skills as a politician and bishop. A later Coptic historian tells us that "in Athanasius's days, there was no disorder or persecution in the Holy Church."[121] Peter passed from the scene just over fifteen hundred years ago, leaving a legacy of reunion achieved through the shrewd exercise of ecclesiastical patronage within a complex local setting—a tradition established by his worthy predecessors on the throne of Saint Mark.

# Ten

# Conclusions

Intercommunal relations in Alexandria had passed through several distinct phases prior to Diocletian's capture of the city in 298. During the early Roman period, tensions remained high between the dominant pagan majority and Alexandria's sizable Jewish community. Although the Romans were able to maintain an uneasy peace in the city, anti-Roman sentiment frequently took the form of anti-Judaism as Alexandrian pagans lashed out at the protected minority. Despite the presence of a Roman garrison, the enforced peace in the city was punctuated by outbursts of intercommunal violence, particularly when one community sensed a shift in the policies of the local Roman authorities. The early second century witnessed the most destructive episode in this violence. The Jewish Revolt of 115–17 did not usher in the dawn of a messianic age, but instead brought about the virtual annihilation of the Alexandrian Jewish community. Henceforth, Alexandria's Jews were a factor of only the slightest political significance, at least until the last half of the fourth century.

Having asserted their undisputed hegemony in the city, Alexandria's pagans were free to work out a modus vivendi with their Roman overlords. As long as the Alexandrians were faced with a sound and unified Roman authority, consistent with traditional notions concerning the relationship between ruler and ruled, Alexandria enjoyed a measure of peace and political stability. This relationship started to break down in the third century, beginning with Caracalla's ill-fated visit to the city in 215. As political authority in the empire tended to become more fragmented and unstable during the middle years of the century, factions emerged within the city supporting rival contenders for the imperial throne. Political stability in Alexandria deteriorated to the point of open civil war during the 260s. Even though Aurelian was able to restore order after a bloody struggle in 272, internecine strife continued to plague the city and was closely linked to the wider political fortunes of the empire. This trend culminated in the usurpation of Domitius Domitianus and later of his lieutenant, Aur. Achilleus in 297–98. This rebellion was crushed by Diocletian in his usual thoroughgoing manner. Malalas's description of Diocletian "entering the city on horseback with his horse trampling on the corpses" serves as a vivid image of imperial authority being forcefully reasserted.[1]

Alexandria in late antiquity was free from the blatant challenges to imperial authority which had been commonplace in the era before the Tetrarchy. However, a new factor proved to be an equally unsettling force within Alexandrian society—the Christian church. Of negligible influence during the second century, the church thrived in the tumultuous years of the mid-third century, growing in numbers and in strength. Christianity brought into question the authority structures of both the hegemonic pagan culture, as well as of its own parent culture, Judaism. Combined with the widely held suspicion that the followers of the new religion were disloyal to the Roman state, these factors ensured that the Christians would suffer persecution as a destabilizing force in society. The resultant strong communal bonds among Alexandria's Christians and the clearly established hierarchy of leadership within the church rendered the Alexandrian Christian community a powerful force during the later empire, especially at those times when the local church was not divided over doctrinal or disciplinary issues.

Alexandria's pagans rose to the challenges posed by this new community, and developed a much more clearly defined communal identity by the mid-fourth century. They were able to lynch a bishop with impunity, combine with some of the city's Jews in persecuting Christians, and hold their own in pitched street battles against the Christians. In the end, the decisive factor in this conflict was the stance of the Roman authorities, either the normal administrative and military apparatus under the Praefectus Augustalis, or specially commissioned imperial representatives sent out from Constantinople. Once imperial policy had turned against both paganism and Judaism by the 390s, it was not long before the Christian community took advantage of its new status and established a virtual hegemony within the city.

Despite our focus on Alexandria's ethno-religious communities, it should be noted that communal identity functioned simultaneously on several levels in late antiquity. The city's inhabitants saw themselves as pagans, Jews, or Christians, but they also saw themselves as Alexandrians. Their allegiance to their city was manifested at those moments when the city at large was perceived to be threatened by outsiders. A prime example of this intercommunal solidarity occurred in September 367, when Valens's designated bishop, Lucius, attempted to establish himself in the city. Once it became widely known that Lucius had ignored long-established protocols for the ceremonial adventus of a notable, "the whole populace of the city, Christians and pagans, and of diverse religions" united in their demand for his expulsion.[2] This opposition differed from the citywide hatred that brought about the lynching of George of Cappadocia in 361. In George's case, each ethno-religious community had its own particular reasons for detesting him. Their functional solidarity arose out of their individual interests.

An important shift in Alexandrian self-identity occurred after the contest for urban hegemony had been decided in favor of the Christians during the patriarchate of Cyril. By the mid-fifth century, the loyalties engendered by the city and by Christianity became identified with one another. This transformation in urban consciousness produced the passions that fed the Monophysite-Chalcedonian strife after the deposition of the patriarch Dioscorus in 451.[3] After the destabilized era of the fourth and early fifth centuries, marked by intercommunal competition, Alexandrian society had achieved a measure of reintegration.

Late antique Alexandrians were acutely aware that they lived in a magnificent city with a glorious past. Yet, for the individual Alexandrian, the city's ethno-religious communities provided a primary group affiliation across this period. The boundaries between these groups were not always impermeable. Indeed a certain fluidity in allegiance was especially noticeable among the city's intellectual elite. In their case, however, their primary adherence was to the values and outlook inculcated by classical paedeia.

Admittedly, there is a danger in subscribing to a model of intercommunal relations predicated on the competition for urban hegemony. In adopting this model, are we simply embracing the views of the respective leadership elites? Are we merely parroting the literature produced after the fact by those committed to a totalizing rhetoric? More to the point, did the man (or woman) in the street understand intercommunal relations in Alexandria to be governed by long-standing conflict between sharply defined groups? Furthermore, if the people of Alexandria seem to adhere to this model, are they doing so only because it has been imposed upon them by their communal leadership—an elite that by its powers of coercion and by the consciously ingrained habits of deference was able to dictate the ways in which urban culture was interpreted, that is, to impose a cultural hegemony?[4]

By answering affirmatively to these questions, we would rob the Alexandrians of their ability to choose, an ability that lies at the heart of the shifting patterns of religious adherence during late antiquity. As we have seen, the eventual success of the Christian community was by no means a foregone conclusion throughout most of the fourth century. The establishment of Christianity as the hegemonic culture in Alexandria resulted, not only from the political acumen of Christian leaders and the intervention of imperial authorities, but on a more fundamental level, from the individual decisions of countless Alexandrians. Some recent commentators have seen this as a "marketplace" approach for understanding cultural change during late antiquity, a model that "gives primacy to the overall pattern of coexistence" and excludes a "monochrome picture of warring parties."[5] I would suggest that this cultural "marketplace" could be intensely competitive as some "retailers" attempted to monopolize the market while others resorted to drastic means simply to preserve their "market share." Pagans, Jews, and Christians fashioned their communal identities by occasionally adopting appealing elements from one another. In the end, however, they did so in order to maximize their position in the competition for cultural hegemony.

The emperor Julian was well aware of these dynamics in Alexandrian society, and he did not like what he saw. Referring to the growing power of the Christian community under Athanasius, he complained that they did not represent "the healthy part of the city," and that "this diseased part [the Christian community] has the audacity to arrogate to itself the name of the whole." His antidote to this deliberate program of identifying Christianity with Alexandrian civic life was to remind the Alexandrians that their exalted status, derived from the great deeds of the Macedonian conqueror, was far superior to the attractions of both Judaism and Christianity. In light of their glorious past, the pagan emperor was "filled with shame . . . to think that even a single Alexandrian can admit that he is a Galilaean."[6]

In late antique Alexandria, a multicultural urban milieu did not foster an easygoing toleration among communal groups—indeed, quite the opposite. Why was this? There was nothing about Christianity and Judaism in late antiquity which made them rigidly exclusive, to the point that insurmountable barriers were erected between them. At Antioch, portions of the Christian community saw nothing wrong with participating in Jewish festivals. Evidence from Aphrodisias indicates that the Jewish community was able to incorporate Gentile "God-fearers" in its self-understanding. In an earlier age, even Alexandria could host Gnostic groups who freely borrowed from a variety of religions as they fashioned their own cosmos.

By the fourth and fifth centuries, those Gnostic groups had all but disappeared. The sharply defined communal boundaries that characterized late antique Alexandria were the result of a particular set of local circumstances inherited from the Ptolemaic and early Roman past. Long-standing hostility between Greeks and Jews which culminated in the Jewish Revolt of 115–17 had left a residue of animosity. During the mid-third century and again during the Tetrarchy, the persecution of Christianity was particularly fierce in Alexandria. Added to this was the heavy hand of imperial authority which intervened continuously, in part to secure the loyalty of a city vital to the supply of the empire. We are becoming painfully aware at the close of the twentieth century that age-old enmities are not easily resolved, and that the clumsy intervention of an outside authority sometimes can fan the flames of these hatreds or even cause the warring factions to close ranks against the outsider.

Alexandria is a particularly instructive setting for observing social structure and intercommunal conflict during late antiquity. The sheer abundance of literary sources, in conjunction with the results of recent archaeological investigations, permit an unusually detailed examination of this major city of the late empire. While comparable in size with Rome, Antioch, or Constantinople, the clear demarcation of communal boundaries in Alexandria as well as the rapidly changing roles of its respective communities set it apart from these other urban centers.

Intercommunal competition is but one approach for mapping out the contours of social life in late antique cities. In the case of Alexandria, this methodology yields particularly rich dividends, as it seems to allow for the fullest exposition of the city's social dynamic. We have seen, however, that other perspectives may also contribute to our understanding of this complex metropolis. A sensitivity to urban design and the interplay between topography and urban society also facilitates our analysis of late Roman Alexandria. By attempting (however haltingly) to "see" the city from the perspective of its inhabitants, we are able to gain a sense of this varied urban environment and, as a result, to understand more fully one of late antiquity's most intriguing cities.

# Eleven

# Epilogue: From Roman Alexandria to Islamic Al-Iskandariyyah

In the parish of Segny [a small town of sixth-century Gaul], a certain girl of high rank in the world was seized upon by a cruel demon; she was not only shut up in a convent but even bound with iron chains. When many people, in the usual attempts to cure her, twined formulas of exorcism round her neck (the authors [of these formulas] being personally unknown to her), she, through the unclean spirit, jeered at their names—sad to say—and claimed that those who had written these texts had exhibited more vices in the past and had been guilty of this and that specific sin, which had been hidden from mens' knowledge. Then one of the bystanders said to the possessed woman: "What are these others' sins to us? You terrify us by your own vices, Unclean One! Truly, in Christ's name, I shall fasten not only the writings of those men whom you slander, but, if I can, of all the saints, round your neck, so that you may be overcome by the crowd of those who command you, if you dare to despise these few." The devil said, "You can load me with cargoes of Alexandrian papyri, if you like, but you will never be able to expel me from the vessel I have got possession of, until you bring me the order of Eugendus, the monk of Jura.[1]

As one might expect, Eugendus was immediately sought out, and his word of command had the desired effect upon the poor girl.

This anecdote, drawn from a Frankish saint's life, testifies to the importance of Alexandria in the early medieval West even after the Germanic invasions. Pirenne, of course, saw the expansion of Islam in the seventh century, rather than the fifth-century invasions, as the great break separating antiquity from the Middle Ages. His thesis has been extensively debated for the half century since the publication of *Mohammed and Charlemagne,* and recent assessments have focused on individual sites and the early medieval remains of ancient economic activity. Surprisingly scant attention has been paid to Alexandria's transition from antiquity to the Middle Ages, and the role that the city played in commercial developments during these crucial centuries. When ʿAmr ibn al-ʿAs and his followers finally rode into the siege-weary city in September of 642, did this capitulation mark an important watershed in the city's long history? Michael Morony has demonstrated in his studies of Iraq in the seventh century that the imposition of a new elite on a conquered region does not necessarily dictate radical alterations in economic or social organization.[2] Nearly a millennium earlier, Alexander's Macedonian troops became rapidly assimilated into the prevailing socioeconomic structures of the regions they conquered while maintaining cultural ties with the Greek motherland—thereby creating the distinct civilization of the Hellenistic age. Although the Arab conquerors of Alexandria expressed wonder at the city's many monuments and the dazzling brilliance of her marble structures (so bright that later chroniclers claimed a tailor could thread a needle during a full moon), can we say that these new masters from the Hijaz significantly altered Alexandria's urban evolution?[3]

It is essential at the outset to take into account several preliminary considerations regarding the form and development of cities—that is to say, urban morphology. First of all, we must exercise great care employing value-laden terms such as "decline," especially when describing the transformation of classical cities into those of the Middle Ages, whether in Europe or in the Near East. Moreover, the form of cities tends to be static, unlike many other human institutions, and changes that do take place are often transgenerational. For these reasons, we normally speak of evolution, not revolution, in urban morphology. Peter Fraser has commented on the difficulty of discerning changes in Alexandria's urban landscape from one stage of classical antiquity to another. This comes as no surprise, given the general continuity in Alexandria of classical society and its particular urban requirements.[4]

Nevertheless, urban form tends to reflect, over time, the society it embraces. Adjustments are made in the urban landscape as society gradually shapes its environment. Thus, a better understanding of urban morphology in late antiquity can be derived from identifying the various factors that transformed Alexandria from the cosmopolitan queen of the eastern Mediterranean to a neglected provincial backwater. The importance of Alexandria as a center for production and trade, the well-spring of new religious and philosophical movements, and its role as the stage for wide-ranging political and social conflict underscore the importance of attempting to piece together this diverse mosaic into an understandable urban milieu.

Several complementary avenues of inquiry serve as trajectories for tracing Alexandria's varied fortunes across late antiquity and the early Middle Ages—from Diocletian's capture of the city in 298 to the Fatimid occupation in 969—with 642 as the traditional divide between the classical and medieval periods. A study of the city's walls provides useful information regarding the growth and contraction of the inhabited precinct throughout these centuries. Ancient writers from the late Ptolemaic to the Byzantine period, as well as depictions on etched glass and in mosaics unite in their praise of Alexandria's lengthy walls.[5] Although precise information regarding the course of the Ptolemaic and Roman walls is lacking, we have seen that they probably enclosed an area of a thousand hectares. A portion of these walls was destroyed in 646 when ʿAmr crushed a short-lived rebellion against Arab rule led by a Byzantine commander named Manuel.[6] We are much better informed as to the exact circuit of the ninth-century wall, which took in an urban area of only three hundred hectares, and barely embraced the waterfront along the Great Harbor.[7] For late antiquity, density estimates based on archaeological and papyrological data, in addition to the testimonies of classical writers, are in broad agreement that the population of the ancient city was in the range of 200,000. This rough estimation of Alexandria's population in late antiquity contrasts dramatically with the early medieval period, in light of archaeological strata suggesting a much sparser distribution of habitation within the city.[8] It seems clear that the population had declined considerably in less than five hundred years, perhaps by as much as two-thirds.

Although there were marked demographic changes across this period, the physical aspect of the city developed much more gradually. In one important respect the city was little changed: the grid system of streets laid out at the city's foundation was maintained well into the Middle Ages. The fourteenth-century historian-geographer Abu al-Fida relates that, "Alexandria is a most beautiful city. It was built in the form of a chessboard and such a structure of the streets makes it impossible for a stranger to be lost in the town."[9] The continuity of this street pattern stands in sharp contrast to many other classical cities in the Near East, whose streets were narrowed and often were blocked entirely by encroaching structures—a tendency that begins to develop as early as the fourth and fifth centuries.[10]

While the persistence of the Ptolemaic street grid demonstrates an important case of continuity with the classical city, significant changes in Alexandria's topography would have astonished Strabo or Diodorus. Undoubtedly, the most notable change in the face of the city was the destruction of the luxurious Bruchion district in the northeastern sector of the city. Bruchion had been the site of the palace complexes of the Ptolemaic kings, and later became the seat of the Roman administration in the city. However, this splendid region suffered irreparable damage during Aurelian's siege of the city in 272. Well over a hundred years later, the historian Ammianus Marcellinus speaks of this quarter as a thing of the past, and his contemporary, Bishop Epiphanius of Cyprus, says that the region was still deserted.[11]

The much venerated tomb of Alexander the Great also perished during these centuries. Unlike Bruchion, however, we have no explicit testimony regarding the cause of its destruction. The last mention in the sources of the Conqueror's mausoleum occurs at the time of the emperor Caracalla's visit in 215.[12] Perhaps it too was lost during the civil wars which racked the city in the mid-third century.

As we have seen, the conversion of many of Alexandria's inhabitants to Christianity had the concomitant effect of Christianizing much of the city's topography. This change in religious allegiance greatly altered the face of late antique cities throughout the Mediterranean world. In Alexandria, many former temples were transformed into churches, thus accommodating the needs of new worshipers and proclaiming the victory of the new religion over the old gods. The structures constituting the great temple of Serapis had been forcibly converted into a series of churches and monasteries at the end of the fourth century. Even after much of the site was demolished, later Muslim geographers were so impressed that they thought that the *jinn* had erected the buildings for Solomon.[13] The new patriarchal cathedral in the fourth century was the former Caesarion, a huge precinct dominating the Eastern Harbor which had been erected by Cleopatra in honor of Caesar. Although it was eventually destroyed by fire in 912, the lofty obelisks that stood in front of it remained until they were carried off to London and New York in the 1870s.

Besides converting older structures, many new churches were erected throughout the city. The most notable was the martyrium church of Saint Mark, built in the suburban region of Boukolia, just beyond the city walls to the east. Various local chronicles mention that it was restored and renovated during the period 670–80.[14] As it was located in the immediate suburbs, it probably suffered from both the Sassanian and the Arab sieges. It is likely that the Persians effected the most destruction, since we have many accounts of churches and monasteries being destroyed during the wars of the early seventh century.[15] Even after the bones of Saint Mark were stolen away to Venice in 823, pilgrims still visited his martyrium.[16] However, by the late ninth century the church was described as situated three kilometers east of the city, an important indicator of urban contraction during late antiquity.[17]

The coming of Islam in the seventh century saw an identical pattern in Alexandria's urban morphology as that attending the ascendance of Christianity three centuries earlier. This time, Alexandria's churches, like the pagan temples before them, became fair game for conversion into mosques. The second largest church in the city, dedicated to the martyr-bishop Theonas, was transformed into what was later known as the Mosque of a Thousand Columns—the name itself speaks of the building's grandeur.[18] And as in the fourth century, the needs of the new religion called for the construction of new houses of worship. By the ninth century, at least five mosques had been built in the city.[19] Yet, one would be minimizing the function of these buildings if they were viewed only as religious structures, for Alexandria's new mosques, as also the churches before them, were prominent foci of the new community and served as important gathering places, much like the temples, theaters, hippodromes, and markets of the classical city.

A remarkably vivid cross section of Alexandria's history throughout late antiquity and the early medieval period can be seen as a result of the excavations at Kōm el-Dikka. The stratigraphy of this site reveals that large Roman houses of the second century were torn down to make way for an urban renewal project in the fourth century. As though reflecting one overall design, a complex of public buildings was erected including large imperial baths, lecture halls, cisterns, and a small theaterlike structure. Near to these buildings there arose a series of workshops and street-front stores, attracted no doubt to the ready market provided by the public buildings. This entire fourth-century level was eventually filled in with debris during the later sixth and seventh centuries. In the eighth century, while burials were taking place in what was once the theater, a spacious Arab house was built near the former workshops. This house was of a similar design to previous dwellings in the city. Yet, it maintained a decidedly rural aspect, considering its relative isolation, the agricultural refuse found on the site, and the sinking of a well within a large adjoining courtyard. By the ninth and tenth centuries, this house too was covered over by debris.[20] The street running in front of it, which had maintained its direction throughout the site's history, now ceased to exist. The area became one of Alexandria's most important cemeteries within the reduced circuit of the city walls.[21] Although the excavated site only represents a small portion of both the ancient and the medieval city, it confirms the picture we have seen in the literary sources: late antique vitality, followed by a rapid contraction of urban life in the ninth century.[22]

Further, the archaeological remains from Kōm el-Dikka, in conjunction with data supplied by literary sources, give us a rather detailed picture of the changing patterns of Alexandrian trade from late antiquity into the early Islamic period. As we have seen, this trade was predicated upon Alexandria's unique geographical position: at the end of trade routes stretching from India and Arabia, across the Eastern Desert to Edfu or Coptos, down the Nile and via canal to the city's bustling docks—whence goods could be shipped to every corner of the Mediterranean. Moreover, the cheap transport afforded by one of the greatest rivers in the world allowed for the efficient exploitation of the fertile lands along its banks.

The wealth generated for the city by this wide-ranging carrying trade must have been enormous. Added to this were numerous import and export tolls levied at the harbors as well as the profits made from currency exchange. Moreover, the profits reaped from the export of Egyptian agricultural products were supplemented by those related to the production and exchange of exquisite luxury items derived from the Nile Valley's rich supply of raw materials.

Judging by the literary sources, this active trade in agricultural and luxury goods continued unabated well into the seventh century. Maintenance work on the harbor moles is attested as late as the reign of Maurice (582–602).[23] Alexandrian merchants are found in a variety of Mediterranean ports, and at times they journeyed as far as Britain in order to exchange grain for tin.[24] Moreover, this far-flung trade apparently was unaffected by Vandalic piracy, even in the western Mediterranean. The excavations at Kōm el-Dikka confirm this picture, as imported pieces of pottery from North Africa, Asia Minor, and Cyprus are found in strata from the third century to the end of the seventh century. Gradually, however, pottery from Middle and Upper Egypt comes to predominate, and by the eighth century, there is a veritable flood of Egyptian tableware. Ivory remains from Kōm el-Dikka exhibit this same pattern, since the eighth and ninth centuries seem to mark a clear shift from the styles and subject matter of antiquity to floral designs and geometric patterns common to much of the Islamic Near East.[25]

Having sketched briefly these changes in urban area, topography, population, and trade, we can advance some tentative explanations for the shift in Alexandrian fortunes taking place in the eighth and ninth centuries. To begin with, it should be noted that the city seems to have recovered remarkably well from a string of natural and military catastrophes which occurred during the course of late antiquity. Plagues in the third and sixth centuries, serious earthquakes in 365 and 551, and protracted sieges of the city in the third and seventh centuries doubtless left their mark on population levels and urban topography.[26] In the early seventh century, Alexandria welcomed a host of refugees from Syria and Palestine who were fleeing the Persian advance.[27] When the Byzantine fleet finally sailed from the Great Harbor in September 642, large numbers of Greeks left their city and embarked for Constantinople.[28] Nevertheless, these seem to have been only temporary fluctuations in population numbers, followed by recovery over the course of a generation or two.

Clearly, 642 did not mark an important watershed in Alexandria's history, except from the standpoint of political control. The continuity in urban life we have observed until the eighth and ninth centuries is a direct result of Mediterranean trade being maintained throughout this period. Unlike other major classical cities, like Antioch or Rome, the lifeblood of Alexandria's prosperity was trade, not agricultural rents. Many of the largest classical cities functioned as cultural and economic centers for a large body of landed gentry who chose to live in an urban setting, thereby producing a ready market for goods and services. When the status of these gentry was broken during the invasions of the fifth, sixth, and seventh centuries, the cities they took as their residences could only decline. Not so Alexandria. Although there were portions of the Alexandrian elite (the wealthy bouleutai) with landholdings in the countryside, many of them had acquired their fortunes from previous successes in trade. The imposition of a new conquering elite did not effect fundamental dislocations in landholding patterns or in the larger context of Egypt's economic life. At most, the profits reaped from Alexandria's lucrative carrying trade were shared out among new merchants coming from the Hijaz.

Moreover, the markets that existed in Alexandria were created by a variety of sources that were not greatly affected by the events of these centuries. A full complement of Byzantine administrators was headquartered at Alexandria, and even after their departure in the seventh century, the new conquerors had to carry out most of the same functions performed by the previous administrative apparatus.[29] To staff this administration and provide for the city's protection against Byzantine seaborne invasion, Alexandria was designated a frontier post (*thaghr*) and as many as twelve thousand men were garrisoned in the city.[30] Continuity across this period is evidenced by the retention of the title *augoustalios* to refer to the governor of Alexandria—nearly a century after the Arab conquest.[31] During the administration of ʿAbd al-ʿAziz ibn Marwān (685–705), brother of caliph ʿAbd al-Malik, the temporary garrison at Alexandria was enhanced by the resettlement of Arabs from Fustāt at sites all along the Mediterranean coastline.[32] Reflecting Alexandria's role in administration, we find that it was also in the time of ʿAbd al-ʿAziz ibn Marwān that one of Egypt's most important state treasuries was located in the city.[33]

In addition to this large body of Arab administrators and militia, and the economic benefits derived from the city's status as an administrative center, Alexandria continued to enjoy the wealth generated by a lively tourist trade. Pilgrims thronged to the city of Saint Mark, often the first stop on their journey to the Holy Places.[34] During the fifth, sixth, and seventh centuries the shrine of Saint Menas southwest of Alexandria attracted large numbers of devoted pilgrims. Although the pilgrimage center enjoyed its peak of popularity in the early sixth century, it was still large enough in the later seventh century to rival many contemporary cities.[35] During this period, Alexandria also maintained its status as an important center for intellectual life, and its reputation was undiminished as the best place in the Mediterranean world to obtain an education in medicine, astronomy, and geometry.

The volume of exchange and manufacture taking place in this urban center generated a wide variety of employment. Doubtless the greatest sources of employment were the city's docks. Aside from the huge labor force needed to transship goods passing through the port, many were employed in shipbuilding. The fame of Alexandrian shipwrights (*technitai*) was widespread, and it comes as no surprise that the caliph Muʿawiya (661–80) had a portion of his great warfleet built in the city's shipyards. Consequently, Alexandria became the staging point for regular raids (*koursa*) against Byzantine coastlines. To fit out this naval force, great quantities of supplies were collected throughout Egypt and sent to the city.[36] Coptic sailors and oarsmen provided much of the manpower for the fleet, even during the periodic sieges of Constantinople.[37] In their proclivity for maritime activities, the Alexandrians of the seventh and eighth centuries were merely following the traditions of their fathers. For in the words of the continuator of Caesar's *Commentaries* (some seven hundred years earlier), "They were seafaring men whose city and native district were by the sea, and they had been trained in sailing from childhood by daily practice; and so they were eager to avail themselves of a resource that was natural to them and part of their daily lives."[38]

The transfer of political power to the Arabs brought no appreciable disruption in the volume of Alexandrian trade since the new elite was generally favorable to mercantile activity.[39] It should be remembered that the Prophet and many of his companions were merchants, including ʿAmr ibn al-ʿAs, the conqueror of Alexandria. A Muslim tradition, much discussed by modern historians, even credits ʿAmr with having visited the city prior to Islam's age of conquest. As we would expect, trade continued to flourish throughout the seventh century—even though it was now largely in the hands of Muslim merchants.[40]

However, this all-important trade which determined Alexandria's continued prosperity after 642 also caused its unavoidable economic decline in the later eighth and ninth centuries. After 750, the capital of the Caliphate shifted from Syria to the plains of Iraq. Umayyad Damascus was supplanted by Abbasid Baghdad, and as a result, new patterns of trade developed when markets sprang up far from the shores of the Mediterranean. Further, the new regime in Baghdad was much more hostile to Byzantine interests in the eastern Mediterranean. Maritime commerce waned as the navies of the great powers fought sporadically for control of the region.

This shift in market dynamics was accompanied by an invasion of Andalusian corsairs, who held sway in Alexandria between 814 and 827—at the same time that a local insurrection broke out in lower Egypt under the leadership of ʿAli ibn ʿAbd al-ʿAzīz al-Jarawī. After a fierce struggle, commanders sent by the caliph al-Ma'mūn extinguished the rebellion and expelled the Andalusian pirates.[41] However, these upheavals had decimated Alexandria's population, left portions of the city in ruins, and had isolated this hub of commerce from the wider world. The shrunken circuit of the ninth-century wall testifies to the city's sufferings.

A final blow to the status of Alexandria was dealt by the emergence of the Tulunid dynasty after 868. Despite the ambiguities of Ahmad ibn Tulun's official role as an Abbasid governor, he was able to craft a fundamental change in Egypt's status. For the first time in over a thousand years a sovereign independent state was established in Egypt. This development spelled an end to the massive exploitation of Egypt's resources by a foreign power—whether it be Roman, Byzantine, Umayyad, or Abbasid.[42] Under the Tulunids (868–905) and later the Ikshidids (935–969), Egypt's principal market for its goods and services developed rapidly at the apex of the Delta—some 180 kilometers upriver.[43] Excavations in the past thirty years have revealed a portion of the rapidly growing urban conglomeration at Fustāt/Misr.[44] Although a "proto-city" had existed on the site since the mid-seventh century, it was mainly after Ibn Tulun came to power there that the urban area expanded, embracing his stately new mosque and his princely dwellings to the northeast of Fustāt, christened al-Qata'i.

From this urban complex of Misr/Fustāt/al-Qata'i, trade routes stretched across the Sahara by caravan or by the newly dredged canal toward the Red Sea, which originally dated from the reign of Trajan.[45] As early as the caliphate of ʿUmar (634–44), Egyptian grain and oil had been shipped regularly to the Hijaz via this canal, which was maintained by requisitioned labor throughout Egypt.[46]

Papyrus receipts of the eighth and ninth centuries testify to the regular flow of goods through the canal to the Red Sea port of Clysma.[47] In addition, as Ibn Tulun expanded his realm to the northeast in the later ninth century, trade with Iraq and Byzantium began to be conducted principally through trading cities in Syria. Thus, commerce was drained away from Alexandria and redirected to either an internal market upriver or to regions east of Egypt.

In Alexandria itself, the condition of the city's canals, which had long served as arteries of prosperity, attest to the fundamental changes taking place during these centuries. This intricate system of canals, constructed during the Ptolemaic and early Roman periods, linked the city with the Canopic branch of the Nile at Schedia, and also allowed waterborne traffic to pass from Lake Mareotis on the south of the city to the Eastern Harbor. Besides joining Alexandria with these important trade routes, the canals also supplied the city with its main source of fresh water and served as protecting moats on the south and east. The defensive capabilities of the canals was recognized by ʿAmr ibn al-ʿAs, for it is said that he drained them following his capture of the city.[48] Even though they were restored during the later seventh century, these all-important canals were allowed to silt up and were dredged only occasionally during the next four hundred years.[49] This progressive neglect can be traced to the mid-fifth century, when the emperor in Constantinople released Alexandrian collegia from the responsibility of cleaning of the canals.[50] Henceforth, the state took responsibility; but only when a strong central authority existed with resources to expend, as during the reign of Justinian, were the canals properly maintained.[51] Moreover, the lengthy Schedia canal lost its raison d'être, when the Canopic branch of the Nile dried up in the ninth and tenth centuries. Nile traffic was thus confined to the two remaining channels running to the sea. As a result, when new ports were needed to accommodate mercantile traffic with Syria and other destinations in the eastern Mediterranean, more favorably situated cities like Rashid and Dumyat were developed. The growth of these ports effectively siphoned off much of the trade which passed through the previously bustling harbors of Alexandria.

The transformation of Alexandria in the seventh, eighth, and ninth centuries is mirrored by contemporary developments in the city's immediate hinterland, especially in the region of Mareotis. A recently excavated villa at Huwariya appears to have been occupied from the fourth through the early seventh centuries. This double peristyle villa was built originally on the pattern of a large urban house. Sometime during the fifth century, the villa was transformed into a waystation for Christian pilgrims journeying to the shrine of Saint Menas. Although the villa site was abandoned in the seventh century, a more diffuse agricultural settlement nearby exhibits an unbroken sequence of habitation throughout the early Middle Ages, with the minor modification that burial customs gradually conformed to contemporary usage evidenced by the Muslim necropoleis at Kōm el-Dikka.[52] This would suggest that the status of elite Byzantine landowners suffered as a result of the Persian or Arab invasions, perhaps to the extent that the landowners retreated to the walled safety of Alexandria or even took flight with the army to Constantinople. However, the broad base of the region's agricultural economy remained intact, at least until the ninth century.

The neighboring port of Philoxenite (sometimes referred to as Marea), located on the western arm of Lake Mareotis, ceased to function in the late seventh or early eighth century.[53] While this apparent cessation of maritime activity may have been caused by a drop in the water level of the lake, it seems more likely that the decline in lake traffic was due to the restricted appeal of Saint Menas's nearby shrine after the Muslim conquest of the Near East. Since the shrine had been in the hands of the pro-imperial (or Melkite) patriarch of Alexandria for nearly a century and a half, it is only natural that it would have suffered a decline following the end of Byzantine administration in Egypt. Although the shrine continued to function on a limited basis during this period, its survival was due more to its appropriation by local Coptic authorities in the late eighth and early ninth centuries than to a continuing stream of pilgrims from abroad.[54] The end of this period witnessed several destructive raids that crippled the shrine and led to its eventual abandonment. Monasteries to the south and west of Alexandria were also devastated at this time. This resulted in the transfer to Cairo during the episcopate of Christodoulos (1047–78) of the

Fig. 26. Heraclius and his son, Heraclius Constantine (613–41). Gold solidus. The last gold coin with an emperor's image minted in Alexandria (613–18). Dumbarton Oaks, inv. 188a.

(Courtesy of The Byzantine Collection, © 1991 Dumbarton Oaks, Trustees of Harvard University, Washington, D.C.)

Coptic patriarchate, an institution that formerly had ruled Egypt and much of the eastern Mediterranean from the city of Saint Mark.

No single event triggered Alexandria's transformation from a cosmopolitan mercantile center into a provincial trading station; rather, a closely linked series of developments contributed to the city's deterioration. Further, Alexandria's decline in status was not irreversible. Once contact with the west increased in the twelfth and thirteenth centuries, Alexandria again took its place as a vital center for exchange between the Near East and Europe. New canals were even dug, and the waters of the Nile once more flowed to the city.

The changing role of the Pharos, that lofty wonder of the ancient world, exemplifies Alexandria's transformation across this period. The Frankish pilgrim, Arculf, gives us an account of the lighthouse (ca. 680) which little differs from depictions going back nearly a thousand years:

> At the right-hand side of the port is a small island, on which there is a great tower which both Greeks and Latins called Farus because of its function. Voyagers can see it at a distance, so that before they approach

> the port, particularly at night-time, the burning flame lets them know that the mainland adjoins them, lest they be deceived by the darkness and hit upon the rocks, or lest they should be unable to recognize the limits of the entrance. Accordingly, there are keepers there who put in torches and other fuel to tend the fire that acts as a presage of landfall and a mark for the harbor mouth.[55]

Later Arab geographers tend to describe the Pharos in very different terms, even taking into account the destruction wrought upon the great lighthouse by earthquakes, notably in the tenth century. In their writings, the Pharos has become a watchtower from which the threatening ships of the men of Rūm (Byzantium) might be seen. The vast mirror, formerly used as a beacon, now becomes a fantastic spyglass which can see as far as the emperor's palace in Constantinople. These geographers also entertained speculations that the Pharos was erected along the axis of the earth and rested upon a foundation of a gigantic crystalline crab sculpted by the ancients in imitation of its counterpart in the heavenly zodiac—notions that confirm our view that Alexandria had become merely a city of unknown marvels and wonders, dimly reflecting its former glory.[56]

# Appendix

Chronological Table of Emperors, Prefects, and Patriarchs: Fourth and Fifth Centuries

| Emperor (Eastern Empire) | Prefect[1] | Patriarch |
|---|---|---|
| Diocletian 284–305 | Aur. Achilleus 297 | Theonas 282–300 |
| Galerius 305–11 | Sossianus Hierocles 307 | Peter I 300–311 |
| Licinius 308–24 | Aelius Hyginus 308–9 | |
| Maximinus Daia 309–13 | | |
| | | Achillas 311–12 |
| | Julius Julianus 314 | Alexander 312–28 |
| Constantine 324–37 | Septimius Zenius 328–29 | Athanasius 328–73 |
| | Flavius Hyginus 331–32 | |
| | Flavius Philagrius 335–38 | |
| Constantius II 337–61 | Antonius Theodorus 338 | |
| | Flavius Philagrius 338–39 (bis) | (Gregory) 339–45 |
| | Longinus 341–43 | |
| | Nestorius 345–52 | |
| | Sebastianus 353–54 | |
| | Cataphronius 356–57 | (George) 357–61 |
| | Faustinus 359–61 | |

*continued*

Chronological Table (*continued*)

| Emperor (Eastern Empire) | Prefect[1] | Patriarch |
|---|---|---|
| Julian II 361–63 | Gerontius 361–62 | |
| | Ecdicius Olympus 362–63 | |
| Jovian 363–64 | Maximus 364 | |
| Valens 364–78 | Flavianus 364–66 | |
| (Procopius) 365 | | |
| | Fl. Eutolmius Tatianus 367–70 | (Lucius) 367 |
| | Aelius Palladius 371–74 | Peter II 373–80 |
| | | (Lucius) (bis) 373–78 |
| Theodosius 379–95 | Hypatius 383 | Timothy I 380–85 |
| | Alexander 388–90 | Theophilus 385–412 |
| | Evagrius 391 | |
| | Hypatius 392 (bis) | |
| Arcadius 395–408 | Paulacius 398–404 | |
| | Euthalius 403/4 | |
| Theodosius II 408–50 | | |
| | Orestes 414/15 | Cyril 412–44 |
| | Callistus 422? | |
| | Charmosynus 443? | |
| | | Dioscorus 444–51 |
| Marcian 450–57 | Theodorus 451 | (Proterius) 452–57 |
| | Florus 453 | |
| | Nicolaus 457 | |
| Leo I 457–74 | | Timothy II, Aelurus 457–77 |
| Leo II 474 | | |
| Zeno 474–91 | Anthemius 477 | (Timothy, Salophacialos) 460–82 |
| (Basiliscus) 475–76 | | Peter III, Mongus 477–90 |
| (Fl. Marcian) 479 | | |
| | Theognostus 482 | (John Talaia) 482 |
| | Pergamius 482 | |
| (Illus and Leontius) 484 | Entrechius 482?–489? | |
| | | Athanasius II 490–94 |
| Anastasius 491–518 | | |

[1] I have included here only those prefects who appear in the text or are otherwise noteworthy. Dates are taken from *PLRE* 1 and 2.

# Abbreviations

The abbreviations listed below are largely of secondary literature or collections of sources contained in the text and notes. Titles of primary sources and journals are abbreviated according to the format found in *The Oxford Classical Dictionary,* 2d ed., ed. N. G. L. Hammond and H. H. Scullard (Oxford: Clarendon, 1970); H. G. Liddell, R. Scott, H. S. Jones, and R. McKenzie, eds., *A Greek-English Lexicon* (Oxford: Clarendon, 1968); G. W. Lampe, *A Patristic Greek Lexicon* (Oxford, 1961); and the *Clavis Patrum Graecorum* (Turnhout, 1979). Abbreviations of papyrological sources are conveniently collected in E. G. Turner, *Greek Papyri: An Introduction* (Oxford, 1968).

| | |
|---|---|
| Adriani, *Repertorio* | A. Adriani, *Repertorio d'arte dell'Egitto greco-roman.* Series C, 2 vols. (Palermo, 1966). |
| *AE* | *L'année épigraphique.* |
| *ANRW* | *Aufstieg und Niedergang der römischen Welt* (Berlin, 1972–) |
| *BASP* | *Bulletin of the American Society of Papyrologists* |
| *BIFAO* | *Bulletin de l'Institut français d'archéologie orientale* |

| | |
|---|---|
| Breccia, *Ins.* | E. Breccia, *Inscriptiones Graecae Aegypti, II: Inscriptiones nunc Alexandriae in Museo* (Cairo, 1911) |
| *BSAA* | *Bulletin de la Société archéologique d'Alexandrie* |
| Calderini, *Dizionario* | A. Calderini, *Dizionario dei nomi geografici e topografici dell'Egitto greco-romano* (Milan, 1935) |
| *CIJ* | *Corpus Inscriptionum Judaicarum*, ed. J. B. Frey (Rome, 1936–52) |
| *CIL* | *Corpus Inscriptionum Latinarum* (1863–) |
| *CoptEncy* | *The Coptic Encyclopedia*, ed. A. S. Atiya, 8 vols. (New York, 1991) |
| *CPJ* | *Corpus Papyrorum Judaicarum*, ed. V. A. Tcherikover and A. Fuks (Cambridge, Mass., 1957–64) |
| *CSEL* | *Corpus Scriptorum Ecclesiasticorum Latinorum* |
| *É&T* | *Études et travaux* |
| *GCS* | *Die griechischen christlichen Schriftsteller* |
| *IG* | *Inscriptiones Graecae* (1887–) |
| *IGRR* | *Inscriptiones Graecae ad Res Romanas Pertinentes* (1906–) |
| *ILS* | *Inscriptiones Latinae Selectae*, ed. H. Dessau (Berlin, 1902–16) |
| *JEA* | *Journal of Egyptian Archaeology* |
| Jones, *LRE* | A. H. M. Jones, *The Later Roman Empire: 284–602* (Oxford, 1964) |
| *JRS* | *Journal of Roman Studies* |
| *JTS* | *Journal of Theological Studies* |
| MIFAO | *Mémoires publiés par les membres de l'Institut français d'archaéologie orientale* |
| *PG* | *Patrologia Graeca* |

| | |
|---|---|
| *PO* | *Patrologia Orientalis* |
| *R-E* | A. Pauly, G. Wissowa, and W. Kroll, *Real-Encyclopädie der classischen Altertumswissenschaft* (Stuttgart, 1894–) |
| Rodziewicz, *Habitations* | M. Rodziewicz, *Les habitations romaines tardives d'Alexandrie à la lumière des fouilles polonaises à Kōm el-Dikka, Alexandrie* 3 (Warsaw, 1984) |
| *ZPE* | *Zeitschrift für Papyrologie und Epigraphik* |

# Notes

*Chapter One. Introduction*

1. True to form, he then followed with twenty-eight detailed laws regulating the administration of the city and the province. Preface to Edict 13, *Corpus Juris Civilis,* vol. 3, ed. R. Schoell and G. Kroll (Berlin, 1954), 780, dated by the editors to the period between September 538 and August 539 (795, n. 3). See also the able survey by E. R. Hardy, "The Egyptian Policy of Justinian," *DOP* 22 (1968): 23–41.
2. G. Dagron, *Naissance d'une capitale: Constantinople* (Paris, 1974); C. Mango, *Le développement urbain de Constantinople: 4e–7e siècles,* Travaux et mémoires du Centre de recherche d'histoire et civilisation de byzance, Monographies 2 (Paris, 1985); also the important collection of articles in H. G. Beck, ed., *Studien zur Frühgeschichte Konstantinopels,* Miscellanea Byzantina Monacensia 14 (Munich, 1973); C. Foss, *Ephesus after Antiquity: A Late Antique, Byzantine and Turkish City* (Cambridge, 1979); J. H. W. G. Liebeschuetz, *Antioch: City and Imperial Administration in the Later Roman Empire* (Oxford, 1972); C. Lepelley, *Les cités de l'Afrique romaine au Bas-Empire,* 2 vols. (Paris, 1979–81). Aphrodisias: K. T. Erim, *Aphrodisias: City of Venus Aphrodite* (New York, 1986); J. de la Genière and K. Erim, eds., *Aphrodisias de Carie* (Paris, 1987); C. Roueché, *Aphrodisias in Late Antiquity* (London, 1989); idem, *Performers and Partisans at Aphrodisias* (London, 1992); C. Roueché and K. T. Erim, eds., *Aphrodisias Papers, Journal of Roman Archaeology,* suppl. 1 (Ann Arbor, Mich., 1990); R. R. Smith and K. T. Erim, eds.,

*Aphrodisias Papers 2, Journal of Roman Archaeology,* suppl. 2 (Ann Arbor, Mich., 1991).

3. A quarter century ago, a flurry of scholarly activity on Alexandria culminated in P. M. Fraser's *Ptolemaic Alexandria,* 3 vols. (Oxford, 1972), and also included Adriani's compendium and A. Bernand's *Alexandrie la Grande* (Paris, 1966). The most important earlier authorities are Mahmoud-Bey "El Falaki," *Mémoire sur l'antique Alexandrie . . .* (Copenhagen, 1872); G. Botti, *Plan de la ville d'Alexandrie à l'époque ptolémaïque* (Alexandria, 1898); O. Puchstein, "Alexandreia," *R-E* 1 (1894): 1376–88; A. J. Butler, *The Arab Conquest of Egypt,* 2d ed., ed. P. M. Fraser (1902; Oxford, 1978), chap. 24, "Alexandria at the Conquest," 368–400, with Fraser's additional bibliographical essay, lxxiii–lxxvi; E. Breccia, *Alexandria ad Aegyptum,* English ed. (Bergamo, 1922); H. I. Bell, "Alexandria," *JEA* 13 (1927): 171–84; Calderini, *Dizionario,* 55–205; W. Schubart, "Alexandria," in *Reallexikon für Antike und Christentum* (Stuttgart, 1950), 1:271–83; A. Adriani, "Alessandria," in *Enciclopedia dell'arte antica: Classica e orientale* (Rome, 1958), 1:204–16. See also G. Caruso, "Alcuni aspetti dell'urbanistica di Alessandriain età ellenistica: Il piano di progettazione," in *Alessandria e il mondo ellenistico-romano: Studi in onore di Achille Adriani,* ed. N. Bonacas, A. DiVita, and G. Barone (Rome, 1983), 4:43–53.

   Early Roman Alexandria has been better served in recent years. See especially D. Delia, *Alexandrian Citizenship during the Roman Principate,* American Classical Studies, no. 23 (Atlanta, 1991); idem, "The Population of Roman Alexandria," *Transactions of the American Philological Association* 118 (1988): 275–92; W. D. Barry, "Aristocrats, Orators and the 'Mob': Dio Chrysostom and the World of the Alexandrians," *Historia* 42.1 (1993): 82–103. See also the superb collection of inscriptional evidence in F. Kayser, *Recueil des inscriptions grecques et latines (non funeraires) d'Alexandrie imperiale* (Cairo, 1994); regrettably, this work appeared too late for me to consult it.

   Surveys of the city's history during late antiquity may be found in H. Heinen, "Alexandria in Late Antiquity," in *CoptEncy* 1:95–103; P. M. Fraser, "Alexandria, Christian and Medieval," in *CoptEncy* 1:88–92.

4. E. Patlagean, *Pauvreté économique et pauvreté sociale à Byzance: 4e–7e siècles* (Paris, 1977), 8.
5. On this issue, see the comments of A. K. Bowman, "Papyri and Roman Imperial History," *JRS* 66 (1976): 160–161.
6. R. S. Bagnall, *Egypt in Late Antiquity* (Princeton, 1993).
7. On the traditional compartmentalization of Egyptian studies and its relation to the discipline of papyrology, see the seminal article of D. Hobson, "Towards a Broader Context of the Study of Greco-Roman

Egypt," *Echos du mond classique / Classical Views* 32.7 (1988): 353–63. For papyrological sources on the city, consult E. G. Turner, *Greek Papyri: An Introduction* (Oxford, 1968), 49–50; W. L. Westermann, "Alexandria in the Greek Papyri," *BSAA* 38 (1949): 36–50. Calderini's monograph-length entry on Alexandria in his *Dizionario* is a mine of information on the city culled from papyri published before 1935.

8. Adrianai, *Repertorio*. See also A. Bernand's review of this work, "Un inventaire des monuments d'Alexandrie gréco-romaine," *Revue des études grecques* 85 (1972): 139–54.
9. Strabo 17.1.6–10; Herodian 4.8.6–4.9.8; Achilles Tatius 5.1–2; Ammianus Marcellinus 22.16.7–23; John of Nikiu *Chronicle*.
10. *Alexandria civitas splendida, populus levissimus, sed amatores peregrinorum*. Antoninus of Piacenza *Itinerarium* 45 (*CCSL* 175, p. 152).
11. Clem. *Strom*. 6.5 (*PG* 9, col. 261b).
12. *M. Polyc*. 3.2; *ad Diog*. 1.5–6; Aristides *Apol*. 2; Tertul. *ad Nat*. 1.8; *Scorp*. 10.
13. On the early history of Christianity in Alexandria, see J. Faivre, "Alexandrie," in *Dictionnaire d'histoire et de géographie ecclésiastiques* (Paris, 1914), 2:290–369; H. Leclercq, "Alexandrie, archéologie," in *Dictionnaire d'archéologie chrétienne et de liturgie* (Paris, 1924), 1:1098–1182; Calderini, *Dizionario*, 165–78; E. R. Hardy, *Christian Egypt: Church and People* (New York, 1952); M. Krause, "Das christliche Alexandrien und seine Beziehungen zum koptischen Ägypten," in *Aegyptica Treverensia: Trierer Studien zum Griechisch-Römischen Ägypten*, vol. 1, *Alexandrien*, ed. N. Hinske (Trier, 1981), 53–62; C. Andresen, "Siegreiche Kirche," *ANRW* 2.23.1 (1979): 387–495; B. A. Pearson, "Earliest Christianity in Egypt: Some Observations," in *The Roots of Egyptian Christianity*, ed. B. Pearson and J. Goehring (Philadelphia, 1986), 132–59; and especially the two articles of A. Martin, "Aux origines de l'église copte," *Revue des études anciennes* 83 (1981): 35–56; and "Les premiers siècles du christianisme à Alexandrie: Essai de topographie religieuse, 3e–4e siècles," *Revue des études augustiniennes* 30 (1984): 211–25.
14. For this turbulent episode in Alexandrian history, see T. E. Gregory, *Vox Populi: Violence and Popular Involvement in the Religious Controversies of the Fifth Century A.D.* (Columbus, Ohio, 1979), 163–201.
15. Isidore of Pelusium *Ep*. 1.152; Leo the Great *Ep*. 120.2; cf. Soc. *HE* 7.7 cols. 749c-752a, 7. 11 col. 757b.
16. Josephus *BJ* 2.385–387, 498; Dio Chrysostom *Or*. 32.27–30; Herodian 4.8.7.

    In the later empire, Julian *Ep*. 21 (378d-79d); *Expositio Totius Mundi et Gentium* 37.1–5; Amm. Marc. 16.15, 23; 22.11.4; *Historia Augusta Tyr. Trig*. 22.1–3; *Quadr. Tyr*. 8.1–5; Ausonius *Ordo Urbium Nobilium* 4.4–5; Socrates Scholasticus *HE* 4.20, 7.13 col. 761a.

17. See now the revisionist work of W. D. Barry, "The Ptolemaic Crowd and the Riot of 203 BC," *Echos du monde classique/Classical Views* 12 (1993): 415–31; idem, "Popular Violence and the Stability of Roman Alexandria, 30 BC–AD 215," *BSAA* 45 (1993): 19–34; idem, "Aristocrats, Orators and the 'Mob': Dio Chrysostom and the World of the Alexandrian," *Historia* 42.1 (1993): 82–103; idem, "Faces of the Crowd: Popular Society and Politics of Roman Alexandria, 30 B.C.–A.D. 215" (Ph.D. diss., University of Michigan, 1988).
18. Even the emperors during this era recognized that the Alexandrian populace was susceptible to mob violence (Constantius II: Soc. *HE* 2.23 col. 259b–c; Julian *Ep.* 21).
19. A visitor to Alexandria in the fourth century, the anonymous author of the *Expositio Totius Mundi,* was puzzled by this incongruity between a city famous for its intellectual achievements and a city often given to violence. Unable to reconcile the two, he finally exclaims (37.6), "It is altogether an incomprehensible city and region" (*et est in omnibus civitas et regio incomprehensibilis*).
20. Richard Krautheimer has used this type of descriptive analysis in his interpretation of the late antique history of Rome, Milan, and Constantinople; see Krautheimer, *Three Christian Capitals: Topography and Politics* (Berkeley, 1983).
21. E. N. Bacon, *The Design of Cities,* 2d ed. (New York, 1974), esp. 15–65.
22. Ibid., 20, 33–36.
23. Ibid., 64–67. "From the time of its first beginning in archaic days, the Panathenaic procession and the sensations of those taking part in it gave the central theme to the development of Athens. From that time on, much of the architectural effort was directed toward providing punctuating points in the experience of its movement, toward adding a note to the rhythm set by previous generations. But the conceiver, the promoter, the architect, and the builder of these injections into a sequence of sensation were themselves the product of the cumulative effect of moving over the Panathenaic Way, and so were automatically attuned to the demands of its accumulated rhythms" (65).
24. M. Girouard, *Cities and People: A Social and Architectural History* (New Haven, 1985); J. E. Vance, *This Scene of Man: The Role and Structure of the City in the Geography of Western Civilization* (New York, 1976), revised as *The Continuing City: Urban Morphology in Western Civilization* (Baltimore, 1990); S. Kostof, *The City Shaped: Urban Patterns and Meanings through History* (Boston, 1991); idem, *The City Assembled: The Elements of Urban Form through History* (London, 1992). Sensitivity to urban design and architecture sets these works apart from earlier urban histories, which are almost entirely preoccupied with socioeconomic factors to the neglect of the physical setting of the cities; see M. Weber,

*The City*, trans. D. Martindale and G. Neuwirth (New York, 1958); G. Sjoberg, *The Preindustrial City: Past and Present* (New York, 1960); L. Mumford, *The City in History* (San Diego, 1961).

25. William MacDonald, *Architecture of the Roman Empire*, vol. 2 (New Haven, 1986). MacDonald often refers to an urban "armature," that is, "a clearly delineated, path-like core of thoroughfares and plazas," or more succinctly, "an architecture of connection" (9). Quite plainly, these armatures are identical to Bacon's movement systems.

While great strides have been made in recent years to assess properly the role of cities within ancient society, these urban histories are perhaps even more dominated by socioeconomic concerns than are the discussions of other preindustrial cities. This neglect of the physical setting's interaction with ancient urban cultures is most likely due to the traditional segregation of fields within classical studies, thereby consigning questions regarding urban design to the purview of archaeologists.

26. An elegant theoretical exploration of these issues may be found in E. V. Walter, *Placeways: A Theory of the Human Environment* (Chapel Hill, N.C., 1988).

27. Most notably, I. H. M. Hendriks, P. J. Parsons, and K. A. Worp, "Papyri from the Groningen Collection I: *Encomium Alexandrae*," *ZPE* 41 (1981): 71–83.

28. P. M. Fraser, "A Syriac *Notitia Urbis Alexandrinae*," *JEA* 37 (1951): 103–8.

29. For a general overview of the site, see W. Kolataj, "Recherches architectoniques dans les thermes et le théâtre de Kōm el-Dikka à Alexandrie," in *Aegyptiaca Treverensia: Trierer Studien zum Griechisch-Römischen Ägypten*, vol. 2, *Das Römisch-Byzantinische Ägypten*, ed. G. Grimm, H. Heinen, and E. Winter (Mainz, 1983), 187–94; and M. Rodziewicz, "Archaeological Evidence on Byzantine Architecture in Alexandria," *Graeco-Arabica* 4 (1991): 287–93. The preliminary reports of the excavations may be found in the journal *Études et travaux*, published by the Center of Mediterranean Archaeology of the Polish Academy of Sciences. The articles commence in 1966, and may be found under the names of the principal excavators of the site, K. Michalowski, L. Lipinska, W. Kubiak, T. Borkowska-Kolataj, Z. Kiss, W. Kolataj, and M. Rodziewicz. Annual reports of the years 1980–84 are in *BSAA* 44 (1991). For a summary of the annual excavations with full bibliography, consult M. Rodziewicz, "A Brief Record of the Excavations at Kom el-Dikka in Alexandria (1960–1980)," *BSAA* 44 (1991): 1–70. Even though final reports are lacking for the theater and the lecture halls, others have been published in the series *Alexandrie*, also under the auspices of the Center of Mediterranean Archaeology: M. Rodziewicz,

*La céramique romaine tardive d'Alexandrie, Alexandrie* 1 (Warsaw, 1975); Z. Borkowski, *Inscriptions des factions à Alexandrie, Alexandrie* 2 (Warsaw, 1981); Z. Kiss, *Sculptures des fouilles polonaises à Kōm el Dikka (1960–1982), Alexandrie* 4 (Warsaw, 1988); idem, *Les ampoules de Saint Ménas découvertes à Kōm el Dikka (1961–1981), Alexandrie* 5 (Warsaw, 1989); W. Kolataj, *The Imperial Baths at Kōm el-Dikka, Alexandrie* 6 (Warsaw, 1992), and, most importantly, Rodziewicz, *Habitations*. This last work is a careful analysis of the site, its stratigraphy, and the variety of its material remains—altogether, the measure against which all future final reports from Kōm el-Dikka must be judged.

30. So Botti, *Plan de la ville,* 117–18; Breccia, *Alexandria ad Aegyptum,* 101; Calderini, *Dizionario,* 136; corrected in Adriani, *Repertorio,* 233.
31. *Alexandria enim vertex omnium est civitatum,* Amm. Marc. 22.16.7.

*Chapter Two. The Urban Setting*

1. Malalas 12.41[308–9]; John of Nikiu 77.1–6; Eutropius 9.23. A compendium of Diocletian's journeys may be found in T. D. Barnes, *The New Empire of Diocletian and Constantine* (Cambridge, Mass., 1982), 49–56. The precise chronology of the revolt and its suppression has been the source of scholarly controversy for several generations, so much so that A. K. Bowman has called it "the most vexed chronological question of the period," in "Papyri and Roman Imperial History," *JRS* 66 (1976): 159. For the most part, I have chosen here to follow the outline of events posited by J. D. Thomas, "The Date of the Revolt of L. Domitius Domitianus," *ZPE* 22 (1976): 253–79; C. Vandersleyen, *Chronologie des préfets d'Égypte de 284 à 395,* Collection Latomus, vol. 55 (Brussels, 1962), 44–61; Bowman, "Papyri," and "The Revolt of Busiris and Coptos," *BASP* 21.1–4 (1984): 33–36.
2. The epithet used as the title of this section is found frequently in papyri and inscriptions: *P.Oxy*. 40.2925; *P.Mich*. 606 inv. 182, 723 inv. 902, 724 inv. 422; *P.Ryl*. 2.110, 4.618; *P.Wisc*. 65; *IGRR* 1.381, 1073; Breccia, *Ins.,* 130.
3. Diodorus Siculus 17.52.2; Strabo 17.1.7; Amm. Marc. 22.16.8. In the winter, these breezes often became raging winds: *M. Petr. Al.* 10, in P. Devos, "Une passion grecque inédite de S. Pierre d'Alexandria et sa traduction par Anastase le Bibliothécaire," *AnBol* 83 (1965): 157–87.
4. *Expositio* 36.9–15, 35.3–5. Graffiti: Rodziewicz, *Habitations,* 219, describes them as the most numerous of all the genre scenes.
5. Strabo 17.1.7; Amm. Marc. 22.16.7–9; *Expositio* 35.1–8, 36.9–16.
6. Even though, in his rather confused account of the city's foundation, John credits Cleopatra VII with the construction of these amenities. John of Nikiu 67.7–8.

7. Plutarch *Alex.* 26.5; Strabo 17.1.6; Amm. Marc. 22.16.7. While we might reasonably question the veracity of this colorful foundation legend, it played an important role in shaping the civic consciousness of Alexandrians for nearly a millennium.
8. A. Bernand, *Alexandrie la Grande* (Paris, 1966), 86–100. P. M. Fraser also follows Strabo's itinerary in his description of the city; see *Ptolemaic Alexandria* (Oxford, 1972), 1:11–32. Strabo's omissions are noted by Fraser, (1:29–32).
9. In the following discussion, I make no claim of presenting comprehensive bibliographical information for each of the topographical features within the city. I only indicate some of the more important references found in late antique literature, or those passed over by the standard compendia. For full annotation, consult Calderini, *Dizionario,* and Adriani, *Repertorio.*
10. Ammianus Marcellinus makes special note of this aspect of the city's design: *Sed Alexandria ipsa non sensim (ut aliae urbes), sed inter initia prima aucta per spatiosos ambitus* (But Alexandria itself, not gradually like other cities, but at its very beginning, attained its wide extent). 22.16.15.
11. Heptastadion: Calderini, *Dizionario,* 111–12; Adriani, *Repertorio,* 220–21. Harbors: Calderini, *Dizionario,* 125–26; Adriani, *Repertorio,* 236–38.
12. Letter of Dionysius in Eus. *HE* 7.21.4. Nautical imagery familiar to Alexandrians pervades a seventh-century Coptic text that praises the pastoral work of Peter I: "[Peter] possessed the rudders of the spiritual ship (and) he made the passengers seated in it equal in the riches of the good God. For he had them sail into good harbors—I mean the holy Gospels—and he made them do business by its holy commandments." Alexander Al. *Encom. Petr. Al.,* Coptic text in H. Hyvernant, *Les actes des martyrs de l'égypte* (Hildesheim, 1977), 257, trans. T. Vivian.
13. Chaereu and Schedia: Gregory Naz. *Oratio* 21.28–29. Goods were transfered from large Nile barges to shallow-drafted canal boats at Chaereu. It was considered the first stopping place on a journey from Alexandria: Athan. *v. Ant.* 86: *Hist. Aceph.* 4.3; *P.Oxy.* 56.3864.

    Alexandrian canals: Calderini, *Dizionario* 84–86; Adriani, *Repertorio,* 212–14. The various canals that linked together the Nile, the lake, and the sea passed so close to the city's walls that defenders could easily hurl stones at enemy ships that ventured into these waterways: John of Nikiu *Chron.* 107.46–48.

    The literary sources attesting the canal between Mareotis and Eunostos are problematic, but the overwhelming need to transship grain efficiently to this harbor argues in favor of this canal's existence. For a discussion of the canals and ports of Alexandria in the context of commercial exchange with the regions bordering the lake, see M. Rodziewicz, "Alexandria and the District of Mareotis," *Graeco-Arabica* 2 (1983): 199–216.

14. These reefs remained a danger to shipping throughout this period: Leont. N. *v.Jo. Eleem.* 26; Athan. *Hist. Ar.* 58; *epit.Phot.* [Damascius] 71 (ed. Zintzen, 100).
15. Pharos: Calderini, *Dizionario,* 156–64; Adriani, *Repertorio* 234–235; Fraser, *Ptolemaic Alexandria,* 1:17–20; P. A. Clayton, *The Seven Wonders of the Ancient World* (London, 1989), 138–57. Achilles Tatius 5.6.2–3.
16. Docks and warehouses: s.v. "Apostaseis," in Calderini, *Dizionario,* 93; Adriani, *Repertorio,* 206; Fraser, *Ptolemaic Alexandria,* 1:24–25. Emporion: Calderini, *Dizionario,* 110–11; Adriani, *Repertorio,* 220. Caesarion: Calderini, *Dizionario,* 218–19; Adriani, *Repertorio,* 214–16; Fraser, *Ptolemaic Alexandria,* 1:24.
17. *Legat. ad Gaium* 22 (trans. Colson and Earp, *LCL*).
18. Bruchion: Calderini, *Dizionario,* 97–100, 105–6, 126–27; Adriani, *Repertorio,* 208–10, 211, 226; Fraser, *Ptolemaic Alexandria,* 1:14–15, 22–23.

    Few questions in Alexandrian topography have generated as much controversy as the location of Alexander's tomb. A persistent tradition during the Islamic period places the tomb in the vicinity of Shari al-Nebi Danyal. Another likely topographical candidate is the area of the palaces. Unfortunately, the ancient literary sources are equivocal on this matter. Calderini, *Dizionario,* 149–51; Adriani, *Repertorio,* 242–45; Fraser, *Ptolemaic Alexandria,* 1:15–17; E. Breccia, "La tomba di Alessandro Magno," *Egitto greco e romano,* 3d ed. (Pisa, 1957), 28–55; R. Bianchi, "Hunting Alexander's Tomb," *Archaeology* 46.4 (July–August 1993): 54–55.

    Museon: Calderini, *Dizionario,* 128–30; Adriani, *Repertorio,* 228–29; Fraser, *Ptolemaic Alexandria,* 1:15, 305–35. See now the thorough study by D. Delia, "From Romance to Rhetoric: The Alexandrian Library in Classical and Islamic Traditions," *American Historical Review* 97.5 (1992): 1449–67. Destruction of Bruchion: Eus. *HE* 7.32.7–12; Amm. Marc. 22.16.15; Epiphanius *de Mens. et Pond.* 9 (*PG* 43, cols. 249c–50c).
19. Theater: Calderini, *Dizionario,* 114–15; Adriani, *Repertorio,* 247–48. See also W. A. Daszewski, "Notes on Topography of Roman Alexandria," in *Alessandria e il mondo ellenistico-romano: Studi in onore di Achille Adriani,* ed. N. Bonacas, A. DiVita, and G. Barone (Rome, 1983), 4:54–69. Height of the temple of Serapis: John of Nikiu 78.46. Paneion: Strabo 17.1.10. Unfortunately, the exact location of the ancient Paneion remains a mystery. Until the excavations carried out by the Polish Center of Mediterranean Archaeology, it was often assumed that

the mound of Kōm el-Dikka corresponded to the Paneion. Ammianus Marcellinus 22.16.12.

20. Inner port: the so-called Cibotos Harbor, or "the box," based on its shape (Strabo 17.1.10); Calderini, *Dizionario,* 121; Adriani, *Repertorio,* 237. North-south avenue: Strabo 17.1.8. Parallel streets: Strabo 17.1.8; cf. Achilles Tatius 5.1.4–5; Athan. *Hist. Ar.* 58 col. 764c. See also Calderini, *Dizionario,* 81–84; Adriani, *Repertorio* 245–47. Street widths: Rodziewicz, *Habitations,* 17–22, 246–51. See also M. Broshi, "Standards of Street Widths in the Roman-Byzantine Period," *Israel Exploration Journal* 27 (1977): 232–36.
21. William MacDonald, *Architecture of the Roman Empire* (New Haven, 1986), 2:3, 5, 17–31.
22. Width of Via Canopica: The Via Canopica measured "more than a plethron in breadth" (Strabo 17.1.8)—roughly equivalent to New York's Fifth Avenue (30 meters). By way of comparison, the Arkadiné of ancient Ephesus was 23 meters in breadth, Rome's Via Flaminia was 21 meters, and the colonnaded boulevard of Palmyra was 27 meters wide. The closest ancient parallel was Antioch's Street of Herod and Tiberius, which measured 29 meters in width. See also MacDonald, *Architecture,* 38–42. Thessaloniki: H. von Schoenebeck, "Die Stadtplanung des römischen Thessalonike," in *Bericht über den 6. Internationales Kongress für Archäologies* (Berlin, 1940), 478–82; Ch. I. Makaronas, "*Via Egnatia* and Thessalonike," in *Studies Presented to D. M. Robinson,* ed. G. E. Mylonas (Saint Louis, 1951), 380–88; J. M. Spieser, *Thessalonique et ses monuments du IVe au VIe siècle* (Paris, 1984).
23. 5.1.1–5, trans. S. Gaselee, *LCL.* Cf. Diodorus Siculus 17.52.3.
24. Adamnanus *de Locis Sanctis* 2.30.23.
25. Length of Via Canopica: D. G. Hogarth, "Report of Prospects of Research in Alexandria," *Egypt Exploration Fund 1895* (1896): 1–33; E. Breccia, *Alexandria ad Aegyptum* (Bergamo, 1914); Adriani, *Repertorio,* 49–83, 245–47. Direction: L. Mayer, *Views in Egypt from the Original Drawings in the Possession of Sir Robert Ainslie* (London, 1804); Adriani, *Repertorio,* pl. 11, fig. 33. For a judicious discussion of the evidence and its modern interpreters, see M. Rodziewicz, "Le dêbat sur la topographie de la ville antique," *Revue de l'occident musulman et la Méditerranée* 46.4 (1987): 38–48.
26. Gate of the Sun: Malalas 11.23 [280]; John of Nikiu *Chron.* 108.1–11. See also Calderini, *Dizionario,* 113–14, 139; Adriani, *Repertorio,* 236. Hostels: Athan. *Hist. Ar.* 58 col. 764b; *P.Jews* 1914.15–16; *Anth. Pal.* 9.787. In the early seventh century, the Chalcedonian patriarch, John the Almsgiver, constructed a hostel specially designated for traveling monks, the so-called Monks' Inn (*pandektēn tōn monachōn*), Leont. N. *v. Jo. Eleem.* 24.

27. Agora: *P.Oxy*. 43.3093; Cassius Dio 50.5.1; Achilles Tatius 5.8.2; Athan. *Hist. Ar.* 58 col. 764b; Jo. Moschus *Prat. Spir.* 77. Calderini, *Dizionario,* 88–89, 137; Adriani, *Repertorio,* 203–204, 227. The Tetrapylon only appears in Christian literary sources from late antiquity. See Calderini, *Dizionario,* 154; Adriani, *Repertorio,* 254. Its central location is suggested by Evagrius in his account of the murder of Proterius, whose body was dragged to the Tetrapylon and exhibited to the populace (*HE* 2.8; also Zach. Mytil. *HE* 4.2). The Tetrapylon probably resembled the roughly contemporary tetrapylon in Thessaloniki (the so-called arch of Galerius), which was also centrally located in the city's design. Cf. the earlier tetrapylon of Gerasa, the freestanding tetrakionion in Palmyra, and the sixteen-columned tetrapylon at Aphrodisias: K. T. Erim, "Recent Work at Aphrodisias, 1986–1988," in *Aphrodisias Papers,* ed. C. Roueché and K. T. Erim, *Journal of Roman Archaeology,* suppl. 1 (Ann Arbor, Mich., 1990), 9–11.
28. Palladius *Hist. Laus.* 21.6.
29. *hoi agoraioi*. Athan. *Hist. Ar.* 55 col. 760b; *M.Pet.Al.* 16., in *AnBol* 83 (1965): 157–87. Cf. Philo *Flacc.* 64, 95; *Leg.* 122; Acts 16:5 (in Thessaloniki).
30. Gymnasium: Strabo 17.1.10. See also Calderini, *Dizionario,* 107–8; Adriani, *Repertorio,* 222.
31. Western suburbs: Strabo 17.1.10; Athan. *Apol. ad Constant.* 27 col. 629c; Palladius *Hist. Laus.* 5.1; *Hist. Aceph.* 5.4; *Festal Index* 37; John of Nikiu *Chron.* 107.14–16. B. Tkaczow, "La topographie des nécropoles occidentales d'Alexandrie," *EOS* 70 (1982): 342–48. Eastern suburbs (Nicopolis and Hippodrome): *P.Jews* 1914.14–16; *Hist. Aceph.* 5.13; *P.Oxy*. 34.2725; Diodorus Siculus 17.51.3. Calderini, *Dizionario,* 116, 134; Adriani, *Repertorio,* 230–31; A. E. Hanson, "Nicopolis, Juliopolis, and the Roman Camp," *ZPE* 37 (1980): 249–54; K. A. Worp, "Observations on Some Military Camps and Place Names in Lower Egypt," *ZPE* 87 (1991): 291–95. The location of Alexandria's hippodrome(s) is largely unknown, owing to a certain imprecision of nomenclature on the part of the ancients, and also to the nearly complete obliteration of any physical remains. See the thorough discussion of J. H. Humphrey, *Roman Circuses: Arenas for Chariot Racing* (Berkeley, 1986), 505–12.
32. Athan. *Hist. Ar.* 58 col. 764b–c (trans. A. Robertson).
33. A similar hierarchy of Alexandrian streets is found in an offhand comment of Bishop Dionysius in the third century. He states that, during the persecutions, "there was no street [*hodos*], no thoroughfare [*leōphoros*], no alley [*stenōpos*] by which we could go." Eus. *HE* 6.41.8.
34. Ptolemy *Geog.* 4.5.46; Strabo 5.1.7; Philo *Quod omnis probus liber sit* 125; *P.Oxy*. 1.35. In the later empire, *Expositio* 34.1; Athan. *Hist. Ar.*

17 col. 712d; *Chronicon Pascale* A.D. 205 (ed. Dindorf, 497, lines 1–2); M. *Chres*. 96 (after A.D. 350); *P.Mich*. 723 inv. 902; *P.Abinn*. 63; *History of the Patriarchs* 1.1 [42]. See also H. I. Bell, "Alexandria ad Aegyptum," *JRS* 36 (1946): 130–33.

35. I. H. M. Hendriks, P. J. Parsons, and K. A. Worp, "Papyri from the Groningen Collection I: Encomium Alexandreae," *ZPE* 41 (1981): 71–83.

36. . . . "civitas opulenta, dives, fecunda, in qua nemo vivat otiosus. Alii vitrum conflant, aliis charta conficitur, omnes certe linyphiones aut cuiuscumque artis esse videntur." *HA Quad. Tyr*. 8.5–6; cf. *Aur*. 45.1. The author of the *HA* displays more than a casual acquaintance with things Egyptian, but his authority should not be taken very far—for example, to furnish historical data on shadowy third-century usurpers from Egypt like Firmus, whom the author describes as so voracious that he would eat an entire ostrich in a single day! Firmus is also depicted swimming with crocodiles and riding hippopotomi. The author's firsthand knowledge of Egypt seems to be limited to the exported Egyptian luxuries he so enjoyed. We hear quite a bit about expensive clothing and glassware, particularly in the last third of the *HA* where the author relies more on his own experience and imagination than on reliable historical sources.

37. Alexandrian glass: Strabo 16.2.25; *HA Verus* 5.3 (one of the more trustworthy earlier lives); S. H. Auth, "Luxury Glasses with Alexandrian Motifs," *JHS* 25 (1983): 39–44. Workshops at Kōm el-Dikka: Rodziewicz, *Habitations,* 127–28, 141–43, 239–42, 303, 331. The rough-and-tumble atmosphere of an Alexandrian workshop is portrayed in Leont. N. *v. Jo. Eleem*. 38 (ed. Festugière). The basic floor plan of the workshop at House D is echoed in a simplified form at the roughly contemporary port on Lake Mareotis, where a row of shops fronting one of the harbors has been excavated (figure 5). F. el-Fakharani, "Recent Excavations at Marea in Egypt," in *Aegyptiaca Treverensia: Trierer Studien zum Griechisch-Römischen Ägypten,* vol. 2, *Das Römisch-Byzantinische Ägypten,* ed. G. Grimm, H. Heinen, and E. Winter (Mainz, 1983), 2:175–86, particularly 179–81. Oven rooms and glass molds at Kōm el-Dikka: Rodziewicz, *Habitations,* 241–42, 249–51; 437, pl. 72; cf. Jo. Moschus *Prat. Spir*. 77.

38. 36.1–9.

39. Papyrus production: Pliny *HN* 13.69, 76; *PSI* 4.333; Strabo 17.1.15; *BGU* 4.1121/*Sel.Pap*. 41 (lease on a papyrus marsh, 5 B.C.). See esp. N. Lewis, *Papyrus in Classical Antiquity* (Oxford, 1974); idem, *Papyrus in Classical Antiquity: A Supplement,* Papyri Bruxellenses 23 (Brussels, 1989). Use of Alexandrian papyrus: Justinian *Nov*. 44.2; Gregory of

Tours *Hist.* 5.5; Gregory the Great *Moral.* 13.10, col. 1024; *Vitae patrum Iurensium: Eugendi* 11 (ed. Krusch, *Monumenti Germanine Historica, Scriptores rerum Merovingicarum,* vol. 3).

40. Epiph. *Haer.* 76.1.5.
41. *Quid? sine lino Aegyptio esse non possumus! HA Gall.* 6.4–5. Alexandrian woven goods: *P.Oxy.* 12.1428; Soc. *HE* 1.27 col. 153a; *Acta SS. Paese and Thecla* (Pierpont Morgan Codex M 591, T. 28, F. 52 R i). Linen workers: *P.Giess.* 40, col. 2, recording their expulsion from Alexandria on the orders of Caracalla. See also H. Braunert, *Die Binnenwanderung: Studien zur Sozialgeschichte Ägyptens in der Ptolemäer- und Kaiserzeit,* Bonner Historische Forschungen, no. 26 (Bonn, 1964), 186–212. Linen merchants: *P.Oxy.* 43.3111; *ILS* 7564.
42. Claudian *In Eutropium* 1.357; Cosmas Indicopleustes *Topographia Christiana* 3.70; *Ed. Diocl.* 26–28; *B.Tal.Mo'ed Katan* 26a–b.
43. Among many other types of specialized crafts, shoemaking appears to have been especially common, although it is possible that the frequency of shoemakers may simply be a random skewing of our extant sources. Leont. N. *v. Jo. Eleem.* 44a; *History of the Patriarchs* 1.2 (ed. Evetts), 142–145 [44–47], Greek version in *PG* 115, cols. 164–69; *Mishna, Aboth* 4.11, *Kelim* 5.5; *P.Tal.Hagiga* 3.1.
44. *Hist. Laus.* 6.5, 13.1, 17.1; *P.Tal.Hagiga* 3.1; *Mir. Apa Mena* (ed. and trans. Drescher, 114–15); *Canons of Athanasius* 103 (ed. and trans. Riedel and Crum); *Expositio* 35.5–6; *P.Fay.* 93/*Sel.Pap.* 44 (A.D. 161).
45. Apollonius: *Hist. Laus.* 13.1–2. A list of agricultural products is presented in *Expositio* 34.5–6. See also Pliny *HN* 14.74, 117; *P.Oxy.* 43.3111; *P.Abinn.* 22. Oil: *P.Mich.* 613 inv. 1939; *P.Tal.Shabbath* 2.2. There seems to have been some small-scale cultivation of olives in the gardens of Alexandria's suburbs; Strabo 17.1.35; cf. *Canons of Athanasius* 16 (ed. and trans. Riedel and Crum). See also R. Bagnall, *Egypt in Late Antiquity* (Princeton, 1993), 29–31; D. J. Mattingly, "Oil for Export?" *Journal of Roman Archaeology* 1 (1988): 33–56. Barley: *P.Oxy.* 14.1652, 43.3091; *P.Cair.Isidor.* 57, 58, 61; *Canons of Athanasius* 69 (ed. and trans. Riedel and Crum). Dates: *P.Tal.Demai* 2.1; *P.Mich.* 657 inv. 957. On requisitioned agricultural goods, see R. S. Bagnall, "Agricultural Productivity and Taxation in Later Roman Egypt," *Transactions of the American Philological Association* 115 (1985): 289–308. Alexandrian vegetable merchant: *Hist. Monach.* 14.18.
46. The abundance of this region was such that many Egyptians from upriver sought sustenance here during a particularly severe famine in the mid-seventh century; *History of the Patriarchs* 1.14 (ed. Evetts), 501 [237].
47. *P.Oxy.* 7.1045, 10.1274, 12.1462; John of Nikiu 94.18. See also Calderini, *Dizionario,* 208–9.

48. On Mareotis, see Kees, "Marea," *RE* 14.2 (1930): 1676–78; A. de Cosson, *Mareotis* (London, 1935); and M. Rodziewicz, "Alexandria and the District of Mareotis," *Graeco-Arabica* 2 (1983): 199–216.
49. Strabo 17.1.14; also de Cosson, *Mareotis,* 70–82.
50. *Hist. Laus.* 7.1.
51. *Expositio* 35.3–5, 36.1–7; *P.Tebt.* 3.867 (third century B.C.); Pliny *HN* 13.76; *v. Jo. Eleem.* 8; *Hist. Monach.* 27.10.
52. Strabo tells us that the lake "contains eight islands, and all the shores around it are well inhabited" (17.1.14).
53. Lake dwellers: Heliodorus *Ethiopica* 1.4; Achilles Tatius 4.12–14; *v. Jo. Eleem.* 8. See also Bernand, *Alexandrie la Grande,* 32–35. At the time of the Arab conquest, particularly wealthy Alexandrians hid out in the lake's marshes in an attempt to avoid the payment of tribute (John of Nikiu *Chron.* 120.69).
54. Soc. *HE* 1.27 cols. 153c–156a. Athanasius calls it the chora of Alexandria, and informs us that the churches in the district were subject directly to the Alexandrian bishop and not to a *chorepiscopos* (Athanasius *Apol. contra Ar.* 85 col. 400b–c). During later centuries, Mareotis was counted as a Byzantine province (John of Nikiu 107.4, 12; Justinian *Edict* 13.1, 9, 17–22).
55. Settlement in Mareotis: a third-century papyrus from Tebtunis mentions a farmstead (*epoikion*) at Alexandria, perhaps referring to this region, (*P.Tebt.* 2.335). A large peristyle villa rustica has been recently excavated in this area at Huwariya, and can be dated on the basis of pottery remains to the fourth through the seventh centuries: Rodziewicz, "Alexandria and the District of Mareotis," 204–7; see also Rodziewicz, "Remarks on the Peristyle House in Alexandria and Mareotis," in *Papers of the Twelfth International Congress for Classical Archaeology in Athens* (Athens, 1983); el-Fakharani, "Recent Excavations at Marea in Egypt," 184–86. Wine production in Mareotis: Strabo 17.1.15; Virgil *Georg.* 2.91; Horace *Odes* 1.37; Athenaeus *Deipnosophistes* 1.33; Jo. Moschus *Prat. Spir.* 162; *History of the Patriarchs* 4 [pp. 56–57]. Although Mareotic wine was much sought after, John the Almsgiver could claim that "its taste is nothing to boast of and its price is low"—doubtless because of its local production (Sophr. H. *v. Jo. Eleem.* 10). See also el-Fakharani, "Recent Excavations at Marea in Egypt," 182–84.
56. I wish to thank Mieczslaw Rodziewicz for bringing this discovery to my attention. On Mareotic wine production, see J.-Y. Empereur and M. Picon, "Les régions de productions d'amphores impériales en Méditerranée orientale," in *Amphores romaines et histoire economique: Actes du colloque de Sienne, 22–24 mai 1986* (Rome, 1989), 223–48; J.-Y. Em-

pereur, "Quelques amphores égyptiennes impériales timbrées," *BSAA* 45 (1993): 81–90.

57. John of Nikiu *Chron.* 109.1–3; Theodoret *HE* 2.13.
58. *Mir. Apa Mena* (ed. Drescher, 112, 114–15); el-Fakharani, "Recent Excavations at Marea in Egypt," 178–81; P. Grossmann, "Die Querschiffbasilika von Hauwarīya," *BSAA* 45 (1993): 107–21. El-Fakharani suggests that this site is to be identified with the city of Marea, but Rodziewicz has argued convincingly for an identification with the Byzantine port of Philoxenite, constructed no earlier than the late fifth century: Rodziewicz, "Alexandria and the District of Mareotis," 202–4; idem, "Taenia and Mareotis: Archaeological Research West of Alexandria," *Annual of the Egyptian Society of Greek and Roman Studies* 1 (1990): 62–78.
59. *P.Sakaon* 24/*P.Thead.* 35; *P.Sakaon* 25/*P.Thead.* 36. At the time of Bishop Peter's martyrdom in 311, the officers in charge of the execution easily found a handful of stonecutters to break into Peter's cell and spirit him away to his death: *M. Petr. Al.* 10. in *AnBol* 83 (1965): 157–87.
60. Tombs east of the city: *M. Petr. Al.* 14.
61. *Apoph. Patr.* Systematic Coll. 237.
62. Epiphanius *advers. Haer.* 69.1 col. 201d, 2 cols. 204d–5a; *Chron. Pasch.* 252 cols. 608c–9a; *Hist. Laus.* 15.1, 24.1, 35.14–15; *P.Jews* 1914. 42–43; *P.Hamb.* 1.39/*Sel.Pap.* 369; W. *Chres.* 19; *HA Ant.P.* 5.5; Malalas 11.23[280]; Athan. *Hist. Ar.* 10 col. 705a–b. For a discussion of the uprising in Boukolia, see J. Winkler, "Lollianus and the Desperadoes," *JHS* 100 (1980): 155–81.
63. *P.Oxy.* 1.141 (A.D. 503); *P.Oxy.* 8.1130 (A.D. 484).
64. Taxation and requisitioned labor: *P.Oxy.* 14.1660, 17.2106, 17.2113, 34.2705, 43.3090, 43.3111, 44.3197, 48.3412, 51.3635, 59.3982. *P.Cair.Isidor.* 72; *P.Amh.* 2.138. Role of the church: *Hist. Monach.* 18.2; cf. *P.Oxy.* 16.1898, 16.1906, 16.2002. Theadelphia document: *P.Sakaon* 25/*P.Thead.* 36.
65. Alexandrian merchandise: *Hist. Laus.* 13.1 (food and medicine); *PSI* 9.1080/*Sel.Pap.* 132 (purple dye); *P.Oxy.* 1.119 (musical instruments), 7.1069 (foodstuffs), 8.1153 (books and jars of oil), 14.1678 (oil and "purple"), *P.Oxy.* 19.2244, 59.4000 (axles, purples, acacia wood, reed baskets); *Hist. Laus.* 32.8 (a monk sent to Alexandria in order to "sell produce and buy the necessities"—*epi to diapōlēsai men autōn ta erga sunōnēsasthai de tas chreias*). *Pragmata* in Alexandria: *P.Amh.* 2.136; *P.Oxy.* 7.1070, 8.1155. Banking and commercial transactions: *P.Oxy.* 1.144, 3.509 (an Alexandrian owing money to an Oxyrhynchite), 8.1130, 20.2269, 41.2983, 43.3146 (funds borrowed

from imperial accounts in Alexandria), 27.2527, 46.3287, 48.3396, 48.3401, 56.3867. A miserly banker-moneychanger (*trapezitēs*) who asks his slave to steal from him and give to the poor: Leont. N. *v. Jo. Eleem.* 38. Judicial affairs: *P.Oxy.* 31.2597, 43.3093. Trophimus: *P.Oxy.* 8.1160.

66. Students: *Sel.Pap.* 133. Tourists and pilgrims: *P.Herm.Rees* 2, 3, 4, 5, 6 (the *Theophanes Archive*—a circle of Hermetics); *P.Tebt.* 2.416 (a pagan traveling to Alexandria in order to pray, *proskynēsai*); *P.Mich.* 3.213 inv. 338, 3.221 inv. 1362, 8.513 inv. 5159, *P.Tebt.* 2.407 (visitors to Alexandria for a variety of reasons, all stopping to venerate Serapis in his temple: on this, consult H. C. Youtie, "Grenfell's Gift to Lumbroso," *Illinois Classical Studies* 3 [1978]: 90–99); *Hist. Monach.* 20.15; *Hist. Laus.* 13.1, 32.8, 35.14–15 (monks).
67. *P.Giess.* 4.40 col. 2/*Sel.Pap.* 215 (trans. Hunt and Edgar).
68. ". . . by chance there were two coming from the countryside, one an elderly man and one an elderly virgin. The two entered the city, the old man to sell a hide covering and to go away again, the old woman to sell a pair of winding sheets. They came to the attention of Peter, the martyr of God. The holy martyr said to them, 'And where are you going?' They answered saying, 'To the city to sell our goods.'" *M. Petr. Al.* 14, in Devos, "Une passion grecque inédite," 157–87, trans. T. Vivian.
69. Grain diverted to Syria in order to supply troops for Constantius's campaign against the Sassanians (*Expositio* 36.16–19); alleviating a famine in Antioch during the reign of Julian the Apostate (Julian *Misopogon* 367b). The population of Alexandria was so dependent on grain from the chora, that a brief interruption in the supply could bring about famine: John of Nikiu *Chron.* 97.7.
70. Josephus *BJ* 2.383–386. See G. E. Rickman "The Grain Trade under the Roman Empire," in *The Seaborne Commerce of Ancient Rome,* ed. J. H. D'Arms and E. C. Kopff, *Memoirs of the American Academy in Rome* 36 (1980): 263–64; G. E. Rickman, *The Corn Supply of Ancient Rome* (Oxford, 1980), 10, 113–18, 231–35.
71. Justinian *Ed.* 13.8/*Corpus Juris Civilis,* vol. 3, ed. R. Schoell and G. Kroll (Berlin, 1954), 783, which specifies 8 million units (probably *artabae*) or 36 million modii. A less reliable figure of 40,000 modii is given by Socrates Scholasticus (*HE* 13.2 col. 209a). On these figures, see Rickman, *Corn Supply,* 232–33; R. Duncan-Jones, "The Choenix, the Artaba and the Modius," *ZPE* 21 (1976): 43–52; D. W. Rathbone, "The Weight and Measurement of Egyptian Grains," *ZPE* 53 (1983): 265–75. On the organization of transport to the two capitals, see B. Sirks, *Food for Rome* (Amsterdam, 1991), 202–17.
72. Sack capacity based on Rickman's estimate of 6.66 modii per sack or 56

liters = 1.58 bushels ("Grain Trade," 263; *Corn Supply,* 20). This accords well with artistic representations of Roman *saccarii* unloading grain ships at the capital's busy ports.

For ship size, I assume an average of 340 tons burden, following L. Casson, *Ships and Seamanship in the Ancient World,* 2d ed. (Princeton, 1986), 170–73, esp. nn. 24, 25; and 183–90.

Grain harvest and transport to Alexandria: shipments beginning to arrive in Alexandria in mid-April (*P.Turner* 45); receipt for grain deposited in granaries of Chaereu in mid-May (*P.Cair.Isidor.* 61). Given the time required to process and transship the grain, I take May 15 as an approximate date for the earliest sailing of fully loaded grain ships from Alexandria's harbors.

Sailing season: 11 March–10 November (Vegetius 4.39); 15 April–15 October (*C.Th.* 13.9.3.3.). For the cumbersome grain ships, I follow the more conservative dates. See J. Rougé, "La navigation hivernale sous l'Empire romain," *Revue des études anciennes* 54 (1952): 316–25. The season is further reduced if one factors in the 10–20 day voyage to Constantinople (Casson, *Ships and Seamanship,* 282–91), yielding a total sailing season of approximately 138 days.

73. E.g., *P.Cair.Isidor.* 38, 57, 58, 61; *P.Mich.* 724 inv. 422; *P.Turner* 45; *P.Sakaon* 11, 12, 82; *P.Ryl.* 413, 652; *P.Amh.* 137, 138; *P.Wisc.* 65; *P.Oxy.* 1.126, 1.142, 10.1254, 10.1259, 10.1260, 14.1660, 16.1906, 16.2022, 17.2125, 22.2347, 43.3091.

74. *Granaries: P.Oxy.* 10.1259; 60.4063, 4064, 4065. For the guarantees accompanying samples of wheat, see e.g., *P.Strassb.* 31.6; *P.Oxy.* 10.1254, 60.4064.

75. *C.Th.* 13.5.32; *P.Oxy.* 51.3634; *P.Turner* 45; *P.Cair.Isidor.* 61; *Homily on the Virgin* 79, attributed to Theophilus, (Michigan Coptic manuscripts [New York, 1923] 369).

76. *C.Th.* 14.26; John of Nikiu *Chron.* 107.8.

77. *Supra caput enim habens Thebaidis Indorum genus et accipiens omnia praestat omnibus. Expositio* 35.6–7. Exports from Alexandria: *Hist. Laus.* 14.1 (Spain); Leont. *v. Jo. Eleem.* 10 (Britain and the Pentapolis), 28 (the Adriatic), 35 (Gaul), 13 and *ILS* 7564 (Sicily), 26 and Jo. Moschus *Prat. Spir.* 77 (Africa). Imports from Egypt and regions beyond: Strabo 17.1.7.

78. Epiph. *Haer.* 66.1.11.

79. *P.Oxy.* 60.4070; John of Nikiu *Chron.* 103.2–3. P. J. Sijpesteijn, "Der *POTAMOS TRAIANOS,*" *Aegyptus* 43 (1963):70–83.

80. *C. Th.* 12.12.2. Alexandrian merchants in Ethiopia: Cosmas Indicopleustes *Top. Christiana* 2.54, 56.

81. J. Schwartz, "Die Rolle Alexandrias bei der Verbreitung orientalischen Gedankenguts," *ZPE* 1 (1967): 197–217.

*Chapter Three. The Social World*

1. Ausonius *Ordo Urbium Nobilium* 4.1–3.
2. Achilles Tatius 5.1.6.
3. Diodorus Siculus 17.52.6. Adamnan *de Locis Sanctis* 2.30.1 (*urbs valde populosa*). In the fifth century, Theodoret described Alexandria as "an immense and populous city" (*HE* 1.1).

   Two factors complicate an analysis of Alexandria's population in antiquity. Although the city was hemmed in by unchanging topographical features, there appears to have been a certain fluctuation in the circuit of the city's walls during the course of the centuries. The construction of modern Alexandria has all but obliterated the scanty traces of wall-like structures, so it is necessary to rely heavily on literary testimony. These sources indicate that the city's walls were extended to the south as a result of periodic restoration and reconstruction. By the late Byzantine period, they bordered the southern canal and/or Lake Mareotis itself (*IGRR* 1.1055–56; *CIL* 3.12046; Cassius Dio 78.23.3; Amm. Marc. 22.16.15; Stephen of Byzantium, s.v. "*Alexandreia*"; John of Nikiu 107.48). See also P. M. Fraser, *Ptolemaic Alexandria* (Oxford, 1972), 1:27; Calderini, *Dizionario,* 152–54; Adriani, *Repertorio,* 227–28.

   Another difficulty in determining population is the lack of precise information regarding the capacity of Alexandria's hippodrome. Although it is possible tentatively to extrapolate population figures from hippodrome capacity in other cities of late antiquity, the Alexandrian hippodrome near the Serapeum was constricted in size by surrounding hills. Even more disappointing is the complete absence of data from the extramural hippodrome to the east of the city. See J. H. Humphrey, *Roman Circuses: Arenas for Chariot Racing* (Berkeley, 1986), 505–12. In addition, the figure for population density is, of course, only a very rough approximation. See J. C. Russell, "Late Ancient and Medieval Population," *Transactions of the American Philosophical Society,* n.s., 48.3 (1958): 63–68; R. Duncan-Jones, *The Economy of the Roman Empire: Quantitative Studies,* 2d ed. (Cambridge, 1982), 274–77.

   Ancient measurements of the city's size: Josephus *BJ* 386; Philo *Flacc.* 92; cf. Strabo 17.1.8.

   A recent attempt at estimating the population of the city during the early principate may be found in D. Delia, "The Population of Roman Alexandria," *Transactions of the American Philological Association* 118 (1988): 275–91, followed in large part by R. Bagnall and B. Frier, *The Demography of Roman Egypt* (Cambridge, 1994), 54. Delia concludes her thoroughgoing study with the observation, "Hence the maximum estimate for the population of Roman Alexandria suggested herein—500,000–600,000—is a mere approximation of a variable which would wax and wane in the course of the next four centuries." This figure is echoed by an estimate of 525,000 adult inhabitants in the sixth century, calculated by M. el Abbadi on the basis of the Alexandrian annona. This seems to be too high, given the stresses on the city's population during the sixth century. M. el Abbadi, "The Grain Supply of Alexandria and Its Population in Byzantine Times," in *Proceedings of the XVIII International Congress of Papyrology* (Athens, 1988), 2:317–23.

4. Fluctuations in population: Eus. *HE* 7.22.7–10, 32.7–11; Soc. *HE* 4.3; Leont. N. *v. Jo. Eleem.* 25; Amm. Marc. 22.16.14; Athan. *Hist. Ar.* 58 col. 764c. Growth of suburban villas: *Hist. Aceph.* 5.4, where Athanasius is depicted hiding in a villa beyond the New Canal to the west of the city. The patriarch's hideout is described elsewhere as "an ancestral tomb" (Soc. *HE* 4.13 col. 495c). This confusion is explained by the gradual encroachment of suburban dwellings into this region of tombs and gardens which originated during the time of the Ptolemies (Strabo 17.1.10). Cf. B. Tkaczow, "La topographie des nécropoles occidentales d'Alexandrie," *EOS* 70 (1982): 342–48.

   Urban agriculture: [libellus of deacon Theodore] *ACO* 2.1.2.47; [libellus of deacon Ischyrion] *ACO* 2.1.2.51; Jo. Moschus *Prat. Spir.* 207.

5. The original is embedded in Michael the Syrian *Chronicle* 5.3 (trans. Chabot), vol. 1, 113–15. For an analysis of this text, see P. M. Fraser, "A Syriac *Notitia Urbis Alexandrinae*," *JEA* 37 (1951): 103–8.

   A mid-fourth-century papyrus from the Abinnaeus Archive concerns a dispute over property in Alexandria, part of which included "a fourth of a small courtyard (*auludrion*)"; see *P.Abinn.* 63, line 5. On Alexandrian housing, see also Soz. *HE* 4.10; [libellus of deacon Ischyrion] *ACO* 2.1.2.51; [libellus of presbyter Athanasius] *ACO* 2.1.2.57; *P.Lond.* 3.1164f28.

6. This assumes that the *Notitia*'s total of 24,296 houses refers to households rather than dwellings. An average household of 7.34 people is computed by D. W. Hobson, "House and Household in Roman Egypt," *Yale Classical Studies* 28 (1985): 220. See also H. Maehler, "Häuser und ihre Bewohner im Fayūm in der Kaiserzeit," in *Aegyptiaca Treverensia: Trier Studien zum Griechisch-Römischen Ägypten*, vol. 2, *Das römisch-byzantinisch Ägypten*, G. Grimm, H. Heinen, and E. Winter (Maine, 1983), 119–37. If actual dwellings are meant, then the population total comes closer to Diodorus's 300,000 (based on 11.27 per house as estimated by Hobson, 221), 24,296 × 11.27 =

273,815. These figures approximate density figures for areas of modern Egypt: cf. D. Panzac, "Espace et population en Egypte," *Méditerranée* 50.4 (1983): 71–80. Bagnall and Frier estimate 5.31 for average household size in the towns of Roman Egypt and 10.36 for houses with multiple families, slaves, and lodgers (*Demography of Roman Egypt,* 66–70). This latter figure would yield a population of just over a quarter of a million. Of course, density estimates for Egypt's chora (both ancient and modern) are not necessarily reliable indicators of density within a major city.

7. Papyrus: *P.Bibl.Univ.Giss.* 46/Musurillo 3, col. 1, line 15. Ibn ʿAbd al-Hakam: translated from Torrey's edition of the *Futūh Misr* by H. E. Omar Toussoun in *BSAA* 20 (1924): 231.
8. *P.Oxy.* 46.3271; Ps.-Callisthenes v. *Alex. Magni* 1.32.9; *BGU* 4.1151, 4.1127; M. *Chres.* 107; Breccia, *Ins.* 71; Josephus *BJ* 2.494–95; Philo *Flacc.* 55; Fraser, "Syriac *Notitia,*" 104; Epiphanius *de Mens. et Pond.* 9 col. 249. For discussions of this geographical division, see Calderini, *Dizionario,* 79–80; Adriani, *Repertorio* 239–40; Fraser, *Ptolemaic Alexandria,* 1:34–35, with 2:108–110, nn. 264–70.

   A newly edited papyrus (*P.Oxy.* 3756) provides the first papyrological reference to the Epsilon quarter. Perhaps more importantly, the writer of the papyrus also mentions a subdistrict called Sigma: "Aurelius Aeithales . . . dwelling in the Epsilon quarter, in the locality called Sigma . . . " (*Aurēlios Aeithalēs . . . oikōn en tō ei gramatos pros topō kaloume[n]ou Sigmatos . . .*). While the papyrus's editors suggest that Sigma refers to a C-shaped portico (citing a tenuous parallel from a Syrian inscription), a more natural interpretation would regard Sigma as one letter in a further alphabetical enumeration of the subdistricts of Alexandria's quarters. However, without more corroborating testimony, the question of the Alexandrian subdistricts remains open for the present.
9. Rome: Suet. *Aug.* 30.1; Pliny *HN* 3.66; *CIL* 6.975/*ILS* 6073.

   Antinoopolis: W. *Chres.* 207; *P.Rein.* 49. One recent commentator has suggested that after the "Syriac *Notitia*" enumerates the well-known Alexandrian grammata, an appended list of "quarters" is, in fact, a catalog of prominent plintheia within the grammata: A. Lukaszewicz, "Nouveaux textes documentaires d'Alexandrie," in *Atti del XVII Congresso Internazionale di Papirologia* (Naples, 1984), 3:879–84. While this second list does contain toponyms of smaller locales in the city (Bendideion, the isle of Anotinos Pandotos, Zephyrion), it also contains larger geographical regions (Canopus, Nicopolis, Lochias) which were surely as large as the grammata. One of these purported plintheia, "the quarter of Hadrianos," is even described as "immense." Fraser, "Syriac *Notitia,*" 104–6.

Constantinople: G. Dagron, *Naissance d'une capitale: Constantinople* (Paris, 1974), 512–30.

10. R. MacMullen, *Roman Social Relations* (New Haven, 1974), 67. *P.Hib.* 28, dating from the Ptolemaic period, indicates that the city had 6 tribes, 120 phratries, and 720 demes. Examples of deme and phratry use: *BGU* 4.1127 (18 B.C.); *P.Oxy.* 1.95/*Sel.Pap.* 32 (A.D. 129); *P.Oxy.* 14.1707/*Sel.Pap.* 33 (A.D. 204); *P.Fay.* 93/*Sel.Pap.* 44 (A.D. 161). For an extended discussion of these matters, see Delia, *Alexandrian Citizenship during the Roman Principate,* American Classical Studies, no. 23 (Atlanta, 1991).
11. Jo. Moschus *Prat. Spir.* 207. On the role of neighborhoods in urban society, see S. Greer, "Neighborhood," in *International Encyclopedia of the Social Sciences* (New York, 1968), 11:121–25.
12. A more common pattern was naming streets after popular sovereigns. See Fraser, *Ptolemaic Alexandria,* 35–36; MacMullen, *Roman Social Relations,* appendix A.2., "Crafts' Localities," 132–35.
13. *PSI* 9.1080/*Sel.Pap.* 132; *P.Oslo* inv. 1621; *P.Oxy.* 14.1678. R. W. Daniel, "Through Straying Streets: A Note on the *CHMACIA*-Texts," *ZPE* 54 (1984): 85–86; D. P. Fowler, "New Directions," *ZPE* 59 (1985): 45–46; R. Ling, "A Stranger in Town: Finding the Way in an Ancient City," *Greece and Rome* 37.2 (1990): 204–14.
14. Lycians and Phrygians: *IGRR* 1.1078; *SEG* 8.359; *OGIS* 658. Rhakotis: Strabo 17.1.6; Ps.-Callisthenes *v. Alex. Magni* 1.31.2; Q. Curtius 4.33; Tacitus *Hist.* 4.83–84; Clement Alex. *Protrepticus* 4.42; John Malalas 8.1 [192]; *P.Giess.* 4.40, col. 2. The Coptic name for Alexandria, Rhakoti, reverts to this native pre-Hellenistic toponymn. The Arab conquerors, like the Greeks and Romans before them, adopted the name of the Macedonian Founder.
15. In a study otherwise notable for the careful use of urban design theory, G. Caruso is so bold as to map out particular zones of land usage within Alexandria. Despite this lack of care and a surprising disregard for recent archaeological work, Caruso's rough schematic analysis of the ancient city is head and shoulders above many of his predecessors in providing a theoretical framework for understanding Alexandria's morphology. G. Caruso, "Alcuni aspetti dell'urbanistica di Alessandria in età ellenistica: Il piano di progettazione," in *Allessandria e il mondo ellenistico-romano: Studi in onore di Achille Adriani,* ed. N. Bonacas, A. DiVita, and G. Barone, *Studi e Materiali* 4, Istituto di Archeologia, Università di Palermo (Rome, 1983), 43–53, esp. 49, fig. 5. For spatial differentiation in urban design, see S. Kostof, *The City Assembled* (London, 1992), 71–121; E. V. Walter, *Placeways: A Theory of the Human Environment* (Chapel Hill, N.C., 1988), 23–43.

This type of analysis has been applied recently by R. Laurence, *Roman Pompeii: Space and Society* (London, 1994).

16. At times, it is possible to identify areas where particular classes tended to congregate. For example, in late antiquity it appears that the poor and the crippled could often be found frequenting the Forum of Augustus, that is, an agora either adjoining the Caesarion or located close by. The attraction of this spot could be explained by the proximity of the patriarchal cathedral in the former temple, and the benefits bestowed upon these groups by their wealthy episcopal patron (Leont. *v. Jo. Eleem.* 27; *Hist. Laus.* 21.3, 6).
17. Rodziewicz, *Habitations,* 330–47. Casual digs along streets R3 and L2 have suggested the presence of wealthy townhouses with peristyles and mosaics during the late Roman period. If confirmed, these would indicate a remarkable degree of socioeconomic differentiation within a relatively small region, since they must have stood cheek-by-jowl with the public structures (baths, theater, lecture halls, cisterns) and the more modest housing along street R4. See the remarks of M. Rodziewicz, "Archaeological Evidence on Byzantine Architecture in Alexandria," *Graeco-Arabica* 4 (1991): 287–97.
18. A succinct expression of the stratified model may be found in W. V. Harris, "On the Applicability of the Concept of Class in Roman History," in *Forms of Control and Subordination in Antiquity,* ed. T. Yuge and M. Doi (Tokyo, 1988), 598–610.

    For a discussion of vertical social ties, see L. S. B. MacCoull, "Patronage and the Social Order in Coptic Egypt," in *Egitto e storia antica dall'Ellenismo all'età araba,* ed L. Crisuolo and G. Geraci (Bologna, 1989), 497–502. One particularly revealing example of these social bonds concerns the Chalcedonian patriarch, John the Almsgiver, in the early seventh century. In this instance, the patriarch's nephew had been insulted by a shopkeeper, and the nephew demanded that the shopkeeper be publicly scourged and humiliated. Instead, John "immediately summoned the overseer of the shopkeepers [*ton epanō tōn kapēlōn*] and ordered him never in future to accept from that shopkeeper either his customary tip/sportula [*tas sunētheias*] or the rent for the shop [*enoikion tou ergastēriou autou*] or the public taxes [*ta dēmosia*], for this shop, too, belonged to the holy church." Leont. N. *v. Jo. Eleem.* 16. Here, John's beneficence casts light upon the various obligations customarily owed to patriarchal patronage.
19. R. Bagnall, *Egypt in Late Antiquity* (Princeton, 1993), 226.
20. On the difficulties of reconstructing the ancient social hierarchy on the basis of testimony from the literary elite, see the remarks of Bagnall, ibid., 227–29.

21. John the Almsgiver provides a revealing list of Alexandrian status indicators when he chides those who say in their hearts, "I am a little better-looking or richer or more distinguished [*eudoxoteros*] or hold some important public office [*archēn ophikiou tinos*]." Leont. N. *v. Jo. Eleem.* 40. See also H. Geremek, "Les *politeumenoi* égyptiens sont-ils identique aux *bouleutai*?" *Anagennesis* 1 (1981): 231–47.

    Edict of 436: *C.Th.* 12.1.191. Despite lengthier tenures of those sitting on the council, its real political power as a deliberative body seems to have declined during the fourth century; A. K. Bowman, "Papyri and Roman Imperial History," *JRS* 66 (1976): 166.

    Exemption of decurions from corporal punishment: *C.Th.* 12.1.190. This exemption was previously an important status indicator which separated them as *honestiores* from *humiliores*. However, during the late empire, this particular privilege was gradually eroded under pressure from successive brutal regimes. See P. Garnsey, *Social Status and Legal Privilege in the Roman Empire* (Oxford, 1970), 260–76; and P. Brown, *Power and Persuasion in Late Antiquity* (Madison, 1992), 48–58.
22. Pagan bouleutai: Athan. *Hist. Ar.* 54 col. 760a, 78 col. 788b. Burial of Peter: *History of the Patriarchs* 1.6 [136]. Death of Hypatia: John of Nikiu *Chron.* 84.100. Well-born men (*eugeneis andras*): Athan. *Ep. Encycl.* 4 col. 232a. Mention is made of certain "believing rulers of the city" in the tenth-century *Homily on the Virgin* 83, attributed to Theophilus (385–412) (Michigan Coptic manuscripts [New York, 1923], 371).
23. Athan. *Hist. Ar.* 78 col. 788c (trans. Robertson).
24. Ibid., col. 788d.
25. Aristocratic landlords: [libellus of deacon Ischyrion] *ACO* 2.1.2.51; [libellus of presbyter Athanasius] *ACO* 2.1.2.57. Moneylending: *P.Oxy.* 46.3287. Aristocrats and business elsewhere: for Rome, see J. H. D'Arms, *Commerce and Social Standing in Ancient Rome* (Cambridge, Mass., 1981); for the East, consult H. W. Pleket, "Urban Elites and Business in the Greek Part of the Roman Empire," in *Trade in the Ancient Economy,* ed. P. Garnsey, K. Hopkins, and C. R. Whittaker, (Berkeley, 1983), 131–44; idem, "City Elites and Economic Activities in the Greek Part of the Roman Empire: Some Preliminary Remarks," in *Acts of the International Congress on Greek and Latin Epigraphy, 3–9 October 1982* (Athens, 1984), 134–43; for Antioch in late antiquity, J. H. W. G. Liebeschuetz, *Antioch: City and Imperial Administration in the Later Roman Empire* (Oxford, 1972), 74–75, 82–83. Pragmateutai: mentioned in a papyrus dated 427, *P.Oxy.* 16.1880. Horion's agent: Calpurnius Eusebius, *P.Oxy.* 40.2925, 2938.

26. *hêmeis heterois echomen kataleipsai tous ponous*. *Hist. Laus.* 14.1 (Paesius and Isaias).
27. Jo. Eph. *HE* 3.1.33. Shipowners who are also bouleutai: *C.Th.* 13.5.7; Jo. Moschus *Prat. Spir.* 193 (a son of one of the city's chief men—*tōn prōtōn tēs poleōs*—who inherits "ships and gold"); *P.Oxy.* 17.2125; Athan. *Ep. Encycl.* 5 col. 233a–b, 7 col. 238b; *P.Oxy.* 1.87 (a ship-owning bouleutes, A.D. 342); *P.Oxy.* 22.2347 (a surety made by a shipper sailing a vessel owned by an unnamed third party), with P. J. Sijpesteijn, "*P.Oxy.* XXII 2347 Reconsidered," *BASP* 15 (1978): 225–26. One example of a relatively poor naukleros is the unnamed ship-owner who deposited with John the Almsgiver his entire savings of 540 nomismata, Leont. N. *v. Jo. Eleem.* 26. Wealthy merchants: *P.Oxy.* 43.3111, *Hist. Monach.* 14.18, and the merchant with Spanish connections described as an "emporos Spanodromos," *Hist. Laus.* 14.1.
28. Bowman and Rathbone attribute this shift to the loss of social status formerly enjoyed by Alexandrian citizens in the wake of the *Constitutio Antoniniana*: A. K. Bowman, "Papyri and Roman Imperial History," 167; Bowman and D. Rathbone, "Cities and Administration in Roman Egypt," *JRS* 82 (1992): 127; Rathbone, *Economic Rationalism and Rural Society in Third-Century A.D. Egypt* (Cambridge, 1991), 50–51.
29. Alexandrian bouleutai owning rural land: second century—*P.Oxy.* 1.100; *P.Oxy.* 3.473; third century—*P.Oxy.* 4.705, 8.1114, 12.1534, 14.1646, 17.2120, 38.2849, 38.2854, 40.2901, 40.2916, 40.2925, 42.3060, *P.Turner* 42, *SB* 6.8999, *P.Tebt.* 2.335, *P.Flor.* 1.50; fourth century—*M.Chr.* 196, *P.Oxy.* 43.3146, 48.3386, *P.Mich.* 15.723 inv. 902, *P.Abinn.* 22, 62, 63, *P.Turner* 37, *P.Sakaon* 69, *BGU* 405/*Sel.Pap.* 56; fifth through seventh centuries—*P.Oxy.* 16.1904; Leont. *v. Jo. Eleem.* 13.; *P.Ant.* 95. Subletting of rural land: *P.Flor.* 1.50; *P.Bour.* 42; *P.Princ.* 37; *BGU* 9.1900. For a discussion of these texts, see A. C. Johnson, *Egypt and the Roman Empire* (Ann Arbor, Mich., 1951), 74–75.
30. *dia ton peri autous plouton kai tēn ek tēs politeias dunasteian*, Athan. *Hist. Ar.* 73 col. 781b; *oi en ploutō diaboētoi*, Athan. *Apol. ad Constant.* 28 col. 632a; *Hist. Ar.* 78 col. 788b.
31. Third-century magistracies in Oxyrhynchus: *P.Oxy.* 10.1252, 12.1412, 17.2108, 17.2120, 40.2898, 49.3498, 50.3568, 51.3612. Later bouleutai appear most commonly as *dekaprotoi*, that is, low-level officials concerned with grain shipments: *P.Cair.Isidor.* 38; *P.Sakaon* 11, 12, 82, 86.
32. Pagan authors: *totam didici levem, pendulam, seditiosissimum, HA Quad.Tyr.* 8.1, 5; *onti tas gnōmas kouphotatō kai epi brachytatois rasta*

*kinoumenō*, Herodian 4.8.7. The author of the *Historia Augusta* seems to take a particularly dim view of lower-class Egyptians and Alexandrians who, "like madmen and fools are led by the most trivial matters to become highly dangerous to the commonwealth" (*Est hoc familiare populi Aegyptiorum ut velut furiosi ac dementes de levissimis quibusque ad summa rei publicae pericula perducantur*), *Tyr. Trig.* 22.1–2; Julian *Ep.* 21 (378d–79d). Christian writers: *staseōs, physei to dēmmodes enthermon*, Soc. *HE* 4.20 col. 505c; *amentis populi male sana tumultu*, Ausonius *Ordo Urbium Nobilium* 4.4–5; cf. Evagrius's lengthy tirade against the violence of the Alexandrian "rabble," *HE* 2.8. See also citations listed in my introduction, n. 16.

33. Philo *Flacc.* 4; (*xystikēs synodou*) *IGRR* 1.1083. Although we seldom hear of actual craft organizations, their presence can be adduced from references in which fellow tradesmen are mentioned as a collective body, either taking a particular action or as the subject of some official pronouncement. This follows the pattern from other cities, such as Rome, Antioch, or Constantinople, where the collegia are sometimes better attested. See J. P. Sodini, "L'artisanat urbain à l'époque paléochrétienne (IVe–VIIe S.)," *Ktēma* 4 (1979): 71–119.

Sailors and dockworkers: *C.Th.* 13.5.32; Philostorgius 2.2; *P.Giss.* 1.11/*Sel.Pap.* 423 (A.D. 118); Soc. *HE* 6.15 col. 709b; linen workers: *P.Giss.* 4.40 col. 2; carpenters: *P.Oxy.* 3.226; *P.Mich.* 513 inv. 5159; bakers: Philostorgius 2.2; *P.Oxy.* 3636; *P.Sakaon* 25 = *P.Thead.* 36 (cf. the fourth-century bakers of Rome who were so well organized that they were able to establish a secretive system of kidnapping unsuspecting persons to serve as workers, Soc. *HE* 5.18); gem cutters: *Hist. Laus.* 6.5; shoemakers: Leont. *v. Jo. Eleem.* 44a; *P. Tal. Hagiga* 3.1 (although this last may refer to a gem cutter); gravediggers: Epiph. *Haer.* 76.1.6–7; water carriers: Leont. N. *v. Jo. Eleem.* 1; shopkeepers: Leont. *v. Jo. Eleem.* 16.

An Egyptian context is provided by L. S. B. MacCoull, "Notes on the Social Structure of Late Antique Aphrodito," *BASC* 26 (1984): 65–77; P. Van Minnen, "Urban Craftsmen in Roman Egypt," *Münstersche Beiträge z. antiken Handelgeschichte* 5.2 (1987): 88–95; I. F. Fikhman, "Sur quelques aspects socio-économiques de l'activité des corporations professionelles de l'Égypte byzantine," *ZPE* 103 (1994): 19–40.

34. Internal organization of Egyptian collegia: *P.Rend.Harris* 73; *P.Oxy.* 1.53, 1.85; *PSI* 3.202. Prostitutes: Leontius speaks of "the chief one of these women" (*tēs prōtēs tōn toioutōn gunaikōn*), Leont. N. *v. Jo. Eleem.* 38 (ed. Festugière), who translates the phrase as "la maîtresse du collège des putains." This may be formalizing a title bestowed more on account of job skills than due to any official status. Social rank of

collegium officers: *C.Th.* 14.27.1. In the collegium of the *navicularii,* we hear of "the first-ranked persons of the Alexandrian grain fleet," *C.Th.* 13.5.32; contrasted with the poorer members, *C.Th.* 16.2.42.1. Great Synagogue: *B.Tal.Sukkah* 51b. Naukleroi: *IG* 14.918; *IGRR* 1.1062.

35. Dredging of canals: *C.Th.* 14.27.2. There is some evidence that cities in Middle and Upper Egypt were also taxed in order to support the upkeep of the Alexandrian canals; *SB* 5.7756 (A.D. 359). On the *collatio lustralis* or *chrysargyron,* see Jones, *LRE,* 431–32, 858–59, with full references; and R. S. Bagnall, "The Periodicity and Collection of the Chrysargyron," *Tyche* 7 (1992): 15–17.

36. Patriarch and naukleroi: in a letter describing a recent persecution in the city, Athanasius writes, "We adjure also the shipmasters [*nauklērous*] to publish these things everywhere, and carry them to the ears of the most religious Augustus, and to the prefects and magistrates in every place, in order that it may be known that a war has been waged against the church." *Hist. Ar.* 81 col. 793b. When the Arian cause gained ascendancy in the city, Gregory the Cappadocian compelled the navicularii to carry also his letters throughout the empire, *Ep. Encycl.* 5 col. 233b, 7 col. 238b. Athanasius also encouraged the readers of his *Life of Antony* to "question those who sail from here, for possibly when all have told their tale, the account will hardly be in proportion to his merits." Athan. *v. Ant.* prol. On the Alexandrian naukleroi, see also B. Sirks, *Food for Rome* (Amsterdam, 1991), 104–5. Sailors as patriarchal supporters: Soc. *HE* 6.15 col. 709b; Soz. *HE* 8.15–16; Pall. *dial. v. Io. Chrys.* 8. Sailors persecuted by Arians: Athan. *Ep. Encycl.* 5 col. 233a (A.D. 339); Theodoret *HE* 4.19 col. 1176b (A.D. 374). Anti-Athanasian tradesmen: Athan. *Apol. contra Arianos* 15 col. 273a.

37. *Hist. Laus.* 20.2; see also Lampe, *Patristic Greek Lexicon,* s.v. "politikos," p. 1114. The "people of Alexandria": Soc. *HE* 1.37 col. 173b, 7.13 col. 761a, 7.14 col. 765c. Caracalla's edict: *P.Giss.* 4.40 col. 2 (A.D. 215). Other enactments seeking to control migration from the chora to the city: *SB* 1.4284; *P.Westminster Coll.* 3; *P.Flor.* 1.6; *P.Gen.* 16; *P.Lond.* 904; *BGU* 2.372. J. D. Thomas, "A Petition to the Prefect of Egypt and Related Imperial Edicts," *JEA* 61 (1975): 201–21, publishes a further example and also provides a discussion of the other papyri. Alexandrian citizenship and the grain dole in Oxyrhynchus: *P.Oxy.* 40.2901, 40.2915, 40.2927, 40.2932 (between 268 and 272). Fourth century: *P.Oxy.* 14.1722 (early fourth), 46.3305 (A.D. 313).

38. Leont. N. *v. Jo. Eleem.* 21 (trans. Dawes and Baynes).

39. Poverty: Leont. N. *v. Jo. Eleem.* 1 mentions one poor Alexandrian who

entreats "some retailer/tavern keeper or workshop foreman [*pros kapēlon ē pros heteron ergastēriakon*] 'Give me a tremissis, and I will work for you for a month or two, as you wish, because my folk at home are very hungry.'" Church subsidies for the poor: Leont. N. *v. Jo. Eleem.* 2.

*Anexodos*: Athan. *Hist. Ar.* 13 col. 708c, 60 col. 765b, 61 col. 768a; Leont. N. *v. Jo. Eleem.* 7; Liddell, Scott, Jones, and McKenzie, *Greek-English Lexicon,* 133; Lampe, *Patristic Greek Lexicon,* 135. This term is not discussed by Patlagean in her careful study of the nomenclature of poverty in late antiquity—perhaps because the sources using the word are principally Egyptian, that is, outside her chosen parameters. See E. Patlagean, *Pauvreté économique et pauvreté sociale à Byzance: 4e–7e siècles* (Paris, 1977), 25–35.

Charitable institutions: Soc. *HE* 2.17; Athan. *Hist. Ar.* 61 col. 768a; Leont. N. *v. Jo. Eleem.* 7; *P.Oxy.* 16.1898 (an offering to a hospital, A.D. 587); *C.Th.* 16.2.42–43.

Beggars in Agora: *Hist. Laus.* 6.5–9, 21.2–14; Leont. N. *v. Jo. Eleem.* 27; cf. Greg. Nyssa *de Pauper.Amandis* 1. On this agora, see also *BGU* 4.1079/*Sel.Pap.* 107 ("in the market of Augustus," *eis Seba(stēn) Agora(n),* A.D. 41), as well as Calderini, *Dizionario,* 88–89, and Adriani, *Repertorio,* 203–4.

40. Slavery: *P.Oxy.* 44.3197 (fifty-nine to seventy slaves in the household of Tiberius Iulius Theon, A.D. 111); *Hist. Laus.* 14.1 (slaves belonging to the estate of a wealthy merchant, fifth century); *P.Abinn.* 64 (sale of two Alexandrian-born slaves, mid-fourth century); [libellus of presbyter Athanasius] *ACO* 2.1.2.57 (three household slaves referred to as *andrapoda,* "base creatures / human cattle"); Leont. N. *v. Jo. Eleem.* 38 (slave managing household accounts, seventh century); *P.XV Congr.* 22 (slaves employed at an inn); *P.Oxy.* 1.95/*Sel.Pap.* 32 (sale of slave from Alexandria, A.D. 129); Leont. N. *v. Jo. Eleem.* 33 (patriarchal admonitions to mercy toward slaves).
41. B. A. van Groningen, *Le gymnasiarque des métropoles de l'Égypte romaine* (Paris, 1924); N. Lewis, "The Metropolitan Gymnasiarchy: Heritable and Salable," *ZPE* 51 (1983): 85–91.
42. While this small structure should, by no means, be confused with the great theater of Alexandria, its form and function as an urban gathering place provide an important link between the two types of entertainment building. J.-C. Balty has argued vigorously that the Kōm el-Dikka "theater" is, in fact, the bouleuterion of post-Severan Alexandria. Although the chronology of the site might suggest this identification, the absence of supporting epigraphic testimony, the paucity of literary evidence, and the lack of the site's final publication together count against such a conclusion. J.-C. Balty, "Le 'bouleuterion' de l'Alexandrie sévérienne," *É&T* 26 (1983): 7–12. See also the com-

ments of E. Rodziewicz, "Late Roman Auditoria in Alexandria in the Light of Ivory Carvings," *BSAA* 45 (1993): 269–79.

43. Theater: Soc. *HE* 7.13 col. 761a–b. *P.Oxy*. 27.2476; *Hist. Laus*. 26.4; *Hist. Monach*. 19.3–8; Soc. *HE* 4.23 col. 513b; *HA Verus* 8.11 (*fidicinas et tibicines et histriones scurrasque mimarios et praestigiatores et omnia mancipiorum genera*); [libellus of deacon Ischyrion] *ACO* 2.1.2.51. Antioch: Libanius *Oratio* 19.28; cf. John Chrysostom *Hom. in Gen*. 6.6. Chatby flute: Greco-Roman Museum inv. 21705. Edict of Justin (A.D. 524/25), Malalas *Chron*. 17.12[417]. Church canons: *Canons of Athanasius* 31, 75 (ed. Riedel and Crum).

    Hippodrome: *Oratio* 32.31; cf. Juvenal *Sat*. 10.81. Philostratus informs us that "the Alexandrians are devoted to horses, and flock into the hippodrome to see the spectacle," (Philostr. *Vit. Apoll*. 5.26). See also the lucid study of W. D. Barry, "Aristocrats, Orators, and the 'Mob': Dio Chrysostom and the World of the Alexandrians," *Historia* 42.1 (1993): 82–103.

44. Prefect and crowd: Soc. *HE* 7.13 col. 761b. Florus: Evagrius *HE* 2.5. Statue of Serapis: Rufinus *HE* 2.23 (*ad ultimum truncus qui superfuerat in amphitheatro concrematur*). In fact, this incident was likely to have occurred in the theater, not the amphitheater. Proterius: Zach. Mytil. *HE*. 4.2 (trans. Hamilton and Brooks).

45. See especially the seminal work on this topic by Alan Cameron, *Porphyrius the Charioteer* (Oxford, 1973); "Heresies and Factions," *Byzantion* 44 (1974): 92–120; and *Circus Factions: Blues and Greens at Rome and Byzantium* (Oxford, 1976). See also J. Jarry, "Hérésies et factions en Égypte byzantine," *BIFAO* 62 (1964): 173–86; idem, *Hérésies et factions dans l'empire byzantine du IVe au VIIe siècle* (Cairo, 1968); J. V. A. Fine, "Two Contributions on the Demes and Factions in Byzantium in the Sixth and Seventh Centuries," *Zbornik radova vizantoloskog instituta* 10 (1967): 29–37.

46. Z. Borkowski, *Inscriptions des Factions à Alexandrie, Alexandrie* 2 (Warsaw, 1981), 72–110, esp. 99, fig. 3, and 101, fig. 4.

47. In most cases employing the formula: *nika ē tychē*.

48. Fourth-century *factionarius*: *P.Cair.Isidor*. 57, 58. Prefectural support for factions: Justinian *Edict* 13.15–16 (ed. Schoell and Kroll, 787–88). Previously, Alexandrian bouleutai were assessed one hundred solidi annually, which helped to underwrite the cost of maintaining races in the hippodrome.

    Factions in seventh century: John of Nikiu 107.25, 46; 108.14; 119.9. Although the inscriptions from the theatre-like building at Kōm el-Dikka date from this same period, I remain skeptical of the political significance ascribed to them by Borkowski. In virtually all cases, the inscribers of the graffiti could have been motivated by nothing more than sporting enthusiasm and team loyalty. Even though the factions had become partially politicized, they did not cease to function as sporting organizations. See also the balanced review of Borkowski by R. Bagnall and Alan Cameron, *BASP* 20 (1983): 75–84.

The only reference to actual hippodrome violence of which I am aware comes from a third-century source claiming to relate events of the late first century, and even here the emphasis is on the passions roused by horse racing (Philostr. *Vit. Apoll.* 5.26).

49. Dio Chrys. *Oratio* 32.32. Riot of 66: Josephus *BJ* 490–91. Although Josephus refers to the site of these events as an *amphitheatron*, Adriani rightly points out that a public meeting is more likely to have taken place in the urban theater, rather than in the amphitheater located at some distance from the city, not far from Nicopolis. Strabo 17.1.10; Adriani, *Repertorio*, 205–6. A generation prior to this incident, the theater crowd "burst into shout after shout of applause," at the mention of "freedom" in a play by Euripides, thereby expressing deeply felt political sentiments (Philo *Quod omnis probus liber sit* 141). Theater violence in 414/15: Soc. *HE* 7.13 col. 761c. Theater violence as spectacle: *Acta SS. Paese and Thecla* (Pierpont Morgan Codex M 591, T. 28, F. 55 V ii, 61 V ii, 81 R ii).
50. Theater claque: Cameron, *Circus Factions*, 234–44; C. Roueché, *Performers and Partisans at Aphrodisias* (London, 1992), 132–33; R. Browning, "The Riot of A.D. 387 in Antioch: The Role of the Theatrical Claques in the Later Roman Empire," *JRS* 42 (1952): 13–20. For the early empire, see R. MacMullen, *Enemies of the Roman Order* (Cambridge, Mass., 1966), 168–76, 338–42; W. J. Slater, "Pantomime Riots," *Classical Antiquity* 13.1 (1994): 120–44. Nero and the "Alexandrian style": Suetonius *Nero* 20.3. Claque in 193: Cassius Dio (Xiphilinus) 74.13.2–5; Herodian 2.7.3–6. Caracalla: Cassius Dio (Xiphilinus) 78.23.3.
51. Monophysite chants in the 450's: Zach. Mytil. *HE*. 4.3. 414/15: Soc. *HE* 7.13 col. 761a–b. *Parabalani*: *C.Th.* 16.2.42.2; 16.2.43.
52. Fourth-century estimates: Fraser, "Syriac *Notitia*," 104, with discussion on 107–8. Letter of ʿAmr ibn al-ʿAs: Ibn ʿAbd al-Hakam, *Futūh Misr wa-Akhbāruhā*, ed. C. Torrey (New Haven, 1922), 82 / Saʿid ibn Batriq (Eutychius) *Ann.* 2.316–17. On the reliability of these figures, see L. I. Conrad, "The Conquest of Arwād," in *The Byzantine and Early Islamic Near East: Problems in the Literary Source Material*, ed. Averil Cameron and L. I. Conrad (Princeton, 1989), 354–58.

Baths at Kōm el-Dikka: Kolataj, "Recherches architectoniques," 187–89; E. Rodziewicz and M. Rodziewicz, "Alexandrie 1976," *É&T* 12 (1983): 241–61; idem., "Alexandrie 1977," *É&T* 12 (1983): 263–

75; Koltaj, *The Imperial Baths at Kōm el-Dikka, Alexandrie* 6 (Warsaw, 1992). It has been suggested, on the basis of two inscribed ostraca found on the site, that this bath complex may be identified with the Baths of Diocletian mentioned in Theophanes *Chronogr*. 107.4. Lacking more substantive evidence, such an identification should be regarded as tentative. A. Lukaszewicz, "Nouveaux textes documentaires d'Alexandrie," in *Atti del XVII Congresso Internazionale di Papirologia* (Naples, 1984), 3, 879–84.

Upkeep of baths: Justinian *Edict* 13.15–16 (ed. Schoell and Kroll, 787–88). Taverns and baths as gathering places: Jo. Moschus *Prat. Spir*. 194; *Canons of Athanasius* 93 (ed. Riedel and Crum). On the social role of public baths in early Byzantium, see C. Mango, "Daily Life in Byzantium," *Jahrbuch für österreichischen Byzantinistik* 31 (1981): 337–53; A. Lumpe, "Zur Kulturgeschichte des Bades in der byzantinischen Ära," *Byzantinische Forschungen* 6 (1979): 151–66.

53. Palladius *Hist. Laus*. 26.4, 35.14.

54. *Expositio* 37.1–5, following the translation of Rougé, who admits that this difficult portion of the text is probably corrupt (267–68).

Among the augustal prefects, Fl. Philagrius and Hypatius each had a second tenure of office, and Faustinus (praef. aug., 359–61) was previously *rationalis Aegypti*. Philagrius was especially popular with the Alexandrian demos, despite his enforcement of Arian hegemony in Alexandria. Indeed, Gregory of Nazianzus (a compatriot of Philagrius) states that Philagrius was "for a second time entrusted with the administration of the city at the request of the people," since he "was honored as much as he was loved" (*Or*. 21.28). Athanasius brands Philagrius as "a man of no respectable character." Yet, Athanasius grudgingly acknowledges Philagrius's popularity, even though he claims that "by means of promises which he afterward fulfilled, he succeeded in gaining over the heathen multitude, with the Jews and disorderly persons" (Athan. *Ep. Ency*. 3). For the careers of these prefects, see entries in *PLRE* 1.

55. A sampling of imperial edicts: *P.Oxy*. 1.34, 6.889, 9.1185, 12.1405, 12.1475, 43.3105; *P.Mich*. 529 inv. 5473. See also F. Burkhalter, "Archives locales et archives centrales en Égypte romaine," *Chiron* 20 (1990): 191–216. Theodosius: *Hist. Monach*. 1.64. Appointment of Maximus: Zosimus 4.37.3. Display of imperial portraits: Julian *Ep*. 59 (ed. Bidez-Cumont); [libellus of layman Sophronius] *ACO* 2.1.2.64.

The seated porphyry statue has sometimes been identified as Diocletian, perhaps because the styling and material seems "Tetrarchic" (Greco-Roman Museum inv. 5934).

56. Athan. *Apol. contra Ar*. 51, 87; *Apol. ad Constant*. 22, 24; *Hist. Ar*. 48–49; Julian *Ep*. 24 (398); Soc. *HE* 3.13, 4.13.

57. Athanasius and the emperors: see now D. Arnold, *The Early Episcopal Career of Athanasius of Alexandria* (Notre Dame, Ind., 1991); and T. D. Barnes, *Athanasius and Constantius: Theology and Politics in the Constantinian Empire* (Cambridge, Mass., 1993). Both of these works should be seen in the light of the comments of C. Kannengiesser, "Athanasius of Alexandria: Some Open Questions," *Coptologia* 12 (1991): 27–40. Constantine's vexation with Athanasius: *eis thymon achtheis,* Soc. *HE* 1.35 cols. 169c–71a; Athan. *Apol. contra Ar.* 87 col. 405a.

    Imperial emissaries to Alexandria: Athan. *Apol. ad Constant.* 19 col. 620b; *Hist. Ar.* 48 col. 752c, 51 col. 756b, 81 col. 793d. After the death of the deposed patriarch Dioscorus in 454, Marcian sent to Alexandria a *silentarius* named John, who was charged with the task of convincing the Alexandrians to support Proterius. Instead, John was won over by the arguments of the Alexandrians and subsequently voiced their complaints before the emperor—who remarked sarcastically, "We sent you indeed, to persuade and exhort the Egyptians to obey our will: but you have returned to us, not according as we wished, since we find you an Egyptian" (Zach. Mytil. *HE* 3.11, trans. Hamilton and Brooks). A useful list, illustrating the variety of officials who represented the emperor's interests, may be found in Athan. *Apol. ad Constant.* 10 col. 607b–c (*duces, katholikoi, comites, palatini, agentes in rebus*). *Comites*: Athan. *Hist. Ar.* 48–49 col. 753a, 54 col. 757c–d, 55 col. 760b.

58. Nicopolis: *P.Jews* 1914; *Hist. Aceph.* 5.13; *P.Oxy.* 14.1666. See also K. A. Worp, "Observations on Some Military Camps and Place Names in Lower Egypt," *ZPE* 87 (1991): 291–95. Libyan tribes: Philostorgius *HE* 11.8; *P.Mich.* 206, inv. 338. Blemmyes: Palladius *Hist. Laus.* 32.10, *Dialogus* 20; Eus. *V. Const.* 1.8; Zosimus 1.71. See also A. M. Demicheli, *Rapporti di pace e di guerra dell' Egitto romano con le popolazioni dei deserti africani* (Genoa, 1976); R. Updegraff and L. Török, "The Blemmyes I," *ANRW* 10.1 (1988): 44–106.

    Dux Aegypti and dux Thebaidis: Several times during the later Roman period these two posts were combined or were divided yet further, cautioning us to avoid a hard and fast hierarchy of military posts at this time: *Annales du Service des antiquités de l'Égypte* 34 (1934): 22–23; *CIL* 3.12073/*ILS* 701; J. Leipolt, *Shenute von Atripe* (Leipzig, 1903), 164. By the mid-sixth century, the authority of the dux Thebaidis was absorbed by that of the prefect in Alexandria (*CJ* 1.57.1; 2.7.13), who also was responsible for requisitioning supplies and furnishing the troops' expenses (Justinian *Edict* 13.13, ed. Schoell and Kroll, p. 787).

    Dux Aegypti and public order: *Hist. Aceph.* 5.12–13; *Acta SS.*

*Paese and Thecla* (Pierpont Morgan Codex M 591, T. 28, F. 55 V i); *P.Lond.* 1914.9–10–"soldiers of the dux and of the camp." For the activities of military *comites* within the city, see *Hist. Aceph.* 2.10; Athan. *Hist. Ar.* 51 col. 756b; Amm. Marc. 22.11.9. Dux Aegypti as persecutor: Socrates *HE* 2.11 col. 205a; Athan. *Hist. Ar.* 81 col. 793d, *Fest. Ind.* a.360; Amm. Marc. 22.11.2–3; Julian *Ep.* 60; Eunapius *v. Soph.* 6.11.2; Sozomen *HE* 7.15.5.

59. Athan. *Ep. Encycl.* 4 col. 232a, *Apol. c. Ar.* 56.; Soc. *HE* 4.22 col. 509a, 4.24 col. 542a. Prefect and *corrector*: *SB* 1.4426; *P.Oxy.* 43.3111. The usurper Fl. Achilleus is styled as *corrector/epanorthētēs* in contemporary documents (*P.Cair.Isidor.* 62; *SB* 6.9167; see Jones, *LRE,* 45). After the defeat of Licinius in 324, the administration of the province reverted back to a strongly prefect-dominated system (*P.Oxy.* 3756, nn. 7–9). See also H. Heinen, "Provincial Organization of Egypt," in *CoptEncy* 6:2022–24. Judicial petitions: *P.Abinn.* 63; *P.Oxy.* 31.2597, 43.3093. On the nature of these petitions, see J. D. Thomas, "A Petition to the Prefect of Egypt and Related Imperial Edicts," *JEA* 61 (1975): 201–21. Full discussions may be found in H. Hübner, *Der Praefectus Aegypti von Diocletian bis zume Ende des römischen Herrschaft* (Munich, 1952); C. Vandersleyen, *Chronologie des préfets d'Egypte de 284 à 395,* Collection Latomus, vol. 55 (Brussels, 1962); B. Verbeeck, "Prefect," in *CoptEncy* 6:2007–10.

60. A terminus ante is now supplied by *P.Oxy.* 54.3756, which indicates that the *praeses Ioviae* exercised authority over Alexandria at least until 325. After that time, the prefect seemed to have jurisdiction over the city. However, the evidence is far from conclusive on this point. See J. D. Thomas, "The Administrative Divisions of Egypt," in *Proceedings of the Twelfth International Congress of Papyrology* (Toronto, 1974), 465–69; A. H. M. Jones, "Egypt," in *The Cities of the Eastern Roman Provinces,* with revisions by J. D. Thomas (Oxford, 1971), 336 and 489, n. 50; and Thomas's further remarks in *BASP* 22 (1985): 25–27. See also the introductory comments to *P.Oxy.* 51.3619, 54.3756.

61. Subordinate financial officials: *P.Oxy.* 1.41, 9.1204, 10.1260, 43.3127; *P.Beatty Panop.* 1.64; Athan. *Apol.ad Constant.* 19 col. 620b; *Hist. Ar.* 55 col. 760b, 58 col. 764a; possibly also in Zach. Mytil. *HE* 3.2 (trans. Hamilton and Brooks). These officials appear to have replaced the pre-Diocletianic *idios logos* and *procurator usiacus*; cf. P. R. Swarney, *The Ptolemaic and Roman Idios Logos* (Toronto, 1970), 133–34. The latest datable reference to the *idios logos* may be found in W. *Chres.* 72 (A.D. 234), which suggests that this post may have disappeared as early as the administrative reforms of Philip I (the Arab). *Procurator rei privatae*: *P.Oxy.* 33.2673 (A.D. 304). *Procurator Phari*: Achilles Tatius 5.7.3; *P.Oxy.* 10.1271, 31.2567, 43.3118; *BGU*

1.162, 165, 167, 171; *C.Th.* 14.27.2; *Gnomon Idios Logos* 68; Strabo 2.101. Cf. *ILS* 1433 from the mid-third century, which speaks of a *Proc(urator) Alex(andreae) Pelusi Par[(aetoni)]*, perhaps another official entrusted with guarding the province's frontiers. *Praepositus monetae*: Amm. Marc. 22.11.9; *Hist. Aceph.* 2.10. M. Paechin argues that Ammianus has mistakenly called Draconitus a *praepositus*, when in fact, the proper designation was *procurator*, "*Praepositus* or *Procurator*?" *Historia* 36 (1986): 248–49.

62. Rank of *praefectus annonae*: (*vir clarissimus*) *P.Turner* 45. Equestrian holders of this office are also known (*diasēmotatos/perfectissimus*), *P.Ryl.* 4.652.

A fascinating glimpse into the inner workings of this bureaucracy can be gleaned from *P.Turner* 45, which details the hierarchy within the department in A.D. 374. Among the officials subordinate to the *praefectus annonae Alexandrinae* there are listed a number of receivers, supervisors, *tabularii*, *oeconomoi*, and auditors. Other, more familiar administrators in the grain trade find little attestation from late Roman sources—for example, the *procurator Neapoli*, the *procurator ad Mercurium Alexandreae*, and the *procurator Alexandreae*, all from earlier documents, *P.Oxy.* 10.1259, 17.2125, 31.2567, 42.3031. Cf. John of Nikiu 107.17 (seventh century).

63. Decline of magistracies and attendant financial burdens: Athan. *Hist. Ar.* 78 col. 788b–d; Libanius *Or.* 49.12. Antioch: Libanius *Or.* 2.35; 48.3, 25; *Ep.* 375.5; Julian *Misopogon* 475. See also P. Garnsey, "Aspects of the decline of the urban aristocracy in the Empire," *ANRW* 2.1 (1974): 229–52.

The honorific office of *stratēgos*, roughly equivalent to a Latin *duovir*, should not be confused with the civic post of the same name which was responsible for police protection in the city. See Bowman, "Papyri and Roman Imperial History," 166 and n. 136.

Alexandrian *cursus*: see the discussion in *P.Oxy.* 12.1412, note on lines 1–3; cf. *IGRR* 1060, 1044; *BGU* 2.578, 1.121; *P.Amh.* 124. For the early imperial period, see the exhaustive treatment by Delia, *Alexandrian Citizenship*, 89–113.

64. Prytanis: *PSI* 12.1225; *P.Oxy.* 1.59; 12.1412 (where the prytanis calls to order a meeting of the *boule* in Oxyrhynchus). During the early principate, Alexandria appears to have been governed by a group of *archontes*—later formalized by Septimius Severus as the city's boule. Prytanis and dux: Athan. *Apol. ad Constant.* 24 col. 625b. The association of the prefect with Alexandrian magistrates is also echoed in Athan. *Hist.Ar.* 81 col. 796b, where the patriarch exhorts unspecified *politeutas* to work with the prefect in restoring peace to the city.

Dikastai: Athan. *Apol. ad Constant.* 33 col. 639b; *Hist. Ar.* 31 col.

728c; *Ep. Encycl.* 2 col. 225c; *Hist. Aceph.* 1.9. A. Martin, in her commentary on the *Hist. Aceph.*, follows Lallemand in assuming that these are members of the prefect's *officium*. The evidence, at least from Alexandria, seems to indicate otherwise. A. Martin, *Histoire "Acéphale" et Index Syriaque des Lettres Festales d'Athanase d'Alexandrie, SC* no. 317 (Paris, 1985), 182 n. 35; J. Lallemand, *L'administration civile de l'Égypte* (Bruxelles, 1964), 72–75. For prefectural courts in an earlier period, see H. Kupiszewski, "The *iuridicus Alexandreae*," *Journal of Juristic Papyrology* 7–8 (1953–54): 187–204. On the shadowy Alexandrian ekklesia during this period, see the tenuous references in Philostorgius *HE* 2.11; Soc. *HE* 7.15 col. 768.

For the structure of civic government in contemporary Oxyrhynchus, see E. G. Turner, "Oxyrhynchus and Rome," *HSCP* 79 (1975): 15–16; and A. K. Bowman, *The Town Councils of Roman Egypt* (Toronto, 1971), 121–27. More broadly, see H. Heinen, "Boule," in *CoptEncy* 2:413–14, with full bibliography.

65. "saepe illi ob neglectas salutationes, locum in balneis non concessum, carnem et olera sequestrata, calceamenta servilia et cetera talia usque ad summum rei publicae periculum in seditiones, ita ut armarentur contra eas exercitus, pervenerunt." *HA Tyr. Trig.* 22.2.

66. Liberatus *Brev.* 18; John of Nikiu *Chron.* 89.35; John Malalas 401. A similar fate threatened John, an otherwise popular prefect under the emperor Maurice (582–602), when the city suffered a serious grain shortage. He was saved only by the intervention of influential Monophysites who valued his former assistance (John of Nikiu *Chron.* 97.7). These incidents should be carefully distinguished from the extraordinary circumstances attending the struggle for Egypt during the revolt of Heraclius against Phocas. In Alexandria, the civil war ended with the victory of Nicetas and the withdrawal of Bonosus in 609. Phocas's unfortunate prefect, named John, was decapitated and his head was displayed above one of the city's main gates. The strife of this period was more characteristic of the usurpations and civil wars of the mid-third century than of the intervening centuries. For popular violence against the prefect in the early principate, see Strabo *Geog.* 17.1.53.

67. Prefectural guards: *ōmous kai agrious*, in *Hist. Monach.* 19.9. Cf. Athan. *Apol. contra Ar.* 14 col. 272c–d, 31 col. 300c, 83 col. 397b. On the use of soldiers in police activities, see R. MacMullen, *Soldier and Civilian in the Later Roman Empire* (Cambridge, Mass., 1963), 50–56. Combinations of imperial troops: in 356, during the disturbances which preceded the installation of George the Cappadocian, Athan. *Apol. ad Constant.* 24 col. 265a; *Hist. Aceph.* 1.10–11.

*Stratēgoi tōn poleōs*: this post undoubtedly evolved from the late

Ptolemaic *nukterinos stratēgos* (Strabo 17.1.12, and cf. *BGU* 729; *P.Oxy*. 1.100, 10.1270). See also Bagnall, *Egypt in Late Antiquity,* 164–65. By the late sixth century, if we can trust the data supplied by John Moschus, it appears as though the prefect's guards ("the men of the Praetorium") had taken over much of the police work in Alexandria (Jo. Moschus *Prat. Spir*. 72, 75). For similarly functioning officials elsewhere, see Liebeschuetz, *Antioch,* 124–25; Jones, *LRE,* 692. On the relation between the strategos and military authorities in the Egyptian countryside, see R. W. Davies, "The Investigation of Some Crimes in Roman Egypt," *Ancient Society* 4 (1973): 199–212.

Use of force by strategoi: Athan. *Hist. Ar*. 63 col. 768d; during the Christian persecution of 257–60 (Eus. *HE* [Dionysius] 7.11.22), and in the turmoil of 356 (Athan. *Hist. Ar*. 81 col. 796b).

68. Florus: *kai tēn stasin pros brachu dialusai,* Evagrius *HE* 2.5. Four years later, a *comes* named Dionysius was less successful in his attempts to suppress Monophysite rioting after the lynching of Proterius. In the end, Dionysius was forced, "being at his wits' end," to acquiesce in the consecration of Timothy Aelurus (Zach. Mytil. *HE* 4.1, trans. Hamilton and Brooks). Some sort of organized bread dole had probably been going on in Alexandria since the end of the first century when the city's food supply is referred to as an imperial beneficence in a letter of Trajan and, shortly afterward, when Dio Chrysostom speaks of Alexandrians, "to whom you need only throw bread and a ticket to the hippodrome"; see *P.Oxy*. 42.3022 (A.D. 98); Dio Chrys. *Or*. 32.31.

Diocletian: Procopius *Hist. Arc*. 26.40–44. Theodosius II: *C.Th*. 14.26.1–2, *de Frumento Alexandrino*. See J. Durliat, *De la ville antique à la ville byzantine,* Collection de l'École française de Rome 136 (Rome, 1990), 323–34.

69. Grain dole in Oxyrhynchus: *P.Oxy*. 40.2892–2940. See J. R. Rea's extensive introduction and notes to these documents in *The Oxyrhynchus Papyri,* vol. 40, Egypt Exploration Society Graeco-Roman Memoirs, no. 56 (London, 1972), 1–117. Also, Turner, "Oxyrhynchus and Rome," 17–18.

Alexandrian dole: Eus. *HE* [Dionysius] 7.21.9; *P.Oxy*. 12.1412; *P.Mich*. 613 inv. 1939; Justinian *Edict* 13.15–16 (ed. Schoell and Kroll, 787–88); *C.Th*. 14.26.2; *P.Abinn*. 63.

70. *tōn anagkaiōn hupospanizontas aphelomenos*: Procopius *Hist. Arc*. 26.43; *C.Th*. 14.26.2; Athan. *Apol. de fuga* 6 col. 651a; *Hist. Ar*. 13 col. 708c.

71. "House and bread" (*Alexandreia oikian te kai artous*): *P.Mich*. 723 inv. 902, line 2. The editor of the papyrus is puzzled by the meaning of *artous,* stating that the obvious meaning of "wheat-bread loaf" makes

"no sense in the above text," and opts instead for a rather tenuous reading of *artous* as "doors." Once *artous* is recognized as a reference to the bread dole, the most natural meaning is also the most logical in this particular context. For parallels, see U. Wilcken, *Grundzüge und Chrestomathie der Papyruskunde* (Leipzig, 1912), 356–67. Abinnaeus: *P.Abinn.* 22. See also T. D. Barnes, "The Career of Abinnaeus," *Phoenix* 39.4 (1985): 368–74. Grain distribution and house ownership: V. Martin and D. van Berchem, "Le *Panis Aedium* d'Alexandrie," *Revue de philologie* 16 (1942): 5–21.

Grain dole as honorific: by the end of the fifth century, when much of the administration of Alexandria's annona was in ecclesiastical hands, the Monophysite patriarch Timothy Aelurus is seen distributing *paxamatia,* "little cakes or biscuits," to "the great men and rulers of the city" (Zach. Mytil. *HE* 5.4, trans. Hamilton and Brooks). Zachariah's translators are bewildered by the Syriac transliteration of the Greek *paxamatia,* stating that "the meaning can hardly be 'little cakes.'" Yet, this most natural translation makes perfect sense if one interprets the bread dole as a largely honorific social institution. Cash bounty: *P.Abinn.* 63. One of the recipients of Timothy Aelurus's bread distribution wanted "a gift of denarii" instead of grain (Zach. Mytil. *HE* 5.4, trans. Hamilton and Brooks). Wealthy recipients: [libellus of presbyter Athanasius] *ACO* 2.1.2.57; *P.Oxy.* 40.2901, 40.2904, 40.2915, 40.2916, 40.2927. See Rea's discussion in the volume containing these papyri, 2–9. Also, N. Lewis, "The Recipients of the Oxyrhynchus Siteresion," *Chronique d'Égypte* 49 (1974): 158–62; Turner, "Oxyrhynchus and Rome," 20–24; J. M. Carter and K. Hopkins, "The Amount of the Corn Dole at Oxyrhynchus," *ZPE* 13 (1974): 195–96.

72. Athan. *Apol. contra Ar.* 18 col. 277b; *Hist. Ar.* 13 col. 708c. The Monophysite patriarch Timothy Aelurus lavishly expended the church's money on "the poor, and the widows, and the entertaining of strangers, and upon the needy in the city" (Zach. Mytil. *HE* 4.3, trans. Hamilton and Brooks). Charitable institutions: Palladius *Hist. Laus.* 6.7–9; *v. Jo. Eleem.* 6. *AP* 9.787 preserves an inscriptional epigram, which adorned a pilgrim hostel built by Eulogius (patriarch, 580–607).

73. M. Rodziewicz, *La céramique romaine tardive d'Alexandrie, Alexandrie* 1 (Warsaw, 1975), 42–47, 68. An epigram on John's tomb described him as having possessed "an abundance of wealth, greater than all the sons of Cyprus, both from his patrimony and from his own honest labors." *AP* 7.679. In the context of late antique aristocratic life, his renowned almsgiving habits could be interpreted as the bestowing of traditional beneficia upon his clients. John's experience in administer-

ing his inherited wealth made him particularly suited to manage the vast resources of the Alexandrian patriarchate. The pottery record from Kōm el-Dikka suggests that this wealthy magnate from Cyprus maintained relations with Cypriot business interests—or at the very least promoted commercial ties between his see and his homeland. On this epigram, see Alan Cameron, "The Epigrams of Sophronius," *Classical Quarterly,* n.s., 33 (1983): 284–92.

74. Church's collection and transport network: Rufinus *v. Patrum* 2.18; *P.Oxy*. 16.1906, 16.2002; *v. Jo. Eleem*. 10 (for the activities of the patriarchal grain fleet in the Mediterranean). Imperial gifts of grain to church: *P.Lond*. 1914.49–51, 56; Athan. *Apol. contra Ar*. 18 col. 277b; *Ep. Encycl*. 4 col. 232a. Oil distribution: *P.Mich*. 613 inv. 1939 mentions an oil shipment of 9,000 sextarii (roughly 1,298 gallons or 4,914 liters) for the *annona civica*. Distributions of oil were so vital in the eyes of the populace that the prefect Theodosius was murdered during an acute shortage in 516 (Malalas 16.15[401–2]). For the church-administered dole, see Athan. *Hist. Ar*. 13 col. 708c. Accusations against Athanasius: Athan. *Apol. contra Ar*. 18 col. 277b. Confiscation of church's grain: Athan. *Hist. Ar*. 31 col. 728c.

75. Recipients of church's dole: Athan. *Ep. Encycl*. 4 col. 232a; *Apol. de fuga* 6 col. 651a; *Hist. Ar*. 13 col. 708c (*anexodōn*; see n. 39), 63 col. 769a. Confiscations in 339: Athan. *Hist. Ar*. 10 col. 705b.

76. Athan. *Hist. Ar*. 54 col.757d.

77. Antioch: Libanius *Or*. 20.7. Constantinople: Soc. *HE* 2.13 cols. 208d—9a; Soz. *HE* 3.7 cols. 1049c–51a.

78. *History of the Patriarchs* 1.13 (ed. Evetts), 466–67 [202–3].

79. An offhand comment of a monk at the suburban monastery of Oktokaidekaton illustrates the central place held by the Via Canopica in contemporary images of Alexandria. While reflecting on the worldliness of recent monks, the ascetic states: "My children, if you wish to be saved, flee men. For today, we do not cease to go to the gates and to traverse through the entire city [*pasan polin*] to the countryside so as to seek to make abundant provision for avarice and vain glory and to fill up our souls with vanity," Jo. Moschus *Prat. Spir*. 110. The only way to journey across the entire city and thence into the countryside was by the Via Canopica. Processions along the Via Canopica are often denoted in the sources by the phrases *per mediam ciuitatem, dia mesēs tēs agoras* or *dia pasēs tēs poleōs*.

80. William MacDonald, *Architecture of the Roman Empire* (New Haven, 1986), 2:29.

81. Kostof, *The City Assembled,* 195–98.

82. On the types and uses of public spaces, see Kostof, *The City Assem-*

*bled,* 123–64. The gradual morphology of public spaces is discussed in R. Krier, *Urban Space* (New York, 1979), 30–62.

Callixenus, quoted by Athenaeus 197c–203b; see also E. E. Rice, *The Grand Procession of Ptolemy Philadelphus* (Oxford, 1983). For processions in medieval Alexandria, see the remarks of P. Kahle, "Die Katastrophe des mittelalterlichen Alexandria," in *Mélanges Maspéro* 3, *MIFAO* 68 (Cairo, 1934–40): 137–54.

83. Cassius Dio (Xiphilinus) 51.16.3–5; *P.Oxy.* 25.2435 recto; 34.2725. On the imperial adventus in Alexandria during the early Roman period, see the comments of W. D. Barry, "Faces of the Crowd: Popular Society and Politics of Roman Alexandria, 30B.C.–A.D. 215" (Ph.D. diss., University of Michigan, 1988), esp. chap. 2 (50–92).

84. Claudius: *P.Lond.* 1912, lines 34–40. On this very important imperial letter, see the extended discussion in H. I. Bell, *Jews and Christians in Egypt* (London, 1924), 1–37; as well as in *CPJ,* 1:36–55. Theodosius: Zosimus 4.37. Seventh-century festival: Sophronius *Vita Cyri et Iohannis* (*PG* 87.3, cols. 3685–88). Sophronius's authorship is disputed, but the context and language place it prior to the mid-seventh century. Cf. T. Nissen "De ss. Cyri et Iohannis Vitae formis," *An Bol* 57 (1939): 65–71. Homily of Theophilus: the phrase "in the midst of the marketplace" can only refer to the Mesonpedion or Agora in the ceremonial heart of the city: "A Homily on the Virgin by Theophilus, Archbishop of Alexandria," 90, cols. 1–2, text and translation in W. H. Worrell, *The Coptic Manuscripts in the Freer Collection,* University of Michigan Studies, Humanistic Series, vol. 10 (New York, 1923), 308–9 (text), 375 (trans.).

85. Severus in 199: Malalas 12.21 [293]. Caracalla in 215: Herodian 4.8.8. For this episode, which eventually led to the massacre of many Alexandrians on the emperor's orders, see W. Reusch, *Der historische Wert der Caracallavita in den SHA, Klio* Beiheft 24 (Leipzig, 1931); P. Benoit and J. Schwartz, "Caracalla et les troubles d'Alexandrie," *Études de papyrologie* 7 (1948): 17–33; the detailed notes to this passage in C. R. Whittaker, trans., *Herodian,* 2 vols., Loeb Classical Library (Cambridge, Mass., 1969–70); and the judicious comments of Barry, "Faces of the Crowd," 136–43.

86. Gregory Nazianzus *Oratio* 21.28–29: *Eō gar legein krotous pandēmous, kai murōn ekchuseis, kai pannuchidas, kai pasan phōti katastraptomenēn tēn polin, kai dēmosias estiaseis kai oikidias . . .* The parallel between the imperial and the patriarchal adventus was further enhanced by the crowd's practice of shouting acclamations. During Germanicus's visit, the Alexandrians frequently interrupted his speech with shouts of: "Hurrah! Lord! Good luck! You will gain blessings!" (*P.Oxy.* 25.2435

recto). At the time of Athanasius's elevation to the episcopate, the crowd exclaimed: "He is a good, pious Christian! An ascetic! A true bishop!" (Athan. *Apol. contra Arianos* 6).

The patriarchal adventus continued even after the Arab conquest. Following thirteen years of persecution and exile under Byzantine rule, the Coptic patriarch Benjamin I returned to Alexandria in 643/44 amid scenes of public rejoicing. As a token of the new state of affairs in Egypt, Benjamin was escorted by the dux to ʿAmr, who received the patriarch "with honor and veneration and love." In a carefully staged ceremony, Benjamin returned the honor by publicly praying a blessing upon ʿAmr and his soldiers before they set out on the conquest of Pentapolis (*History of the Patriarchs* 1.14, ed. Evetts, pp. 496–97 [232–33]. Fifty years later, the newly elected patriarch, Isaac (690–93) was escorted in triumph from Babylon to Alexandria: "With him walked crowds of bishops who had all gathered together to set him over the churches. . . . And it happened that when they reached the city of Alexandria, the whole multitude came out to meet him, the clerics carrying the gospels and crosses, sweet-smelling censers and burning tapers, and they sang psalms before him until they had brought him into the city." Mena of Nikiu *The Life of Isaac of Alexandria,* trans. D. N. Bell (Kalamazoo, Mich., 1988), 63–64; Coptic text and French trans. in E. Porcher, *Vie d'Isaac, Patriarche d'Alexandrie, PO* 9.3 (Paris, 1914).

87. Apollonius: Philostratus *Life of Apollonius* 5.26. The quasi-fictionalized nature of Philostratus's biography (early third-century account of late first-century events) does not mitigate the value of his work for this discussion. If anything, the fact that Philostratus needed to provide a believable context for Apollonius's visit to Alexandria underscores the typicality of these processions.
88. Lucius probably sought to avoid the violent death meted out to his Arian predecessor at Alexandria, George of Cappadocia. Since he was ordained to the priesthood by George, it is likely that Lucius feared the Alexandrians would equate him with his hated mentor (*Historia Acephala* 4.7).
89. Ibid. 5.13.
90. . . . *aplē gar eisodō tēs poleōs epibainein ouk ēdunato* . . . Theodoret *HE* 4.19; Soc. *HE* 4.21.
91. *Apoph. Patr.* Systematic Coll. 237. A beloved ascetic in the early seventh century (Leont. N. *v. Jo. Eleem.* 38, ed. Festugière) was buried after a lengthy procession which was illuminated with candles and torches and resounded with the honorific acclamations of the mourners. Epiph. *Haer.* 76.1.6–7; Jo. Moschus *Prat. Spir.* 77.
92. Achilles Tatius 5.1.2; Philostratus *Life of Apollonius* 5.26. Serapeum

riots: Rufinus *HE* 2.22–30 (ed. Mommsen), *GCS* 9.2 (Leipzig, 1908). Quotation from Soc. *HE* 5.15 col. 604c.

93. Evagrius *HE* 2.5. Cf. an episode over a century and a half later, when the authorities placed four tyrannical officials "on a camel, and had them conducted throughout all the city of Alexandria in the sight of all men," prior to their imprisonment and eventual execution: John of Nikiu 97.25. Third-century persecution: Eus. *HE* [Dionysius] 6.41.15. A variant form of this procession type took place during the pagan-Jewish violence of A.D. 38, when several dozen Jewish leaders were taken into custody. Flaccus the prefect, "having ordered them to be put in bonds, straightway marshaled a fine procession of these elderly men through the middle of the Agora [*steilas kalēn pompēn dia mesēs agoras*], trussed and pinioned, some with thongs and others with iron chains, and then taken to the theatre" (Philo *in Flaccum* 74). On these events, see E. M. Smallwood, *The Jews under Roman Rule* 2d ed. (Leiden, 1981), 235–50, and the analysis of Barry, "Faces of the Crowd," 103–18.

Riot of 361: *Hist. Aceph.* 2.10; Amm. Marc. 22.11.8–10; Epiph. *Haer.* 76.1.1–2. A late source supplies the detail that after the murder of Proterius, his body was paraded on a camel to the hippodrome; see Eutychius [Sa'id ibn al-Batriq] *An.* 102—*PG* 111, col. 1055.

At the end of antiquity, in the struggle for Alexandria during the revolt of Heraclius (609), the rebels slew the imperial commander, Apulon (Apollonius ?), "cut off his head, and suspending it on a lance they carried it into the city." It was later placed over an important gate "for all that went in and out to see." John of Nikiu *Chron.* 107.16, 21 (trans. Charles). Public chastisement in Agora: ". . . *kai bouneurizei kai pompeuei auton dia tou epanō tēs agoras*." Leont. N. *v. Jo. Eleem.* 16.

The classic examination of ritual communal cleansing in comparative societies is M. Douglas, *Purity and Danger* (London, 1966). The theatricality of executions in the Roman world is surveyed by K. M. Coleman, "Fatal Charades: Roman Executions Staged as Mythological Enactments," *JRS* 80 (1990): 44–73, and G. W. Bowersock, *Martyrdom and Rome* (Cambridge, 1995), 41–57.

94. Proterius: Evagrius *HE* 2.8. Zach. Mytil. *HE* 2.4, adds the detail that Proterius's body was burned in the hippodrome. Anti-Jewish riots of 38: Philo *in Flaccum* 65. In a later passage (71), Philo states that the pagans "dragged the bodies of their victims through almost every lane of the city" and then burned the remains. Decian persecution: Eusebius *HE* [Dionysius] 6.41.3–9. Dionysius singles out for mention one woman named Quinta who refused to sacrifice. The pagans then "bound her by the feet and dragged her through the whole city [*dia pasēs tēs poleōs surontes*], and dashed her against the millstones, and at

the same time scourged her; then, taking her to the same place, they stoned her to death."

Martyrdom of Saint Mark: *History of the Patriarchs* 1.1 (ed. Evetts), 146–47 [48–49]. The precise date of the formation of this tradition is still disputed, but the presence of an underlying Greek original is indicated by a typically Alexandrian pun chanted by the pagan mob: "Drag the serpent through the cattle pasture!" (*Surōmen ton boubklon en tois Boukolou*). Boukolia was an eastern district of Alexandria and an early center of Christianity in the city. Although the apocryphal nature of this martyrdom renders it difficult to date with precision, the requirements of verisimilitude argue for the typicality of the incident.

95. During the violence of 373, several virgins were "dragged in triumph . . . through all the town," and a deacon from Rome "was led publicly through the town by executioners, with his hands tied behind his back like some notorious criminal" (Theodoret *HE* 4.19). On Hypatia's murder, the principal sources are John of Nikiu 84.100–102; Soc. *HE* 7.7.

96. Theodoret *HE* 5.22; Rufinus *HE* 9.23 (ed. Mommsen), *GCS* 9.2 (Leipzig, 1908), 1028–29. Cf. an incident at Caesarea Philippi during the reign of Julian, when a statue of Christ was torn down, dragged around the city, and then mutilated by pagans: Sozomen *HE* 5.21.

97. For the following incident, see Zachariah Scholasticus *Vita Severi Antiocheni* (ed. and trans. Krugener), *PO* 2 (Paris, 1907), 14–39. Zachariah's identity and career have been matters of dispute. Evagrius refers to a Monophysite history of the church composed by a Zachariah Rhetor, surveying the period 450–91. This Zachariah is generally held to be identical to the Zachariah who studied with Severus of Antioch and later wrote his biography. He likewise composed a vita of a Monophysite monk named Isaiah. Is this the same Zachariah who, in 536, is listed as the Chalcedonian bishop of Mytilene and attended a synod at Constantinople? The current consensus, which I follow here, argues for this identification and for Zachariah's conversion to Chalcedonian theology sometime in the first quarter of the sixth century. The texts and translations of Zachariah's works are frequently cited with a variety of appellations (Rhetor, Scholasticus, of Mytilene, etc.). I simply abbreviate him as Zach. Mytil.

The *Historia Ecclesiastica,* in its surviving Syriac epitome, is edited and given a Latin translation by E. W. Brooks in *CSCO,* Scriptores Syri, ser. 3, vols. 5–6 (Louvain, 1921–29). There is also an English translation by Brooks and F. J. Hamilton, *The Syriac Chronicle Known as that of Zachariah of Mitylene* (London, 1899). Books 3–6 of the *HE* seem to be preserved intact by the epitomizer, and as they are the principal sources for my discussion, I do not feel the need to distinguish between Zachariah and the epitomizer—normally referred to as ps.-Zachariah.

On Zachariah, see E. Honigmann, "Patristic Studies," *StudTest* 173 (1953): 194–204; K. Wegenast, "Zacharias Scholastikos" in *R-E* 9.2 (1967): 2212–16; W. H. C. Frend, *The Rise of the Monophysite Movement* (Cambridge, 1972), 202 n. 5; P. Allen, "Zachariah Scholasticus and the *Historia Ecclesiastica* of Evagrius Scholasticus," *JThS*, n.s., 31.2 (1980): 471–88; R. A. Darling Young, "Zacharias: The Life of Severus," in *Ascetic Behavior in Greco-Roman Antiquity,* ed. V. L. Wimbush (Minneapolis, 1990), 312–28.

98. Zach. Mytil *v. Sev.* (ed. and trans. Kugener), 32–35.
99. Philostratus *Life of Apollonius* 5.26.
100. *Alexandria autem civitas est valde maxima et eminens in dispositione et abundans omnibus bonis et escis dives. Expositio* 35.1–3.

*Chapter Four. The Jewish Community*

1. This episode is discussed in full in chapter 9, pp. 299–304.
2. On this important Diasporan community, consult C. H. Kraeling, "The Jewish Community at Antioch," *Journal of Biblical Literature* 51.2 (1932):130–60; W. A. Meeks and R. L. Wilken, *Jews and Christians in Antioch in the First Four Centuries of the Common Era* (Missoula, Mont., 1978); R. L. Wilken, *John Chrysostom and the Jews* (Berkeley, 1983).
3. *B.Tal.Yebamoth* 80a, quoting R. Eliezar, a second-century *Tanna*; Socrates *HE* 7.13 (*PG* 67, col. 764a); Damascius *Vita Isidori* fr.190 (ed. Zintzen, 163).
4. H. A. Green, *The Economic and Social Origins of Gnosticism,* SBL Dissertation Series, no. 7 (Atlanta, 1985), has painted a remarkably lucid and penetrating portrait of Alexandrian Jewry in the first centuries B.C. and A.D. However, his social history of the community neglects the basic question of continuity arising from the revolt of 115–17. Although Green suggests that Gnosticism grew up in the turmoil following the disasters of 70 and 135, perhaps a more likely stimulus for Egyptian Gnosticism could easily be found closer to home during the upheaval and social dislocation brought about by the revolt in Egypt. The revolt in Egypt might also hold the key to understanding the shift from predominantly Jewish forms of Gnosticism in the first century to the nearly exclusive Gentile makeup of Egyptian Gnostic groups in the following centuries—an issue that Green does not address (see esp. 262–65).
5. A. H. M. Jones characterizes this fluctuation in the amount of historical

evidence as "a dark tunnel, illumined from either end, and by rare and exiguous light wells in the interval. One cannot do much more than follow out the known tendencies of the Severan age, at the same time looking forward to the state of affairs that appears under Diocletian, and thus hope to grope one's way through the intervening darkness" (*LRE*, 23).

6. Most surveys of the Alexandrian Jewish community in antiquity restrict themselves to the late Ptolemaic and early Roman periods, only rarely making brief comments on the later Roman era: A. Bludau, *Juden und Judenverfolgungen im alten Alexandria* (Münster, 1906); L. Fuchs, *Die Juden Aegyptens in ptolemaischer und römischer Zeit* (Vienna, 1924); H. I. Bell, *Juden und Griechen im römischen Alexandreia,* Beiheft zum Alten Orient, no. 9 (Leipzig, 1926); idem, "Anti-Semitism at Alexandria," *JRS* 31 (1941):1–18; A. Kasher, *The Jews in Hellenistic and Roman Egypt:The Struggle for Equal Rights,* Texte und Studien zum Antiken Christentum, no. 7 (Tübingen, 1985); J. Méléze-Modrzejewski, *Les juifs d'Égypte de Ramsès II à Hadrien* (Paris, 1991); P. Bilde, *Ethnicity in Hellenistic Egypt* (Aarhus, 1992). For a wealth of information concerning Jews in Egypt and Alexandria, consult the still standard prolegomena, introductions, and notes contained in *CPJ*. The epigraphic material is now collected and analyzed in W. Horbury and D. Noy, *The Jewish Inscriptions of Graeco-Roman Egypt* (Cambridge, 1992), though one should keep in mind the cautions of R. S. Kraemer, "Jewish Tuna and Christian Fish: Identifying Religious Affiliation in Epigraphic Sources," *HTR* 84.2 (1991): 141–62. See also the relevant chapters of E. M. Smallwood, *The Jews under Roman Rule,* 2d ed. (Leiden, 1981), 220–55, 364–68, 389–412.
7. Jewish emigration from Palestine: Josephus *Ap.* 1.186–89, 194; *AJ* 12.8. Tombs: concentrated in the areas of Chatby, El-Ibrahimiya, and el-Hadra. See Horbury and Noy, *Jewish Inscriptions,* xiii-xvi, nos. 1–12/*CIJ* 2.1424 31. Reasons for emigration: Aristeas 12–14; Josephus *BJ* 1.31–33; *P.Tal.Yoma* 6.3; *CPJ* nos.1–6.
8. All such estimates must be regarded with caution, since demographic figures provided by ancient writers are notoriously inexact. Philo *In Flacc.* 43; Josephus *BJ* 2.385:Diod. Sic.1.31.8, 17.52.6.
9. Josephus states that the quarter called Delta was the sector of the city "where the Jews were concentrated," probably in the eastern part of Alexandria since the garrison camp of Nicopolis seems to have been close at hand (*BJ* 2.494–95). Elsewhere he says that the Jewish quarter was along the shore and near the palace, again in the eastern portion of Alexandria (*Ap.* 2.33–36). Later Christian sources state that the martyrium of Saint Mark was located close to the shore, in the easternmost sector of the city. Since the earliest propagation of Christianity was

among the Diaspora communities of the Mediterranean, the martyrium may provide another link for establishing the site of the Alexandrian Jewish quarter. However, this identification of the Delta sector with the probable Jewish quarter near Bruchion is called into question by a papyrus dating from the reign of Augustus which places the Delta quarter in the western part of the city, embracing the small Cibotos Harbor within the Eunostos Harbor (*BGU* 1151, verso, col. 2 line 40; Strabo 17.110). Philo relates that two of Alexandria's five quarters were considered Jewish and that Jews settled throughout the city, with synagogues "in each sector" (*kath hekaston tmēma*) *Leg.* 132, 124; *Fl.* 55). This diffusion of Jewish settlement is confirmed by epigraphic evidence for two synagogues in widely divergent areas of the city, el-Hadra in the east and el-Gabbari by the Eunostos Harbor (*CIJ* 2.1433, 1432). On these geographical questions, see H.Box, *Philonis Alexandrini: In Flaccum* (Oxford, 1939), 99–100; A. Fuks in *CPJ* vol. 1, 69–72; E. M. Smallwood, *Philonis Alexandrini: Legatio ad Gaium* (Leiden, 1961), 20–21, 215–16; P. M. Fraser, *Ptolemaic Alexandria* (Oxford, 1972), 1:26, 55–56, with 2:78, 182, 2:109–10, n. 270; A. Martin, "Les premier siècles du christianisme à Alexandrie: Essai de topographie religieuse, IIIe–IVe siècles," *Revue des études augustiniennes* 30 (1984): 211–25; B. A. Pearson, "Earliest Christianity in Egypt: Some Observations," in *The Roots of Egyptian Christianity*, ed. B. A. Pearson and J. E. Goehring (Philadelphia, 1986), 145–48, 151–54; idem, "The *Acts of Mark* and the Topography of Ancient Alexandria," *BSAA* 45 (1993): 239–46.

10. Range of occupations: *CPJ* 142–45, 149, 152; *CIJ* 2.1435, 1442, 1447; *B.Tal.Sukkah* 51b; Philo *Fl.* 57; 3 Macc. 3:10. See also *CPJ* vol. 1, 48–52. Cf. Antioch: *B.Tal.Kethuboth* 67a; Josephus *BJ* 7.45. Government officials: *CPJ* 125, 127; Josephus *AJ* 17.159, 259; 20.100, 147. See also T. Rajak, "The Jewish Community and Its Boundaries," in *The Jews among Pagans and Christians in the Roman Empire*, ed. J. Lieu, J. North, and T. Rajak (London, 1992), 9–28.
11. Organization of *politeuma*: Josephus *AJ* 14.117, 12.108, *BJ* 7.412; Philo *Fl.* 74; *B.Tal.Sukkah* 51b. Cf. Antioch: Josephus *BJ* 7.47; *P.Tal.Sanhedrin* 3.21a.
12. Philo *Leg.* 132; *B.Tal.Sukkah* 51b.
13. *B.Tal.Sukkah* 51b; *B.Tal.Yoma* 38a; *P.Tal.Yoma* 3.11; *CIL* 6.10099; *IGRR* 4.1414; *IG* 12, pt. 3, 1243.
14. *P.Tal.Hagiga* 3.1; *Mishnah Aboth* 4.11.
15. Much of the current scholarship on the Alexandrian Jewish community is taken up with these questions. See *CPJ* vol.1, 57–74; Smallwood, *The Jews under Roman Rule*, 224–55; Kasher, *The Jews in Hellenistic and Roman Egypt*.
16. Among the modern literature on the revolt, pride of place should be

given to the remarks of Tcherikover and Fuks in the relevant sections of *CPJ*. See also A. Fuks, "The Jewish Revolt in Egypt (A.D. 115–117) in the Light of the Papyri," *Aegyptus* 33 (1953):131–58; idem, "Aspects of the Jewish Revolt in A.D. 115–117," *JRS* 51 (1961): 98–104; A. Tcherikover, *The Jews of Egypt in the Hellenistic-Roman Age,* 2d ed.(Jerusalem, 1963), 160–66 (in Hebrew); Smallwood, *The Jews under Roman Rule,* 389–427; A.Kasher, "Some Comments on the Jewish Uprising in Egypt in the Time of Trajan," *Journal of Jewish Studies* 27.2 (1976): 147–58; S. Applebaum, *Jews and Greeks in Ancient Cyrene* (Leiden, 1979); M. Pucci, "*Alexandria ad Aegyptum*:117–119 A.D.," *Scripta Classica Israelica* 5 (1979–80): 195–205; idem, *La rivolta ebraica al tempo di Traiano,* Biblioteca di Studi Antichi 33 (Pisa, 1981); idem, "La revolta ebraica in Egitto (115–17 d.C.) nella storiografia antica," *Aegyptus* 62 (1982): 198–202; idem, "Greek Attacks against Alexandrian Jews during Emperor Trajan's Reign," *Journal of Jewish Studies* 40.1 (1989): 31–48; T. D. Barnes, "Trajan and the Jews," *Journal of Jewish Studies* 40.2 (1989): 145–62.

17. The most important literary accounts of the revolt are: Eusebius *HE* 4.2.1–5, *Chron.* 2.164; Cassius Dio 68.32.1–3; Appian *B.Civ.* 2.90, *Arabicus Liber* fr. 19; Orosius *Hist.* 7.12, 27; George Syncellus 347d–349b; *HA Hadr.* 5.2, 8; John of Nikiu 72.14–16. Supplementing these are a number of pertinent papyrological sources: *CPJ* 157/*P.Oxy.* 1242; *CPJ* 158a/*P.Par.* 68 and *P.Lond.* 1.227; *CPJ* 158b/*BGU* 341; *CPJ* 435; *CPJ* 436/*P.Giss.* 19; *CPJ* 437/ *P.Giss.* 24; *CPJ* 438/*P.Brem.* 1; *CPJ* 439/*P.Giss.* 27; *CPJ* 440/*P.Bad.* 36; *CPJ* 441/ *P.Bad.* 39; *CPJ* 442/*P.Brem.* 63; *CPJ* 443/*P.Giss.* 41; *CPJ* 444/*P.Brem.* 11; *CPJ* 445/ *P.Oxy.* 1189; *CPJ* 446/*P.Brem.* 15; *CPJ* 447/*P.Oxy.* 707; *CPJ* 448/ *P.Oxy.* 500; *CPJ* 449/*BGU* 889; *CPJ* 450/*P.Oxy.* 705 cols. 1–2; *P.Mich.* 8.471 inv. 5393); *P.Mich.* 8.477 inv. 5399; *P.Mich.* 8.478 inv. 5400; *PSI* 1063; *BGU* 140; Köln inv. 5.941/*ZPE* 51 (1983): 80–84.
18. An undercurrent of zealotry and restiveness among Egyptian Jews can be detected in portions of the *Oracula Sibyllina,* bk. 5, most of which was composed between A.D. 70 and the outbreak of the revolt in 115. See J. J. Collins, *Sibylline Oracles,* in *The Old Testament Pseudepigrapha,* vol. 1, *Apocalyptic Literature and Testaments,* ed. J. H. Charlesworth (Garden City, N.Y., 1983), 317–472, esp. 390–92. Text in J. Geffcken, ed., *Die Oracula Sibyllina* (Leipzig, 1902), 103–32. For the chronology of the revolt's early stages, consult Fuks, "Aspects of the Jewish Revolt," 100; modified by Barnes, "Trajan and the Jews." Though I agree with Barnes that the war in the chora between Jewish rebels and regular Roman army units should be dated to 116–17, the brief but vicious stasis in Alexandria should be placed slightly earlier, towards the end of 115.
19. The other being legio XXII Deiotariana, later destroyed in Palestine

during the Bar Cochba war. These garrison legions were normally supported by at least three auxiliary cohorts: cohors I Ulpia Afrorum equitata, cohors I Damascenorum, and cohors I Augusta Pannoniorum. Evidence for the transfer of legio III Cyrenaica, either in whole or in part, to the Syrian front at the time of the Parthian War is provided by two inscriptions, one from Dura Europos in 115 and the other from Judaea in 116. P. V. C. Baur, M. I. Rostovtzeff, and A. R. Bellinger, eds., *The Excavations at Dura Europos: Fourth Season, 1930–1931* (New Haven, 1933), 56–59; *CIL* 3.13587. Kasher admits that "we have no precise details about military man-power in Egypt in the years A.D. 115–17, nor sufficient information about the location of the different units" ("Jewish Uprising," 151). Consequently, assertions regarding these matters are, at best, plausible conjectures based on the fragmentary evidence. For a full discussion, see Kasher, "Jewish Uprising," 150–54, and more exhaustively, J. Lesquier, *L'armée romaine d'Egypt d'Auguste à Dioclétien* (Cairo, 1918), 73–96.

20. Eusebius *HE* 4.2.3–4, where Lucuas is called the *hēgoumenos* of the rebels as well as their *basileus*. The language employed by the chroniclers and the papyrological writers reflects the escalation of the revolt from scattered disturbances to a full-scale war. Occasionally, the revolt is referred to as "civil strife" (*stasis, CPJ* 244/*P.Brem*.11.30), more often as a "disturbance" (*thorubos*, ibid., line 26; *P.Mich*. 8.477 line 29; *P.Mich*. 8.478 line 14), or an "attack" (*ephodos, CPJ* 443/*P.Giss*. 41 col. 2.4–5). In Cyrenaica, the official designation appears to have been *tumultus/tarachos* (*Africa Italiana* 1 [1927]: 321; *SEG* 9.168; P. M. Fraser, "Hadrian and Cyrene," *JRS* 40 [1950]: 77–90). *Tumultus/tarachos* seems to denote a particularly serious rebellion or insurrection. In Egypt, however, the alliance of rebelling local Jews with an invading army of Cyrenaican Jews earned for the revolt its most common designation, "war" (*polemos, CPJ* 158a/*P.Par*. 68 col. 2.3, 6; Appian *Arabicus Liber* fr. 19; *CPJ* 450/*P.Oxy*. 705 col. 2.33). This term is most often used by later writers (Artemiodorus *Oneirokritika* 4.24; Syncellus 347d; "*atrocissima bella*," Orosius 7.12.6). The escalation of the conflict is best seen in the terminology employed by Eusebius: "increasing the scope of the rebellion [*stasin*] . . . they started a great war [*polemon*] while Lupus was governor of all Egypt." *HE* 4.2.2. In this, Eusebius seems to echo Claudius' letter to the Alexandrians, dated to A.D. 41, in which the emperor discusses the responsibility "for the riots and feud [*tarachēs kai staseōs*], or rather, if the truth be told, the war [*polemou*] with the Jews" (*P.Lond*. 1912.73–74). See the comments of Fuks, "Jewish Revolt," 155–56, and Applebaum, *Jews and Greeks*, 308–10.

21. Applebaum marshals an impressive body of evidence in support of his

thesis that the revolt was primarily a movement of militant, anti-Roman, Zionism: *Jews and Greeks*, 242–344.

22. Eus. *HE* 4.2.3. Turbo had risen from the rank of *primus pilus*, had held several urban posts, and by 114 was the commander of the classis Misenensis. His familiarity with naval operations probably served him well during his campaign against the Jewish rebels in the Nile Delta. *AE* (1946): 113; *CIL* 16.60. For an analysis of his career, see R. Syme, "The Wrong Marcius Turbo," *JRS* 52 (1962): 87–96.
23. Appian *Arabicus Liber* fr. 19; *CPJ* 438/*P.Brem*. 1.

    The archives of Apollonius and his family constitute some of the most vivid sources for the events surrounding the revolt. Of the nearly 150 papyri in this collection, 10 of these are family letters and official documents concerned with the revolt. The personal letters are an especially poignant witness to the upheaval of these years.

    For a convenient table indicating the geographical extent of the revolt in the chora as well as the sources related to each site, see Fuks, "Jewish Revolt in Egypt," 149.

    Coins: S. H. Webber, "An Egyptian Hoard of the Second Century, A.D.," *Numismatic Notes and Monographs* 54 (1932): 1–14. Of the denarii in this hoard, the vast majority (138) are Trajanic, the last datable issues belonging to the period of his sixth consulship (A.D. 112).

    Atrocities: *CPJ* 437/*P.Giss*. 24.3–4. Cassius Dio, normally not an author to indulge in anti-Judaic slander, alleges that the Cyrenaican Jews "would eat the flesh of their victims, make belts for themselves of their entrails, anoint themselves with their blood and wear their skins for clothing; many they sawed in two, from the head downwards; others they gave to wild beasts, and still others they forced to fight as gladiators." He adds, "In Egypt, too, they perpetrated many similar outrages" (68.32.1–2 trans. Cary). These shocking charges have naturally puzzled modern commentators. Some have attributed the acerbity of these remarks to Dio's eleventh-century Byzantine epitomizer, Xiphilinus. Others have viewed these atrocities as no more than a literary *topos* that is commonly ascribed to outlaws or to other rebels like Viriathus or Boudicca. Yet, in conjunction with the letter of Apollonius's mother, perhaps it is best to follow Wilcken, who interprets these passages as evidence for a *Kriegspsychose* among the Greek populations of the affected provinces. The veracity of these allegations is not as important as the fact that they were widely believed to be true. See U. Wilcken, *P.Brem*.15; A. Fuks in *CPJ*, vol. 2, pp. 235–36; J.Schwartz, "Aspects politiques du Judaisme au début du IIIe siècle a.c.," *L'antiquité classique* 39 (1970): 147–58; Applebaum, *Jews and Greeks*, 332–33; M.

Stern, *Greek and Latin Authors on Jews and Judaism* (Jerusalem, 1980) 2:347–48, 387.

24. Eusebius *HE* 4.2.3. Battle near Memphis: *CPJ* 439/*P.Giss*. 27.5–7. On these strategic considerations, see Kasher, "Jewish Uprising," 155–56. Reinforcements: *CPJ* 438/*P.Brem*. 1.15–16, where the writer says he has heard "that another legion of Rutilius arrived at Memphis" (*hoti allē legeōn Rou[ti]liou elthousa eis Mem[ph]in*). By this time, Rutilius Lupus apparently considered the situation in Alexandria to be under control sufficiently so that he could take to the field with part of the Nicopolis garrison.

    A terminus ante quem for the military campaign is provided by *CPJ* 443/*P.Giss*. 41 in which Apollonius requests leave from the prefect to attend to his estates in the Hermopolite nome. Evidently, peace has been established, and since this is Apollonius's second application, we may conclude that the cessation of hostilities occurred some months before the second request's date of 28 November 117. Further, one of Hadrian's earliest military appointments was the transfer of Turbo to Mauretania, where an insurrection had broken out in Trajan's last years. This would suggest that Turbo was no longer needed in Egypt and Cyrenaica (*HA Hadr*. 5.8).

25. Orosius: *in Alexandria autem commisso proelio victi et adtriti sunt, Hist*. 7.12.7 (*CSEL* vol. 5, ed. K. Zangenmeister). Edict of Lupus: *pro tēs Rōmaiōn p[r]os Ioudaious machēs, CPJ* 435 col. 3.26–4.1. Applebaum argues that the *machē* mentioned in this papyrus was not associated with the revolt, but was simply an episode "of intercommunal street-rioting of the type long known in Alexandria." He bases this conclusion on the assumption that "the entire atmosphere reflected in this papyrus . . . is not that of the rebellion itself." He likewise finds *CPJ* 158a–b (the *Acta Pauli et Antonini*) to be lacking a similar war "atmosphere" (*Jews and Greeks*, 267). However, it should be pointed out that the *Acta* are dated to a period early in Hadrian's reign, probably 119–20. Consequently, the *Acta* were composed shortly after the extensive destruction and acute loss of life in Alexandria resulting from the Jewish revolt. It would appear, then, that "atmosphere" is not a suitable criterion for determining the sequence of events in Alexandria.

    Eusebius emphasizes the contrasting fortunes of the rebels in Alexandria and those in the Egyptian chora, who continued the revolt without the aid of their Alexandrian brethren (*HE* 4.2.3).

26. Most notably in A.D. 66, when Tiberius Alexander used the garrison legions to quell a riot, giving them permission "not merely to kill the rioters but to plunder their property and burn down their houses" (Josephus *BJ* 2.493–98).

27. *P.Mich.* 8.478 inv. 5400, in which Terentianus, a common soldier, writes to his relatives that none of the soldiers "were able to pass the camp gate" (*oude tēn pul[ēn] tēs p[arambolēs] exelth[ein] esch[ē]ke tis hēmon*), lines 11–13. He received his wound while fighting in this disturbance/uproar (*thorubos,* line 14)—the same word he used in another letter to describe the "uproar and anarchy in the city" (*thorubos kai akatastasia tēs poleōs*) which the soldiers with difficulty were attempting to suppress; see *P.Mich.* 8.477 inv. 5399, lines 29–30. Roman losses during the revolt appear to have been severe. One unit, the cohors I Lusitanorum, was reduced by nearly a third and had to make up for this shortage by enrolling recruits from Asia Minor, signifying a lack of suitable recruits within Egypt itself: *PSI* 1036/Hunt and Edgar 368; J. F. Gilliam, "An Egyptian Cohort in A.D. 117," in *Bonner Historia-Augusta-Colloquium 1964/1965* (Bonn, 1966), 91–97. The same proportion of casualties appears in a fragmentary list of soldiers from legio III Cyrenaica and legio XXII Deiotariana: R. O. Fink, *Roman Military Records on Papyrus* (Cleveland, 1971), 160–63; Kasher, "Jewish Uprising," 156–58; J. Schwartz, "Où a passé la *legio XXII Deiotariana*?" *ZPE* 76 (1989): 101–2. Although there is no precise record as to the place where these losses occurred, they all appear to have happened in Alexandria or in Egypt during the course of the rebellion, not in Syria during the Parthian War. Applebaum takes several lines from the *Oracula Sibyllina,* bk. 14 (incorrectly ascribed to bk. 12) as a reference to the defeat of III Cyrenaica "by the dikes of the Nile" 14.326–29. However, some commentators suggest that bk. 14 is concerned instead with the Arab conquest in the seventh century! This would counsel that a certain skepticism should attend historical reconstructions based on passages in apocalyptic literature. See the introductory comments of J.J.Collins to bk. 14 in *The Old Testament Pseudepigrapha,* 1:459–60.
28. Appian *B.Civ.* 2.90. The British excavators of the Serapeum concluded that it had been mostly destroyed during the reign of Trajan and later rebuilt under Hadrian: A. Rowe and B. R. Rees, "The Great Serapeum of Alexandria," *Bulletin of the John Rylands Library* 39.2 (1957): 496. The extent of the damage to the Serapeum as well as the chronological framework posited by the excavators is brought into question by two papyrus letters of Terentianus, the soldier stationed at Nicopolis. During the height of the fighting, he writes to his father that he prays for him daily "in the presence of our lord Serapis and the gods who share his temple" (*para tō kuriō Sarapidi kai tois sunnaois theois*), *P.Mich.* 8.477 inv. 5399 line 5, and 8.478 inv. 5400 lines 5–6. Perhaps a plausible solution to this apparent contradiction would be that there

was a local Serapeum within the garrison camp itself, situated on the other side of the city from the great temple of Serapis.

29. In Cyrene alone, the rebels damaged the temples of Zeus, Apollo, Artemis, Isis, Hecate and the Dioscuri. See Applebaum's thorough discussion of the archaeological evidence from the province in *Jews and Greeks,* 269–94. Gentile observers clearly recognized that the destruction of pagan cults and temples was an important goal of the Jewish rebels. This is best seen in the epithet *anosios,* "impious," which became the standard characterization of the Jews after the revolt. The epithet was evidently associated with the Jews' activities during the revolt, as it was a relatively uncommon designation prior to 115–17 (*CPJ* 438/*P.Brem.* 1.4; *CPJ* 443/*P.Giss.* 41 col. 2.4–5, an official communication; *CPJ* 158a/*P.Par.* 68 col. 6.13–15; *CPJ* 157/*P.Oxy.* 1242.42–43).
30. Philo *Leg.* 132. This intensity of antipagan sentiment among the Alexandrian rebels of 115 perhaps betokens the breadth of support that the revolt had within the Jewish community. In 115, the *isopoliteia* question, which was so important to the Hellenized upper classes within the community, fades completely from view—a somewhat surprising fact given the prominence which the issue had throughout the first century.
31. Nile: *CPJ* 440/*P.Bad.* 36; *CPJ* 441/*P.Bad.* 39; Appian *Arabicus Liber* fr. 19.1–4. Roads: *CPJ* 446/*P.Brem.* 15, in which Herodes asks Apollonius for permission to visit his brother in Alexandria. Herodes makes his request when he is presented with an opportunity to make the journey by boat, since he would "not be able to go on foot through the country because of its devastation" (*ou d[unē]somai pezeuein tous topous* [. . .] *dia tē ekporthēsin tōn top[ōn]*), lines 21–23. More explicit testimony concerning this type of destruction comes from Cyrene, where milestones near the city and dated to the Hadrianic era speak of roads "which had been overturned and broken up in the Jewish revolt" (*tumultu Iudaico eversa et corrupta*); see *SEG* 9.252; Applebaum, *Jews and Greeks,* 236–37.
32. Eus. *Chron.* Hadr. 1, in the *Versio Armenica.* Jerome's *ad Chron. Euseb.* follows this, but with an important difference: *Hadrianus Alexandriam a Romanis subversam publicis instauravit expensis* (ed. Helm, p. 197). The *a Romanis* may be simply a scribal error, but it could also signify that the Roman forces were compelled to destroy portions of the city in their attempt to root out the Jewish rebels.

    Hadrian's extensive (re)building program within the city is further substantiated by several papyri (*P.Oxy.* 7.1045; *BGU* 1084; *SB* 7239, 7561) and by the Syriac *Notitia Urbis Alexandrinae,* found in the *Chron-*

*icle* of Michael the Syrian (5.3 = vol. 1, pp. 113–15, ed. Chabot); and P. M. Fraser, "Syriac *Notita Urbanis Alexandrinae*," *JEA* 37 (1951): 103–08. One of the quarters mentioned in the catalogue is "the Quarter of Hadrianos which is immense." This quarter probably grew up around a temple constructed during the reign of Hadrian (the *Hadrianeion*) and dedicated to the Imperial cult. (An inscription dated to A.D. 170 of unknown provenance within the city refers to an *archiereus Hadrianeiou kai Sebastōn*, *IGRR* 1.1060. See also Calderini, *Dizionario*, 89–90; Adriani, *Repertorio*, 222–23.) Fraser suggests that both the temple and the quarter were on the city's periphery and Calderini places the temple in the vicinity of the Caesarion. Adriani is even more specific, arguing on the basis of the inscription that the temple stood to the east of the Caesarion. If their suggestions are correct, this would locate the temple and the quarter in the northeast portion of the city, the very region commonly regarded as having the highest concentration of Jewish inhabitants prior to the revolt (see n. 9). The construction of a temple dedicated to the imperial cult in this locale is in keeping with Hadrian's later establishment of the imperial cult on the Temple Mount in Jerusalem following Bar Cochba's revolt (to be distinguished from the emperor's earlier founding of Aelia Capitolina—see L. Mildenberg, *The Coinage of the Bar Kokhba War*, *Typos* 6 [Zurich, 1984], 102–9). It appears in both cases that the emperor set out to purposely offend Jewish sensibilities and demonstrate the supremacy of imperial might and authority over provincial rebellion.

33. Eus. *Chron.* 2.223 (*PG* 19, col. 544), *HE* 4.2.3. Greek reprisals in A.D. 38: Josephus *BJ* 2.490–98. Prefect's edict: *CPJ* 435 col. 2.21–27, col. 3.1–8. Chronology of reprisals: *CPJ* 158a/*P.Par.* 68 col. 2.5–7. These lines, though fragmentary, speak of a *kurios* (probably the prefect) who left the city on official business elsewhere (*apodēmia*). It was during his absence that these incidents occurred (*tauta egeneto*). See the notes on these lines in *CPJ* vol. 2, p. 96. Also M. Pucci, "*CPJ* II, 158, 435 e la rivolta ebraica al temp di Traiano," *ZPE* 51 (1983): 95–103. Slaves and mime show: *CPJ* 158a/*P.Par.* 68 col. 1.5–7, col. 3.9–12; *CPJ* 158b/*BGU* 341.13–15. Destruction of Great Synagogue: *B.Tal.Sukkah* 5.1.

34. Talmudic estimates on loss of life: *B.Tal.Gittin* 57b; *Sukkah* 51b. Emigration from Egypt: R. Yohannan, a fourth-generation *Tanna* and "the sandalmaker from Alexandria"—*Mishna Aboth* 4.11, *Kelim* 5.5, *Yebamoth* 11.5; *P.Tal.Hagiga* 3.1; R. Zakkai, a Palestinian *Tanna* from Alexandria—*P.Tal.Kethuboth* 4.4; *Yebamoth* 6.1, 7.5; *'Abodah Zarah* 2.6. Several second-century tomb inscriptions from Joppa are of former Alexandrians: *CIJ* 918, 928, 934 (two individuals). For a broader perspective on this topic, see A. Kasher, "The Nature of Jewish Migra-

tion in the Mediterranean Countries in the Hellenistic-Roman Era," *Mediterranean History Review* 2.1 (1987): 46–75.

35. Tcherikover's suggestion, after expressing initial puzzlement: "But why did the prefect adopt so strange a measure?" *CPJ* vol. 2, p. 98. Also see Smallwood, *Jews under Roman Rule,* 408–9 (following Tcherikover).

36. Martialis would have been particularly suited for the task of maintaining order in a large city since he had served previously as prefect of the *vigiles* in Rome during 111 and 113, (*CIL* 6.221, 222/*ILS* 2160, 2161). Greek reaction to resettlement: *CPJ* 158a/*P.Par.* 68 col. 4.12–18. That the new district was extramural is implied by *proskatoikein,* "to settle opposite/by the side of" in lines 14–15. See Tcherikover's discussion in *CPJ* vol. 2, p. 98.

    Egyptian Jews in Alexandria: although Alexandria itself might not have been the goal of Jewish refugees from upriver, the city's docks probably served as a transit point for émigrés bound for Joppa, Palestine's main port. One of the Joppa inscriptions from this period includes the funerary marker of Isaac, "priest of Egypt" *iereos (E)gip[ti]o[u]* (*CIJ* 930). R.Hanan, "the Egyptian," appears in Palestine during the second century as a respected *Tanna,* and was even considered one of "the Sages" (*B.Tal.Sanhedrin* 17b).

    The new Alexandrian settlement may have been located on the site of Jewish habitation before the events of 115, perhaps even the original Jewish district mentioned by Philo and Josephus. If the Jewish quarter was, in fact, beyond the eastern edge of the city, Martialis's policy could be interpreted as the forcible segregation of the Greek and Jewish communities and the concentration of Jewish population in this area. On the topography of previous Jewish settlement in Alexandria, see n. 9.

37. The so-called *Acta Pauli et Antonini*: *CPJ* 158a/*P.Par.* 68; *CPJ* 158b/*BGU* 341.

38. Jewish Diaspora and the Bar Kochba war: Smallwood, *Jews under Roman Rule,* 441–42. Cassius Dio is the only ancient writer who asserts that the rebels in Judaea were joined by Diasporan Jews, who were "everywhere showing signs of disturbance, were gathering together, and giving evidence of great hostility to the Romans, partly by secret and partly by overt acts" (69.13.1, trans.Cary). See the discussion of this passage in Stern, *Greek and Latin Authors on Jews and Judaism,* 2:402–5.

    Palestinian *sicarii* in Alexandria: Josephus *BJ* 7.409–20. The gerousia was roused to action after the *sicarii* had murdered "certain Jews of rank" who had opposed the spread of the zealots' ideology. Although the gerousia worked in concert with the Jewish ecclesia, the gerousia clearly took the lead in the suppression of the *sicarii*. By contrast, the

Diasporan communities in Cyrenaica were very receptive to "the madness of the *sicarii,*" with tragic and bloody consequences (*BJ* 7.437–46).

39. The post-Trajanic *Acta* (according to Musurillo) include *P.Oxy*. 2177; *P.Yale* inv. 1536 and *P.Oxy*. 33; as well as the more fragmentary *BGU* 588; *P.Fayum* 217; *P.Bouriant* 7; and *P.Oslo* 170. The only mention of Jews occurs in *P.Aberdeen* 136, an inconclusive fragment described as a "tiny scrap" by the editor. All are conveniently collected in H. A. Musurillo, *The Acts of the Pagan Martyrs* (Oxford, 1954). Cassius Dio, whose history contains comparably full information on Jewish affairs, does not mention the Jews in his account of the events of 215. The absence of the Jews is all the more conspicuous since Dio was a contemporary of the Severi, and is usually well-informed on the events of his day as well as on the history of the Jews. For Caracalla's visit to Alexandria and the subsequent massacre, see Dio 78.22.1–78.23.4; Herodian 4.8.6–4.9.8; *HA Car*. 6.2–3; and the so-called *Acta Heracliti* in Musurillo, 77–79, 229–32.
40. For Roman-Jewish relations during the second and third centuries, see P. Schäfer, *Geschichte der Juden in der Antike* (Stuttgart, 1983), 177–90; Smallwood, *Jews under Roman Rule,* 467–538.

    Jews in Jerusalem: *P.Tal.Ma'aser Sheni* 3.6; *B.Tal.Bathra* 75b. Circumcision: *Dig*. 68.8.11.1, where Antoninus Pius lifts Hadrian's ban on the circumcision of Jews but retains the prohibition against the circumcision of Gentiles. Proselytism: *Gerim* "Proselytes," a minor tractate of the Babylonian Talmud, was compiled during these centuries in order to codify procedures for the reception of converts. See M. Goodman, *Mission and Conversion: Proselytizing in the Religious History of the Roman Empire* (Oxford, 1994).
41. Caracalla's journey through Palestine in 215 may provide the setting for a number of amusing anecdotes which are often known under the heading, "Antoninus and the Rabbi," in which an emperor engages in a lively dialogue with a Jewish patriarch. See the discussion in M. Avi-Yonah, *Geschichte der Juden im zeitalter des Talmud* (Berlin, 1962), 38–41. Later tradition in Palestine regarded Septimius Severus and Caracalla as having "greatly esteemed the Jews" (*Iudaeos plurimum dilexerunt*), according to Jerome *In Dan*. 11.34.

    Dio's brief account of Jewish monotheism during the Second Commonwealth is characterized by a tone of reverence and moderation (37.17.1–4), and lacks any reference to tales of Jewish lepers expelled from Egypt under the leadership of Moses, or to allegations of Jewish ass-worship; cf.Tacitus *Hist*. 5.2–5. The same impartial tone is found in other second-century writers such as Galen and Numenius of Apamea.

42. R. W. Wilken, *Judaism and the Early Christian Mind* (New NHaven, 1971), 43. Clement: fr. 7 in *GCS* 17 (1909), 225; Eus. *HE* 6.13.7. Origen: N. R. M. de Lange, *Origen and the Jews* (Cambridge, 1976), 8–9, 23–28; H. Bietenhard, *Caesarea, Origenes und die Juden* (Stuttgart, 1974); R. Kimelman, "Rabbi Yohanan and Origen on the Song of Songs: A Third Century Jewish-Christian Disputation," *HTR* 73.3–4 (1980): 567–95. Wilken, *Judaism and the Early Christian Mind,* 42–44; J. A. McGuckin, "Origen on the Jews," in *Christianity and Judaism,* ed. D. Wood, Studies in Church History no. 29 (Oxford, 1992), 1–13.

43. *Epistle of Barnabas*: Recent discussions may be found in R. S. MacLennan, *Early Christian Texts on Jews and Judaism* (Atlanta, 1990), who rightly stresses that all such documents must be read in light of the specific local circumstances in which they were written; W. Horbury, "Jewish-Christian Relations in Barnabas and Justin Martyr," in *Jews and Christians: The Parting of the Ways,* ed. J. D. G. Dunn (Tübingen, 1992), 315–45; L. W. Barnard, "The Epistle of Barnabas and its Contemporary Setting," *ANRW* 2.27.1 (1993): 159–207.

*Dialogue of Timothy and Aquila*: F. C. Conybeare, ed., *The Dialogue of Athanasius and Zacchaeus and of Timothy and Aquila, Anecdota Oxoniensia* (Oxford, 1898); see also the extensive discussion of A. L. Williams in his *Adversus Judeos* (Cambridge, 1935), 67–78.

44. *Oracula Sibyllina*: J. J. Collins, "The Sibylline Oracles," in *Jewish Writings of the Second Temple Period,* ed. M. E. Stone (Philadelphia, 1984) 357–81, esp. 379–80; idem, *Sybylline Oracles,* in *The Old Testament Pseudepigrapha,* 1:443–58; D. S. Potter, *Prophecy and History in the Crisis of the Roman Empire* (Oxford, 1990), 95–140, argues for a largely pagan authorship of these books. Text in Geffcken, *Die Oracula sibyllina,* 189–210.

Judas: *hos kai tēn thruloumenēn tou antichristou parousian ēdē tote plēsiazein ōeto,* Eus. *HE* 6.7.1. The *History of the Patriarchs* calls him a "Jewish scribe" (1.4, ed. Evetts, *PO* 1 [Paris, 1904], 164), and both sources report that he composed commentaries during the reign of Septimius Severus identifying the tribulations depicted in Daniel with the present age. The subject of his commentaries, as well as his name, together count against his being a Christian.

45. Landowners and shippers: *CPJ* 455/*PSI* 883; *CPJ* 453/*P.Würzburg* 14; *CPJ* 462a–h/*O.Bodl.* 778, 784, 1433, 1435–37, 1455; *CPJ* 469/*P.Princet.* 73. Farmers and peasants: *CPJ* 452a; *CPJ* 451/*P.Rendel Harris* 142; *CPJ* 460/*P.Ryl.* 594 col. 1; *CPJ* 464; *CPJ* 478a/*O.Mich.* 565; *CPJ* 466/*P.Vars.* 16. It is not possible to conclude, however, that Egyptian Jews were predominantly agricultural, at least not any more than their Egyptian neighbors. The extant papyri are largely made up of receipts related to the leasing and taxing of land. Soldiers: *CPJ*

465/*P.Oxy*. 735 col. 3.19, dated to 205. There are a number of Semitic names in this list of soldiers, but these individuals could hail from a variety of locales throughout the Levant. Only Barichius possesses a name clearly identifiable as Jewish; cf. *CIJ* 953 (Joppa), *CIJ* 1438 (Alexandria). Jewish festivals: *CPJ* 452a col. 2.15–16; *CPJ* 467/*P.Gron*. 3.13.

46. Great care must be exercised, however, when using such statistical data in order to demonstrate the decline of Egyptian Jewry following the revolt. Both Applebaum and the editors of *CPJ* point to the evidence afforded by the 254 ostraca from Edfu (Apollinopolis Magna) which record the payment of taxes by Jews. The overwhelming majority (217) date from the period A.D. 70–116, after which there is a complete break in the sequence until 151, when they resume again but only in greatly reduced quantities. Tcherikover and Fuks account for the thirty-five-year lacuna by assuming that it "was due to the annihilation of the Jewish community of Edfu after the failure of the Jewish revolt of A.D. 115–117" (*CPJ* vol. 2, p. 109). Applebaum likewise associates the break in tax payments with the Jewish revolt (*Jews and Greeks*, 267–68). However, this evidence appears to be wrenched out of context, since an examination of the non-Jewish ostraca from Edfu reveals an almost identical chronological distribution in the volume of ostraca receipts. This would indicate that the entire town went into a period of decline in the immediate post-Trajanic era, caused by some factor perhaps unrelated to the revolt. A plausible explanation for this decrease in material evidence is supplied by the fact that the terminus of the main caravan route leading from Berenike on the Red Sea was transferred from Edfu to Coptos during the reign of Trajan. It is not surprising then that Edfu suffered, and that this decline was reflected in the population decrease of an ethnic community usually associated with trade (*Fouilles Franco-Polonaises II: Tel Edfu 1938*, ostraca nos. 290–304, 152–54; *Fouilles Franco-Polonaises III: Tel Edfu 1939*, ostraca nos. 388–471, 348–60).

47. The status of Egyptian Jewry during this period is surveyed by J. Mélèze-Modrzejewski, "Ioudaioi apheiremenoi: La fin de la communauté juive d'Egypt (115–117 de n.e.)," *Symposion 1985: Vortage zur griechischen und hellenistischen Rechtsgeschichte*, ed. G. Thur (Köln, 1989), 337–61.

    Depopulation: *CPJ* 454/*P.Oxy*. 100.9 (Oxyrhynchus); *CPJ* 468/*P.Amh*. II. 98.8–10 (Hermoupolis); *CPJ* 471/*BGU* 585 (Sebennytos), for Paabos, son of Abramos; *CPJ* 460/*P.Ryl*. 594 col. 1 (Karanis), indicating that there was only one adult male Jew out of a total population of over a thousand adult males in the town. However, the import of this data for determining the effects of the revolt should be considered with a certain amount of caution, since the Karanis tax records are all post-Trajanic, and therefore fail to provide the necessary comparable data from the period prior to the revolt.

Confiscations: one official document, circulated among several strategoi, suggests that Jewish property was confiscated in the Herakleopolite, Oxyrhynchite, and Kynopolite nomes—three districts within the Heptanomia (*CPJ* 445/*P.Oxy*. 1189). There is also evidence that confiscations took place in the Athribite nome, a region in the upper Delta near Leontopolis (*CPJ* 448/*P.Oxy*. 500).

Jews in Greco-Egyptian literature: a papyrus of the late second or early third century speaks of a Jewish character in a mime who carries a burden and apparently elicited gales of laughter from his audience (*CPJ* 519). In a different vein, a third-century fragment of the apocalyptic "Oracle of the Potter" contains prophecies of doom for the Jews, who are labeled "lawbreakers," *paranomoi* (*CPJ* 500). The most vivid example of this anti-Jewish feeling is a papyrus from Oxyrhynchus which states that an annual festival was held to celebrate the victory over the Jews at the time of the revolt—some eighty years before (*CPJ* 450/*P.Oxy*. 705 cols. 1–2). Oxyrhynchus was also the find site of several important fragments of the *Acta Alexandrinorum*, a genre replete with anti-Jewish sentiment. It appears that hatred toward Jews was not necessarily an Alexandrian phenomenon. See D. T. M. Frankfurter, "Lest Egypt's City Be Deserted: Religion and Ideology in the Egyptian Response to the Jewish Revolt (116–117 CE)," *Journal of Jewish Studies* 43 (1992): 203–20.

Guard at Serapeum: *CPJ* 475/*P.Oxy*. 43.

48. An inscription commemorating the reconsecration of a synagogue reflects the improved status of the Egyptian Jewish communities. Although of unknown provenance, this inscription on an alabaster *tabula* probably comes from the upper Delta, as it was discovered near Cairo. Mommsen (and later commentators) date the reconsecration plaque to the era of Palmyrene ascendancy in Egypt c. 270–71 since it clearly states that REGINA ET REX IVSSER(VN)T, probably a reference to Zenobia and her son Vaballathus (*CIJ* 1449); Mommsen, in *Ephemeris Epigraphica* 4 (1881): 25–26.

Another indication of the revival of Jewish status in the chora is a papyrus from Oxyrhynchus, dated to 291, in which Aurelius Dioskoros represents "the community/synagogue of the Jews" (*tēs suna[g]ōgēs tōn Ioudaiōn*) in the manumission of a Jewish woman named Parome along with her two children. The Jewish community pays fourteen talents as the fee for Parome's enfranchisement, a sum that attests a certain level of wealth within this community of the Heptanomia (*CPJ* 473/*P.Oxy*. 1205).

49. Eusebius *HE* 4.2.3. Severity of punishment in Alexandria: underscored by Syncellus's laconic statement that "Hadrian inflicted punishment upon the Jews who revolted against the Alexandrians" (*Adrianos Ioudaious kata Alexandreōn stasiazontas ekolasen*), *Chronographia* 348d. The identification of Hadrian as the avenging emperor poses something of a problem if one regards this passage as a reference to the reduction of the rebels in 115. The most plausible solution would be to view the emperor's actions as an aspect of the reconstruction and reorganization program carried out by Martialis. One aspect of Hadrian's punishment of the Alexandrian Jews was the construction during his reign of a temple for the imperial cult, probably located in a portion of the city with a previously dense concentration of Jewish inhabitants. On Syncellus, see R. A. Laquer, "Synkellos," *R-E* 4 (1932): 1388–1410.

The absence of any comment concerning the Jewish community in the *Gnomon* of the *Idios Logos,* dated to the middle of the second century, is an eloquent testimony of the community's decline after the revolt. One would expect at least some reference to the Jews among the 115 laws regulating Alexandria's diverse population. Although originally composed during the principate of Augustus, the extant *Gnomon* dates from the reign of Antoninus Pius (*BGU* vol. 5).

50. For the historiographical impact of more numerous sources concerning the Jewish community of fourth-century Antioch, see R. L. Wilken, *John Chrysostom and the Jews* (Berkeley, 1983), 43–44.
51. Financial duties of synagogues: *C.Th.* 16.8.14; 16.8.29.

Archisynagogoi: Bodleian Library MS. Heb. c.57(P); A. E. Cowley, "Notes on Hebrew Papyrus Fragments from Oxyrhynchus," *JEA* 2 (1915): 210; *CPJ* vol. 1, 101–3. An *archisynagogus Iudeorum* of Alexandria is mentioned in a purported letter of Hadrian which probably was composed during the 390s (*HA Quad. Tyr.* 8.3). On this passage, see R. Syme, *Emperors and Biography* (Oxford, 1971), 25–27; Stern, *Greek and Latin Authors on Jews and Judaism,* 2: 636–41. Archisynagogi also appear in an imperial rescript dated to 399 (*C.Th.* 16.8.14). In the early Roman period archisynagogoi are mentioned in an honorific decree from A.D. 3, but there is some question whether the office in this particular instance is associated with the Jewish community (Horbury and Noy, *Jewish Inscriptions,* no. 18). Archisynagogoi in 414/15: Socrates *HE* 7.13 (*PG* 67, col. 764a). A plurality of synagogues in the city is attested by the phrase *tas sunagōgas tōn Ioudaiōn,* occurring in the same passage (col. 764b). John of Nikiu (84.98) closely follows Socrates in his account of the same incident, and adds that after the outbreak of intercommunal violence, the

Christian crowd "marched in wrath to the synagogues of the Jews and took possession of them, purified them, and converted them into churches."

"Elders of the Kneseth": Bodleian Library MS. Heb. c.57(P). Another fragment from the same collection mentions the "leaders" of a Jewish community, using a transliterated Hebrew word for the Greek, *prostatai,* MS. Heb. d.83(P)b.

Antiochene archisynagogoi: Two dedicatory inscriptions from a late fourth-century synagogue at Apamea refer to one of these archisynagogoi, named Ilasios (*CIJ* 803, 804). Antiochene *gerousiarchos*: M.Schwabe and B.Lifshitz, *Beth She'arim* (New Brunswick, N.J., 1973–74), no. 114. For a discussion regarding the leadership of the Antiochene community, see W. A. Meeks and R. L. Wilken, *Jews and Christians in Antioch* (Missoula, Mont., 1978), 6–10; C. Kraeling, "The Jewish Community at Antioch," *Journal of Biblical Literature* 51 (1932): 137.

52. Archisynagogoi as patrons and benefactors: T. Rajak and D. Noy, "*Archisynagogoi*: Office, Title and Social Status in the Graeco-Jewish Synagogue," *JRS* 83 (1993): 75–93. R. Abbahu: *P.Tal.'Erubin* 3.8. On various modes of synagogue leadership, see A. T. Kraabel, "Social Systems of Six Diasporan Synagogues," in *Ancient Synagogues: The State of Research,* ed. J. Gutmann (Providence, R.I., 1981), 79–91.
53. Although this institution itself owed much to its Greco-Roman environment: A. T. Kraabel, "The Diaspora Synagogue," *ANRW* 2.19.2 (1979): 477–510; idem, "Unity and Diversity among Diaspora Synagogues," in *The Synagogue in Late Antiquity,* ed. L. I. Levine (Philadelphia, 1987), 49–60; G. Foerster, "The Art and Architecture of the Synagogue in Its Late Roman Setting," in Levine, *Synagogue in Late Antiquity,* 139–46.
54. Antiochene synagogues: Kraeling, "Jewish Community at Antioch," 140–45; Meeks and Wilken, *Jews and Christians in Antioch,* 8–9. Alexandria: Soc. *HE* 7.13 (*PG* 67, col. 764b); John of Nikiu 84.98. Apamea: V. Verhoogen, *Apamée de Syrie aux Musées royaux d'art et d'histoire* (Brussels, 1964); E. L. Sukenik, "The Mosaic Inscriptions in the Synagogue at Apamea on the Orontes," *Hebrew Union College Annual* 23 (1950–51): 541–51. Galilee: A.Kloner, "Ancient Synagogues in Israel: An Archaeological Survey," in *Ancient Synagogues Revealed,* ed. L. I. Levine (Jerusalem, 1981), 12–15; S. Loffreda, "The Late Chronology of the Synagogue of Capernaum," in Levine, *Ancient Synagogue,* 52–59; E. M. Meyers, "The Current State of Galilean Synagogue Studies," in Levine, *The Synagogue in Late Antiquity,* 127–37.
55. Alexandrian stelai: Horbury and Noy, *Jewish Inscriptions,* nos. 15–17,

possibly 19, 127–28/*CIJ* 2.1436–38, 1446, 1435. Letter of ʿAmr: Ibn ʿAbd al-Hakam, *Futūh Misr* (ed. Torrey), p. 82; Eutychius (Saʿid ibn Batriq) *Ann*. 2.316–17 (*PG* 111, col. 1107). *Plethos*: Soc. *HE* 7.13 (*PG* 67, col. 764a). Aside from these two standard definitions, among Christian authors the term often took on the meaning of "congregation" or "body of the faithful," that is, *to plēthos tōn pistōn, Hom.Clem.* 3.61; *agiou Christianikou [p]lēthous, P.Lond.* 1913.7.

56. Jewish intellectuals: Zeno, an Alexandrian Jew who renounced Judaism and became a teacher of philosophy. His enemies claimed that he was both ignorant and forgetful—Damascius *V.Isidori* fr. 239 (ed. Zintzen, p. 197); Acoluthos, another teacher of philosophy, but outspoken in his defense of Judaism—Anastasius Sinaita *Viae Dux Adversus Acephalos* 14 (*PG* 89, col. 249c). Doctors: Jacob and Hesychius—*v. Isidori* fr. 194 (ed. Zintzen, p. 167); Adamantios—Soc. *HE* 7.13 (*PG* 67c, col. 764c); Domnus—*v. Isidori* fr. 335 (ed. Zintzen, p. 265).

    Alexandrian medicine: . . . *licet opus ipsum redoleat, pro omni tamen experimento sufficiat medico ad commendandam artis auctoritatem, Alexandriae si se dixerit eruditum,* Amm. Marc. 2.16.18. Other late antique testimonies of the fame of Alexandrian medical training can be found in Eunapius *VS* 498; Theodoret of Cyrus *Ep*. 114, 115; *Expositio* 37; Palladius *Hist. Laus*. 35.12. Cf.the list of requirements enacted by Valentinian in 368 in order to secure qualified doctors for the *regiones* of Rome, *C.Th*. 13.3.8. See also J. Scarborough, "Ammianus Marcellinus 22.16.18: Alexandria's Medical Reputation in the Fourth Century," *Clio Medica* 4 (1969): 141–42; and the reply of V. Nutton, "Ammianus and Alexandria," *Clio Medica* 7 (1972): 165–76. A broader context is provided by V. Nutton, "From Galen to Alexander: Aspects of Medicine and Medical Practice in Late Antiquity," *Dumbarton Oaks Papers* 38 (1984): 1–14; J. Duffy, "Byzantine Medicine in the Sixth and Seventh Centuries: Aspects of Teaching and Practice," ibid., 21–28.

57. Jewish slave owners: *C.Th*. 3.1.5; 3.7.2. Urbib: Eutychius (Saʿid ibn Batriq) *Ann*. 2.132. A Coptic homily (attributed to Cyril but probably dating from the late sixth century) recounts the conversion of an *archisynagogos* named Philoxenos. The homily describes him as very rich in gold, silver, servants, and flocks. However, the reliability of this account is doubtful due to its long discussion of Philoxenos' most notable virtue, his outstanding charity and hospitality. Although the name Philoxenos is not altogether uncommon in Alexandria and Egypt (Athan. *Apol. c. Ar*. 21; Marin. *v. Procli*. 11; *P.Lond*. 3.780; *Papiri greci e latini* 1.77; *P.Erl*. 67), it seems just a bit too coincidental in the context of this conversion story, given that his remarkably apt name is otherwise unattested among Egyptian Jews—*Philoxenos* / "Mr.Hospitality!" *Ser-*

*mo de Paen.*, ed. P. M. Chaîne, *Mélanges de la Faculté Orientale, Université Saint-Joseph, Beyrouth* 6 (1913): 493–528.

Jewish landowners and merchants in the chora: *CPJ* 480/*O.Mich.* 216; *CPJ* 504/*P.Lond.* 5.1904; *CPJ* 477/*P.Oxy.* 1429; *CPJ* 500/*P.Bad.* 4.53. Josep: *CPJ* 479/*P.Goth.* 114. A sixth-century papyrus letter refers to the harsh and exacting reputation of Jewish creditors, thereby providing evidence for continuity from the early Roman period in the practice of Jewish moneylending within Egypt; see *CPJ* 507/*Wiener Studien* 12 (1890): 82, and cf. *CPJ* 152 (A.D. 41), which contains an allusion to Jewish creditors. Jewish landowners from Alexandria: *CPJ* 142/*BGU* 1132 (14 B.C.); *CPJ* 145/*BGU* 1129 (13 B.C.).

58. *[Hup]er sōtōrias kuras Rouas thugatros [tou ma] / karistatou Entoliou Borouch Barachia Shalom* ("Borouch, son of Barachias: For the safety / well-being of the lady Roua, daughter of the most blessed Entolios. Peace"). Horbury and Noy, *Jewish Inscriptions*, no. 15 /*CIJ* 1438, with photo; *CPJ* vol. 3, p.141. There has been some discussion among scholars as to the interpretation of the last three Greek words, some taking *Entoliou* as a proper name, and others reading *Borouch Barachia* as a Hebrew benediction written in Greek letters. Even though Entolios may simply describe Barouch as "law-abiding," it is attested as a Jewish name from inscriptions in Cyprus and Caesarea, thus allowing for its use as a proper name here.
59. Roman Tower: Adriani, *Repertorio*, 66–68. It is possible, however, that the column base was originally located in another sector of the city and was later moved to the harbor area. Dockyards and warehouses: Strabo 17.1.9; Adriani, *Repertorio*, 220, 236–37; P. M. Fraser, *Ptolemaic Alexandria* (Oxford, 1972), 1:21–25.
60. "The group of Jews and Samaritans is recognized as not lawfully summoned to the compulsory public service of shipmasters. For if any assessment is clearly levelled upon an entire group, it can obligate no specific person. Whence, just as poverty-stricken persons and those occupied as petty tradesmen must not undergo the compulsory public service of transportation as shipmasters, so those persons suitable because of their property, who could be selected from such groups for the performance of the aforesaid compulsory public service, must not be held exempt" (Iudaeorum corpus ac Samaritanorum ad naviculariam fuctionem non iure vocari cognoscitur; quidquid enim universo corpori videtur indici, nullam specialiter potest obligare personam. Unde, sicut inopes vilibusque commerciis occupati, naviculariae translationis munus obire non debent, ita idoneos facultatibus, qui ex his corporibus deligi poterunt ad praedictam functionem, haberi non oportet immunes). *C.Th.* 13.5.18, dated 18 February 390, trans. Pharr.
61. Synesius *Ep.* 4 (*PG* 66, cols. 1328–41), now often numbered 5 after the

edition of A. Garzya, *Synesii Cyrenensis Epistolae* (Rome, 1979). I retain the old citation, since the Migne text is more accessible to the majority of readers.

The exact date of this voyage has been a point of controversy ever since the work of Tillemont in 1707, resulting in a wide range of purported dates: Tillemont—396, 402, or 413; Druon—397; Seeck and Grützmacher—404; Lacombrade—402; Vogt, Cameron, and Long—401; Roques—407. These varying chronologies, however, do not substantially modify the import of the epistle for this discussion, since they all fall between the date of *C.Th.* 13.5.18 (390) and the crisis in Alexandrian Jewish history occasioned by the events of 414/15. Among the more recent literature treating this letter, see J. Vogt, "Synesius auf Seefahrt," in *Kyriakon: Festschrift J. Quasten,* ed. P. Granfield and J. A. Jungmann (Münster, 1970), 400–408; D. Roques, "La Lettre 4 de Synésios de Cyrène," *Rev.Ét.Grec.* 90.430–31 (1977): 263–95; C. Lacombrade, "Encore la Lettre 4 de Synésios et sa Nouvelle Lune," *Rev.Ét.Grec.* 91.435 (1978): 564–67; J. Long, "Dating an Ill-Fated Journey: Synesius, *Ep.* 5," *Transactions of the American Philological Association* 122 (1992): 351–80.

Amarantus: "*ho kubernētēs nomodidaskalos,*" *Ep.* 4 (*PG* 66, col. 162d).

62. Duties of navicularii: *C.Th.* 13.5.1–38. The Eunostos Harbor was Alexandria's main emporium for goods originating in the interior by way of Lake Mareotis and the canals. Consequently, Eunostos served as the transit point for Egyptian grain bound for other Mediterranean ports. See Fraser, *Ptolemaic Alexandria,* 1:26, n. 180; Adriani, *Repertorio,* 237. Sailors in grain fleet as patriarchal supporters: in 380, when sailors backed the patriarch Peter in his attempt to influence episcopal succession in Constantinople; in 403, during Theophilus's conflict with John Chrysostom in Constantinople; and in 431, when sailors made up a portion of Cyril's crowd of supporters at the turbulent Council of Ephesus.

63. Caracalla's edict: *P.Giess.* 40 col. 2/ Hunt and Edgar, 2.215. Jewish weavers: J. Juster, *Les Juifs dans l'empire romain* (Paris, 1914), 2:306–7. "Alexandrian mending": *B.Tal.Mo'ed Katan* 26a–b, dated to the early fourth century. Claudian *In Eutropium* 1.357; Cosmas Indicopleustes *Topographia Christiana* 3.70. After describing the craftsmanship of the priestly garments and the dividing curtains used in the wilderness tabernacle, Cosmas states, "It is a sure fact that up to this very day one can find most of these crafts practiced, especially by the Jews" (*Amelei heōs tēs sēmeron hēmeras tas pleistas tōn technōn toutōn para Ioudaiois hōs epi to pleiston eurēseis*).

64. Amarantus: "*Ho men nauklēros ethanata katachreōs ōn.*" *Ep.* 4 (*PG* 66, cols. 1328d–29a).

"If Jews should be harassed by some criminal charge or by debts and should pretend that they wish to be joined to the Christian law, in order that they may be able to avoid criminal charges or the burden of debts by taking refuge in the churches, they shall be driven away, and they shall not be received until they have paid all their debts or have been cleared of criminal charges by proof of their innocence" (Iudaei, qui reatu aliquo vel debitis fatigati simulant se Christianae legi velle coniungi, ut ad ecclesias confugientes vitare possint crimina vel pondera debitorum, arceantur nec ante suscipiantur, quam debita universa reddiderint vel fuerint innocentia demonstrata purgati). *C.Th.* 9.45.2, dated 17 June 397, trans. Pharr.

65. R. Abbahu: *P.Tal.ʿErubin* 3.8. *Apostoli*: their activities are described in *C.Th.* 16.8.14, 17. A garbled allusion to *apostoli* visiting Alexandria can be found in *HA Quad.Tyr.* 8.4, "Even the patriarch himself, when he comes to Egypt, is forced by some to worship Serapis, by others to worship Christ" (*Ipse ille patriarcha cum Aegyptum venerit, ab aliis Serapidem adorare, ab aliis cogitur Christum*). See Juster, *Les Juifs dans l'empire romain,* 1:388–94; R. Syme, *Ammianus and the Historia Augusta* (Oxford, 1968), 60–65; idem, *Emperors and Biography* (Oxford, 1971), 17–29. Inquiries from Alexandria: *P.Tal.ʿErubin* 3.8. This continues a pattern established in the second century, when a delegation was sent to Palestine in order to question R. Joshua ben Hananiah on a wide range of religious matters (*B.Tal.Niddah* 69b). Sabbath observance: *P.Tal.Pesahim* 3.1; *P.Tal.Shabbath* 2.2; *B.Tal.Shabbath* 26a.

66. Hebrew papyri: edited by A. E. Cowley in "Notes on Hebrew Papyrus Fragments from Oxyrhynchos," *JEA* 2 (1915): 209–13. For a thorough treatment of this little-known branch of Egyptian papyrology, see C. Sirat, *Les papyrus en caractères hébraiques trouvés en Égypte* (Paris, 1985). Tcherikover's comments in *CPJ* vol. 1, pp. 101–2. The broader Mediterranean context is provided by T. Rajak, "Jews and Christians as Groups in a Pagan World," in *"To See Ourselves As Others See Us": Christians, Jews, "Others" in Late Antiquity,* ed. J. Neusner and E. S. Frerichs (Chico, Calif., 1985), 247–62; F. Millar, "The Jews of the Graeco-Roman Diaspora between Paganism and Christianity, AD 312–438," in *The Jews among Pagans and Christians in the Roman Empire,* ed. J. Lieu, J. North, and T. Rajak (London, 1992), 97–123.

67. Libanius *Ep.* 914, 917, 973, 974, 1084, 1097, 1098, 1105. As one would expect from the correspondence of this urbane rhetor, Libanius's letters are replete with erudite allusions to classical literature. This would suggest that the Jewish recipient was trained in the tradi-

tional paideia, as it was understood in the fourth century. On this correspondence, consult M. Stern, *Greek and Latin Authors on Jews and Judaism,* 2:580–83.

68. Oxyrhynchus Hebrew papyrus: F. Klein-Franke, "A Hebrew Lamentation from Roman Egypt," *ZPE* 51 (1983): 80–84. Antinoopolis funerary inscription: *CIJ* 1534. Although undated, a Hebrew label from a mummy case found in Middle Egypt is further evidence of Hebrew usage among Egyptian Jews in a cultural context not necessarily "Hebraic" in orientation (*CIJ* 1536, with line drawing). Karanis: *CPJ* 474a, b/*P.Cair.Isidor.* 114, 115. Marriage contract from Antinoopolis: C. Sirat, P. Cauderlier, M. Dukan, and M. A. Friedman, *La Ketouba de Cologne: Un contrat du mariage juif à Antinoopolis* (Opladen, 1986).

    Alexandrian Jews and the theater: Socrates *HE* 7.13 (*PG* 67, col. 761a). Even the scholarly Philo was not averse to attending the theater or going to the stadium for the fights of pancratiasts (Philo *Quod omnis probus* 26, 141). During late antiquity, Jews elsewhere appear to have been avid spectators at the amphitheater, circus, and theater (John Chrys. *Jud.* 1.4; Augustine *Sermo* 17.9). See also Juster, *Les Juifs dans l'empire romain,* 2:240–41.

69. *CPJ* vol. 1, p. 107.

70. J. Parkes, *The Conflict of the Church and the Synagogue* (London, 1934), 234–35; M. Simon, *Verus Israel,* trans. H. McKeating from the 3d French ed. (Oxford, 1986), 224–25; Tcherikover in *CPJ* vol. 1, pp. 98–99.

71. Peter Brown's phrase in *The Making of Late Antiquity* (Cambridge, Mass., 1978), 4. See also G. Alföldy, *Römische Sozialgeschichte,* 2d ed. (Wiesbaden, 1979), 118–21, 182–84; R. MacMullen, *Roman Social Relations* (New Haven, 1974), 62–67. Jewish participation in civic life and the consequences for communal boundaries are discussed in J. Neusner, "The Experience of the City in Late Antique Judaism," in *Approaches to Ancient Judaism,* vol. 5, *Studies in Judaism and Its Greco-Roman Context,* ed. W. S. Green, Brown Judaic Studies, no. 32 (Atlanta, 1985), 37–52; P. Trebilco, *Jewish Communities in Asia Minor* (Cambridge, 1991), 173–85; W. Kinzig, "'Non-Separation': Closeness and Cooperation between Jews and Christians in the Fourth Century," *Vigiliae Christianae* 45.1 (1991): 27–53; Rajak, "Jews and Christians as Groups in a Pagan World," 247–62; idem, "The Jewish Community and Its Boundaries," in Lieu, North, and Rajak, *The Jews among Pagans and Christians in the Roman Empire,* 9–28.

72. Ambrose *Ep.* 41 (preached before Theodosius in 388); Epiphanius *Haer.* 14–20; Aphrahat *Hom.* 1, 11, 12; Basil of Caesarea *Hom.* 24; Council of Elvira (ca. 306), Canons 49, 50, 16, 78; Council of Antioch (341), Canon 1; *Canons of Laodicaea* (ca. 365) 29, 37, 38. This ongoing

contact is corroborated by archaeological material: L. V. Rutgers, "Archaeological Evidence for the Interaction of Jews and Non-Jews in Late Antiquity," *American Journal of Archaeology* 96 (1992): 101–18. For the perceptions of one another which grew out of this interaction, see J. Lieu, "History and Theology in Christian Views of Judaism," in Lieu, North, and Rajak, *The Jews among Pagans and Christians in the Roman Empire,* 79–96.

73. *C.Th.* 3.7.2/9.7.5.
74. The edicts are addressed to the praetorian prefect of the East, Maternus Cynegius, who was probably in Alexandria at the time (*C.Th.* 10.10.19, dated to 387, and *ILS* 1273, an inscription in his honor dedicated by the Alexandrians).
75. *C.Th.* 16.9.1 (dated 336), 16.9.2 (339), 3.1.5 (384 to Cynegius), 16.9.3 (415), 16.9.5 (423).
76. H. Schreckenberg, *Die christlichen Adversus-Judaeos-Texte und ihr literarisches und historisches Umfeld (1.–11.Jh.),* 2d ed. (Frankfurt am Main, 1990); M. Waegeman, "Les traités *adversus* Judeos: Aspects des relations judéo-chrétiennes dans le monde grec," *Byzantion* 56 (1986): 295–313. The late antique background is provided now by R. Lim, *Public Disputation, Power, and Social Order in Late Antiquity* (Berkeley, 1995); idem, "Religious Disputation and Social Disorder in Late Antiquity," *Historia* 44.2 (1995): 205–31.
77. Edited by F. C. Conybeare in *Anecdota Oxoniensia,* Classical Series (Oxford, 1898); trans. by Conybeare in *The Expositor,* 5th ser., 5 (1897): 300–20, 443–63. For questions of date and provenance, see A. L. Williams, *Adversus Judaeos* (Cambridge, 1935), 117–22.
78. Jewish-Christian debate: Jerome *Ad Titum* 3.9; *v. s.Epiphani* 1.52; Theodoret *Ep.* 113, 115. Cyril's *On the Apostasy of the Synagogue*: mentioned by Gennadius *De Vir. Ill.* 57. Collected fragments in *PG* 76 cols. 1421–24. Isidore of Pelusium: *Ep* 1.141 (*PG* 78); 2.94, 99; 3.94, 112; 4.17, 26.
79. Jewish proselytism: Tertullian *Ad Nat.* 1.13; Damasus *Ep.* 4.24 (*PL* 13); Jerome *Ep.* 93; *C.Th.* 16.8.1 (dated 315); 16.8.7 (352); 16.7.3 (383); 16.8.25, 27 (423); *N.Th.* 3.3–5.

    Judaizing Christians: Isaac of Antioch *Hom. de Magis*; Epiphanius *Haer.* 28.5; Aphraates *Hom.*11, 15; Jerome *Ep.* 121; *Canons of Laodicaea* 16, 29 (Sabbath observance), 35 (worship of angels), 36 (Jewish magical practices), 37–38 (participation in Jewish feasts and rites); Augustine *Ep.*196; Council of Elvira *Canon* 16, 26, 49, 50, 78. Reaction of Christian hierarchy: Wilken, *John Chrysostom and the Jews*; and G. Dagron, "Judaïser," *Travaux et mémoires* 11 (1991): 359–80. Text of John Chrysostom's sermons against Judaizers in *PG* 48, cols. 843–942. Eng. trans.: P. W. Harkin, *Saint John Chrysostom: Discourses against*

*Judaizing Christians*, The Fathers of the Church, vol. 68 (Washington, D.C., 1979).

80. Athanasius confirms the absence of real Judaizing practices in Alexandria by applying the term to the perceived legalistic bent of Arian theology (Athan. *de Decretis* 2). On the relation between Judaizing controversies and the status of Jewish communities, see the comments of N. R. M. de Lange, "Jews and Christians in the Byzantine Empire," in *Christianity and Judaism*, ed. D. Wood Studies in Church History, no. 29 (Oxford, 1992), 20–21.
81. *Jud.* 1.6.5 (trans. Harkin).
82. *C.Th.* 16.8.1, 5. Cf. *C.Th.* 9.45.2, the only evidence of Jews desiring to become Christians in Alexandria/Egypt (the regions under the augustal prefect's authority). The broader context of intercommunal representation is provided by R. Kalim, "Christians and Heretics in Rabbinic Literature of Late Antiquity," *HTR* 87.2 (1994): 155–69.
83. *Acta Donati, Macarii, et Theodori* 3.11–14 (*Acta Sanctorum* 22 May).
84. John Chrysostom notes the compatibility of Arianism with Judaism and Judaistic forms of Christianity at Antioch (*Jud.* 1.1.8). This is not to say, however, that Arians looked favorably upon Jews, even though they shared a common enemy in Homoousion Christianity. The laws of the Arian emperor Constantius are every bit as harsh toward Jews as those of his father or his Nicene successors like Theodosius (*C.Th.* 16.9.2; 16.8.6; 16.8.7).
85. ". . . *tous te Ioudaious kai tous ataktous* . . . ," Athan. *Ep.Encyl.* 3 (*PG* 25, col. 228a); ". . . *hōsper epathlon kai misthon tēs toiautēs paranomou nikēs parechousa tois ethnikois kai tois Ioudaiois* . . . ," *Ep.Encyl.* 4 (col. 229b); "*heneken tōn Areiomanitōn kateskeusan hupo ethnikōn kai Ioudaiōn genesthai,*" *Ep.Encyl.* 7 (col. 237c); " . . . *euthus ho tou ethnous hēgoumenos, ton Hellēnikon kai Ioudaikon* . . . ," Theod. *HE* 4.18 (*PG* 82, col. 1164c); ". . . *poluōnētōn sunēthōs epaphiemenōn kat' autōn tōn boiōn para tōn eidōlolatrōn kai tōn Ioudaiōn,*" Theod. *HE* 4.19 (col. 1176c), quoting a letter of Peter II, Athanasius's successor as patriarch.
86. Theod. *HE* 4.18–19 is the fullest account. These events are also echoed in Soc. *HE* 6.22 and Soz. *HE* 6.20.
87. The conversions recorded are predominantly those of Alexandrian Jews from the highest social and economic levels within the community. Perhaps they had the most to lose as a result of confiscations and the degradation of status which followed the events of 415. Adamantios, teacher of medicine (Soc. *HE* 7.13); Jacob and Hesychius, physicians (Damascius *v. Isidori* fr. 194, ed. Zintzen, p. 167); Zeno, teacher of philosophy (Damascius *v. Isidori* fr. 239, ed. Zintzen, p. 197). Regarding the latter, Damascius states that Zeno went to great lengths to demonstrate his complete repudiation of Judaism, regularly profaning

the former synagogues in the city by riding a white ass through them on the Sabbath. Late fifth and early sixth centuries:Domnus, teacher of medicine (Damascius *v. Isidori* fr. 335, ed. Zintzen, p. 265); Urbib, *Judaeus opulentus* who cared for the poor (Eutychius / Saʿid ibn al-Batriq *Ann.* 2.132); Philoxenos, *archisynagogos* (see n. 57).

88. Leont. N. *v. Jo. Eleem.* 24; John of Nikiu *Chron.* 91.1–9; "Homily on the Virgin by Theophilus, Archbishop of Alexandria" in *The Coptic Manuscripts in the Freer Collection,* ed. W. H. Worrell (New York, 1923), 368–74.
89. Michael the Syrian *Chron.* 8.12. Apparently they were denied this permission since the city's Jews are still without a synagogue nearly 100 years later (*History of the Patriarchs* 1.13, p. 467 [203]). At about the same time, there is mention of a family of Jews living "in the eastern quarter of the city" during the patriarchal reign of Timothy III, 517–35 (John of Nikiu *Chron.* 91). A contemporary Coptic source makes a brief but tantalizing reference to a "Jewish street": *Sermo de Paen.*, ed. Chaîne.
90. Acoluthos: Anastasius Sinaita *Viae Dux Adversus Acephalos* 14 (*PG* 89, col. 249c). Jewish teachers: Jo. Moschus *Prat. Spir.* 172. Treaty between ʿAmr and Cyrus: John of Nikiu 120.2; Ibn ʿAbd al-Hakam, *Futūh Misr* (ed. Torrey), p. 82. See also A. J. Butler, *The Arab Conquest of Egypt,* 2d ed., ed. P. M. Fraser (1902; Oxford, 1978), 310–27.

*Chapter Five. The Pagan Community*

1. Funeral of Heraiskos: Damascius fr. 174 (ed. Zintzen, p. 147). Tegran Tomb: Adriani, *Repertorio,* 145–46; M. Krause, "Mummification," in *CoptEncy* 6:1696–98.
2. Damascius frs. 161, 163–64, 172, 174 (ed. Zintzen, 135, 137, 145, 147); [Damascius] *Epit. Photiana* 95–96 (ed. Zintzen, p. 140).
3. Sophronius *Nar. mirac. ss. Cyri et Iohannis* 46; Leont. *v. Jo. Eleem.* 2.
4. For the later stages of polytheistic belief and practice in Egypt, see J. Maspero, "Horapollon et la fin du paganisme égyptien," *BIFAO* 11 (1914): 163–95; A. D. Nock, "Later Egyptian Piety," in *Essays on Religion and the Ancient World,* ed. Z. Stewart (1944; Cambridge, Mass.: 1972), 2: 566–72; B. R. Rees, "Popular Religion in Graeco-Roman Egypt: II, The Transition to Christianity," *JEA* 36 (1950): 86–100; R. Rémondon, "L'Égypte et la suprême résistance au Christianisme (Ve–VIIe siècles)," *BIFAO* 51 (1952): 63–67; D. Bonneau, *La crue du Nile* (Paris, 1964), 421–39; H. D. Saffrey, "Quelques aspects de la piété populaire dans l'antiquité tardive," *Revue des études augustiniennes* 31 (1985): 3–19; G. Fowden, *The Egyptian Hermes: A Historical Approach to the Late Pagan Mind,* 2d ed. (Cambridge, Mass., 1993); G. Bower-

sock, *Hellenism in Late Antiquity* (Ann Arbor, Mich., 1990), 15–28, 55–69; R. Bagnall, *Egypt in Late Antiquity* (Princeton, 1993), 261–75; F. Dunand and C. Zivie-Coche, *Dieux et hommes en Égypte, 3000 av. J.-C.–395 apr. J.-C.: Anthropologie réligieuse* (Paris, 1991), 199–329; F. R. Trombley, *Hellenic Religion and Christianization: c. 370–529,* 2 vols. (Leiden, 1993–94); P. Athanassiadi, "Persecution and Response in Late Paganism: The Evidence of Damascius," *JHS* 113 (1993): 12–22; L. Kákosy, "Probleme der religion im römerzeitlichen Ägypten," *ANRW* 2.18.5 (1995): 2894–3049.

5. An *archierosuna* is mentioned in *C.Th.* 12.1.107 (A.D. 386). *Archiprophētēs*: *P.Ryl.* 110 (A.D. 259) and 4.618 (A.D. c.317). See also A. Bülow-Jacobsen, "The Archiprophetes," in *Actes du XVe Congrès International de Papyrologie,* (Brussels, 1979), 4:124–31; K. Rigsby, "On the High Priest of Egypt," *BASP* 22 (1985): 279–89.
6. See G. Weckman, "Community," in *The Encyclopedia of Religion,* ed. M. Eliade (New York, 1987), 566–71; R. Robertson, *The Sociological Interpretation of Religion* (New York, 1970); B. Wilson, "The Sociology of Sects," in *Religion in Sociological Perspective* (Oxford, 1982), 89–120.
7. For a sampling of this syncretistic outlook, see the diverse collection of amulets in C. Bonner, *Studies in Magical Amulets, Chiefly Graeco-Egyptian* (Ann Arbor, Mich., 1950); also, M. Naldini, "Testimonianze cristiane negli amuleti greco-egizi," *Augustinianum* 21 (1981): 179–88.
8. R. Grant, "The Religion of the Emperor Maximin Daia," in *Christianity and Other Greco-Roman Cults,* ed. J. Neusner (Leiden, 1974), 4:143–66.
9. J. J. O'Donnell provided a much needed corrective to a misleading pagan-Christian dichotomy in "The Demise of Paganism," *Traditio* 35 (1979): 45–88. By the early fifth century, the political victory of Christianity gave rise to a "totalizing discourse" in which Christian interpretations of the recent past swept away competing historiographies—a theme taken up with verve and elegance by Averil Cameron in *Christianity and the Rhetoric of Empire* (Berkeley, 1991). See also the incisive remarks of Peter Brown in *Power and Persuasion in Late Antiquity* (Madison, Wis., 1993), 126–33.
10. Cf. the comments of Soz. *HE* 5.15. On these matters, see now O. Nicholson, "The 'Pagan Churches' of Maximinus Daia and Julian the Apostate," *Journal of Ecclesiastical History* 45.1 (1994): 1–10.
11. Epiph. *Haer.* 51.22.9–10, trans. P. Amidon, in *The Panarion of St. Epiphanius, Bishop of Salamis* (New York, 1990).
12. This should be set against the broader Egyptian evidence of documentary papyri which points to a general decline in traditional polytheistic religious practice across the third and early fourth centuries, a decline

that seems to have been largely unrelated to the rise of Christianity. See Bagnall, *Egypt in Late Antiquity,* 261–68, who cogently argues for a history of later Egyptian paganism written with reference to its own internal dynamic—not simply an inversion of the history of Egyptian Christianity. Unfortunately, it is even more difficult to construct a history of Alexandrian paganism independent of Christian sources, since Alexandria lacks the papyrological context provided for the Egyptian chora. Yet, this background urges a degree of caution on the use of Christian testimonies of pagan belief and practice.

13. Bowersock, *Hellenism in Late Antiquity,* 22–28, quotation from p. 27.
14. Epiph. *Haer.* 51.22.8. Serapis: P. M. Fraser, *Ptolemaic Alexandria* (Oxford, 1972), 1:246–54.
15. *nusquam enim deorum mysteria sic perficitur quomodo ibi ab antiquo et usque modo, Expositio* 34.7–9; earlier quotation from 36.19–27. Although the author may be referring, in fact, to the whole of Egypt, it can be argued that he never progressed beyond the confines of Alexandria and its immediate hinterland. See Rougé, in *Expositio,* 30–31.
16. This, in fact, is the methodology followed by Fraser in his lengthy chapter on religion in *Ptolemaic Alexandria,* 1:189–301; and also by C. E. Visser in *Götter und Kulte im ptolemäischen Alexandrien* (Amsterdam, 1938).
17. Translation of the Syriac text in P. M. Fraser, "Syriac *Notitia Urbis Alexandrinae,*" *JEA* 37 (1951): 104. The statistics are as follows: Quarter Alpha: 308 temples, 1,655 courts, 5,058 houses, 108 baths, 237 taverns, 112 porticoes; Quarter Beta: 110 temples, 1,002 courts, 5,990 houses, 145 baths, 107 taverns; Quarter Gamma: 855 temples, 955 courts, 2,140 houses, . . . baths, 205 taverns, 78 porticoes; Quarter Delta: 800 temples, 1,120 courts, 5,515 houses, 118 baths, 178 taverns, 98 porticoes; Quarter Epsilon: 405 temples, 1,420 courts, 5,593 houses, . . . baths, 118 taverns, 56 porticoes.
18. As does Fraser, "Syriac *Notitia,*" 107.
19. Rodziewicz, *Habitations,* 332. While numerous rooms in the houses of Kōm el-Dikka have wall niches that could easily have been utilized for religious objects, Rodziewicz rightly points out that such a conclusion is not necessarily warranted since the niches could have been used to hold lamps or other objects of everyday use (79).
20. Gamma also contains a large number of taverns—perhaps an indication that the social functions of Alexandrian temples and the conviviality found in its taverns are somehow related.
21. The major evidence: Ps.-Callisthenes *v. Alex. Magni* 1.32.9; *BGU* 1151, 1127; M. *Chres.* 107; Breccia *Ins.* 71; Josephus *BJ* 2.494–95; Philo *Flacc.* 55; Epiphanius *de Mens. et Pond.* 9 col. 249. Gamma and Epsilon

in papyri recently edited as *P.Oxy*. 46.3271 and 55.3756. See also Calderini, *Dizionario,* 79–80; Adriani, *Repertorio* 239–40; Fraser, *Ptolemaic Alexandria,* 1:34–35, with 2:108–10, nn. 264–70.

R. Tomlinson, *From Mycenae to Constantinople* (London, 1992), 99–100, argues that "the *klimata* were strips across the width of the city, rather than 'quarters,' and presumably labelled from west to east." However, the only evidence he cites for this arrangement is the uncertain ancient testimony for the position of Delta. His otherwise illuminating discussion of the city (97–108) is based on a sensible comparison with the Macedonian capital of Pella, a city that shares many features with Alexandria.

22. The *Notitia* likewise displays a studied lack of interest in the location of synagogues or churches within the city, suggesting perhaps the religious sentiments of its compiler.
23. The evidence for individual deities and their respective temples is conveniently collected in Adriani, *Repertorio*; Calderini, *Dizionario*; and Fraser, *Ptolemaic Alexandria,* 189–301.
24. Agathos Daimon: S. Handler, "Architecture on the Roman Coins of Alexandria," *AJA* 75 (1971): 68–69; Fraser, *Ptolemaic Alexandria,* 1:209–11. Tychaion and Tyche: Libanius *Descr*. 25; *AP* 9.180. Fraser, *Ptolemaic Alexandria,* 242–43; J. G. Milne, *Catalogue of Alexandrian Coins* (Oxford, 1933), lv, xc, nos. 444, 600, 726, 970, 973, 1075, 1529, 1708, 1887, 2135, 2324, 2523, and many other examples that demonstrate the importance of this goddess in the civic consciousness of the city from the first century through the reign of Diocletian. Kybele: Fraser, *Ptolemaic Alexandria,* 1:277–78.
25. Poseidion: Synesius *Ep*. 4. Temple of Aphrodite: Breccia *Ins*. 58.
26. Canopus: Strabo 17.1.16–17; Amm. Marc. 22.16.14; Eunapius *v. Soph.* 471; Rufinus *HE* 2.26. See esp. A. Bernand, *La delta égyptien d'après les textes grecs,* vol. 1, *Les confins libyques* (Cairo, 1970), 153–328.
27. Eunapius *v. Soph*. 471. Rufinus: ". . . opere forniceo constructa, quae inmissis desuper luminaribus et occultis adytibus invicem in semet distinctis usum diversis ministeriis et clandestinis officiis exhibebant. iam vero in superioribus extreme totius ambitus spatia occupant exedrae et pastoforia domusque in excelsum porrectae, in quibus vel aeditue vel hi, quos appellabant agneuontas, id est, qui se castificant, commanere soliti erant. porticus quoque post haec omnem ambitum quadradis ordinibus distinctae intrinsecus circumibant. in medio totius spatii aedes erat pretiosis edita columnis et marmoris saxo extrinsecus ample magnificeque constructa. in hac simulacrum Serapis ita erat vastum, ut dextera unum parietem, alterum laeva perstringeret . . ." *HE* 11.23, in E. Schwartz, *Eusebius Werke,* vol. 2, (ed. Mommsen), *GCS* 9 (Berlin, 1909).

Ammianus Marcellinus: "post Capitolium, quo se veneralibis Roma in aeternum attolit, nihil orbis terrarum ambitiosius cernat." 22.16.12.

28. On Dionysus, see Fraser, *Ptolemaic Alexandria,* 1:201–12; W. A. Daszewski, *Dionysos der Erlöser* (Mainz, 1985); Bowersock, *Hellenism in Late Antiquity,* 41–53.
29. The evidence from Egypt seems to point to a gradual decline in Isis worship across the Roman period: D. Bonneau, "Les fêtes Amesysia et les jours épagomènes," *Annales du Service des antiquités de l'Égypte* 70 (1985): 365–70; Bagnall, *Egypt in Late Antiquity,* 261–68.
30. Gnostics: their presence in the Egyptian chora seems to have endured well into the fifth century. T. Orlandi, "A Catechesis against Apocryphal Texts by Shenute of Atripe and the Gnostic Tests of Nag Hammadi," *HTR* 75 (1982): 85–95; A. E. Samuel, "How Many Gnostics?" *BASP* 22 (1985): 297–322; A. Veilleux, "Monasticism and Gnosis in Egypt," in B. A. Pearson and J. E. Goehring, eds., *The Roots of Egyptian Christianity* (Philadelphia, 1986), 271–306.

    Hermetics: The collection of letters referred to is the so-called Archive of Theophanes published as *P.Herm.Rees* 2–6. See the discussion in G. Fowden, *The Egyptian Hermes: A Historical Approach to the Late Pagan Mind,* 2d ed. (Cambridge, 1993), 175–76.

    Manichaeans: S. N. C. Lieu, *Manichaeism* (Manchester, 1985), 74–75; L. Koenen, "Manichäische Mission und Klöster in Ägypten," in *Das römisch-byzantinische Ägypten: Akten des internationalen Symposions 26.–30. September 1978 in Trier, Aegyptiaca Treverensia: Trierer Studien zum Griechisch-Römischen Ägypten,* ed. G. Grimm, H. Heinen, and E. Winter (Mainz, 1983), 2:93–108. Aphthonius and Aetius: Philostorgius *HE* 3.15. Didymus: *PG* 39, cols. 1085–1110.
31. R. Ze'iri: *B.Tal.Sanhedrin* 67b. Athanasius: Soc. *HE* 1.27.
32. *Historia Augusta: nemo illic archisynagogus Iudaeorum, nemo Samarites, nemo Christianorum presbyter non mathematicus, non haruspex, non aliptes, HA Quad. tyr.* 8.3–4. Athanasius was noted by contemporaries for his skill in the interpretation of omens: Amm. Marc. 15.7.8—echoed by *Apoph. Patr.* Epiphanius 1.

    *Expositio,* quoted at 36.23–24. Magic and Alexandrian Christians: *Canons of Athanasius* 25, 41, 71 (ed. Riedel and Crum).
33. Ammianus: . . . *et recalet apud quosdam adhuc—licet raros—consideratio mundani motus et siderum . . . pauci super his scientiam callent, quae fatorum vias ostendit,* 22.16.17. Paul and Theon: Paul's *Eisagōgika* in the Teubner edition by Boer, 1958. The *Suda* ascribes to Paul an *Apotelesmatika,* "astrological teaching" that is no longer extant (*Suda* Pi 810). Theon's *On Omens* mentioned in *Suda* Theta 205. Penalties for divination: *C.Th.* 9.16.1–12. Christians and astrology: Athan. *Ep.*

39.1, in L. Th. Lefort, ed., *S. Athanase. Lettres festales et pastorales en Copte, CSCO* 150–51 (Louvain, 1955). See also Bagnall, *Egypt in Late Antiquity,* p. 274 for a discussion of a cache of horoscopes, dated to the 380s, which were used by Christians. Penance of astrologers: *Canons of Athanasius* 72, 73 (ed. Riedel and Crum).

34. Asclepiodotus: *politikēs philotimias . . . tō oikō sunēthous,* Damascius fr. 189 (ed. Zintzen, p. 163). Ammonius: Damascius fr. 124 (ed. Zintzen, p. 107). In the Greek East, the honor of public banqueting was traditionally accorded to acclaimed benefactors of the city, like victorious athletes or generals. Horapollon: *P.Cair.Masp.* 67295, with translation and commentary in J. Maspero, "Horapollon et la fin du paganisme égyptien," *BIFAO* 11 (1914): 163–95. See also *PLRE* 2, s.v. "Fl. Horapollon 2"; R. A. Kaster, *Guardians of Language* (Berkeley, 1988), 295–97.
35. "The Pagan Holy Man in Late Antique Society," *JHS* 102 (1982): 33–59.
36. Themistius *Or.* 28.341d. Kinship bonds among philosophers: witness the families of Hermeias (*PLRE* 2, stemma 29), Fl. Horapollon (*PLRE* 2, stemma 31), Isidore (*PLRE* 2, stemma 31), and the earlier father-daughter dynasty of Theon and Hypatia. Fowden, *The Egyptian Hermes,* p. xxi.
37. Aphthonius: Zach. Mytil. *v. Sev.* (ed. and trans. Kugener), *PO* 2 (Paris, 1907), 25. Groups of teachers and students: a discussion of the social dimensions of this phenomenon may be found in Fowden, *Egyptian Hermes,* 177–95.
38. Aetius: Epiph. *Haer.* 76.2.1–2. Philoponus's theological inclinations: see now the foundational article of L. S. B. MacCoull, "Another Look at the Career of John Philoponus," *Journal of Early Christian Studies* 3.1 (1995): 47–60.
39. In lieu of a final report of the excavation, see the valuable remarks of E. Rodziewicz, "Late Roman Auditoria in Alexandria," *BSAA* 45 (1993): 269–79.
40. The wider context of this cultural *koinē* is supplied by Kaster, *Guardians of Language,* 70–95.
41. Asclepius and Hygeiea: *BMC Alex.* nos. 13–15, 703, 705, 1611–13, 1708, 1813, 1867, 2109, 2174; Milne, nos. 3041–42, 3060, 3117, 3237, 3377; W. A. Daszewski, "A Statuette of Hygieia from Kom el-Dikka in Alexandria," *Mitteilungen des Deutschen Archäologischen Instituts Abteilung Kairo* 47 (1991): 61–66, with brief catalog of known types.
42. Zach. Mytil. *v. Sev.* (ed. and trans. Kugener), 29, 34–35, though some of these images had been brought from other threatened sanctuaries.
43. See chapter 9.

44. Athanasius on Julian: Soz. *HE* 5.13. Julian and Alexandrian cults: *Apoph. Patr.* (alphabetical series) Epiphanius 1; Julian *Ep.* 60, 111 (ed. Bidez-Cumont).
45. Athanasius: *History of the Patriarchs* 1.8 (ed. Evetts), pp. 419 [155], 423 [159]. Bishops and cessation of pagan practices: *C. Th.* 16.10.19.3. Mark of Arethusa: Soz. *HE* 5.10. Gaza: Marc. Diac. *v. Porphyrii* 1–75.
46. Theophilus: *History of the Patriarchs* 1.8, p. 419 [155]. See also T. Orlandi, "Un frammento copto Teofilo di Alessandria," *Rivista degli studi orientali* 44 (1969): 23–26. Cynegius: Libanius *Or.* 18.214; 30.22, 44–46. See also J. F. Matthews, "A Pious Supporter of Theodosius I: Maternus Cynegius," *JTS* 18 (1967): 438–46; idem, *Western Aristocracies and the Imperial Court: A.D. 364–425* (Oxford, 1975), 140–44; *PLRE* 1, s.v. "Maternus Cynegius 3"; B. Gassowska, "Maternus Cynegius, Praefectus Praetorio Orientis and the Destruction of the Allat Temple in Palmyra," *Archaeologica* 22 (1982): 107–23. Marcellus: Theodoret *HE* 5.21. Libanius on defense of temples: *Or.* 30.55.
47. Cynegius in Egypt: Zosimus 4.37; *Consul. Constan.* 1.244–45. It was during the first visit that a statue was erected in his honor by the Alexandrians, *ILS* 1273.
48. Paulinus of Nola *Carm.* 19.98–116. Cf. Soc. *HE* 5.16; Theodoret *HE* 5.22. Modern assessments of the episode may be found in T. Orlandi, "Uno scritto di Teofilo di Alessandria sulla distruzione del Serapeum?" *ParPas* 121 (1968): 295–304; J. Schwartz, "La fin du Sérapeum d'Alexandrie," in *American Studies in Papyrology,* vol. 1, *Essays in Honour of C. Bradford Wells* (New Haven, 1976), 97–111; F. Thelemon, *Païens et Chrétiens au IVe siècle: L'apport de l'"Histoire ecclésiastique" de Rufin d'Aquilée* (Paris, 1981), 245–79; A. Baldini, "Problemi della tradizione sulla 'distruzione' del Serapeo di Alessandria," *Rivista storica dell'Antichità* 15 (1985): 97–152; E. A. Clark, *The Origenist Controversy* (Princeton, 1992), 52–56.
49. *dia mesēs tēs agoras,* Soc. *HE* 5.15 col. 604c; Rufinus *HE* 2.22–30 (ed. Mommsen), *GCS* 9.2 (Leipzig, 1908).
50. *Igitur gentiles . . . velut draconum calice potato insanire omnes ac palam furere coeperunt, HE* 2.22.
51. Helladius: Soc. *HE* 5.15.50; Kaster, *Guardians of Language,* 289. Sallies against Christians: Rufinus *HE* 2.22. Gessius had even entertained hopes of a future consulate, *Anth. Pal.* Palladas 7.687–88. On Gessius, see Alan Cameron, "Palladas and the Fate of Gessius," *Byz. Zeit.* 57 (1964): 279–92; *PLRE* 1, s.v. "Gessius 1."
52. *de Romani imperii potestate, de vindicta legum et de his quae talia solerent subsequi.* Rufinus *HE* 2.22.
53. Theod. *HE* 5.17; Soz. *HE* 7.25.

54. *terra dehiscens ilico solveretur in chaos caelumque repente rueret in praeceps*. Rufinus *HE* 2.23.
55. On the use of this technique in Alexandria, see figure 25, and E. Rodziewicz, "Remains of a chryselephantine statue in Alexandria," *BSAA* 44 (1991): 119–30.
56. *ac per singula loca membratim in conspectu cultricis Alexandriae senex veternosus* [Serapis] *exuritur*. Rufinus *HE* 2.23.
57. Rufinus *HE* 2.28; John of Nikiu *Chron*. 78.42–47; *History of the Patriarchs* 1.8, p. 419 [155], 1.11, p. 426 [162]. The Serapeum long remained a formidable structure. Decades afterward, during a riot connected with the Monophysite controversy, some beleaguered imperial troops sought refuge from the mob "in the old temple of Serapis"; see Evagrius *HE* 2.25 = Priscus fr. 28 (ed. Blockley, 324–25).
58. Palladas on Gessius: "When Baukalos saw Gessius just after his death, / and lamer than ever, he spoke thus: / 'Gessius, what made thee descend into Hell, / naked, without funeral, in new burial guise?' / And to him in great wrath Gessius at once replied: / 'Baukalos, the pride of wealth may cause death.'" *Anth. Pal*. 7.686.1–6.

    Career of Palladas: *Anth. Pal*. 9.171.1–4; 9.175. Also, Alan Cameron, "Palladas and Christian Polemic," *JRS* 55 (1965): 26–27; Kaster, *Guardians of Language*, 327–29. Blaming Serapis for his subsequent hard times, Palladas seems to have regarded the god as the unfaithful patron deity of Alexandrian grammarians, *Anth. Pal*. 9.174.1–12.
59. Soc. *HE* 5.16. For their careers, see Kaster, *Guardians of Language*, 241, 289.
60. Rufinus *HE* 2.22. Rufinus also styles him the "standard bearer" (*antesignanus*) of the pagan crowd. Sozomen relates that the pagans "were instigated to revolt by the inflammatory discourses of a man named Olympius," and that his speeches boosted the flagging morale of the pagans, so that "he retained the multitude with him in the Serapeum" (*HE* 7.15).

    Olympius does not appear in either *PLRE* 1 or 2, save for a bare mention of a priest and rhetor known as "Olympus 2" in *PLRE* 1, whom the editors do not identify with the famous Alexandrian religious leader—though the quoted source begins Zintzen's collection of fragments (Damascius fr. 92, p. 69).
61. *toiade tis epekathēto peithō tois cheilesi tou andros, ouk anthrōpeion to chrēma, alla theioteron,* [Damascius] *Epit. Photiana* 48 (ed. Zintzen, p. 70) = Damascius fr. 92 (ed. Zintzen, p. 71).
62. (*oudeis d' houtōs ēn tēn psuchēn ateramôn kai barbaros, hos ouk epeitheto kai katekēleito tois apo tou hierou stomatos ekeinou hreousi logois*. [Damascius] *Epit. Photiana* 48 (ed. Zintzen, p. 68) = Damascius fr. 92 (ed. Zintzen, p. 69).

63. *ho de sunageirōn hekastote tous paratugchanontas edidaske ta archaia nomima kai tēn toutois ephepomenēn eudaimonian, hosē te kai hoia theothen apēnta tois akribōs tauta diaphulattousin.* Damascius fr. 97 (ed. Zintzen, p. 73). With regard to his religious preferences, it was said that Olympius had originally "come to Alexandria in order to worship Serapis" (*eis Alexandreian epi tên therapeian tou Serapidos*), Damascius fr. 91 (ed. Zintzen, p. 69).
64. Hierodidaskalos: Damascius fr. 97 (ed. Zintzen, p. 73). Social status of Olympius's followers: [Damascius] *Epit. Photiana* 51 (ed. Zintzen, p. 72) = Damascius fr. 99 (ed. Zintzen, p. 73).
65. Antoninus's students: Eunapius *v. Soph.* 470–71. Students and magic in Berytus: Zach. Mytil. *v. Sev.* 66 (ed. and trans. Kugener).
66. Eunapius *v. Soph.* 471. A sampling of tourists and pilgrims visiting the shrine: *P.Oxy.* 2.283; *P.Mich.* 213 inv. 333, 221 inv. 1362, 513 inv. 5159; *P.Tebt.* 416.
67. *C.Th.* 16.10.11 (trans. Pharr). It should be noted that while the edict banned pagan cult, it did not explicitly order the destruction of temple property. The legal difficulties surrounding this edict and the earlier rescript that ended the standoff at the Serapeum are discussed by O. Seek, *Geschichte des Untergangs der antiken Welt* (Berlin, 1920), 5:233–34; A. Favale, *Teofilo d'Alessandria* (Torino, 1958), 62–65.
68. Zosimus 5.23.3. A synodical letter from the Alexandrian church, included in the correspondence of Jerome, indicates that Theophilus himself was sensitive to charges that he had been responsible for the temple's destruction. In it, he criticizes the Origenists for trying to "stir up the heathen by denouncing the destruction of the Serapeum" (Jerome *Ep.* 92.3).
69. *P.Goleniscev* 6 verso, published in A. Bauer and J. Strygowski, "Eine alexandrinische Weltchronik," *Denkschriften der Kaiserlichen Akademie der Wissenschaften: Wien* 51.2 (1906): 1–204.
70. Unlike many other incidents of temple destruction during this period, there is no evidence that monks played an active role in the demolition of Serapis's temple. There is only the oblique reference, found in the *Apoph. Patr.,* that "Theophilus the archbishop summoned some Fathers to go to Alexandria one day, to pray and to destroy the heathen temples there" (Theophilus 3). Monks do not appear in either Rufinus or Socrates Scholasticus. On the role of monks in temple destruction, see the remarks of P. Brown, *Authority and the Sacred* (Cambridge, 1995), 50–51.
71. Public feasts in honor of Nile: Libanius *Or.* 30.35. Transfer of Nilometer: Rufinus *HE* 2.30. See also Thelemon, 273–79; D. Bonneau, "Continuité et discontinuité notionale dans la terminologie religieuse du Nil, d'après la documentation grecque," in *Mélanges Étienne Bernand,*

ed. N. Fick and J.-C. Carrière (Paris, 1991), 23–35; idem, "La divinité du Nil sous le principat en Égypte," *ANRW* 2.18.5 (1995): 3195–215.

72. Palladas on Tyche: *Anth. Pal.* 9.180–83, quoted at 183.3–4 (trans. Paton, *Loeb Classical Library*). Statues in Tychaion: one night in 602, they were seen to come down from their pedestals and utter prophecies concerning the impending death of the emperor Maurice, Theophylact Simocatta *Hist.* 7.13.10. Destruction of other statues: *Anth. Pal.* 9.441.1–6, 528.1–3; cf. Soc. *HE* 5.16; Firm. Mat. *de Err. Prof. Rel.* 28.6. See also Alan Cameron, "Notes on Palladas," 223–25. Palladas on Eros: *Anth. Pal.* 9.773.1–2.
73. Rufinus *HE* 2.29.
74. Theodoret *HE* 5.22—though one should not put too much weight upon the the veracity of this account, given the programmatic nature of ecclesiastical chronicles.
75. Sozomen *HE* 7.20; Rufinus *HE* 2.30.
76. On the role of miracles and demonstrations of power in religious conversions during antiquity, see R. MacMullen, *Christianizing the Roman Empire* (New Haven, 1984), esp. 25–42, 59–67.
77. Damascius fr. 97 (ed. Zintzen, p. 73).
78. Ibid.
79. *Apoph. Pat.* (alphabetical series), Bessarion 4.
80. *de Div. Daem.* 1.1, dated to the period 406–8.
81. *sed post occasum Serapis, quae iam alterius daemonis stare delubra potuerunt?* Rufinus *HE* 2.28.
82. A broader discussion of the role of sacrifice and its prohibition may be found in K. Harl, "Sacrifice and Pagan Belief in Fifth- and Sixth-Century Byzantium," *Past and Present* 128 (1990): 7–26.
83. Rufinus *HE* 2.24–25.
84. See chapter 9.
85. Two centuries later, Sophronius ensured the lasting fame of these two saints with his delightful *Narratio miraculorum ss. Cyri et Iohannis,* composed in thanks for the healing of an eye disease. Saint Cyrus gave his name to the locale which today retains his memory, Father Cyrus = Abū Qir.
86. Damascius fr. 100 (ed. Zintzen, p. 75). Zach. Mytil *v. Sev.* (ed. and trans. Kugener), 18, 20–21, 29.
87. The full narrative may be found in the *v. Severi* (ed. and trans. Kugener), 14–39. See my discussion in chapter 9, pp. 325–30.
88. Damascius fr. 34 (ed. Zintzen, p. 33).
89. Damascius fr. 117 (ed. Zintzen, p. 97). Severus's consulship, as well as urban prefecture, occurred during the turbulent reign of Anthemius (Augustus 467–72). See *PLRE* 2, s.v. "Severus 19."

90. *Epit. Photiana* [Damascius] 67 (ed. Zintzen, p. 96).
91. Damascius fr. 118 (ed. Zintzen, p. 97).
92. Damascius fr. 276 (ed. Zintzen, p. 219).
93. Damascius fr. 276 (ed. Zintzen, p. 219); *Epit. Photiana* [Damascius] 163 (ed. Zintzen, p. 218).
94. Damascius fr. 100 (ed. Zintzen, p. 75).
95. Damascius fr. 174 (ed. Zintzen, p. 147).
96. *Hieroglyphica,* ed. F. Sbordone (Naples, 1940); G. Boas, trans., *The Hieroglyphics of Horapollo* (Princeton, 1993). See also S. L. Karren, "Horapollon," in *CoptEncy* 4:1255–56; and Kaster, *Guardians of Language,* 295–97, who is cautious about ascribing the *Hieroglyphica* to Horapollon.

*Chapter Six. The Christian Community*

1. John Moschus *Prat. Spir.* 72.
2. In light of long-standing Alexandrian religious epithets, it is intriguing to note that Serapis's devotee in the story is simply styled an "old man" (*gerōn*), a name ascribed in the past to Serapis himself (Rufinus *HE* 11.23).
3. Leont. N. *v. Jo. Eleem.* 2; Sophronius *SS. Cyri et Johannis Miracula* 46, *PG* 87.3, col. 3596.
4. Mena of Nikiou, *Martyrdom of St. Macrobius,* ed. with French trans. by H. Hyvernant, in *Les Actes des martyrs de l'Égypte* (Paris, 1886; reprint, New York, 1977), 225–46; English trans. by D. N. Bell, *Mena of Nikiou: The Life of Isaac of Alexandria and the Martyrdom of St. Macrobius* (Kalamazoo, Mich., 1988), 111–27.
5. P. M. Fraser, "John of Nikiou," in *CoptEncy* 5:1366–67; A. S. Atiya, "Ibn al-Bitrīq, Saʿīd," in *CoptEncy* 4:1265–66; J. Den Heijer, "History of the Patriarchs of Alexandria," in *CoptEncy* 4:1238–42, with full bibliography.
6. *P.Lond.* 1914 (H. I. Bell, *Jews and Christians in Egypt* [London, 1924]), 53–71).
7. See, however, the judicious comments of D. W. H. Arnold, "Sir Harold Idris Bell and Athanasius: A Reconsideration of *London Papyrus* 1914," in *Studia Patristica,* vol. 21, ed. E. A. Livingstone, Papers presented to the Tenth International Conference on Patristic Studies held in Oxford, 1987 (Leuven, 1989), 377–83; idem, *The Early Episcopal Career of Athanasius of Alexandria* (Notre Dame, Ind., 1991). Broader issues of Athanasian scholarship are cogently discussed in C. Kannengiesser, "Athanasius of Alexandria: Some Open Questions," *Coptologia* 12 (1991): 27–40.
8. A. S. Atiya, in *CoptEncy* 1: 298–302; T. D. Barnes, *Athanasius and*

*Constantius: Theology and Politics in the Constantinian Empire* (Cambridge, Mass., 1993).

9. "The Career of Athanasius," in *Studia Patristica,* 21:391.
10. Recent studies have argued that the triumphalism which so permeates the histories of Rufinus, Socrates, Sozomen, and Theodoret (all within a couple of generations of the victory of Christianity) calls into question their historical judgment. In this view, the historians' portrait of the church's conquest over paganism is simply a skillful literary construct that celebrates the ideology of the new regime over the errors of the pagan past. While the interpretation of near contemporary events offered by these ecclesiastical chroniclers certainly needs to be taken with a grain of salt, their attention to detail—particularly on a local stage—confirms the value of their works. P. Canivert, *Histoire d'une entreprise apologétique au Vème siècle* (Paris, 1958), 118–25; B. Croke, "City Chronicles of Late Antiquity," in *Reading the Past in Late Antiquity,* ed. G. Clarke (Rushcutters Bay, New South Wales, 1990), 165–203; Averil Cameron, *Christianity and the Rhetoric of Empire: The Development of Christian Discourse* (Berkeley, 1991), 120–54; P. Brown, *Power and Persuasion in Late Antiquity* (Madison, Wis., 1992), 126–30; idem, *Authority and the Sacred* (Cambridge, 1995), 24–26, 65.

    Miniature of Theophilus and Serapeum in *P.Goleniscev* 6 verso, published in A. Bauer and J. Strygowski, "Eine alexandrinische Weltchronik," *Denkschriften der Kaiserlichen Akademie der Wissenschaften: Wien* 51.2 (1906): 1–204.
11. From the Martyrdom of Saint Mark, embedded in the *History of the Patriarchs* 1.2 (ed. Evetts), 142–45 [44–47]; Greek version in *PG* 115, cols. 164–69. A useful discussion of the text may be found in Pearson, "Earliest Christianity in Egypt: Some Observations," in B. A. Pearson and J. E. Goehring, *The Roots of Egyptian Christianity* (Philadelphia, 1986), 137–45, esp. n. 37.
12. R. MacMullen, *Christianizing the Roman Empire* (New Haven, 1984), p. 104.
13. Some of Origen's curious pagan inquirers later became bishops and martyrs: Eus. *HE* 6.3.1–2. Origen's activities as underground teacher: 6.3.5–6.
14. Peter I: *M. Petr. Al.,* Latin text in W. Tefler, "St. Peter of Alexandria and Arius," *AnBol* 67 (1949): 127. Julian on Athanasius' sermons: Julian *Ep.* 111 (ed. Bidez-Cumont); Sozomen *HE* 5.15. Cyril and notaries: T. Orlandi, ed. and trans., *Storia della Chiesa di Alessandria* (Milan, 1970), 2:77. Staff of copyists: *History of the Patriarchs* 1.12 (ed. Evetts), p. 431 [167]. Cf. Geo. Al. *v. Chrys.* 41 (in *S. Joannis Chrysostomi Opera,* ed. H. Savile [Etonae, 1613], 8:217.25); and Aug. *Ep.* 213 on the presence of *notarii* at church assemblies.

15. Christians and plague victims: letter of Dionysius in Eus. *HE* 7.22. This may be compared with a similar occurrence in Carthage a decade earlier, when Cyprian organized relief for the afflicted. He even considered it a Christian obligation to care for their former persecutors: Cyprian *ad Dem*. Interestingly enough, Dionysius makes no mention of care for dying pagans, perhaps a testimony to rigidity of communal boundaries in Alexandria.

    Church as mediator during stasis: Eus. *HE* 7.32.7–12. The best discussion of these incidents is still S. I. Oost, "The Alexandrian Seditions under Philip and Gallienus," *Classical Philology* 56 (1961): 1–26. A new study of this period in Alexandrian history is a desiderata, in light of recent source-critical work and a clearer understanding of Alexandrian topography. See also C. Andresen, "Siegreiche Kirche," *ANRW* 2.23.1 (1979): 387–495.

    On Alexandrian processions, see the exhaustive study of H. Brakmann, "*Synaxis Katholikê* in Alexandreia: Zur Verbreitung des christlichen Stationsgottesdienstes," *Jahrbuch für Antike und Christentum* 30 (1987): 74–89.
16. Athan. *v. Ant*. 70.
17. Athan. *Apol. ad Constant*. 33; Libanius *Or*. 30.8; Eunapius *v. Soph*. 472.
18. Evagrius: *Hist. Monach*. 20.15 (cf. Palladius *Hist. Laus*. 38). Copres and the Manichaean: *Hist. Monach*. 10.30. R. Lim (*Public Disputation, Power and Social Order in Late Antiquity* [Berkeley, 1995], 79) takes the unnamed city to be Hermopolis Magna. Peter I and Diogenes: D. Spanel, "Two Fragmentary Saʿidic Coptic Texts Pertaining to Peter I, Patriarch of Alexandria," *Bul.Soc.Arch.Copte* 24 (1979–82): 89–90.
19. Soz. *HE* 7.20.
20. *History of the Patriarchs* 1.8 (ed. Evetts), 407–8 [143–44]; Leont. N. *v. Jo. Eleem*. 38 (36 in Gelzer's ed.); Jo. Moschus *Prat. Spir*. 207; *S. Pachomii vita bohairice scripta* 89.
21. Zach. Mytil. *v. Sev*. (ed. and trans. Kugener), *PO* 2 (Paris, 1907), 12–38.
22. Zach. Mytil. *v. Sev*. (ed. and trans. Kugener), p. 15.
23. By the time of Paralios's conversion in the later fifth century, another type of conversion becomes increasingly prominent in the sources—conversion from nominal Christianity to monasticism. These two types of conversion exist side by side in the *vita Severi*, so that one needs to distinguish very carefully a character's former religious predilections in order to determine under which rubric the conversion falls. Some individuals, such as Paralios's brother Stephen, a medical student, are even converted from paganism directly to monasticism. Even though Zachariah was among the zealous philoponoi of the Alexandrian church, Paralios thought it necessary to remove Stephen from

Zachariah's care, "because, to tell the truth, [Paralios] found me too weak," Zach. Mytil. *v. Sev.* (ed. and trans. Kugener), p. 39.

24. R. S. Bagnall, "Religious Conversion and Onomastic Change in Early Byzantine Egypt," *BASP* 19.3–4 (1982): 105–24; E. Wipszycka, "La valeur de l'onomastique pour l'histoire de la christianisation de l'Égypte," *ZPE* 62 (1986): 173–81; R. S. Bagnall, "Conversion and Onomastics: A Reply," *ZPE* 69 (1987): 243–50; G. H. R. Horsley, "Name Change as an Indication of Religious Conversion in Antiquity" *Numen* 34 (1987): 1–17; E. Wipszycka, "La christianisation de l'Égypte au ive–ve siècles: Aspects sociaux et ethniques," *Aegyptus* 68 (1988): 117–64.
25. Martyrs under Decius: letter of Dionysius in Eus. *HE* 6.41. Alexandrian clergy in early fourth century: Athan. *Apol. c. Ar.* 64, 71, 73, 75; Soc. *HE* 1.6.
26. *HM* 5.4.
27. *Liturgy of Saint Mark*, Greek version, in *Liturgies Eastern and Western*, ed. F. E. Brightman (Oxford, 1896), 1:143, lines 20–26.
28. Theophylact Simocatta *Hist.* 8.13.7–14.
29. *Liturgy of Saint Mark*, 126, lines 18–20.
30. Summaries of each season, along with bibliographical references, may be consulted in M. Rodziewicz, "A Brief Record of the Excavations at Kom-el-Dikka in Alexandria (1960–1980)," *BSAA* 44 (1991): 1–70. Early Roman villas: Rodziewicz, *Habitations*, 17–58. Later evolution of the site: M. Rodziewicz, "La stratigraphie de l'antique Alexandrie à la lumière des fouilles de Kom el-Dikka," *É&T* 14 (1990): 145–51. Baths: see now W. Kolataj, *The Imperial Baths at Kōm el-Dikka*, 2 vols., *Alexandria 6*, (Warsaw, 1992).
31. Workshops: Rodziewicz, *Habitations* 241–42, 249–51. These were similar in form to the contemporary shops at Marea/Philoxenite, as yet unpublished. For other useful comperanda, see J. S. Crawford, *The Byzantine Shops at Sardis* (Cambridge, Mass., 1990); and the review of the same by J. Russell, "Shops for a Small Industry and Retail Trade in a Late-antique City," *Journal of Roman Archaeology* 6 (1993): 455–60.

    John Moschus *Prat. Spir.* 78. See also J. P. Sodini, "L'artisanat urbain à l'époque paléochrétienne (IVe–VIIe S.)," *Ktēma* 4 (1979): 71–119; P. van Minnen, "Urban Craftsmen in Roman Egypt," *Münstersche Beiträge z. antiken Handelgeschichte* 6.1 (1987): 31–88.
32. Ivory and bone production: E. Rodziewicz, "Bone Carvings Discovered at Kōm el-Dikka, Alexandria, in 1967," *É&T* 3 (1969): 147–52; idem, "Reliefs figurés en os des fouilles à Kōm el-Dikka," *É&T* 10 (1978): 317–36. Terracottas: M. Martens, "Figurines en Terre-Cuite Coptes," *BSAA* 43 (1975): 53–77.

    Menas flasks: Z. Kiss, *Les ampoules de Saint Ménas découvertes à Kōm el-Dikka (1961–1981), Alexandrie* 5 (Warsaw, 1989); idem, "Ampulla," in *CoptEncy* 1: 116–18. A local source for this production is suggested by the great number of the Menas ampoules, in quantities that appear to surpass even the fervent piety of one restricted urban neighborhood. Further, the majority of the ampoules are of a virtually identical type produced in the period 610–42, showing Saint Menas between two camels with two crosses in the field above (Kiss, *Les ampoules de Saint Ménas,* 15–18). It may be conceded, however, that some shrewd Alexandrian entrepreneur may have brought the ampoules in bulk from the Mareotis to Alexandria to sell to pilgrims.

Alexandrians and pilgrims: Antoninus of Piacenza *Itinerarium* 45 (*CCSL* 175, p. 152); Sophronius *v. S. Mariae Aegyptiae* 18–21 (*PG* 87.3, cols. 3709–12).

33. House D is described in exhaustive detail by M. Rodziewicz, *Habitations,* 66–128, 194–245; amplifying an earlier report found in idem, "Un quartier d'habitation gréco-romain à Kōm el-Dikka," *É&T* 9 (1976): 169–210. Walls: their strength puts into better perspective the observation of Agathias, who studied in Alexandria in the mid-sixth century: "people's houses there are not at all strongly-built and quite incapable of standing up to even a small amount of seismic vibration, being frail and flimsy structures consisting of a single thickness of stone" (Agathias *Hist.* 2.15.7, trans. J. D. Frendo). Second-floor balustrade: Rodziewicz, *Habitations,* 67, 70, 115–16, 330. Inscriptions over entries: unfortunately, other inscriptions of this *tabula ansata* type from R4 survive in mere fragments, so it is impossible to speculate as to their content. Rodziewicz, *Habitations,* 210. Other religious images and symbols: Rufinus *HE* 2.29.
34. Palladius *Hist. Laus.* 6.5; *P.Tal.Hagiga* 3.1.
35. Rodziewicz, *Habitations* 87.
36. Ibid. and fig. 95 on p. 93 for the lock plate. The coins come from roughly the same period as other coin-finds throughout Kōm el-Dikka: B. Lichocka, "Un tresor de monnaies byzantines à Kom el-Dikka (Alexandrie)," *É&T* 16 (1992): 67–79.
37. Rodziewicz, *Habitations,* 330.
38. Multistoried Alexandrian dwellings: in the course of the proceedings against the patriarch Dioscorus at the Council of Chalcedon in 451, Athanasius, a priest and nephew of Cyril, accused the patriarch of confiscating his house (*oikos*) which sat upon a fourth floor (*tetartēi stegēi*): [libellus of presbyter Athanasius] *ACO* 2.1.2.57. The offhand manner in which Athanasius describes his "house" may have implications for understanding various texts relating house totals in a city or an *insula*. Also, *P.Lond.* 3.1164f28 (third century A.D.); ivory of Saint Mark, Louvre OA.3317.

Number of inhabitants: aside from the question of house height, there is also the matter of determining density of occupation in such a house. Evidence from the Egyptian chora approximates an average of 11.27 occupants per house, strikingly similar to ratios from rural houses in modern Egypt showing 10.5 occupants per house. However, House D has an area of nearly 100 square meters, almost double the average area of houses from Karanis—archaeologically, the best-known town in the chora. Moreover, one would expect domestic residency patterns to be markedly different in the teeming metropolis. Altogether, this makes for a set of unknown variables that prohibits any firm estimates for urban density. Essentially, one encounters in small scale at House D the same problems inherent in any estimation of population for the entire city.

39. Rodziewicz, *Habitations,* 70, 195–204.
40. Directly opposite from the fresco, on the south wall of D12, two large spikes of iron with eyelets were driven into wedges of wood set into the limestone wall. Their exact role is unclear, since they stood too close to the wall to carry lamps. Moreover, their size suggests that they were designed to carry heavy objects. Their careful placement, however, shows them to be in relation to the scene on the opposite wall (Rodziewicz, *Habitations,* 70, 204).
41. Rodziewicz points out that, in the space allotted, it would have been an easy matter to paint in several more figures, providing all of the figures were reduced in size (*Habitations,* 204, 332). This lends weight to the idea that the painting was intended to be viewed by a fair number of worshipers at one time.
42. M. Rodziewicz, "Remarks on the Domestic and Monastic Architecture in Alexandria and Surroundings," in *Archaeology of the Nile Delta,* ed. E. C. M. van den Brink (Amsterdam, 1988), 267–77; idem, "Alexandria and the District of Mareotis," *Graeco-Arabica* 2 (1983): 199–216; idem, "Remarks on the Peristyle House in Alexandria and Mareotis," *PRAKTIKA: Papers of the Twelfth International Congress for Classical Archaeology in Athens* (Athens, 1988): 175–78.

    At the other end of the empire, renovation of the villas at Lullingstone in Britain and Fraga in Spain created similar interior chapels toward the end of the fourth century: G. W. Meates, *Lullingstone Roman Villa* (London, 1955); J. de C. Sera Rafols, "La Villa Fortunatus de Fraga," *Ampurias* 5 (1943): 6–35; M. C. Fernandez Castro, *Villas Romanas en España* (Madrid, 1982). The entire phenomenon of the Christianization of rural villas is discussed in J. Percival, *The Roman Villa* (Berkeley, 1976), 166–99.
43. R. Krautheimer, *Corpus Basilicarum Christianarum Romae* (Vatican City, 1939), 1:267–303.

44. The morphology of religious building types in the first four centuries A.D. is carefully examined in L. M. White, *Building God's House in the Roman World* (Baltimore, 1990), esp. 111–26 for the *domus ecclesiae*.
45. Ascetic withdrawal within Alexandria: *Apoph. Patr.* Systematic Coll. 43, 237; *Apoph. Patr.* Anon. Coll. 67; *Apoph. Patr.* Anthony 24; John Moschus *Prat. Spir.* 60, 73, 75, 105, 106, 171, 172; Palladius *Hist. Laus.* 21.2–4, 6; Serapion of Thumis *Ep. ad Monachos*. Oratories under John the Almsgiver: Leont. N. *v. Jo. Eleem.* 42. Cf. Justinian *Nov.* 131.7 for regulations concerning the foundation of oratories.
46. The Donatists in North Africa regularly met in private houses to escape detection or as an alternative to the official church: W. H. C. Frend, *The Donatist Church* (Oxford, 1952), 53–54. See also now the useful comparative material collected by H. O. Maier, "Private Space as the Social Setting of Arianism in Ambrose's Milan," *JTS*, n.s., 45.1 (1994): 72–93; idem, "The Topography of Heresy and Dissent in Late-Fourth-Century Rome," *Historia* 44.2 (1995): 232–49; idem, "Religious Dissent, Heresy and Households in Late Antiquity," *Vigiliae Christianae* 49 (1995): 49–63.

    Within Alexandria itself, both hostels and private houses are mentioned as meeting places for heretical groups: Melitians—*P. Lond.* 1914 (Bell, *Jews and Christians in Egypt*, 53–71); Arians—Soz. *HE* 5.7; Philostorgius *HE* 3.20; Monophysites—letter of Marcian in Mansi, vol. 7.517–20; John Moschus *Prat. Spir.* 106.
47. Eusebius *v. Const.* 3.65; *C.Th.* 16.5.11. By the end of the seventh century, the status of private oratories was addressed by a council of eastern bishops brought together in Constantinople by Justinian II. An early canon of this so-called Council in Trullo had prohibited clerics from offering eucharist or baptizing in domestic oratories without the permission of the local bishop, whereas a later canon of the same council forbade all baptisms whatsoever within the oratory of a house (*C. in Trull.* can. 31, 59).
48. *mē . . . tois toioutous euktēriois prospsausēte*. Leont. N. *v. Jo. Eleem.* 42.
49. *History of the Patriarchs* 1.14 (ed. Evetts), 501–2, [237–38].
50. Rodziewicz, *Habitations*, 210. Similar representations of the cross are found rather frequently in early Christian iconography from the region, for example, in the cathedral of Faras, the hermitages of Esna in Upper Egypt, and in the monasteries of Kellia.
51. Ibid., 87, 211, 219–22, 398, 421.
52. Rodziewicz, "Reliefs figurés en os," 326–30; Rodziewicz, *Habitations*, 243–44.
53. A similar process can be seen in the use of traditional renderings of the seasons in paintings: K. Kolodziejczyk, "Fragments d'enduits peints

des fouilles polonaises a Kōm el-Dikka (Alexandrie)," *É&T* 15 (1990): 193–202.

54. Rodziewicz, "Reliefs figurés en os," 319–20.
55. Serapis and Dionysius: Rodziewicz, *Habitations,* 43, 48. Isis: M. Martens, "Figurines en Terre-Cuite Coptes," *BSAA* 43 (1975): 53–77, although it seems to me that their Isiac identification is at best problematic, in light of their fragmentary state of preservation. Sphinx: Z. Kiss, "Un sphinx sur un plat romain tardiff de Kōm el-Dikka, Alexandrie," *É&T* 16 (1992): 29–34.
56. Rufinus *HE* 2.29.
57. D. B. Spanel, "Theophilus," in *CoptEncy* 7:2247–53, with full bibliography.
58. Three thetas: Saʿid ibn al-Batriq (Eutychius) *Annales, PG* 111, col. 1025; *History of the Patriarchs* 1.11 (ed. Evetts), p. 426 [162]. Isidore and the widow's bequest: Soz. *HE* 8.12. Contemporary assessments of Theophilus: Soz. *HE* 8.18; Palladius *Dial. de Jo. Chrys.* 22; Isid. Pel. *Ep.* 1.152 (*PG* 78, col. 284).
59. R. Krautheimer, *Three Christian Capitals* (Berkeley, 1983), 93–121.
60. Adriani, *Repertorio,* 35, 98, 201–59; Calderini, *Dizionario,* 165–78; H. Leclercq, "Alexandrie" in *Dictionnaire d'archéologie chrétienne et de liturgie* 1.1:1107–25. A. Martin, "Les premiers siècles du christianisme à Alexandrie: Essai de topographie religieuse (IIIe–IVe siècles)," *Revue des études augustiniennes* 30 (1984): 211–25. The scant material remains are surveyed by B. Tkaczow, "Archaeological Sources for the Earliest Churches in Alexandria," in *Coptic Studies,* ed. W. Godlewski (Warsaw, 1990), 431–35.
61. Epiph. *Haer.* 69.2.4.
62. *Hist. Aceph.* 5.7 (February 366), in which civic officials escort Athanasius from a suburban villa to the nearby church of Dionysius.

    The excavations at Kōm el-Dikka have revealed that large-scale urban renewal projects were possible in the center of the city, but they required the demolition of previous structures. Such a project was more feasible in the semiresidential areas to the south of the Via Canopica than along the boulevard itself.
63. George: *Hist. Aceph.* 2.3. Church of Pierius: Epiph. *Haer.* 69.2.4.
64. Athan. *Apol. ad Constant.* 15; *Festal Index* 11, 28; *Hist. Aceph.* 1.10–11.
65. Saʿid ibn al-Batriq (Eutychius) *Annales* 433–35, *PG* 111, col. 1005; *Copto-Arabic Synaxarion,* 12 Baʾūnah. M. van Esbroeck, "Michael the Archangel," in *CoptEncy* 5: 1616–20.
66. Soc. *HE* 7.13; wrongly identified as the church of Saint Athanasius by John of Nikiu *Chron.* 84.96–97.

67. *Festal Index* 41–42; Synesius *Ep.* 4; Strabo 17.794; Ps. Callisthenes 1.31.
68. *Festal Index* 37–38, 40; Epiph. *Haer.* 69.2.2; Soc. *HE* 7.15; John of Nikiu *Chron.* 119.14, 120.12; Athan. *Apol. ad Constant.* 14–15, *Hist. Ar.* 55.
69. A comparable shift can be seen in Aphrodisias: R. Cormack, "The Temple as the Cathedral," in *Aphrodisias Papers* ed. C. Roueché and K. T. Erim, *Journal of Roman Archaeology,* suppl. 1 (Ann Arbor, Mich., 1990), 75–84; idem, "Byzantine Aphrodisias: Changing the Symbolic Map of a City," *Proceedings of the Cambridge Philological Society* 216 (1990): 26–41.
70. Isis Pharia and Agia Sophia: John Moschus *Prat. Spir.* 105, 106; *Epit. Phot.* [Damascius] 71 (ed. Zintzen, p. 100). Martyrdom of Metras: Eus. *HE* 6.41.3. Vitalios: Leont. N. *v. Jo. Eleem.* 38 (36 in Gelzer's ed.). Milan: Krautheimer, *Three Christian Capitals,* 68–92; N. B. McLynn, *Ambrose of Milan* (Berkeley, 1994), 223–37.
71. *Anth. Pal.* 9.183.3–4.
72. Parish churches: Epiph. *Haer.* 69.2.2–7. Presbyters in parishes: Epiph. *Haer.* 68.4.2; Soc. *HE* 5.22. Letter of Alexander: *Arii depos.* in Athan. *de Decret.* 34.1–4.
73. Soz. *HE* 1.15; Soc. *HE* 1.6. Cf. Athan. *Apol. c. Ar.* 73.
74. Epiph. *Haer.* 69.2.6.
75. Cemeteries: Eus. *HE* 7.10. Martyrium of Saint Mark: *M. Petr. Al.* 11–14, 16; John of Nikiu *Chron.* 95.8–11, 108.8 (trans. Charles); *History of the Patriarchs* 1.14 (ed. Evetts), 495, [231]; Palladius *Hist. Laus.* 45.
76. *Hist. Laus.* 15.1, 35.14–15.
77. Cyrus and John at Canopus: *Copto-Arabic Synaxarium* 4 Abib; Sophron. Hier. *Mir. Cyr. et Jo.* (*PG* 87, cols. 3424–3676), *Laudes Cyr. et Jo.* (*PG* 87, cols. 3380–3421). Daphne: Soz. *HE* 5.19–20; Soc. *HE* 3.18; Theodoret *HE* 3.6.
78. Orlandi, *Storia della Chiesa di Alessandria,* 2:61–62.
79. The most thorough examination of these monasteries during the period of their greatest influence remains P. van Cauwenberg, *Études sur les moines d'Égypte depuis le Councile de Chalcédoine jusqu'à l'invasion arabe* (Louvain, 1914), 63–81.
80. MacMullen, *Christianizing the Roman Empire,* 67.

*Chapter Seven. The Inner Life of the Christian Community*

1. *Canons of Athanasius* 57, ed. and trans. W. Riedel and W. E. Crum (London, 1904). On these, see W. Reidel, *Die Kirchenrechtsquellen des Patriarchat Alexandrien* (Leipzig, 1900; reprint, Aalen, 1968); H.

Munier, "Mélanges de littérature copte 3: Les Canons de saint Athanase," *Annales du Service des antiquités de l'Égypte* 19 (1920): 238–41; R.-G. Coquin, "Canons of Pseudo-Athanasius," in *CoptEncy* 2: 458–59.

2. Soc. *HE* 5.8; Greg. Naz. *Or.* 42.23, 43.37; *C.Th.* 16.1.3; Just. *Nov.* 123. In these pages, I employ the terms bishop and patriarch interchangeably, as I do not see any appreciable difference in the exercise of episcopal authority on either side of the 380s.
3. *Apoph. Patr.* Anon. Coll. 81.
4. The enumeration of offices includes bishop, presbyters, deacons, subdeacons, readers, singers, and doorkeepers: *Canons of Athanasius* 10 (ed. and trans. Riedel and Crum).
5. Recent reconstructions of patriarchal chronologies may be found in G. Fedalto, *Hierarchia Ecclesiastica Orientalis,* vol. 2, Patriarchatus Alexandriae, Antiochae, Hierosolymitanae (Padua, 1988), 581–90; and A. S. Atiya, "Patriarchs, Dates and Succession of," in *CoptEncy* 6:1913–20.
6. Eus. *HE* 6.29.5; 7.32.30. T. Vivian speculates on the possibility that Peter directed the catechetical school, and rightly points out the paucity of evidence for this view. The major literary sources for the history of the patriarchate normally make a point of trumpeting the esteem garnered by the newly elected patriarch in his previous post as head of the catechetical school. Their silence in the case of Peter seems telling. T. Vivian, *Saint Peter of Alexandria: Bishop and Martyr* (Philadelphia, 1988), 11–12.
7. Eus. *HE* 7.32.30; Alexander Al. *Encom. Petr. Al.*, Coptic text in H. Hyvernant, *Les actes des martyrs de l'Égypte* (Hildesheim, 1977), 249, 252; *History of the Patriarchs* 1.6 (ed. Evetts), p. 209 [111].
8. *History of the Patriarchs* 1.8 (ed. Evetts), 407–8 [143–44]; John of Nikiu *Chron.* 79.1–10. John Moschus preserves the oft-quoted story of Alexander taking a stroll by the seashore one day when he chanced to overhear some boys playing at church. He was so impressed with the demeanor and wisdom of the boy playing the bishop (Athanasius) that he took him under his care from that time forward (Jo. Moschus *Prat. Spir.* 197).
9. Promotion of patriarchal protégés: *Hist. Aceph.* 5.14; *History of the Patriarchs* 1.6 (ed. Evetts), p. 383 [119]; 1.11, pp. 425–26 [161–62]; 1.13, p. 448 [184]. Ascetics as patriarchs: *History of the Patriarchs* 1.14, p. 473 [209]; 1.14, p. 487 [223].
10. *History of the Patriarchs* 1.8 (ed. Evetts), pp. 407–8 [143–44]; Soz. *HE* 6.12; Athan. *Hist. Ar.* 13; Soz. *HE* 5.6.
11. Wealth of patriarchs' families: Soz. *HE* 8.12; *ACO* 2.1.2.57. John: Sophr. H. *v. Jo. Eleem.* 2, 12, 16; Sophr. H. *v. Jo. Eleem.* 4. On Nicetas,

see *PLRE* 3.2.940–43. Anastasius: *History of the Patriarchs* 1.14 (ed. Evetts), 478–79 [214–15]. Andronicus: *History of the Patriarchs* 1.14 (ed. Evetts), p. 484 [220].

12. Kinship ties among patriarchs: *Hist. Aceph.* 5.14; *History of the Patriarchs* 1.13 (ed. Evetts), p. 449 [185]. Athanasius and Theophilus: John of Nikiu *Chron.* 79.1–10 (trans. Charles).
13. Cyril at Nitria: *History of the Patriarchs* 1.11 (ed. Evetts), p. 427 [163]. Election of Cyril: Soc. *HE* 7.7.
14. *ACO* 2.1.2.57. The size of the family's fortune is indicated by references to income-producing buildings (*oikodomēmata kai prosodia*), houses, several hundred pounds of gold, and numerous slaves.
15. *ACO* 2.1.2.47, 51. One deacon named Theodore summed up Dioscorus's policy as follows: "Dioscorus excluded me from the clergy at the beginning of his episcopate . . . and likewise threatened to expel me from this great city without any other reason than the intimacy and favor [*tēs oikeiotētos kai eumeneias*] with which Cyril of holy memory had honored me. For his plan was to expel from this city or even to kill, not only the members of the family of Cyril, but also those who had been his close associates [*prosoikeiōthentas*], in the hatred which he bore against the orthodoxy of Cyril's faith."
16. Gaianus and Theodosius: *History of the Patriarchs* 1.13 (ed. Evetts), 456–57 [192–93]; John of Nikiu *Chron.* 92.1–6; Zach. Mytil. *HE* 9.19. The fact that there was no clear road to the succession is also demonstrated by Athanasius's passing over his trusted secretary, Theophilus, and choosing an elderly presbyter named Peter (*Hist. Aceph.* 5.14).
17. Eutychius (Saʿid ibn al-Batriq) *Annales, PG* 111, col. 982; Jerome *Ep.* 146; Severus of Antioch *Ep.* 6.2.3; Epiph. *Haer.* 69.2.5–7; *History of the Patriarchs* 1.6 (ed. Evetts), p. 383 [119]; 1.9, pp. 423–24 [159–60]; 1.13, p. 456 [192]; Evagrius *HE* 2.9; Sophr. H. *v. Jo. Eleem.* 4. Athanasius provides a backhanded description of the authority for episcopal ordination in mid-fourth-century Alexandria when he excoriates the Arian intruder, Gregory of Cappadocia, "a stranger to the city, not having been baptized there, nor known to the general body, and desired neither by presbyters, nor bishops, nor laity—that he should be appointed at Antioch, and sent to Alexandria, accompanied not by presbyters, nor by deacons of the city, nor by bishops of Egypt, but by soldiers." Athan. *Apol. c. Ar.* 30.
18. Liberatus *Brev.* (*PL* 68, cols. 1036–37). The ritual is described in reference to the conflict between the supporters of Gaianus and Theodosius for the succession from Timothy III (d. 535).

    Some hint of these practices may be found in accounts of the martyrdom of Peter I in 311, when his body was placed upon the patriarchal throne, with his successor Achillas receiving the *pallium*

(*History of the Patriarchs* 1.6 [ed. Evetts], p. 400 [136]); *M. Petr. Al.* 16–18. These events, however, may not represent traditional Alexandrian practice, since Peter's death was both unexpected and violent, and also afforded the Alexandrians the opportunity finally to place on the *synthronos* a beloved patriarch who, in life, humbly refused to sit on the seat of Saint Mark.

On the questions surrounding patriarchal succession, see E. W. Brooks, "The Ordination of the Early Bishops of Alexandria," *JTS* 2 (1901): 612–13; W. Telfer, "Episcopal Succession in Egypt," *Journal of Ecclesiastical History* 3 (1951): 1–13; E. W. Kemp, "Bishops and Presbyters at Alexandria," *Journal of Ecclesiastical History* 6 (1955): 125–42; M. Shoucri, "Patriarchal Election," in *CoptEncy* 6: 1911–12.

19. Residence at church of Saint Dionysius: Athan. *Ep. Ency*. 5; *Hist. Aceph.* 2.3, 5.7. "Four months and twenty-four days after, that is on the 8th of Phaōphi (5 October 365), the bishop Athanasius left the church secretly by night, and retired to a villa near the New River [*recessit in villa iuxta fluvium novum*]. But the prefect Flavianus and the *dux* Victorinus not knowing that he had retired, on the same night arrived at the church of Dionysius with a force of soldiers. And having broken the back door, and entered the upper parts of the house in search of the bishop's apartment [*ingressi atrium et partes superiores domus ospitium episcopi querentes*], they did not find him, for, not long before, he had left this place." *Hist. Aceph.* 5.4. Cf. Sozomen *HE* 6.12.
20. Leont. N. *v. Jo. Eleem.* 12.
21. Leont. N. *v. Jo. Eleem.* 11, 42. This phrase may also reflect Alexandrian topography, since it may refer to the patriarch descending from some residence along the limestone ridge running through the city to a church, like the Caesarion, located near the shore.
22. Oratory: Leont. N. *v. Jo. Eleem.* 26, 39, 42; Jo. Moschus *Prat. Spir.* 146. Consistory: *M. Petr. Al.* 17; Leont. N. *v. Jo. Eleem.* 2, 15, 18, 28, 40. It was probably here that the patriarch also took meals with his clergy; see *Canons of Athanasius* 66 (ed. and trans. Riedel and Crum). Library: *Encom. Apa Mena* (ed. Drescher, p. 129), probably written between 680 and 790; also a notice contained in a Coptic dormition of the Virgin, in F. Robinson, *Coptic Apocryphal Gospels* (Cambridge, 1896), 220. Baths: *ACO* 2.1.2.51; John of Nikiu *Chron.* 92.8; cf. *P.Oxy.* 1.148 (sixth century). A late antique private bath complex has been excavated at Kōm el-Dikka: M. Rodziewicz, "Private Roman Bath at Kōm el Dikka in Alexandria," *É&T* 2 (1968): 143–54; K. Kolodziejczyk, "Remarques sur les thermes privés à Kōm el-Dikka (Alexandrie)," *É&T* 16 (1992): 57–65.
23. Although this reflects the concurrent expansion of imperial bureaucracy, the growth of clerical offices in Alexandria can best be explained

in reference to local needs. One should not rule out, however, the broader climate of opinion which tacitly accepted the proliferation of officialdom. For the Egyptian evidence, see E. Wipszycka, "La chiesa nell'Egitto del IV secolo: Le strutture ecclesiastiche," in *Miscellanea Historiae Ecclesiasticae* 6, *Congrès de Varsovie 1978* (Warsaw, 1983), 182–201.

24. Senior presbyter: Soc. *HE* 6.9; Soz. *HE* 8.12.3; Leont. N. *v. Jo. Eleem.* 15; cf. Jerome *Ep.* 125.15. Archdeacon: Soc. *HE* 7.7; Soz. *HE* 7.19. Subdeacons: *Canons of Athanasius* 11, 43 (ed. and trans. Riedel and Crum).
25. Readers in ante-Nicene Church: Justin *I Apol.* 67; Tertullian *de praesc. haer.* 41; Cyprian *Ep.* 38. Patriarchal protégés as readers: Peter—Alexander Al. *Encom. Petr. Al.*, Coptic text in Hyvernant, *Les actes des martyrs de l'Égypte*, 252; Theophilus—John of Nikiu *Chron.* 79.13; Cyril—*History of the Patriarchs* 1.11 (ed. Evetts), p. 427 [163].
26. Basil of Caesarea began his career as a lector; see Greg. Naz. *Orat.* 43.27. Cf. Greg. Naz. *Ep.* 11; Ambrose *de excessu fratis* 61; Soc. *HE* 7.41.
27. Readers above subdeacons: *Canons of Athanasius* 35 (ed. and trans. Riedel and Crum). On the clerical status of the Alexandrian lectorate, see Leont. N. *v. Jo. Eleem.* 44a in which a reader, clearly ranked as one of the clergy, is later ordained to the priesthood. Cyril: *History of the Patriarchs* 1.11 (ed. Evetts), p. 427 [163]. Episcopal regulation of readers: *Canons of Athanasius* 12, 18, 58 (ed. and trans. Riedel and Crum). Pay of readers: Jo. Mos. *Prat. Spir.* 171; John of Nikiu *Chron.* 92.9. Shoemaker/reader: Leont. N. *v. Jo. Eleem.* 44a.
28. Theophilus *Canon* 10, in P.-P. Joannou, *Discipline générale antique*, part 2, *Les canons des pères grecs* (Rome, 1963), 270; *Canons of Athanasius* 89 (ed. and trans. Riedel and Crum). This last canon speaks of the officials required to enter the treasury of the church. While the archpresbyter's presence is mandated, the archdeacon is conspicuously absent—something of a surprise given the diaconate's former function of administering the resources of the church.
29. Duties and authority of oikonomos: *Canons of Athanasius* 61, 80, 81, 89 (ed. and trans. Riedel and Crum); Leont. N. *v. Jo. Eleem.* 2.
30. Two possible exceptions to this rule, sometimes cited by older authorities, are the Chalcedonian bishops Proterius (452–57) and John Talaia (482). The sole source for Proterius holding the office of Alexandrian oikonomos is a textual gloss on the libellus of Ischyrion against Dioscorus at the Council of Chalcedon (Mansi 4.1017). However, both Zachariah of Mytilene (*HE* 3.2) and Liberatus (*Brev.* 14.99) identify him as senior presbyter/archpriest of the Alexandrian church. In the case of John Talaia, Evagrius (*HE* 3.12) and Liberatus (*Brev.* 16.107)

style him both priest and oikonomos. However, Evagrius provides the added detail that his service as oikonomos was limited to a minor post as steward of only one parish church in Alexandria.

31. Chalcedon: *ACO* 2.1.2.51. Clergy and avarice: Theophilus *Canon* 11, in Joannou, *Discipline générale antique,* 270.
32. Leont. N. *v. Jo. Eleem.* 3, 5, 11, 14, 35, 37; *Canons of Athanasius* 11, 13, 21 (ed. and trans. Riedel and Crum).
33. *Canons of Athanasius* 26, 31, 75, 93 (ed. and trans. Riedel and Crum).
34. *Canons of Athanasius* 38, 41, 44, 49, 71, 75 (ed. and trans. Riedel and Crum); *C.Th.* 9.16.4 (A.D. 357).
35. Leont. N. *v. Jo. Eleem.* 42 (trans. Dawes and Baynes).
36. The classical evidence is elegantly presented in R. MacMullen, *Paganism in the Roman Empire* (New Haven, 1981), 18–48.
37. *C.Th.* 16.2.42.
38. Didymus: Soc. *HE* 4.25; Soz. *HE* 3.15; Rufinus *HE* 2.7; Palladius *Hist. Laus.* 4. If the catechetical school indeed lasted until the time of Didymus, the Origenist tendencies of the great teacher certainly would have spelled the end to this institution by the time of Theophilus. An earlier date for its demise is posited by G. Bardy, "Pour l'histoire de l'école d'Alexandrie," *Vivre et Penser* (= *RevBib*) 2 (1942): 80–109.

    Ammonius: *PLRE* 2.71–72; L. G. Westerink, *Anonymous Prolegomena to Platonic Philosophy* (Amsterdam, 1962), x–xiii. Elias and David: *PLRE* 3a.389, 438; Westerink, xx–xxiv.
39. Theodore: Jo. Moschus *Prat. Spir.* 171; cf. 77. Zach. Mytil. *v. Sev.* (ed. and trans. Kugener), p. 12 (cf. p. 43 for the conversion of John the Sophist).
40. Zach. Mytil. *v. Sev.* (ed. and trans. Kugener), p. 24.
41. Jo. Moschus *Prat. Spir.* 172.
42. Aristocrats in mid-third-century persecutions: Eus. *HE* 6.41.11; 7.11.24. Philoromus: Eus. *HE* 8.9.6–7. See also *PLRE* 1.698; T. D. Barnes, *The New Empire of Diocletian and Constantine* (Cambridge, Mass., 1982), 183. Dorothea: Eus. *HE* 8.14.15–16. Her name is supplied by Rufinus, in his version of Eusebius.
43. Eus. *HE* 6.2.13–14.; Jo. Moschus *Prat. Spir.* 75; *Apoph. Patr.* Systematic Coll. 237; *Canons of Athanasius* 103, 104 (ed. and trans. Riedel and Crum).
44. Palladius *Hist. Laus.* 21.2–4.
45. Paesius and Isaias: Palladius *Hist. Laus.* 14.1, 3. Cf. the fifth-century widow Peristeria, who directed in her will that vast sums of gold be given to "the monasteries, as well as to the hostels, hospitals, and the poor people of Egypt [*kai tois xeneōsi kai ptōcheiois kai heterois penēsi tēs Aiguptiakēs chōras*]"—[libellus of Ischyrion] *ACO* 2.1.2.51. Almsgiving banker: Leont. N. *v. Jo. Eleem.* 38. Quantities of gold: *Apoph. Patr.*

Anon. Coll. 47; Leont. N. v. *Jo. Eleem.* 11. One landowner, who sought to receive a clerical office from John the Almsgiver, offered as a bribe 200,000 bushels of grain and 180 pounds of gold (Leont. N. v. *Jo. Eleem.* 13).

46. Constantius's threats: Athan. *Ep. Ency.* 4; *Hist. Ar.* 31, 48–49, 54. Bouleutai and notarius in 365: *Hist. Aceph.* 5.1–7; Soz. *HE* 6.12.
47. Expulsion of Lucius: *Hist. Aceph.* 5.11–13. Diogenes: *Hist. Aceph.* 1.9.
48. Peter Mongus: Zach. Mytil. v. *Sev.* (ed. and trans. Kugener), pp. 33–35. Aristocrats and patriarchal elections: *History of the Patriarchs* 1.6 (ed. Evetts), p. 400 [136]; 1.13, p. 456 [192]; 1.14, 478–79 [214–15]; John of Nikiu *Chron.* 78.42–44 (trans. Charles); Evagrius *HE* 2.9; Athan. *ep. Ency.* 2; *Apol. ad Constant.* 28.
49. *thumelikais kai theatrikois heterois prosōpois,* in the [libellus of Ischyrion] *ACO* 2.1.2.51.
50. Both groups are listed in a revealing inventory of offices and persons connected with the church of Oxyrhynchus, dating to the late sixth or early seventh century. This list, which designates recipients of a wine distribution, does not appear to be in any hierarchical order. The parabalani are listed after the gravediggers, but before the readers. The philoponoi follow the readers: *P.Iand* 8.154.
51. *C.Th.* 16.2.42. Their function as hospital attendants is spelled out in *C. Th.* 16.2.43, which describes them as those "assigned to care for the suffering bodies of the sick" (*qui ad curanda debilium aegra corpora deputantur*) and "are experienced in the practice of healing" (*qui pro consuetudine curandi gerunt experientiam,* trans. Pharr). For modern literature, see A. Philipsborn, "La compagnie d'ambulanciers 'parabalani' d'Alexandrie," *Byzantion* 20 (1950): 185–90; W. Schubart, "Parabalani," *JEA* 40 (1954): 97–101; J. Rougé, "Les débuts de l'épiscopat de Cyrille d'Alexandrie et le *Code Théodosien,*" in *Alexandrina: Hellénisme, judaïsme et christianisme à Alexandrie, Mélanges offerts au P. Claude Mondésert* (Paris, 1987), 339–49.
52. In a law promulgated less than two years later, the number of parabalani was increased to six hundred and all attempts at placing them under secular authority were abandoned. Henceforth, they "shall be subservient to the commands and regulations of the most reverend priest [i.e., the patriarch] and shall continue under his supervision." *C.Th.* 16.2.43.
53. *Quibus neque ad quodlibet publicam spectaculum neque ad curia locum neque ad iudicium adcedendi licentiam permittimus.*
54. Parabalani at Ephesus: *ACO* 2.1.1.176. Danger of hospital work: noted in *The Oxford Dictionary of Byzantium* (New York, 1991), s.v. "Parabalani," by T. E. Gregory. Libellus of Ischyrion: *ACO* 2.1.2.51.
55. Zach. Mytil. v. *Sev.* (ed. and trans. Kugener), pp. 12, 24. In many

respects, the philoponoi differed very little from the more widely attested *spoudaioi* ("zealous ones"); cf. *Canons of Athanasius* 93 (ed. and trans. Riedel and Crum). Although the philoponoi are not attested as profusely in legal texts as the parabalani, this is more than made up for by the narrative of Zachariah of Mytilene's *vita Severi*. While studying In Alexandria during the 480s with Severus of Antioch, Zachariah and many of his fellow students joined the philoponoi, thereby providing a vivid window on the inner life of this group. A thoroughgoing analysis which catalogs documentary evidence from the chora may be found in E. Wipszycka, "Les confréries dans la vie religieuse de l'Égypte chrétienne," in *Proceedings of the Twelfth International Congress of Papyrology* (Toronto, 1970), 511–25; idem, "Confraternity," in *CoptEncy* 2:586–88. See also S. Pétridès, "Spoudaei et Philopones," *Echoes d'Orient* 7 (1904): 341–48; P. J. Sijpesteijn, "New Light on the *Philoponoi*," *Aegyptus* 69 (1989): 95–99. The broader topic of lay confraternities is ably surveyed by P. Horden, "The Confraternities of Byzantium," in *Voluntary Religion*, ed. W. J. Sheils and D. Wood, Studies in Church History, vol. 23 (Oxford, 1986), 25–45.

56. Menas: Zach. Mytil. *v. Sev.* (ed. and trans. Kugener), p. 12. Charitable work of *philoponoi*: Soph. H. *mir. Cyr. et Jo.* 5 (*PG* 87.3, col. 3432c). Dialogue with patriarchs: Leont. N. *v. Jo. Eleem.* 19; Geo. Al. *v. Chrys.* 41 (in *S. Joannis Chrysostomi Opera*, ed. H. Savile [Etonae, 1613], 8:217.25).

    Philoponoi as lay representatives: illustrated by a late (10th century) text which claims to relate an incident from the episcopate of Demetrius (189–231). The bishop was admonished by an angel in a dream to repent before "the clergy and the *philoponoi*" for keeping a wife after his elevation to the patriarchal throne, "The Encomium of Flavianus, bishop of Ephesus, on Demetrius, bishop of Alexandria," BM.MS.O.6783 fol. 35b, in *Coptic Martyrdoms in the Dialect of Upper Egypt*, ed. and trans. E. A. Wallis Budge (London, 1914), 143.

57. Though there is also the possibility that the name was given to John as a testimony to his intellectual zeal and industry. Modern authorities on both sides of the issue are enumerated in R. Sorabji, "John Philoponus," in *Philoponus and the Rejection of Aristotelian Science*, ed. R. Sorabji (Ithaca, N.Y., 1987), 4–6. See also R. A. Kaster, *Guardians of Language* (Berkeley, 1988), 334–38.

58. Leaders of *philoponoi*: "Martyrdom of Saint Mercurius the General," BM.MS.O.6801 fol. 20a, in *Miscellaneous Coptic Texts in the Dialect of Upper Egypt*, ed and trans. E. A. Wallis Budge (London, 1915), 277; T. Orlandi, *Storia della Chiesa di Alessandria* (Milan, 1968), 1:46, line 16. *Philoponion*: Sophr. H. *mir. Cyr. et Jo.* (*PG* 87) cols. 3432, 3544, 3628. Whenever a *philoponion* is mentioned in later documentary

texts, it seems to refer to a building which has evolved into a monastic house. See the discussion, with full references, in Wipszycka, "Confréries," 517–19. Hierarchy within philoponoi: Zach. Mytil. *v. Sev.* (ed. and trans. Kugener), 26, 56.

59. L. Clugnet, "Vies et récits d'anachorètes, II: Textes grecs inédits extraits du Ms. Grec de Paris 1596," *Revue de l'orient chrétien* 1 (1905): 47–48.
60. Stephen: Zach. Mytil. *v. Sev.* (ed. and trans. Kugener), p. 39. Conversion of fellow townsmen: cf. Severus of Antioch's "Discourse on the Compassion of God and on the Archangel Michael," BM.MS.O.7597 fol. 30a, in Budge, *Coptic Texts in the Dialect of Upper Egypt,* 174. *Agōnistai*: Zach. Mytil. *v. Sev.* p. 26. Berytus: Zach. Mytil. *v. Sev.* 57–75.
61. Zach. Mytil. *v. Sev.* (ed. and trans. Kugener), 23–24; Aug. *Conf.* 3.6, 5.14. Cf. Libanius's description of student rowdies in Antioch: *Or.* 58.4–5.
62. Zach. Mytil. *v. Sev.* (ed. and trans. Kugener), 26–27.
63. Opposition to emperor and magistrates: *Hist. Aceph.* 5.1–3. Athanasius: "A document was then read, containing popular complaints [*kai grammateion aneginōsketo dēmotikōn ekboēseō*] that the people of Alexandria could not continue their attendance at church on his account," Soz. *HE* 2.25 (*PG* 67, col. 1004a). Defense of prefect: Soc. *HE* 7.14.
64. Zach. Mytil. *HE* 4.3.
65. Consent of populace: mentioned explicitly at the elevation of Theodosius I in 535, *History of the Patriarchs* 1.13 (ed. Evetts), p. 456 [192]. Dioscorus II: Theophanes *Chron.* AM 6009. Acclamations: Athan. *Apol. c. Ar.* 6. Denuncuations: *History of the Patriarchs* 1.13 (ed. Evetts), p. 466 [202]. Lucius: *Hist. Aceph.* 5.13.
66. Peter I: *M. Petr. Al.* 2–3, in P. Devos, "Une passion grecque inédite de S. Pierre d'Alexandria et sa traduction par Anastase le Bibliothécaire," *AnBol* 83 (1965): 157–87, trans. T. Vivian. Nearly two hundred and fifty years later, the Alexandrian laity responded in an almost identical manner to the expulsion of Theodosius, and cried out to the authorities, "Why hast thou removed the good shepherd Theodosius from us?" *History of the Patriarchs* 1.13 (ed. Evetts), p. 459 [195]. Athanasius: Soz. *HE* 6.12; *Hist. Aceph.* 1.8, 5.2; Athan. *Apol. ad Constant.* 24. Chants forwarded to emperor: *C.Th.* 8.5.32. Cf. *History of the Patriarchs* 1.13 (ed. Evetts), p. 459 [195]: "Then the governor was afraid of them, and dreaded lest the affair should be reported to the prince; and so he sent Gaianus, the heretic, out of the city."
67. This stance hardly constitutes an anti-imperial "nationalism," since it also explains the populace's vigorous defense of the prefect Orestes against a band of seditious monks who had come into the city at the behest of Cyril (Soc *HE* 7.14).
68. Popular agitation in 458: Evagrius *HE* 2.9. Imperial sanctions: Priscus

of Panium fr. 28 (Evagrius *HE* 2.5) in R. C. Blockley, *The Fragmentary Classicising Historians of the Later Roman Empire* (Liverpool, 1983), 2:325; *History of the Patriarchs* 1.13 (ed. Evetts), 466–67 [202–3].

69. *Hist. Aceph.* 5.11–13; Zach. Mytil. *HE* 5.5. While all three of these bishops had doctrinal points against them (at least in the eyes of the Alexandrians), other bishops like Gregory of Cappadocia (4th century) or John the Almsgiver (7th century) were able to maintain their position despite their identification with theological views deemed heterodox by most Alexandrians.
70. John of Nikiu *Chron.* 120.14–16 (trans. Charles).
71. *M. Petr. Al.* 17, in Devos, "Une passion grecque inédite," 157–87, trans. T. Vivian.
72. *History of the Patriarchs* 1.13 (ed. Evetts), p. 456 [192].

*Chapter Eight. Community and Factionalism in the Christian Community*

1. *History of the Patriarchs* 1.13 (ed. Evetts), p. 456 [192].
2. Burial of bishops: *M. Petr. Al.* 13, 18; Alexander Al. *Encom. Petr. Al.*, Coptic text in H. Hyvernant, *Les actes des martyrs de l'Égypte* (Hildesheim, 1977), 247. Theophilus and Timothy I: *P.Goleniscev* 6 recto, published in A. Bauer and J. Strygowski, "Eine alexandrinische Weltchronik," *Denkschriften der Kaiserlichen Akademie der Wissenschaften: Wien* 51.2 (1906): 1–204. See also M. Krause, "Mummification," in *CoptEncy* 6:1696–98. Ivory of Saint Mark: Louvre OA.3317. A discussion with bibliography may be found in W. F. Volbach, *Elfenbeinarbeiten der Spätantike* (Mainz, 1976), 96, no. 144.
3. Ordination: *History of the Patriarchs* 1.11, 12 (ed. Evetts), 427, 430 [163, 166]; *M. Petr. Al.*, Latin text in W. Tefler, "St. Peter of Alexandria and Arius," *AnBol* 67 (1949): 128; *Canons of Athanasius* 5, 10, 17, 52 (ed. and trans. Riedel and Crum).

   List of clergy: at the third session of the Council of Chalcedon, the priest Athanasius complained that Dioscorus had "deprived me of the priesthood and has excluded me from the ecclesiastical hierarchy [*tou ekklēsiastikou katalogou*—literally "list"), without having produced any accusation against me." *ACO* 2.1.2.57. Cf. the letter of Constantius to the Alexandrians, wherein the emperor refers to "all those of the sacred register" (*pantas tous tou hierou katalogou*), in Athan. *Apol.Sec.* 54.

   Ratification of orthodoxy and obedience: *Canons of Athanasius* 18; Sophr. H. *v. Jo. Eleem.* 5; *History of the Patriarchs* 1.13, 460–61 [196–97].
4. Petr. Al. *Ep. Can.* (*PG* 18, cols. 467–508).
5. Athanasius and coercion: Epiph. *Haer.* 68.7.5, 69.11.7; *P.Lond.* 1914.

A catalog of the charges against Athanasius put forward at the Council of Tyre is contained in Soz. *HE* 1.25. All the more ironic, then, is Athanasius's assertion that "the truth is not preached with swords or with arrows, nor be means of soldiers; but by persuasion and counsel," in Athan. *Hist. Ar.* 33.

Later patriarchs: Soz. *HE* 8.12; *History of the Patriarchs* 1.12 (ed. Evetts), p. 437 [173]; Soc. *HE* 7.7; *ACO* 2.1.2.38–64; Evagrius *HE* 3.22; Zach. Mytil. *HE* 6.1. *Ekklēsiekdikoi*: Leont. N. *v. Jo. Eleem.* 24, 37, 38.

Judicial violence: R. MacMullen, "Judicial Savagery in the Roman Empire," *Chiron* 16 (1986): 43–62, reprinted in *Changes in the Roman Empire* (Princeton, 1990), 204–17; idem, *Corruption and the Decline of Rome* (New Haven, 1988), 137–42; P. Brown, *Power and Persuasion in Late Antiquity* (Madison, 1992), 50–54. As Brown describes this propensity toward judicial violence, "a tide of horror lapped close to the feet of all educated persons" (52).

6. Bishops and sacraments: Jo. Moschus *Prat. Spir.* 207; *History of the Patriarchs* 1.6 (ed. Evetts), p. 387 [123], 1.11, p. 427 [163]. Bishops and relics: John of Nikiu *Chron.* 78.42–47, 120.12–13 (trans. Charles); *History of the Patriarchs* 1.8, p. 419 [155]; Jo. Moschus *Prat. Spir.* 146.
7. This important transformation of late antique urban life is portrayed in vivid terms by Brown, *Power and Persuasion,* 78–117.
8. Wealth of patriarch: Leont. N. *v. Jo. Eleem.* 13, 28, 45; Gregory *Regist.epist.* 6.58, 8.28, 9.175, 10.21. John's gifts to Modestus: Leont. N. *v. Jo. Eleem.* 20. Sophronius adds that John also contributed quantities of oil, clothing, and pack animals: Sophr. H. *v. Jo. Eleem.* 9.
9. Cyril's *eulogiae*: Cyril *Ep.* 96; letter of Archdeacon Epiphanius, text in *ACO* 1.4.293, trans. by J. I. McEnerney, *St. Cyril of Alexandria: Letters 51–100,* FOTC 77 (Washington, D.C., 1987), 188–92. Discussion in Brown, *Power and Persuasion,* 15–17; P. Batiffol, "Les présents de Saint Cyrille à la cour de Constantinople," *Bulletin d'ancienne littérature et d'archéologie chrétienne* 1 (1911): 247–64. Theophilus: Palladius *Dial. J. Chrys* 8 (trans. Meyer). Athanasius: *Apol. c. Ar.* 9.
10. Soz. *HE* 6.12; *ACO* 2.1.2.57. Notwithstanding the declaration of John the Almsgiver that "the property of humble John has never amounted to more than this one coin," the revenues he possessed from his ancestral lands on Cyprus must have been considerable: Leont. N. *v. Jo. Eleem.* 45; Sophron. H. *v. Jo. Eleem.* 2; *Anth. Pal.* 7.679.
11. Exemptions for clergy: Eus. *HE* 10.7.2. Church as conduit for subsidies: Athan. *Apol. c. Ar.* 18.2, 60.2; Soc. *HE* 1.27; Soz. *HE* 1.22.

Tithes and revenues from chora: as but one example, a monastic community near Arsinöe in the Fayyūm was famous for sending entire boatloads of clothing and grain down the Nile for the patriarch to distribute among the poor in Alexandria: *Hist. Monach.* 18.1–2; cf. Leont. N. *v. Jo. Eleem.* 45. The evidence is collected and analyzed in E. Wipszycka, *Les resources et les activités économiques des églises en Égypte du IVe au VIIIe siècle,* Papyrologica Bruxellensia, no. 10 (Brussels, 1972); R. Monks, "The Church of Alexandria and the City's Economic Life in the Sixth Century," *Speculum* 28 (1953): 349–62.

Legacies: Soz. *HE* 8.12; Leont. N. *v. Jo. Eleem.* 11; *ACO* 2.1.2.57. "Gifts" for offices: Gregory *Regist. epist.* 13.44. John and simony: Leont. N. *v. Jo. Eleem.* 5, 13.

12. *Canons of Athanasius* 89 (ed. and trans. Riedel and Crum); Athan. *Ep. Ency.* 4. John refers to his large money chest as "the storeroom of Christ" (*apothēkē tou Christou*); see Leont. N. *v. Jo. Eleem.* 12.
13. Alexander Al. *Encom. Petr. Al.* 250–51 (the text itself is from the sixth or seventh century and may reflect later practice); Leont. N. *v. Jo. Eleem.* 5, 9, 31; *History of the Patriarchs* 1.6 (ed. Evetts), p. 387 [123]; cf. 1.8, 407–8 [143–44]. The ease with which the future lector Theodore gained an interview with Athanasius may speak more of Theodore's social rank than of the bishop's accessibility: *S. Pachomii vita bohairice scripta* 89.
14. *ACO* 2.1.2.47, 51, 57.
15. *Canons of Athanasius* 14, 15, 47, 80 (ed. and trans. Riedel and Crum).
16. Leont. N. *v. Jo. Eleem.* 2. "A bishop shall not be any Sunday without almsgiving. And the poor and orphans shall he know as doth a father, and shall gather them together at the great festival of the Lord [Pascha], vowing and distributing much alms and giving unto each whereof he hath need. And at the feast of Pentecost he shall refresh all the people. . . . And on the feast of the Lord's Epiphany, which was in the month Tūbah, that is the feast of Baptism, they shall rejoice with them. The bishop shall gather all the widows and orphans and shall rejoice with them, with prayers and hymns, and shall give unto each according to his needs; for it is a day of blessing. . . . God hath established the bishop because of the feasts, that he may refresh them at the feasts. For thus is God merciful and would not that any of mankind should suffer." *Canons of Athanasius* 16 (ed. and trans. Riedel and Crum).
17. Patriarchal charity: Leont. N. *v. Jo. Eleem.* 2, 7. These gifts are bestowed in the context of a "daily distribution" (*diadosis*), probably a nontechnical designation as it is also used frequently with reference to eucharistic bread. Bishops and grain dole: Soc. *HE* 1.35, 2.17; Athan. *Apol. c. Ar.* 18, *Ep. Ency.* 4, *Apol. de Fuga.* 6, *Hist. Ar.* 31; *ACO* 2.1.2.51; *Canons of Athanasius* 89.
18. Eus. *HE* 7.22; Palladius *Hist. Laus.* 6.5–9; *ACO* 2.1.2.51; Sophr. H. *v. Jo. Eleem.* 6, 7, 9; Leont. N. *v. Jo. Eleem.* 7, 11, 27, 45. Another method

John employed to display his concern for the sick was to go out of his way to visit the city's hospitals two or three times a week: Leont. N. *v. Jo. Eleem.* 9.

19. Monophysite and Chalcedonian "gifts": Zach. Mytil. *HE* 3.3; *History of the Patriarchs* 1.13 (ed. Evetts), 456–57 [192–93], 1.14, p. 491, [227]; John of Nikiu *Chron.* 92.10 (trans. Charles). Apollinaris: Jo. Moschus *Prat. Spir.* 193; cf. Leont. N. *v. Jo. Eleem.* 30.
20. Athan. *Ep. Ency.* 5, *Hist. Ar.* 81; Soc. *HE* 6.15; Soz. *HE* 8.17; Palladius *Dial. J. Chrys* 6, 8; *ACO* 1.1.5; Evagrius *HE* 2.9; Leont. N. *v. Jo. Eleem.* 11, 21, 35 (twenty pounds of gold to a merchant in the Gallic trade), 10 (fifteen pounds of gold plus a cargo of grain).
21. *Apoph. Patr.* Anon. Coll. 47; Jo. Moschus *Prat. Spir.* 60, 75; Sophr. H. *v. Jo. Eleem.* 6; Leont. N. *v. Jo. Eleem.* 11.
22. Palladius *Hist. Laus.* 14.1, 3; Jo. Moschus *Prat. Spir.* 207; Leont. N. *v. Jo. Eleem.* 1, 11, 38.

    Isidore and Theophilus: Palladius *Dial. J. Chrys.* 6; Soz. *HE* 8.12. On these larger issues, see E. A. Clark, *The Origenist Controversy: The Cultural Construction of an Early Christian Debate* (Princeton, 1992), 37–60; J. H. W. G. Liebeschuetz, *Barbarians and Bishops: Army, Church, and State in the Age or Arcadius and Chrysostom* (Oxford, 1990), 157–208.

    Dioscorus: "No one is ignorant . . . of the affair of Peristeria of illustrious memory. As this one had set forth in her will, for the good of her soul, that very great sums of gold should be supplied to the monasteries, as well as to the hostels, hospitals and to the poor people of Egypt [*kai tois xeneōsi kai ptōcheiois kai heterois penēsi tēs Aiguptiakēs chēras*), this money—taken with violence from those who had been personally bequeathed it in the will—this very reverend one [Dioscorus] determined that it should be distributed, instead of as alms, to actresses and to the people of the theatre" [libellus of Ischyrion] *ACO* 2.1.2.51.
23. Athan. *Apol. c. Ar.* 9, *Apol. ad Constant.* 19. Letter of Constantius contained in Athan. *Apol. ad Constant.* 30.
24. Soc. *HE* 7.6—speaking of Cyril.
25. *hōsanei idiou ktēmatos autou ousēs,* in [libellus of Ischyrion] *ACO* 2.1.2.51. Leont. N. *v. Jo. Eleem.* 3, 13, 16, 39.
26. Diversion of grain: Athan. *Apol. c. Ar.* 9; *ACO* 2.1.2.51. Removal of imperial portraits: [libellus of layman Sophronius] *ACO* 2.1.2.64. Support of usurpers: Soc. *HE* 2.26, 6.2; Athan. *Apol. ad Constant.* 6; Petr. Patr. fr. 16 in *FHG* 4:184–91; John of Nikiu *Chron.* 105.2–3 (trans. Charles). John's vision: Leont. N. *v. Jo. Eleem.* 44b. Cf. Constantine VII *de Ceremoniis* 1.60 and Gelzer's commentary on this passage in Leontius.

27. Eus. *HE* 6.2.13–14.
28. Evagrius *HE* 2.5; *M. Petr. Al.*, Latin text in Tefler, "St. Peter of Alexandria and Arius," 127; Athan. *Hist. Ar.* 10, 19, 31; *Hist. Aceph.* 1.9, 5, 1–7; *Festal Index* 32; Soz. *HE* 6.12; *History of the Patriarchs* 1.13 (ed. Evetts), p. 457 [193]. John: "And Apollinaris bishop of the Chalcedonians died in Alexandria, and a man, named John, an ex-military man, was appointed in his stead. And he had a goodly presence and forced none to forsake his faith. But he glorified God in His Church in the midst of all the assembled people, and they gave thanks to the emperor for the noble acts he had done." John of Nikiu *Chron.* 94.24 (trans. Charles).
29. R. Bagnall, *Egypt in Late Antiquity* (Princeton, 1993), 148–80.
30. *S. Pachomii vita bohairice scripta* 201 (trans. Vielleux).
31. In fact, several stories in the *Apoph. Patr.* seem to take great delight in recounting the various sins of bishops (e.g., *Apoph. Patr.* Anon. Coll. 70).
32. To this interpretation, it may be objected that many of the monks of late antique Egypt were, in fact, transplanted townsmen. This was especially the case with the monks of Alexandria's suburban monasteries. Hagiographical sources and papyri detail the monks' numerous ties with their hometowns. Moreover, as the Anthropomorphite and Chalcedonian controversies demonstrated, some of the monks possessed considerable erudition. Nonetheless, the ideology of the desert demanded a certain renunciation of urban values, to say nothing of urban comforts. The monastic vision was profoundly antiurban, perhaps expressing more the sentiments of alienated townsmen than any deep-seated rural opinions. While this may temper any wooden urban-rural dichotomy, it is still possible to speak of monasticism as largely a rural phenomenon. This representation of monasticism as antiurban permeated the multifaceted relations between the monks and their urban contemporaries.
33. Athan. *v. Ant.* 91. Even the best-intentioned patriarch could be rebuffed in his attempt to establish ties with the monks. In 329/30 Pachomius went into hiding to avoid seeing Athanasius (*S. Pachomii vita bohairice scripta* 28)—a tradition followed by many hermits who fled from recognition by the great and powerful (*Apoph. Patr.* Moses 8, Arsenius 31; Palladius *Hist. Laus.* 34.2–4). This compulsion to flight was all the more pressing when the hermit was being sought for ordination (Palladius *Hist. Laus.* 11.1–2).

    A body of anecdotes later grew up about ascetics who snubbed Theophilus. Two of the most striking: "Blessed Archbishop Theophilus, accompanied by a magistrate, came one day to find Abba Arsenius. He questioned the old man to hear a word from him. After a short silence the old man answered him, 'Will you put into practice what I say to you' They promised him this. 'If you hear Arsenius is anywhere, do not go there'" (*Apoph. Patr.* Arsenius 7). "The same Abba Theophilus, the archbishop, came to Scetis one day. The brethren who were assembled said to Abba Pambo, 'Say something to the archbishop, so that he may be edified.' The old man said to them, 'If he is not edified by my silence, he will not be edified by my speech'" (*Apoph. Patr.* Theophilus 2). See also T. Orlandi, "Theophilus of Alexandria in Coptic Literature," *Studia Patristica* 16 (1985): 100–4.

34. From the monastic standpoint, the worst of the Arian bishops was Lucius, who contested the see with Athanasius and his successor, Peter II. Though remaining in Alexandria, Lucius determined to break monastic opposition to him by sending troops to Nitria. The scenes that followed were predictably violent, with many ascetics wounded in the fray, and others forcibly expelled from their monastic retreats (Rufinus *HE* 2.3–4; Soc. *HE* 4.24; Soz. *HE* 6.20; Jerome *Chron.* anno 379). In light of these circumstances, it is no wonder that a hermit named Moses the Saracen refused ordination "by Lucius laying his hand upon me, for it has been filled with blood" (Soc. *HE* 4.36). On this persecution and its effects on the monks of the desert, see H. G. Evelyn White, ed., *Monasteries of the Wadi 'n Natrūn,* vol. 2, *New Coptic Texts from the Monastery of Saint Macarius,* Metropolitan Museum of Art Egyptian Expedition Publications (New York, 1926), 77–83.

35. Theophilus: see n. 32, and *Apoph. Patr.* Theophilus 3, where the patriarch induces some unsuspecting monks to eat meat contrary to their rule of life. Peter Mongus: in late 477, Peter withdrew before the introduction of troops in the city, who forcibly reinstated the imperial appointee, Timothy Salophaciolos. Rather than find a monastic retreat upriver (the usual method in such circumstances), Timothy went into hiding within the city, "moving about from one house to another" (Zach. Mytil. *HE* 5.5).

36. Zach. Mytil. *HE.* 5.9; 6.1–2; Evagrius *HE* 3.16, 22.

    John Moschus serves as another important witness of the gulf which could open up between urban ecclesiastics and rural ascetics. He and his associate Sophronius were Chalcedonians, and as such, they remained within the restricted boundaries of the Melkite patriarch's authority. Consequently, these eager tourists of asceticism stayed in Alexandria and only ventured out as far as a few of the suburban monasteries which were firmly under the Chalcedonian patriarch's control. The rigidity of the confessional boundary between Monophysite and Chalcedonian is cast in high relief by the fact that Moschus, for all his fascination with the ascetical life, completely shunned the great monastic center of Nitria—little more than a day's journey from Alexandria.

37. Cyril: in contrast to Theophilus, Cyril is favorably regarded in the *Apophthegmata Patrum*. He is praised for his spiritual discernment, and on one occasion, for his "guile" in leading an elderly and respected ascetic out of a false interpretation of the Old Testament priest/king, Melchizedek (*Apoph. Patr.* Anon. Coll. 70; *Apoph. Patr.* Daniel 8). This high regard was probably a product of Cyril's own ascetical training at Nitria and his extraordinary knowledge of the Scriptures (*History of the Patriarchs* 1.11, p. 427 [163]).

    Patriarchal residence at Enaton: *History of the Patriarchs* 1.13–14, 470–74 [206–10]. At Saint Macarius: Eutychius (Saʿid ibn al-Batriq) *Annales* 156 (*PG* 111, cols. 169d–70a). By the time John Moschus and Sophronius (both Chalcedonians) visited Enaton in the early seventh century, the resident monks no longer appeared to be Monophysites. See also the extended discussion in Evelyn/White, *Monasteries of the Wadi 'n Natrūn,* 2:236–39.

38. Urban asceticism: *S. Pachomii vita bohairice scripta* 89; *Storia della Chiesa di Alessandria,* ed. and trans. T. Orlandi (Milan, 1968–70), 1:66–67, 2:61–62; Palladius *Hist. Laus.* 21.6; *Apoph. Patr.* Systematic Coll. 237; Serapion of Thumis *Ep. ad Monachos* (*PG* 40, cols. 923–42); John Moschus *Prat. Spir.* 60, 73, 75, 105, 106, 171, 172. On the topos of desert withdrawal, see J. E. Goehring, "The Encroaching Desert: Literary Production and Ascetic Space in Early Christian Egypt," *JECS* 1.3 (1993): 281–96. On the cultural context of the ascetical movement in Alexandria, see J. A. McGuckin, "Christian Asceticism and the Early School of Alexandria," *Studies in Church History* 22 (1985): 25–39. The relationship between the suburban monasteries and the city's religious history is surveyed in the excellent study by E. Wipszycka, "Le monachisme égyptien et les villes," *Travaux et memoires* 12 (1994): 1–44, a work that appeared too late for me to profit by in these pages.

    Dorotheus: Palladius *Hist. Laus.* 2.2. Earlier use of Alexandrian cemeteries: Eus. *HE* 7.10. Monastic re-use of cemeteries: Palladius *Hist. Laus.* 5.1, 7.1; *Hist. Monach.* 1.37–44. See also R.-G. Coquin and M. Martin, "Monasteries in and around Alexandria," in *CoptEncy* 5: 1645–46. One small group of late antique structures, possibly monastic, was excavated in the region of Sidi Bishr, approximately halfway between Alexandria and Canopus: W. A. Daszewski, H. el Sheikh, and S. Medeksza, "An Unknown Christian Complex at Alexandria," in *Coptic Studies,* ed. W. Godlewski (Warsaw, 1990), 87–105.

39. An unnamed ascetic inhabited a cell for many years near the military camp at Nicopolis (*Apoph. Patr.* Systematic Coll. 237). Arsenius at Canopus: *Apoph. Patr.* Arsenius 28, 42.

A pagan reaction to monks and relics at Canopus: "They settled these monks at Canopus also, and thus they fettered the human race to the worship of slaves, and those not even honest slaves, instead of the true gods. For they collected the bones and skulls of criminals who had been put to death for numerous crimes, men whom the lawcourts of the city had condemned to punishment, made them out to be gods, haunted their sepulchers, and thought that they became better by defiling themselves at their graves." Eunapius *V. Soph.* 472.

40. J. B. Ward-Perkins identified this monastery within the enclosure walls of the Ptolemaic temple at Taposiris Magna, "The Monastery of Taposiris Magna," *BSAA* 36 (1945): 48–53. M. Rodziewicz has kindly pointed out to me that this identification should be called into question by comparing the purported monastery's architecture with recent excavations of similar structures in both Alexandria and in the Mareotis region which are undoubtedly domestic in nature. More likely sites for the monastic community include a church just to the west of Taposiris Magna, and a church discovered in 1990 situated in the southeastern section of Taposiris Magna itself. See P. Grossmann, "Die Kirche extra muros von Taposiris Magna," *Mitteilungen des Deutschen Archäoligischen Instituts Kairo* 38 (1982): 152–54; idem, "A New Church at Taposiris Magna-Abusir," *Bulletin de la Société d'archéologie copte* 21 (1992): 25–30; M. Rodziewicz, "Remarks on the Peristyle House in Alexandria and Mareotis," in *Papers of the Twelfth International Congress for Classical Archaeology in Athens* (Athens, 1983).
41. Enaton: among its more frequently mentioned leaders are Lucius and Longinus, both of the fourth century, and Salomon of the fifth century. (Lucius and Longinus appear in the *Apoph. Patr.* and Salomon in Zach. Mytil.*v. Sev.*, ed. Kugener, *PO* 2 [Paris, 1907], 14–35). John Climacus (ca. 600) recounted his memorable sojourn at Enaton in his *Scala Paradisi* 4.20–39. See also Jo. Moschus *Prat. Spir.* 145, 146, 171, 178.
42. Anthony and Athanasius: Athan. *v. Ant.* 69–71. Several years later, Flavian of Antioch followed an identical policy by persuading a desert ascetic named Julianus to denounce Arianism publicly in Antioch (Theodoret *HE* 4.24). See G. J. M. Bartelink, "Les rapports entre le monachisme égyptiene et l'épiscopat d'Alexandrie," in *Alexandrina: Hellénisme, judaïsme et christianisme à Alexandrie, Mélanges offerts au P. Claude Mondésert,* (Paris, 1987), 351–63; D. Brakke, *Athanasius and the Politics of Asceticism* (Oxford, 1995); and C. Kannengiesser, "Athanasius of Alexandria and the Ascetic Movement of His Time," in *Asceticism,* ed. V. Wimbush and R. Valantasis (New York, 1995), 479–92.

    Pambo in Alexandria: *Apoph. Patr.* Pambo 4. Conduct of monks: *Canons of Athanasius* 49, 92 (ed. and trans. Riedel and Crum).
43. *Apoph. Patr.* Theophilus 3. In his account of the Tall Brothers, Socrates

Scholasticus relates: "They were moreover distinguished both for the sanctity of their lives and the extent of their erudition, and for these reasons their reputation was very high at Alexandria. Theophilus in particular, the prelate of that city, loved and honored them exceedingly; insomuch that he constituted one of them Dioscorus, bishop of Hermopolis against his will, having forcibly drawn him from his retreat. Two of the others he entreated to continue with him, and with difficulty prevailed upon them to do so; still by the exercise of his authority as bishop he accomplished his purpose" (Soc. *HE* 6.7, trans. Zenos).

Isidore: Soc. *HE* 6.2, 9; Jerome *in Johannem* 37 (*PL* 23, col. 390).

44. Cassian *Coll.* 10.2. The episode in Alexandria is recounted by Soc. *HE* 6.7.
45. Soc. *HE* 6.7 (trans. Zenos).
46. Soz. *HE* 8.9; *C.Th* 12.1.63; 16.3.1–2; *C.I.* 1.3.22, 26, 29. Marcian's formulary was addressed to the sixth session of the Council of Chalcedon and was adopted as part of Canon 4, Mansi, vol. 7. 174–78.
47. Orestes and the monks: Soc. *HE* 7.14. Perhaps Cyril attempted to counterbalance monastic influence through his cultivation and deployment of parabalani. Letter of Marcian: Mansi, vol. 7. 481–84.
48. From the "Life of Timothy Aelurus" in Evelyn White, *Monasteries of Wadi 'n Natrūn,* 2:165.

    This alliance was first brought together during the patriarchate of the imperial appointee, Proterius: "the priests, and the monks, and many of the people, perceiving that the faith had been polluted, both by the unjust deposition of Dioscorus and the oppressive conduct of Proterius and his wickedness, assembled by themselves in the monasteries, and severed themselves from his communion" (Zach. Mytil. *HE* 3.2).
49. Soz. *HE* 4.10; Theodoret *HE* 4.18; *S. Pachomii vita bohairice scripta* 89; Soc. *HE* 7.14; Zach. Mytil. *HE* 6.2.
50. The following is a revised version of a study first presented to the 1991 Byzantine Studies Conference and subsequently published in *Vig.Chr.* 47 (1993): 234–45.
51. J. M. Leroux, "Athanase et la seconde phase de la crise arienne (345–73)," in *Politique et théologie chez Athanase d'Alexandrie,* ed. C. Kannengiesser (Paris, 1974), 145–56; and the valuable collection of articles in M. R. Barnes and D. H. Williams, eds., *Arianism after Arius* (Edinburgh, 1993). See also C. Stead, "Arius in Modern Research," *JTS,* n.s., 45.1 (1994): 24–36.
52. Epiph. *Haer.* 69.2.2–7; Athan. *Apol. ad Constant.* 15: *M. Petr. Al.* 16, in *AnBol* 83 (1965): 157–87; Soc. *HE* 2.11.6; *Hist. Aceph.* 2.3, 5.4.
53. Epiph. *Haer.* 69.1- 2; *Chron. Pasch.* 252 cols. 608c–9a; *M. Petr. Al.* 11.

R. Williams, *Arius: Heresy and Tradition* (London, 1987), 264, n. 107, suggests that the church in Baucalis derived its name from the Greek word for a wine or water cooler, and that the church was formerly used as a vintner's warehouse. Given the economic differentiation of Alexandria's topography, it seems more likely that vintners' warehouses would be located on the opposite side of the city, near the famous wine-growing regions of Taenia and Mareotis: Strabo 17.1.15; Pliny *HN* 14.74, 117; Virgil *Georg.* 2.91; Horace *Odes* 1.37; Athenaeus *Deipnosophistes* 1.33; *v. Jo. Eleem.* 10.

54. Palladius *Hist. Laus.* 15.1, 35.14–15; Cyril *Ep. Fest.* 8 (420); Achilles Tatius 3.15; Heliodorus 1.5–30; Cassius Dio 71.4. On the evolution of the *boukoloi* as a literary type, see J. Winkler, "Lollianos and the Desperadoes," *JHS* 100 (1980): 155–81, esp. 175–79.
55. Epiph. *Haer.* 69.1.2, 2.6.
56. Athan. *Hist. Ar.* 10.
57. Greg. Naz. *Or.* 21.16; Athan. *de Syn.* 12; *ad Episcopos* 7; *Hist. Ar.* 75.
58. Epiph. *Haer.* 76.1.5–7. An analogous relationship between urban topography and religious dissent is explored by H. O. Maier, "The Topography of Heresy and Dissent in Late-Fourth-Century Rome," *Historia* 44.2 (1995): 232–49.
59. *M. Petr. Al.* 11–14; Palladius *Hist. Laus.* 45. Thorough discussions of the traditions connecting Mark with Boukolou/Boukolia may be found in B. A. Pearson, "Earliest Christianity in Egypt: Some Observations," in *Roots of Egyptian Christianity,* ed. B. A. Pearson and J. E. Goehring (Philadelphia, 1986), 132–59; idem, "The *Acts of Mark* and the Topography of Ancient Alexandria," *BSAA* 45 (1993): 239–46. Ascetics at martyria: *Canons of Athanasius* 91–92, 98–99 (ed. and trans. Riedel and Crum). Destruction of Saint Mark's martyrium: *History of the Patriarchs* 1.14 (ed. Evetts), p. 495 [231].
60. *M. Petr. Al.* 14 indicates that Peter's executioners took him "from the south side of the commemorative chapel of the holy evangelist Mark, and stood him in a deep valley where there were tombs." On these cemeteries, see A. Bernand, *Alexandrie la Grande* (Paris, 1966), 210–16, 222–28.
61. Palladius *Hist. Laus.* 5.1, 15; Athan. *v. Ant.* 49.
62. Epiph. *Haer.* 69.3.1–2; letter of Alexander in Theodoret *HE* 1.3; letter of Athanasius in Theodoret *HE* 2.11; Libanius *Or.* 30.8; Rutilius Namatianus *de Reditu Suo* 439–52, 517–26.
63. Epiph. *Haer.* 69.11.7; cf. 68.7.5.
64. Soc. *HE* 1.6–7; Soz. *HE* 2.23, 25; Philostorgius *HE* 2.2.
65. Athan. *Ep. Ency.* 4; *Hist. Ar.* 31, 48–49, 54, 73; *Apol. ad Constant.* 28.
66. *Eukoloi*: Athan. *Hist. Ar.* 78 col. 788d.

    Aside from a strong pagan element among the bouleutai, the urban elite undoubtedly included some Homoousians since Athanasius himself mentions certain "well-born men" (*eugeneis andras*) who were persecuted during the Arian conflict in 339: Athan. *Ep. Ency*. 4 col. 232a.

67. Athan. *Hist. Ar*. 55–56.
68. Ibid. 73. Athanasius's attempt to portray these two groups of young Alexandrians as identical is demonstrably tendentious. It is more likely that upper-class Alexandrian youth exhibited the same religious inclinations as their aristocratic elders.
69. *Neoi*: for the Alexandrian evidence, see D. Delia, *Alexandrian Citizenship during the Roman Principate*, American Classical Studies, no. 23 (Atlanta, 1991), 71–88. Letter of Constantius: in Athan. *Hist. Ar*. 48. Massacre of youths in 215: Herodian 4.9.6–7; Cassius Dio 78.23.
70. Athan. *Ep. Ency*. 4; *Hist. Ar*. 13, 31, 54, 60–61, 72; *Apol. de Fuga*. 6; Evagrius *HE* 2.5.

    There are hints that other groups within Alexandrian society gave their allegiance to the Arian (or more precisely, the imperial) cause during the 340s and the 350s. Cryptic remarks of Athanasius speak of certain unspecified collegia that were incited to anti-Homoousian violence by imperial agents: Athan. *Apol. c. Ar*. 15; *Hist. Ar*. 55.
71. Athan. *Ep. Ency*. 6; *Festal Index* 18.
72. Theodoret *HE* 4.18–19: *Festal Index* 39; *Hist. Aceph*. 5.11–13.

*Chapter Nine. Intercommunal Conflict during Late Antiquity*

1. Evagrius *HE* 2.8; *HA Tyr. Trig*. 22.1–3.
2. *Expositio* 37.6 (ed. Rougé).
3. The following section is a revised version of a study published in *GRBS* 32.3 (1991): 281–301.
4. The principal sources for Gregory's episcopate and Philagrius's prefecture(s) are *Festal Index* 11–18; Athan. *Ep. Ency., Apol. c. Ar*. 30, *Hist. Ar*. 10–21, *Fest. Ep*. 10; Gregory Naz. *Or*. 21.28; Soc. *HE* 2.11, 14; Soz. *HE* 3.6, 12.
5. *Hist. Aceph*. 1.1; *Or*. 21.29; Soc. *HE* 2.24.
6. Diogenes: Athan. *Hist. Ar*. 31; *Hist. Aceph*. 1.7–8; *Festal Index* 25; *Populo uero resistente Diogeni uehementer et iudicibus, reuersus est Diogenes sine effectu, Hist. Aceph*. 1.9. Syrianus and Hilary: Athan. *Apol. ad Constant*. 22–24; Soz. *HE* 4.9. Attack on church of Saint Theonas: *Festal Index* 28; *Hist. Aceph*. 1.10–11; Athan. *Apol. ad Constant*. 25; *Apol. de Fuga*. 24. George: Soz. *HE* 4.10.
7. See M. Simonetti, *La crisi ariana del IV secolo* (Rome, 1975), 226–30, 326–33; E. D. Hunt, "Christians and Christianity in Ammianus Marcellinus," *CQ*, n.s., 35 (1985) 186–200; J. Matthews, *The Roman*

*Empire of Ammianus* (Baltimore, 1989), 441–44; and M. Caltabiano, "L'assassinio di Giorgio di Cappadocia," *Quaderni catanesi di studi classici e medievali* 7 (1985): 17–57. Caltabiano's study rightly emphasizes the way in which the fifth-century church historians reinterpreted the events of 361 as a simple manifestation of theological conflict, thereby discounting social and political factors. Consequently, the near contemporary sources take on an even greater importance in understanding George's episcopate.

8. Annik Martin, in her otherwise outstanding analysis of Athanasius's episcopate, relegates these events to a brief notice in a section discussing "Alexandrie la violente," in *Histoire "Acéphale" et index syriaque des lettres festales d'Athanase d'Alexandrie, SC* no. 317 (Paris, 1985), 102–3.
9. *Hist. Aceph.* 2.1–2; *Festal Index* 18–19. The chronology of this period is carefully reconstructed by Martin, *Histoire "Acéphale,"* 89–97. Cf. W. Bright, "Georgius of Cappadocia," in *DCB* 2: 637–40 (London, 1880).
10. Zosimus 2.51–52; *Epit. de Caes.* 42.4–8; Eutropius 10.12. On Constantius's relations with Athanasius, see K. M. Girardet, "Constance II, Athanase et l'édit d'Arles (353): A propos de la politique religieuse de l'empereur Constance II," in C. Kannengiesser, *Politique et théologie* (Paris, 1974), 65–91; and L. W. Bernard, "Athanase et les empereurs Constantin et Constance," in ibid., 127–43. A thoroughgoing analysis may be found in Barnes, *Athanasius and Constantius* (Cambridge, Mass., 1993), esp. 165–75. Constantius's antipagan legislation: *C.Th.* 16.10.2–6; Libanius *Or.* 72.8. Altar of Victory: Ambrose *Ep.* 18.22; Symmachus *Rel.* 3.7.

    Athanasius and Magnentius: Soc. *HE* 2.26. Marcellinus (Magnentius's *magister militum*) and Nunechius (a senator and possibly a praetorian prefect) sent to Constantinople via Alexandria: Petr. Patr. fr. 16 in *FHG* 4:184–91. Athanasius neglects to mention them, and only speaks of ecclesiastical envoys: *Apol. ad Constant.* 6–11. See also Barnes, *Athanasius and Constantius,* 102–6.
11. Heraclius, Cataphronius, and Faustinus: *Hist. Aceph.* 2.1–2; Athan. *Hist. Ar.* 55, 58. Syrianus: Athan. *Apol. ad Constant.* 27. Pagans threatened: *bouleutas kai dēmotas ethnikous neōkorous tōn eidōlōn,* Athan. *Hist. Ar.* 54 col. 760a. Collegia: *tines tōn ergasiōn, Hist. Ar.* 55 col. 760a.
12. Athanasius's account of the riot: *Hist. Ar.* 55–56. *Hoi Agoraioi*: *Hist. Ar.* 55 col. 760b. Cf. Acts 17:1–9, where a tumult in Thessaloniki occurs after "the Jews . . . rounded up some bad characters from the marketplace [*tōn agoraiōn andras tinas ponērous*], formed a mob, and started a riot in the city." In a near contemporary text to Acts, Plutarch

describes Scipio Africanus "rushing into the Forum attended by men who were of low birth [*agenneis*], and former slaves, who were frequenters of the forum [*agoraious*] and able to gather a mob," Plut. *Aem*. 38.3. Hence, *agoraios* becomes a synonym for "common," "rowdy," or "vulgar." Earlier references include Philo *in Flaccum* 64, 95; *Legatio ad Gaium* 122. This same social grouping is also referred to as "those of the Dromos" (*Acts of Peter*, in *Bibliotheca Hagiographica Graeca* [Bruxelles, 1957], 1502, 1502a).

Athanasius singles out the katholikos, Faustinus, as the principal agent who incited *hoi agoraioi*. The Arians "found that Faustinus, who is the *katholikos* by style, but is an *agoraion* in habits, and profligate in heart, was ready to play his part with them in these proceedings, and to stir up the heathen." *Hist. Ar*. 58.

13. Caesarion: Epiph. *Haer*. 69.2.3; Athan. *Apol. ad Constant*. 14–17.
14. Athanasius's description of pagan actions: *Hist. Ar*. 56–57, 59. Dionysiac background: Callixenus, quoted by Athenaeus 197c–203b. Adriani, *Reportorio*, 191–97; A. Bernand, *Alexandrie la Grande* (Paris, 1966), 206–9; Fraser, *Ptolemaic Alexandria*, 1:205–6.
15. It should be recalled that during their long tenure in the episcopate, most late Roman bishops were able to develop extensive networks of local patronage and considerable influence in local affairs. This contrasts sharply with the revolving door of imperial appointments. In the five years discussed here (356–61), there were no fewer than seven prefects and three duces/strategoi who administered Alexandria.
16. Riots of 339: Athan. *Ep. Ency*. 3–4; *Apol. c. Ar*. 30; *Hist. Ar*. 10–13. Patronage of Gregory and Philagrius: ordination and tax exemption —*Apol. ad Constant*. 28; grain dole—*Ep. Ency*. 4, *Hist. Ar*. 31, 54; gifts of oil and other alms—*Hist. Ar*. 13, 72; unspecified "promises" —*Ep. Ency*. 3.
17. Church and king riot: the best discussion of the taxonomy of this riot is E. P. Thompson, "The Moral Economy of the English Crowd," *Past and Present* 50 (1971): 76–136. Also consult N. Z. Davis, "The Rites of Violence: Religious Riot in Sixteenth-Century France," *Past and Present* 59 (1973): 53–91; M. Mollat and P. Wolff, *Ongles bleus, Jacques et Ciompi: Les révolutions populaires en Europe aux XIVe et XVe siècles* (Paris, 1970); and S. Desan, *Reclaiming the Sacred: Lay Religion and Popular Politics in Revolutionary France* (Ithaca, N.Y., 1990).

Pagan slogans: *Hellēn gegone Kōnstantios, kai hoi Areianoi ta hēmōn*, Athan. *Hist. Ar*. 56 col. 761a. Caesarion: D. Fishwick, "The Temple of Caesar at Alexandria," *American Journal of Ancient History* 9.2 (1984): 131–34; E. Huzar, "Emperor Worship in Julio-Claudian Egypt," *ANRW* 2.18.5 (1995): 3092–3143. *Expositio*: *nusquam enim deorum mysteria sic perficitur quomodo ibi ab antiquo et usque modo,* 34.7–9.

A similar incident occurred some fifty years later in the North African town of Calama, when a crowd of pagans celebrating a festival (contrary to a recent law of Honorius) assaulted a church with the tacit support of the local administration: Aug. *Ep.* 91.

18. George's arrival: *Festal Index* 19. Previous career: *hupodektēs en Kōnstantinoupolei tamiakōn genomenon,* Athan. *Hist. Ar.* 75. Transfer from the imperial service to the episcopate was not unusual under Constantius, as in the case of Eleusius of Cyzicus (Soz. *HE* 4.20). Library: Julian *Ep.* 106 [411c], (ed. Bidez-Cumont). See also A.-J. Festugière, "Julien à Macellum," *JRS* 47 (1957): 53–58. Character: Amm. Marc. 22.11.4; Epiph. *Haer.* 76.1.1–8; Greg. Naz. *Or.* 21.16; Athan. *de Syn.* 37, *ad Episcopos* 7; Constantius quoted in Athan. *Apol. ad Constant.* 30.
19. Athan. *Apol. de Fuga.* 6–7.
20. Julian *Ep.* 60 [379b] (ed. Bidez-Cumont); Soz. *HE* 4.30; Amm. Marc. 22.11.6.
21. *"quam diu," inquit "sepulcrum hoc stabit?"* Amm. Marc. 22.11.7.
22. Artemius in Alexandria: Theod. *HE* 3.14; *Passio Artem.* 4, 8, 18 (ed. Bidez), *GCS* 21 (Leipzig, 1913). On Artemius's career, see J. Dummer, "F. Artemius dux Aegypti," *ArchPF* 21 (1971): 121–44; and *PLRE* 1, s.v. "Artemius 2." Reaction to Artemius's attack on Serapeum: Julian *Ep.* 60 [378–80] (ed. Bidez-Cumont). Artemius also employed force to promote the emperor's Arian policies within Alexandria, at one point engaging in a violent house-to-house search in order to discover the hiding place of Athanasius (*Festal Index* 32).
23. *id quoque ad deorum cultum existimans pertinare.* Amm. Marc. 22.11.9.
24. *Pe'ot*: although the wearing of *pe'ot* is best known in the modern period from certain Jewish communities of eastern Europe and the United States, there is evidence of the usage from late antiquity: *B.Tal.Mak.* 20b, following the injunction found in Leviticus 19:27. Jews in violence of 339 and 373: Athan. *Ep. Encyl.* 3, 4, 7; Theodoret *HE* 4.18, 19—quoting a letter of Bishop Peter, Athanasius's successor. Revolt of Patricius: Aur. Vict. *Caes.* 42.11; Jerome *Chron.* s.a. 352; Soc. *HE* 2.23; Soz. *HE* 4.7. Constantius and the Jews: *C.Th.* 16.8.7. Text and extended discussion in A. Linder, *The Jews in Roman Imperial Legislation* (Detroit, 1987), 151–54; Julian *Ep.* 204 [396–98] (ed. Bidez-Cumont); Linder, 154–60.
25. Soc. *HE* 1.35; Athan. *Apol. c. Ar.* 9; *Ep. Ency.* 5.
26. Epiph. *Haer.* 76.1.5–7.
27. Arianism and extramural regions: Epiph. *Haer.* 69.3.1–2; Athan. *Hist. Ar.* 10. George: Greg. Naz. *Or.* 21.16; Athan. *de Syn.* 12; *ad Episcopos* 7; *Hist. Ar.* 75. Economy in suburbs: Epiph. *Haer.* 76.5;

*Expositio* 36.1–9; Strabo 17.1.15; *BGU* 1121/*Sel. Pap.* 41; Pliny *HN* 13.76; *P.Sakaon* 24/*P.Thead.* 35; *P.Sakaon* 25/*P.Thead.* 36. Tax immunity for gravediggers: *C.Th.* 16.2.15.1.

28. Attack on George in 358: *Hist. Aceph.* 2.3. The anonymous author's simple use of the term *plebs* does not allow us to speculate on the composition of the crowd and its specific religious sympathies, either Homoousian or pagan. Departure of George: *Festal Index* 30. George's activities outside of Alexandria: Soz. *HE* 4.6, 16; Theodoret *HE* 2.23–24; Soc. *HE* 2.39–40. Accusations at Council of Arminium: *harpagōn kai hubreōn*, Soz. *HE* 4.17; cf. Soz. *HE* 2.23–25. A balanced treatment of the theological issues during this period may be found in R. P. C. Hanson, *The Search for the Christian Doctrine of God* (Edinburgh, 1988), 348–86, 557–637.
29. *Hist. Aceph.* 2.4; Soz. *HE* 4.10.
30. Paul: *Hist. Aceph.* 2.5; Amm. Marc. 19.12.3–16. Paul's prefecture (357–59) followed that of Cataphronius, the initiator of Constantius's hard-line policies in 356. It may be conjectured that a pagan had been chosen, in part, to mollify the pagan crowds that rioted in the summer of 356. If so, Parnasius's rapid fall from imperial favor suggests that Constantius considered his softened policy to have gone too far—especially when his hand-picked bishop had been thrown out of the city, and the prefect had failed to support the bishop with sufficient force. Indeed, the vindictive George may have had some hand in targeting Parnasius for trial. The *Hist. Aceph.* goes so far as to claim that Paul's activities in Alexandria were motivated solely by a policy to exact vengeance on George's enemies: *Paulus . . . proposuit imperiale preceptom pro Georgio et domuit multos ob eius uindicta*. Parnasius: Amm. Marc. 19.12.10; Lib. *Ep.* 29; *Or.* 14.15–16. Andronicus: Amm. Marc. 19.12.11; Lib. *Ep.* 77. Demetrius: Amm. Marc. 19.12.12.
31. Faustinus: Athan. *Hist. Ar.* 55, 58. Artemius: *Festal Index* 32; Julian *Ep.* 60 [379b] (ed. Bidez-Cumont); Greg. Naz. *Or.* 21.20.
32. Return of George: Soz. *HE* 4.10. Ensuing persecution: Soz. *HE* 4.30. Pagan reaction: Soz. *HE* 5.7. The celebrated pagan physician and teacher, Zeno, was exiled from Alexandria during this period, later restored by Julian: Julian *Ep.* 58 [426] (ed. Bidez-Cumont); Libanius *Ep.* 171.
33. Death of Constantius: Amm. Marc. 21.15.1–6; *Consul. Const.* s.a. 361; Jerome *Chron.* s.a. 361—testimony to the slowness of communications within the empire. Attack on George: Soz. *HE* 5.7. Imprisonment: *Hist. Aceph.* 2.9.
34. Soc. *HE* 3.3.
35. *Passio Artem.* Anhang 3, 167–75 (ed. Bidez). Ammianus claims that

the Alexandrian pagans rioted against George upon hearing that Artemius was dead (22.11.8). However, the *Passio Artem.* states that Artemius was beheaded in Daphne, the luxury suburb of Antioch. Julian, who presided over his trial, did not arrive in Antioch until July of 362.

36. Death of George: the events are described with slight variation in Amm. Marc. 22.11.8–11; Soz. *HE* 5.7; Soc. *HE* 3.2–3; *Hist. Aceph.* 2.8–10; *Chron. Pasch.* (ed., Dindorf, p. 546). Sozomen and Socrates both attribute George's murder to insults he offered to pagan cult objects discovered during the construction of a church. However, the same story is repeated for the pagan-Christian clashes of 391 where the sequence of events seems to fit far better. The announcement of Constantius's death provided more than sufficient motivation for an Alexandrian crowd to rise up against the hated bishop, finding legitimation for its actions in the accquiescence of the imperial authorities. Julian on George: *tō theois echthrō,* Julian *Ep.* 60 [379c] (ed. Bidez-Cumont).
37. Julian *Ep.* 106 [411], 107 [377–78] (ed. Bidez-Cumont).
38. Amm. Marc. 22.11.5 (trans. Rolfe). Authority of George: Julian *Ep.* 60 [379a] (ed. Bidez-Cumont)—a concentration of powers which prefigured the combined prefecture-patriarchate of the hated Melkite appointee Cyrus (630–42): *History of the Patriarchs* 1.14 (ed. Evetts), p. 489 [225].
39. Return of Athanasius: *Festal Index* 34; Soc. *HE* 3.7; Soz. *HE* 5.6; Greg. Naz. *Or.* 21.27. Exile under Julian: *Festal Index* 35; *Hist. Aceph.* 3.5–6, 4.3–4. Authority of Athanasius: it was so great within Alexandria that the Arian emperor Valens was unable to install an antibishop to his liking until after Athanasius's death: *Hist. Aceph.* 5.1–7; *Festal Index* 37; Soc. *HE* 4.20. Lucius: he had made an abortive attempt to take up the episcopate of the city in September of 367: *Festal Index* 39; *Hist. Aceph.* 5.11–13. Character of Lucius's episcopate: Soc. *HE* 4.20–21; Theodoret *HE* 4.18–19; Soz. *HE* 6.19–20.
40. Palladius *Dial. de v. J.Chrys.* 6; Soc. *HE* 6.7.
41. Recent assessments of these events may be found in J. Rougé, "Les débuts de l'épiscopat de Cyrille d'Alexandrie et le *Code Théodosien,*" in *Alexandrina: Hellénisme, judaïsme et christianisme à Alexandrie, Mélanges offerts au P. Claude Mondésert* (Paris, 1987), 339–49; idem, "La politique de Cyrille d'Alexandrie et le meurtre d'Hypatie," *Cristianesimo nella storia* 11 (1990): 487–92; P. Évieux and W. H. Burns, *Cyrille d'Alexandrie: Lettres Festales, I–VI, SC* no. 372 (Paris, 1991), 43–72; M. Dzielska, *Hypatia of Alexandria,* trans. F. Lyra (Cambridge, Mass., 1995), 85–100.
42. Soc. *HE* 7.7 (trans. Zenos).

43. Rougé argues that Abundantius's inability to secure the candidate of his choice indicated that he acted only as a private person, without instructions from Constantinople and without armed support ("La politique de Cyrille," 486–87). This is an argument from silence, and there were several instances in late antique Alexandria when imperial directives proved unenforceable in the face of popular opposition: Soz. *HE* 6.12, *Hist. Aceph.* 1.7–8; *Festal Index* 25, *Hist. Aceph.* 1.9; *Festal Index* 27, *History of the Patriarchs* 1.13 (ed. Evetts), p. 459 [195].
44. *History of the Patriarchs* 1.12 (ed. Evetts), p. 430 [166].
45. Soc. *HE* 7.7. Cf. Nicephorus Callistus *HE* 14.14 (*PG* 146, col. 1100c).
46. *C.Th.* 16.5.48–52; Soc. *HE* 7.9; *History of the Patriarchs* 1.11 (ed. Evetts), p. 427 [163].
47. *History of the Patriarchs* 1.12 (ed. Evetts), p. 430 [166]; *Ep. Fest.* 1.1.10–21, P. Évieux and W. H. Burns, *Cyrille d'Alexandrie: Lettres Festales, I–VI, SC* no. 372 (Paris, 1991), 142–45.
48. *History of the Patriarchs* 1.11, 12 (ed. Evetts), 427–28 [163–64], 431 [167].
49. R. W. Wilken, *Judaism and the Early Christian Mind* (New Haven, 1971), p. 60.
50. *PG* 77, cols. 420a, 853c; 70, col. 229c; 69, col. 565c. I am indebted to Wilken, *Judaism and the Early Christian Mind,* 61, for this catalog. *Ep. Fest.* 1.5.27–29, 1.6.110–12 (ed. Évieux and Burns, 172–73, 180–81). This is echoed by a passage in his commentary on the Gospel of John: "Let the ignorant Jews who harden their minds to complete stubbornness, realize that they pour self-invited destruction upon their own heads. They will be under divine wrath, receiving the total loss of good things as the wages of their rage against Christ," (*in Jo.* 5.46, trans. Wilken, *Judaism and the Early Christian Mind,* 65–66).
51. *C.Th.* 16.8.8–9, 11–12, 14–16, 18, 20. See also Avi-Yonah, 225–29; G. Alon, *The Jews in Their Land in the Talmudic Age,* trans. and ed. G. Levi (Cambridge, Mass, 1989), 705–37; R. Syme, *Emperors and Biography* (Oxford, 1971), 17–29.
52. *C.Th.* 9.40.22; Soc. *HE* 7.1.
53. On Aurelian's career, see *PLRE* 1, s.v. "Aurelianus 3"; and A. Cameron and J. Long, *Barbarians and Politics at the Court of Arcadius* (Berkeley, 1993), 161–90. His religious leanings are examined with great care by Cameron and Long, 71–84, 305–7.
54. *C.Th.* 16.8.22.
55. Soc. *HE* 7.13 (*PG* 67, cols. 760–65). Derivative accounts may be found in Theophanes *Chron.* AM 5905; Cassiodorus *Hist. Eccl. Tripartita* 11.11; George Cedrenus *Compendium Historiarum* 1.589; Nicephorus Callistos *HE* 14.14; Michael the Syrian *Chron.* 8.3. A

variant local tradition is contained in John of Nikiu *Chron*. 84.89–99. There are also ambiguous echoes of these events in Augustine *Sermo* 5.5; Isidore of Pelusium *Ep*. 3.128; and *History of the Patriarchs* 1.12 (ed. Evetts), p. 434 [170].

56. John of Nikiu *Chron*. 84.95 (trans. Charles).
57. *C.Th*. 16.8.22—the same law which encouraged the destruction of synagogues "in desert places" as long as it can be done "without sedition." The edict also stripped the Jewish patriarch in Palestine of his authority, forbade the circumcision of Christians, and freed Christian slaves belonging to Jewish masters.
58. *Ep.Fest*. 4.4.1–4.6.130 (ed. Évieux and Burns, 256–75); 6.6.1–6.6.11.105 (ed. Évieux and Burns, 362–93).
59. Independent witnesses toward the end of the fourth century say that there were some five thousand monks dwelling at Nitria: Jerome *Ep*. 22; Palladius *Hist. Laus*. 7, 13. See also A. Guillaumont, "Nitria," in *CoptEncy* 6: 1794–96.
60. Rufinus *HE* 2.22.
61. Gibbon sums up his assessment of these events by stating: "The murder of Hypatia has imprinted an indelible stain on the character and religion of Cyril of Alexandria" (chap. 47 in *Decline and Fall of the Roman Empire*, ed. J. B. Bury [London, 1909], 5:117).

    Cyril's supporters: *DCB*, s.v. "Cyrillus 7," by W. Bright; F. Schaefer, "St. Cyril of Alexandria and the Murder of Hypatia," *Catholic University Bulletin* 8.4 (1902): 441–53; L. R. Wickham, ed. and trans., *Cyril of Alexandria: Select Letters* (Oxford, 1983), xvi–xvii; A. S. Atiya, "Cyril I, Saint," in *CoptEncy* 3: 671–75; J. A. McGuckin, *St. Cyril of Alexandria: The Christological Controversy* (Leiden, 1994), 12–14.

    Political interpretation: Soc. *HE* 7.15. K. Praechter, "Hypatia," *R-E* 9 (1914): 242–49; J. Geffcken, *The Last Days of Greco-Roman Paganism*, trans. S. MacCormack (Amsterdam, 1978), 243; J. M. Rist, "Hypatia," *Phoenix* 19.3 (1965): 214–25; P. Chuvin, *A Chronicle of the Last Pagans*, trans. B. A. Archer (Cambridge, Mass., 1990), 85–90; Dzielska, *Hypatia*, 103–4.
62. Sometimes, even stronger prejudices serve to counterbalance Socrates' partial estimate of Cyril. His narrative of Cyril's conflict with the Jewish community is marked by the same anti-Semitic sentiment found in other passages, such as 3.20 (Julian and the temple), 5.22 (on Judaizing tendencies).
63. Rist, Praechter, and Chuvin fail to draw upon the information supplied by John of Nikiu. For recent assessments of Hypatia's teaching and influence, see now Cameron and Long, *Barbarians and Politics*, 39–62; Dzielska, *Hypatia*.
64. *Ep. Fest*. 1.6.116–21 (ed. Évieux and Burns, pp. 180–81); *contra Jul*.

508c–d; cf. *History of the Patriarchs* 1.12 (ed. Evetts), p. 431 [167]. For the date and occasion of Julian's treatise and of Cyril's reply, see W. J. Malley, *Hellenism and Christianity,* Analecta Gregoriana vol. 210 (Rome, 1978); *Cyrille d'Alexandrie, Contre Julien,* ed. and trans. P. Burgeuière and P. Évieux, *SC* no. 322 (Paris, 1985).

Relics of Cyrus and John: Cyril Al. *hom* 18 (*PG* 77, cols. 1100–1105); Copto-Arabic Synaxarion 4 Abib (*PO* 17 [Paris, 1904], 621–62); Sophronius *Passio et laud. Cyr. et Iohan.* (*PG* 87.3, cols. 3693, 3696). On this episode, see McGuckin, *St. Cyril,* 16–20; idem, "The Influence of the Isis Cult on St. Cyril of Alexandria's Christology," *Studia Patristica* 24 (1992): 191–99.

65. Damascius fr. 102, (ed. Zintzen, p. 102); Philostorgius (Photius) *HE* 8.9. In a later passage, Damascius denigrates her background in mathematics, saying: "Isidorus was very different from Hypatia, not only in that she was just a woman and he a man, but also in that she was a geometrician and he a philosopher"; [Damascius] *Epit. Photiana* 52 (ed. Zintzen, p. 76). Cf. John of Nikiu (84.87): "she was devoted at all times to magic, astrolabes, and instruments of music." On Theon, consult *PLRE* 1, s.v. "Theon 3."

66. Both Socrates (*HE* 7.13) and Damascius (fr. 102) emphasize the public nature of her instruction, the latter stating that "she publicly expounded (*exēgeito dēmosia*) the doctrines of Plato, Aristotle, and the works of the other philosophers." See also H. I. Marrou, "Synesius of Cyrene and Alexandrian Neoplatonism," in *The Conflict between Paganism and Christianity in the Fourth Century,* ed. A. Momigliano (Oxford, 1963), 128–50; Dzielska, *Hypatia,* 56–57. Cameron and Long, *Barbarians and Politics,* 40–41, urge caution on the question of her public appointment, since Damascius's statements may simply reflect his contempt for anyone who did not restrict his or her teaching to a select group of initiates.

    Synesius: *Ep.* 4, 10, 15, 16, 33, 81, 124, 154, according to the numbering system adopted in the edition of R. Hercher (Paris 1873).

67. For Synesius's sojourn in the city, see *Ep.* 145; cf. *C. Th.* 11.24.3. On Hypatia: *Ep.* 16; *tēs gnēsias kathēgemonos tōn philosophias orgiōn, Ep.* 137 col. 1525a (trans. Fitzgerald). Hypatia's students: Synesius *Ep.* 4, 11, 16, 54, 137–46. See also *PLRE* 2, s.v. "Herculianus" and "Cyrus 7."

68. An additional irritant to Cyril may have been the recently issued law that exempted "grammarians, orators and teachers of philosophy, and likewise physicians" and their families from taxation and compulsory public services (*C.Th.* 13.3.16–17, dated 11 November 414).

69. Libanius serves as perhaps the best example of this practice: *Ep.* 56, 83, 105, 110, 267, 288, 394, 400, 838, 1443, 1496.

70. *Ep.* 81 col. 1453a (trans. Fitzgerald).

71. Damascius frs. 102, 104 (ed. Zintzen, 77, 79); Soc. *HE* 7.15.
72. Damascius fr. 104 (ed. Zintzen, p. 79).
73. John of Nikiu *Chron*. 84.88, 100; Soc. *HE* 7.14–15. Although we may rightly disagree with John's assessment of the relationship between Orestes and Hypatia, his sometimes garbled narrative preserves the context of Alexandrian politics better than Socrates' ordered chronicle. According to Socrates, the Jewish-Christian violence of 415 appears largely unconnected with the events leading up to Hypatia's death (*HE* 7.13–15). John of Nikiu, on the other hand, embeds his account of the Jewish plot and expulsion within the story of Hypatia. It seems clear from John's narrative that Cyril and the Christians held Hypatia responsible for creating a political climate in which the violence perpetrated by elements of the Jewish community might otherwise have gone unpunished. Perhaps it would not be stretching the evidence too far to suggest that Hypatia counseled the prefect to support the Jewish community as a useful counterbalance against the growing power of the Christians.
74. Soc. *HE* 7.7, 13.
75. John of Nikiu *Chron*. 84.88. John adds the tantalizing detail: "But he once went [to church] under circumstances of danger." Such circumstances were numerous, but which one would induce Orestes to join as one of the faithful, under the authority of the patriarch?
76. Soc. *HE* 7.14.
77. Damascius fr. 104 (ed. Zintzen, 79, 81). Peter: Socrates briefly identifies him as a "reader" (*anagnōstēs*), but John of Nikiu (84.100) dwells upon the character of Peter, "a perfect believer in all respects in Jesus Christ," after first indicating that he was a magistrate.
78. Soc. *HE* 7.15; Damascius fr. 105 (ed. Zintzen, p. 81); Malalas 14.12 [359]; John of Nikiu *Chron*. 84.100–2; Theophanes *Chron*. AM 5906a.
79. Perhaps these fanatical Christians are an early appearance of the philoponoi, prior to their formal organization as a lay confraternity over the course of the fifth century.
80. *C.Th*. 16.2.42.2 (trans. Pharr).
81. A broader context for the antipagan violence of this period is suggested by John of Nikiu's remark that "in those days [i.e., after Cyril's enthronement in 412 and before the death of Atticus in 425], the orthodox inhabitants of Alexandria were filled with zeal and they collected a large quantity of wood and burned the place of the heathen philosophers" (*Chron*. 84.45, trans. Charles). This comment is set apart quite distinctly from John's account of the death of Hypatia (84.87–103) and must refer not to her ritual cremation, but to some otherwise unreported attack on pagan institutions.
82. *C.Th*. 12.12.15.

83. *C.Th.* 16.2.42, prologue.
84. *C.Th.* 16.2.43; John of Nikiu *Chron.* 84.103.
85. The accusations against Dioscorus were presented at the Council's third session on 13 October: *ACO* 2.1.2.38–64.
86. This section is a revised version of a study first published in *JECS* 1.3 (1993): 297–316.
87. *History of the Patriarchs* 1.13 (ed. Evetts), p. 445 [181]; Evagrius *HE* 2.5. A useful discussion of the events in Alexandria is provided by T. E. Gregory, *Vox Populi: Violence and Popular Involvement in the Religious Controversies of the Fifth Century A.D.* (Columbus, Ohio, 1979), 163–201. Two works foundational to any study of this period are W. H. C. Frend, *The Rise of the Monophysite Movement* (Cambridge, 1972), and the collection of articles in A. Grillmeier and H. Bacht, *Das Konzil von Chalkedon: Geschichte und Gegenwart,* 3 vols. (Würzburg, 1953–62). On Dioscorus, see M. P. Roncaglia, "Dioscorus," in *Copt-Ency* 3: 912–15.
88. Evagrius *HE* 2.8; Zach. Mytil. *HE* 4.2; Theophanes *Chron.* AM 5950; Eutychius (Saʿid ibn al-Batriq) *Annales* 101–3 (*PG* 111, col. 1055). Eutychius adds the detail that Proterius's body was later burned in the hippodrome (108, col. 1056).
89. Elevation of Timothy Aelurus: Evagrius *HE* 2.8; "Life of Timothy Aelurus," ed. and trans. H. G. Evelyn White, in *The Monasteries of the Wadi 'n Natrūn, vol. 1, New Coptic Texts from the Monastery of Saint Macarius,* Metropolitan Museum of Art Egyptian Expedition Publications (New York, 1926), 164–65. Arrest and exile of Aelurus: "Life of Timothy Aelurus," 166–67; Theophanes *Chron.* AM 5951–52. Early career of Peter: Saʿīd ibn al-Bitrīq (Eutychius) *Ann.* 105, col. 1056; Liberatus *Brev.* 16 (in E. Schwartz, ed., *ACO* part 2, [Berlin, 1936], 5:98–141). Elevation of Timothy Salophacialos: Evagrius *HE* 2.11.
90. Zach. Mytil. *HE* 4.10.
91. Aelurus's use of patronage: Zach. Mytil. *HE* 4.3, 5.4. He was supported in his bid for the patriarchal throne by a broadly-based coalition of Alexandrian dignitaries (*axiōmatikoi*), magistrates (*politeuomenoi*), monks, the urban demos, and the naukleroi of the grain fleet (Evagrius *HE* 2.9).

    Some measure of Aelurus's popularity can be gleaned from Zachariah's account of his return to Alexandria: "Timothy arrived in Alexandria, and he was received with great state, with torches, and also songs of praise by the various peoples and languages there, and even by the members of the Proterian party, who beheld the affection for him displayed by the citizens. But the band of the priests, and the monks, and the sisters in Christ, and all the people in a body, chanting their hymns, and saying, 'Blessed is he that cometh in the name of the

Lord,' conducted him into the Great Church" (Zach. Mytil. *HE* 5.4, trans. Brooks, p. 110).

In his otherwise penetrating analysis of factionalism in fifth-century Alexandria, Gregory interprets the division of the Alexandrian population during the Christological controversies as one determined almost exclusively by socioeconomic class. Despite his assertion that "the rich of the city generally supported Proterius, while the majority of the population remained loyal to Dioscorus" (*Vox Populi,* 190), there are clear indications that a Monophysite patriarch like Timothy Aelurus was able to gain enthusiastic support among the upper classes (Zach. Mytil. *HE* 4.3).

92. Zeno: Theophanes *Chron.* AM 5965–66; John Malalas *Chron.* 376; Malchus fr. 16 (ed. Blockley); Evagrius *HE* 2.17. On Zeno and his reign, see the exhaustive study of A. Lippold in *R-E,* 2d ser., 19 (1972): 149–213; and the judicious reconstruction of the sources by E. W. Brooks, "The Emperor Zeno and the Isaurians," *English Historical Review* 30 (1893): 209–38. His career is outlined with full references in *PLRE* 2, s.v., "Fl. Zenon 7," and in W. Barth, *Kaiser Zeno* (Basel, 1894).

Basiliscus: Theophanes *Chron.* AM 5967; Malchus frs. 8–11 (ed. Blockley); John Malalas *Chron.* 377–78; Evagrius *HE* 3.3–6; Zach. Mytil. *HE* 5.1–4. See also Lippold, *R-E,* 2d ser., 19 (1972): 160–62; Brooks, "Emperor Zeno," 216–18; and G. M. Bersanetti, "Basilisco e l'imperatore Leone I," *RAP,* ser. 3, 20 (1943–44): 331–46. E. Schwartz, *Publizistische Sammlungen zum Acacianischen Schisma,* Abhandlungen der Bayerischen Akademie der Wissenschaften, n.s., 10 (Munich, 1934), has a relevance far beyond that suggested by its title. Besides collecting the major texts concerned with inter-episcopal relations, Schwartz also provides an extensive background discussion which frequently casts light on political affairs. On Zeno and Basiliscus, see 181–85.

Return of Zeno: John Malalas *Chron.* 379–80; *Chron. Pasch.* (ed. Dindorf, 1832), 600–602; Zach. Mytil. *HE* 5.5; Evagrius *HE* 3.8; John Malalas *Chron.* 380. Schwartz, *Acacianischen Schisma,* 189–93.

Death of Timothy: Zach. Mytil. *HE* 5.5; Evagrius *HE* 3.11; *History of the Patriarchs* 1.13 (ed. Evetts), p. 445 [181].

93. Elevation of Peter: *History of the Patriarchs* 1.13 (ed. Evetts) p. 445 [181]; Zach. Mytil. *HE* 5.5. Zeno's reaction: *Hoper eis Zēnōna diaban exetaraxe kai tō men ho Zēnōn thanatou zēmian prosetimēse,* Evagrius *HE* 3.11 (trans. E. Walford). Reinstatement of Salophacialos: Evagrius *HE* 3.11; Zach. Mytil. *HE* 5.5; *History of the Patriarchs* 1.13, p. 447 [183]; Theophanes *Chron.* AM 5969; Theodoros Anagnostes *HE,* ed. G. Hansen (Berlin, 1971), p. 115. Peter in hiding: Zach. Mytil. *HE*

5.5. Salophacialos' reaction: *quia latitabat Alexandriae et insidiabatur ecclesiae,* Liberatus *Brev*. 16.

94. Zach. Mytil. *HE* 5.5.
95. 5.6 (trans. Brooks, p. 116).
96. Jerome *Praef. Reg. Pachom*. 1. On Metanoia, see now the thorough treatment by J. Gascou, "Metanoia," in *CoptEncy* 5 (1991): 1608–11. Gascou (1609) questions Metanoia's tendency to follow the theological direction of Constantinople on the grounds that there were traces of Monophysite opinion at Metanoia. However, most of this evidence comes from the sixth and seventh centuries, and simply reflects the changing fashions of imperial theology.

    Athanasius's accusations against Dioscorus: Mansi, vol. 6, cols. 1021–29 and *ACO* 2.1.2.56–58. Cf. Liberatus *Brev*. 13; Evagrius *HE* 2.18. Salophacialos: Theophanes *Chron*. AM 5967. John: Zach. Mytil. *HE* 5.6; Evagrius *HE* 3.12. Theophanes *Chron*. AM 5973 adds the biographical detail that John was oikonomos of an Alexandrian church—undoubtedly during the patriarchate of Salophacialos.
97. Death of Salophacialos: Simplicius *Ep*. 17. John and the prefect: *History of the Patriarchs* 1.13, p. 447 [183]; Zach. Mytil. *HE* 5.6. Monastic support for Peter Mongus: Zach. Mytil. *HE* 5.6.
98. By 482, Zeno desperately needed to restore religious unity since he was faced with the twin challenges of Illus's imminent rebellion and the incursions of Theoderic and his Goths in Thessaly and Macedonia. Illus: Liberatus *Brev*. 17; Evagrius *HE* 3.27; Theophanes *Chron*. AM 5972. Theoderic: John of Antioch fr. 213; Marcellinus comes *Chron*. s.a. 481, 482; Michael the Syrian *Chron*. 9.6. Various texts of the Henotikon may be found in Liberatus *Brev*. 17; Nicephorus Callistus *HE* 16.12; Zach. Mytil. *HE* 5.8; Evagrius *HE* 3.14.
99. Liberatus *Brev*. 18; Evagrius *HE* 3.15; Zach. Mytil. *HE* 5.9.
100. Return of Peter Mongus: *History of the Patriarchs* 1.13 (ed., Evetts) p. 447 [183]. Chalcedonian withdrawl to Canopus: Zach. Mytil. *HE* 5.9. Though at one time a supporter of Dioscorus, Cyrus went over to the Chalcedonian faction and bitterly opposed Dioscorus and his successors. Popular opinion in Alexandria held that Cyrus switched loyalties due to his ambition for ecclesiastical office and for his adulterous behavior (Zach. Mytil. *HE* 5.7). Pergamius and Apollonius: Evagrius *HE* 3.13.
101. Zach. Mytil. *HE* 5.7; Evagrius *HE* 3.13–14; Theophanes *Chron*. AM 5976.
102. Zach. Mytil. *HE* 5.7. Despite their loss of influence within the Alexandrian church, the Chalcedonians at Canopus continued to wage a propaganda campaign, "crying out evil words" against Peter (Zach. Mytil. *HE* 5.9).
103. *History of the Patriarchs* 1.13 (ed. Evetts), 446–47 [182–83].

104. Zach. Mytil. *HE* 3.2, 6.1–2; Arabic-Jacobite *Synaxarium* ᶜAmshīr 2 (ed. and trans. Basset), *PO* 11.5 (Paris, 1915), [732] 766. Zachariah quoted at *HE* 6.1. *Vite dei monaci Phif e Longino,* ed. T. Orlandi (Milan, 1975), pp. 79–83, describes one violent confrontation between the monks of Enaton and the prefect's troops. There was considerable discussion among the schismatics concerning the appointment of a patriarch in opposition to Peter. They were dissuaded from this course of action by a former episcopal associate of Peter's named Theodore. Hence, the schismatics were called the Acepheloi by adherents of Peter (*History of the Patriarchs* 1.13 [ed. Evetts], p. 447 [183]; Zach. Mytil. *HE* 6.2).
105. Zach. Mytil. *HE* 6.1.
106. Peter's evolving theological stance receives the caustic comment from Evagrius that he "never abided by one opinion, being a double-dealer, a waverer, and a time-server, now anathematizing the synod at Chalcedon, at another time recanting and admitting it with entire assent" (*Houtos ho Petros, ōs kothornos kai palimbolos kai tois kairois sundiatithemenos, hēkista pros mian estē gnōmēn, nun men anathematizōn tēn en Kalchēdoni sunodon, nun de palinōdian legōn kai tautēn psēphois hapasais dechomenos*), *HE* 3.17 (trans. Walford).
107. Peter Mongus's abjuration of Chalcedon: Liberatus *Brev.* 18; Zach. Mytil. *HE* 6.2; Evagrius *HE* 3.22. Sanctions against schismatics: Evagrius *HE* 3.22; Zach. Mytil. *HE* 6.1. Felix and Zeno: Mansi, vol. 7, cols. 1066, 1078.
108. Revolt of Illus: John of Antioch fr. 214.2–11; Theophanes *Chron.* AM 5972–77; John Malalas *Chron.* 388–89; Evagrius *HE* 3.27. Brooks, "Emperor Zeno," 221–31. John and Illus: Liberatus *Brev.* 16–17.

    In Antioch, the end of the rebellion resulted in the expulsion of Calandio from his bishopric. Calandio had been the eventual Chalcedonian nominee of Acacius, after Zeno had forcibly deposed Peter the Fuller. Since the rebellion broke out in Cilicia and Antioch, Calandio undoubtedly found it politic to throw in his lot with the usurpers and erase Zeno's name from the Dyptichs. In Zeno's eyes, Calandio's support for the rebels far outweighed his theological opinions, and Zeno had him banished to the Great Oasis in 485. Consequently, Peter the Fuller was brought back into power through an ecclesiastical revolving door reminiscent of the events in Alexandria (Liberatus *Brev.* 17–18; John Malalas *Chron.* 388–89; Evagrius *HE* 3.16; Gelasius *Ep.* 13; Zach. Mytil. *HE* 5.9).
109. Christianity of Illus and Leontius: Liberatus *Brev.* 16; Theophanes *Chron.* AM 5974; Zach. Mytil. *HE* 5.9; Theodorus Lector *Epit.* 435. Pagan support for the revolt: *Epit. Phot.* [Damascius] 294 (ed. Zintzen, p. 237); Zach. Mytil. *v. Sev.* p. 40. On the religious dimensions of the revolt, see the perceptive remarks of Chuvin, *Chronicle of the Last*

*Pagans,* 96–100. The relation between paganism and imperial usurpation in the fifth century is surveyed in R. von Haehling, "Damascius und die heidnische Opposition im 5. Jahrhundert nach Christus," *Jahrb. für Ant. und Christ.* 23 (1980): 82–95.

110. Malchus fr. 23 (ed. Blockley); Rhetorius in *Catalogus codicum astrologorum Graecorum* 8.4, pp. 221–24. On Pamprepius and his career, consult *PLRE* 2, s.v., "Pamprepius," and the indispensable study of A. Delatte and P. Stroobant, "L'horoscope de Pamprépius," *Bull. Acad. Roy. de Belg., Classe des Lettres,* 5th ser., 9 (1923): 58–76. See also H. Grégoire, "Au camp d'un Wallenstein byzantin: La vie et les vers de Pamprépios, aventurier païen," *Bull. Assoc. G. Budé* 24 (1929): 22–38; R. Keydell, "Pamprepius," *R-E* 18.3 (1949): 409–15; and R. Asmus, "Pamprepios: Ein byzantinischer Gelehrter und Staatsmann des 5. Jahrhunderts," *Byzantinische Zeitschrift* 22 (1913): 320–47; R. A. Kaster, *Guardians of Language,* (Berkeley, 1988), 329–32.

111. Alexandrian pagans and Pamprepius: Damascius *v. Isid.* frs. 298–300 (ed. Zintzen, p. 239). Nicomedes: his precise office is not detailed in the sources, where he is simply styled Zeno's *apostaleis*. It is likely that he held the post of either *agens in rebus* or *notarius*. Damascius *v. Isid.* frs. 313–14 (ed. Zintzen, p. 251), fr. 328 (p. 261). Nicomedes' initial investigation: Damascius *v. Isid.* frs. 313–15 (ed. Zintzen, 249–51). Nicomedes eventually cast his net of investigation yet wider by the denunciations of certain informers and his interception of incriminating letters (frs. 314, 329, pp. 251, 261). A somewhat different reconstruction of these events is found in P. Athanassiadi, "Persecution and Response in Late Paganism: The Evidence of Damascius," *JHS* 113 (1993): 1–29.

112. Damascius *v. Isid.* frs. 314–15 (ed. Zintzen, p. 251), 320 (p. 255), 328 (p. 261), 334 (p. 265); *Epit. Phot.* [Damascius] 180–84 (ed. Zintzen, p. 252), 185 (p. 254), 190 (p. 260). There even appears to have been a violent scuffle at the docks, during which one philosopher (Isidore?) ordered his servants to take up scraping tools from the baths to defend themselves (Damascius fr. 319—p. 253; *Epit. Phot.* [Damascius] 182–83—p. 252).

113. Ammonius: *Epit. Phot.* [Damascius] 292 (ed. Zintzen, p. 251). The sincerity of Ammonius's conversion may be questioned if he was, in fact, the author of the lines traditionally ascribed to him: "Though (the soul) may be forced by tyrants to profess an impious doctrine, (it) can never be forced to inner assent and to belief" (in Philoponus *de Anima* 126.29–31; see L. G. Westerink, *Anonymous Prolegomena to Platonic Philosophy* (Amsterdam, 1962), xii, and Alan Cameron, "The Last Days of the Academy at Athens," *Proceedings of the Cambridge Philological Society,* n.s., 15 [1969]: 14–15).

Horapollon: Damascius fr. 317 (ed., Zintzen, p. 253). On Horapollon, see M. J. Maspero, "Horapollon et la fin du paganisme égyptien," *BIFAO* 11 (1914): 163–95; and Kaster, *Guardians of Language,* 295–97.

114. *kai tauta tōn peri thanatou phrontidōn hupoleipomenōn, Epit. Phot.* [Damascius] 177 (p. 248). In Constantinople, Zeno put to death the pagan epic poet, Pelagius, perhaps due to perceived treasonous activities (Theophanes *Chron.* AM 5983; John Malalas *Chron.* 390).

115. *anēr itamos ōn kai periponēros, Epit. Phot.* [Damascius] 170 (ed. Zintzen, p. 236). The assessment of Peter Mongus articulated here contrasts markedly from that of Frend, *Monophysite Movement,* p. 187, who claims, "Peter lacked Cyril's ability to weld his doctrinal and political aims into a coherent whole." The doctrinal vacilation deplored by observers throughout the empire makes better sense when Peter is analyzed as a local leader, especially in view of his calculated weaving together of Christological and antipagan disputes.

116. Damascius *v. Isid.* fr. 100 (ed. Zintzen p. 75); Zach. *v. Sev.* (ed. and trans. Kugener), 18, 20–21, 29. A careful analysis of the literary evidence concerning Canopus and the surrounding area may be found in A. Bernand, *La delta égyptien d'après les textes grecs,* vol. 1, *Les confins libyques* (Cairo, 1970), 153–328.

117. The full narrative may be found in Zach. Mytil. *v. Sev.* (ed. and trans. Kugener), 14–39. The incident may be placed confidently within a relative chronology, since one of the principals, Paralios, is found still in Caria at the outbreak of Illus's rebellion (*v. Sev.* 40). Another principal, Asclepiodotus, fled to Caria from Alexandria following the collapse of the rebellion and Zeno's subsequent persecution of pagan intellectuals (*v. Sev.* 41–42).

Chuvin (*Chronicle of the Last Pagans,* 111) argues that the police action described by Damascius cannot be conflated with Peter Mongus's antipagan campaign found in Zachariah's *v. Sev.,* since both the agents and targets of the two official actions are quite different. Aside from the fact that our two main sources for these events have radically different interests, I would suggest that these episodes are closely related, and that Peter Mongus's antipagan actions are simply a natural outgrowth of the changed imperial climate against paganism. These local initiatives must have very shortly preceded Zeno's concerted pogrom against Alexandrian pagans.

118. Zach. Mytil. *v. Sev.* 33. At about the same time, Damascius speaks of the difficulties encountered by sailors entering the harbor without divine protection, "certain people having secretly destroyed the holy image." In the previous passage, Damascius had been discussing the

worship of Isis and Osiris. This, in conjunction with the location and function of this unnamed cult, leads me to conclude that the image destroyed was that of Isis Pharia, the patroness of sailors, whose shrine was close to the great lighthouse of Pharos: *Epit. Photiana* [Damascius] 71 (ed. Zintzen, p. 100).

A possible echo of these events in the archaeological record was unearthed in 1982. In a spot just to the east of the principal north-south street of the city and some meters south of the Via Canopica, a mixed group of cult objects and religious inscriptions was broken up and burned. The statuary was of ivory and was probably decorated with gold, gilded stucco, and semiprecious inlays. Despite the fragmentary nature of the find, it appears that the statuary depicted Serapis and Isis. The objects were first hacked to pieces and then were deliberately burned on a limestone pavement, even though they were made from valuable materials (figure 25). Nearby pottery, which can be dated from the end of the fourth century through the fifth century, provides a general chronological context. When were the objects destroyed? While there is a good chance that the destruction occurred in 391, following the end of public cult at the Serapeum, a date during Peter Mongus's episcopate cannot be excluded. There is also the possibility that the destruction occurred during some incident unrecorded by our literary sources. A full description of the find is contained in E. Rodziewicz, "Remains of a Chryselephantine Statue in Alexandria," *BSAA* 44 (1991): 119–30. A broader archeological context is provided by M. Rodziewicz, "Report on the activities of the Archaeological Mission at Kom el-Dikka (Alexandria) in 1982," ibid., 84–102.

119. Zach. Mytil. *HE* 6.2. Zachariah underscores Peter's support among the Alexandrian populace in a later passage in the same chapter: "The people, however, since they received Peter without dispute when he anathematised the Synod (of Chalcedon), were greatly incensed against the monks. But they were restrained by the chief men of the city and by Peter, so that there was no public tumult."
120. Theophanes *Chron.* AM 5981; Zach. Mytil. *HE* 6.4–6; Evagrius *HE* 3.23.
121. *History of the Patriarchs* 1.13 (ed. Evetts), p. 448 [184]. Evagrius quotes a letter of some Chalcedonian monks who relate that, after the death of Peter, "Alexandria, Egypt, and Africa remained at unity among themselves" (3.31).

*Chapter Ten. Conclusions*

1. Malalas *Chron.* 12.41, (trans. Jeffreys, Jeffreys, and Scott).
2. *Hist. Aceph.* 5.13.
3. This, of course, reflects on the question of Egyptian "nationalism"

during this period. See G. Fowden, *Empire to Commonwealth* (Princeton, 1993); J. Meyendorff, *Imperial Unity and Christian Divisions* (Crestwood, N.Y., 1989); F. Winkelmann, "Ägypten und Byzanz vor der arabischen Eroberung," *Byzantinoslavica* 40 (1979): 161–81.

4. T. J. Jackson Lears, "The Concept of Cultural Hegemony: Problems and Possibilities," *American Historical Review* 90.3 (1985): 567–93.
5. J. Lieu, J. North, and T. Rajak, eds., *The Jews among Pagans and Christians in the Roman Empire* (London, 1992), 2–6; P. Brown, *Authority and the Sacred* (Cambridge, 1995), 68–9. Earlier adumbrations of this model may be found in the important collection of articles edited by J. Neusner and E. S. Frerichs, *"To See Ourselves as Others See Us": Christians, Jews, "Others" in Late Antiquity* (Chico, Calif., 1985).
6. Julian *Ep.* 111 (ed. Bidez-Cumont).

*Chapter 11. Epilogue*

1. *Vitae Patrum Iurensium: Eugendi* 11, *Monumenta Germaniae Historica, Scriptores rerum Merovingicarum* vol. 3, 158–59, ed. and trans. in J. N. Hillgarth, *Christianity and Paganism: 350–750,* rev. ed. (Philadelphia, 1986), 14–15.
2. M. G. Morony, "Conquerors and Conquered: Iran," in *Studies on the First Century of Islamic Society,* ed. G. H. A. Juynboll (Carbondale, Ill., 1982), 73–87; idem, *Iraq after the Muslim Conquest* (Princeton, 1984). On the issue of cultural transformation in another contemporary society, see the observations of A. Kazhdan and A. Cutler, "Continuity and Discontinuity in Byzantine History," *Byzantion* 52 (1982): 429–78.
3. Ibn Gubayr *Rihla,* ed. W. Wright, 42–43, quoted in S. K. Hamarneh, "The Ancient Monuments of Alexandria according to Accounts by Medieval Arab Authors," *Folia Orientalia* 13 (1971): 79.

   For late Byzantine and medieval Alexandria, consult A. J. Butler, *The Arab Conquest of Egypt,* 2d ed., ed. P. M. Fraser (1902; Oxford, 1978), chap. 24, "Alexandria at the Conquest," 368–400, and Fraser's bibliographical essay, lxxii–lxxvi; P. Kahle, "Zur Geschichte des mittelalterlichen Alexandria," *Der Islam* 12 (1921): 29–84; E. Combe, *Alexandrie Musulmane* (Cairo, 1933); idem, "Inscriptions arabes du Musée d'Alexandrie," *BSAA* 30 (1936): 56–78; S. Labib, "al-Iskandariyya," in *Encyclopedia of Islam,* 2d ed. (Leiden, 1980) 132–37; W. Kubiak, "Stèles funéraires arabes de Kom el Dick," *BSAA* 42 (1967): 17–26; idem, "Inscriptions arabes de Kom el Dick," *BSAA* 43 (1975): 133–42; E. Prominska, *Investigations on the Population of Muslim Alexandria* (Warsaw, 1972); Rodziewicz, *Habitations,* 336–47; idem, "Graeco-Islamic Elements at Kom el Dikka in the Light of the New Discoveries," *Graeco-Arabica* 1 (1982): 35–49; idem, "Archaeological

Evidence on Byzantine Architecture in Alexandria," *Graeco-Arabica* 4 (1991): 287–93; H. Heinen, "Alexandria in Late Antiquity," in *CoptEncy* 1:95–103; P. M. Fraser, "Alexandria, Christian and Medieval," in *CoptEncy* 1: 88–92; M. Müller-Wiener, *Eine Stadtgeschichte Alexandrias von 564/1169 bis in die Mitte des 9./15. Jahrhunderts* (Berlin, 1992); P. M. Fraser, "Byzantine Alexandria: Decline and Fall," *BSAA* 45 (1993): 91–106.

4. "The development of Alexandria as a city largely escapes us" P. M. Fraser, *Ptolemaic Alexandria* (Oxford, 1972), 1:36–37.
5. Late antique mosaics showing Alexandria: at Gerasa, see C. H. Kraeling, *Gerasa: City of the Decapolis* (New Haven, 1938), 341ff; at Qasr el-Lebia in Cyrenaica, see A. Grabar in *Cahiers archéol.* 12 (1962): 135–39.
6. Ibnʿ Abd al-Hakam, *Futūh Misr wa-Akhbāruhā*, ed. C. Torrey (New Haven, 1922), 80, 175–76. A partial French translation may be found in O. Toussoun, "La conquête de l'Egypte par Ibn Abd-el-Hakam," *BSAA* 19 (1923): 213–38; Ahmad ibn Yahyā al-Balādhurī, *Kitāb Futūh al-buldān* 221, trans. P. K. Hitti as *The Origins of the Islamic State* (New York, 1916), 347–48.
7. See Adriani, *Repertorio,* 228.
8. Rodziewicz, *Habitations,* 336–47.
9. *Takwim al-Buldān* (ed. Reinaud), p. 230, quoted in Hamarneh, "Monuments of Alexandria," 79.
10. Apparently controlled in Alexandria; cf. *C.Th.* 15.1.9, to the prefect, Ecdicius, which speaks of private construction on civic property (A.D. 362).
11. Amm. Marc. 22.16.15; Epiphanius *de Mens. et Pond.* 9 (*PG* 43, cols. 249c–50c).
12. Cassius Dio 75.13; Herodian 4.8.9.
13. Al-Garnati, *Tuhfat al-Albab* (ed. Ferrand), p. 73, quoted in Hamarneh, "Monuments of Alexandria," p. 83.
14. Ibn al-Batrīq (Eutychius), *Annales* 328–36 (*PG* 111, col. 906b); John of Nikiu *Chron.* 95.10, 108.8.
15. Theophanes *AM* 6105–7; Leont. *v. Jo. Eleem.* 6, 9, 20; Sebeos *History of Heraclius* 23, 25.
16. Adamnanus *de Locis Sanctis* 2.30.25; Bernard the Wise *Itinerarium* 6.
17. *Expliciunt peregrinationes totius terre sancte* 175 (ca. 1350), trans. J. H. Bernard as *Guide-Book to Palestine,* Palestine Pilgrim Text Society (London, 1894), 6:33.
18. Calderini, *Dizionario,* 169–70; E. Breccia, *Alexandria ad Aegyptum,* English ed. (Bergamo, 1922), 55.
19. Ibn ʿAbd Al-Hakam, *Futūh Misr* (ed. Torrey), p. 41.
20. Rodziewicz, *Habitations,* 336–47; idem, "Graeco-Islamic Elements at Kom el Dikka."

21. For the necropoleis at Kōm el-Dikka, see E. Prominska, *Investigations on the Population of Muslim Alexandria* (Warsaw, 1972); idem, *Variations de taille des habitants d'Alexandrie au cours des siècles* (Warsaw, 1985).
22. Some measure of the city's physical deterioration can be gleaned from the unfortunate demise of the poet al-Butayn in 825, who perished when an underground drain or cistern caved in, engulfing both him and his horse: Al-Tabarī, *Tārikh al-Rusul wa al-Mulūk* 1091 (ed. Bosworth), vol. 32, p. 164.
23. John of Nikiu *Chron.* 97.18.
24. Leont. v. *Joh. Eleem.* 10, 13, 26, 28, 35; *ILS* 7564.
25. Rodziewicz, *Habitations*; idem, "Graeco-Islamic Elements at Kom el Dikka"; idem, *La céramique romaine tardive d'Alexandrie, Alexandrie* I (Warsaw, 1975); G. Majcherek, "The Late Roman Ceramics from Sector G—Alexandria (1986–1987)," *É&T* 16 (1992): 81–117.
26. Soz. *HE* 6.2.14–15; Amm. Marc. 26.10.15; Eus. [Dionysius] *HE* 7.21; Agathias 2.15.7; Malalas 18.90 [481].
27. Leont. v. *Joh. Eleem.* 6, 9, 20.
28. John of Nikiu *Chron.* 120.17–21.
29. Al-Balādhurī, *Kitāb Futūh al-buldān* 223 (trans. Hitti), p. 350.
30. Ibn ʿAbd Al-Hakam, *Futūh Misr* (ed. Torrey), 130–31, 192.
31. *P.Lond.* 1392 (A.D. 710/11). See also V. Christides, "Continuation and Change in Early Arab Egypt as Reflected in the Terms and Titles of the Greek Papyri," *BSAA* 45 (1993): 69–75.
32. Al-Kindi, *Governors and Judges of Egypt* (ed. Guest), p. 49.
33. *P.Lond.* 1412 (A.D. 702/3).
34. Adamnanus *de Locis Sanctis* 2.30 (ca. 683); Bernard the Wise *Itinerarium* 6 (ca. 870). Cf. the earlier pilgrim, Antoninus of Piacenza *Itinerarium* 45 (ca. 570). See also, M. Martin, "Pilgrims and Travelers in Christian Egypt," in *CoptEncy* 6:1975–77.
35. P. Grossmann, *Abu Mina: A Guide to the Ancient Pilgrimage Center* (Cairo, 1986), 10; idem, "Abū Mīnā," in *CoptEncy* 1:24–29.
36. *P.Lond.* 1353, 1392, 1393; P. Rem 32. See also H. I. Bell, "Two Official Letters of the Arab Period," *JEA* 12 (1926): 265–81; A. Allouche, "Umayyad Fleet, Coptic Contributions to," in *CoptEncy* 7:2286.
37. Al-Tabarī *Tārikh al-Rusul wa al-Mulūk,* (ed. de Goeje), vol. 2, p. 1346; *P.Lond.* 1349, 1353, 1374, 1434; *P.Rem.* 9, 52.
38. *B.Al.* 12 (trans. Gardner).
39. Patricia Crone has supplied a much needed corrective to unsupported assumptions regarding the mercantile role of the pre-Islamic Hijaz and the commercial activities of its inhabitants in her *Meccan Trade and the Rise of Islam* (Princeton, 1987).
40. On this subject, see A. S. Ehrenkreutz, "Another Orientalist's Remarks

concerning the Pirenne Thesis," *Journal of the Economic and Social History of the Orient* 15 (1972): 94–104.

41. Al-Tabarī, *Tarīkh al-Rusul wa al-Mulūk* 1091–92 (ed. Bosworth), vol. 32, pp. 164–65; *History of the Patriarchs* 1.19 (ed. Evetts), 428–36, 459–65 [543–50, 573–79].
42. The annual tribute paid to the Abbasid treasury should be viewed as token recognition of caliphal authority, especially when it is set against the total revenues of this wealthy land.
43. Al-Balādhurī, *Kitāb Futūh al-buldān* 212–13, (trans. Hitti), 335–37.
44. The preliminary reports, written by G. T. Scanlon and W. B. Kubiak, may be found in the *Journal of the American Research Center in Egypt* 4 (1964)–6 (1965). Final reports: G. T. Scanlon, *Fustāt Expedition Final Report,* vol. 1, *Catalogue of Filters* (Winona Lake, Ind., 1986); W. Kubiak and G. T. Scanlon, *Fustāt Expedition Final Report,* vol. 2, *Fustāt—C* (Winona Lake, Ind., 1990). See also W. B. Kubiak, *Al-Fustat: Its Foundation and Early Urban Development* (Cairo, 1987).
45. "The Moslem forced [the Egyptians] to excavate anew the canal of Trajan, which had been destroyed for a long time, in order to conduct water through it from Babylon in Egypt to the Red Sea" John of Nikiu *Chron.* 120.31 (trans. Charles). For the early history of this canal, see P. J. Sijpesteijn, "Der *POTAMOS TRAIANOS,*" *Aegyptus* 43 (1963): 70–83.
46. *P.Lond.* 1336; Ibn abd al-Hakam, *Futūh Misr* (ed. Torrey), 158–65; Al-Balādhurī, *Kitāb Futūh al-buldān* 216 (trans. Hitti), 340–41.
47. *P.Lond.* 1346/*Sel.Pap.* 432; *P.Lond.* 1386, 1387. There are indications, however, that the caravan route from Fustāt to Clysma was also used. See V. Christides, "Misr," in *Encyclopedia of Islam,* 2d ed. (Leiden, 1991), 7.158.
48. John of Nikiu *Chron.* 121.3.
49. *P.Lond.* 1353. line 11 (A.D. 710), one of the very few references to this canal following the Arab conquest.
50. *C.Th.* 14.27.2 (436).
51. Procopius *Aed.* 6.1.1–5.
52. M. Rodziewicz, "Alexandria and the District of Mareotis," *Graeco-Arabica* 2 (1983): 204; idem, "Remarks on the Peristyle House in Alexandria and Mareotis," in *Papers of the Twelfth International Congress for Classical Archaeology in Athens* (Athens, 1983); idem, "Archaeological Evidence on Byzantine Architecture in Alexandria," *Graeco-Arabica* 4 (1991): 287–93.
53. A terminus post quem for the demise of the port is suggested by the presence of Cypriot pottery, which was not imported into Egypt until the first quarter of the seventh century; a terminus ante by the complete absence of the Coptic glazed ware found in abundance elsewhere

after the eighth century. See Rodziewicz, "Alexandria and Mareotis," 203.

54. Grossmann, *Abu Mina,* 10, 14–16, 18; idem., "Abū Mīnā," in *CoptEncy* 1:24–29.
55. Adamnanus *de Locis Sanctis* 2.30.8–9.
56. Various texts are collected and translated in Hamarneh, "Ancient Monuments of Alexandria," 85–93, 104–8. See also the perceptive comments of F. de Polignac, "Al-Iskandariyya: Oeil du monde et frontière de l'inconnu," *Mélanges d'archéologie et d'histoire de l'École française de Rome* 96 (1984): 425–39; idem, "L'imaginaire arabe et le mythe de la fondation legitime," *La revue de l'occident musulman et de la Mediterranée* 64 (1987): 55–63.

# Index

*Page references to illustrations are printed in italic type.*

# ANCIENT SOCIETY AND HISTORY

The series Ancient Society and History offers books, relatively brief in compass, on selected topics in the history of ancient Greece and Rome, broadly conceived, with a special emphasis on comparative and other nontraditional approaches and methods. The series, which includes both works of synthesis and works of original scholarship, is aimed at the widest possible range of specialist and nonspecialist readers.

*Published in the Series:*

Eva Cantarella, *Pandora's Daughters: The Role and Status of Women in Greek and Roman Antiquity*
Alan Watson, *Roman Slave Law*
John E. Stambaugh, *The Ancient Roman City*
Géza Alfödy, *The Social History of Rome*
Giovanni Comotti, *Music in Greek and Roman Culture*
Christian Habicht, *Cicero the Politician*
Mark Golden, *Children and Childhood in Classical Athens*
Thomas Cole, *The Origins of Rhetoric in Ancient Greece*
Maurizio Bettini, *Anthropology and Roman Culture: Kinship, Time, Images of the Soul*
Suzanne Dixon, *The Roman Family*
Stephen L. Dyson, *Community and Society in Roman Italy*
Tim G. Parkin, *Demography and Roman Society*
Alison Burford, *Land and Labor in the Greek World*
Alan Watson, *International Law in Archaic Rome: War and Religion*
Stephen H. Lonsdale, *Dance and Ritual Play in Greek Religion*
J. Donald Hughes, *Pan's Travail: Environmental Problems of the Ancient Greeks and Romans*
C. R. Whittaker, *Frontiers of the Roman Empire: A Social and Economic Study*
Pericles Georges, *Barbarian Asia and the Greek Experience*
Nancy Demand, *Birth, Death, and Motherhood in Classical Greece*
Elaine Fantham, *Roman Literary Culture: From Cicero to Apuleius*
Kenneth W. Harl, *Coinage in the Roman Economy, 300 B.C. to A.D. 700*
Christopher Haas, *Alexandria in Late Antiquity*

**Library of Congress Cataloging-in-Publication Data**

Haas, Christopher.
Alexandria in late antiquity : topography and social conflict / Christopher Haas.
p. cm. — (Ancient society and history)
Includes bibliographical references and index.
ISBN 0-8018-5377-X (alk. paper)
1. Alexandria (Egypt)—Civilization. 2. Alexandria (Egypt)—Social conditions. 3. Alexandria (Egypt)—Ethnic relations. 4. Alexandria (Egypt)—Religion. I. Title. II. Series.
DT154.A4H36 1997
932—dc20 96-21424
CIP